D1567140

Crime Scene Forensics

A Scientific Method Approach

Crime Scene Forensics

A Scientific Method Approach

Robert C. Shaler

CRC Press is an imprint of the
Taylor & Francis Group, an **informa** business

CRC Press
Taylor & Francis Group
6000 Broken Sound Parkway NW, Suite 300
Boca Raton, FL 33487-2742

Printed and bound in India by Replika Press Pvt.Ltd.
Version Date: 20110714

International Standard Book Number: 978-1-4398-5995-7 (Hardback)

Library of Congress Cataloging-in-Publication Data

Shaler, Robert C.
Crime scene forensics : a scientific method approach / Robert C. Shaler.
p. cm.
Includes bibliographical references and index.
ISBN 978-1-4398-5995-7 (hbk. : alk. paper)
1. Crime scenes. 2. Crime scene searches. 3. Criminal investigations. 4. Forensic sciences. I. Title.

HV8073.S42243 2012
363.25'2--dc23 2011028482

Visit the Taylor & Francis Web site at
http://www.taylorandfrancis.com

and the CRC Press Web site at
http://www.crcpress.com

Contents

Part VII

MISCELLANEOUS CONSIDERATIONS AND SPECIALIZED SCENES

Acknowledgments

I want to thank my students at the Pennsylvania State University for suffering through the various iterations of incomplete and badly formatted chapters that formed the basis of their crime scene investigation course and this text. I want to thank my forensic colleagues to whom I owe my continuing educations, forensic insights, and acumen. I also want to acknowledge Becky Masterman and David Fausel at Taylor & Francis who stuck with me through self-imposed deadlines that I continually missed. Most importantly, I want to thank my lovely wife who still thinks it is cute that I cannot "see" something in plain sight, such as a flash drive with all of my chapters, and who sticks by and supports me as I remain "sort of" retired.

Author

Robert C. Shaler received his doctoral degree from the Pennsylvania State University in 1968 and over his career held academic appointments at the University of Pittsburgh School of Medicine, the University of Pittsburgh School of Pharmacy, the City University of New York, New York University School of Medicine, and most recently, at the Pennsylvania State University.

He joined the scientific staff of the Pittsburgh and Allegheny County Crime Laboratory in 1970, where, as a criminalist, he practiced forensic science, testified in court, and investigated crime scenes. In 1977, he joined the Aerospace Corporation staff and managed four Law Enforcement Assistance Administration (precursor of the National Institute of Justice) contracts, one of which resulted in the bloodstain analysis standard of the nation's crime laboratories until the mid-1980s. In 1978, he joined the staff of the New York City Medical Examiner's Office as the head of its serology laboratory, a position he held until 1987 when he moved to the Lifecodes Corporation, the nation's first forensic DNA typing laboratory. There, he introduced "DNA fingerprinting" to the nation's legal and law enforcement communities through a series of nationwide informational lectures. Dr. Shaler returned to the Medical Examiner's Office in 1990, where he created a modern Department of Forensic Biology, helped design its current 300,000-square-foot building, and established the city's first crime scene reconstruction team, which still operates from within the Medical Examiner's Office.

In the wake of the terrorist attacks on the World Trade Center, he assumed responsibility for the DNA identification effort, designing the testing strategy, and coordinating the work of six different laboratories. In 2003, he was awarded an honorary doctoral degree from the State University of New York at Stony Brook for his work for the citizens of New York and for his effort to identify the missing in the World Trade Center rubble. In 2005, he published *Who They Were: Inside the World Trade Center DNA Story: The Unprecedented Effort to Identify the Missing*, which told the story of the medical examiner's staff and scientists working behind the scenes of the DNA identification effort.

He retired from the Medical Examiner's Office and accepted a professorship at the Pennsylvania State University in 2005, where he started and was the first director of the university's forensic science program. At Pennsylvania State University, he taught the principles of crime scene investigation to undergraduate and forensic science graduate students. His crime scene investigation course attracted national attention and was featured on *The Today Show*, *Hollywood Heat*, and *Crime Scene University*—a Discovery Channel six-part miniseries broadcast in 2008. He was a member of two National Academies' NRC committees that published the 2009 report *Strengthening Forensic Science: A Path Forward* and the 2011 report *Review of the Scientific Approaches during the FBI's Investigation of the 2001 Anthrax Letters.* His online course, "The Principles of Crime Scene Investigation," taught through the Pennsylvania State University's World Campus, reaches students, law enforcement, and criminal justice professionals worldwide.

Dr. Shaler's research and professional interests focus on applying science and technology to crime scene investigation. His current research is related to identifying human and bacterial DNA in fingerprints and to quantify the biological response to trauma and stress by analyzing postmortem blood and tissue. He has taught workshops to law enforcement in crime scene investigation, crime scene reconstruction, and bloodstain pattern analysis. He is the recipient of a U.S. patent for a novel method for developing fingerprints, a continuing project for which he recently received funding from the National Institute of Justice. He is the author of over 40 publications and chapters in four books.

The Philosophy and Essentials of Crime Scene Forensics

I

Crime Scene Forensics Philosophy, Practice, and Teaching

1

There are no perfect crimes, merely imperfect investigations [1].

1.1 Introduction

The premise of this text is that crime scene investigations are joint scientific and investigative endeavors, the success of which requires experience, creative thinking, logic, and the correct application of the science and the scientific method. These investigations are intensely intellectual exercises. To disagree is ignorance, inexperience, or stupidity. It is much like what the legendary golf pro Bobby Jones thought about his profession and is credited with saying, "Competitive golf is played mainly on a five-and-a-half-inch course . . . the space between your ears." So it is with crime scene investigation and reconstruction. In fact, a competent crime scene investigation is as cerebral an exercise as any scientific endeavor in forensic science. Students need to understand that scene investigations are comprehensive, tedious, and difficult scientific exercises that dovetail experience, training, and education.

Police officers and scientists who investigate crime scenes are variably called crime scene investigators, forensic investigators, or technicians, depending on the jurisdiction in which they work. The term "crime scene technician" is neither used nor appropriate in this text because the term demeans the scientists and specialized investigators who do this work. The terms "scene scientist" and/or "investigator" or "scene investigator" are more appropriate, depending on the role the individual plays. For example, if the person conducting the investigation is a police officer/detective, a nonscientist, this person is considered to be a scene investigator. If the person working at the scene is a scientist, this person is considered to be a scene scientist and may or may not be a scene investigator. In this text, individuals who investigate crime scenes will be called scene scientists/investigators or scene investigators. At times, too, the terms "students" and/or "novice investigators" will be used to differentiate them from the more experienced scene scientists/investigators.

Lawyers, law enforcement officials, politicians, and even forensic scientists fail to understand the delicate balance between science and the investigative activity required to successfully work a crime scene, believing that crime scene investigation is a simple, nonscientific process requiring minimal expertise that anyone can be trained to do. Crime scene unit composition illustrates the inherent belief that scene investigation is simply a matter of spreading dusting powder around; shining an alternate light source (ALS) or laser to find fingerprints, biological fluids, and fibers; collecting the evidence; and packaging and delivering it to an appropriate location, perhaps a crime laboratory. Unfortunately, however widely held a belief this may be, such an investigative paradigm is wrong.

Many texts discuss the principles of crime scene investigation and reconstruction. These are written primarily for police investigators and eschew or minimize the science underlying the process. Here, we are concerned with teaching the philosophy of crime scene investigation by emphasizing the necessary thought processes required to ensure the appropriate application of science to the investigation. This text is designed as a first-level course of instruction for undergraduate and graduate students in forensic science programs. It is also appropriate for police, crime scene investigators, emergency medical technicians, forensic nurses, medical investigators, and prosecuting and defense attorneys who need to understand the basic philosophy of crime scene investigation and how science is applied in the field. Nonscience professionals need to understand the basics and dynamics of crime scene investigation in order to properly do their job.

The course of instruction and its philosophy as presented in this text have been taught to forensic science majors (undergraduate and graduate) and criminal justice majors at Penn State University as well as online at the university's World Campus.

1.2 Why Investigate the Crime Scene?

A reasonable but almost flippant response to the question, "Why investigate the crime scene?" might be "To find evidence." This is certainly what happens during an investigation, but is that all? Is that the sole reason for investigating a crime? For a text aimed at providing instruction in crime scene investigation, the question is definitely appropriate, and finding evidence is but one important product of crime scene investigation. The overriding purpose, of course, is to solve the crime and related crimes, which also seems self-evident. The scene investigation per se, however, does not normally solve the crime immediately, which is why the scene investigation is just the initial step in the process. The five reasons for investigating the crime scene, with the finding of evidence being a by-product of the process, are to

- Develop investigative leads for detectives
- Develop specific information—in the form of evidence or investigative logic—to enable a successful prosecution
- Locate probative evidence, exculpatory or inculpatory, that is, to provide evidence of innocence or guilt
- Locate significant information in the form of evidence to allow a successful and accurate reconstruction
- Link crimes through the evidence

Texts of crime scene investigation and those specifically devoted to forensic science often pose the following series of investigative questions concerning the objectives or purpose of crime scene investigations:

- What happened?
- When did it happen?
- Where did it happen?
- Who was involved?
- How was it done?
- Why was it done?

Although these are important, they seem too obvious. Perhaps a better set of investigative questions dig deeper into the mechanism of the crime in order to uncover greater investigative information, as Fisher [2] writes,

> The objectives of a crime scene investigation are to
>
> - Reconstruct the incident
> - Ascertain the sequence of events
> - Determine the mode of operation
> - Uncover a motive
> - Discover what property was stolen
> - Find out all that the criminal may have done
> - Recover physical evidence of the crime

Some of these abovementioned reasons seem redundant and others more specific, but each requires critical thinking as it relates to a specific scene investigation. For some scene investigators, answering these could be impossible because responding appropriately requires in-depth knowledge and experience in criminalistics and crime scene investigation.

1.3 Who Should Investigate Scenes of Crimes?

The answer to "Who should investigate scenes of crimes?" is the question "Which of the arbitrarily listed categories of investigators below would you choose, given a choice, to investigate the scene of your mother's brutal murder?"

- Experienced police/scene investigator/detective leading the forensics unit, where the forensics unit is defined as a crime scene investigative team
- A criminalist with a strong scientific background and scene investigative experience
- A forensic scientist working in a trace/serology unit in a crime laboratory who was assigned to the investigation

An honest, unbiased police investigator might choose the experienced scene investigator—the first category—who has investigated numerous scenes and is probably not a scientist but instead a "forensics" expert who applies scientific techniques at the scene, correctly or incorrectly. As a scientist, I would choose representatives from the first two categories. My preference would be to have the criminalist lead the scientific aspect of the scene investigation, which would include interpreting scientific evidence and applying science at the scene. How this works in practice is clear, however, and choosing the criminalist—the second category—to be an integral part of the investigative team might also be an intellectual exercise. The reason is that mixing science and investigators has not been widely popular or accepted by police agencies, although that paradigm is slowly changing.

However, this has been a point of controversy for decades. In an article titled "Science versus practical common sense in crime detection," in 1931, Al Dunlap [3], then the editor of *The Detective*, reported his address at the annual convention of the 17th International Association of Identification (IAI) in Rochester, New York. At the same convention,

Captain Duncan Mathewson, the Chief of Detectives of the San Francisco Police Department, said,

> In truth, there is no real cause for a misunderstanding between the exponents of modern science and those who emphasize the need of practical common sense methods of crime detection. Science should simply confine its efforts to the solution of all problems that call for special scientific treatment, and never undertake to steal the show, so to speak, by underrating the importance of practical common-sense methods in the general investigation of nearly all cases. . . . Science is not, by the wildest stretch of the imagination, a substitute for practical methods, as the public has often been led to believe; instead it is just a most valuable acquisition and potent aid which should go hand in hand with plain practical common sense and good judgment in a combined effort to cope with the difficult crime situation that confronts the law-enforcement agencies in every section of the land. (pp. 326–327)

In 1931 scientific applications to law enforcement were in their infancy, and, the inflammatory rhetoric aside, Dunlop understood the need for a cooperative effort between science and the police investigator. The police-versus-science at crime scenes controversy continues, though, as illustrated by an attack in Gardner and Bevel's [4] commentary on Chisum and Turvey's [5] statements in *Crime Reconstruction*:

> Throughout this text, the authors incorporate a class-based ad hominem attack that is directed against anyone associated with law enforcement. Some of these attacks are indirect and veiled as a discussion of objectivity, but others are clear statements that show the authors come with their own very distinct personal bias. (p. 800)

Chisum and Turvey [5] responded, clearly illustrating their thoughts:

> The harsh reality is that crime scene processing and documentation efforts are often abysmal if not completely absent. . . . The in-service training available to law enforcement typically exists in the form of half-day seminars or short courses taught by nonscientists who, on their own, in no way impart the discipline and expertise necessary to process crime scenes adequately for the purposes of reconstruction. (p. 118)

These controversies are unfortunate. This text promotes the premise that the combined efforts of police investigators and crime scene scientists are critical in our technologically expanding world of crime scene investigation. This applies not only to a single investigation but also to the global question of a scene's relatedness to other crimes of a similar nature or crimes of a dissimilar nature but committed by the same perpetrator. This text considers that logic and the scientific method play the most critical roles in the successful investigation of the crime scene.

1.3.1 Crime Scene Investigative Paradigms*

In the context of the above discussion, it is instructive to examine the current crime scene investigative paradigm in the United States and then compare it with an idealized upgrade.

* "Example, pattern; *especially*: an outstandingly clear or typical example or archetype: an example of a conjugation or declension showing a word in all its inflectional forms: a philosophical and theoretical framework of a scientific school or discipline within which theories, laws, and generalizations and the experiments performed in support of them are formulated; *broadly*: a philosophical or theoretical framework of any kind" [6].

1.3.1.1 The Current Paradigm

Does a crime scene investigation paradigm exist? The answer is, "Sort of, although it is complex." A modern composite paradigm might read as follows:

> Police secure, investigate, and assume responsibility for the integrity and security of the crime scene and its investigation. They document the scene and search for, preserve, and package evidence, ensuring it reaches the appropriate individuals or agencies.

Most, if not all, crime scene investigations are more complicated than that, and certainly individual scene investigative paradigms are prevalent, depending on the jurisdiction in which a crime scene occurs. Because of failures in scene investigations, it was realized that standardization of crime scene investigation procedures was necessary. In 1996, the U.S. Department of Justice began publishing a series of pamphlets that included *Crime Scene Investigation: Guide for Law Enforcement* (2000), *Death Investigation: A Guide for the Scene Investigator* (1996), *A Guide for Explosion and Bombing Scene Investigation* (2000), *Electronic Crime Scene Investigation* (2001), and *Fire and Arson Scene Evidence* (2000). Additionally, several books on the subject are available as are scene checklists. These publications assume the police are the prime scene investigators. Certainly, using such reference sources and checklists of investigative activity, the quality of scene investigations has improved. However, one can argue that upgrading has come at a price—the repression of creative thought and logic.

Responders to crime scenes have varied experience, education, expertise, and resources. Most crime scenes are investigated by smaller agencies by sworn police officers having varied training and experience, likely in specialty workshops, the annual IAI meetings, the Federal Bureau of Investigation (FBI), or during police academy training. Scene investigators in large cities might have more experience and more extensive training by in-house experts or by hired outside experts who give specific training sessions. In some jurisdictions, forensic scientists respond to scenes, especially violent crimes, such as in Suffolk County, New York, and Pittsburgh, Pennsylvania. In others, crime scene investigators call the crime laboratory for help in specific investigations, such as searching for semen in vehicles or for help in locating cleaned-up blood.

As Attorney General Janet Reno [7] stated in *Crime Scene Investigation*: *Guide for Law Enforcement*,

> Actions taken at the outset of an investigation at a crime scene can play a pivotal role in the resolution of a case.... While many agencies have programs in crime scene processing, the level of training and resources available varies from jurisdiction to jurisdiction, as does the opportunity to practice actual investigation. (p. iii)

1.3.1.2 An Evolving Paradigm

A new paradigm is required to accommodate our modern, high-tech world. Applicable science and technology are expanding exponentially at crime scenes at what almost seems a feverish, uncontrolled pace that matches the level of scientific advancement. A current thought is that relevant information at the scene should be made available as soon as possible to investigators so that the investigation cannot only be concluded but corollary investigations can be linked.

Although a relevant and new scene investigative paradigm seems impossible—the existing paradigm is entrenched in the operative mind-set of law enforcement—the need for change is of paramount importance. Exceptions to the current paradigm do exist, but generally, outsiders are discouraged from participating or afforded minor roles as subject matter experts in the investigative process. What follows is arguably the form a modern scene investigative paradigm should take. Before elucidating such a form, it is important to consider six arguable premises that embody the underlying philosophy of this new paradigm.

1.3.1.2.1 Premise 1: Crime Scene Investigation Is a Scientific Endeavor Lay police investigators perform most, if not all, of the administrative aspects of the investigation. These same investigators apply science at the scene often without scientific supervision, an in-depth understanding of the technology they are using, an understanding of the science behind that technology or its limitations, and little or no true understanding of how the scientific method works or how it should be used. Because this is a scientific endeavor, scene-trained forensic scientists and criminalists should be present or, with the appropriate scene investigative credentials, manage the scene investigation to ensure that these techniques are applied properly, that the data obtained are reliable, and that the data are interpreted correctly. This would mean a shift from a completely experience-based investigation to one of experience, science, and logic through the application of the scientific method.

Additionally, as Thornton [8] wrote,

> Logic is the science that evaluates arguments. An argument as used here does not mean a verbal fight but, rather, a group of premises that claims to support a conclusion. Premises are statements that set forth the reasons or evidence for an idea. Conclusions are the statements that the evidence is claimed to support or imply. For logic to work properly the parent premises must be valid and the conclusion must follow from valid premises. (p. 39)

Currently, the investigative paradigm is justice-based. That is, the intent is to capture evidence that leads to a trial and conviction. By considering the scene as a scientific process, the investigation becomes science-based, where the investigation not only collects important evidence but also considers the information and data obtained holistically so that connections to other investigations can be explored. If the result is a correct conviction, society wins.

1.3.1.2.2 Premise 2: Performed Correctly, a Crime Scene Investigation Is as Difficult and as Complex as Any Forensic Endeavor Many might consider the next statement a stretch, one from a delusional imagination: a crime scene investigation is not unlike forensic DNA analysis in that the vast majority of individual manipulations is deceptively simple but the underlying foundation is complex. Certainly, a lay person, that is, a police investigator, *can* be trained to perform hands-on laboratory work. Data interpretation can also be straightforward, and a lay person can interpret the raw DNA data in simple cases and arrive at a correct interpretation and conclusion. The same is true for crime scene investigations. Almost anyone can be trained to dust for fingerprints, package evidence, and carry out the fundamental activities at the scene.

The courts would likely look askance at lay police officers testifying as experts to DNA test results. If, however, in a moment of insanity, the court was to permit such testimony, even in error, the defense would have a field day during the *voir dire*! In crime scene investigations, however, the courts routinely allow nonscientists to testify to the application of scientific procedures without objection from opposing counsel.

All or most DNA cases are not that simple, and problems and interpretive errors occur by qualified forensic DNA scientists because the data can be complex and ambiguous, such as with mixtures and low levels of DNA where stochastic effects are prevalent. As in the DNA example, some crime scenes can be elementary and the data obtained straightforward and easily interpreted by someone with experience. Even apparent simple crime scenes *can* be complex and complicated, perhaps more so than most DNA cases. This is so because crime scene investigation requires the integration of multiple disciplines, expertise, specialized training, and experience; it is the juxtaposition of science, scene investigative skills, critical thinking, logic, and an unbiased open mind. Forensic DNA analysis is, well, just science, although not simple. Crime scene investigation is more; it is both investigation and science.

Complex crime scenes occur more frequently than complicated DNA cases. The investigation of the scene, the interpretation of the evidence, and an eventual reconstruction is anything but straightforward. It should be analyzed by individuals having strong scientific backgrounds, scene interpretative skills, and investigative experience. The competent scene scientist/investigator is a rare and special individual because the person needs to have the unique ability to perform the work flawlessly. In fact, most forensic scientists—although they would probably argue the point—would likely fare no better than the untrained police investigator when piecing together the facts obtained from a scene investigation.

A complete, effective, and efficient crime scene investigation is an amalgamation of several unique skills. It is an intellectual endeavor that requires scene experience, attention to detail, a skeptical perspective, developed powers of observation, in-depth knowledge of criminalistics, and the ability to apply deductive and inductive reasoning as embraced in the scientific method. Not everyone, including some forensic scientists, has the intellect, the experience, the credentials, or the ability to investigate a crime scene effectively. Although the steps listed in the scientific method seem straightforward, applying them correctly during a scene investigation is not easily done. Forensic scientists having only a singular expertise, for example, forensic DNA analytical skills, who rarely, if ever, venture into the "real" forensic world, likely do not have the requisite credentials to be a competent crime scene investigator. This person would likely be relegated to evidence collection, packaging, and preservation.

In any scientific endeavor, work is split between important though necessary administrative functions and the application and interpretation of the scientific data. Under proper scientific supervision, lay scene investigators are trained to apply the science at the scene, for example, developing fingerprints, recognizing bloodstain patterns, chemically enhancing footwear prints, lifting impression prints, and so on. In fact, this is how most scenes are investigated. However, when decisions need to be made with regard to applying the science in a specific circumstance or interpreting data as they are obtained, it is advantageous to have a scientist make the decision or recommend methodologies because s/he would have a deeper understanding of the limitations of the methods.

1.3.1.2.3 Premise 3: Criminalists and Experienced Scene Investigators Should Work Together to Interpret and Draw Inferences from Scene Data Where is the line in the sand between the scientist, in this instance the criminalist, and the experienced scene investigator? The answer should be easy, but it is not. The vast majority of scene investigations are conducted by lay investigators and inexperienced forensic scientists who do not have the credentials to investigate crime scenes. Additionally, data interpretation should not occur in a vacuum. The logical solution is for criminalists and experienced scene investigators to share the responsibility using their collective and divergent experience, education, training, and expertise to collaborate as a single training vehicle. However, even experienced investigators lack the appropriate scientific credentials to interpret all scene data properly because they do not know or understand the limitations of the tests used or how to correctly interpret the data developed.

Take, for example, the presumptive chemical tests for blood that have been around for over 150 years. These tests involve chemical reagents available from commercial forensic sources. Two of the most common are prepared in acidic solutions—3,3′,5,5′-tetramethybenzidine (TMB) and leucomalachite green—and two are prepared in basic solutions—luminol and Kastle–Meyer (KM). Though rare, in treating a surface to determine whether a particular stain might be blood, it is possible to obtain divergent results: a negative result with one and a positive result with the other. If the testing surface is sufficiently acidic, testing with KM can give a negative result, even though the stain tested is blood. Understanding the chemistry involved is the key to understanding why this occurs. If only the KM reagent was used, the lay investigator might interpret the negative test result as proof that blood was not present, especially if the stain was off-color. An experienced scene investigator, by applying logic and experience, *might* consider the look and location of the stain and ignore the divergent test results and collect the stain anyway.

1.3.1.2.4 Premise 4: Scene Scientists/Investigators Should Never Masquerade as Something They Are Not: Lay Investigators Should Not Attempt to Be Criminalists, Scientists, or Police Investigators without the Appropriate Credentials In addition to sketching, documenting, and securing the scene, investigators dust and fume fingerprints, lift dust prints, enhance bloodstains, recognize bloodstain patterns, and so on. For reasons other than those discussed in Chapter 2 in this volume—bias, these same investigators should not pretend to be criminalists, although they can make presumptive matches based on class characteristics of pattern evidence in order to obtain an idea concerning the minimum number of people who might have been at the scene. Making definitive statements, however, is beyond their expertise.

Born from the O. J. Simpson murder case, crime scene investigators follow scripts and procedures, some written and others based on word-of-mouth, to minimize mistakes. This is not unlike a forensic DNA laboratory that has manuals for standard operating procedures. Using written procedures is certainly a proper method and a mandatory one in order to be accredited, but these can never be substitutes for observational skills, scientific knowledge, and scene investigative skills. The following quote from the Crime Scene Forensics website [9] illustrates the fact that a qualified expert should make the scientific interpretations:

> Crime scene interpretations, crime scene reconstructions and eventual expert opinions, should always be left to qualified experts. In any given case, it will be impossible for a forensic expert to give such an opinion, if the crime scene is not properly documented.
>
> In the everyday context in which the word forensics is used, it implies an advanced degree of training, education, experience, and very expensive equipment.

1.3.1.2.5 Premise 5: Certification Should Be Mandatory—Instead of Voluntary—and Should Be Restructured So That Scientists and Police Scene Investigators Can Be Rigorously Certified: Crime Scene Units Should Be Accredited and Its Individuals Certified A recent publication by the National Research Council [10], the research arm of the National Academies, recommended (Recommendation 7) that all forensic science professionals (this should include crime scene investigators) should be certified. Certification does not guarantee excellence, but it does raise the bar with respect to training, education, and practice. All crime scene investigations, regardless of the crime, deserve the very best investigators because they are the most critical aspect of any investigation. The problem is that there are few consequences for incompetent investigators.

Crime scene investigation is much like live TV of the 1950s. Mistakes or "bloopers" are there for all to see. Unlike live TV, however, mistakes at crime scenes are not recorded, they are not funny, and there is no incentive to "own up" to making them. After all, who will know? Mechanisms to censure incompetence or mistakes made at the scene do not usually exist, and peer review is akin to the fox watching the hen house!

For instance, if an investigator loses an electrostatic lift of a dust print, who will know or chalk it up to something other than investigator error? If an investigator over dusts a fingerprint, smudges important evidence, or chooses an incorrect enhancement technique, who will know? If an investigator misses important, potentially exculpatory, evidence, who will know? And if such a mistake is uncovered, the only censure might be an embarrassing day in court or a scolding by an unhappy prosecutor before trial or by a supervisor, assuming the supervisor learns about the mistake. Rarely does the investigator face dismissal, get placed on administrative leave, or get transferred to another unit. The investigator will likely remain in the crime scene investigation unit, and no one will re-examine his/her past work to check for similar mistakes, unlike what happens when errors occur in a forensic laboratory. This is because few second chances exist at crime scenes.

Certification should be mandatory and layered. The IAI's layered crime scene certification program is a great start, but it is not rigorous enough because it is geared toward non-scientist crime scene investigators. However, an additional certification should be available for more advanced investigators and scene scientists, which includes an in-depth understanding of the scientific concepts used at crime scenes and how and when to apply the science in specific circumstances. In other words, knowing when the technology fails; it should stress the limitations of the science including when it can be used and when it will result in ruined or compromised evidence.

1.3.1.2.6 Premise 6: Investigation of the Crime Scene Is the Most Critical Part of a Competent Forensic Investigation Usually, this premise is where the crime and the participants—the victim(s), the assailant(s), and the scene(s)—coincide in time and space. Here, the seemingly silent, though perhaps loudest, participant in the crime from a scientific perspective, the scene, offers the human participants a physical plant for their activities.

French scientist Edmond Locard is credited with the (perhaps overstated and overused) statement "Every touch leaves a trace" (see Chapter 4). Simply, this means that an exchange of material—physical evidence—large or small, macroscopic or microscopic, takes place among the participants. This is the premise of the forensic scientist who believes that if this evidence can be located and analyzed, a physical connection among the participants can be identified. Hopefully, this will lead to an outcome that helps to solve the crime and benefit society. This is also the mantra of the crime scene investigator who believes that this evidence is present and must be found, packaged, and preserved. Known contemporarily as the Locard Exchange Principle, this idea, this paradigm of criminalists, forensic scientists, and crime scene investigators, is the essential ingredient of forensic science, and, as experience confirms, is well in operation at crime scenes.

By examining the six premises above, one can conclude the following:

- Scientists who have experience as crime scene investigators and are criminalists should play a prominent role in a scene investigation because s/he can apply the scientific method properly, understands the limitations of the science, and will approach the scene without bias.
- Scientists and lay investigators should not work in a vacuum—an absurdly stupid thought. Criminalists are, well, scientists. Investigators are, well, investigators. They have different expertise and should work together. They should be the bookends of the investigation.

The Locard Exchange Principle is where law enforcement investigators and forensic scientists or criminalists are on the same page. It is also where they part company in their approach to scene investigations. Police investigators understand that evidence can be transferred from person to person and from person to scene. Police training, however, is nonscientific and process-based—a mechanism to minimize mistakes in the field. It is, in effect, a check-list approach to scene investigation. The reason is that police are the keepers of the crime scene, the agency in charge, saddled with the responsibility of performing a competent and thorough investigation.

There is no doubt that police investigators are dedicated and take their work seriously. These investigators have real-world experience that is not taught in chemistry or biology laboratories, even in the best universities. While crime scene investigation needs a serious upgrade, criminalists should not replace scene investigators as this would be counterproductive and a tragic loss of experience and expertise. It is, however, abundantly clear that the rapid advance in the application of highly sophisticated technology and the employment of more rigorous scientific procedures at the scene require or will require a scientific presence at the scene.

As discussed above, many forensic scientists look at crime scene investigation as a mindless, nonscientific, and almost rote process, an endeavor that can and should be practiced by those without a scientific background. Their motto seems to be to "keep the lab coats in the lab and put the uniforms in the field." Such a philosophy is idiotic and fallacious, of course. It fails to realize that, without the proper application of science and the scientific method during the investigation, the evidence received by the forensic laboratory represents the bias of the scene investigators and that exculpatory or inculpatory evidence may have been left behind and lost forever.

Is this fantasy? Absolutely not! All diligent forensic scientists bear witness to crime scene units that have overlooked important and probative of evidence. The following are only illustrations from my experience.

- Bloody palm print of the perpetrator that was misinterpreted by investigators and subsequently found by scientists during a reinvestigation of the scene
- A murder weapon left under a sofa found by scientists reinvestigating a scene
- A dead body lying in the basement under a pile of rubbish missed by crime scene investigators
- Failure of police bloodstain pattern analysis (BPA) experts to use the simple concept of significant figures while testifying to impact angles from bloodstains at the scene
- Failure to collect probative bloodstain evidence at the scene

These are hardly isolated events. The question "What level of scientific expertise is necessary for scene investigations?" spawns an argument that ventures far and wide. For the purposes of this discussion, the following new paradigm should be considered:

> Police should control and assume the responsibility for the integrity and security. They should work cooperatively with scene scientists who should lead the scientific aspects of the scene investigation. Together they should search for, preserve, and package evidence and ensure that it reaches the appropriate individuals and/or agencies for subsequent analysis and interpretation by criminalists and other forensic-related professionals. Together, they should interpret scene data as a basis for the logical reconstruction of scene events.

1.4 Definitions: Crime Scene, Forensic Science, Criminalistics, Forensics

1.4.1 Crime Scene

The discussion above touched on several terms without defining them. One, of course, is the crime scene, taken for granted that it does not need a definition. The others are forensics, forensic science, and criminalistics. Everyone understands that crime scenes exist and intuitively know what they are. Still, no one has taken the time to define the crime scene per se. For this and subsequent discussions, it is important to define the scene, if for no other reason than to put it into perspective as a starting point for a forensic investigation. To proceed with this text without defining the crime scene would be inappropriate. Thus, the crime scene might be defined as

> The place where the participants of the crime meet in time and space.

From this definition, it seems the crime scene is *the* place where the event takes place. The definition of participants includes the scene itself. Thus, a typical homicide scene would involve the murderer, the scene, and the victim; a burglary would involve the burglar and the scene. However, there can be more complicated scenes that might not follow such a strict definition. For example, a dumped body scenario would involve several "scenes": the place where the murder took place, which includes the murder scene, the perpetrator, and the victim, the transportation vehicle, and the dump location. In each, there is a place (murder location, transportation vehicle, and dump location), a perpetrator, and a victim. But does the definition consider all circumstances? Is it broad enough, especially considering scenes where the participants do not meet at the same place at the same time?

Consider a bioterrorism event, such as the anthrax mailings of 2001. Here the perpetrator mailed the lethal *Bacillus anthracis* to his victims, which means the perpetrator might not have ever been in the same location as the victim or the death location. The participants were never in the same place at the same time, which makes identifying the "crime scene" elusive: Was it the postal boxes in which the anthrax-laced envelopes were mailed, the place where they (New York, Washington DC) were delivered, or the place where the anthrax was prepared? Could the "scene" be all three? Perhaps, a more comprehensive definition of the crime scene is necessary to account for such scenarios. Thus, the following definition is proposed: *The place where the participants meet in time and space or where the instrument of the crime (biological, explosive, etc.) is prepared and delivered regardless of the route it takes.*

This definition takes into consideration the more complex crime scenes as well as the routine simple ones: The bioterrorism or explosive device event in which the biological agent is prepared at one location and then delivered to another, the homicide resulting from spousal argument, the abducted sexual assault case, or the burglary. The bioterrorism/explosive device scenes that challenge the first definition are covered as are the more common single-location crimes.

1.4.2 Forensic Science

Several texts on forensic science are available, many of which offer superb introductions to the practice of the profession. Kirk's original text *Crime Investigation* updated by Thornton [11] was the first important American treatise. More recent works by Saferstein [12], DeForest et al. [13], Chisum and Turvey [5,14,15], and Inman and Rudin [16–18] are also illustrative. With the exception of the works by Kirk and Thornton [11] and Chisum and Turvey [5,14], these texts use the term "criminalistics" in their title. It seems the terms criminalistics and forensic science are used interchangeably. So, if anything, what is the difference?

To arrive at the answer, working definitions of both terms are necessary. Unfortunately, finding a satisfactory definition for either, especially criminalistics, is elusive. Complicating this is a third term, "forensics" that has recently gained in popularity and usage. Because of popular TV programs, the public probably confuses forensic science with those who practice forensics. Criminalistics, it seems for some, is an alternative for either. These terms and the concepts they embody should be clarified for students, who need to understand what defines each in practice.

Interestingly, scientists who practice forensic science are not confused. A recent *ad hoc* survey conducted by Penn State University forensic science majors as a class assignment found noteworthy results [19]. When asked, "Are you a criminalist?" a forensic drug chemist or forensic biologist would likely reply in the affirmative. Likewise, if the same scientists were asked, "Are you a forensic scientist?" the response would be identical. One of the crime laboratory scientists considered the exercise "academic" because he knew what his job was. Generally, scientists who analyzed physical evidence in crime laboratories considered the terms synonymous. Police officers who practiced forensics knew they were neither a scientist nor a forensic scientist. And while they did not know the difference between a forensic scientist and a criminalist, they understood that they were neither although they were employed in forensics units. So, it seems, the professionals in the field understand there are differences. As DeForest et al. [13] wrote,

> The term forensic science is sometimes used as a synonym for criminalistics. Both terms encompass a diverse range of activities. (p. 4)

What DeForest et al. [13] wrote is certainly true, although they suggest the two terms may not be synonymous, defining forensic science as

> Forensic science is also defined in a broader sense to include forensic medicine, odontology, anthropology, psychiatry, toxicology, questioned documents examination, and firearm and toolmark, and fingerprint examinations, as well as criminalistics. Criminalistics is concerned with the recognition, identification, individualization, and evaluation of physical evidence, using the methods of the natural sciences in matters of legal significance. (p. 4)

Importantly, too, they realize that criminalistics does not necessarily require a criminal association [13]:

> Despite the implications of the name, criminalistics' activities are not limited to criminal matters. They are used in civil law cases and in regulatory matters as well. (p. 4)

So, what are the differences, if any, between forensic science and criminalistics? Bell [20] defines forensic science as

> In the broad sense, the application of the techniques of science to legal matters, both criminal and civil. (p. 142)

Bell's [20] definition is in conflict with the major American professional societies. The American Academy of Forensic Scientists (AAFS) is a group of professionals, physicians, lawyers, scientists, engineers, and so on working under the broad umbrella called the forensic sciences. As DeForest et al. [13] wrote, many in the academy are not scientists. In fact, some of the sections in the academy are populated by nonscientists, jurisprudence and forensic medicine being examples. The underlying impression is that the term forensic science is an amalgam of professions and thus simply an umbrella designation. In this context, the thoughts of DeForest et al. [13] are appropriate. Under this umbrella, criminalistics falls into one section, which leads one to opine that forensic science is not a profession but simply a term encompassing a diverse group of scientific and nonscientific professionals who apply the underlying principles of their profession to understand and elucidate questions of criminal and civil concern. The National Institute of Justice categorizes 12 disciplines in the forensic sciences [21]:

- General toxicology
- Firearms/toolmarks
- Questioned documents
- Trace evidence
- Controlled substances
- Biological/serology screening (including DNA analysis)
- Fire debris/arson analysis
- Impression evidence
- Blood pattern analysis
- Crime scene investigation
- Medicolegal death investigation
- Digital evidence

For arguments sake, the following working definition of forensic science might be considered:

> A discipline comprised of a diverse group of forensic professionals who employ and adhere to the rigorous standards of their respective professions, who consider matters under consideration in order to ascertain the truth of a set of alleged facts, criminal or civil.

1.4.3 Criminalistics

With the above as a working definition of forensic science, we turn to criminalistics. As far as the AAFS is concerned, criminalistics is a subsection, a branch, of forensic science, with each subsection a stand-alone profession. It seems reasonable that a forensic scientist might identify with being a criminalist and vice versa. Inman and Rudin [16] opine that a scientist working in crime laboratories might be "... properly referred to as an analyst, a forensic scientist or a criminalist" (p. 10).

These authors believe a criminalist is also a forensic scientist. However, if one considers this analytically, a forensic scientist is not necessarily a criminalist. In the Inman and Rudin [16] definition, their inclusion of an "analyst" is vague, and in truth, an analyst is not necessarily a scientist; political pundits are often referred to as analysts. A criminalist is *always* a scientist. Legal scholars also seem confused by the terms. Saks and Koehler [22] lump forensic scientists and criminalists together in their discussion of what they term the "individualization fallacy."

The term "criminalistics" was derived from the German *Kriminalistic* and likely coined by Hans Gross in the late 1800s to describe scientists working on physical evidence in police laboratories at about the same time as the term "police science" was popular. The latter stuck, morphing into "forensic science" in the twentieth century, while the former evoked only confusion, sometimes becoming synonymous with a social science or criminology—in the late nineteenth century, scientific criminal investigators were known as criminologists. However, "criminalistics" did not die or morph into criminology. Instead, embracing Kirk's philosophy, as discussed in *Crime Investigation* [11], it became the preferred term to describe scientists in crime laboratories in California and in a few laboratories in the eastern United States. Even today, civil service classifications for crime laboratory scientists are blurred. Some jurisdictions advertise job openings for forensic scientists and others for criminalists, seemingly equating the two, while describing the qualifications of successful candidates similarly.

The California Association of Criminalists (CAC) does not define criminalistics but gives examples of some types of criminalistics [23].

The *Merriam-Webster Online Dictionary* [24] likewise incorrectly defines criminalistics, not directly implying a legal connection but indirectly as only associated with criminal cases: "Application of scientific techniques in collecting and analyzing physical evidence in a criminal case." This definition equally applies to many AAFS subdisciplines.

Forensic text authors believe forensic science and the law are integrally bound. This seems true, perhaps, because most forensic analyses are conducted in crime laboratories by scientists, although neither the results nor the scientist conducting the tests may see the courtroom. The CAC definition, too, implies a court relationship, suggesting that the result of criminalistics analyses "***may*** [emphasis added] be significant in legal cases," implying that a courtroom appearance or relevance is not absolute. In fact, DeForest et al. [13] agree. The reason criminalists are involved in an investigation is to examine physical evidence that may or may not have legal implications (see the discussion in Section 1.5). Thus, if criminalistics is not exactly forensic science, and vice versa, what is it? As Inman and Rudin [16] state,

> This practical definition of criminalistics—the person who analyzes evidence in a crime laboratory may be referred to as an analyst, a forensic scientist or a criminalist—has taken on a life of its own, expanding to encompass a more general philosophy and cognitive framework. (p. 10)

This idea approaches the essence of criminalistics. Criminalistics, then, is not simply a profession made up of scientists who examine evidence by applying the principles of science and using the scientific method. Nor is it simply the science of comparison. In fact, it is as much a science as it is a philosophy, a holistic approach with respect to an analytical strategy with results obtained and interpreted from within the framework of an entire case; that is, piecing together fragments of scientific fact to eventually arrive at testable hypotheses. Without this blend of the holistic and scientific, it is impossible to investigate a crime scene properly, to evaluate correctly an analytical strategy in the laboratory, or to reconstruct the events of a crime. This is true because criminalistics considers all the information in a case, not merely the analysis of a single piece of evidence. As such, it is an amalgam of the principles of science, logic, critical thinking, and experience. From this, perhaps, the following working definition of criminalistics might be proposed:

> A discipline that embraces a holistic philosophy, the principles of science, the scientific method, and logic as it relates to the analysis and interpretation of evidence and its relationship to a set of alleged facts.

As stated above, criminalistics—as a profession—is as much a philosophy as it is a science. Does this differ from forensic science, as an umbrella term? Of course! Can a forensic biologist be a criminalist? Certainly, but only if the forensic biologist's analytical approach is holistic, involves the principles of science, uses the scientific method to arrive at interpretive conclusions, and works within the framework of the incident case. Before considering specific examples, it is important to examine the traits a criminalist must have. Consider Figure 1.1.

Extrapolating, a criminalist, then, is a scientist who, while using the scientific method, considers both the hard and soft facts in a case, for example, examines physical evidence, performs scientific tests, studies autopsy reports and hospital records, investigates crime scenes and/or studies the crime scene investigative reports and photographs, evaluates witness statements, and so on, before arriving at conclusions, preparing reports, or testifying in court. Applying the definition above, it is clear that a scientist working in a crime laboratory is not necessarily a criminalist. Consider the examples below.

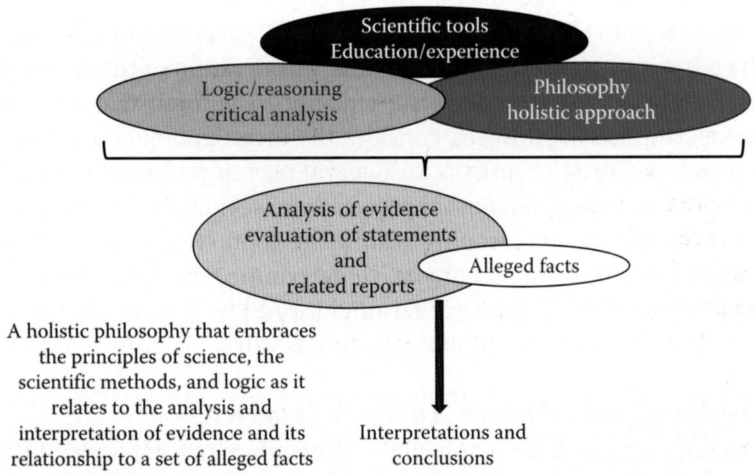

Figure 1.1 Criminalistics: a marriage of science, logic, and philosophy.

1.4.3.1 The Forensic DNA Biologist

The forensic DNA biologist who accepts a cut-out from a scientist (or scene investigator), who first screened the evidence for the presence of, say, semen, and then performs DNA analysis is not a criminalist. In fact, the individual who conducts scientific tests on samples received by the laboratory, though it is evidence, is a scientist. This is not unlike the medical technologist in a clinical laboratory who is given a sample to determine cholesterol blood levels. For the forensic DNA biologist there may be little or no thought or a lot of thought concerning the factual information in the case. However, the scientist who screens the evidence for the presence of biological data may practice criminalistics because, during the examination of that evidence, the origin of the evidence, its relationship to the case history, an evaluation of a stain's location and pattern, and finally a determination of the appropriateness for DNA analysis should be considered. The location of biological and physical evidence might dictate other analyses. Although the resulting DNA profile might be critical for a successful prosecution, generating the DNA profile is not the practice of criminalistics.

1.4.3.2 The Medical Examiner

Another example is the medical examiner. Is routine forensic medicine the practice of criminalistics? The medical examiner performs a scientific (medical) investigation with respect to cause and manner of death and may conduct a medicolegal investigation to ascertain the circumstances of the death. Usually, though, this is where forensic medicine ends. There is little or no consideration of all the facts of the case with respect to reconstructing the events of the crime. However, the medical examiner works in a different world and, while not necessarily approaching death holistically with respect to the what, where, why, and how of all of the evidence, his or her practice of forensic medicine may be more akin to criminalistics than that practiced by either DNA analysts or the forensic street drug chemists (see Section 1.4.3.3).

1.4.3.3 The Forensic Street Drug Chemist

The forensic street drug scientist is a chemist who specializes in the analysis of illicit drugs, usually without considering the holistic aspects of the case. Drug evidence comes to the laboratory and is given to the forensic drug chemist to determine whether there is a violation of the drug statutes. Normally, there is little consideration of the case history because the goal is to determine whether there is a violation. The forensic drug chemist, in this context, is not a criminalist. However, consider the investigation of a clandestine laboratory. Here, the forensic drug chemist is an integral part of the investigation and must be familiar with the case history and must approach the case holistically, using a logical investigative process and inductive reasoning within the context or framework of the case to determine the presence of drug precursors, to determine whether danger exists to other investigators, or to identify substances that might lead investigators to the originators of the clandestine laboratory. In this context, the forensic drug chemist is a criminalist.

1.4.3.4 The Bloodstain Pattern Analysis Expert

What about the BPA expert (see Chapter 14)? Although many self-styled BPA experts are not scientists and, by definition, are not criminalists either, some BPA experts are criminalists. Chapter 14 discusses whether criminalists or forensic scientists who specialize in BPA should perform these interpretations, if BPA has a basis in science. This arena of investigation has attracted a slew of experts who use their years as police investigators, a 40-hour bloodstain pattern course, and an IAI certification to establish "expert" credentials. Experience shows that many of these individuals often over interpret bloodstain pattern evidence, and, although there are likely many reasons, one is that they are not scientists. Some profess applying the scientific method in their work but have little understanding of how to do so properly. There are, however, scientists and perhaps nonscientists who perform BPA investigations and are skilled at interpreting bloodstain evidence. These scientists should understand the underlying science and apply it holistically. They are criminalists.

1.4.3.5 The Crime Scene Investigator

The police crime scene investigator may or may not be a scientist and, therefore, not necessarily a criminalist. These lay investigators—once the scene is secure and the injured cared for—are given the task of locating, collecting, and preserving evidence. A criminalist could be part of this process and should consider the scene from a holistic perspective. Thus, determining whether a scientist is a criminalist is ascertained by how the individual approaches their casework. If the approach is holistic and embraces the logic and reasoning of the scientific method, then the individual is probably a criminalist.

1.4.4 Forensics

Another confusing term is "forensics," coined from a modern adaptation inspired by popular TV programs. The public equates it with forensic science and criminalistics (if they are aware of the term). Those who have heard the term criminalistics often equate it with criminology. Still, the term has become an integral part of the modern forensic lexicon. Clearly, though, those who practice forensics in the TV sense are not scientists and, by definition, are neither criminalists nor forensic scientists. Mostly, they are police investigators who apply forensic science at crime scenes to locate and enhance evidence as part of the scene investigation. The off-scene analysis of pattern evidence, such as fingerprints or footwear impressions, takes place either in the forensics unit of the police department, which is not necessarily a section of the crime laboratory and may not be analyzed by scientists, or in the crime laboratory, where scientists perform the analysis. The term "forensics," as discussed above, applies to lay professional investigators who process crime scenes.

Sometimes, these investigators are also criminalists or forensic scientists. For example, the New Jersey State Police's crime scene unit conducts most of the forensic investigations. However, if the unit needs a forensic biologist, a crime laboratory scientist is dispatched. This person is a scientist (a forensic scientist) who performs a specific service, such as a search for semen or cleaned-up blood. In the context of this example, this person does not approach the scene holistically in the sense that a criminalist would.

Thus, one might define forensics as

> The application of standard investigative techniques to the processing of crime scenes by those police and/or scientific investigators skilled in the art.

Or, perhaps more appropriately, to accommodate the schematic in Figure 1.2, as

> A broad term applied to disciplines whose members are professionals who apply accepted investigative and/or scientific techniques to questions related to the criminal justice system.

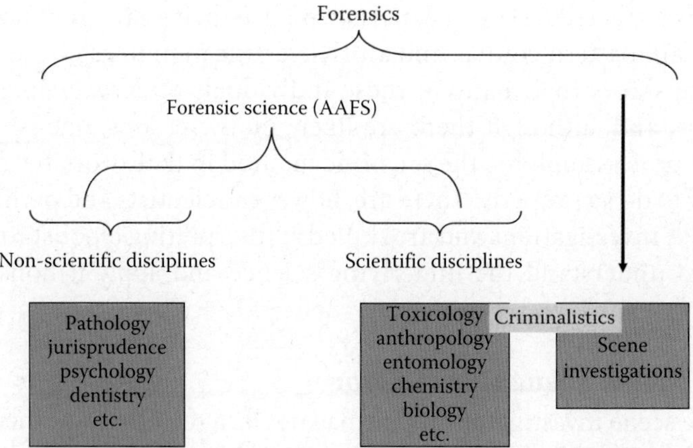

Figure 1.2 Forensics: an umbrella term embracing forensic investigations.

In the evolving lexicon of everyday usage, even this may not suffice, as "forensics" has become an umbrella term that seems to supersede even forensic science, encompassing all forensic activity including forensic science. In this respect, a schematic of forensics is shown in Figure 1.2, which captures the essence of "forensics" as an all-encompassing term embracing the categories and subdisciplines of forensic science as defined by the AAFS. Notice how criminalistics bridges the gap between the scientific and nonscientific aspects of crime scene investigation. Such a placement captures the role that criminalistics does and should play in scene investigation.

1.5 The Concept of Evidence

Students should thoroughly understand the theoretical and conceptual basis of evidence: what it is, how it is manifested, how it occurs, and its dynamics (Chapter 4). The discussion of the concept of evidence is critical because evidence is the fundamental reason why crime scenes are important. Defining evidence from the perspective of crime scene investigation should be a prime consideration for any text dedicated to the topic, and one would assume that authors writing about crime scene investigation and/or crime reconstruction would go to great lengths to include it in their discussion. However, with the exception of seemingly token coverage, the concept of evidence is almost universally considered self-evident.

1.5.1 Perceptions of Evidence

In the context of this text, scientific evidence is typically used to support or reject hypotheses. Notwithstanding input from legal scholars, this section is concerned with how crime scene investigators and forensic scientists/criminalists perceive evidence. Interestingly, the authors of most of the widely read texts on forensic science, crime scene investigation, and crime reconstruction fail to include an in-depth discussion of evidence, choosing instead to offer overly simplistic definitions, if at all. Some examples will suffice. Saferstein [12], for example, offers a single sentence:

> Any object that can establish that a crime has been committed or can provide a link between a crime and its victim or between a crime and its perpetrator. (p. 35)

Other authors discuss evidentiary characteristics without defining them carefully. In the *Encyclopedia of Forensic Science*, Bell [20] defines physical evidence as

> Broadly speaking, any type of tangible evidence as opposed to something such as the testimony of an eyewitness. Physical evidence can be anything, from a microscopic trace of dust to a car, but there are some generalizations that can be made. Physical evidence must be documented, collected, marked, transported, and stored in a manner consistent with its type. (p. 284)

The definition above is inadequate because it uses the word to define itself, which leaves the reader with little understanding of what evidence is. Fisher [25] assumes Bell's [20] position by dividing evidence into broad categories:

> Physical evidence can take any form. It can be as large as a house or as small as a fiber. It can be fleeting as an odor or as obvious as the scene of an explosion. In fact, the variety of physical evidence that may be encountered in an investigation is infinite. (p. 1)

Eckert [26] takes the Saferstein [12] view:

> Physical evidence may be generally defined as any material either in gross or trace quantities that can establish through scientific examination and analysis that a crime has been committed. (p. 33)

Lee et al. [27] consider evidence in the general sense, discussing the different types, their characteristics, and their importance, and offer readers no clear definition of what it is. They portray it differently, much of which seems to come from the definition by DeForest et al. [13]:

> Physical evidence can be classified according to its physical state, by the type of crime, by the nature of the evidence, by its composition, or by the types of question to be resolved *[investigative question not legal question]*, etc. Each of these classifications is useful for offering conceptual ideas and practical means in the crime scene search and any other investigational assistance. (p. 6)*

Lee et al.'s [27] concepts of evidence, although important, do not constitute a definition. But, as they state, what they propose is a classification. However, their thoughts expand on previous ones as it is more holistic.

Geberth's [28] approach is essentially similar to that of Bell [20]. He writes,

> Anything and everything should be considered as evidence. Whether this evidence is physical or testimonial, it must be preserved, noted, and brought to the attention of the investigators. (p. 1)

He also considers evidence transfer:

> There is a principle that in homicide investigation refers to a theoretical exchange between two objects that have been in contact with one another. This theory of transfer or exchange is based on the following facts: 1. the perpetrator will take away traces of the victim and the scene. 2. The victim will retain traces of the perpetrator and may leave traces on the perpetrator. 3. The perpetrator will leave traces at the scene. (p. 2)

* Emphasis added.

After a poignant discussion of "forensics" and "forensic science," Inman and Rudin [17] introduce the concept of evidence, citing what they refer to as a "unifying paradigm of forensic science," "divisible matter," which they believe is a prerequisite to the Locard Exchange Principle (p. 87). They imply that evidence, and any discussion about it, is really a conversation about forensic science, because considering one necessarily implies a discussion about the other. One could take this concept a step further by stating that evidence may well be profession-defining, that is, evidence defines the profession of forensic science. Put another way, without evidence, forensic science cannot exist. Similarly, without forensic science, evidence cannot be interpreted correctly by the trier of fact. Although Inman and Rudin [18] ask: "What is evidence?" they never offer an in-depth discussion except to consider that "the law defines evidence only by its relevance" (p. 103).

This is an interesting statement because it considers the concept of evidence as something that has meaning but only in a legal context, which might not be entirely true. Gardner [29] defines evidence as: ". . . anything that tends to prove or disprove a fact in contention" (pp. 7–8). This concept is similar to that of Lee et al. [27] who address the investigative question as compared with Gardner who addresses the legal question, although this is not entirely clear. Gardner [29] continues, saying that,

> whether evidence is collected or not, . . . it is real, it is tangible, and it cannot be denied. The physical evidence never lies. It is what it is, although we can certainly misinterpret its meaning. . . . The concept of physical evidence involves more than the mere collection of things. Each scene encountered tells a story. Each scene demands consideration of issues evident through observations made by the investigator's senses of sight, smell and touch. Thus a complete consideration of physical evidence demands that investigators be critically observant. (pp. 7–8)

Gardner's [29] concept of evidence, without attribution, parrots that of Kirk and Thornton [11], and places it squarely within his investigational comfort zone, the practicum. To him, evidence is related to the crime scene; however, he does hint at its psychological nature during the scene investigative process by stating "... whether evidence is collected or not ..." (pp. 7–8). He does not consider evidence with respect to its admissibility in legal proceedings, as do Fisher [2,25] and Eckert [26], but from the investigational perspective. In the context of crime reconstruction, Chisum and Turvey [14] refer to their previous work in which they coined the concept of evidence dynamics:

> [Evidence dynamics] ... refers to any influence that adds, changes, relocates, obscures, contaminates, or obliterates physical evidence, regardless of intent. (p. 1)

Chisum and Turvey [15] chose the term because ". . . all forms of physical evidence are at the mercy of environmental change, activity, and time" (p. 161).

These perceptions dovetail nicely with Inman and Rudin's [17] concept of divisible matter (see Chapter 4). Chisum and Turvey [5,14,15], like Gardner [29], refer to the practicum and, by extension, hint at something more than an irrevocable legal obligation.

1.5.2 Divisible Matter and the Transfer of Evidence

In their text, Inman and Rudin [17] introduce the principle of divisible matter. Succinctly, this refers to evidence that splits or fractures after being subjected to some force. Each part of the split evidence goes its separate way, one transferring to the scene and/or its participants, the other remaining with its original source. The importance of this concept is the recognition that evidence has a life that begins in one form and ends in another. Importantly, for this discussion, they consider something as evidence whether or not it is recognized by investigators (see Chapter 4 for a more in-depth discussion).

1.5.3 The Human Mind and the Recognition of Evidence

Consider the question: "Can evidence be defined in terms of the human psyche's ability to recognize it?" Gardner hints at the issue of investigator psychology at the crime scene without mentioning bias specifically. Further consider the questions: "Can an investigator's bias cause a failure to recognize important evidence because it could upset a preconceived notion of what happened?" or "Can an investigator's skill at interpreting evidence at the scene go uncompromised, regardless of bias?"

For example, say an investigator locates an item at the crime scene, perhaps a knife lying a short distance from the deceased at a particularly bloody homicide scene. S/he examines it visually for blood and, seeing none, considers it in the context of his interpretation of other evidence at the scene. S/he decides the knife has no evidentiary value. In the end, s/he does not collect it. At this juncture, the investigator made a decision—the knife did not meet the investigator's personal standard as probative evidence.

A second investigator conducting a second search of the same scene also sees the knife. S/he considers the wounds on the body, evaluates the relative size of the cuts in the victim's shirt, and decides the knife might have probative value and collects it. S/he considers what has been learned from experience, namely, that blood on a knife is not always readily apparent.

Each investigator applied their personal criteria to evaluate the knife as evidence. One noticed that it had no obvious blood and decided not to collect it. The other correlated the knife's blade width to cuts in the victim's clothing and, applying knowledge from experience with "bloody" knives, decided differently.

The medical examiner and the forensic biologist are the arbiters of the knife's true relevancy. The medical examiner examines the knife for consistency with the wounds on the deceased, much like the second investigator, but with a more exacting approach. The forensic biologist determines whether there is blood on the knife. The latent print examiner might be asked to examine the knife for fingerprints. If any of these forensic professionals find something connecting the knife to the crime, the prosecutor might decide the knife has evidential value and incorporate it into a trial strategy.

Critical decisions such as those made at the crime scene to either ignore or recognize something as evidence can determine the success or failure of an investigation. Neither investigator in the knife scenario knows how important the knife might be; others decide that for them. The difference between them reflects their personal biases, experience, incompetence, laziness, and the various human traits that make people different. The same is true of the crime lab scientist, where one forensic biologist may examine the knife visually and decide there is no blood. Another might examine the knife microscopically and then chemically.

In a case from New York City, the Forensic Analysis and Reconstruction Unit (FARU) of the Office of the Chief Medical Examiner of New York City responded as a second responder to a homicide scene. One FARU scientist found a palm print in blood that detectives of the New York Police Department (NYPD) crime scene unit had missed. When confronted with this, the crime scene detectives, presumably not to be embarrassed, indicated their "expert" opinion was that the palm print had insufficient ridge detail in order to make a comparison. The FARU supervisor disagreed. He alerted the sergeant in charge who instructed his team to collect the print. The incident created hard feelings between the two teams. Eventually, the NYPD latent print unit matched the palm print to a suspect, who was eventually convicted. The crime scene detective who opined that the palm print had no evidential value and refused, at first, to collect it believed the palm print was not "evidence" in the case. The FARU investigator, however, thought differently. In his mind, the palm print was probative evidence (Ralph Ristenbatt III, April 2010, pers. comm.).

What was it that convinced one investigator and not the other that there was sufficient ridge detail: experience, bias, laziness, psychological mindset? It was not experience because the crime scene detective had significantly more hands-on experience than the FARU scientist. Anecdotally, the crime scene detective subsequently tried to claim credit for finding the palm print. This was refuted by his colleagues.

Certainly, there are a plethora of reasons explaining why one investigator "finds" evidence while the other "finds" nothing. Still, the discussion illustrates a point. Evidence can be as much psychological as physical.

1.5.4 The Legal Perspective/Connection

Legal evidence differs from scientific evidence. The former requires a legal proceeding to determine whether what has been found is evidence; this is defined by state and federal rules of evidence that govern the admissibility of what has been admitted into a legal proceeding. In this context, evidence is used to prove or disprove a point at issue. In the law, policies require evidence that tends to prove or disprove that an assertion or fact must nevertheless be excluded from consideration based on indications related to reliability or to other concerns. Testimony (oral presentation) and exhibits constitute the main categories of evidence presented at trials or other legal proceedings.

Evidence certainly plays a critical role in legal proceedings as they cannot occur without it. Much like in the examples of forensic science and criminalistics, evidence is the defining entity for legal proceedings. However, can evidence exist outside the boundaries of a legal proceeding or legally related investigation? Fisher and Eckert do not believe so because they define evidence by imbedding it in terms of legal relevance. Fisher [25] defers to the dictionary, which agrees, hinting at the role of evidence in finding the ground truth:

> . . . something submitted to a competent tribunal as a means of ascertaining the truth of any alleged matter of fact under investigation before it. (p. 1)

Eckert [26] suggests that evidence exists only in the legal setting:

> Thus physical evidence is always derivative of some sort of testimony. (p. 72)

After reading these perspectives, one is left with the impression that evidence is really only derivative of some sort of testimony. Is this true? The ultimate question is: "When does something (other than testimony) become evidence?" When an investigator perceives it as evidence, when it is collected at the scene or when it is introduced into a legal proceeding? Certainly, the crime scene investigator has an opinion because one purpose of being at the scene is to search for, collect, and package evidence. A forensic scientist testifies, that is, offers opinion testimony or testimonial evidence, about evidence examined in the laboratory. On the witness stand, the crime scene investigator testifies about the chain of custody of evidence collected at the crime scene before it is "admitted into the legal proceeding." From a legal perspective, then, evidence begins life in a legal proceeding. A forensic scientist testifies about the scientific analysis of something that has been introduced as evidence, although it had been collected as evidence with the expectation that it *might* be used in a legal setting. An item offered as evidence and, subsequently, admitted by the court is considered admissible evidence. In a sense, then, we are differentiating that which is "admissible" from that which is outside the legal setting. Although from a legal perspective, evidence begins life in a legal proceeding. From a forensic investigative perspective, it begins life when it is *perceived* as evidence by the investigator.

Evidence can probably wear two defining hats—one when it is perceived as evidence during the scene investigation and the other when it is admitted into a legal proceeding. The investigator believes it is evidence because it might have relevance for the legal proceeding, where it becomes admissible evidence. After being admitted, the importance of the evidence rises because then it is recognized by the trier of fact. This has a different feel than when it was still lying in a corner at the crime scene waiting for an investigator to "see" it as evidence. However, once the scene investigator does see the evidence, and collects it, it begins its journey up the ladder of evidentiary importance. In fact, by assigning two defining roles for evidence, its definition clarifies.

Once admitted, the evidence reaches its pinnacle of importance. It is still that same physical, tangible something found in a corner at some bloody crime scene, but it has now met the appropriate legal standards applied to admissible evidence. Having passed the Locard Exchange Principle and divisible matter tests, the investigator's recognition test, the trial strategist's test, and the admissibility standard, it is officially evidence.

1.5.5 Defining Evidence

Many terms are applied to evidence: scientific, physical, testimonial, relevant, circumstantial, direct and indirect, exculpatory or inculpatory, probative, and admissible. Each has a specific, although different, interpretation depending on who uses which descriptive adjective. Crime scene scientists/investigators are concerned with locating physical evidence at the scene and preserving it for future admissibility into a legal proceeding. The forensic scientist is concerned mostly with physical evidence and developing relevancy through scientific analysis. Attorneys are concerned with winning or losing a case and thus consider evidence as direct or indirect (circumstantial), probative or not, exculpatory or inculpatory, and admissible or not. The courts are concerned with finding the truth of allegations, the point at issue, so their concern is with relevancy and admissibility as defined by the law. Interestingly, with the sole exception of "physical," each of the adjectives listed above describes evidence in functional terms. Physical, however, does not have a function. It simply exists.

Perhaps we should examine evidence more from a conceptual basis and try to unite these seemingly diverse concepts with the understanding that considering evidence as something solely tangible is superficial. This ignores the fact that evidence must be recognized, as discussed above, and the admissibility context, which is its storytelling role (from Gardner's [29] perspective) or its role to question and answer (from Fisher's [25] perspective).

In its most obvious form, evidence may not be just something tangible. It is, in fact, the vehicle used to identify the ground truth of an issue (Fisher-like). Isn't this how jurors see it? More appropriately, though, it should encompass the universality of the Locard Exchange Principle, the concept of divisible matter, the reality of evidence dynamics, the human psychological condition, and legal admissibility.

Returning to the crime scene, the genesis of physical evidence occurs where the Locard Exchange Principle and the principle of divisible matter are the primary factors. From an investigative perspective, evidence is in the mind of the investigator, which does not at all imply something that does not exist or is not tangible such as a vaporous thought. It means that the human mind perceived it for what it was. That is what "remains." If an analyst or investigator perceives something as unimportant, even if documented correctly, its value at ascertaining the ground truth is useless, and it ceases to be evidence until another's perception revives it.

Consider two friends who are arguing about some fact, perhaps the number of people who drive a red Corvette. One states that 4 out of every 10 Corvette drivers drive a red Corvette. The other challenges the statement saying, "Show me your evidence?" Clearly, there is no court issue here, only the concept that evidence can solve the argument. What about evidence that is more of a thought or a hypothesis? Consider the criminalist who attempts to reconstruct the events of a crime by examining the appropriate documentation? Much of what is examined is tangible, but the thought process is not. In fact, it might be vaporous. However, in the court, these thoughts become opinions, which can be admissible.

Considering the discussion above, the following is a working definition of evidence derived solely for this text:

> Anything associated with a crime scene, incident or argument; whether or not it has been collected, described, photographed, analyzed scientifically, or reasoned about and which might be introduced into a legal proceeding in order to ascertain the truth of an issue.

1.6 Instruction: A Philosophy

This text is geared toward junior through senior undergraduate science students and entry-level forensic science graduate students. It is also designed as a first course in a forensic science curriculum because the crime scene is where crimes take place. The scene is also where the formal education of forensic scientists and scene investigators should begin, because that is where the concept of physical evidence and its importance makes the most sense, initially. This text is also appropriate for practicing professionals who have the requisite scientific and or investigative backgrounds. It introduces students to the concept of criminalistics—applying thoughtful science to crime scene investigation through the proper application of the scientific method. It is the quintessential entry-level course of study, marrying the principles of forensic science and crime scene investigation.

After completing a guided course of instruction, students will acquire an understanding and appreciation of the role forensic science plays in crime scene investigations. The workshops will provide hands-on experience so that students can bridge the gap between the academic and the practicum. They will learn how the scientific method leads to a logically organized scene investigation and to recognizing physical evidence. They will learn the techniques used at scenes to enhance evidence, collect it, and preserve it. They will learn how to screen data and decide how to use it to reconstruct the events of the crime. This text is the underlying basis of a course that is a logical gateway to more rigorous courses in criminalistics, forensic chemistry, and forensic biology.

College-level courses designed to train police officers and crime scene investigators in the way this text is structured do not exist. Although it is geared to college-level and graduate students studying science, which means they should already have a basic understanding of the scientific method, it is also appropriate for students studying criminal justice who are headed toward law enforcement. These students will benefit by developing logical investigative skills consistent with the tenets inherent in the scientific method. Law enforcement needs entry-level personnel trained in the logic that science and the "method" offers.

The learning principle for forensic science students, investigator trainees, and criminal justice students is similar. Experience has shown that when students in criminal justice and forensic science programs enroll for the same course where the instruction is geared toward the science students, the former students are faced with concepts they do not understand because they do not have the requisite scientific background. However, they traditionally perform well and have little difficulty understanding the concepts, the hands-on aspects, and the process of investigating mock scene scenarios.

Crime scene investigation, like all forensic practice, is both intellectual and vocational. This text reinforces both. The learning process is adapted from the military model: tell them what they need to know, tell them again, and then tell them a third time. The mechanism of each "telling" is the key. In this text, each is in a different format. For example, didactic instruction—formal lectures—is balanced with a triple dose of hands-on, in-class problem-solving discussions, homework, examinations, and mock scene experience.

1.6.1 Structure of the Instruction

As all instructors understand, there are realities to teaching and learning.

- Students react to grades and accountability. It helps if they also enjoy the learning process, which is almost guaranteed in a crime scene investigation course. Still, they are students and they must balance one course against another. If they are doing well in one course and poorly in another, they typically spend more time on the more difficult course. This hinders some instructional activity in the other course, especially one that has a team concept because other members of the team tend to suffer.
- Most students work only when they have to, typically at the last possible moment.
- Instructive activities that result in the highest comprehension and retention should be used in teaching. The following were used as a guide in putting together the course. Clearly, the pontificating professor standing in front of a classroom is not how students learn.
  - 5% listening to lectures
  - 10% reading information
  - 20% from audiovisual materials
  - 30% when a demonstration is added
  - 50% when discussing facts in groups
  - 75% from practicing by doing
  - 90% by teaching others at the same time they are learning

Most college-level instructors lecture from Powerpoint™ slides made available to students through online services. Unfortunately, these slides become a student's crutch. Taking notes has become a historical exercise, one performed by only the best students although not extensively; students perceive that the Powerpoint™ slides reflect the entire content of the course, forgetting that they really are only outlines of topics that must be supplemented by reading and note-taking. Powerpoints are not the meat and potatoes of the course and are not necessarily the basis of examination questions.

The text is divided into definable parts. Part I covers material related to the general scene investigation process, covering, as in this chapter, definitions and philosophy as well as hands-on considerations. Chapter 2 has a discussion of the scientific method, bias, and logic and how reasoning and the proper application of the scientific method is the only way to minimize bias in an investigation. Chapter 3 tackles the concept of scene management and presents the role the scientific method plays in managing the scene investigation. Chapter 4 covers the important concept of how evidence originates through a discussion of the Locard Exchange Principle and the principle of divisible matter. Chapter 5 considers the scene search and the intellectual ingredients necessary for successfully finding probative evidence.

Part II has several chapters devoted to preserving the crime scene. Chapter 6 covers the basics of photography as they relate to forensic investigations. It also considers why the forensic photographer is an integral part of an active scene investigation. Chapter 7 defines the role sketching plays in archiving the scene, while Chapter 8 considers the scene video and the topic video as complements to photography and sketching to competently archive the crime scene. Three workshops, with exercises, conclude Part II, two devoted to digital forensic photography and one to sketching.

Part III begins the discussion of various types of impression/pattern evidence most commonly found at crime scenes. Chapters 9 and 10 consider fingerprints. Chapter 9 presents the intellectual ingredients necessary to successfully find and develop fingerprints at crime scenes. Chapter 10 considers the practical on-scene issues necessary as well as a general discussion of impression evidence in blood. After Chapter 10, two workshops provide hands-on experience designed to help students learn fingerprinting methods for porous and nonporous surfaces. Chapters 11 and 12 consider two commonly occurring types of impression evidence, footwear impressions and tire track impressions, respectively. After Chapter 12, one workshop guides students through impression casting and lifting, and enhancing footwear impressions.

Part IV, The Biological Crime Scene, considers the various types of biological evidence found at scenes. Chapter 13 discusses biological evidence as the multitasking category of evidence, its forensic relevance, how to recognize, collect, and preserve it. Chapter 14 continues with a discussion of bloodstain patterns as evidence. After Chapter 15, microbial forensics, two workshops with exercises, introduce students to the chemical and physical methods for finding biological evidence at the scene. The second workshop presents the basics of how blood leaves the human body and the patterns it forms. Chapter 16 is an introduction to the value of insects (bugs) at the crime scene and how they relate to ascertaining the postmortem interval.

Part V considers other types of evidence. Chapter 17 is a discussion of the micro scene, and can be considered an extension of Chapter 4, The Origin of Evidence. After Chapter 17, a workshop presents exercises that demonstrate the Locard Exchange Principle. The exercises also introduce students to the methods used to collect trace: picking, taping, and vacuuming. Chapter 18 considers glass as another type of multitasking evidence. The ensuing workshop guides students through a window-breaking exercise.

Part VI covers shooting incident scenes. Chapter 19 considers shooting scenes, bullets, ricochet, and bullet holes as examples of the Locard Exchange Principle. It discusses how to determine bullet paths, identify bullet wipe, test for gunshot residue (GSR), and understand how and why bullets ricochet. The ensuing workshop allows students to determine the angular components of the bullet path: vertical and azimuth. Chapter 20 focuses on vehicles involved in shooting scenes.

Part VII, Miscellaneous, discusses three separate topics: Chapter 21 discusses fire scenes, Chapter 22 considers quality assurance issues, and Chapter 23 presents methods for collecting and preserving various evidence types not necessarily covered in other chapters.

References

1. L. Lofland. *The Graveyard Shift*. Available at: http://www.leelofland.com/wordpress/?p = 6646 (accessed January 13, 2011).
2. B. A. J. Fisher. 2004. Chapter 3: The crime scene investigator. In: *Techniques of Crime Scene Investigation*, 7th edn. Boca Raton, FL: CRC Press, p. 48.
3. A. Dunlap. 1931. Science versus practical common sense in crime detection. *The American Journal of Police Science*, 2(4):323.
4. R. M. Gardner and T. Bevel. 2007. Commentary: crime reconstruction. *Journal of Forensic Identification*, 57(6):800.
5. W. J. Chisum and B. E. Turvey. 2007. Practice standards for the reconstruction of crime. In: W. J. Chisum and B. E. Turvey (eds), *Crime Reconstruction*. New York, NY: Elsevier Academic Press, p. 118.
6. *Merriam-Webster Online Dictionary*. Paradigm. Available at: http://www.merriam-webster.com/dictionary/paradigm (accessed February 28, 2011).
7. J. Reno. 2000. *Crime Scene Investigation: A Guide for Law Enforcement. Research Report.* Washington, DC: U.S. Department of Justice, Office of Justice Programs, p. iii.
8. J. I. Thornton. 2007. Chapter 2. Crime reconstruction—ethos and ethics. In: W. J. Chisum and B. E. Turvey (eds), *Crime Reconstruction*. New York, NY: Elsevier Academic Press, p. 39.
9. T. Martin. 2008. *Crime Scene Forensics Handbook: A Field Guide for the First Responder*, Crime Scene Technician Edition. Flushing, NY: Looseleaf Law Publications, Inc. Available at: Crime Scene Forensics, LLC, New York; www.crimescene-forensics.com.
10. Committee on Identifying the Needs of the Forensic Science Community, Committee on Science, Technology and Law Policy and Global Affairs, Committee on Applied and Theoretical Statistics, Division on Engineering and Physical Sciences, National Research Council of the National Academies. 2009. Summary. In: *Strengthening Forensic Science in the United States: A Path Forward*. Washington, DC: The National Academies Press, p. 25.
11. P. L. Kirk and J. I. Thornton. 1974. *Crime Investigation*, 2nd edn. New York, NY: John Wiley and Sons.
12. R. Saferstein. 2004. *Criminalistics: An Introduction to Forensic Science*, 8th edn. Upper Saddle River, NJ: Pearson, p. 35.
13. P. DeForest, R. Gaensslen, and H. C. Lee. 1983. *Forensic Science: An Introduction to Criminalistics*. New York, NY: McGraw Hill p. 9.
14. W. J. Chisum and B. E. Turvey. 2000. Evidence dynamics: Locard's exchange principle and crime reconstruction. *Journal of Behavioral Profiling*, 1:1–15.
15. W. J. Chisum and B. E. Turvey. 2007. Evidence dynamics. In: W. J. Chisum and B. E. Turvey (eds), *Crime Reconstruction*. New York, NY: Elsevier Academic Press, p. 161.

16. K. Inman and N. Rudin. 2000. Introduction. In: *The Principles and Practice of Criminalistics: The Profession of Forensic Science*. Boca Raton, FL: CRC Press, p. 10.
17. K. Inman and N. Rudin. 2000. Chapter 4: The origin of evidence—Divisible matter and transfer. In: *The Principles and Practice of Criminalistics: The Profession of Forensic Science*. Boca Raton, FL: CRC Press, pp. 87–99.
18. K. Inman and N. Rudin. 2000. Chapter 5: The recognition of physical evidence. In: *The Principles and Practice of Criminalistics: The Profession of Forensic Science*. Boca Raton, FL: CRC Press, p. 103.
19. R. C. Shaler. 2007. Class assignment for senior and graduate students in the Forensic Science Program at Penn State University. Unpublished results. University Park, PA: Penn State University.
20. S. Bell. 2008. *Encyclopedia of Forensic Science*, 2nd edn. New York, NY: Facts on File Science Library, pp. 142, 284.
21. National Institute of Justice. 2006. Status and needs of forensic science service providers: a report to Congress. Available at: http://www.ojp.usdoj.gov/nij/pubs-sum/213420.htm (accessed August 28, 2007).
22. M. J. Saks and J. J. Koehler. 2008. The individualization fallacy in forensic science evidence. *Vanderbilt Law Review*, 61:199–220.
23. California Association of Criminalists. Criminalistics Information. Available at: http://www.cacnews.org/membership/criminalistics.html (accessed July 26, 2011).
24. *Merriam-Webster Online Dictionary*. Criminalistics. Available at: http://www.merriam-webster.com/dictionary/criminalistics (accessed September 27, 2010).
25. B. A. J. Fisher. 2004. Introduction. In: *Techniques of Crime Scene Investigation*, 7th edn. Boca Raton, FL: CRC Press, p. 1.
26. W. Eckert. 1997. *Introduction to Forensic Science*, 2nd edn. Boca Raton, FL: CRC Press, pp. 33, 72.
27. H. C. Lee, T. Palmback, and M. T. Miller. 2005. *Henry Lee's Crime Scene Handbook*. San Diego: Elsevier Academic Press, p. 6.
28. V. Geberth. 2006. *Practical Homicide Investigation: Tactics, Procedures, and Forensic Techniques*, 4th edn. Boca Raton, FL: CRC Press, pp. 1, 2.
29. R. M. Gardner. 2005. *Practical Crime Scene Processing and Investigation*. Boca Raton, FL: CRC Press, p. 7–8.

The Scientific Method, Bias, and Reasoning

2

Truth is sought for its own sake. And those who are engaged upon the quest for anything for its own sake are not interested in other things. Finding the truth is difficult, and the road to it is rough.*

2.1 Introduction

The hallmark of any successful crime scene investigation is a team effort whose director, like the maestro of an orchestra, is its leader. How well the team performs is related to how well its leader uses the scientific method, thinks critically and creatively, opens lines of communication with subordinates, and applies inductive, deductive, and abductive logic. If done properly the culture of science wraps its arms around the team and protects it from making critical mistakes, introducing subjectivity, and conducting a biased investigation. This is true because science itself is self-correcting. Mistakes, when found, are corrected, and biases, through team effort and the application of the scientific method, are avoided. As Chisum and Turvey [2] wrote,

> Evidence interpretation is a complex process, and the less one understands about the nature of physical evidence, the principles of forensic science, analytical logic, and the scientific method, the simpler crime reconstruction may seem. (p. 92)

When asked how the crime was solved or the most probative evidence located, no crime scene investigator would consciously say,

- "I used the scientific method to solve this crime."
- "The scientific method pin-pointed the most important evidence at that scene."
- "My creative employment of induction and deduction led me to the killer."
- "I ensured that I had an open line of communication with my subordinates."

That is not how science and scene investigation work. Most if not all crime scene investigators never consciously consider their cognitive thoughts, that is, the reasoning process they employ after or during the investigation. It becomes and should be second nature. Their approach is based on education, intuition, training, and experience. The scene scientist's approach is different, however, because it is based on deductive and inductive reasoning buttressed by education, intuition, training, and experience.

Chapter 1 suggested that crime scene investigation is not simply the application of science but actually a complex scientific endeavor. As such, it is, like all science, a step-wise

* Stated by Alhazen (Ibn Al-Haytham) in his *Critique of Ptolemy*, translated by S. Pines, *Actes X Congrès internationale d'histoire des sciences*, Vol. I. Ithaca, 1962, as quoted in Reference [1].

process of knowledge and information-building about understanding what happened, who might have done it, and what probative evidence is available. It is also a problem-solving exercise. For example, why did this happen and in what sequence? Obtaining as precise an answer as possible illustrates why crime scene investigation is particularly suited to the application of the scientific method. If we delve further into the reasons, the explanation of why this is true is plainly clear. Scientists attempt to explain observations through a series of constantly tested and revised hypotheses, the ultimate feedback mechanism, using what is called the scientific method. And so should scene scientists/investigators.

2.2 The Scientific Method: Scene Scientists and Scene Investigators

Authors of science text books nearly invariably include a discussion of the scientific method, by typically listing the so-called steps inherent in the method, often offering an appropriate diagram spiced with an example or two. Over the years, there have been scholarly articles on the subject. As Cohen says [3],

> According to the currently fashionable view, it is of the very essence of the scientific method to distrust all reason to rely on the facts only. The motto, "Don't think; find out," often embodies this attitude. The scientific method is supposed to begin by banishing all preconceptions or anticipations of nature. In the first positive stage it simply collects facts; in the second, it classifies them; then it lets the facts themselves suggest a working hypothesis to explain them. It is only in the last stage, in the testing or verifying of hypotheses (so as to transform them into established laws) that the rational deduction of consequences plays any part. Such deduction, it is maintained, brings us no new information. It only makes explicit what experience has already put into our premises. (p. 76)

Most scientific texts list five to seven steps inherent in the scientific method. Edmund lists eleven on his Web site [4]. While his is one person's opinion, students of science will recognize the following widely accepted list, which tracks Cohen's explanation quoted above.

- Observe a phenomenon that has no good explanation (potential evidence, which we label as observable phenomena)
- Formulate a hypothesis
- Design an experiment(s) to test the hypothesis
- Perform the experiment(s)
- Accept, reject, or modify the hypothesis

By itself, this list offers little insight to its application to a specific scene investigation. To illustrate, consider an example of a homicide scene examined applying the scientific method. The following are the gross observations—the macroscene (Chapter 4). The microscene is not considered in this discussion.

- A deceased male is lying face up on the floor in his bedroom, the victim of a single stab wound to the chest.
- He has an incised wound (a deep cut) on his right forefinger.
- His shirt, which is torn, has drip pattern in blood on the chest.
- The front door is open.

- The living room window is open.
- A sneaker print in dust is on the floor under the window.
- Dried droplets—not blood—mar some of the sneaker print detail.
- A dry but diluted drop of blood is in the kitchen sink.
- A crumpled paper towel with dried blood sits on the kitchen sink.
- A shattered drinking glass is on the kitchen floor near the sink.
- A wicked storm with high winds passed through the town several hours earlier.

All scenes have multiple gross observable phenomena (macroscene elements), much of which has no immediate, simple, reasonable, or seemingly logical explanation. Additionally, each might have many explanations of which only one rests in the ground truth. Frustratingly, most explanations will never be known with absolute certainty because, other than the participants of the crime, investigators were not present when the event took place. Thus, the essence of all scene investigations is sorting fact from fiction, identifying what is crime-related and eliminating what is not.

One can generalize the observable phenomena and place them into arguable categories. It would be instructive for novice investigators and students to place these observations into usable categories such as

- People living their lives
- Activity of the crime that spawned the investigation
- Activity or events unrelated to neither of the above
- Unknown at this time

All observable scene phenomena must be interpreted correctly, that is, put into a category correctly, or risk being misinterpreted. If misinterpreted, the result can be a botched investigation leading to the arrest and conviction of an innocent person. Scene investigators use their experience and intuition to understand these macroscene elements. Certainly, using experience to interpret new phenomena is a normal extension of an engaged mind, and it is reasonable. It is, however, the seed of experience-based bias, which is the natural consequence of living and working in the real world. Bias happens subconsciously and, while not necessarily bad if controlled, it can lead the scene scientist/investigator down an incorrect interpretive path. Called the "I've seen it a million times" syndrome, everyone pigeonholes their experiences and past scene observable elements they use to interpret scene elements in each new setting. The result is a mixture of correct and incorrect interpretations of what the scene is trying to tell them.

What differentiates scene investigators from scene scientists is how they use their experience and intuition to arrive at final interpretations or conclusions. Scene investigators trust their experience and draw final conclusions based on their observations over time. This seems reasonable but, in truth, is a myopic approach because the process automatically arrests the mental exercise once they have "decided" what happened. The scene scientist, however, never offers a "final" interpretation or conclusion until all hypotheses have been "tested" and alternative explanations exhausted. The word "final" is in quotes because even the final conclusion offered can change if new evidence is located. It is this "testing" of alternate explanations that separates scene investigators from scene scientists. Table 2.1 illustrates the first thought processes leading to hypotheses based on observable phenomena at the scene.

Table 2.1 First Hypotheses Based on Scene Observations

Gross Observable Phenomena	Initial Interpretation (*Hypothesis)*
Deceased on floor with single stab wound to chest	Deceased stabbed by assailant and died quickly
Deep incised wound to right forefinger	Defensive wound—deceased knew what was happening and was fighting for his life
Drip pattern of dried blood on the shirt of the deceased	Result of stab wound or blood dripping from knife
Storm passed through hours earlier	No immediate causal relationship to crime
Living room window is open	Perpetrator entered the house through window
Dry residue sneaker print on floor under window	Perpetrator's sneaker print
Dried droplets mar sneaker pattern	Window was open before storm
Front door open	Perpetrator's exit route
Dried, diluted drop of blood in kitchen sink	Perpetrator was injured and went to sink to wash after committing crime
Paper towel with dried blood on kitchen sink	Perpetrator used towel to clean and dry wound
Shattered drinking glass on kitchen floor	Altercation began in the kitchen with perpetrator struggling with deceased here

These explanations of observable phenomena seem reasonable and they may be all the explanation needed. However, a scene scientist considers these as testable hypotheses, each having an alternative explanation. Thus, this is the first round of observational explanations, some of which might be correct and others incorrect. If this is as far as an investigator goes, which is essentially jumping to conclusions without considering reasonable alternatives, the scene is open to missing important probative evidence.

The next step requires the formulation of alternative hypotheses, which is the essence of the scientific method. Returning to the homicide scenario, the scene scientist formulates alternative scenarios. The result is shown in Table 2.2, an expansion of Table 2.1. Here, the third column offers alternative explanations of the macroscene observation scenarios, different from those in the first column and also perhaps more reasonable.

These alternative explanations also have merit but, regardless, the ground truth remains unknown. In fact, it might lie somewhere between the two hypotheses. Or, a third as yet unconsidered alternative might be closer to what actually happened. At this point, these are competing hypotheses. New evidence could trigger a third set of hypotheses or eliminate one of the original two. The point is that the best fact-fit can be only determined through experimentation, step 3 of the scientific method. For students and novice investigators, the concept of experimentation is often frightening because it forces them into unknown intellectual territory. Experimentation, however, does not necessarily require or necessarily imply actual laboratory experiments, although that is certainly a possibility. From a crime scene perspective, some experimentation can be done at the scene, which might result in a change of one of the hypotheses or even create new ones. Laboratory testing might be done on evidence collected and transported to the forensic laboratory. If laboratory experimentation is necessary, the best interpretation of what happened and the sequence of events would be put on hold.

Table 2.3 proposes possible experiments (see the last column), not all of which are laboratory-based. The idea is not to design a way to prove the original or alternative hypotheses but to disprove them. In fact, the scientific method requires that the experiment's intended design is to disprove projected hypotheses. This not-so-subtle fact is lost

Table 2.2 Alternative Scenarios Based on Observable Phenomena at the Scene

Gross Observable Phenomena	Initial Hypothesis	Alternative Hypothesis
Deceased on floor with single stab wound to chest	Deceased stabbed by assailant and died quickly	Deceased fell on knife and died quickly
Deep incised wound to right forefinger	Defensive wound—deceased knew what was happening and was fighting for his life	Deceased cut finger picking up shards of glass from floor
Drip pattern of dried blood on the shirt of the deceased	Result of stab wound or blood dripping from knife	Result of blood dripping from cut finger
Storm passed through hours earlier	No immediate causal relationship to crime	Storm blew open front door
Living room window is open	Perpetrator entered the house through window	Deceased opened window to cool house before crime took place
Dry residue sneaker print on floor under window	Perpetrator's sneaker print	Victim's sneaker print
Dried droplets mar sneaker pattern	Window was open before storm	Window was open before storm. Droplets might have happened during storm
Front door open	Perpetrator's exit route	Blown open by storm
Dried, diluted drop of blood in kitchen sink	Perpetrator was injured and went to sink to wash after committing crime	Deceased tried to clean wound after cutting finger on glass shards
Paper towel with dried blood on kitchen sink	Perpetrator used towel to clean and dry wound	Deceased tried to stop bleeding with paper towel
Shattered drinking glass on kitchen floor	Altercation began in the kitchen with perpetrator struggling with deceased here	Deceased dropped glass when storm blew open front door

on most lay investigators [3]. It is also expected that these experiments might create new hypotheses, which trigger more testing.

After all data have been analyzed, hypotheses tested and retested, a point will be reached when no more testing seems reasonable or warranted. Then, a truth of some sort will emerge. This truth may not represent the actual ground truth, but will be closer than if the process had been stopped after the first set of hypotheses. The process may have led to new evidence that should have elicited additional questions and perhaps new hypotheses.

In the example above, what would the investigative result have been if the investigator solely relied on the initial interpretation of the events? Possibly, the evidence collected and subsequently analyzed by a forensic laboratory would have represented that investigator's experience-based bias, which would be myopic in scope. By considering all alternative scenarios, the scene scientist/investigator permits the self-correcting mechanism inherent in the scientific method to dictate the flow of the investigation and the evidence discovery process.

This is why the scientific method, applied correctly, is the only way to eliminate bias in an arena where there are few, if any, checks and balances. By its very nature, the scientific method conducts those checks and balances through the hypothesis, experimentation, and feedback process. For science students, this process makes sense. For novice and many

Table 2.3 Proposed Experiments to Disprove Advanced Hypotheses

Gross Observable Phenomena	Initial Hypothesis	Alternative Hypothesis	Possible Experiments
Deceased on floor with single stab wound to chest	Deceased stabbed by assailant and died quickly	Deceased fell on knife and died quickly	• Examine report of the medical examiner • Look for other signs of struggle • Check fingerprints
Deep incised wound to right forefinger	Defensive wound—deceased knew what was happening	Deceased cut finger picking up shards of glass from floor	• Examine medical examiner's report • Look for shards of glass with blood • DNA analysis of blood
Drip pattern of dried blood on the shirt of the deceased	Result of stab wound or blood dripping from knife	Result of blood dripping from cut finger	• Interpretation of drip pattern • DNA testing on blood
Storm passed through hours earlier	No immediate causal relationship to crime	Storm blew open front door	See entry "Front door open" below
Living room window is open	Perpetrator entered the house through window	Deceased opened window to cool house before crime took place	• Check for pry marks • Check fingerprints not matching deceased • Check victim/other footprints on ground
Dry residue sneaker print on floor under window	Perpetrator's sneaker print	Victim's sneaker print	Check sneaker of victim
Dried droplets mar sneaker pattern	Window was open before storm	Window was open before storm. Droplets might have happened during storm if storm blew open window	Check storm wind direction
Front door open	Perpetrator's exit route	Blown open by storm	• Check storm wind direction • Check jimmied or broken locks • Check impact area where door should have hit wall
Dried, diluted drop of blood in kitchen sink	Perpetrator was injured and went to sink to wash after committing crime	Deceased tried to clean wound after cutting finger on glass shards	DNA analysis of blood
Paper towel with dried blood on kitchen sink	Perpetrator used towel to clean and dry wound	Deceased tried to stop bleeding with paper towel	• Bloodstain pattern • DNA of blood
Shattered drinking glass on kitchen floor	Altercation began in the kitchen with perpetrator struggling with deceased here	Deceased dropped glass when storm blew open front door	• Check glass for blood • Check for crushed shards on shoe of deceased

experienced investigators, this is a foreign concept. For scene investigators as opposed to scene scientists, the approach is not necessarily satisfying because it offers only a sketchy roadmap of how to conduct a competent scene investigation. This is the reality of the scientific method. Scientific processes are complex. Scene investigations, too, are complex and without question a scientific endeavor. Using a cut-and-dried method for conducting a scene investigation is ludicrous.

The above homicide example was intentionally simplistic because it was intended to illustrate the scientific thought process. In the current paradigm of crime scene investigation (Chapter 1), police investigators apply scientific methods at crime scenes without using the scientific thought process. Like researchers, scene scientists create new understanding because they use what is known to uncover the truth of the unknown, that is, the truth underlying alleged facts. Researchers question the unknown and use the scientific method to uncover more basic truths. Despite these disparate missions, scene scientists and basic researchers use a common approach to accomplish their goals.

The foregoing discussion makes it seem as though scene scientists and scene investigators exist on different planets. Nothing could be further from the truth. The discussion is not meant to imply that scene scientists and police investigators do not and cannot play on the same field, even if their individual roles and missions are decidedly different. In fact, they are complementary. At the crime scene, the scene scientist conducts the business of science distinct from but complimentary to the investigative role of the police scene investigator. The scientific mind places a premium on precision, objectivity, repeatability, experimentation, uncertainty management, peer review, and experience in order to arrive at reliable interpretations of clues left at the scene because these methods have a history of successfully relating information while correcting misunderstandings.

The scene scientists' approach is radically different from that of the scene investigator, whose mission is to find and arrest the perpetrator. The scene scientist has no mission or allegiance except to the facts. The scene investigator searches for facts (evidence) to fit a scenario or an "idea" of what happened based on experience or on information relayed by messengers—witnesses, other officers, and so on. Still, they play on the same team. One is the pitcher and the other the catcher. Is the scene scientist the pitcher or the catcher? The reader should decide.

2.3 Bias in Scene Investigations

Scene scientists judge facts, understanding that one must define facts carefully; some facts are hard and others are soft. The competent scene scientist remains loyal to the hard facts, such as scientific data, observable phenomena, and so on, and seriously considers only undeniably supportable soft facts, such as witness statements. Each new fact must pass muster by testing against an appropriate hypothesis. Only when all of the facts are known can a scenario of what happened be reliably expressed. New facts that do not fit must have an explanation, which means a new or modified hypothesis. Without this process, investigations are prone to bias. According to Dror (an expert studying human behavior) and Rosenthal [5],

> Human judgments are affected by a variety of factors. These effects stem from our initial perceptual mechanisms to higher cognitive functions. Given such variability and individual differences, the question arises: How reliable are human judgments? The variability across

> individuals reflects that people are different; they have different past experiences, mental representations and abilities, as well as different motivations, personalities, and so forth. (p. 900)

Scene investigators will likely bristle at the suggestion that they are biased in their work. They correctly believe crime scene investigation is a critical process and, as such, they strive to find evidence to support a successful prosecution. They would likewise challenge the suggestion that they do not actively search for exculpatory evidence even though their subconscious is focused on prosecutions. This should not come as a surprise. Scene investigators in the United States mostly represent the investigative arm of law enforcement and, thus, are an integral part of the prosecution team. Their mission is to find probative evidence to prove someone committed the crime, which they do through a process of deductive reasoning, where, if their premises are true, the conclusion must also be true. By definition, then, they are as biased as the crime scene expert hired by the defense team.

The prosecutor, who is an integral player and arguably the most critical member of the prosecution's adversarial team, is by definition also biased. But the prosecutor, as an advocate, is supposed to be biased, and so is the defense attorney. The scene scientist who responds to the scene and who is likely employed by the prosecution's team must resist the inherent biases and should have no stake in the investigative process. The reason is that science should bring objectivity to the investigative process. That is not to imply that a scene scientist cannot be swayed by reason.

Science researchers use the scientific method to eliminate the bias. If the researcher conducts experiments to arrive at a preconceived result, the process is not science. Researchers work at a frontier of the unknown, an area of uncertainty, where the work is a continual process of discovery propelled by the scientific method as the guiding principle. The scientific community conducts research and presents and/or publishes the work in scientifically acceptable venues. There, the review process takes place and sanctions occur, albeit usually at a later time. The researcher is, in essence, saying, "Look what I've done. Take your best shot." This is the process by which science tests itself and reveals errors before they are widely disseminated. In this way, too, science finds scientific fraud and thus is self-correcting through the process of peer review, publication, and collegial interactions (e.g., sharing at conferences). Unlike law enforcement, the culture of science encourages critical questioning of past results and its colleagues. The scientific culture encourages cautious, precise statements and frowns on statements that venture beyond facts; it is acceptable for colleagues to challenge one another, even if the challenger is junior. This is not what happens in the scene investigative arena.

The issue is that each scene investigation should be thought of much like a research project. At crime scenes, scene scientists/investigators are working at the frontier of the unknown, of uncertainty. But unlike scientific research, there is no fall-back position and rarely peer review. In fact, most criminal cases have no contemporary review process, no peer review, and thus no mechanism to uncover shoddy, biased, or fraudulent work. The scientific process is the antithesis of what happens in real-life crime scene investigations. Unfortunately, the following are real-life events:

- Planting evidence at a crime scene to point to a defendant
- Collecting evidence without a warrant by claiming exigent circumstances
- Ignoring evidence at a scene that might exonerate a suspect
- Failing to report a colleague, superior, or subordinate for inappropriate activity

Many types of bias exist to which investigators and scientists are prone. Examples are shown in Table 2.4. Forensic examples are included to illustrate the relevance.

With respect to bias in the forensic sciences, which is equally true for crime scene investigation, Risinger and Saks [6] wrote,

> When everyone from Nobel prize winners to average citizens . . . take steps to make sure their judgments are not distorted by extraneous context information, then it is hard to conceive of what it is that makes forensic scientists think they are immune from the same effects. (p. 51)

Of particular relevance is that these ideas with respect to crime scene investigation are not new. May wrote in 1936 [7], and Cooley and Turvey [8] reported later,

> . . . often the most significant bit of evidence is overlooked or misinterpreted because someone has jumped to a premature conclusion. . . . To face a crime with an open mind—a mind willing to believe and disbelieve even its own senses, sometimes willing to admit and desert one line of investigation for another, is one of the most difficult tasks of the detective. (p. 71)

Uncertainty is the breeding ground for bias and two factors are at work: ambiguity and subjectivity. In the former, if the evidence or the circumstances are incomplete, murky, or equivocal, the scene scientist—or the crime scene investigator—is free to develop opinions, which can represent personal bias; slanting interpretations toward the prosecution's view of a case or searching for scene evidence based on an arrest or a colleague's description of the assailant. When subjectivity is the issue, scene interpretations rest on an examiner's experience or beliefs which results in bias. Prejudices and biases occur during decision-making situations where the decisions represent a gray area, typically where there is ambiguity and subjectivity [8,9]. In black-and-white situations, decisions are typically straightforward and easy: Where do we cordon off the broadcast and print media during the investigation? Who on the team is the spokesperson for the media? Where is the command center? When should we look for fingerprints? Such ground-ball questions have definite answers.

Table 2.4 Forensically Important Categories of Bias

Bias Name	Bias Description	Forensic Example
Bandwagon effect (also groupthink, herd behavior, manias)	Tendency to do or believe things because many other people do	The prosecutor or detectives are *certain* a suspect is the killer because he is a "bad guy." At the scene, this knowledge could sway the course of the investigation especially if the scene investigators know who the "bad guy" is.
Confirmation effects	The tendency to search for or interpret information in a way that confirms one's preconceptions	The crime scene investigator who has a preconceived idea of what happened or who committed the crime and searches the scene to uncover evidence to support that notion.
Observer–expectancy effect (also observer effects, context effects, expectancy effects)	The expectation of a given result with the unconscious manipulation of an experiment or misinterpretation of data in order to find it	An analyst expects a result but does not get it, and then creates scenarios so that the correct results are not obtained. The crime scene investigator ignores evidence that does not fit a specific theory of the case.

Some decisions are not straightforward, however: What does the bloodstain spatter pattern on a wall mean? What technique will best visualize latent prints on a door knob—super glue fuming or dusting with powders? How should we enhance a wet residue footwear impression? Can we lift it? Is it really a wet residue print? How do we know? Which enhancement chemicals should we use? Should we do it at the scene or should we try to collect it? What is the bullet path through the car? Where was the shooter standing?

No one corners the market on making bad decisions, certainly not scene scientists, forensic scientists, or crime scene investigators. Everyone has biases and everyone makes decisions based upon them. But bias does not belong at crime scenes or in the forensic laboratory. Thus, it must be controlled. The first example comes not from a crime scene investigation but from what has been termed the "Gold Standard" [10] of forensic science—DNA.

2.3.1 Case Example 1

An example of ambiguity involved a decision made with respect to the reporting of DNA statistics. The deceased was found naked on his bedroom floor. The crime scene unit (laboratory scientists) found a hair on the body of the deceased, and the laboratory's microscopic analysis reported that the hair was different from that of both the deceased and the defendant. This must have been a blow to the prosecution because it meant that physical evidence found at the scene did not belong to the person the prosecutor had on trial: believed to be a lone killer. The ensuing DNA analysis was critical for the prosecution because, had the DNA conclusively matched either the defendant or the victim, the microscopic analysis would not have mattered.

The first analytical decision the laboratory made after the microscopic examination was incorrect. At that time, and at the time of writing this text, the first line of DNA attack after microscopic analysis of hair was to perform mitochondrial DNA typing. Instead, the laboratory chose to analyze for nuclear DNA, the results of which were not a typical DNA match; according to the laboratory, the DNA results matched the victim but the statistics were not stellar: 1 in 493 or almost 1 in 500. Still, the statistics clearly favored the prosecution's view of the case. A closer look at the statistics showed that the laboratory tailored the statistics to favor the prosecution, whether intentionally or not. Had the DNA calculations been made in an unbiased way, the statistics would have been 1 in 6, a huge difference in determining whose hair it was or was not [11]. The second example is a crime scene example [12].

2.3.2 Case Example 2

The brutal murder of a 20-year-old woman, presumably by her ex-boyfriend, is an example of extreme on-scene bias and incompetence. The prosecution's alleged factual history as follows:

- Ex-boyfriend breaks down glass door to the house to come after his ex-girlfriend, who is dating someone else.
- He grabs a chef's knife from a knife holder in the kitchen and chases his ex-girlfriend to an upstairs bathroom.
- He butchers the ex-girlfriend, slashing her head and throat with the knife.
- He stabs himself in the chest and leaves the bathroom, goes down the stairs and falls at the foot of the stairs next to the kitchen where he remains until found by the police.

- The ex-girlfriend's sister calls her father who calls the police.
- The father is first on the scene. He finds his daughter and then the ex-boyfriend. He begins kicking the ex-boyfriend in the head.
- One of the officers on the scene is the uncle of the deceased. He does not leave the scene.
- The father is still at the scene.
- The on-scene investigation is incomplete, presumably because the police conclude that the ex-boyfriend is the murderer.
- In addition to the above, the on-scene work was shoddy or simply not considered important since the "actor" was in custody.
- They photographed evidence of the scene without scales and without using a tripod. Most photographs were taken at an angle.
- Bloody footprints in the bathroom were not photographed properly nor were they enhanced (see Figure 2.1).
- Bloody footprints in the hallway outside the bathroom and in the kitchen were not enhanced. No on-scene comparisons were made of the class characteristics of the bloodstained footwear impression prints to the shoes of the deceased, the ex-boyfriend, or the father.
- No fingerprinting was performed at the scene.
- The ex-boyfriend's clothing and shoes were not examined at the scene or by the crime laboratory for glass shards.
- The bloodstain spatter patterns in the bathroom were not interpreted.
- A bloody knife found in the bathroom was processed by the police latent print laboratory using Amido black. Stained friction ridge detail is observed, but the laboratory reports an inability to raise the latent prints (see Figure 2.2).
- BPA of the staining on the knife does not support the contention that the ex-boyfriend stabbed himself after murdering the ex-girlfriend.

Figure 2.1 Bloodstained footprint at scene. (Photograph by Robert C. Shaler.)

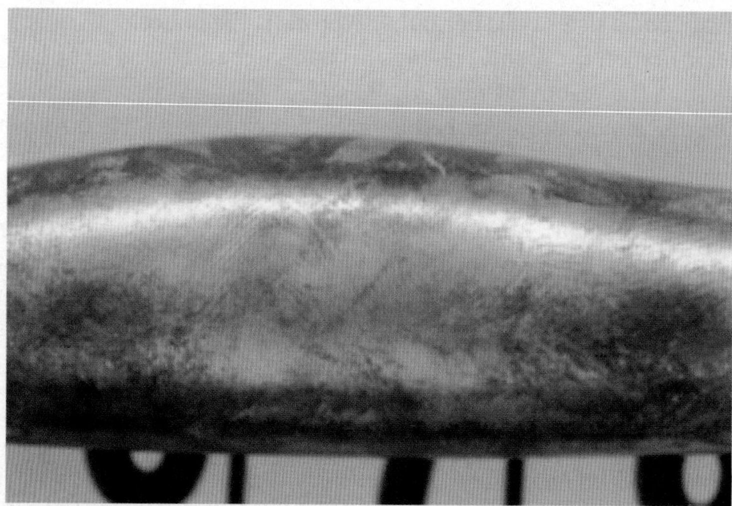

Figure 2.2 Amido black stained bloody knife handle. (Photograph by Robert C. Shaler.)

So how can biases be eliminated or at least minimized at the crime scene? One way is to change the existing crime scene paradigm (see Chapter 1). The reason is that science is self-correcting because of the inherent challenges built into the scientific method and the need for peer review. Such a process does not exist during or after a crime scene investigation. However, if each crime scene is considered a research project unto itself, the self-correcting process must be completed within a timeframe dictated by the case situation. Certainly investigators can and do return to crime scenes, but unlike scientific research, where additional experiments can be run and laboratory notebooks preserved, when the crime scene is released, it is finished.

How does one integrate the self-correcting aspect of science into the scene investigation process? Science does it by challenging hypotheses developed by the scientific method and by peer review. Challenging investigative hypotheses at a crime scene is difficult because scene investigators are usually from the same agency, and this may require challenging a supervisor. In a paramilitary organization such as the police, this can lead to professional suicide. The ideal is a team leader who is willing and open to having intellectual discussions concerning alternative hypotheses during the investigation. Hopefully, the discussion would be openly challenging. Theoretically, this ideal is certainly possible, and in some jurisdictions it may well happen. How well it works will depend on the team leader because the personality of each team is different, and each team leader has different relationships with subordinates.

The openness of such discussions depends on the ego, self-esteem, and self-assuredness of the team leader. If the team leader's ego and/or decisions are not at least open for discussion, his/her evolving emotions may get in the way of a competent investigation, as the team leader's opinions and ideas become the final arbiter in how the investigation proceeds. Figure 2.3 illustrates how a meaningful investigation can be severely compromised. The team leader is not open to suggestions that might call into question his authority or his ego. The dark arrows indicate closed or minimally open lines of communication. In these situations, opposing hypotheses may not be seriously considered or might even be considered a threat to the team leader's authority, even though the purpose is to solve the crime. This emotional blockage of information between the team leader and subordinates is illustrated in Figure 2.3.

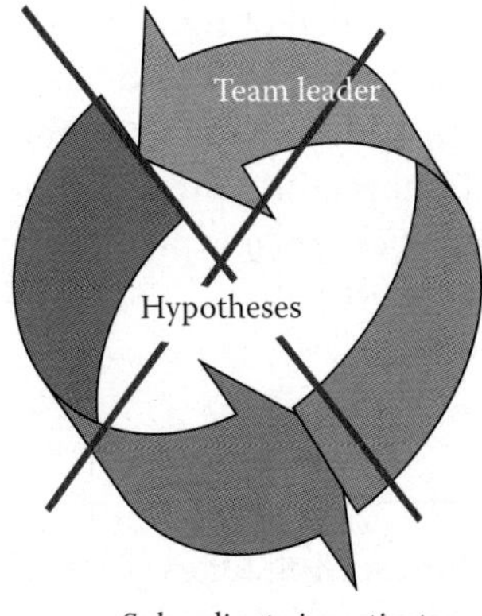

Figure 2.3 Truncated information flow between subordinates and team leader.

However, a scientist at the scene can change the dynamics of the team's personality. The scientific presence automatically brings a sense of objectivity that should not be challenged. Certainly there will be personality conflicts and differences in authority, but the scientist should not be the team leader's subordinate. In time, conflicts will be minimized as scientists and investigators establish a healthy working relationship. Individual team members might feel apprehensive about challenging their superior, but the scientist should not, as the palm print example in Chapter 1 illustrated.

When the scientist enters the investigative arena, Figure 2.3 changes and should appear more like Figure 2.4. The green arrows show open lines of communication. The yellow arrows represent a partially open communication path. The dark arrows, as in Figure 2.3, indicate minimal effective communication, such as the team leader instructing subordinates with respect to the scene investigative process.

The subordinate-to-team leader openness might still be truncated, but the scientist and the team leader should have an open dialog. In fact, the scientific presence can open lines of communication such that an open forum can occur among all scene investigators: scientist, team leader, and subordinates. Certainly this is the ideal. It opens the possibility that the scene will be processed as it should: as a research project amid uncertainty and chaos.

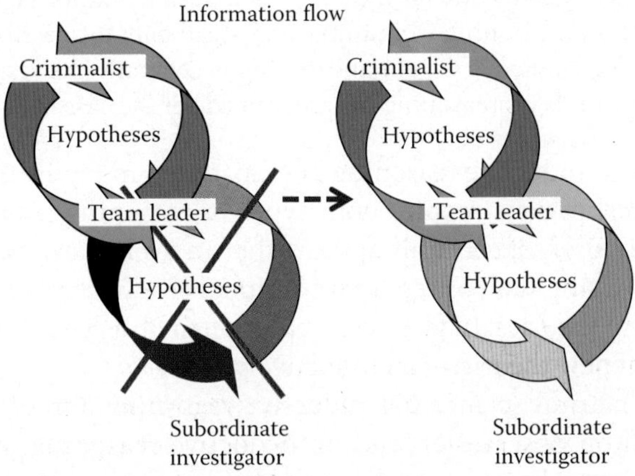

Figure 2.4 Lines of communication among team members.

The forgoing underscores the self-correcting, bias-mitigating capabilities of the scientific approach in crime scene investigations. Without a scientific presence at the scene, the investigation is prone to bias, error, and subjectivity, none of which has a place in an environment in which ambiguity and uncertainty prevail. Since many if not most scene investigations have no contemporaneous peer review process, the scientific approach is the only way to protect the integrity of the investigation.

2.4 Reasoning

There is little doubt that a form of reasoning takes place during any crime scene investigation. And since crime scene investigation is a scientific process and the direct application of the scientific method, there must be logic and reasoning. Is it a deductive or an inductive process? To explore these possibilities, definitions are in order.

Deductive reasoning works from the general to the more specific and is often referred to as a "top-down" process of logic. It begins with a theory and moves to a testable hypothesis. Testing or verification requires observations or experiments that address the hypothesis which is ultimately either confirmed or not. This feels like what happens at crime scenes. Concerning deductive criminal profiling, Turvey [13] says,

> The advantages of the Deductive Criminal Profiling model are very important. This model requires specialized education and training in forensic science, crime scene reconstruction, and wound pattern analysis. . . . Deductive Criminal Profiles tend to be more specific than Inductive Criminal Profiles, assisting greatly in the major goal of the profiling process, which is to move from a universal set of suspect characteristics to a more unique set of suspect characteristics.

Inductive reasoning begins with an observation and moves to a testable tentative hypothesis, which is more open-ended. This also feels like what happens at crime scenes. From there, a theory is derived, which must be confirmed. In short, it moves from the specific to the general and is thought of as a "bottom-up" process of logic or reasoning. Inductive criminal profiling, Turvey [13] says, is

> The process of profiling criminal behavior, crime scenes, and victims from the known behaviors and emotions suggested by other criminals, crime scenes, and/or victims. In essence, as the term suggests, this is reasoning from initial statistical data to specific criminal offender behavior. In any event, Inductive Criminal Profiling is generally the result of some kind of statistical analysis, or finds it's reasoning in cases outside of the case at hand.

Both deductive and inductive reasoning are illustrated in Figure 2.5.

Crime scene investigations require both types of reasoning simultaneously. And by examining the above closely, it certainly appears that an overlap exists. It might be possible to assemble both into a singular concept that continuously cycles from theories to observations and back again to theories. In fact, researchers often observe patterns in data that lead to the development of new theories—an inductive process.

All branches of natural science use inductive reasoning and establish theories and laws of nature based on observation and on deductive reasoning to draw conclusions. There are circumstances where observations come first. One might observe certain facts that form a pattern that eventually leads to tentative hypotheses, which are tested to form

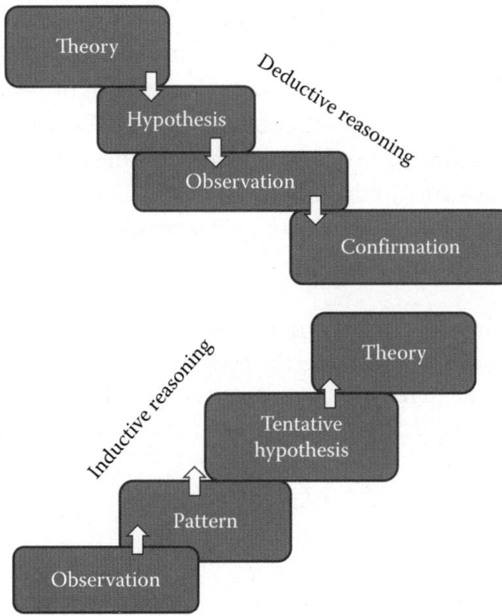

Figure 2.5 Illustration of deductive and inductive reasoning.

the basis of a theory. Still, the theory must be confirmed, which would be abduction. Gudwin [14] wrote,

> We propose understanding abduction not as the process of anomaly detection (which would be deduction), neither as the process that generates hypothesis (which would be induction) but as the test selection of those hypotheses.

In this context, confirmation is a process that invokes another type of reasoning—abductive reasoning. A combined process of inductive, deductive, and abductive reasoning appropriate for crime scene investigation is illustrated in Figure 2.6.

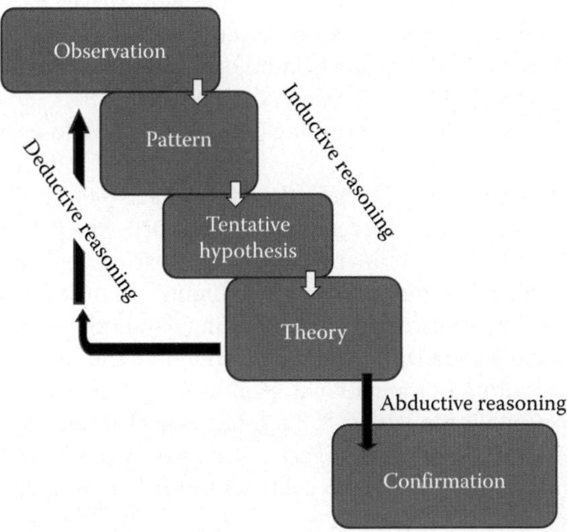

Figure 2.6 Inductive/deductive/abductive reasoning as applied in crime scene investigations.

From a practical perspective, does defining how reasoning fits the crime scene investigation help? Many believe the process is intuitive and subject to experience. The truth is that reasoning is applied but likely not as a conscious thought process. The scientist does this as a matter of education, training, and experience. Investigators—the good ones—do it as a matter of intuition, training, and experience. As these mental processes are at work at the crime scene, there is little doubt that the investigation is a scientific endeavor. Thus, the scientific method is the best tool to ensure a successful scene investigation.

As Sherlock Holmes [15] said,

> In solving a problem of this sort, the grand thing is to be able to reason backward. That is a very useful accomplishment, and a very easy one, but people do not practice it much. In the everyday affairs of life it is more useful to reason forward, and so the other comes to be neglected. There are fifty who can reason synthetically for one who can reason analytically. (p. 83)

References

1. S. Sambursky (ed.) 1974. Section II, The middle ages. *Physical Thought from the Presocratics to the Quantum Physicists*. UK: Pica Press, p. 139.
2. W. J. Chisum and B. Turvey. 2007. Practice standards for the reconstruction of crime. In: W. J. Chisum and B. E. Turvey (eds), *Crime Reconstruction*. New York, NY: Elsevier Academic Press, p. 92.
3. M. R. Cohen. 1931. *Reason and Nature: An Essay on the Meaning of Scientific Method*. Harcourt, Brace & Co., New York.
4. N. W. Edmund. *The Scientific Method Today*. Available at: http://www.scientificmethod.com/index.html (accessed February 7, 2009).
5. I. Dror and R. Rosenthal. 2008. Meta-analytically quantifying the reliability and biasability of forensic experts. *Journal of Forensic Sciences*, 53(4):900–903. Available at: http://www.cci-hq.com/Dror_JFS_expert_reliability_and_biasability.pdf (accessed February 8, 2009).
6. D. M. Risinger, M. J. Saks, W. C. Thompson, and R. Rosenthal. 2002. The *Daubert/Kumho* implications of observer effects in forensic science: hidden problems of expectation and suggestion. *California Law Review*, 90(1):1–56.
7. L. S. May. 1936. *Crime Nemesis*. New York, NY: The Macmillan Company.
8. C. M. Cooley and B. E. Turvey. 2007. Observer effects and examiner bias: Psychological influences on the forensic examiner. In: W. J. Chisum and B. E. Turvey (eds), *Crime Reconstruction*. New York, NY: Elsevier Academic Press, pp. 58–60, 71.
9. V. J. Phillips and M. Saks. 2001. The application of signal detection theory to decision making in forensic science. *Journal of Forensic Sciences*, 46:294–298.
10. M. J. Saks and J. J. Koehler. 2005. The coming paradigm shift in forensic identification science. *Science*, 309:892–895.
11. People of the State of New York v. Daniel Pelosi, Ind. No. 746-04 (supreme court, suffolk co.).
12. Commonwealth of Pennsylvania v. Frederick Cleveland, 2010, CR# 000001-09, OTN#K 696 4753.
13. B. E. Turvey. 1998. Deductive criminal profiling: Comparing applied methodologies between inductive and deductive criminal profiling techniques. *Knowledge Solutions Library*, Epub. Available at: http://www.corpus-delicti.com/Profiling_law.html (accessed Jully 25, 2011).
14. R. R. Gudwin. On the generalized deduction, induction and abduction as , the elementary reasoning operators within computational semiotics. Available at: ftp://ftp.dca.fee.unicamp.br/pub/docs/gudwin/publications/isas98_3.pdf (accessed February 9, 2009).
15. A. C. Doyle. 1887. *A Study in Scarlet*, Part 2, Chapter 7, p. 83. In: Electronic Text Center, University of Virginia Library, p. 119. Available at http://etext.virginia.edu/toc/modeng/public/DoyScan.html (accessed Jully 25, 2011).

Management Basics
The Investigative Glue

3

3.1 Introduction

Learning to manage a crime scene is a critical skill, and students of forensic science and law enforcement should understand the principles of scene management if they are to become successful crime scene scientists/investigators. They must have a grasp and understanding of the investigation sequence in order to understand how these elements fit together. This makes an efficient and coordinated investigation and, if the team leader is also effective, it generally leads to a successful scene investigation. The key ingredients a successful team manager must possess include the following: A broad experience in scene investigation, knowledge of scene forensics/criminalistics, knowledge of police and legal procedures, understanding the value of physical evidence, knowing the limitations of the science, applying the scientific method, recognizing, collecting and preserving evidence, and how to effectively blend the investigative sequence.

Contemporary scene investigative philosophy must embrace the rapidly changing dynamics of scene investigation as it relates to modern scene science and technology. More than ever, a firm foundation in science is rapidly becoming a critical prerequisite for successful scene investigations. However, if a crime scene unit or team leader, regardless of the experience base or the scientific backgrounds of the scene members, has little or no scene management expertise, the investigation can be botched and critical probative evidence present might be lost forever. This is why competent management is the glue that holds the scene investigation together.

The contemporary scene manager—the team leader—must possess the appropriate credentials in order to work efficiently and appropriately within an intense environment that gives the physical surroundings an aura of chaos. Putting this into perspective, the modern team leader must be almost a super person of sorts, and possess in depth scene experience, knowledge of police procedures, understand the science and criminalistics and their limitations, where to obtain scarce resources in unusual situations and how to expedite the investigation without compromising quality. In short, scene management is a dauntingly complex responsibility.

It is not axiomatic that an experienced scene investigator will automatically be a competent scene manager. Such reasoning is fallacious. It's like having processed, that is, been at a thousand scenes without knowing whether they were done correctly. The scene manager is someone who can multitask and work well with people, understands the intricacies of the investigation and its ancillary activities.

3.1.1 Teaching Crime Scene Management

Authors of several crime scene investigative texts typically discuss how to manage scene resources so that evidence is collected and preserved appropriately. Mostly, these discussions are general overviews geared toward law enforcement and not to students who have little or no knowledge or experience with scene investigations. They gloss over the scientific aspects and concentrate on explaining the "how-to" of investigations, broadly covering the basics of the scene investigation. Virtually none provide an in-depth mechanism from which students can learn to manage the scene investigation. Students, whether enrolled in the university or at the police academy, need to understand more about the role of scene management as well as the intricacies involved in bringing the scene to a successful completion. This means understanding the science of the scene as well as when and how to apply the vocational aspects the investigation.

As presented in Chapter 1, it is axiomatic that learning requires multiple sensory inputs, which is why this text suggests instructors use a combination of theory and intensive practice. In universities, chemistry is taught exactly in this way; lectures are followed by laboratory exercises. Medicine has become a problem-based learning process. Likewise, the philosophy here embraces the problem-based concept. The same is true for scene management. Students must do more than read about it in a text or listen about it in a lecture. Learning scene management requires a multitiered approach that provides needed experience in applying scene science while directing team members (classmates) in scene investigations of varying complexity.

Mostly, law enforcement professionals learn scene management on-the-job, which can be good or bad. If the instructor is a world-class instructor who has the correct knowledge and experience, the training can top notch. However, the sad truth is that on-the-job training is notoriously inadequate because it perpetuates bad habits, poor skills, and faulty knowledge. That does imply that appropriate models of scene management do not exist. After all, investigators have been managing scenes for hundreds of years, and it would be stupid to imply that none have been done correctly. However, it would be ludicrous to suggest that all scenes have been managed correctly. My experience, with large police crime scene units, suggests that many scenes are managed poorly.

3.1.2 The Learning Process

The management philosophy presented here has been taken from others as well as this author's experience. Mostly, however, is based on the management process presented by Gardner [1] spiced up a notch with the scientific method. His format is based on the U.S. Army model and offers students and investigators a roadmap on how to proceed in step-by-step sequence. The hallmark of the process is a series of checks and re-checks designed to ensure that nothing is overlooked. While not the direct application of the scientific method, it is a mechanism for students to learn the basics of scene management. In no way does this suggest that the Army method is the only way to manage a scene or is it necessarily the best way. It is simply a place for students to being the learning process.

Scene management cannot be done properly without practice because it is as much vocational as theoretical, and it is dictated by the specific circumstances of the scene. Many might even argue that scene management is entirely vocational, which was likely true until sophisticated science and technology became an integral part of the scene investigator's repertoire. So, learning scene management is treated in this text from both the theoretical and vocational aspects.

In this course, the structure provided by Gardner [1] is bolstered by having instructors ask students for their rationale for choosing to manage a mock scene in a particular way.

After the mock scene investigation, the team leader (manager) prepares an in depth report of the scene investigation. The report summarizes the scene investigative sequence, how the technology was employed, whether it was successful and if not the reasons why. The report also includes a section on the interpretation of the evidence collected and its relative importance to the investigation. Students are graded on their approach as well as the unit's success in finding probative evidence and how well the hands-on aspects were performed, for example, fingerprinting, enhancement and collecting impression evidence, bloodstain pattern interpretations, photography, sketching, and so on. The other team members prepare a report describing how well their classmate managed the scene investigation. Thus, all the students taking part in the investigation are required to consider and think about how the investigation progressed from a management perspective. This is the essence of the learning process. Students learn from their classmates' mistakes. They also learn from how well their classmates approach the management responsibility. As the course progresses, the scenes become more complicated and the students typically manage those scenes more effectively than they did at the beginning of the course.

Scene management is a progressive sequence beginning with the first official or responding officer at the scene. Texts geared toward law enforcement typically begin with an explanation of crime scene management by first explaining the first responder's responsibility. This is appropriate because the first officer is usually the first official there. The first responder's role is critical to a successful investigation because he/she must preserve life, secure and preserve the scene and document as much as possible about the scene as it was found until relieved by an investigator in charge.

3.2 The Responding Officer

This course is not concerned with the responsibilities of the first officer but more with how to investigate the scene after the first officer hands it off to the team leader or to the detective in charge of the investigation. However, the first official on the scene has critical responsibilities that can dramatically affect the subsequent scene investigation. As a crucial first step in any scene investigation, these responsibilities are outlined in a National Institute of Justice pamphlet [2]. Without going into exhaustive detail, a first officer's responsibilities can be placed into discrete categories:

- Observations
- Actions taken
- Documentation

3.2.1 Observations

Generally, the observations lead to a documentable action. Such first-level observations require the first office to answer questions in order for the investigation to proceed smoothly. Among others, these can include: What happened here? Who should respond? The answers come from responses to other questions listed below, which are intuitive or a part of the responding officer's academy or on-the-job scene preservation training.

- Is the scene active—is the perpetrator on the scene?
- Is the scene clear?

- Are victims injured?
- Are victims deceased?
- Are there witnesses? Are they available? Are they separated?
- Are the witnesses potential suspects?
- What is the scope of the scene?

A determination of the scope of the scene is necessary: Is this an indoors only crime or does it have an outdoor component? Even in indoor scenes, for example, a homicide, the perpetrator entered somehow.

Second-level observations reflect aspects of the scene itself and include those subtle details that are obvious only after entering the scene. These, like all observations, should be archived using a digital or tape recording device or by using a note pad. The digital era has elevated the potential for information gathering. Point-and-shoot cameras are readily available and are capable of providing important as-the-scene-was-first-seen information and can archive impressions and observations. Although these cameras are capable of giving fairly high-resolution photographs and are certainly helpful, they are not a substitute for the subsequent official archiving by the crime scene unit. The first officer must be cognizant of the following:

- Fleeting evidence
  - Odors—cooking, gunshot, cigarette/cigar smoke
  - Ice cubes melting
- Entry/exit points
  - Doors—locked unlocked—tampered
  - Windows—locked unlocked—tampered
- Signs of activity
  - Struggle
  - TV/radio on
  - Meals—dishes in the sink
  - Food on the table
  - Partially eaten food
- Date/time indicators
  - Newspapers
  - Stopped clocks
  - Spoiled food
  - Hot/cold items
  - Wet blood

Other observations might include:

- Accounting for moved or out of place objects (furniture)
- Monitoring evidence moved/altered by emergency medical technicians (EMT's) as they attend to living victims
- Protecting obvious critical evidence
- Fingerprints* on dusty surfaces or dry residue prints on the floor or furniture

* Fingermark: The North American term for Fingerprints found at crime scenes is latent fingerprints. Most of the rest of the world uses the term fingermark.

- Cartridge cases
- Spent bullets
- Wet and dry residue footwear impressions
- Broken glass

3.2.2 Actions

If the scene is active, that is, a suspect/perpetrator is still there, the responding officer will require police backup. If people are wandering around, in an out of the scene, they must be removed and taken to separate locations. Their contact information must be obtained. Ideally, they will remain in a sequestered area in order to answer questions. If the victims are injured and still alive, Emergency Medical Services will be necessary, and if there are deceased victims, the medical examiner should be called.

Witnesses can also be suspects. They must be segregated and separated from other witnesses, so that they cannot exchange information. Potential suspects should be detained and their contact information obtained.

Additionally, responding officers should be extremely diligent to ensure that evidence is not compromised, damaged, or destroyed. This means having a hands-off policy. Some do-nots include

- Moving anything
- Touching anything unnecessarily
- Using toilets and sinks
- Turning on water
- Eating, drinking, or smoking

The foregoing is simply a short checklist and is far from exhaustive, as each scene is different and it will be determined by the scene. Much of what the responding officer must do and observe is dictated by the circumstances and scene common sense. Since, by definition, no crime scene is uncontaminated, the responding officer's responsibility is to turn over to investigators as virginal a scene as possible, which means protecting and securing the scene. Generalities with respect to accomplishing this exist, but, for example, a murder in an apartment in a high-rise apartment building in New York City will have significantly different approaches to scene security than the field where a small plane crashed or a highway where there was a pedestrian hit-and-run fatality. The responding officer must protect the scene until relieved by the investigator in charge who accepts the official responsibility for the subsequent on-going investigation. With respect to security, the following are possible considerations for indoor scenes:

- Establish scene boundaries
- Protect possible entrance/egress points
- Protect possible probative evidence or evidence location points

For outdoor scenes, a short list might include

- Protect entrance/exit points
    - Along paths, tire tracks on driveways, and so on

- Be cognizant of weather restrictions
- Cordon off large areas
  - Get help from others

Protecting the scene means establishing boundaries and removing witnesses and other voyeurs. The media is also a concern, and it should be moved far enough from the scene so that sophisticated listening devices cannot tune into discussions among investigators and so that cameras with powerful lenses cannot capture salacious material. The investigation does not need dead bodies ending up on the evening news. A general schematic of a hypothetical scene might appear as shown in Figure 3.1.

In the schematic, three levels of security are illustrated [3]: Level 1, Level 2, and the target area. Level 1 restricts access to the scene by passersby, the general public, and the media. Notice that the media would be sequestered to a specific area that is near but not close enough to permit capturing photographs or taping conversations. They are not permitted to wander around even into the Level 1-restricted area. The media should understand that they are free to move anywhere and photograph from where it pleases in areas that not specifically designated as part of the crime scene. Barrier tape is critical. If barrier tape is present and members of the media cross, they risk being arrested and their cameras/video equipment could be confiscated. Unprotected areas or those not designated as "official" are fair game for the media and from which reporters and photographers cannot be legally removed.

Notice, too, that witnesses must be segregated from investigators and the media. Eye witness accounts are notoriously inaccurate, so it would be a mistake to permit reporters to interview witnesses, one or more of which might turn out to be the perpetrator.

The Level 2 area is closer to the target area and is set aside for official business. Only law enforcement, other officials, and dignitaries allowed access to the scene are permitted inside this area. This area should be marked or designated specifically by the first officer, although with the understanding that boundaries established by the first officer are subject to change by the investigators in charge of the investigation. Ideally, a command center would be in the Level 2–designated area. This is where the crime scene unit sets up its

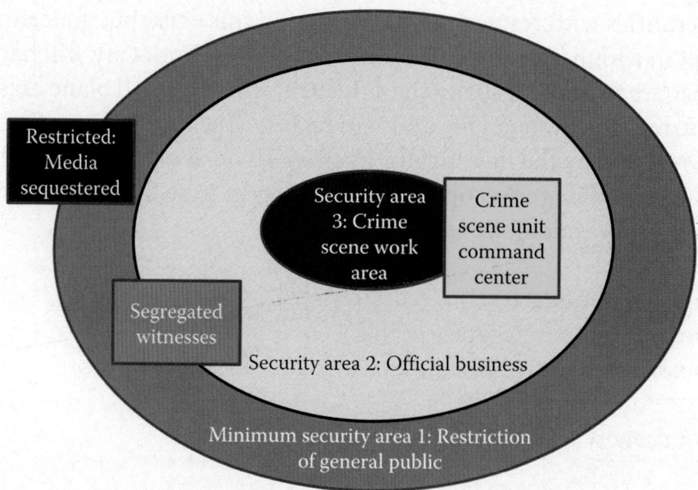

Figure 3.1 Scene security Levels 1–3.

equipment, packaging areas, holds meetings, and so on. It is typically outside the target area, which is where the activity of the crime took place.

Figure 3.1 schematic is an example because no single scheme is adequate for all crime scenes. Certainly, there might be multiple possibilities potentially applicable to a specific scene, but the best of them will be dictated by the scene itself. For example, a scene circumstance might have the command center inside the target area while another would more logically position it outside. Generally, though, the responding officer should establish the initial areas.

When the detective in charge of the investigation takes over, the final responsibility of the responding officer is to debrief the investigator and to conduct what is known as the "walk-though." The debriefing and walk-through is like handing the baton to a teammate in relay race. This is when the responding officer and the investigator examine the scene together, exchange critical information, and exchange control. The responding officer points out observations made, details of the scene that seem important, such as fragile evidence, and what else is known about the scene, such as thoughts, impressions, observations, details, photographs, notes, recordings, and so on. There should be no secrets.

3.2.3 Documentation

The first officer must document everything discussed above. Whether this is means recording into an audio recorder or writing in a notebook is not important. Most important is that this information is not trusted to one's memory and is not lost to the investigation.

3.3 The Team Leader: Managing the Scene Investigation

After the official transfer of scene control, the systematic and analytical process of ascertaining what the scene has to offer in evidentiary terms begins. This is when the team leader takes charge of the investigation. This is the individual who understands that unlike the "detectives" on TV's CSI, no one person does it all, and that the successful scene investigation is a team endeavor, the composition of which is determined by the scene itself and the resources available.

Most crime scene units are comprised of police officers trained to process crime scenes, but some include individuals having diverse expertise, for example, criminalists, as needed. Mostly, these hard-working and dedicated men and women are not scientists. Sometimes, however, additional specialized expertise is required, and those who might become adjunct or part-time members of the unit will be contacted on an as needed basis. For example, if bones are uncovered, an anthropologist may be needed, although this scientist is usually not a member of the responding team. If decomposing bodies are found, a forensic entomologist may be needed, and if there are critical bloodstain patterns, a forensic biologist with bloodstain pattern analysis (BPA) expertise should be called. If the unit finds a clandestine laboratory, a chemist experienced with these situations should be called.

Crime scene units are comprised of detectives and/or police officers, investigators trained to document a scene and to recognize, collect and package evidence. To be certain, this is a minimally singular expertise. Units having large caseloads or scarce resources may assign as few as two or three investigators to work scenes. From any perspective, two-unit crime scene teams inherently lack the expertise and efficiency to effectively do justice to most scenes, not to mention that they run the very real risk of missing critical evidence that could botch the investigation.

The responding officer turns over the scene to the team leader in a process called the preprocessing phase, see Section 3.4. This is an important juncture in the investigation, as everything the responding officer did and observed is relayed to the team leader. In this hand-off phase, the responding officer briefs the team leader until he/she is satisfied that all preliminary work has been completed or started satisfactorily: victims taken car of? Medical examiner (ME) been called? Media sequestered? Witnesses separated and contact information obtained? Command center established? Security in place? Critical and fragile evidence location?

Even after armed with this information, the team leader should never assume that everything has been completed satisfactorily or even begun. It might be that this was the responding officer's first homicide scene, which inexperience and emotional trauma can lead to mental lapses. Double checking, then, is essential to ensure the essentials were completed correctly or begun. During the debriefing, the team leader must consider the legal issues that give the crime scene unit the right to enter the scene because the scene investigation cannot begin until the legal process is complete. If it enters before this is obtained, any and all evidence that was observed and/or collected may not be admissible in court. In a legal sense, then, it is lost.

The debriefing continues in the form of a "walk-through," where the responding officer and the team leader together examine the scene. This is when the team leader gets a first look at the scene and begins to consider an investigative strategy. After the walk-through and the legal right to enter has been confirmed, then and only then can the scene investigation begin.

At this point, the team leader has control of the scene and will pick up where the responding officer left off. If preliminary work is needed, this is the time to do it. For example, if the responding officer neglected or did not have time to set aside space for the command center, the team leader must consider where it should be, or perhaps the walk-through led the team leader to believe the command center should be moved to another location. The same holds true for the media. These are important considerations. The team must be able to work in an area that is close, efficient, and not be where evidence could be destroyed. For example, the command center should not require investigators to trample though the entrance and egress points of the assailant, which would certainly ruin footwear impressions. Similarly, the prying eyes and ears of the media must be absent the main activity of the investigation. An inexperienced responding officer could place the media too close to the investigative activity.

The team leader must consider anything that can interfere with the efficient processing of the scene, such as time constraints. If these exist, they should be evaluated carefully for their effect on the team's ability to effectively and efficiently complete its work. An example might be the scene location. If it is a hit-and-run on a major roadway, blocking it for an extended time may be impossible and involve political aspects out of the team leader's control. Another constraint might be the weather. A homicide in the woods, where there is the threat of rain, will force the team leader to consider how to protect fragile evidence. Or the team leader might order large tents to protect areas of the scene so that the team can complete the investigation without rushing.

All of this occurs before the team sets foot inside the scene. There are also specific scene-processing responsibilities to be coordinated and addressed from within the

Table 3.1 Overview of Team Leader Responsibilities

- Design the investigation plan
- Document the scene
  - Sketching
  - Photography
- Protect the fragile evidence
- Search the scene
- Collect the evidence
- Dust for prints
- Enhance the prints
- Reconstruction
- Case file management
- Crime scene report

constraints of the scene itself. Like all scene activity, they must be completed within a reasonable period of time and done correctly. For example, Table 3.1 lists several activities that occur at scenes. Each of these must be considered by the team leader: Who will do which and in what phase?

From the beginning until its completion, the team leader will be coordinating the activity of the team as well as working with the detectives investigating the crime. There should be a continuous exchange of information, See Chapter 2. From a scene perspective, the investigation begins when the team leader designs an investigative plan and strategy. This includes the how, who, and when of the typical activities taking place: archiving, searching, collecting, packaging, and so on. During this activity, the team leader tracks the progress of the investigation and ensures that the work is done correctly; nothing is missed. Additionally, the team leader should be thinking how to wrap up the investigation, put together the case file, and the write the investigative report.

3.3.1 Subteams

The how, who, and when of the activity is of prime importance. While there is theoretically no absolute correct way to process a scene, there are certainly incorrect ways. Without doubt, certain activities should take place before others. For example, fragile evidence should be marked and protected and/or collected before much activity takes place. The team leader needs to create teams within the crime scene unit itself, each having specific responsibilities for working certain necessary activities. Several activities are listed in the graphic in Table 3.2.

Subteams can have one or more members. For example, a one member subteam might be an individual who does the establishing photography. A second subteam might have two members who sketch and another single member subteam might be searching for evidence. As the scene work progresses, the responsibilities of subteams and their composition might change. A two-member subteam might be searching for evidence, collecting, and packaging while the team leader could be performing the first re-check (discussed below) and another two-member team might be beginning the second Touch phase (discussed below) and begin dusting for fingerprinting on walls, door knobs, and so on. When the first two-member team finishes sketching, it might be assigned to the second re-check.

Table 3.2 Subteam Activities

• Documenting	• Bloodstains
• Sketching	• Testing
• Photography	• Photography
• Logs	• Pattern interpretation
– Evidence	• Enhancement
– Scene attendance	• Shooting incidents
– Photography	• Locating
– Chain-of-custody	• Bullet path trajectories
• Evidence search/package	• Reconstruction
• Fingerprints	• Hypotheses
• Locating/enhancing	• Testing
• Photography	• Case files/reports
• Lifting	

Most teams within the crime scene unit do double-duty in order to complete the necessary tasks. To someone examining the list in Table 3.2, it appears that there should be seven separate teams, each responsible for an individual listed task. If the unit had been split into two member subteam, this would translate into a crime scene unit of 14 members. No crime scene unit has, nor should have 14 team members. First it is a waste of human resources. Second, the team would be tripping over itself as the work progresses. The list is for students so that they realize that specific tasks must be considered, and that the resources available must be utilized to ensure that each is completed properly, expeditiously without delaying the investigation. This is a scheduling problem for the team leader.

An optimum team would have from three to five members, including the team leader. If the team had five members, two-member subteams would perform specific tasks, moving from one activity to another, and the team leader would monitor and perform specific duties as well. An example of how a team leader of a five-member crime scene unit might divide responsibilities is illustrated in Figure 3.2 for only the first two phases of a scene investigation.

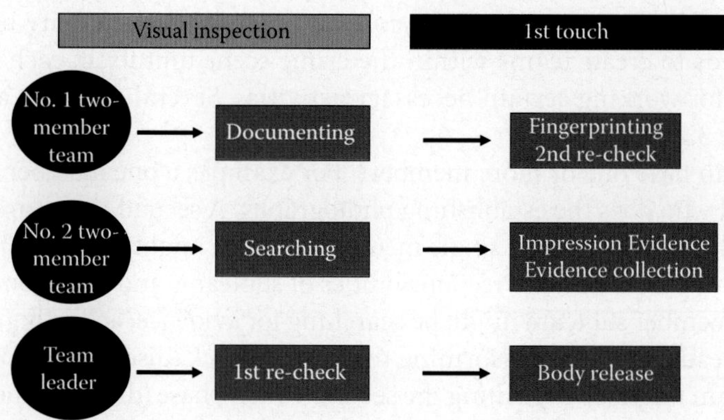

Figure 3.2 Changing subteam responsibilities in a five-member unit.

Generally, the team leader fills-in when necessary. For example, once responsibilities are decided, the team leader might decide to handle establishing photography so that a two-member subteam can begin sketching. After documenting the scene, one of the sketchers might begin packaging collected evidence while the other might begin taking the mid-range and close-up photographs of targeted evidence. There should be an overall logical flow that moves forward until the investigation is completed.

In the hypothetical illustration in Figure 3.2, the No. 1 two-member subteam is tasked with documenting the scene, for example, photography (establishing initially) and sketching. This should begin in the area where the most activity took place because this is where most of the scene investigative activity will take place. When the photography (establishing) in this area is complete the subteam could dust for fingerprints and complete the 2nd re-check. See Figure 3.3.

The No. 2 two-team subteam might be searching for evidence, and protecting fragile evidence. The team leader might be performing the 1st re-check to ensure that nothing had been missed during the first pass through the scene. The second phase of processing, the 1st Touch (Figures 3.2 and 3.3), involves other activities in sequence. The final stage is the 2nd Touch, which is also discussed as part of Section 3.4, *The Scene Processing Cascade.*

Generally, the composition of the crime scene unit as well as its subteams is determined by the resources available. Regardless of the number of team members, at no time should a team member be standing around with nothing to do. All scene investigations have tedious moments, exacting times, and busy work to do. There are also times when it is necessary to wait for a task to be completed before moving into an area. Generally though, there is a lot to do and little down time. It is the team leader's responsibility to keep the team members busy and focused.

3.4 The Scene Processing Cascade

The team leader must determine the team's scene investigative strategy. For students, this is always a problem because they have the urge to do it all at once and get it done. Those not having organizational skills are quickly overwhelmed because crime scene work is

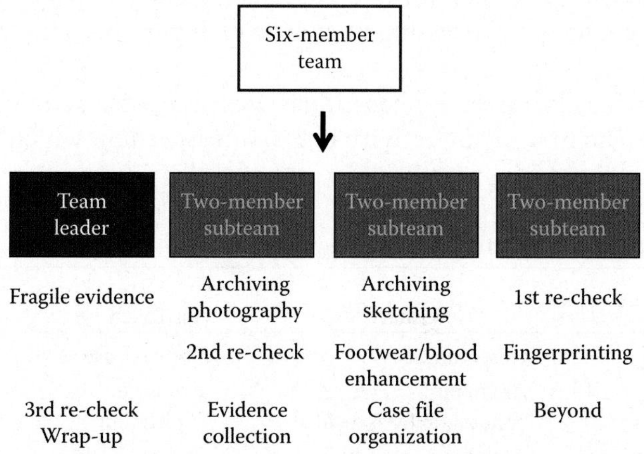

Figure 3.3 Six-member team: hypothetical subteam responsibilities.

daunting and keeping track of activity happening simultaneously is an exercise in frustration. It is also exhausting. Near the end of the second day of managing a mock homicide, one student team leader student sat down in the middle of the floor, put his head in his hands and mumbled, "I just want to slash my wrists." Their overriding concern is to locate and collect *all* probative evidence, which on paper seems like a simple task. As they soon learn, it is not. They also must ensure to protect evidence and preserve it properly.

The investigative work should take place in logical steps so that no probative evidence is missed, damaged, or obliterated. Completing an initial scene investigation is no guarantee that the work is over, and it is not unusual for a crime scene unit to re-visit a scene several times. Additionally, even after a scene is released, questions might arise and additional theories proffered. Therefore, the initial investigation must thoroughly archive the scene in order to preserve the scene in as "virginal" a state as possible.

The general steps of a scene investigation are shown in Table 3.3. While the concept appears simple, students often have trouble identifying which activity occurs when. They aspire to complete the "mundane" archiving chores quickly because they are anxious to dive into the fun stuff: fingerprinting, electrostatic lifting of dust prints, enhancing bloodstains, and so on. They quickly realize, however, that an over anxious investigator makes mistakes, and that the best approach is slow and easy. The labels on following chart emphasize that the first two steps or activities of the scene investigation involve visual activity only and that the actual physical activity, that is, touching or hands on, occurs in the middle and end of the investigative sequence.

The four steps, preprocessing, visual inspection, first touch, and second touch, illustrate a general sequence or stages of the investigation. The only exception to not touching immediately concerns fragile evidence, for example, cartridge cases, and so on, which the team leader must ensure is protected and/or collected as soon as possible.

One should envision crime scene investigative work as a cascade of sequential events, left-to-right in Table 3.3. Preprocessing occurs before the crime scene unit members set eyes or feet inside the scene. This critical step is essentially the process of the responding officer turning the scene over to the team leader, see Section 3.2. After preprocessing is complete, the team leader has decisions to make, some of which will be made after a meeting with the crime scene team after it has an opportunity to walk-through the scene. The first decision is to categorize the scene into its central theme: homicide, sexual assault, burglary, hit-and-run, mass fatality, and so on. A general scene processing cascade after preprocessing is shown in Figure 3.4 and then expanded in Figure 3.5.

The label associated with each phase illustrates a general activity that might take place at that time. The first major activity is *Visual Inspection*, which is exactly what it

Table 3.3 Overview of Scene Investigative Sequence

Phase 1 Preprocessing	Visual	1st Touch	2nd Touch
Legal issues	Observations	Body release	Chemistry
Debrief investigator	Archiving photography and video	Evidence collection	3rd re-check
Victims—alive and dead	Archiving—sketching	2nd re-check	Beyond
1st walk-through	1st re-check		Wrap-up

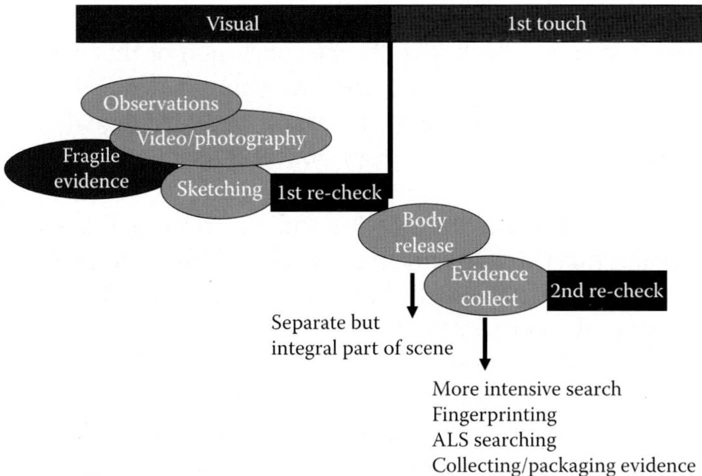

Figure 3.4 Scene processing cascade: visual and 1st touch.

means; only visual observations are made, which might be translated into future action. This is when the scene is archived. The three light blue balloons on the left are labeled *observations*, *video/photography*, and *sketching*. These illustrate the major activities taking place. Observations should be written on a note pad or spoken into a digital recorder so that nothing is left to future memory. Video/photography includes the three basics of forensic photography, although midrange and close-up photography might be taken during other phases of the cascade. This is the time when the scene video is recorded (Chapter 8).

The dark blue box labeled *1st re-check* is a critical reassessment of what the team has accomplished. Here, a subteam or the team leader reviews what has been done and checks to see whether something had been missed. Still, this is a visual process; nothing is touched

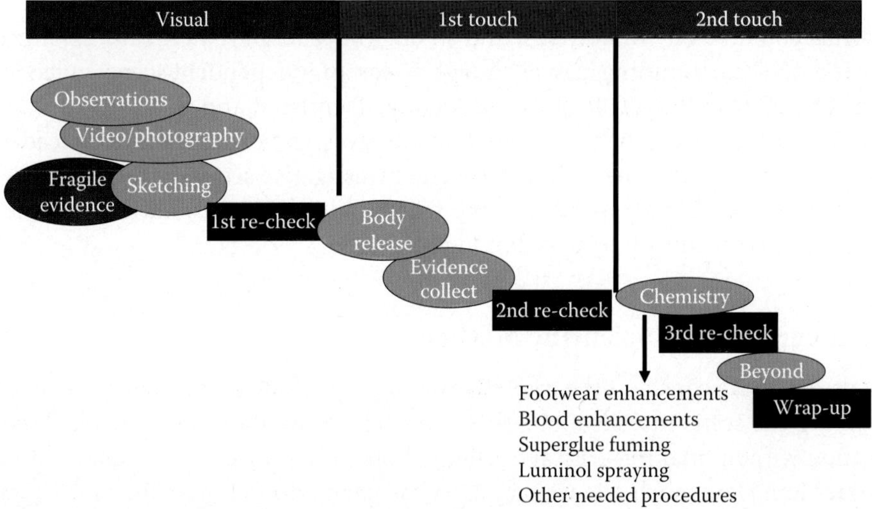

Figure 3.5 Scene processing cascade visual, 1st and 2nd touches.

except perhaps fragile evidence. Missed evidence must be documented as though being catalogued for the first time, which it is. At the conclusion of this phase, the first phase of archiving, establishing photography, and sketching is complete. See Chapter 6. Additionally, the scene has been described in notes or recorded digitally.

The next phase in the cascade is to begin touching evidence and other items at the scene, Figures 3.4 and 3.5.

The section of the cascade in Figures 3.4 and 3.5, *1st touch*, is labeled in order to emphasize for students that this is the first time hands actually touch anything at the scene. The team leader might release the body, but only after the ME has examined it and the team has been considered it as a scene unto itself, for example, archiving, collecting micro-scene elements (Chapter 4), BPA (Chapter 14), and so on.

In the *1st Touch* phase, several tasks are occurring simultaneously: the subteams are busy-performing multiple tasks, such as dusting and lifting fingerprints on walls and other surfaces, another subteam might be examining shoeprints to determine whether they are dry or wet in origin (Chapter 12), and the team leader might be moving furniture searching for other evidence. Midrange and close-up photographs document these activities. The topic video might be recorded (Chapter 8), and new found evidence documented, marked, collected, and packaged. Finally, one or more members or a subteam would perform the 2nd re-check, another critical review of the team's activity to this point.

After the 2nd re-check, the team leader is working toward concluding the scene investigation. In this phase, *2nd Touch* in Figure 3.5, the unit progresses to the chemistry phase of the investigation where chemical enhancement of evidence takes place on items that cannot be removed from the scene. This might include enhancing bloodstains, super glue fuming fingerprints, bullet path determinations, and so on. These activities occur last in the sequence because the evidence associated with these activities is generally not fragile and will not be obliterated or destroyed during the previous scene activity.

After completing the chemical phase, the team does the *3rd re-check*, the final review. This review checks everything yet again. In the *2nd touch* phase, the balloon labeled *Beyond* is a reminder that crime scenes might not necessarily be relegated to the immediate surroundings, for example, the place where a body was found. Activity could have taken place outside the set boundaries of the scene. The driveway might have tire tracks. Fingerprints could be on windowsills, and so on. The label *Beyond* means examining the boundaries of the surrounding area as though it was an independent scene: video, photography, sketching, searching, collecting, packaging, chemistry, and so on.

After the 3rd re-check, the team wraps-up the investigation, and the team leader needs to consider when to release the scene. The entire investigative sequence beginning with the first officer/responder's responsibilities, the team leader's responsibilities, and the crime scene processing cascade are reviewed in Figure 3.6.

3.4.1 Integrating the Scientific Method

The discussion above considers the rote, step-by-step, approach to managing the sequence of events during the scene investigation. This approach allows the team to work through the investigation without making critical mistakes, hopefully. However, an important contemporary question: How much science and logic has gone into the investigation? Certainly, it has been applied, such as enhancing bloodstains, fingerprints, footwear impressions, photography, and so on. But criminalistic logic as embodied in the scientific method is missing.

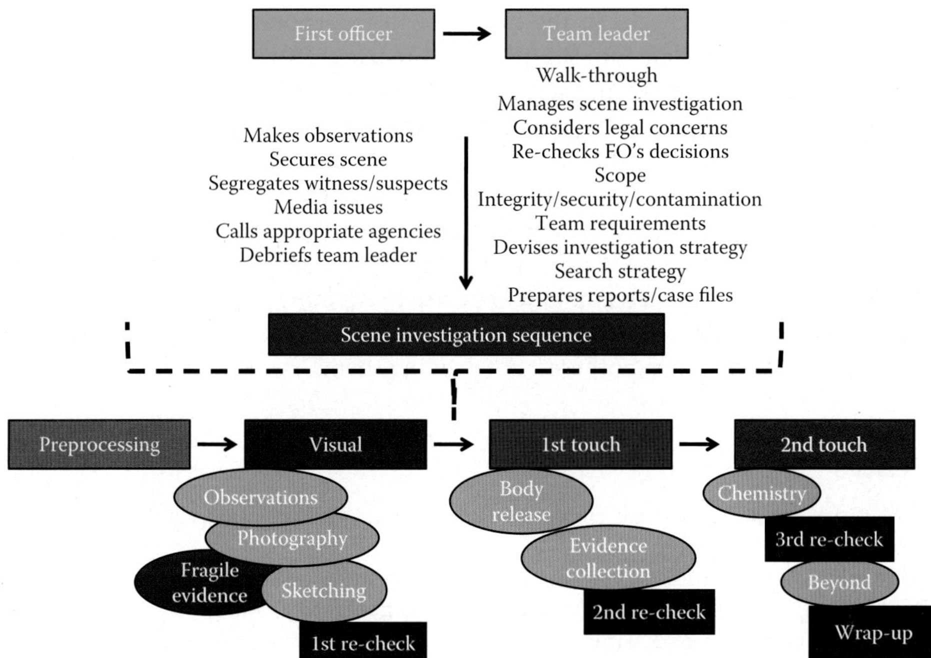

Figure 3.6 The scene investigative sequence: overview.

Integrating the scientific method and the criminalistic approach into the step-by-step process will be the true glue that ensures that any investigation will be successful. As it stands, the scene processing cascade is an outline, of sorts, where the there is only a hint of scientific method feedback mechanism: The 1st, 2nd, and 3rd re-checks. Doubtless, investigators exhibit reason and logic during the investigative sequence. The way in which the Cascade works is that the re-checks are observational checks to ensure that nothing has been missed. This is certainly a good approach, but, alone, is insufficient. So, what's the problem?

As Chapter 2 implies, the scientific method should be the bedrock, the foundation, of the investigation, much like the criminalist employs it to investigate and analyze a set of alleged facts. In fact, as defined in Chapter 1, "Criminalistics is an holistic process that embraces the scientific method, reasoning and critical thinking with respect to the analysis and interpretation of evidence associated with a set of alleged facts."

While not implying that *The Scene Processing Cascade* is an invaluable method because it is absent the scientific method. However, marrying the cascade with criminalistic logic will automatically utilize the principle of the scientific method that, if employed properly, will guarantee the investigation will move forward using a depth of reasoning necessary for ultimate success. Thus the re-check steps in *The Scene Processing Cascade*, when they embody hypothesis testing, rejection and and so on, inherent in the scientific method, will protect the investigation from mistakes, such as missing evidence, and from introducing bias (Chapter 2). Now, the re-check process will reflect not just evidence that had been missed but will focus on its interpretation and analysis, with the goal of building of a body of knowledge based on information and data obtained from the scene. In the process, additional testable hypotheses should develop which, in-turn, should spawn a new set of testable hypotheses or re-checks.

The original three re-checks in the cascade will incorporate a time-tested, scientific process, which might translate into the original three, four, 10 or more "re-checks" as new testable hypotheses develop. As an exercise, students should develop examples of how an investigation might incorporate the scientific method in a scene investigation. The scene example provided in Chapter 2 should be reviewed because it illustrates the point.

In their article on crime reconstruction, Gardner and Bevel [4] point out that the scientific method is inherent in their approach to evidence interpretation. Certainly, their argument is persuasive because it presents a roadmap for lay investigators. Their logic is flawed, however because the terminology they use to *explain* (proving) hypothetical facts is not how scientists employ the scientific method. Instead, scientists concern themselves with a process of *disproving* hypotheses, not proving them.

References

1. R. M. Gardner, 2007. *Practical Crime Scene, Processing and Investigation*. Chapter 4. Boca Raton, CRC Press, pages 75–86.
2. National Institute of Justice, 1995. The first officer's responsibilities. In *The Responding Officer*. Washington, DC, Department of Justine, Government Printing Office.
3. Adapted from: H. C. Lee, P. Timothy, and M. T. Miller, 2005. Chapter 3, General crime scene procedures. In *Henry Lee's Crime Scene Handbook*. Elsevier Academic Press, pages 49–70.
4. R. M. Gardner and T. Bevel, 2007. Theoretical and practical considerations in crime scene reconstruction. *Journal of Forensic Identification*, 57(6):891–911.

The Fundamental Principles of Evidence

4

4.1 Introduction

In Chapter 1, a broad working definition of evidence was proposed, as it relates specifically to crime scene investigation.

> Anything associated with a crime scene, incident, or argument; whether or not it has been collected, described, photographed, analyzed scientifically, or reasoned about and which might be introduced into a legal proceeding in order to ascertain the truth of an issue.

The purpose of such a broad definition is to bring the concept of evidence out of its traditional legal realm into the world of the practicum. In Chapter 1, Section 1.5, titled "The Concept of Evidence," introduced the idea that evidence is not a simple concept and that its definition might have a psychological—some might say investigative—component unrelated to its legal relevance. Also suggested was the possibility that unrecognized "evidence" might still be evidence as defined above.

This chapter expands the discussion of evidence in Chapter 1 as it relates to scene investigation. We will begin with the historical perspective, which implies that any meaningful discussion of crime scene evidence must begin with the most well known and perhaps the founder of modern criminalistics, the French physician and lawyer Edmond Locard. His philosophy embodies the following statement attributed to him—"Every touch leaves a trace," which is also the basic tenet of criminalists and the creed of crime scene investigators.

4.2 The Locard Exchange Principle: "Every Touch Leaves a Trace"

Although Locard probably never said it precisely like that, the Exchange Principle ascribed to him forms the basic philosophy of and the reason for conducting a crime scene investigation. Locard's writings never explicitly mentioned something that he termed an exchange principle (*principe de l'echange*) but he did certainly embrace the concept. For example, writing about the analysis of dust in 1930 [1–3], Locard [1] stated [emphasis in quote added]:

> Among recent researches, the analysis of dust has appeared as one of the newest and most surprising. Yet, upon reflection, one is astonished that it has been necessary to wait until this late day for so simple an idea to be applied as the collecting, in the dust of garments, of the evidence of the objects rubbed against, and the contacts which a suspected person may have undergone. *For the microscopic debris that covers our clothes and bodies are the mute witnesses, sure and faithful, of all our movements and of all our encounters.* (p. 276)

Inman and Rudin [4] believe Locard's publications from 1920 and 1923 represent "slightly different insights into his thinking on the issue of material transfer" (p. 93). While perhaps true, there is also the possibility that their term "insights" might more properly represent a normal progression one takes with maturity and experience. Certainly, by 1930, Locard was convinced that microscopic evidence formed the essence of evidence transfer and, hence, his exchange principle. As the forensic microscopist Richard Bisbing [5] wrote, reporting what the forensic scientist Duayne Dillon said,

> Duayne Dillon recently lamented that authors over the years have offered varying statements that they identified as "Locard's Exchange Principle" and much has been made of the importance of this "principle." He noted that Locard's publications make no mention of an "Exchange Principle," although Locard did make the observation, "Il est impossible au malfaiteur d'agir avec l'intensit que suppose l'action criminelle sans laisser des traces de son passage," translated as, It is impossible for a criminal to act, especially considering the intensity of a crime, without leaving traces of this presence.

Although Locard likely never explicitly referred to his thoughts or beliefs as an exchange principle, others did, as Bisbing [5] also wrote,

> The Locard Exchange Principle was reiterated by L.C. Nickolls, . . . thereby confirming it as a lasting principle . . . I commonly express the principle this way: whenever two objects come in contact with each other, they transfer material from one to the other. The Locard exchange produces the trace evidence of interest from fingerprints to mud.

One might wonder what drove Locard down that specific scientific path. It certainly was not on the minds of his contemporaries. His education in science and the law demonstrated that he had an interest and the background to apply science to the law. Perhaps this juxtaposition of disciplines was the seed that sprouted in his mind. And then there is the most interesting question of who influenced Locard the most. Perhaps surprisingly, he attributes his revelation with respect to trace evidence's importance in criminal investigation to two seemingly divergent historical figures [1].

> I must confess that if, in the Police Laboratory of Lyon, we are interested in any unusual way in this problem of dust, it is because of having absorbed the ideas found in Gross and in Conan Doyle . . . (p. 277)

Hans Gross was a forensic giant, so it is little surprise that Locard studied Gross' 1893 *Manual for Examining Magistrates as a System of Criminology* [6]. From Locard's perspective, this arguably formed the basis of modern criminalistics, if he thought of it as that, because this was the first publication describing the marriage among science, the crime scene investigation, and the law, all of which were Locard's passions. Gross combined, for the first time, fields of knowledge that had not been integrated previously. As Locard [1] wrote in 1930,

> It would be a mistake to believe that the idea of studying dust for the purpose of discovering criminological evidence is of modern origin. By seeking diligently we may trace it to the old masters of legal medicine. However, the first author who clearly described cases where this research has been made is Hans Gross. . . . In his "Manual for Examining Magistrates" Gross grouped together everything in these various teachings that would contribute to the building up of a good criminal investigation. (pp. 276–277)

Locard's second expressed influence was Sir Arthur Conan Doyle, the author of *The Adventures of Sherlock Holmes*. This connection, however, really should not be such a huge surprise. Doyle was a University of Edinburgh-educated physician who learned analytical reasoning from his professor Joseph Bell, an army surgeon and hospital physician. He skillfully applied his medical training and acute mind to create the fictional Holmes, a highly egocentric yet contemplative master scientific sleuth. As Locard [1] wrote,

> For, in the adventures of Sherlock Holmes, the detective is repeatedly asked to diagnose the origin of a speck of mud, which is nothing but moist dust. (p. 277)

Whereas the above discussion suggests that Locard was inspired by Gross and Doyle, Robertson and Roux [7] state, ". . . Locard himself referred to a German chemist (Liebig) for his initial ideas" (p. 89). Regardless of whether it was Gross, Doyle, or Liebig, they were not the only well-known forensic investigators—criminologists as they were called at the time—who might have influenced Locard's thinking. Clearly, his high opinion of Gross affected him greatly, but Locard lived in Lyon and Gross was in Prague. A close and early association in Lyon was a heavyweight criminologist in the early 1900s, Alexandre Lacassagne, the founder of the Lacassagne School of Criminology and a major force in criminal investigations in Lyon. One might speculate that Locard's disillusionment with Lacassagne, if that is what it was, might be that Lacassagne was a devotee of German physicist Franz Joseph Gall's theories of phrenology, a defunct trade once thought to be a science. Did Locard recognize that phrenology was fraudulent and, if so, would that have been reason sufficient enough to look more askance at Lacassagne?

After passing the bar exam in 1907, Locard traveled to Paris to study with Alphonse Bertillon, the founder of the first scientific method for identifying criminals—anthropometry, commonly known as Bertillonage. Like Locard, Bertillon was a forensic renaissance man who dabbled in numerous forensic arenas and believed fervently in the application of science to criminal investigation. It seems surprising, then, that Locard failed to mention Bertillon as someone who helped shape his beliefs with respect to the transfer of evidence. Perhaps, Bertillon never considered the topic or they never discussed the subject or Bertillon did not believe it was important. Bertillon did go to crime scenes and, as Bertillon's student, Locard would have benefitted from his mentor's belief in the application of science to the investigation of crime.

4.3 Divisible Matter

Although not expressed explicitly by him, the concept of the Exchange Principle attributed to Locard was certainly entrenched in his mind and demonstrated in his work. Inherent, too, in his belief that microscopic evidence could be transferred between and among people and between and among inanimate objects, such as a crime scene, was that such transfers required energy. Locard believed that it was the nature of a violent crime to provide the force necessary to affect an evidence transfer. Thus, a fiber from a sexual assault victim's blouse would undergo a force such that, when the assailant's shirt rubbed against it, it would come loose and transfer to the assailant's shirt. Similarly, fibers from the assailant's shirt would transfer to the victim's blouse. For Locard, the operative word was "force," which implies energy, which he believed was required to make such transfers happen. However, the theory might not explain reality. For example, certain fabrics "give up" their fibers easier than others and whereas some require more energy to release fibers than others. If the energy is not there, a transfer might not occur. Still, Locard's ideas represent the reality of what forensic scientists observe in the laboratory today.

Inman and Rudin [8] accepted Locard's idea that it takes energy (force) to affect evidence transfer, making it what they refer to as one of two guiding principles concerning the generation of evidence: divisible matter and transfer (Locard's Exchange Principle). For them, divisible matter implies a source of energy. They argue that something happens to evidence (their premise is that it is not evidence until this happens) which gives it the ability to transfer. They call this a "fracture" that requires energy. Once transferred, however, they define this transferred material as evidence, whether or not discovered [4]:

> If the crime is never discovered or the evidence is never detected, matter has still divided and transferred, and traits have still transferred. (p. 87)

They argue that transfer occurs with only certain kinds of evidence, excluding impression and physical match evidence. According to Inman and Rudin [8], Locard's transfer principle might not explain these types of evidence:

> Recognize that divisible matter does not account for a large category of evidence, that of pattern transfer evidence, such as prints and impressions. The transfer of matter requires its prior division; the transfer of "traits" may not. (p. 78)

Defining a new fundamental principle while excluding a large category of evidence types, a priori, seems problematic. If divisible matter is really a new *fundamental* principle of forensic science, one would expect it to apply to all evidence, regardless of type. Otherwise, it cannot be defined as fundamental. Logically, then, Inman and Rudin's concept would require a separate fundamental principle for each subcategory of evidence. When Inman and Rudin [8] discuss impression evidence, they state:

> Although small amounts of physical matter may be transferred, it is the pattern of transfer that concerns us, not the substance. Therefore divisible matter does not apply. (p. 77)

Irrespective of whether it is a fundamental principle, criminalists and scene scientists/investigators believe in and are concerned with the transfer of patterns or traits that have identification potential because of the individualizing characteristics present. However, pattern evidence is created because a division from the original takes place, which requires energy, albeit slight, and it occurs regardless of whether the transferred pattern has individualizing characteristics. The mechanism is the same. In fact, Locard would likely disagree that the "substance" transferred has little or no value. As Locard [3] wrote when he described a case in which the pattern (trait) itself had little individualizing value,

> The silverware of a restaurant had disappeared. Whoever had taken it must have mounted a chair in order to reach the shelf where it was kept. As chance would have it, there was on the seat of the chair a forgotten napkin. A shapeless mark had been left on the napkin, not distinct enough to indicate the kind of shoe worn by the individual. There was, however, a trace of mud on it, and this was examined under the microscope. In the midst of various animal and vegetable waste matter, there were discovered a superabundance of fine granulations which were recognized as fecal material. This fact was a reminder that during the same night scavengers had been working in a neighboring alley. Consequently, the investigation was directed to these men. (p. 509)

Fingerprints are another category of pattern evidence for which there might not be sufficient individualizing characteristics to make specific identifications. However, that does not imply that the only value of a latent print is to make identifications. Fingerprints come from people, and while it might not take much energy to divide the fingerprint residue from a finger to a physical substrate, there is certainly a division process that takes place of not just the pattern but also the constituents of the print itself. These constituents have investigative value. For example, recent work by Leggett et al. [9], which they term "lifestyle fingermarking," suggests that drugs and drug metabolites can be identified from fingerprints. Additionally, if during the commission of a crime, a perpetrator strangles the victim and then subsequently touches a surface, say on the way out of the scene, the epithelial cells and hence DNA of the victim would be incased in the perpetrator's fingerprint residue. By limiting one's criminalistic activities to simply identifying who left the print, a valuable source of information would be missed.

It seems, then, that defining divisible matter should not be so restrictive. As science advances, the potential exits that a class of evidence not seemingly falling into Inman and Rudin's [4] definition of divisible matter, as quoted below, might convert to one that does:

> Matter divides into smaller component parts when sufficient force is applied. The component parts will acquire characteristics created by the process of division itself and retain physicochemical properties of the larger piece. (p. 98)

The division of matter is shown schematically in Figure 4.1. The original source of the evidence comes from the participants in the crime—the scene, the victim, the perpetrator—and the divided evidence goes in two directions, each exposed to varying and likely different influences.

From the concept of divisible matter, Inman and Rudin [4] describe three corollaries which they believe follow logically:

> **Corollary 1:** Some characteristics retained by the smaller pieces are unique to the original item or to the division process. These traits are useful for individualizing all pieces to the original item.
>
> **Corollary 2:** Some characteristics retained by the smaller pieces are common to the original item as well as to other items of similar manufacture. We rely on these traits to classify the item.

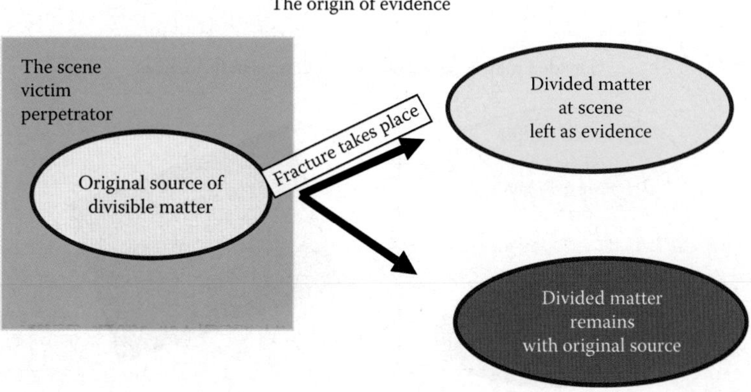

Figure 4.1 Divisible matter.

Corollary 3: Some characteristics of the original item will be lost or changed during or after the moment of division and subsequent dispersal; this confounds the attempt to infer a common source. (p. 98)

4.4 Evidence Dynamics

Corollary 3 considers that once division (fracture) has taken place, the uncertainty of a new environment intercedes. This concept was first espoused by Chisum and Turvey [10] in their concept of evidence dynamics:

> The process of crime reconstruction is often built on the assumption that evidence left behind at a crime scene, . . . is pristine. This assumption involves the belief that the process of taping off an area, limiting access, and setting about the task of taking pictures and making measurements ensures the integrity of the evidence found within. Subsequently, any conclusions reached through forensic examinations and reconstructions of that evidence are assumed to be a reliable lens through which to view the crime. This assumption is not always accurate. (p. 6)

Evidence dynamics refers to those influences that "change, relocate, obscure, or obliterate, the physical evidence, regardless of the intent" (p. 6) [10]. Generally, the dynamic process begins at the instant that forces, during a struggle, create a transfer (divisible matter and the Locard Exchange Principle) and ends when the evidence reaches the courtroom. The thought that the process ends there is not necessarily true either, as evidence used or not used in a legal proceeding might be required for subsequent hearings or trials. Each time the evidence is used or touched, the potential exists for it to change or be obliterated, subjected to the process of evidence dynamics—a process that can continue until it is finally destroyed under some authority.

Chisum and Turvey [10] list several influences of evidence dynamics and caution that each should be considered carefully when evidence is examined. Their list, while seemingly comprehensive, is not meant to be all-inclusive. Figure 4.2 schematically illustrates the process of evidence dynamics.

Here, the divided evidence goes in one of two directions, one with the participants of the event and the other remains with its original source, and each becomes subjected to a new environment—wear, interaction with chemicals, pollutants, and so on—with the potential for obliteration and/or contamination. Table 4.1 shows a list of those influences Chisum and Turvey [10] considered important.

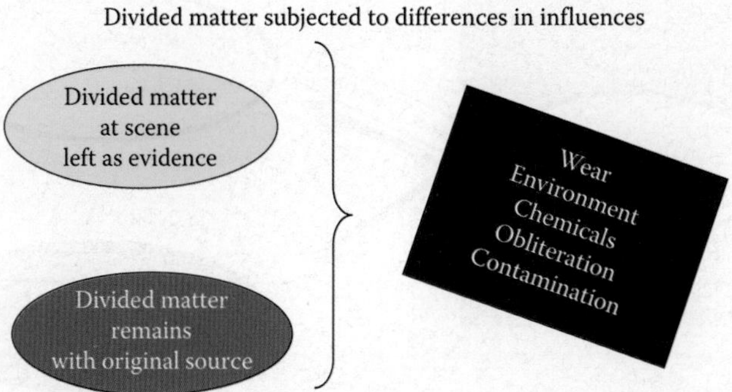

Figure 4.2 Evidence dynamics.

Table 4.1 Influences on Evidence Dynamics

- Offender actions
- Victim actions
- Secondary transfer
- Witnesses
- Weather/climate
- Decomposition
- Insect activity
- Animal predation
- Fire
  - Suppression efforts
- Police
- EMTs
- Scene investigators
- Forensic scientists/forensic entomologist/criminalists
- Medical examiners/coroners

It is not necessary to discuss each, except to point out generally that these must be prime investigative considerations, and scene scientists/investigators should realize that these influences exist and actively consider whether any might have affected the evidence at that scene. If so, then appropriate action should be considered carefully and implemented. The implications should be abundantly clear. Although Chisum and Turvey [10] were writing specifically about crime reconstruction, scene scientists/investigators must understand the resultant effect they can have on the investigation, reconstruction not withstanding.

> The failure to consider Evidence Dynamics as a part of any crime reconstruction [*crime scene investigation*] has the potential to provide for misinterpretations of physical evidence, and inaccurate or incomplete crime reconstruction. (p. 14)

Students and beginning investigators should always consciously consider the effect extraneous forces can have on evidence. In fact, they should actively not only be aware of the above, but also consider the ramifications each might have on the investigation while the investigation is active.

4.5 Crime Scene Elements

Before considering evidence transfers in more detail, it is important to discuss the interrelated parts of the scene as they relate to categories of evidence and where it might be found. This, then, is a focus on subscenes within the larger context of the whole, the whole being the scene itself.

The general concept espoused for finding probative evidence goes something like this: "Evidence leads to evidence." Many crime scene texts ignore this topic, except as a passing comment on searching. Instead, they focus on the various classes of evidence—trace evidence, impression evidence, DNA evidence, and so on—without considering the necessary preamble that places evidence into its proper perspective. This is an oversight because understanding the subcontext of evidence is the critical underlying thought process behind locating it, which is the fundamental reason for conducting crime scene investigation. As such, it is the proper scientific approach and ultimately dictates whether the investigation will be successful.

In their text, Lee et al. [11] consider the subject tangentially, briefly discussing microscopic and macroscopic aspects of crime scenes. Their discussion with respect to the macroscopic point of view refers to a scene they described earlier in their text:

> The macroscopic point of view of the crime scene above would include not just a location, but the victim's body, the suspect's body, the houses, and the vehicle involved. Essentially, this definition is looking at variously sized crime scenes within a crime scene—all are important and should be treated and investigated as crime scene. (p. 4)

They only mention that such a thing as a microscopic point of view exists in the following: ". . . any specific object or piece of physical evidence related to the crime being investigated." (p. 4)

This critical concept of the microscopic scene is typically ignored or considered lightly, as in the above definition. Scene scientists/investigators and students need to understand that a scene, in reality, is many scenes, subscenes, embedded within the whole. Each subscene is a macroscene having one or more microscenes (microscopic scenes) associated with it. Students and scene scientists/investigators need to understand this concept because the two, macroscenes and microscenes, are entirely interrelated, which forms the basis of a holistic* approach guaranteeing a competent and complete scene investigation.

4.5.1 The Macroscene

The macroscene is what an investigator sees on entering the scene, whether a homicide or a burglary. It is what assaults the visual, olfactory, and psychological senses through the assimilation of a plethora of sensory stimuli. A homicide scene might have a body, a pool of blood, obvious signs of a struggle, and spattered blood. A sexual assault might have evidence of a break-in, rumpled bed sheets, and blood. A burglary might have a broken window, a jimmied door, or an obviously disturbed jewelry case. A stalking case might have impression shoeprints outside a window or a forehead imprint on a windowpane. A plane crash might have bodies, luggage, and plane debris strewn across a field. Depending on the scene, the macroscene is the investigator's first visual impression.

The author's first scene was a homicide that occurred over 40 years ago. It took place in a dark alley outside a bar in Pittsburgh. While the scene is not a recurring memory, it easily surfaces. A young woman, lying face up, had been rendered unrecognizable by a large rock, her face bashed in and her head turned into a fleshy pulp of blood, tissue, and bone; blood and brains spilled onto the gravel. There was no odor, just a mess of face, brains, and blood.

* Holistic is a term used throughout this text. It is defined by the *Merriam-Webster Online Dictionary* [12] as: "2. relating to or concerned with wholes or with complete systems rather than with the analysis of, treatment of, or dissection into parts <*holistic* medicine attempts to treat both the mind and the body> <*holistic* ecology views humans and the environment as a single system>."

After literally hundreds of scenes later, that scene still lives; it never goes away, while others, many more violent, are pushed further from the conscious mind. The reason for mentioning this is that our senses are easily assaulted and overwhelmed, and it is easy to lose focus.

The scene diagram depicted in Figure 4.3, a mock shooting incident, was an in-class exercise for students. First consider the obvious scene details listed in the diagram—the macroscene elements: a body, a bullet hole in a window, blood on the entrance doorknob on the exterior surface, blood trail on the floor and small, what some might consider high velocity, spatters on the floor and to the right of where the blood trail begins. A gunshot wound to the deceased, not part of the immediate macroscene, is hidden because of the deceased's position on the floor, although a pool of blood has formed under him suggestive of what might have happened.

Although the macroscene includes obviously visible aspects, other more subtle macroscene elements are also defined for this discussion as part of the macroscene. The reason is that these subtle elements can be made visual by simple techniques. For example, the window has submacroscene elements, the bullet hole the most obvious. Others might include features (elements) that do not immediately stand out: fingerprints on the windowsill, shoeprints in dust on the pavement underneath the window, forehead prints and/or fingerprints on the glass from pressing against the window. These evidentiary elements represent the window's subscene, its macroscene, and they are critical in understanding the window's role in the context of what happened during the commission of the crime. They, too, are part of the macroscene and must be defined as macroscene elements because they can be easily visualized using common scene investigative tools—ALS, flashlight, dusting powder, and so on.

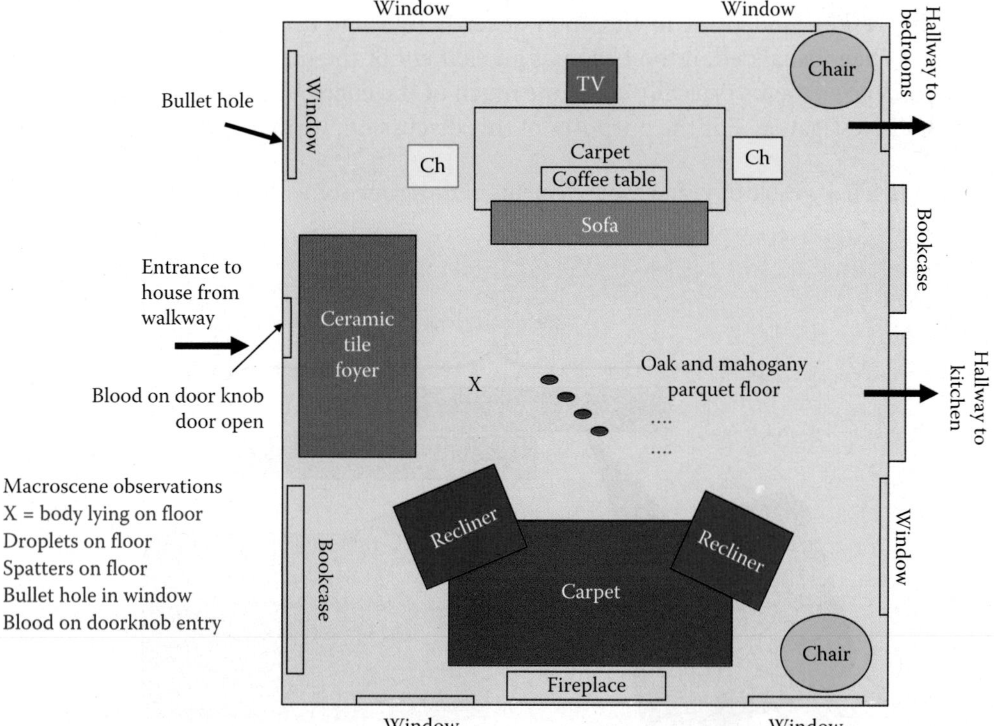

Figure 4.3 Hypothetical crime scene diagram.

The body is another part of the macroscene, itself a macroscene element. Because it is a dead body, however, it evokes a visceral response and tends to become the focal point of the investigation. Novice scene scientists/investigators quickly equate the body with the scene, and ignore other macroscene and microscene elements. This is a natural reaction, but a dead body should never overshadow other elements of the macroscene. Like the window, the body has its own set of macroscene elements: bloodstains and bloodstain patterns on clothing that are both visible and interpretable, GSR in the form of fouling or stippling on the skin, hands, or clothing, and contusions, sharp force wounds, and so on will be defined by the medical examiner during the autopsy.

The scene scientist/investigator must consider each macroscene element individually and as a part of the whole. A schematic of macroscene elements is shown in Figure 4.4.

Although Figure 4.4 is not an all-inclusive list of possible visible and visualizable elements, scene scientists/investigators should never fail to include the elements listed in their search. Considering the scene diagram in Figure 4.3, the important investigative questions seem obvious: What is the direction of the bullet—was its path going inside the house? If so, where is it? Did investigators miss bullet defects or was it a fatal shot that is inside the body? Where was the shooter standing? If the bullet path was toward the outside of the house, where is it and where is the gun? What was the target?

As mentioned, the macroscene includes evidence that is invisible to the naked eye but can be made visible at the scene. Thus, a fingerprint on a doorjamb is invisible until dusted, when it becomes an element of the macroscene. On the other hand, a fingerprint that is not visualized at the scene is latent evidence that is part of the microscene; hopefully, someone develops it in the latent print laboratory, but there is the possibility that it might never be developed, if the surface on which it lies is not collected.

A dry residue shoeprint in the entry foyer is invisible until highlighted by oblique lighting. When visualized, it too becomes an element of the macroscene. These examples of macroscene elements typically consume much of the energy, thought and time of scene scientists/investigators. For the purposes of this discussion, we define the macroscene as

> The individual, visible or visualizable elements of the crime scene, each of which is a part of the whole.

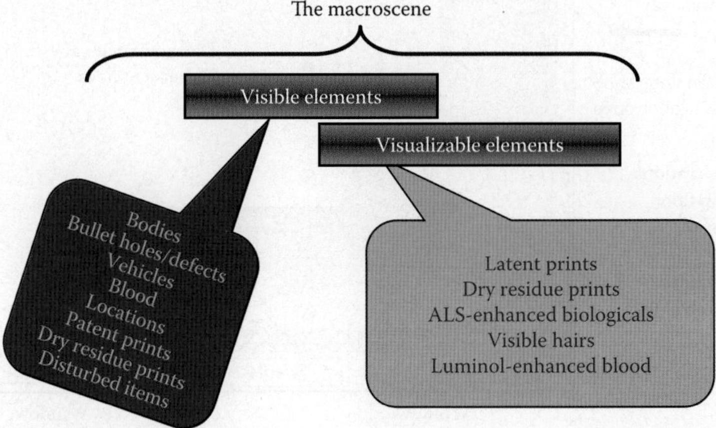

Figure 4.4 Macroscene elements.

4.5.2 The Microscene: Trace Evidence or Locard Elements

Although macroscene elements are visible or can be made visible at the scene, another equally important class of evidence that is not visually apparent and cannot yet be made visible at the scene is the microscene or microscopic scene. Nevertheless, the microscene elements hold no less importance for the investigation, and, like macroscene elements, they must be collected and preserved. Microscene elements are those tiny microscopic traces, divisible matter transferred during the commission of the crime. Scene scientist/investigators typically call microscene elements trace evidence; they must, however, be also correctly thought of as Locard Elements, in honor of the scientist who considered them such a crucial part of the overall investigation. They are the traces, the dust, that likely consumed much of Locard's attention and which formed the basis of his thoughts about the transfer of evidence.

The line between macroscene elements and microscene elements is obviously blurred and not clearly defined. For example, a hair that is visible on a victim's clothing—a blond hair on a black T-shirt—might correctly be considered a macroscene element. However, another hair might not be so easily visible—black hair on a black T-shirt—depending on color, size, location, and background contrast, and might rightly be thought of as a microscene element. Such restrictive definitions are not as important as the concept and how it is thought of at the scene.

The difficulty in locating and collecting these microscene elements lies in the fact that they are invisible; collecting them requires the application of the scientific method through diligence and a systematic and logical approach. Logic requires the consideration of which macroscene elements should be present, given the scene, the crime type, and the type of trace evidence—microscene elements—associated with them. For example, the scene depicted in Figure 4.4 has several macroscene elements: body, blood trail, bullet hole, and so on. Associated with each macroscene element are microscene elements or trace evidence. Although this evidence is invisible to the naked eye, fortunately there are standard collection techniques. In order to properly investigate the macroscene elements at a scene, investigators should ensure that all of the microscene elements present are collected.

It must be absolutely clear that there is an integral relationship between the macroscene and the microscene because the creation of one, by definition, creates the other; the microscene elements are the consequence of activity that created macroscene elements. For example, a struggle between two people might result in one of the two ending up dead. The body is one element of the macroscene. It has macroscene subelements, such as bloodstains, knife wounds, contusions, and so on, and also microscene elements, such as hairs, fibers, fingerprints, GSR, and so on. The knife lying next to the body at the scene is another macroscene element, with a subset of macroscene elements, such as blood, patent bloody fingerprints, imbedded fibers, and so on. It also has microscene elements, such as fiber traces, DNA, and so on.

Figure 4.5 illustrates the obvious interrelationship between the macroscene and the microscene, the macroscene being the visible and the visualized elements—bodies, bullets, and so on—and the microscene being anything microscopic—dust, hairs, fibers, DNA, and so on. One can define the microscene as

> Invisible, microscopic or latent traces intimately associated with the macroscene and commonly called trace evidence but can be considered Locard Elements.

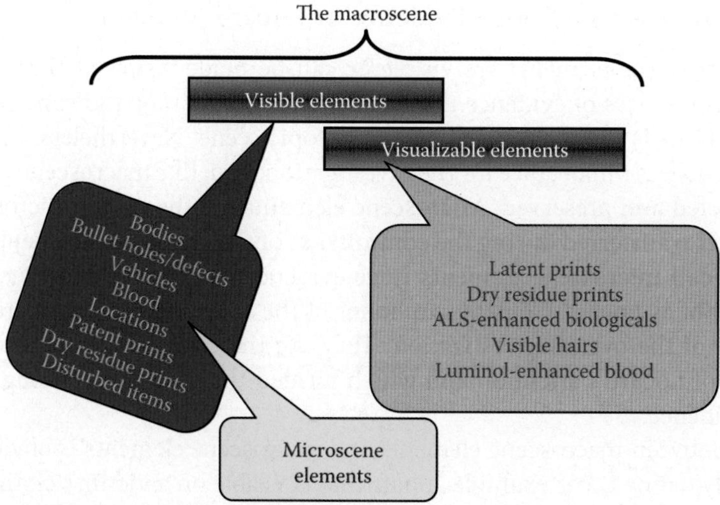

Figure 4.5 Macroscene and microscene elements.

It seems obvious, now, that when two participants interact, such as in a violent crime, physical material will transfer from one to the other and also to the location where the activity takes place—the scene. This is a theory, but to what extent does this really happen? Can such transfers occur a second or more times? What evidence (debris) is normally present in that area (of, say, the struggle) of the macroscene? The first question harks back to the discussion concerning the energy it takes to transfer, for example, fibers from one garment to another during the commission of a crime.

Cwiklik [13] considered the second question, a phenomenon called "secondary transfer," how often it occurs, and what the effect of such transfers might have on an investigation:

> . . . particles and fibers abraded, flaked, broken, or torn from the items themselves as well as other particles and fibers that have collected on the surface of each item prior to their contact. The latter particles and fibers are non-component debris: not an intrinsic (component) part of the items themselves. Their transfer is referred to as secondary, tertiary, and higher degrees of transfer: indirect transfer from the source item. (p. 1136)

Cwiklik also considered the third question and defined sets of microscene elements [the author's terminology applied to Cwiklik's] intrinsic and exogenous to macroscenes. She placed them into specific categories, defining each. See Figure 4.6 which has been adapted from Cwiklik's discussion.

The microscene elements (evidence) of a particular macroscene environment are divided into families. Each family comprises a set of debris (particles and fibers) and an associated subset of debris (particles and fibers). There are also stray particles and fibers and small subsets that hold little investigative value. Each set also shares a common condition, such as a common site, a means of production, and a means of transport. This set represents a record of the daily life of that specific macroscene environment.

The subsets within each set occur from a diverse set of origins including hairs and skin flakes from the occupants, fibers indigenous to that specific environment (e.g., feathers

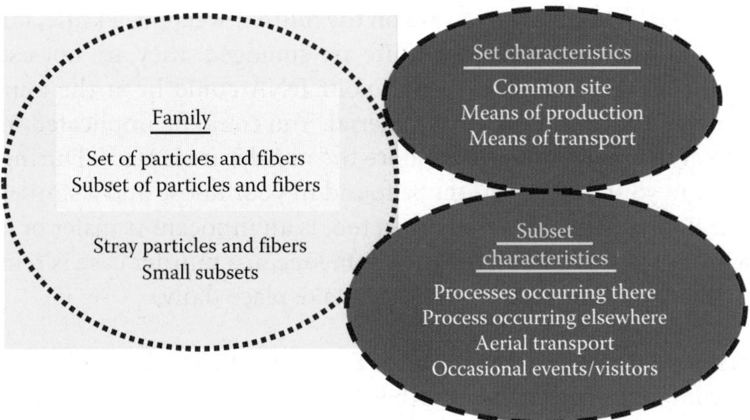

Figure 4.6 Microscene element families.

from pillows in a bedroom or carpet fibers), clothing fibers (e.g., from a wardrobe), processes that occurred elsewhere (e.g., debris shed from clothing or footwear), and aerial transport (e.g., soil, traffic dust, insect parts, botanicals such as pollen and/or spores). These, too, represent part of the daily record of the macroscene.

Different from these is a subset of debris from occasional events that define a timeline for activity taking place within the part of the macroscene that defines the crime scene. Thus, examining a single macroscene environment at a crime scene reflects two important facts: the daily record of that environment and a timeline of transient events taking place within that environment. Scene scientists/investigators must be cognizant that each microscene holds this information and then tailor the search and recovery of evidence so that the daily record and the occasional record are not lost. The challenge is differentiating the daily from the transient records, which is not necessarily the responsibility of the investigation. The responsibility of the investigation, though, is to ensure that microscene elements of the daily record *and* elements present because of the scene activity are both collected. Simply, scene scientists/investigators must collect the appropriate exemplars during the investigation.

4.5.2.1 The Transfer of Microscene Elements

Before we begin a practical discussion on how easy or difficult it is to transfer evidence, it might be interesting to consider how much "stuff" there is in the world that theoretically could be transferred in an environment that is not usually associated with a crime. This is an overwhelming thought because the amount of transferrable material is probably limitless. Certainly, all transferrable material will not end up at a particular crime scene, but each of us is each exposed to a significant amount of transferrable material everyday, which we bring back to where we live and which becomes part of the daily record in our own environment. So what is the implication of environments having a limitless supply of transferrable material?

Well, let us consider an example with only one transfer of material. Suppose one day, in your daily travel, you shake hands with someone who then visits a mutual friend. They end up arguing and a murder takes place—the visited mutual friend is dead. What is the probability that your skin cells (DNA) are on the murder weapon, a knife, taken from the friend's kitchen? If fingerprints on the knife are smudged, they are not useful for purposes of comparison. But innocent or not, your DNA could be at the murder scene, a consequence of an innocent transfer of material. You could be implicated in the murder if you had been at the scene sometime before the murder took place. During the investigation, a fiber from your sweater might be found in your house and a similar fiber might be found in the house of the deceased. This, too, is an innocent transfer of material. The chance of such transfers falsely implicating someone in a murder case is remote, but this example does illustrate that material transfers take place daily.

4.5.2.1.1 Primary Transfer The Locard Exchange Principle explains the transfer of evidence from one person to another. There are, however, instances, such as those suggested above, when transfer does not easily or ever take place. Consider footwear impressions at a scene as an example. Some footwear impressions fall into the macroscene element category because they are either immediately visible, for example, wet origin impressions, or are latent and can be made visible, for example, dry origin impressions highlighted using oblique lighting. For the impression pattern to be transferred, the shoe and the receiving surface characteristics must be able to produce or accept an impression transfer. Importantly, not all surfaces equally accept impression evidence, a topic Bodziak [14] discusses in his comprehensive text on footwear impression evidence. Figure 4.7, adapted from Bodziak, illustrates this principle for footwear evidence [14].

From Figure 4.7, it is clear that certain surfaces have a higher likelihood of accepting footwear impressions than others. For example, a wet shoe will likely leave a print on most surfaces except a carpet perhaps. A dry shoe with dust on the sole will not likely leave a print on a floor that is already dirty, and a clean dry shoe will not likely leave detectable prints on a dirty floor, a carpet, or a clean unwaxed floor. So, while the Locard Exchange Principle theoretically guarantees a transfer of evidence, there are practical considerations scene scientists/investigators must take into account logically.

Surface	Wet Shoe	Blood/Oil/Grease	Dry w/Dust	Clean Dry
Carpet	+	++++	+++	+
Dirty floor	+++	++++	+	+
Clean unwaxed floor	+++	++++	++++	+
Relatively clean unwaxed	+++	++++	++++	+++
Waxed desk top	+++	++++	++++	+++
Glass	++++	++++	++++	+++
Kicked in door	++++	++++	++++	+++
Paper/cardboard	++++	++++	++++	+++

Figure 4.7 Likelihood of two-dimensional footwear transfer on various surfaces.

With regard to the transfer of fibers, Pounds and Smalldon [15] showed that the number of fibers transferred depends on several factors, most of which make sense and others that a priori do not.

- The size of the surface area in contact
- The number of contacts
- The force/pressure applied during contact is directly related to the number of fibers transferred up to a maximum number
- The pressure causes fiber fragmentation resulting in the preferential transfer over larger fibers
- Cotton, acrylic, or wool fibers transfer easier than polyester or viscose fibers, with 80% of polyester or viscose fibers transferred being <5 mm
- Differential shedding results in fiber transfer for mixed blends; the transfer does not occur in proportion to the stated blend (weight) of fibers present
- Most fibers in blends transfer the minor component of the blend
- Morphology and thickness of fibers affect transfer
- Some microfibers transfer larger numbers of fibers than cotton, while others do not transfer as well
- Age and/or wear affects fabric transfer

This list of factors affecting the transfer of fibers might seem somewhat esoteric, especially to crime scene investigators unfamiliar with the concept of fabric/fiber transfer or those experienced investigators who never thought much about evidence transfer in this context. Crime scene scientists/investigators should understand and examine, at the scene if possible, the composition of fabrics—garments, furniture, and so on—situated in areas where transfers might take place—areas of contact during a struggle. The clothing of the deceased should be evaluated to ascertain the potential for the primary fiber transfer from the crime scene and/or the victim to a perpetrator during a violent event. This can be crucial because favorable shedding fabrics are a source of important associative evidence (fibers) that can transfer to the clothing of an assailant. The crime laboratory scientist will search the garment, find the transferred fibers, and compare them to exemplars. This is important because the crime laboratory scientist and the scene scientist/investigator become partners in the investigation.

An important category of multitasking evidence is glass, which, when it breaks, spews fragments or chards in a 360° variable pattern. Essentially, glass fragments fly backward and forward after the break, which means glass shards might be found on a burglar's clothing. See Figure 4.8, adapted from Pounds and Smalldon [15], for an illustration of the distribution of glass shards.

For a burglar breaking a window to enter a residence, small shards of glass should lodge in his clothing, depending on the characteristics of the fabric. Importantly, shards will be found in a 360° circle in the area of the broken window up to a distance of at least 10 ft., with most shards in the approximately 3–5 ft. area of the break. Also, the highest distribution of fragments would be expected in the area between the 45° angle on either side of the impact point. Certainly, the higher the impact force, the smaller the fragments. These small shards have extremely sharp edges, which theoretically can become imbedded in the soles of shoes or in the weave of fabrics, again depending on the composition of the shoe sole and the fabric.

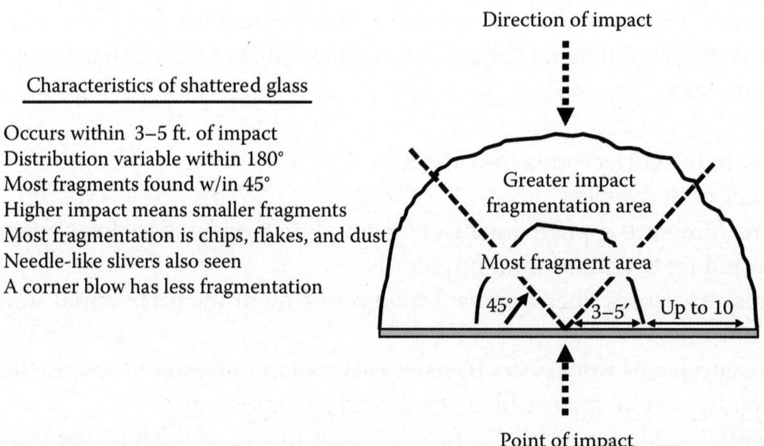

Figure 4.8 Backward distribution of breaking glass.

From a scene perspective, the investigation team should determine the radius of the distribution pattern and locate the area with the highest density of shards. Within the glass distribution pattern, there might be a void, which should alert the scene scientist/investigator that shards might have impacted the clothing of the burglar. Representative samples of glass from the scene should be collected so that an appropriate scientific comparison can be made.

In an in-class exercise, students divided the floor into sections, as shown in Figure 4.9. Then they broke a double-pane basement window using a hammer and tracked and counted fragments and shards on both sides of the break. The shards traveled at least 10 ft. in both directions (essentially the length of the room). The diagram on the slide below

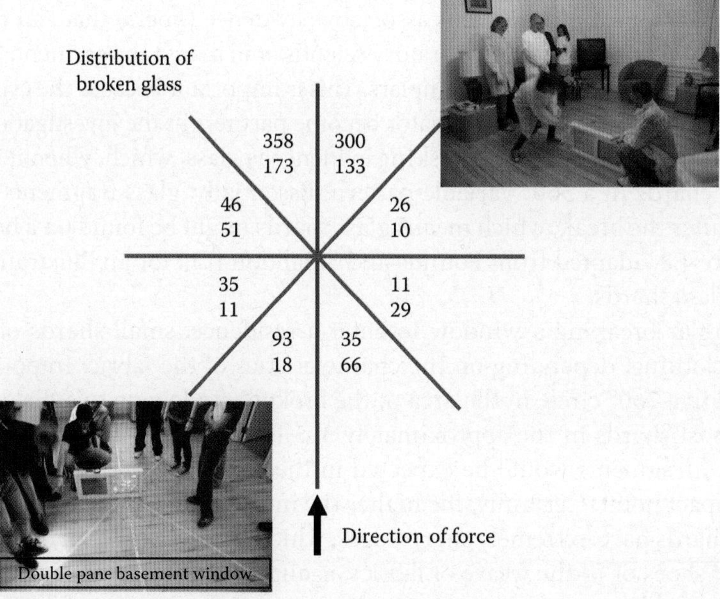

Figure 4.9 Class experiment of breaking windowpane glass.

shows the number of shards counted and their distribution in the eight divided sections. The two numbers in each section represent two separate sections of the class performing the same exercise. The difference in the numbers probably represents the various forces used to break the window.

The exercise clearly illustrated the distribution of glass shards and the direction that the shards took after the break. Importantly, it was noted that glass moved backward as well as forward, suggesting the real possibility of finding glass shards on the clothing of the person breaking the glass.

4.5.2.1.2 Secondary Transfer Secondary transfer happens when trace evidence (e.g., fibers) from a primary target transfers to a secondary target. The concept is illustrated in Figure 4.10.

Assume that a primary transfer has taken place from one fabric to another—blue garment to green garment in Figure 4.10. If the receiving garment (green) subsequently contacts another receiving garment (yellow), fibers can (not a guarantee) transfer from the green garment to the yellow garment resulting in a small percent of fibers being transferred from the blue garment to the yellow garment. This is an example of secondary transfer. This topic has been the subject of conjecture and laboratory studies for several years. Much of the research has been in the form of mock situations and much of it relates to garment-to-garment transfers. Certainly, casework examples exist.

From a crime scene perspective, the scene scientist/investigator should not lose sight of the fact that secondary transfers are possible. It is possible to envision how fibers might be transferred from one garment to another in random fashion as one moves from place to place, sits on fabric chairs, rubs against surfaces, gets jostled in public transportation or in places where other people have been. It would be ludicrous to think we are not picking up trace material from the places we frequent and the objects we touch in our daily lives. Isn't this the Locard Exchange Principle in action? We are, in fact, a living history of our daily environment. If someone attacks us in our home and physical contact occurs, there is a reasonable chance that there will be a transfer of fibers and other trace evidence, both ways. Some of these transfers might involve secondary or higher transfers.

If we consider the transfer of Locard Elements as axiomatic, it is their persistence, then, that should be a concern, although clearly not the main concern, of the scene scientist/investigator.

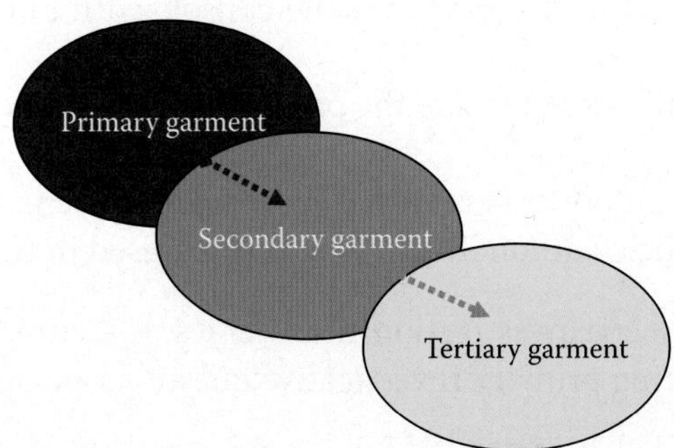

Figure 4.10 Primary, secondary, and tertiary transfers of trace evidence.

4.5.2.1.3 The Persistence of Locard Elements Studies have been done to ascertain how persistent fibers are after transfer. That is, the length of time transferred fibers might remain on a particular surface after an event. It is beyond the scope of this chapter to consider this topic further except to point out that persistence is the concern of the laboratory criminalist with respect to interpreting the meaning of the trace evidence found. See Chapter 17, Section 17.3 transfer and persistence of hair.

4.5.2.1.4 Putting It Together: Asking Investigative Questions Investigative questions are important in the beginning of an investigation and throughout. Initially, there should be at least three investigative questions that lead the team forward. As the investigation continues, other questions will arise and guide the investigation to its next logical step. Let us examine a case to illustrate, in a simple way, how the origin of evidence and appropriate investigative questions can be thought of from a practical sense.

4.6 Scene Scenario

Assume you are the crime scene reconstruction supervisor, and your crime scene unit was dispatched by the prosecutor's office as a secondary responder in the investigation into the death of a 45-year-old man found shot in the head inside his vehicle. The vehicle, found at the end of a dead-end alley, had been taken to the police precinct-processing garage, where your team was to examine it. The police believed the shooting was a homicide and had started the investigation. The following facts are relevant:

- The victim had been removed by emergency medical service (EMS) personnel before the first responding crime scene team arrived.
- Bloodstains were found on the seat and on the console (Figure 4.11 shows the blood patterns present). They suggest the victim was in the driver's side of the car when he died—the largest pool of blood is in the driver's seat (see Figure 4.11). This was confirmed by the EMS supervisor, whose team removed the deceased from the driver's side of the car.
- The windows were up and the doors were shut and unlocked.
- The seats of the car were made of microfiber acrylic.
- The autopsy showed a single gunshot to the head with the entrance just behind the right ear. The projectile had an upward path and did not exit.
- The weapon was not recovered at the scene.
- The deceased was found slumped over the console with blood dripping onto the console.
- A witness saw an individual inside the passenger's side of the car. He did not hear the gunshot.
- The passenger's side door was removed by the crime scene unit in order to gain entrance to the vehicle without disturbing the deceased in the driver's seat.

During the original scene investigation and after it was secured, the information above was available. The following primary investigative questions are apparent:

- Was the manner of death homicide, suicide, or accident?
- Was the car the primary or only scene—was this staged?

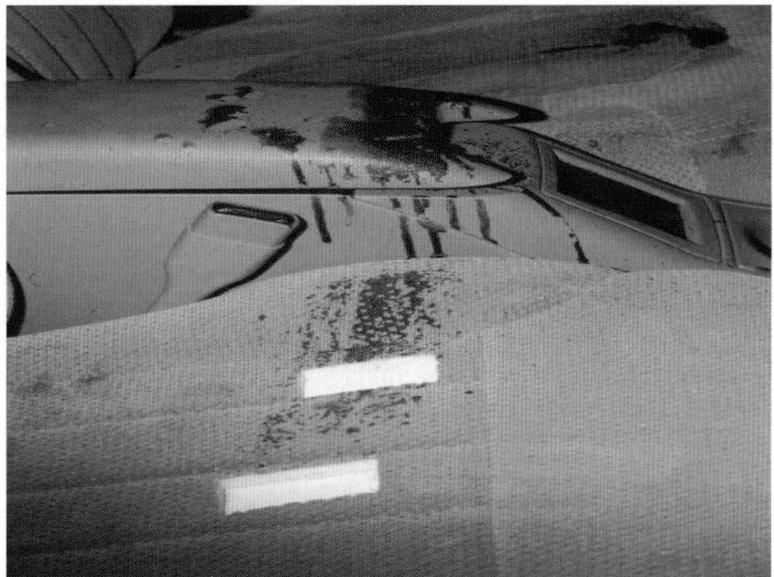

Figure 4.11 Bloodstains on front seats of vehicle.

- A related question might be: If the manner of death is a homicide, what was the origin of the fatal bullet and/or where was the shooter sitting/standing? Where is the weapon?

These questions initiate the scene investigation. Others become apparent as the investigation continues, and as long as questions occur, the scene investigation is incomplete. The primary investigative question is the most important. In this instance, it concerns the manner of death: homicide, suicide, or accident. This is critical because the ground truth can differ from what the macroscene presents or suggests. Certainly, beginning the investigation without formulating the primary investigative questions is a mistake because then it becomes an investigation-lacking leadership, logic, and science. Not surprisingly, students have difficulty formulating investigative questions partly because of inexperience, but also because some questions might not have immediate answers. Another reason is that students have trouble pinpointing what is important given the chaos of the scene.

In the example above, assuming that the manner of death is a suicide is a mistake because that makes the medical examiner the prime investigator, which does not happen except during the autopsy. The scene scientist/investigator should consider all manners of death but should focus on the one that requires the most rigorous investigative effort.

Here, the weapon is missing, which leads to the logical hypothesis that the case is a homicide. Working through the questions is important, but evaluating the scene for what it has to offer can often answer seemingly evasive questions. In considering the scene, the scene scientist/investigator should consider the following:

- What are the important macroscene elements?
- What microscene elements are critical to this investigation, where are they, and with which macroscene elements are they associated?

Table 4.2 Outside the Car: Hypothesis Testing

Macroscene Element	First Hypothesis	Testing the First Hypothesis	Second Hypothesis
Outside the car	This is a homicide, so blood and fingerprints of assailant might be on the outside of the car.	• Fingerprints on driver's side window do not match deceased. • No blood found.	• Assailant touched driver's side window during or before struggle with deceased. • Assailant not injured outside the car.

- Which crime scene investigative techniques are necessary to answer the most important investigative questions?
- What is missing?

Searching for evidence in this case begins with encompassing the above questions into the framework of the scientific method. For example, as defined above, macroscene elements are the most visible elements of the scene. One obvious element is the car, which can be split into outside and inside. Let us consider an example using two elements on the outside of the car, fingerprints, and blood (see Table 4.2).

From the above, the logic requires continuing the investigation as though it is a homicide, even though the unknown fingerprints might be from an innocent passerby. Inside the car, the most visible macroscene elements (minus the body) are the seats, the steering wheel, the dashboard, the console, and the blood. Each should be considered logically using the self-correcting—hypothesis/testing/feedback—mechanism of the scientific method. Eventually, the true scene will come into perspective.

The seats, front and back, require an interesting thought process because they have a microfiber fabric that can accept and shed fibers readily, and might have microscene elements that should be collected by picking and tape lifting. The logic shown in Table 4.3 might be followed.

Certainly, new hypotheses will develop as the investigation continues. And although these findings can provide investigative guidance, there are no concrete answers. The question of the characteristics of the assailant is still not answered and a new hypothesis is necessary to drill closer to that information. The purpose of the above discussion has

Table 4.3 Inside the Car: Hypothesis Testing

Macroscene Element	First Hypothesis	Testing the First Hypothesis	Second Hypothesis
Seats inside the car	This is a homicide, so if assailant sat on seats, fibers from clothing and hairs might be present.	• Tape lifting passenger's seat revealed grossly visible fibers different from shirt and pants of deceased. Not seen on other seats. • Black kinky hair found on passenger's seat. Deceased is Caucasian and has brown hair.	• Assailant sat in passenger's seat during murder. • Assailant might be African-American.

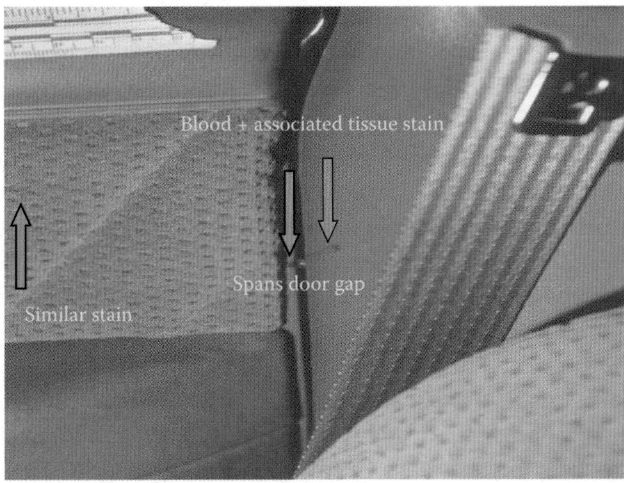

Figure 4.12 Replaced passenger's side door showing positions of blood/tissue.

been to illustrate the logic involved and how it leads the investigation further. That said, where should the investigation go from here? Well, we know that we have someone or more than one person at the scene not including the deceased. We have a witness who saw someone in the passenger's seat, which seems to confirm the finding of hairs, fibers, and fingerprints different from those of the deceased. One investigative question that comes from what we know so far might be: Are there fingerprints on the passenger's side door, inside or outside, that match the fingerprints on the driver's side door? Figure 4.12 should help answer some of the questions.

Thus far, we have not interpreted the blood or the blood patterns inside the car. Do they support the finding that someone was sitting on the passenger's seat when the murder took place? Notice we're still investigating the scene as though it was a murder for the reason already cited.

The inside of the passenger's door had bloodstains on it (see Figure 4.12). If we query the bloodstain patterns on the passenger's side door, considering the discussion above concerning fibers and hairs, we arrive at the data interpreted in Table 4.4.

Each macroscene element should be considered separately and logically in much the same manner as the discussion above. Eventually, an accurate working hypothesis of the true manner of death will emerge. Certainly, the medical examiner plays a critical role in determining how the case gets signed out. As one can see, however, proceeding on the premise that the death is anything but a homicide would be a mistake because that

Table 4.4 Data Interpretation: Hypothesis Testing

Macroscene Element	Second Hypothesis from Table 4.3	Testing the Second Hypothesis	Third Hypothesis
Bloodstain pattern on passenger's side door inside the car.	Assailant sat in passenger's seat during murder.	Bloodstain pattern on door is not interrupted and a mucous-like bloodstain with brain matter spans between the seat and the door.	Assailant did not sit in passenger's seat to commit the murder. Door was closed when deceased was shot.

makes macroscene elements and associated microscene elements irrelevant. Assuming the death is a homicide, whether or not it is, requires scene scientists/investigators to evaluate the external and internal macroscene and microscene elements carefully and completely.

This example is purposely simple, but it provides a glimpse into how the investigation should proceed logically by considering macroscene and microscene elements within the context of the feedback mechanism provided by the scientific method. The initial real-life investigation concluded with the death being signed out as a homicide. Interestingly, the death turned out to be a suicide. A second investigation of the vehicle was conducted as though the death was a homicide, and correctly interpreted the bloodstain evidence. The first investigation ignored the bloodstains on the passenger's door even though the investigators assumed the death was a homicide. Their approach was correct, but they mishandled the investigation. The scientific investigation captured the critical evidence by applying the scientific method throughout the investigation.

References

1. E. Locard. 1930. The analysis of dust traces, Part I. *American Journal of Police Science*, 1(3):276.
2. E. Locard. 1930. The analysis of dust traces, Part II. *American Journal of Police Science*, 1(4):401–418.
3. E. Locard. 1930. The analysis of dust traces, Part III. *American Journal of Police Science*, 1(5):496–514.
4. K. Inman and N. Rudin. 2000. Chapter 4: The origin of evidence—Divisible matter and transfer. In: *Principles and Practice of Criminalistics: The Profession of Forensic Science*. Boca Raton, FL: CRC Press, pp. 83–100.
5. R. E. Bisbing. 2004. Fractured patterns: Microscopical investigation of real physical evidence. Available at: http://www.modernmicroscopy.com/main.asp?article=11, (accessed October 21, 2010).
6. H. Gross. 1893. *Handbuch für Untersuchungsrichter als System der Kriminalistik* (*Manual for Examining Magistrates as a System of Criminology*), 2 vols. By General Books LLC, Memphis (2010).
7. J. Robertson and C. Roux. 1999. Part 5: From the crime scene to the laboratory. In: J. Robertson and M. Grieve (eds), *Forensic Examination of Fibres*, 2nd edn, Taylor and Francis Forensic Science Series. London, UK:Taylor and Francis, p. 89.
8. K. Inman and N. Rudin. 2000. Chapter 3: Overview—A unifying paradigm of forensic science. In: *Principles and Practice of Criminalistics: The Profession of Forensic Science*. Boca Raton, FL: CRC Press, pp. 75–82.
9. R. Leggett, E. E. Lee-Smith, S. M. Jickells, and D. A. Russell. 2007. Intelligent fingermarking: Simultaneous identification of drug metabolites and individuals using functionalized antibody nanoparticles. *Angewandte Chemie International Edition*, 46:4100–4103.
10. W. J. Chisum and B. E. Turvey. 2000. Evidence dynamics: Locard's exchange principle and crime reconstruction. *Journal of Behavioral Profiling*, 1:1–15.
11. H. C. Lee, T. Palmbach, and M. T. Miller. 2001. *Henry Lee's Handbook of Crime Scene Investigation*. London, UK: Academic Press, p. 4.
12. *Merriam-Webster Online Dictionary*. Holistic. Available at: http://www.merriam-webster.com/dictionary/holistic (accessed October 17, 2010).
13. C. Cwiklik. 1999. An evaluation of the significance of transfers of debris: Criteria for association and exclusion. *Journal of Forensic Science*, 44(6):1136–1150.

14. W. J. Bodziak. 2000. *Footwear Impression Evidence—Detection, Recovery, and Examination.* Boca Raton, FL: CRC Press, pp. 17–20.
15. C. A. Pounds and K. W. Smalldon. 1978. The distribution of glass fragments in front of a broken window and transfer to individuals standing nearby. *Journal of the Forensic Science Society,* 18:197–203.

Searching the Scene
Logic in Action

5

Oh, how simple it would all have been had I been here before they came like a herd of buffalo and wallowed all over it.*

5.1 Introduction

The crime scene is the aftermath of individuals participating in an event in point and time. In a hit-and-run case, there might be two cars, one hitting the other, a single vehicle hitting a pedestrian, or a single vehicle hitting an object. In each case, a vehicle leaves the scene. In a sexual battery case, the assailant may break into an apartment or house or may abduct the victim off the street. A homicide may be a violent dispute between spouses, the wake of, perhaps, a bludgeoning resulting in death. In each instance, the crime may or may not define the type of evidence present, but the scene scientist/investigator understands that certain crime types spawn specific types of evidence. Finding the evidence that links the participants to the scene is why crime scene investigations exist and why searching is critical. From a philosophical perspective, we can logically split the crime scene search into two parts:

- The mental approach, the logic required to devise a strategy for the search as well as the processes that will be used
- The by-product of two activities: the original walk through and archiving (Chapter 6)

A searching philosophy and examples are illustrated in Figure 5.1.

Why the Walk through? This is when the team leader sees the macroscene elements for the first time and begins to consider them in the context of the overall scene investigation, mentally gathering information about the scope, size, and location of obvious evidence and perhaps the not-so-obvious fragile evidence.

Archiving is included because it, too, presents a pictorial perspective of how the macroscene relates to the relative location of evidence. During these activities, the relative location of evidence and its interrelatedness and possibly probative value should take shape. Reviewing digital photographs from the archiving process in the last phase of the investigation can help pinpoint the relatedness of evidence that had been missed. If the archivist(s) and the team leader are in synch, this information will slowly emerge from the chaos that defines the crime scenes. Using this collaborative information, the team leader should devise a search strategy based solely on logic, not necessarily a "method" published in a text book. Devising the search strategy requires an understanding of and then acting on

* A. Conan Doyle, The Boscobel Valley Mystery, 1892.

The crime scene

The place where individuals participated in an event at a point in time that resulted in the creation of evidence.

Finding the evidence linking these participants to the scene is why crime scene investigations exist and why searching is critical.

Scene type examples

1. Hit and run cases:
   a. Two cars—one hitting the other–one leaves the scene.
   b. A single car hitting a pedestrian and leaving the scene.

2. Sexual battery case:
   a. Assailant breaks into apartment or house.
   b. Assailant abducts the victim off the street.

3. Homicide cases:
   a. Violent dispute between spouses
   b. A shooting in a drug case

Searches Split into Two Parts

The logic required to devise a strategy for the search and the processes employed.

The byproduct of two activities: The original walk through and archiving.

Figure 5.1 Searching: A philosophy.

the scene information. The mental and physical activities required to conduct a proper search are inextricably joined, such that, if crime scene management is the glue that holds the investigation together, the scene search is the meat and potatoes. It is, in truth, the right arm of scene management and an integral aspect of archiving. Figure 5.2 illustrates the interrelatedness of these activities.

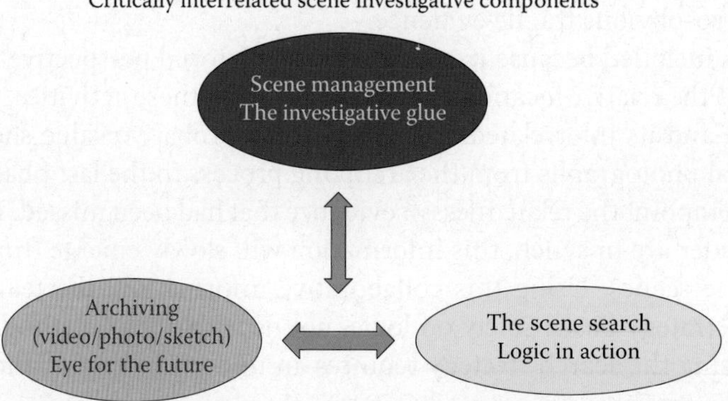

Figure 5.2 Management, archiving, and searching relationship.

The team leader devises the search strategy and the mechanism for archiving and searching the scene. Thus, the team leader is truly the glue that holds the investigation together. She decides who will photograph, sketch, and search, and she is the maestro who directs all the scene activity. This single individual understands why videoing, photographing, and sketching are also eyes of the search team.

5.2 Processing versus Investigation

Modern books on crime scene investigation lull students, novice investigators, and seasoned investigators into believing that searching is a simple, thoughtless process that anyone can perform. Police agencies often call it "processing the scene," which is an simplistic term for what happens. Law enforcement agencies typically fund the detective or investigator to take a workshop or training session, where there is an explanation of the type of evidence that exists, how to find it, how to preserve it, and how to package it. The trainee is given a title, perhaps "Crime Scene Technician" or some other official sounding moniker and then assigns the trainee to a crime scene unit to gain experience. The term processing, as the *Merriam–Webster Online Dictionary** defines it, smacks of mindless simplicity, an exercise of minimal thought to what is being done or why. In contrast, the definition of an investigation is clearly more rigorous†. For this reason the term "processing" should be replaced with something that projects cognizant thought, such as investigation. Scene "processing" is more than a "process." It is a scientific endeavor, a scientific investigation, and it is certainly far from a simple "process."

In truth, searching the scene is the crux of the investigation and likely the most important. Certainly archiving is important, for if done badly, anyone examining the scene after the fact will not "see" the original scene. A poor approach to searching leads to second guessing, which happens if the search is not conducted logically and systematically. If the search is conducted logically and systematically, it will be comprehensive and results in success—finding probative evidence. Chapter 3 gave an overview of the US Army's approach to managing the scene, a system of rechecks in which the scene is searched three times [1]. The discussion suggested that the method minimizes errors. The discussion demonstrated why that approach is not a true application of the scientific method and can lead to investigative failure because the system of three, "rote" re-checks fails to consider the logic and the feedback mechanisms required by the scientific method. The example presented in that discussion illustrated how logically based hypotheses formulated during the investigation can force additional rechecks based on feedback inherent in the scientific process of disproving hypotheses. In truth, the crime scene investigation must be treated like any scientific investigation/research project, the difference being that it involves the law enforcement's investigative arm. Thus the scene investigation is NOT a blind process but one of immense complexity. The above discussion is summarized in Figure 5.3.

* Process–Definition: *Merriam–Webster Online Dictionary.* "a series of actions or operations conducing to an end; especially a continuous operation or treatment especially in manufacture." http://www.merriam-webster.com/dictionary/process, accessed 9/7/2010.

† Investigation–Definition: *Merriam–Webster Online Dictionary.* "Transitive verb: to observe or study by close examination and systematic inquiry. Intransitive verb: to make a systematic examination; *especially* to conduct an official inquiry." http://www.merriam-webster.com/dictionary/investigation, accessed 9/7/2010.

"Processing the scene"

Modern texts lull students, novice investigators, and seasoned investigators into believing that scene searching is a simple process.

Process:

"a series of actions or operations conducing to an end; especially a continuous operation or treatment especially in manufacture"

Processing evokes mindless activity and simplicity. The term should be replaced with something that projects cognizant thought.

Investigation:

"Transitive verb: to observe or study by close examination and systematic inquiry.

"Intransitive verb: to make a systematic examination; especially: to conduct an official inquiry."

Scene investigation and searching is more than a "process." It is a scientific endeavor and as an investigation, it is certainly more than a simple "process."

Figure 5.3 Processing versus investigation.

5.3 Defining the Search

We assume the crime scene team has the legal right to enter the scene and collect evidence. The crime scene search begins when the investigator in charge (team leader) walks through the scene for the first time with the first or responding officer and "sizes up" or takes inventory of the scene, assimilating first impressions. This is when the initial investigative strategy and precautions take shape, as the macroscene elements and other scene nuances distill in the team leader's mind. Examples of scene considerations by the team lead are listed in Table 5.1.

The team leader should be considering specific search parameters to ensure the team does not miss important and/or critically probative evidence. This logical approach contrasts with modern crime scene investigation texts that consider the scene search as a methodical process presented as a "method." That is, they promulgate specific search or "named" procedures designed for specific crime scene types, such as for indoor and/or

Table 5.1 First Scene Considerations

Scene Considerations	Other Issues
Size—physical terms	Obstacles
Relevant—obvious evidence	Additional resources required
Fragile evidence	Media
Scope—crime type primary/secondary/staged	Command center/containment

Table 5.2 Hallmark of a Successful Search

Hallmarks of Successful Searches	Elements
Effective management	Experience—knowledge—leadership
Understanding the nature of the scene	Size, scope, weather, obstacles, on-scene environment, lighting, and so on
Appropriate Logic	Employing the scientific method
Systematic approach	Not random
Creative thinking	Relative associations of scene elements

outdoor scenes. Such a simplistic approach is as ridiculous as the term "processing" because it conveys the impression that scene investigations are mindlessly simple.

To be fair, the intent of these "methods" is not to convey simplicity but to present inexperienced and experienced investigators a roadmap for avoiding serious mistakes, such as missing probative evidence. As Gardner points out [2], "The specific method that the crime scene team chooses is really *unimportant* [emphasis added] so long as the method employed is methodical and systematic." Certainly, this is one objective. However, the search should also be logical.

Minimizing errors can be accomplished, but whether searching is a "method" approach or some hybrid, general guidelines exist to which each scene investigative search must adhere. Table 5.2 lists the hallmarks of successful scene searches.

5.3.1 Effective Management

Simply said, without a strong, experienced manager, scene searches, and the entire investigation will likely be chaotic and doomed to fail. Students, novice investigators, and seasoned investigators tend toward conducting individual, sometimes random, searches without rhyme or reason except to "follow their nose." A strong leader keeps the team focused, assigning roles when required, and keeping the investigation on track. As already mentioned, scene management is inextricably intertwined with archiving and searching. The bottom line is this: effectively managed teams are efficient and thorough.

5.3.2 Nature of the Scene

Each scene presents investigators with a different "look." Homicides in large cities often occur in apartments. While many may have the same set of circumstances, the truth is that they are not the same. Each is different and each has a different geography, different clutter, and so on. Some might have air conditioning and be comfortable in the summer while others may be stiflingly hot, sticky, and uncomfortable. As obvious as this might seem, the difference in temperature and humidity can dramatically affect the success and efficiency of the investigation. As an example, a scene in the middle of July when the temperature is 97°F and the humidity 92%, unpleasant odors coming from a decomposing body will be oppressive. If the scene has air conditioning, these same oppressive odors can be manageable. In hot scenes, excessive perspiring makes investigators work unintentionally faster which can result in a flawed investigation.

Outdoor scenes have a Pandora's box of environmental obstacles, each of which can affect the investigation. A scene in the woods differs from a shooting in a parking lot.

A scene in the mountains in the middle of winter with the temperature hovering in the 10°F range and after a snow storm has obstacles different than the same scene in spring with the temperature in the 60s. A field in May is different than the same field in late July or September. The landscaped back yard of a residential house is different from an unmowed field of knee high wheat. Each has obstacles and each requires a strategy born from logic in order to search it correctly and efficiently.

5.3.3 Logic

All scene searches must embrace a logical approach. What exactly does that mean? Simply said, it means reasoning properly to recognize *relevant* evidence [3]. Finding relevant evidence requires a systematic approach. As Gardner points out, searches must be methodical and systematic. He defines methodical as "marked by ordered and systematic habits or behavior," which he considers the "application of established procedures and practices"[2]. In the context of this discussion, however, this is not necessarily true. The fact is, ideally the crime (not just the crime type) defines the evidence that is present. This does not mean that all homicides have the same evidence; a stabbing may not have the same fact basis or physical evidence present as someone strangled or a stray bullet through the window hitting a child in a large city. However, two homicides in which each deceased is the victim of blunt force trauma may have similar types of evidence present—signs of a struggle, impact spatter, bloody footprints, and so on, but there will also be differences.

What this means is that the approach to the scene search should be guided by the question of relevance, and the guiding principle refers to the relevant investigative questions for that specific scene. Answering them determines how the search for that scene should be conducted. As Inman and Rudin put it, searching is looking with purpose [4], which means, locating probative evidence relevant to the specific crime in a particular place and circumstance. This is not a method approach. It is a reasoned approach.

Certainly, there are expectations during the scene investigation that translate to the search. If someone, a boyfriend, who is a suspect and was detained shortly after the murder of his girlfriend, the scene investigation must continue, ideally scientifically. Knowing who is arrested can present a problem because it is human nature to unintentionally use that context in the investigation by inadvertently searching for specific suspect-related evidence. For example, the scene scientist/investigator may be aware of the physical characteristics and the clothes the boyfriend was wearing and might inadvertently limit the search for those items and ignore evidence that someone else had been at the scene. The scientific method eschews that approach and employs a reasoning process based on promulgated hypotheses that are compared with other hypotheses, tested, and accepted or rejected.

Accepting or rejecting evidence should be based on the totality of evidence at the scene. Thus looking for long blond hairs on the deceased's clothing because the boyfriend has long blond hair is not a reasoned approach. However looking for hairs, in general, on the deceased's clothing is reasonable, and if they turn out to be long black hairs, so be it. If they turn out to be long blond hairs, that is alright, too. An investigator bowing to context bias might not "see" or collect the long black hair on the deceased's blouse because the "suspect" has long blond hairs. Whether the search employs a deductive process [5] or a combination of deductive/inductive where there is the search is a combined inductive/deductive process [5] is important to how the search is conducted and the reasoning employed to locate probative evidence.

5.3.4 Systematic

Gardner suggests that a crime scene search should be methodical and systematic, and defines systematic as "purposefully regular" [3], which implies the application of a search "method." For military and paramilitary agencies, this is easy to implement because it gives their investigators a way to standardize the search in order to accomplish a specific goal. Accountability is easier to ascertain and standardization gives the appearance of thoroughness. In fact, the opposite may be the case. A method search is exactly that: a way to do something that is rote, repeatable, and efficient. However, unless logic is employed, evidence will be missed and evidence that is *not relevant* will be collected.

An example is an New York City (NYC) homicide case in which the New York City Police Department (NYPD) crime scene detective collected the vast majority of blood droplets in a trail leading from an apartment, where a man had been stabbed to another apartment two floors below, a total of 52 droplets. The prosecutor demanded that all 52 droplets be analyzed for DNA. First, the detective correctly assumed that the trail was important, probative evidence, which he surmised had been left by the perpetrator. Second, he methodically and systematically collected nearly every droplet without giving a thought to why he was collecting so many. Not only was collecting and packaging so many droplets an inefficient waste of valuable time, it presented the laboratory with an issue that translated into an argument between the laboratory director (me) and the concerning prosecutor. The question was not the relevance of the droplets, but the necessity to analyze all 52. A thinking crime scene investigator would have considered the droplet trail, realized it came from a single source, and then collected a representative number (beginning, middle, and end) for the laboratory. Thoughtless searches and evidence collection are examples of a "method" approach that are repeated at crime scene investigations throughout the United States and thus become immortalized in crime scene texts. Another example is outdoor scenes, which have unique challenges, different from those in indoor scenes which have cramped space and/or multiple rooms.

Rather than just methodical and systematic, the crime scene search should be logical and systematic. Gardner includes "systematic" in his definition of methodical. But then saying that a crime scene search is methodical and systematic would be redundant. Logical and systematic implies a reasoned approach without being a "method."

5.3.5 Creative Thinking—Out of the Box

The most successful scene detectives and criminalists have an innate ability to think creatively. It is a skill that some learn over time through experience. However, some "see" connections where others, even experienced investigators do not. Those possessing this ability are the best crime scene investigators.

5.4 Scene Search Methods

Although the "method" search as presented in crime scene texts and discussed above is not always appropriate. There is a certain truth in them, however. After all, crime scene investigators have successfully searched scenes using a particular method. And by passing these methods to others on-the-job, in workshops, training exercises, or in a written form, they are in their own way simply teaching others how to be proficient crime scene searchers.

As mentioned, outdoor and indoor searches have unique challenges. In outdoor searches, the investigator must consider the terrain and other physical obstacles. The grid search, as a proposed method for outdoor searching, is certainly one that should be considered seriously. Additionally, the type of crime might dictate the search type, so that looking for human remains in a public park in a wooded area outside Washington, DC might involve a different search strategy than documenting the fragments and body parts from an airplane that had crashed in a farmer's field in Pennsylvania on 9/11. Each outdoor scene scenario presents a particular set of obstacles and challenges and each can be adequately searched using the grid method or a version of it. In a sense, then, variations of the grid search are not fundamentally different because although the grid method might be employed, it might not be employed in exactly the same way in both examples. Searching a wooded area where trees and shrubs offer challenges to maintaining the line of searchers is different from the obstacles in an open field. Regardless, each requires a logical and systematic process that milling around, for example, cannot deliver.

In an indoor search, the layout of the premises, the different constraints of furniture and tight spaces present challenges more often not encountered in outdoor scenes. Vehicle scenes are an example of yet another kind of scene search that presents challenges of another kind: two scenes in one; the inside and outside of the vehicle.

Scene scientists/investigators understand the importance of the scene search but sometimes, it seems, treat it as a chore. Students are no exception. They wander off, eschewing logic and a systematic approach. A proper search requires a constant thought of what the scene is saying. To many, searching is not the sexy part of the investigation: it is not bloodstain pattern interpretation, enhancing tire track impressions, or dusting and lifting fingerprints. However, it should be thought as sexy because this is when the scene leads you to the promised land of evidence. This is the part where the investigator has that "Ah ha!" moment after finding critical evidence that leads to a successful prosecution or exoneration of a suspect.

Logic, then, is the mechanism for finding probative evidence so that the jury and/or the Trier of fact can evaluate the evidence in order to ascertain as closely as possible the ground truth of a case, if such a thing exists. If done incorrectly or haphazardly, the team risks missing important probative evidence or, equally important, in appropriately assessing the scene correctly, such as defining motive, linking evidence, interpreting the sequence of events, and so on. Searching is when investigators display more than an ability to use their hands. This is when their powers of observation, tendencies for bias, attention to detail, and experience are on display.

As mentioned, searching is one of the more critical functions of a scene investigation. Does the word "critical" fit? Is it appropriate? Does it adequately describe the importance of the scene search? The *Merriam–Webster Online Dictionary* defines critical,* "1: of, relating to, or being a turning point of an important juncture." Certainly this explains how important the scene search is. When searching begins, the team enters a make or break point of the investigation because it is looking to "make" the case.

* Critical. *Merriam Webster Online Dictionary.* "of, relating to, or being a turning point or specially important juncture <a *critical* phase>. http://www.merriam-webster.com/dictionary/critical?show=0&t=1283880494, accessed 9/7/2010.

Historically crime scene texts and scene instructors devote space (and time) to "method" searching that represents search experience by investigators who share their experiences because of their personal successes. That is, they have located evidence that has led to successful prosecutions. Over the years, these methods have morphed into a mantra and have attained an almost sacred status among authors. Certainly no self-respecting crime scene text would omit these "methods." Each author or instructor discusses the correct way to approach these methods and usually provides examples of where and when specific methods should be employed.

These methods and their associated diagrams are actually efficient guides because they effectively instill meaning and understanding to a critical aspect of the scene investigation. In other words, a picture is worth a thousand words. Because of that, the following is a discussion of some "methods" with the understanding that applying them in specific situations without logic is a recipe for failure.

5.4.1 The Line (Grid) Methods

One variation of the line method is the grid search. Illustrated in the diagram in the slide below, it is pretty much self-explanatory, so there is really little to need to explain the mechanism of how a search of this type might take place. Like all "method" searches, it, too, is a roadmap, which if followed will likely be conducted properly. The key phrase is, "conducted properly." The grid search is a more powerful variant of simpler search types, such as the line and parallel methods. The reason is that the grid search is in reality a perpendicular search because it happens in two directions. The grid search is illustrated in Figure 5.4 [6].

In class, students are presented with an outdoor area to search as an exercise to illustrate how to conduct a grid search. The search is usually in the woods or in a field. A small amount of evidence is planted, for example, knives, paper, bones, and so on, not to overwhelm the students but to present a challenging exercise. In one exercise, the class was asked to ascertain the distribution of bones at the conclusion of a research project

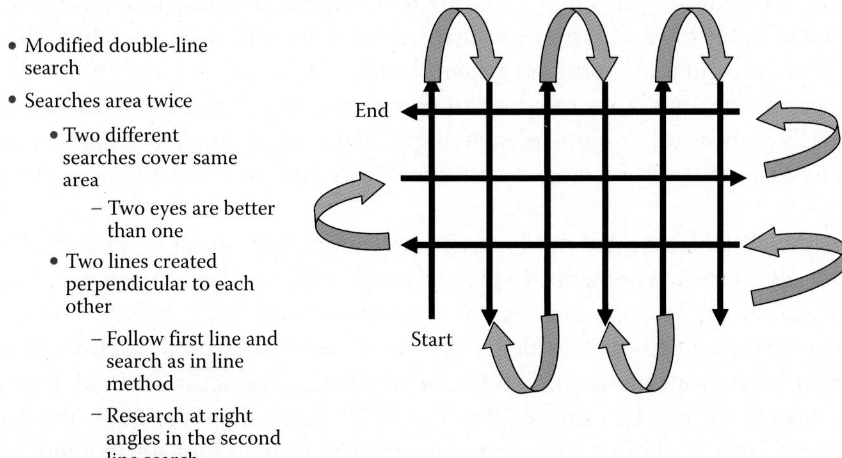

Figure 5.4 Schematic illustration of the grid search.

designed to collect volatiles from decomposing pig carcasses. Over time, the bones were carried off by predators. Pinpointing their distribution relates to finding bones of missing persons in outdoor spaces. The students received a scene scenario so that they know the crime type, but had no knowledge of how much evidence, if any, was present. They were not even certain that the field (or woods) was the crime scene. The instructor assumed the responsibility of the team leader in order to demonstrate how to manage the search and collect evidence. Soon, though, a student was put in charge of the search.

After learning how to conduct a grid search, the line of searchers moved in one direction until they had searched the entire area. Next, they searched perpendicular to the first pass. Typically, they missed evidence on the first pass but almost invariably found it on the perpendicular. Invariably, they were surprised that they had missed evidence on the first pass because they felt that they were doing a thorough job of searching. The exercise cements in their minds the need to conduct a thorough search.

This lesson is lost on investigators who do not routinely or have ever conducted such searches. Another learning principle of the exercise is management. When the assigned student takes over the search, the line immediately turns ragged with students forging ahead and others falling behind. The student in charge must get the line back in shape, which is typically difficult because "ordering" classmates around is outside their comfort zone. Still, the responsibility is to keep the line moving straight without laggards and ensuring the line stopped when evidence was located and marking it with an evidence flag.

The difficulty is to keep the team moving in a straight line. Some students normally tend to move faster or slower, so this becomes a challenge. Communication, at first, is also a problem, because when a student finds evidence, one end of the line stops but the other end keeps moving, which creates an undulating line moving forward. On the second pass, they get it right. From an instructional perspective, students first learn the grid search during an in-class workshop. Later in the semester they are faced with a real scene (mock) and must decide how to search the area; the grid is really their only choice.

Added to their burden is the environment: weather, time (this occurs at 4 a.m., so it is dark), temperature, rain, and/or snow are often present. Bringing the environment into the learning process is important because it gives students a feeling of reality. In the exercise, the team leader must organize her team, search the area immediately without waiting until daylight, and mark, photograph, and collect the evidence. They must also sketch and photograph the area. They are deep in the woods, so generators are not available, so they use flashlights or other high-intensity lights to highlight the search area. It is a difficult exercise executed under trying conditions. Mostly, they do well, but importantly, they learn.

The grid method illustrated in Figure 5.4 is the most appropriate variation of line/grid searches for outdoor environments. In fact, it is applicable to all environments. A variation of the grid search, the line search, or single-pass search is NEVER appropriate, as they are inherently constructed to miss evidence. For large outdoor scenes, such as an airplane crash, it may be appropriate to grid the scene and then conduct individual grid searches within each major grid. An example was the WTC scene after the 2001 attacks on the World Trade Center buildings. The scene was gridded into 70 foot squares and each grid searched systematically. That scene was different than most because each grid had 3D characteristics, surface, and depth [7].

The following list provides a checklist sequence concerning how to conduct a grid search.

5.4.1.1 *The Sequence of an Outdoor Search—Archiving and Searching Using the Grid Method*

- Establishing photography.
- Determine and establish scene boundaries.
- Identify an appropriate search method.
  - Outdoor searches of large areas typically include a variation of the two-dimensional grid method (see Figure 5.4).
- Searchers are at arm's length distance apart in a line.
  - Walk in a straight line until an item of evidence is found. The line stops until the evidence is marked with an evidence marker flag.
  - The line continues in this fashion until the search has been conducted.
  - Search in the perpendicular direction to give the scene a duplicate search.
- Midrange photography of marked evidence.
- Close-up photography of marked evidence.
- Collect and package marked evidence.
- Transport the packaged evidence to the police department and/or crime laboratory.
- Sketch the scene and mark the location of evidence.

Other outdoor line search methods are diagrammed below. Under most circumstances, these lead to missed evidence, especially in complicated areas where evidence might be difficult to see, for example, woods, fields, and so on. On flat, uncovered small surfaces, such as concrete and paved parking lots where the line-of-sight is unhindered, these methods are appropriate. However, nothing is ever lost, except time, by performing a perpendicular search—as in a grid. Figure 5.5 illustrates the line or strip search [8]and Figure 5.6 illustrates the parallel search [9].

- Team leader coordinates search
- Mostly applicable to outdoor scenes
  - Useful for a few or a large number of searchers
  - May use untrained searchers
  - No boundaries make it difficult to search systematically
    - Large areas
      - Parks
      - Yards
      - Parking lots
      - Highways
      - Fields

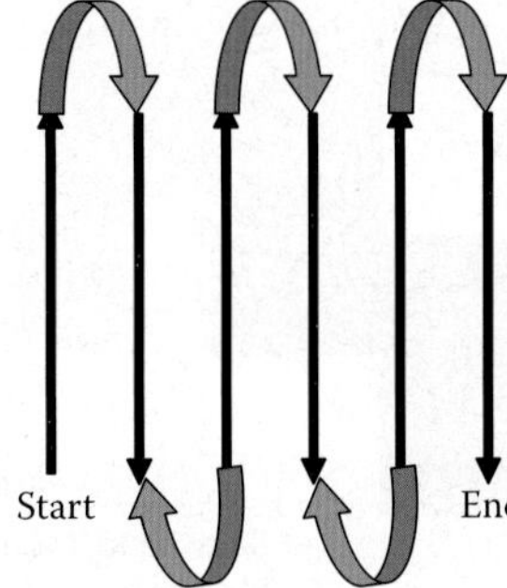

Figure 5.5 Schematic of line or strip search.

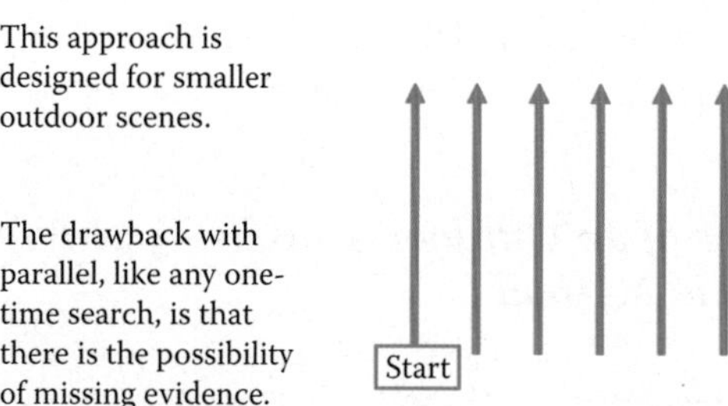

Figure 5.6 Schematic of the parallel search.

5.4.1.2 Zone and Point-to-Point Searches

Zone and point-to-point searches are fundamentally different approaches for searching indoor scenes. For example, the zone method illustrated in Figure 5.7 is a method for prioritizing search areas at an indoor scene. Areas having the most obvious activity become the primary search areas. In Figure 5.7, Zones A, B, and C have obvious macroscene elements (visible evidence). And Zone B—Foyer—has broken glass and footwear impressions suggesting an entry point. These would be the prime areas. Zones D, E, and F might not appear important, but there should be a discussion concerning whether they might have probative evidence and how much effort should be put into searching them. No part of the scene should be ignored.

The point-to-point search illustrated as a cartoon in Figure 5.8 is similar to the zone method because it splits the scene into specific search areas. The difference lies in the reason for making the splits, which depends on the location of evidence instead of dividing an area, such as a house, into zones. In other words, the found evidence dictates the

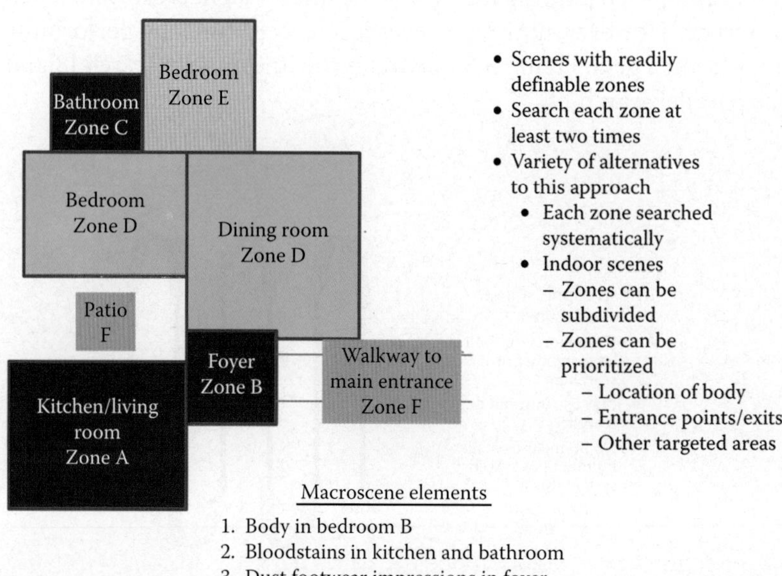

Figure 5.7 Schematic of the zone method.

Small, confined areas and when a potential route of travel has been detected or is suspected.

- Identify key locations or areas within the crime scene.
    - Points of entry/exit, location of the victim, location of weapons, and so on.
- Thoroughly examine the pathways or routes.
    - Connect the key locations to other areas where evidence may be found.
- Fragile evidence
    - Evidence on the floor.
        - Footwear impressions, trace evidence, and so on and make every effort to avoid altering or destroying the evidence.
    - Maintain a narrow path into and out of the scene.
        - Be cognizant of fragile evidence.
- Search each area by at least two investigators (in pairs and one after the other).

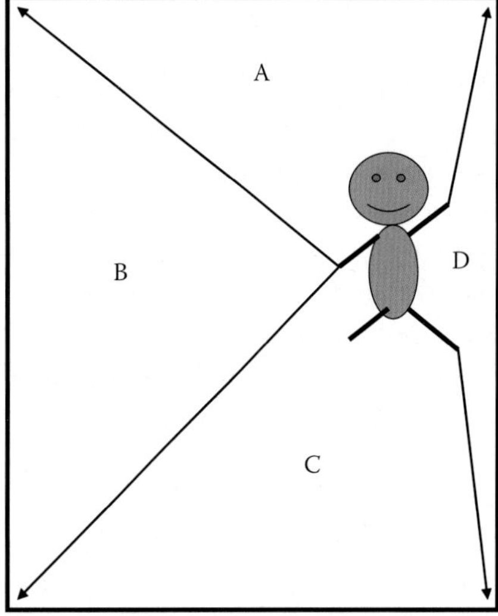

Figure 5.8 Schematic of point-to-point search.

areas to search. Logic also plays a part in targeting areas where evidence might be: entrance or egress points, impression evidence, weapons, and so on. Thus, this search type employs a form of logic. In the cartoon in the slide below, the ant-like body represents something found at the scene, from which searchers fan. The cartoon is facetious, but the concept is not.

The goal of the search, of course, is to find probative evidence without making mistakes. Not a bad idea, actually. The problem is that a competent crime scene search is not simple, and it would be a mistake to employ a method simply because someone wrote about it in a book.

A key word is systematic,* which would be a search characterized by thoroughness and regularity. The bottom line is this. Any systematic search is appropriate as long as it is done correctly and logically. Everyone has seen reality crime shows on television demonstrating incorrectly searched scenes. News programs have filmed police using incorrect scene searches, which would make anyone question how much of the probative evidence present at the scene had actually been recovered. Success is determined by how well the lead investigator/team leader manages the team. When crime scene investigators brag about the hundreds of scenes they have investigated, there is always the temptation to ask: "How many have you done correctly?" The only truthful answer is, "I don't know" because there is no way to know with certainty.

With respect to crime scene investigations, certainty is not the test of certitude. That is, someone being certain the crime scene was investigated properly does not make it so. The

* Systematic. *Merriam–Webster Online Dictionary.* "relating to or consisting of a system 2.: presented or formulated as a coherent body of ideas or principles <*systematic* thought> 3. *a* : methodical in procedure or plan <a *systematic* approach> <a *systematic* scholar> *b* : marked by thoroughness and regularity <*systematic* efforts>. http://www.merriam-webster.com/top-ten-lists/top-10-commonly-confused-words-vol-2/flush-out-flesh-out.html?&t = 1283878175, accessed 9/7/2010.

reason is that quality procedures, as in quality assurance, at most scenes are mostly nonexistent. Another barometer of crime scene search competence is often pointed out that a suspect had been convicted. This is a fallacious reasoning. The court system is not an effective arbiter of quality or competence. It simply means that evidence collected had been admitted into evidence and suggested that the defendant was the guilty person. No one knows whether exculpatory evidence had been missed. By then, though, it is too late to go back.

Certainly, though, "method" searches have been useful because they tend to minimize errors, although sometimes at the expense of creative thinking and logic. A competent search should uncover ALL probative evidence. Certainly "method" scene search diagrams provide a systematic roadmap, but most FAIL to provide the logic needed to successfully conduct a competent, thorough, and systematic search.

5.4.1.3 *The Link Method*

The link method illustrated in Figure 5.9 is another "method" approach. However, unlike the methods described above, it is not a roadmap per se, but instead it relies on logic to lead the investigator to critical evidence. The investigator works to understand and exploit evidentiary associations at the scene. This is based on findings or observations and then applying logic as the tool to proceed. In a sexual assault scene, certain evidence types are common, for example, blood, semen, bite marks, and so on, but other evidence might also be present, such as footwear impression, discarded weapons, or ski masks. The position of the body, the location of a knife, and other specific evidence types dictate how, and perhaps, to proceed.

5.4.1.4 *Ray or Wheel Search*

Another widely illustrated method is the wheel or ray. Any thinking person would take one look at this diagram and wonder who had the original idea. Why would anyone seriously consider using this approach for any scene except for one with an incredibly small footprint. In a large area, this method is a recipe for failure. This concept is illustrated schematically in Figure 5.10.

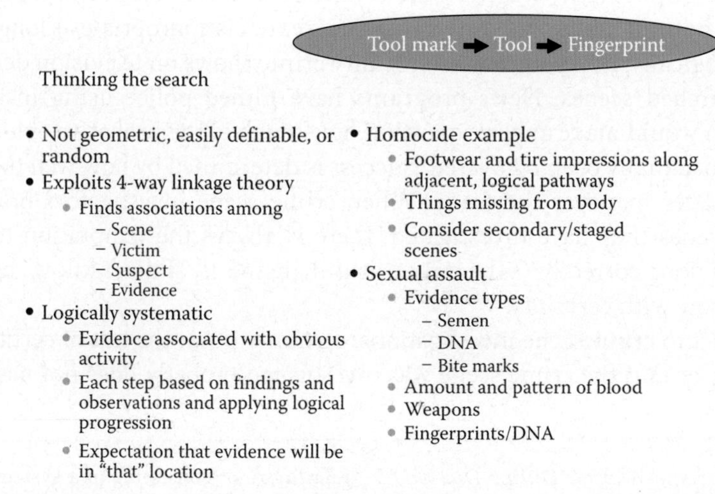

Figure 5.9 Characteristics of the link method.

- Essentially a circular search
  - Star at critical point
    - Travel outward along straight lines (rays)
- Difficult for searching large areas
  - Used only for special situations w/limited applications

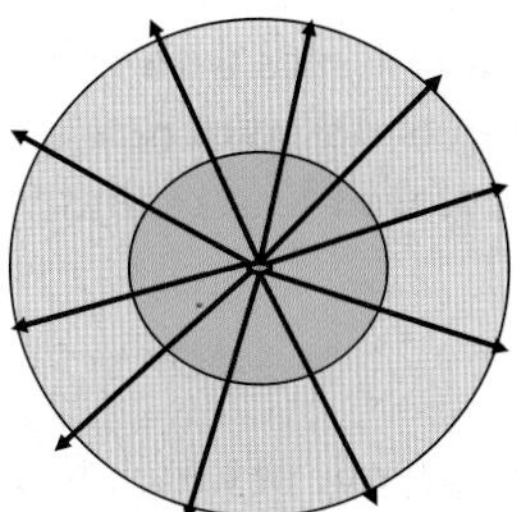

Figure 5.10 Schematic of wheel or ray search method.

5.5 Employing On-Scene Technology and/or Statements

Logic in action means taking advantage of everything available to narrow the search area. An example might be a burglar caught on a surveillance camera that captured the individual's path through the scene and the areas he touched. This dramatically narrows the search area because the investigator knows exactly how the burglar got inside the premise and what he touched. Most of the logic of determining where to search is gone. Areas not captured by the video, however, cannot be dismissed easily, and they must be searched. Statements by witnesses and/or victims can also help narrow the search area. If the victim of the robbery tells investigators that the robber was not in certain areas of his store, searching them is waste of time. For these areas, archiving should suffice.

5.6 Pressures at the Scene

Ideally, pressures of the search—and for the entire scene investigation—would relate only to those associated with finding probative evidence and archiving the scene properly. However, the reality is that pressures exist on a multitude of levels. Certainly, there is an internal pressure to locate evidence, but pressure can come from outside and usually does.

- The media exerts its own brand of pressure, such as hounding the team leader for information.
- The team leader can be tied up with detectives, which places a burden on the other team members.
- The size of the team can create other pressures. A small team may work well together, but each member of the team will have more work to do than those in a larger team. This creates a situation where rushing can create errors. This is a pressure with which the team leader must deal carefully.
- Demanding superiors—police chief, the Mayor, and so on—create pressure to speed the search and provide investigative information quickly.

- Environmental insults create pressures on outdoor scenes. The threat of rain in a wooded scene creates issues with the destruction of evidence.
- Political pressure gets raised to new levels in high profile cases, for example, police shootings, deaths of well-known individuals, and cases of bias.

5.6.1 Constraints

All scenes have constraints, one of which is time. Whether it has to do with workload, where the investigating unit has other scenes to investigate, the weather, or the geography, the scene imposes constraints. An example might be a hit-and-run on a major thoroughfare in rush hour, where there is not only time but also other constraints: traffic, pedestrians, and so on.

5.7 Archiving and Searching Common Scene Types

Investigators encounter certain crime scene types routinely, and students, novice scene scientists/investigators, and experienced investigators should understand the nuances of each. Burglaries have evidence commonly associated with them and so do homicides and sexual assaults. Still, each crime scene is unique and each presents challenges different from the so-called norm for that crime type. The truth is, with respect to evidence, different crime types present overlapping categories of evidence because, what starts as a burglary may well end up as a homicide or a sexual assault. Certainly, specific attributes may occur more frequently with a particular crime type, such as semen in sexual assault cases.

As discussed, searching and archiving are overlapping exercises. The forensic archivist's responsibility is to capture the scene photographically or by sketching which should ultimately lead to evidence, which is collected. During the archiving process, the investigator who "finds" evidence should alert the search team and team leader. Table 5.3 gives an overview of common evidence types associated with certain crime types. Recognize that some of these commonly overlap.

5.8 Technology to Aid Searching

Most search activity employs a visual examination of the scene. As discussed in Chapter 14, finding biological evidence is easier using technology designed to highlight certain kinds of biological evidence. Figure 5.11 illustrates the wavelengths used on an alternate light source (ALS) for locating specific types of evidence.

5.9 Searching for Trace Evidence—Overview Considerations

Chapter 4 describes evidence from various perspectives, one of which is invisible evidence defined as elements associated with the microscene. The search for evidence does not end with picking up items of only the visible elements of the macroscene. The search team must also consider the invisible evidence. Figure 5.11 illustrated how an ALS helps locate invisible evidence, for example, UV light (300–400 nm) aids in finding hairs and fibers and

Table 5.3 Evidence in Selected Case Types

- Vehicle searches
  - Hit and run
    - Exterior/undercarriages/grill/headlights/bumper/windshield
    - Injuries to victim and operator of the vehicle
      - Tissue/blood on vehicle
    - Fingerprints—outside and inside
    - Paint transfers—on clothing, to vehicle
    - Fabric pattern transfers—to vehicle
    - Trace evidence transfer—glass, hairs, fibers
    - Blood, blood spatter
- Homicides and sexual assaults
    - Interior for blood/semen/trace evidence
    - Blood and blood spatter
    - GSR/bullet path determination
    - Fingerprints
    - Trace evidence
    - Saliva
    - Vehicles often involved
  - Suicide
    - Blood spatter/bullet path determination
    - GSR
    - Notes/family history
    - Scene characteristics

light at 450 nm will help locate fibers and some biological evidence. Chapter 4 also discusses primary and secondary transfer of fibers and how glass shard evidence from broken windows, for example, can be important.

The purpose of this section is to alert the reader that collecting trace evidence is critically important. Since it is mostly invisible to the naked and aided eye, collecting it requires

Wavelength (nm)	Principle Use	Viewing Lens
White Light	General scene scanning Fingerprints on shiny surfaces	Clear
UV–365	Hair, fiber, fluorescent material-powders Body fluids/bruises/bite marks/ Food stains	Clear or Yellow
415	Bloodstains Food stains	Clear
450	Body fluids, semen blood Powders/teeth/bones Paint/fibers/accelerants	Orange
465–485	Fluorescent materials/powders Body fluids	Orange
515–535	Super glue-fumed fingerprints	Red
570	Inks	Red

Figure 5.11 Using the ALS to locate evidence.

employing a logical thought process of knowing where to look and then using standard techniques for collecting it. The reader is referred to Chapter 17 for the details.

Knowing where to look, while not difficult, is elusive if there is not a clear understanding of the scene characteristics: Logic in action. Table 5.4 is a limited checklist of places where microscene evidence might logically be found. It also explains why these are places to begin searching. The list is far from exhaustive because it is impossible to know all of the hiding places where trace evidence might be without being at the specific scene. Suffice to say, each scene represents a unique challenge.

The flip side of the search coin for trace evidence relates to knowing where not to search. It would be ridiculous for the scene scientist/investigator to vacuum or tape lift all items of furniture at the scene in order to find that one piece of furniture that has fiber evidence from a perpetrator's shirt. Remember, the subsequent laboratory work is time consuming and tedious, and submitting hit-or-miss evidence in bulk to cover a shoddy scene investigation will incur the wrath of the crime laboratory scientist. Obviously, finding and collecting probative evidence is critical, but collecting evidence without a valid reason is stupidity in action.

A relationship should exist between the scene scientist/investigator and the laboratory scientist, so that the evidence collected and submitted to the laboratory, even if the scientist suspects it is superfluous, can be rationalized. For example, for tape lifts of trace material from furniture in a living room, a conversation might go something like this; this could be a phone conversation or could take place face-to-face. Understand that a phone conversation like this might take place days or weeks after the evidence had been submitted to the laboratory.

Scientist: You sent 50 tapes to the lab taken from furniture at the Dracula scene. I gotta tell ya, there's no way I can do all of the analyses in my lifetime. Why did you collect so many?

Table 5.4 Locations of Trace Evidence

Location	Reason
Points of entrance and egress	These are areas where the perpetrators might have been and can be locations of fibers, hairs, and so on.
Areas of a struggle	These areas are prime targets for hairs fibers, blood, and saliva. They include furniture and carpets and should not be overlooked.
The clothing and shoes of participants in the crime (victims and suspects)	The clothing of victims and suspects in direct contact with each other should have fiber, hair, saliva, and blood evidence present.
Furniture—understanding the transfer potential of certain fabrics	Fabric furniture involved in a struggle (turned over chairs and so on) has the potential of attracting fibers and hairs. The likelihood depends on the characteristics of the fabric—whether it accepts and/or gives up its fibers readily. These can also have saliva and blood.
Bodies of decedents	The body, its clothing.
Fingernails	Anyone involved in a struggle has the possibility of having trace evidence under the fingernails: hairs, fibers, saliva, and blood.
Areas searched by perpetrator	If a perpetrator, for example, a burglar, is searching for valuables, the areas searched are prime targets for trace evidence.

Investigator: I took the ones I thought were important for the investigation.
Scientist: I understand that (thinking the investigator is covering his butt), but is there some priority here?
Investigator: They were in the room where the murder took place.
Scientist: OK, so I notice each piece of furniture is marked with an evidence item number and that you collected lifts from 10 pieces of furniture. Were all 10 directly involved in the struggle or only some of them?
Investigator: Let me check the scene photos.
Scientist: OK.
Investigator: It appears that the struggle mostly took place in one area of the living room, probably on the sofa, Item number 4.
Scientist: OK. I'll start there. Where else?
Investigator: There's a chair near the sofa that had been knocked over. It, too, might be a possible. Item number 7.
Scientist: Thanks, I'll look at both of them. I'll let you know what I find, and we can decide where to go from there.
Investigator: OK, sounds good.

In this scenario, the scene scientist/investigator collected more than the scientist could analyze in a reasonable timeframe. Luckily, they had worked together on cases in the past, so they were able to work out a reasonable starting point for the scientist. A conversation between individuals who had not worked together might not have gone as smoothly, and a disagreement could lead to supervisory involvement, which in these circumstances leaves a sour taste in everyone's mouth. What is eventually analyzed might also depend on whether the laboratory scientist is independent of the police department. A police chief or chief of detectives might order the scientist to analyze all of the evidence. A scientist in an independent laboratory, such as a medical examiner's laboratory, is in a better position to negotiate the analytical sequence. In high profile cases, everyone realizes that more evidence will be collected than normal that will have to be analyzed, even when logic says differently.

References

1. R. M. Gardner. 2005. *Practical Crime Scene Processing and Investigation.* Boca Raton, FL: CRC Press, pp. 75–86.
2. R. M. Gardner. 2005. *Practical Crime Scene Processing and Investigation.* Boca Raton, FL: CRC Press, p. 101.
3. K. Inman and N. Rudin. 2000. Chapter 5: The recognition of physical evidence. In: *The Principles and Practice of Criminalistics: The Profession of Forensic Science.* Boca Raton, FL: CRC Press, p. 101.
4. K. Inman and N. Rudin. 2000. Chapter 5: The recognition of physical evidence. In: *The Principles and Practice of Criminalistics: The Profession of Forensic Science.* Boca Raton, FL: CRC Press, p. 106.
5. K. Inman and N. Rudin. 2000. Chapter 5: The recognition of physical evidence. In: *The Principles and Practice of Criminalistics: The Profession of Forensic Science.* Boca Raton, FL: CRC Press, pp. 107–108.
6. R. M. Gardner. 2005. *Practical Crime Scene Processing and Investigation.* Boca Raton, FL: CRC Press, p. 110.

7. R. C. Shaler, 2005. Chapter 28. Out of the box. In *Who They Were Inside the DNA Story: The Unprecedented Effort to Identify the Missing*. New York, NY: Free Press, pp. 277–291.
8. R. M. Gardner. 2005. *Practical Crime Scene Processing and Investigation*. Boca Raton, FL: CRC Press, p. 108.
9. R. M. Gardner. 2005. *Practical Crime Scene Processing and Investigation*. Boca Raton, FL: CRC Press, p. 109.

II
Forensic Archiving: Today's Eye for the Future

The Principles of Forensic Photography

6

—CRIME SCENE—DO NOT CROSS—CRIME SCENE—DO NOT CROSS—

6.1 Introduction to Forensic Archiving

The term "forensic archiving" is a departure from the usual terminology used to refer to preserving a scene's record. From a contemporary perspective, it is also more appropriate than the more frequently used term: documentation. Archiving has a broader scope and encompasses more than simply applying photographic, sketching, or imaging techniques because it connotes a modern relationship with a digital world. Although subsequent discussions may use the older terminology—documentation—one should not be confused with the broader, more relevant term forensic archiving.

One might inquire why forensics should embrace a new semantic standard. The simple reason is that the current standard no longer reflects current practice. Times change and so does the professional lexicon. The *Merriam-Webster Online Dictionary* [1] considers "archive" a noun, and defines it as: "1. A place in which public records or historical documents are preserved, and 2. A repository or collection especially of information."

Modern computer usage considers "archive" a verb in the context of backing up digital files, and *PC Magazine* [2] defines "active archiving" as "Moving data to a secondary storage medium that can be readily accessed if required." While *PC Magazine* is a specific reference in context, in light of current crime scene practice as well as what happens afterward, it is appropriate.

With respect to preserving a crime scene, information is put into an archive, which can be a case file, a file cabinet, and/or digital photographs on a computer hard drive or a CD backup or both. In contemporary investigations, archiving usually employs a form of digital media, whether photographs taken using a digital single-lens reflex (SLR) camera, a Digicam video recorder, a computer-aided design (CAD) system, software to enhance images, or three-dimensional (3D) digital imaging systems. Even the hand sketch of the scene as well as the handwritten notes of an investigator can be captured in digital format. Archiving, then, is an adequate and timely replacement that brings the practice of scene preservation into modern vernacular. The crime scene archive is, in fact, a place where the historical record of the crime scene exists. The mechanism used to archive the scene can and should include multiple techniques.

Archiving is the critical responsibility of the crime scene investigative unit, which must preserve the scene as found, so that investigators, attorneys, scientists, and so on can "see" in some nebulous future timeframe what the original investigators saw. Thus, capturing the essence of the scene is critical because it is impossible to predict *a priori* when another pair of eyes will need to review the "original." Importantly, too, no single archiving method is sufficient, and the approaches vary from the simple process of taking notes and [illegible]ng reports to using increasingly complex technology. An agency using only 35 mm or [illegible]al cameras coupled with sketching and measuring is not doing its job properly. [illegible]larly, videography alone is insufficient and inadequate as are the newer 3D archiving systems, though they are certainly capable of providing more accurate measurements. Each archiving method has attributes and deficiencies such that a complete and competent record of the scene requires a battery of techniques.

The bottom line is that pictures are not enough. The reason requires a brief discussion of passive and active archiving and why the active process is the most appropriate approach for archiving a scene.

6.1.1 Passive Archiving

Many authors of crime scene investigation texts use the term "scene processing" to describe what happens during the scene investigation. When the crime scene unit enters a scene for the first time and starts getting a "feel" for what happened, a myriad of thoughts echo through each investigator's mind. Questions like those raised in Chapter 1 are relevant. However, once the team begins the archiving process, the actual steps involved may seem rote and removed. This is the connotation of what the term "scene processing" seems to imply, a passive process of taking pictures. All scene investigators know they must photograph and sketch the scene, which includes measuring critical items of evidence in order to fix their location. Experienced scene investigators realize that photography, sketching, and videography are techniques that complement each other and should not stand alone as the only visual representation of the scene.

The investigator who goes into the scene and begins taking photographs without thinking about what the scene is saying with respect to how the macroscene elements fit together is not truly an active part of the investigation and, truthfully, is hardly engaged mentally. He is simply taking pictures or sketching. This is a passive activity. Then, what else, is there? The answer is to engage the brain and make it an active partner in the process, which, with respect to this discussion, is termed active archiving.

6.1.2 Active Archiving

Active archiving is the process of combining the "rote," the passive aspect of archiving, with an engaged brain. Taking establishing photographs (i.e., overviews) of a room with a dead body, while simply moving from one perspective to another, is passive archiving. What is wrong with this? Nothing, if the investigator is a robot.

For example, the forensic photographer should think about the scene elements being captured. Is it enough to record the body lying on the floor in a pool of blood or is it also important to ensure that the photograph also includes, say, the tip of the knife sticking out from under the forearm of the deceased? Is the depth of field (DOF) sufficient to capture that information *and* the knife sticking out from under the sofa 6 ft. behind the body of the deceased? Missing the knife from either perspective might be a critical part of the eventual scene reconstruction because subsequent photographs might miss that angle. The single line of blood droplets on the wall behind where the body lies might have come from blood castoff from a knife. This blood pattern must be captured in the same perspective as the body and the knives, because it is important to understand the relationship of all items of potentially probative evidence. This means thinking carefully about each and every photograph.

In every sense, the forensic photographic process is the visible investigation of the scene, and it is an essential part of an active investigation, where artistic and forensic photography part ways. The artist wants to be creative and capture the scene from an artistic sense. The forensic photographer should not care about being artistically creative but being creative in the forensic sense. Each photograph must capture the best perspectives at the scene in order to capture its story. Like the artistic photographer who allows the landscape to guide the artistic process, the forensic counterpart permits the scene to guide the continuum of photographs from relevant evidence to relevant evidence. Indeed, this might seem paradoxical because the forensic photographer must capture *everything*.

The following list reviews the differences between passive and active archiving. The most important is that the photographer/sketcher uses the scientific method to ensure success during the process.

- Passive
  - Unthinking documentation of a crime scene using photography, sketching, and other archival media
  - No distinct evidence recognition process occurs before or at this point
  - The scene is archived as found
- Active
  - Rigorous use of the scientific method yields greater thoroughness, objectivity, and evidence recognition
  - A process to record physical evidence but which transcends rote archiving
  - Uses the criminalist's holisitic approach
    - Recognize physical evidence
  - Answers relevant investigative questions
  - Guarantees the most complete archive
  - Minimizes bias in the investigation

6.2 Techniques of Forensic Archiving

Archiving is classified into technology types: SLR digital photography, digital/high-definition videography, manual sketching, CAD systems that render scenes in 3D, and 3D imaging systems that use infrared (IR) lasers to make the measurements. An emerging method that has not yet gained widespread application to crime scene work utilizes 3D printing technology. Here, the data from a 3D imaging system is sent to a ceramic printer that prints a 3D ceramic mold of the original scene.

6.2.1 Digital Forensic Photography (Photographic Archiving)

It might seem like a mistake to consider only digital applications because it does not consider the vast history of photography in a forensic context. Modern scene investigators, though, mostly use digital photography. For this reason, it is important that students and novice investigators understand the basic functions of the digital camera and how it is used to photograph scenes of crimes. Certainly, any forensic student should be aware of this interesting history, but digital applications are considered because they are more relevant for students; digital is the present and the future.

Photography is an essential skill, and all scene scientists/investigators must be familiar with its principles as they relate to forensic archiving. Several texts have been written on the subject [3–7], and students should be aware of specialized texts on the subject as well as published material on specialized aspects, for example, ultraviolet (UV) and IR applications.

After reading several of these texts, one can come away with the impression that forensic photography is magical or a mystical manifestation of the medium. This is far from true. It is photography pure and simple, and, like any worthwhile endeavor, expertise takes time and practice. The purpose of this chapter is to acquaint the forensic student and novice investigator with the basics of photography and forensic applications so that they can learn to archive scenes competently. One caveat, though. This discussion will not consider digital evidence comparisons, software enhancements of images, or image processing except, perhaps, as simple examples.

6.2.2 The Purpose of Forensic Photography

When asked what the purpose of forensic photography is, students generally respond with a puzzled expression, maybe a shrug. Maybe the question is too simple or naive. Often, the reply is, "To document the scene." The true response is not quite that simple. Forensic photography has much more far-reaching implications. The most obvious are straightforward and listed below:

- Record and preserve the as-found condition of the scene.
- Show the relative position of evidence at the scene.
- Establish the relative dimensions of evidence.
- Cross-complement other archiving techniques.
- Preserve the as-found scene for future reference.

Certainly the above are important reasons, but there are others. Consider the hypothetical case where the defendant is convicted of a murder and sentenced to life imprisonment or even the death penalty. If, on appeal, the defense finds potentially exculpatory evidence and if a judge rules that the convicted defendant should be granted a new trial, the investigation begins anew. The investigators—defense and prosecution—will be looking for anything supporting the original conviction or an acquittal. This starts with the original scene photographs. One might say, "Well, those photographs were standard operation procedures for documenting the scene." Maybe, but those photographs should bring the scene back to life and thus play an integral part in the second investigation.

But what if the photographs were not good? Maybe at trial, the only photographs of the body shown to the jury had been taken by the medical examiner during the autopsy. This means the jury did not see the position of the deceased at the scene relative to the evidence. In light of the judge's ruling, scene scientists/investigators will be scrambling to examine all of the original scene photographs in order to find something that had not been considered carefully during the first investigation. Maybe that something turns out to be a bloodstain pattern that had been ignored during the original investigation. Since that bloodstain pattern is no longer available, the photograph is the only record available, and if the photograph did not have the proper forensic perspective it might be worthless as an investigatory tool or as evidence. If captured properly, it could play a pivotal role in a retrial.

The importance of scene photography/archiving relates to the overriding responsibility of the investigator to capture the details of the scene without missing anything and the integral relationships of evidence. The paradox is that forensic photography, per se, is an insufficient medium to capture everything. This is the challenge.

6.2.3 Critical Aspects of Forensic Photography

Since this discussion focuses solely on digital photography, discussing categories of digital cameras might seem important, but only two digital camera types should be used in forensic work: the SLR digital camera with interchangeable zoom lenses. One other example of a digital camera, which really is not a different category of camera, is one that has been modified for IR and/or UV photography. Most of the commercially available digital cameras can be modified for IR photography.

The first step for the student and the novice investigator is to become familiar with the camera's functions. Experience shows that even students who have had a course in photography are not prepared to photograph crime scenes. For appropriate forensic photography, the following photographic equipment is necessary:

- An SLR digital camera having, minimally, the capability to take burst photos, adjustable white balance (WB) choices, and a menu for manipulating the International Standards Organization (ISO) ranging from 100 to 6400, manual override modes (aperture, shutter, and manual and program priorities), and exposure compensation. It should also have an external flash attachment.
- Close-up (macro) lens—*f*/1.4 or *f*/2.8, 60 mm.
- Zoom lenses: *f*/2.8, 18–70 and 70–200 mm, or *f*/3.5, 18–200 mm.
- Polarizing lenses to eliminate glare.
- Ball-head tripod.
- External flash.
- Lighting slaves.
- Light towers.
- Appropriate filters for use with an ALS: yellow, orange, and red.
- Ring flash attachment.
- Scales.

6.3 The SLR Digital Camera

Several SLR cameras are available in the marketplace, most of which are upgraded periodically or discontinued as new models arrive. Once a camera is chosen, there is no need to continually upgrade. But, why are SLR digital cameras appropriate for forensic photography? In a word, they are versatile; their specific attributes are listed below:

- Changeable lenses to meet specific photographic challenges
- The investigator sees exactly what the lens "sees" unless the camera is modified for IR photography

- Higher-quality digital SLRs have large image sensors and produce higher-quality photos
- Near-zero lag time

Operating digital SLR cameras is not complicated, although students sometimes struggle to learn its functions. The basic camera operation is rather simple, as explained below, although its advanced functions are typically software-controlled. The basic operational aspects of the digital SLR camera are easily found on the Internet [3,4]. In most professions, technology and techniques have a specialized lexicon, and digital cameras and photography are no exception, so it is important to understand and use the terminology. See Table 6.1 for a list of terms commonly used in digital applications.

Table 6.1 Common Terms Used in Digital Applications

Term	Explanation
Megapixels	More megapixels give you the ability to make larger prints and to crop your photos. They *do not* necessarily have higher image quality.
ISO (and image noise)	Increasing the ISO, say from 200 to 800, lets you take clear photographs in dim light without a flash, but at the expense of image degradation.
Dust control	Dust on an SLR sensor appears as small black spots in photographs. Dust control systems attempt to prevent and eliminate this.
Image stabilization	Two types of stabilization: one that is included inside the camera and one that is inside the lens.
Live view	Composing photographs using the LCD screen on the back and the viewfinder.
Dynamic range	SLR cameras do not match the human eye with regard to seeing details in a scene, even when there is extreme contrast.
Crop factor [4]	A digital SLR sensor is smaller than a frame of 35 mm film, so only a portion of the image that passes through the lens is captured digitally. The effect is an artificial zoom of the image. The eye captures everything. Crop factors are manufacturer-specific, but generally a wide-angle lens on a Nikon digital camera (e.g., 28 mm) will be similar to having a 42 mm lens camera (28 × 1.5) (see Figure 6.1).
Autofocus systems	Autofocus systems can include anywhere from three to more focus points. Number of focus points reflects the accuracy of the SLR digital system.
Continuous drive	A continuous drive allows multiple photographs in rapid succession.
File formats	Forensic photography should be shot in dual format—RAW and JPG. When a digital camera captures images in the RAW format, it does not process the data; the images remain unedited. When a camera captures image data in the JPG format, the camera processes the files such that information is lost: color saturation, sharpness, and contrast. Processing cannot be undone [5].
Aspect ratio	Aspect ratio is the reason for why digital prints never turn out exactly like the image on the computer monitor.
Digital sensor	Light hits a digital sensor that varies in type and expense. The two most common sensors are the CCD and the CMOS. The CCD is the most common and is typically found in lower-end SLR cameras. Most higher-end SLR digital cameras use the CMOS sensor. Benefits of the latter are lower power consumption, less expensive to produce, and, since each pixel has a linked amplifier, it can transfer data easier. Other digital sensors include the super CCD found on Fuji Film's cameras and the Foveon found in the Sigma range of digital SLRs [5].

Students marking pitch on powder-dusted exemplar tread

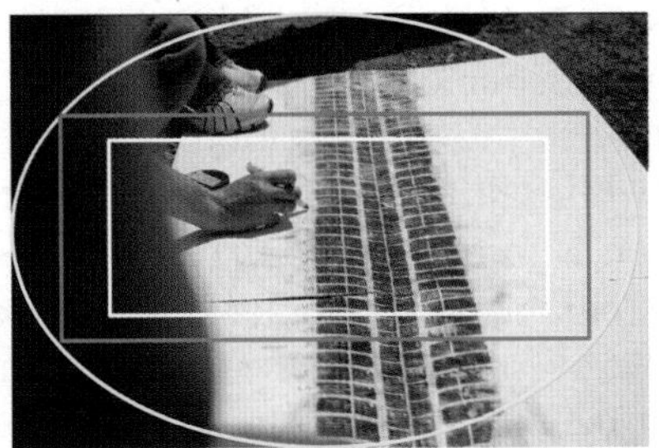

Inside yellow circle is what the human eye sees.
Inside the orange box is what the 35 mm camera shows.
Inside the white box is what the digital cameral shows.

Figure 6.1 Crop factor photograph.

Workshop on forensic photography introduces students to the digital camera. Expectedly there is a progression or learning curve. At the end of the first afternoon, the students are unsure of their photographic abilities because they have not yet established a relationship with the camera. Unknown to them, they are taking baby steps toward archiving mock crime scenes. In the ensuing weeks, they learn several scene-related topics (e.g., fingerprinting, etc.), and some forget some of the camera basics. Instructors reinstruct them as they work through the mock scenes, and, by the end of the course, they are as proficient as many professionals forensic archivists. The students encounter several purposefully set photographic challenges and explore the forensic aspects of IR photography that can have important applications in forensic investigations. By the end of the course, the students have taken giant steps in proficiency, but they still need practice before becoming experts.

6.4 Essential Skills of Forensic Photography

6.4.1 Focus: "If It's Not in Focus, the Rest Doesn't Matter"

Gone are the days when the photographer has to wait for the film to be developed before learning whether a photograph is in sharp (tack sharp) [6] focus because the liquid crystal display (LCD) viewer on digital cameras allows for immediate inspection of the results. However, the LCD viewer on the digital camera can fool you. Its images are small, and photographs may appear in focus on the LCD but out of focus on the computer screen. Thus, the LCD is a useful guide but not the final arbiter of whether a photograph is in focus. Having photographs in sharp focus, called "tack sharp," is vitally important to professional and forensic photographers. Blurry photographs have little use to either, and serve no legitimate investigative purpose in forensic archiving. The following guidelines listed are designed to help ensure that photographs are, "tack sharp."

- Use a tripod with a ball-head mount or at least a monopod. Hand-held photography is for amateurs, and forensic archivists are not supposed to be amateur photographers. There are times during investigative situations where a hand-held procedure is the only way to get the correct photograph. In these situations, the photographer must be extra careful.

- Pressing the shutter while taking the photograph moves the camera. The solution is not to press the shutter. Instead, use a cable release, the self-timer function on the camera, or an IR wireless remote shutter.
- Lock the camera's mirror in the "up" position. Normally, the camera moves the mirror up and locks it while taking the photograph. This causes movement inside the camera. The solution is to move the mirror up manually using the camera's "exposure delay mode" (Nikon) or "mirror lockup" (Canon) before taking the photograph. According to Kelby [6], this is the second most important precaution next to the use of a tripod to keep photographs tack sharp.
- Vibration reduction (VR) (Nikon) or image stabilization (IS) (Canon) is designed to minimize the vibration that comes from pressing the shutter on the camera. This function is resident in either the lens or the camera. Regardless, it works by looking for a vibration and tries to minimize it. If the camera is on a tripod, where there is no vibration, the VR system searches for it, during which it causes a slight vibration. The rules of thumb: If the camera is hand-held, activate the VR system. If the camera is on a tripod, inactivate the VR system.
- Shoot at the sharpest aperture of the lens. Generally, this is about two full stops smaller than wide open. So, if the lens being used is *f*/2.8, the sharpest apertures for that lens would be *f*/5.6 and *f*/8 (two full stops down from 2.8). Not always absolute, this is a general rule; a place to start. Each lens has a sweet spot from which it delivers its sharpest images. The photographer ascertains the characteristics of the lenses used at scenes.
- High-quality lenses make a difference. Use high-quality "glass" for tacking the sharp photographs.
- Avoid high ISOs if possible. When shooting on a tripod in dim light, do not increase the ISO. Keep the ISO at the lowest possible setting. The resulting photographs will be sharper. If the camera is handheld in dim light, it may be impossible to get the photograph without using a higher ISO.
- Because the LCD on the camera back is an unreliable gauge of focus, use the zoom feature on the camera to examine the photograph detail for focus.
- Out-of-camera image manipulation (e.g., Photoshop) can help with focus. Software manipulation of images for forensic purposes is not necessarily bad, but the original image must remain without modification. In fact, there is a trend to avoid or not even allow software manipulation of photos. If this continues, the burden is on the photographer to capture forensically perfect and relevant photographs every time.
- Hand-holding the camera in anything but direct sunlight increases the likelihood of obtaining out-of-focus photographs. A trick is to use the camera's burst function. The chances are good that one of the resulting photographs will be in focus.
- In hand-holding situations, bracing the camera against something (e.g., a wall, a railing, etc.) can steady it sufficiently to obtain sharp photographs.

6.4.2 The Correct Forensic Exposure

Exposure refers to the amount of light entering the camera and has been defined as, "The duration and amount of light needed to create an image" ([7], pp. 32–33) or "The subjection of sensitized film to the action of light for a specific period" ([8], p. 266). The first definition makes more practical sense. The basic unit of exposure is the "stop," where one stop is the equivalent of doubling or halving the amount of light entering the camera, which the photographer controls by adjusting the aperture, shutter speed settings on the camera or the ISO. The ISO setting plays a role in how the digital sensor handles light.

The difference between a shutter speed of 1 and 2 s is one stop and between 1 and 4 s, two stops. Controlling exposure allows the photographer to obtain that perfect forensic perspective, the one that tells the best forensic story. Only then does the photograph have the correct forensic exposure. Said in another way, the correct forensic exposure allows the perfect amount of light into the camera so that the scene can tell its "story." A challenge is that different camera settings allow the *same* amount of light to enter the camera. These are known as equivalent exposures.

6.4.2.1 Equivalent Exposures

The following camera settings allow the same amount of light into the camera, so they are considered equivalent exposures:

- *f*/8—*f*/stop and 1/4 s shutter speed
- *f*/11—*f*/stop and 1/2 s shutter speed
- *f*/16—*f*/stop and 1 s shutter speed

Photographs taken at each of the above exposures vary subtly. Interestingly, the photograph telling the best forensic story may not be the one chosen by a casual viewer. The reason is that a casual viewer does not consider forensic detail but instead how the overall photograph appeals esthetically. The sets of photographs in Figure 6.2, of a bloodstain spatter at a mock scene, were purposely shot using identical exposures using an 18–55 mm zoom lens without a flash.

In Figure 6.2, photograph no. 1—blood spatter on a tile floor, the camera (Nikon D50) was set on aperture priority and an appropriate *f*/stop chosen; the camera selected the shutter speed. For photograph nos. 2–4, the camera was set to manual priority and then adjusted so that each *f*/stop and shutter combination resulted in the same amount of light entering the camera as for photograph no. 1. A quick glance shows that the photographs are similar but not identical. The most obvious difference is the color of the tile floor and the overall darkness of the photograph. From a forensic perspective, photograph no. 2 has the best forensic exposure. First, the color of the floor is the closest to the actual color. Second, the detail in the photograph is the best, and, third, the overall complexion (darkness) of the photograph, although photograph no. 3 appears slightly lighter, is more appropriate for forensic purposes.

So, what makes this photograph more forensically relevant? None of the photographs were shot at the lens extremes; however, the *f*/11 photograph is better because the shot is closer to the middle of the range of the lens, about two stops down from the maximum of the lens. The lens is an 18–55 mm zoom with two maximal apertures: *f*/3.5 and *f*/5.6. This is a kit lens that compromises the ability of the lens to work in minimal light at low *f*/numbers. Thus, the *f*/3.5 maximal aperture at the low end of the range is not optimum for forensic work (see above discussion on focus in Section 6.4.1).

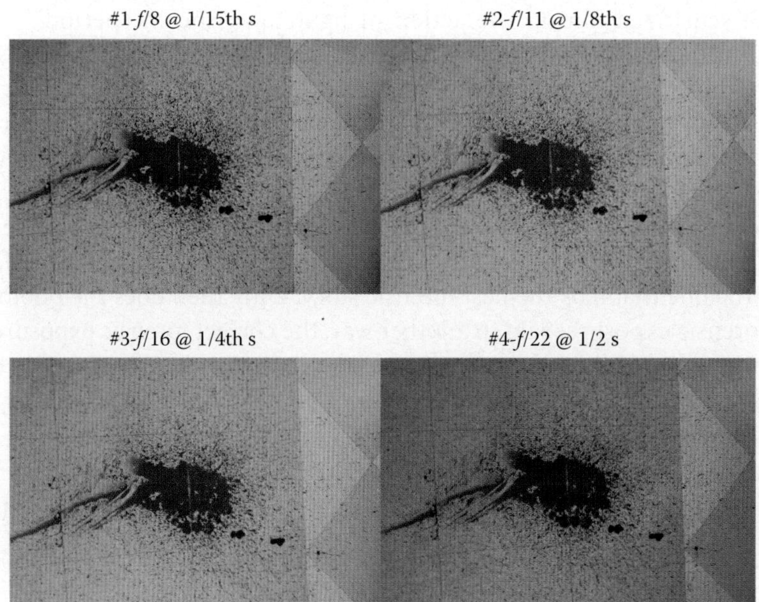

Figure 6.2 Photographs of bloodstain spatter using equivalent exposures. (Photograph by Robert C. Shaler.)

Keep in mind that the photographs in Figure 6.2 were not taken with a flash and they were purposely shot using equivalent exposures. A darker exposure, though not the darkest, was chosen as the best for forensic work. The reason is that slightly darker photographs are often better forensic choices because software enhancements can lighten the photograph without losing detail, but darkening them is usually not as successful. Additionally, overexposed photographs often loose detail, which is critical for properly archiving the crime scene. Kelby believes the opposite, reasoning that overexposure produces less noise, which is usually present in shadows. He believes that lightening the photograph using software increases noise in the resulting photograph [9]. For artistic purposes, this is probably true, but forensic archiving is all about detail and overexposed photographs can lose important forensic information that is not always easily recovered. The following discussion centers on the camera functions that students must master in order to control the exposure.

6.4.3 Aperture

Aperture refers to the size of the hole through which light enters the camera. This opening to the camera's external world is covered by a mechanical shutter that closes more quickly or more slowly (shutter speed), which limits the time the digital sensor is exposed to the light. The camera settings used to adjust the size of the hole are called *f*/stops or *f*/numbers. For most students, the two terms are confusing and counterintuitive because the larger the *f*/number, say *f*/11 or *f*/22, the smaller the hole, and vice versa. Aperture settings are the forensic equivalent of gold. It is the first camera setting that the photographer considers when photographing anything at the crime scene because it controls the most important perspective: What is in focus? This is another way of referring to DOF (see Section 6.8.3.4 below).

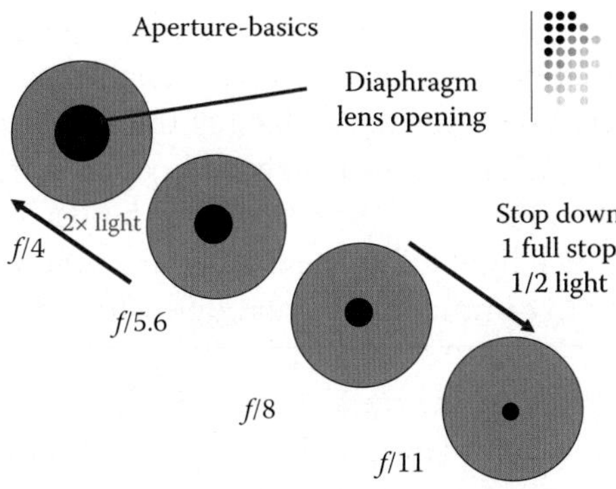

Figure 6.3 Aperture basics.

The relationship between aperture opening and *f*/number is illustrated in Figure 6.3. As shown, the *f*/number or *f*/stop, *f*/4, has a larger opening than the *f*/number *f*/11.

In older 35 mm and digital cameras, the *f*/stops were available in only what was termed "full stops," and moving from one to the other either doubled or halved that amount of light entering the camera. Moving from *f*/11 to *f*/8 opens the aperture (the hole) sufficiently to allow twice the amount of light into the camera. Similarly, cutting the *f*/stop from *f*/4 to *f*/5.6 decreases the amount of light entering the camera in half. Newer digital cameras give photographers more control over light entering the camera. The Nikon D50 and D40 cameras used in this course have *f*/stops stops in one-third and one-half stop numbers: *f*/numbers—5, 5.6, 6.3, 7.1, 8, 9, 10, 11, 13, 14, 16, 18, 20, 22, 25, 29, and 32. Instead of moving a full stop, say from *f*/5.6 to *f*/4, called "stopping down," the photographer can move from *f*/5.6 to *f*/6.3, which gives the photographer finer control over the final exposure.

The "*f*/" designation can also be confusing, but it shouldn't be. As shown in the list below (Definitions), the "*f*" is the focal length in millimeters (mm) and the "/" is the "divided by" function used in mathematics. The *f*/stop is related to the size of the lens opening, which means that there is a mathematical relationship between the size of the lens opening in millimeters (mm) and the *f*/number, as shown below.

- Definitions
  - *f* = focal length (in millimeters—mm)
  - *f*/ = divided by
  - *f*/number = the specific stop setting on the camera
- Calculating the size of the lens opening in millimeters
  - A 50 mm lens (focal length) with an aperture of *f*/1.4
  - Divide the focal length by the *f*/number
  - Lens opening = 50/1.4 or 35.7 mm

The aperture is thought of as either "wide" or "narrow." For example, an *f*/stop or aperture of *f*/2.8 is wide, meaning the "hole" is larger, whereas an *f*/stop of *f*/22 is a narrow opening, meaning the hole is smaller. The digital SLR camera communicates with the lens via electronic contacts, which open and close the aperture depending on what the investigator wants to capture. In contrast to the one-third *f*/numbers above, a standard set of full-stop aperture numbers would be *f*/2.8, *f*/4.0, *f*/5.6, *f*/8, *f*/11, *f*/16, and *f*/22.

The lens is an important player in determining the lens opening because the quality of the lens can limit the effective maximum opening available, called the "maximum aperture." An example compares two zoom lenses having the same focal zoom, the 18–55 mm zoom, but different maxima *f*/numbers. At their wide open settings, one is *f*/3.5 and the other *f*/2.8 (usually labeled on the lens). The latter is the better of the two lenses because it can allow nearly twice as much light to hit the digital sensor at its most wide open setting. Thus, the *f*/2.8 lens is useful in dimmer light situations, which can have important forensic implications.

Some lenses have two aperture maxima. The 18–55 mm zoom lens packaged with less expensive Nikons is known as a kit lens and is typically of lower quality than higher-end lenses. In the kit lens, the 18 mm focal length (wide angle) has an *f*/stop maximum of *f*/3.5 and the 55 mm (zoom) of *f*/5.6. Known as a variable maximum aperture, it is typical of the less expensive lenses sold in camera kits. These lenses typically lose sharpness at the extremes, such as at 18 mm (*f*/3.5) *and* at 55 mm (*f*/5.6). This is important for the forensic photographer because photographing in dimmer light can compromise the clarity and thus the quality of the photograph.

6.4.3.1 Telling the Scene's Story: The Importance of Aperture

Although only one of the big three players in solving the correct forensic exposure puzzle, aperture should be the *first* setting chosen. The reason is that each crime scene has its own story to tell and each photograph has a specific forensic perspective to capture. This is a question of focus, not as in tack sharp, but "What at the scene and in this photograph should be in focus?" The aperture setting determines this. By choosing the aperture first, the photographer is not only determining what should be in focus but is also making a decision after critically evaluating the scene. This is an example of active archiving.

The concept of what is in focus refers to a concept known as "depth of field" or DOF. In evaluating the crime scene, the photographer must consider the DOF because it tells the scene's story. The reason for discussing DOF at the same time as aperture is that the size of the opening controls what is in focus. In simple terms, the DOF refers to "what is in focus." An illustration of how aperture controls what is in focus is shown in the photographs in Figure 6.4 [7].

In the photographs in Figure 6.4a–d, the American flag is the focal point. The tree, the writing on the street, the vehicle behind the tree, the white building to the right of the vehicle, and the brick building in the left top segment of the photograph are important background elements. The photographer determines what should be in focus by changing the lens opening—the aperture. Generally, the larger the *f*/stop (larger *f*/numbers), the narrower the DOF and more of the background will be in focus. Conversely, smaller *f*/stops mean a shallower DOF and, thus, progressively less of the background will be in focus. In Figure 6.4a, all of the background elements are blurry because the *f*/stop, *f*/4, offers minimal DOF; the photograph's focal point, the American flag, is in focus. In Figure 6.4b, the aperture has been narrowed (1 stop) to *f*/5.6 which increases the DOF slightly and brings the tree and the writing in the street more in focus. The vehicle and the buildings, though better, are still rather blurry. A further narrowing of the aperture to *f*/11 (2 stops) is shown in Figure 6.4c. Here, the tree, the writing on the street, the vehicle, and the white building are in focus. The focus of the brick building is better, but close examination (arrow) shows that it is still not as crisp as the white building. In Figure 6.4d, the photographer has narrowed the opening to *f*/22. This improves the DOF and brings

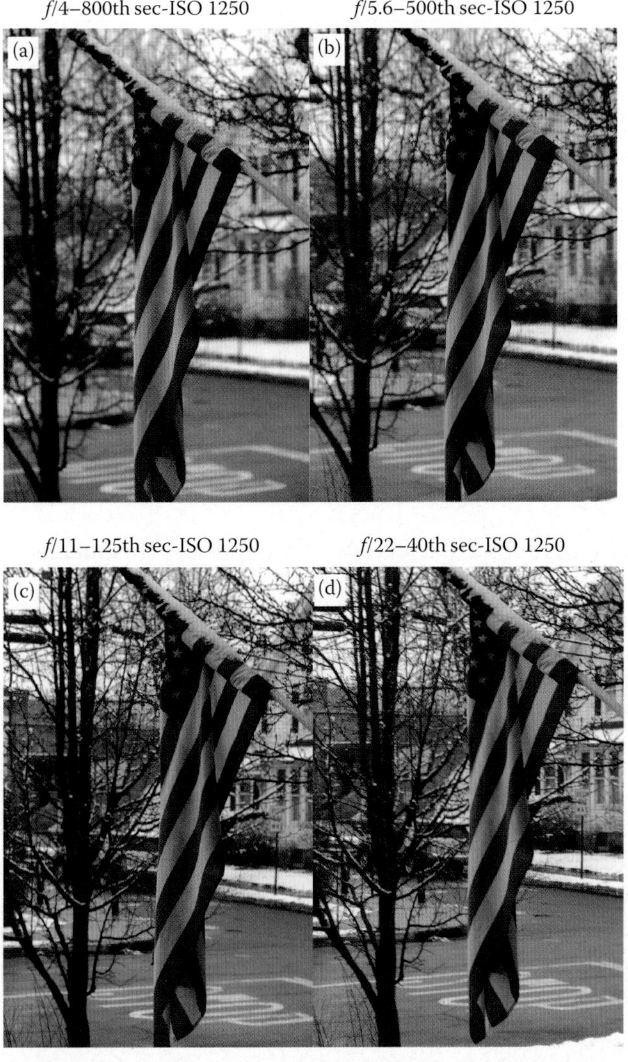

Figure 6.4 Illustration of aperture and depth of field (DOF). (a) *f*/4 wide aperture, background blurry. (b) *f*/5.6 narrower aperture by 1 stop increases DOF slightly. (c) *f*/11 narrower aperture and greater DOF. (d) *f*/22 narrower aperture, maximum DOF.

most of the background elements into focus. At first glance, Figures 6.4c and d appear very similar with respect to focus. However, a close examination of the brick shows that the narrower opening in Figure 6.4d has brought the building into better focus. With the exception of close-up photographs (Table 6.2), a rule of thumb for forensic photography requires a maximum DOF. For other photographs, this means shooting using large *f*/stops so that the aperture is as narrow as possible. However, where DOF is unimportant or nonexistent, such as in close-ups, smaller *f*/stops (larger openings) are permissible, even necessary.

Crime scene photographers take three obligatory types of photographs (some argue there are four [10]). The commonly used types and the reasons for using them are shown in Table 6.2.

Table 6.2 Obligatory Forensic Photographs

Category of Photograph	Reason for the Photograph
Establishing	Continuous, overlapping perspective of the scene. No scales are necessary. Maximum depth of field (*f*/11–22).
Midrange	Capture immediate surroundings and relative relationship of items of potentially probative evidence. Scales may be necessary depending on subject. If so, photographs should be with and without scales. Maximum depth of field (*f*/8–16).
Close-up or microphotography	Capture detail of potentially probative evidence. Photographs with and without scales. Shallow depth of field (*f*/1.4–4). Weiss [10] characterizes close-up images as a way to capture evidence in relation to its discovered location, which for this text is also considered as midrange photography. Weiss considers microphotography a way to "document the evidence itself."

Establishing photographs are overviews of the scene. This means that as much of the scene should be in focus as possible. In other words, there must be a broad DOF, and larger *f*/numbers (smaller aperture). The purpose of establishing photographs is to present the investigator with a continuous, overlapping perspective of the entire scene, which can be accomplished only by ensuring that everything in the photograph is in focus. Midrange photographs are designed to capture specific areas of the scene, where potentially probative evidence is in the immediate area. Again, the *f*/stop must be chosen so that everything in the photograph is in focus. Close-up photographs capture critical detail of specific items of potential evidence that might have probative value. All on-scene close-up photographs must be the last in a series of photographs that show the evidence in the context of its original (scene) environment.

With zoom lenses, determining the DOF by examining the markings on the lens is difficult if not impossible. It can be determined on fixed focal length lenses, however. Figure 6.5 illustrates how to estimate the DOF from fixed focal length lenses.

In the upper part of the diagram, the camera is set at 7 ft. from the object of interest and the camera is set on an *f*/stop of 16 (*f*/16), a midlevel opening. The brackets illustrate what will be in focus: Everything from 5 ft. in front of the camera to a depth of 15 ft. will be in focus. The lower diagram shows the *f*/stop set at *f*/5.6, a wider aperture opening and typically a shallower DOF. In fact, the objects in focus will have a narrow range: 5–10 ft.

The aperture opening is the gateway to light entering the camera, which makes it an important player in determining the exposure. How long that gateway remains open to the outside world is also important. This is known as the shutter speed, and it, too, plays a role in determining the correct exposure.

6.4.4 Shutter Speed

As discussed above, the aperture controls the size of the opening, which is critical, but that hole must close in order to capture the correct amount of light. Regardless of the size of the opening, if the digital sensor is exposed too long, the resulting photograph will be overexposed and meets neither forensic nor artistic standards. The role of the shutter is

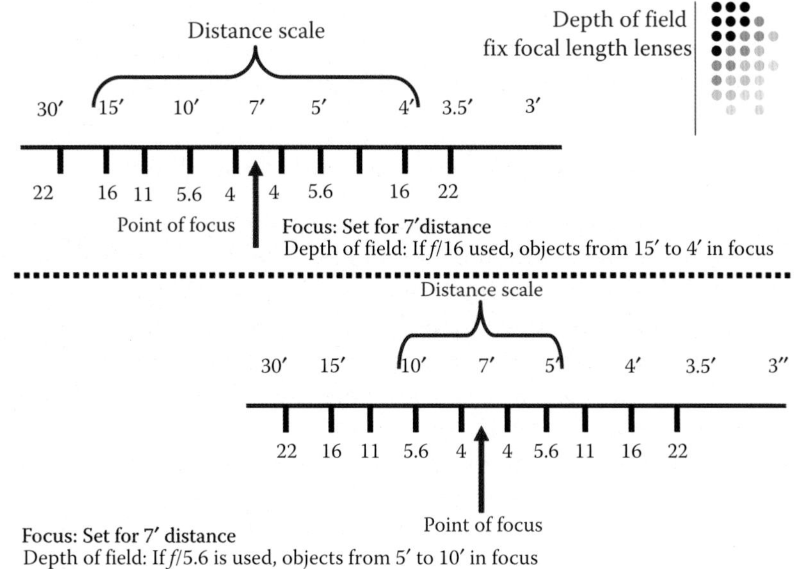

Figure 6.5 Estimating the depth of field (DOF) from fixed focal length lenses.

to shut off the light reaching the digital sensor, which it does by opening and closing the door (diaphragm) over the aperture. The speed at which this happens determines the specific amount of light entering the camera. The markings in the viewfinder or on the LCD of the digital camera displays to the photographer how quickly the diaphragm (shutter) is opening and closing in front of the lens opening, a measure of the shutter speed. The shutter is, in essence, a door to the outside world that remains open for fixed periods of time.

Like aperture settings (*f*/stops), shutter speeds follow a standard scale: 1/8000, 1/4000, 1/2000, 1/1000, 1/500, 1/250, 1/125, and so on, where the denominator refers to fractions of a second. Thus 1/8000 means that the shutter is open for 1/8000th of a second. This list shows progressively longer shutter speeds, each changing by one-half, which means that one-half the amount of light enters the camera with each change in shutter speed. This is equivalent to one full stop. Modern cameras have shutter speeds in less than one full stop increments, such as 1/2, 1/3, 1/4, 1/6, and so on. The viewfinder of the camera displays the shutter speed by showing only the denominator, such as 2, 3, 4, and 6, of the fractions listed above.

The length of time the shutter is open is a concern for photographers because the longer it is open the longer the photographer must hold the camera. A rule of thumb is that a shutter speed of 1/60th of a second is necessary to feel confident that there is no camera movement (camera shake). Modern digital cameras and lenses sometimes have an anti-shake function, which can lower the holding time (shutter speed) from 1/60th to near 1/15th of a second. Below this value, the photographer should use a tripod or some other way to keep the camera from moving.

6.4.5 Exposure Values

Each combination of aperture and shutter speed has what is known as an exposure value (EV), which is essentially the value of equivalent exposures. Thus, 1/60th at *f*/4 has the same EV as 1/125th at *f*/2.8. Different photographs can have the same exposure, but the photographs can have subtle differences (6.4.2.1). These subtle differences make a particular scene photograph better than another for capturing specific detail.

6.4.6 International Organization for Standardization (ISO)

The ISO rating is the third leg of the exposure puzzle, and is a measure of the digital sensor's sensitivity to light. The higher the ISO number, the more sensitive the sensor is to light. For forensic work, the practical implication is that larger ISO numbers offer an opportunity to shoot in dim light. The trade-off is that, as the ISO numbers increase, say 800 and higher, the resulting photograph begins to deteriorate or acquire noise, in digital terminology. In practical terms, the more noise, the less opportunity there is to "blow up" the photograph in order to observe fine detail.

ISO settings affect the exposure like aperture and shutter speed because a change in ISO from 100 to 200, for example, effectively doubles the light available to the photograph, or a full stop. Although more light does not come into the camera, the digital sensor is more sensitive to light entering the camera, which in essence changes the sensitivity of the camera significantly, a full stop.

6.4.7 Focal Length

The focal length is lens dependent and, for practical applications, refers to how far (distance) an object must be from the camera lens in order for it to fill the viewfinder (photograph). Figure 6.6 illustrates the point. The three lenses used in the course are zoom lenses with focal lengths of 18–55, 55–200, and 12–24 mm. The diagram shows that the "normal" zoom lens—18–55 mm (55 mm is the closest to what the human eye perceives) is in the middle of the range. This lens may be most appropriate for midrange photographs. The wide-angle zoom (12–24 mm) allows the photographer to capture more of the scene

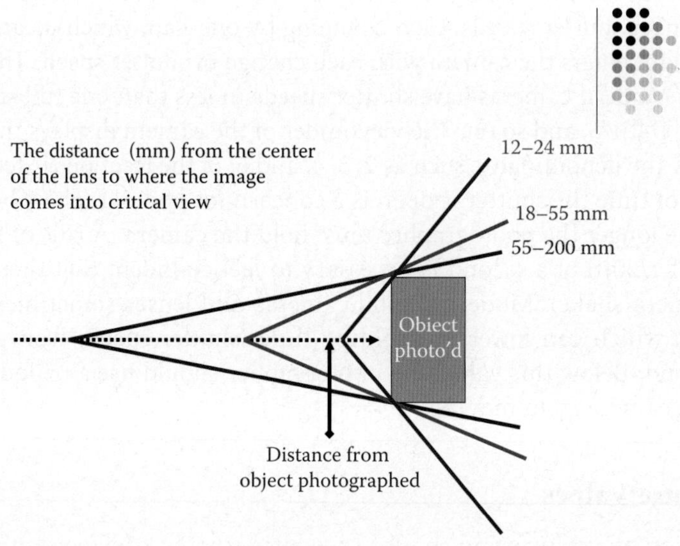

Figure 6.6 Illustration of lens focal length.

without moving back and may therefore be more appropriate for establishing photographs. Also, it may be appropriate in a tight space. The telephoto lens (55–200 mm) captures detail from further away from the object photographed. These lenses have value at outdoor scenes used as either or both a midrange/establishing (55 mm) and midrange (200 mm) setting.

Digital cameras have lenses with focal lengths that based on 35 mm camera equivalents, supposedly based on "film size." Actually, the focal lengths are based on the size of the charge-coupled device (CCD) or complementary metal-oxide-semiconductor (CMOS) digital sensor, which differs by manufacturer. Still, the photographic industry uses 35 mm equivalents for digital lenses, although digital focal lengths are not equivalent to 35 mm camera focal lengths. There is a formula, however, that can convert digital focal lengths into approximate 35 mm equivalents: Digital lens "focal length/0.19" = 35 mm equivalent.

6.4.8 Metering

Cameras need to know how much light is reflected from an object in order for it to decide what an appropriate exposure should be. Modern digital cameras accomplish this using through-the-lens (TTL) metering systems, which means the camera measures the amount of light that is reflected from an object or the light that hits the digital sensor. The light that should be measured is the incident light that hits an object.

As mentioned, typically the light entering and measured by the camera is reflected light, which is only an approximation of the incident light. It is important to remember that the incident light is the important light. If all objects reflected the same amount of light, the TTL system would work perfectly. However, that is hardly the case, and the TTL system often forces the camera into making poor decisions, the result being underexposed or overexposed photographs. Older cameras did not have built-in metering systems, which is why photographers needed a hand-held meter to measure the incident light hitting the object. Figure 6.7 illustrates reflected versus incident light.

In addition to the metering system, the digital SLR camera typically gives the photographer choices to tell the camera how to measure light hitting the digital sensor. Less expensive,

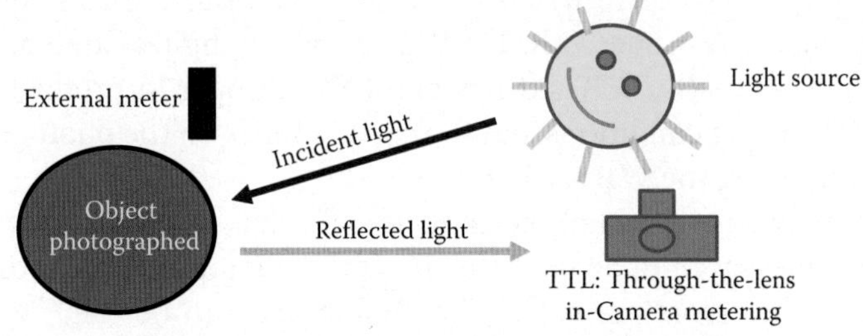

If all objects reflected the same percentage of incident light, the TTL would work just fine. Real-world subjects vary greatly in their reflectance.

In-camera metering is standardized based on the light reflected from an object appearing as middle gray.

Camera aimed directly at any object lighter or darker than middle gray, in-camera light meter will incorrectly calculate under or over-exposure.

Hand-held light meter calculates the same exposure for any object under the same incident lighting.

Figure 6.7 Measuring light: Metering.

beginner SLR cameras often have three metering choices: matrix, center-weighted, and spot. In the matrix mode, the camera meters a wide area of the frame and sets the exposure according to the distribution of brightness, colors, distance, and composition. In the center-weighted mode, the camera meters the entire frame but assigns the greatest weight to the center area. In spot metering, the camera meters the center focus area only. This ensures that the subject is correctly exposed even when the background is brighter or darker.

For most forensic shooting situations, the matrix mode gives the most consistent results. However, situations may exist that require the photographer to use a different type of metering. An example is backlighting, such as photographing someone standing in front of a sunlit window, where the person ends up looking like a silhouette in front of an overexposed window. In these situations, the photographer can fool the camera into using a better exposure by changing the camera settings after using spot metering on either a gray card or a darker area in the focus area. The camera responds to the spot metering by opening the lens and letting in more light. In this instance a flash is appropriate.

6.4.9 Exposure Compensation

This camera function alters the exposure up to +/–5 EV (depending on the camera) to make the photograph brighter or darker. It is available only for user priority modes (manual, shutter, program, aperture) and is most effective with center-weighted or spot metering. Generally, positive (+EV) values lighten a photograph when the main subject is darker than the background and negative (–EV) values darken a photograph when it is lighter. Digital SLR cameras have a function button for adjusting the exposure compensation, which is displayed in the viewfinder to alert the photographer when a photograph might be underexposed or overexposed.

6.4.10 White Balance

There is nothing more frustrating than sorting through students' crime scene photographs that have a blue cast. It signifies sloppy work, someone simply going through the motions of taking pictures without paying attention to the business of forensic photography—passive archiving. It means there was little or no thought to the consequences of selecting—or not selecting—the proper WB. The WB setting on digital cameras tells the camera how to "see" white. Actually, WB settings allow the camera to produce accurate colors under a variety of lighting conditions, but the camera relies on the photographer to specify the lighting condition via the WB setting.

The concept of WB is important because all color has what is known as a color temperature, which is measured in degrees Kelvin. If the photographer chooses the incorrect color temperature, the colors present in the photograph can be "off," which for forensic work is unacceptable (WB can only be corrected using software if the original photograph was taking using the RAW setting). Table 6.3 illustrates how the color temperature changes with the color photographed.

Table 6.3 Color Temperature: Degrees Kelvin and Visible Color

Color temperature (K)	1800	4000	5500	8000	12,000	16,000
Visible color	Red	Yellow	White	Light blue	Blue	Dk. blue

Figure 6.8 Inappropriate white balance setting.

The blue cast in the photograph in Figure 6.8 occurred because the student failed to set the WB properly. The wall in the photograph should appear white. The floor is actually gray.

Luckily, modern digital camera manufacturers do not rely on photographers to memorize or even understand the Kelvin temperature scale. Instead, the camera makes a menu of either icons or described situations available, with the choices based on common shooting situations. Those available on a Nikon D40 camera are shown in Table 6.4 [11].

The auto setting allows the camera to determine what is "white" and it sets the camera's WB automatically. On the incandescent or fluorescent settings, the operator chooses it from the menu function on the back of the camera, selected when the scene has either

Table 6.4 Nikon D40 White Balance Settings

Camera Option	Description
Auto	The camera sets the white balance.
Incandescent	Majority of the light comes from incandescent light (common light bulbs).
Fluorescent	Majority of the light comes from fluorescent lights.
Direct sunlight	Subjects lit by sunlight.
Flash	When using the built-in flash—mimics daylight.
Cloudy	Daylight when the sky is overcast.
Shade	Daylight for subjects in the shade.
Custom	Use a gray or white object at the scene as a reference for the camera to set the white balance.

dominant incandescent or fluorescent light. If two rooms are linked in the scene where one room has, say, fluorescent light and the other incandescent, the result can appear strange. The WB will be correct in one room but the other will be "off." This can be corrected using photographic tricks, but, for most scenes, the WB should be set for the particular area of the scene of interest for that specific perspective. The linked area can be photographed at a later time.

The outdoor settings on the Nikon D40 menu are self-explanatory. The "custom" setting is the only one that gives the photographer control over the specific coloring in the scene. In this mode, the photographer must "train" the camera to recognize "white," accomplished by showing the camera something white in that light at that location or by using a gray card exposed to that specific lighting condition. This is the most accurate way to capture the correct color temperature of the scene. Most photographers begin by setting the camera on "auto" because this usually produces acceptable photographs.

Some digital cameras allow WB bracketing, which means the photographer can shoot a sequence of three images. One frame will be at the WB setting chosen by the photographer, one will be slightly warmer and the other slightly cooler. This gives the photographer a better chance of accurately capturing the colors at the crime scene. Another way of setting WB is to shoot the photograph using the RAW file setting and then alter the WB using appropriate photo-editing software.

6.4.11 Capturing Forensic Content Properly

After learning the basic functions of the camera, mastering the craft of forensic photography requires practice. There is a way to speed up the learning process. The illustration in Figure 6.9 presents a step-wise approach to acquiring properly exposed, forensically relevant photographs. The process begins with choosing the proper perspective.

As discussed, this is more than simply pointing the camera and taking a photograph. There must be a reason for taking the photograph and the perspective considered carefully before pushing the shutter release button. This is when the scene photographer decides what the scene, as reflected in that specific photograph, is going to say to future investigators.

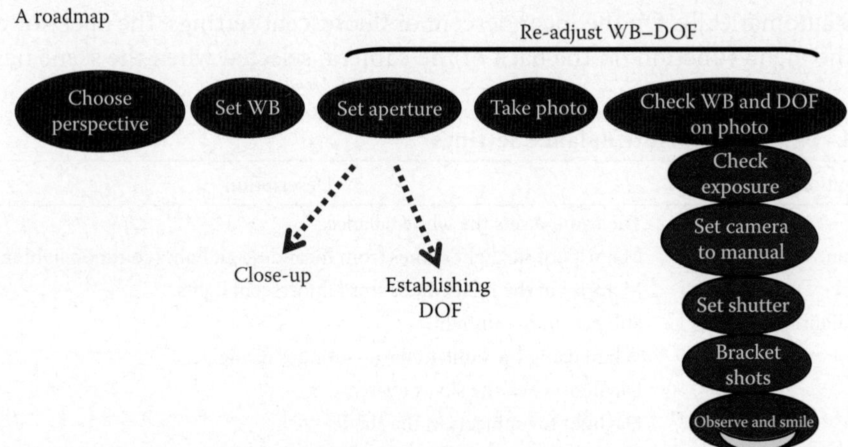

Figure 6.9 Capturing the perfect forensic photograph.

The second step is to examine the lighting at the scene (incandescent, outdoors, fluorescent, etc.) and set the WB. With the WB set, the aperture is next, typically accomplished by moving a selector knob to the "A" aperture priority (a first photograph taken on "auto" can provide a first approximation for setting the aperture and shutter speed). This is when the photographer considers and decides the type of photograph needed—establishing, midrange, or close-up—and hence the DOF required. After the aperture is set, the camera chooses what it believes is an appropriate shutter speed based on the reflected light entering the TTL metering system. The resulting photograph tells the photographer whether the camera is reading the scene properly.

The next step is to examine the WB and exposure in the viewfinder. If they appear perfect, no other adjustment is necessary, and the photographer can move on. However, this is rarely the case. If the WB and the exposure are correct, the next step will likely require setting the camera on "manual" priority and changing the shutter speed to get the best forensic exposure, which can take some trial and error and a few photographs. The forensically perfect photograph is the photographer's reward. The final step is to bracket the shots at different shutter speeds and/or the WB as well.

6.5 Forensic Aspects of Photography

Although forensic photography is simply the application of photographic principles to forensic situations, there are archiving rules that are inviolate.

- The first photograph in a series must have an incident photographic worksheet or cover sheet. This is usually a gray card with colored stripes, the case number, date, location, and name of the photographer.
- Photographs must be listed in a photographic log. As shown in Text Box 6.1, the log must have all of the relevant photographic data.

Text Box 6.1 Photography Log

PSU Case No.			**Date/Time Started:** **Date/Time Completed:**			**Criminalist(s)**	**Camera**
Exp. No.	**Item No.**	***f*/stop**	**Shutter**	**ISO**	**WB**	**Description**	
1							
2							
3							
4							
5							
6							
7							
8							
9							
10							
11							
12							
13							

- Scenes must be preserved using establishing, midrange, and close-up photographs
- Close-up photographs must include one with scales and another without.
- Illumination (metering) should be appropriate to capture impression evidence detail.
- There should be a continuity of overlapping establishing photographs.
- Tripods should be used for all photographs where the camera must be steady: close-ups, certain midrange photos, luminol (BlueStar™) photography, and dim-light situations.
- The camera (and tripod) should be perpendicular to the plane in which the evidence lies and horizontal (parallel).
- Scales must be in the same plane as the object photographed.
- Photographs should be taken before and after each on-scene manipulation (enhancement attempts) of evidence.
- The pop-up flash on the camera should never be used except in specific circumstances. An example would be in a back lit situation or when triggering slaves in at a dark scene.

6.5.1 Scene Incident Photographic Worksheet

The scene incident photographic worksheet is the cover for a book of photographs; each book or series of photographs has a separate cover sheet. The cover sheet has specific data including the date, time, case number, and the name of the photographer. It also has color stripes used to determine whether the camera is "seeing" colors correctly.

6.5.2 Photographic Log

The photographic log is a list of all the photographs taken in a specific series. Each entry contains the specific photographic and forensic information needed about a specific photograph: camera settings, description of what the photograph was, and the type of photograph—establishing, midrange, close-up. In addition, it has other case-specific information. An example of a photographic log used for the Penn State Forensic Science Program is shown in Text Box 6.1.

6.5.3 Types of Photographs

Forensic investigations require complete coverage. Unlike artistic photography where the landscape, the portrait, or the action scene are the objects of interest, the forensic photographer must comprehensively cover the entire crime scene as though filming a documentary (Chapter 8). This means wearing several photographic hats ranging from that of a landscape photographer to that of a close-up photographer. The forensic archivist must be an expert in not only recognizing evidence at the crime scene, but also capturing it in three principle photographic types: establishing, midrange, and close-up.

6.5.3.1 Establishing—Overview or Overall—Photographs

Establishing photographs are overviews of the scene and the first stage of the archiving process. These are designed to depict the general orientation of the scene. This job begins when the crime scene team initiates its investigation, typically before evidence collection.

Photography (or videography) represents the first archived sense of the scene and is a form of archival visual investigation. During the walkthrough with the first officer, the team leader may mark fragile evidence in order to prevent anyone from inadvertently destroying it. Certainly this is important and proper, but it should not interfere with the photographic and overall archiving process.

The scene view should be photographed as found, ideally before evidence markers are placed (fragile evidence excluded), which is often portrayed incorrectly as photographing from the four corners of, perhaps, a room. More importantly, the photographs taken should be shot in sequence so that the end result is a series of overlapping images of the scene.

Gardner [12] recommends taking establishing shots a second time after markers are in place in order to position the relative location of evidence found in areas of interest (see p. 140 in [12]). The reasoning is to capture first the unaltered scene and then to show the relationship of the scene to the marked evidence. For midrange photographs too, it is appropriate to have evidence markers in place.

Importantly, it is critical that the photographer takes proper establishing photographs. While not necessarily archiving the scene as found, protecting fragile evidence is a critical investigative function, which means that there may be situations in which the fragile evidence markers will be in the photograph. Anyone looking at the photographs at a later time should be able to orient themselves to how the scene originally appeared, even with a few evidence markers in place.

A problem with photographing a scene with evidence markers in place may occur at a later time. Evidence markers are placed at the scene to mark obvious potential evidence, and investigators might sometimes "over mark" what they consider evidence on first blush. Sometimes, a marker may be removed because what had been marked might be no longer considered important. However, if the marker is in a photograph and the item relating to that marker is not collected, someone will likely question the "missing evidence discrepancy" during testimony. Avoiding the problem is simple: Evidence markers in photographs must tally with a photographic evidence log indicating any uncollected evidence and the reason for not collecting it.

Capturing all that a scene has to offer is not easy. The relative position of all evidence (not necessarily marked with evidence markers), even evidence not yet found, should be in the photograph unless obscured somehow. Schematics on establishing shots designed for photographers to capture the essence of the scene exist. These are guides and roadmaps used for searching a scene and are designed to minimize the mistakes. Regardless of how it is accomplished, the team leader has the responsibility to archive the scene properly and completely. The photographer does the work of visual archiving, which means, because each scene is unique, careful and critical thought is important and necessary before embarking on a photographic campaign.

For example, photographing from the corners or middle points in a room might capture the overview of the room's dimensions, but this may not be sufficient to capture the front and back of furniture. Areas with a lot of clutter will require more than four-corner photography. The photographer decides how the essence of that room will be archived. Generally, scales are not required for establishing photographs.

For most establishing photographs, the photographer aims to obtain maximum DOF. This means using an appropriate lens, one capable of allowing the photographer to set the DOF so that, when focusing about one-third of the way into the scene, the first third and the final two-thirds are in focus. This is illustrated in the scene schematic Figure 6.10. For

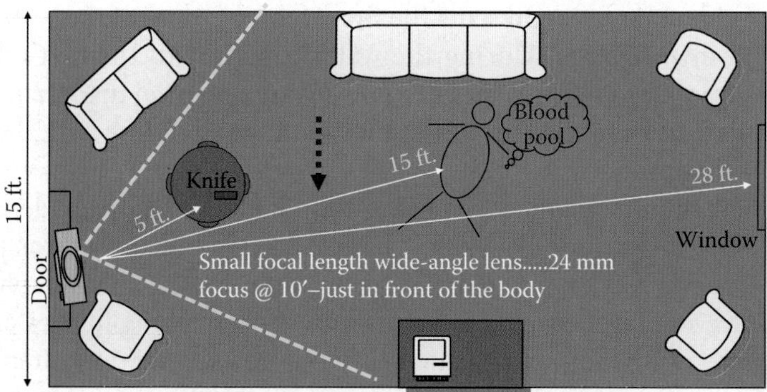

Strive for maximum depth of field
1. Shorten focal length (wide angle lens)
2. Smaller aperture opening (larger *f*/number)
3. Greater distance to point of focus (evidence)

Figure 6.10 Photographic log: Focusing at the scene.

this scene, the focus should be approximately 10 ft. into the scene, which is in front of where the body lies. Focusing on the body may bring other areas of the scene out of focus. As an establishing shot, this photograph is not just about the body but about the relationship of the body to everything in the specific area. The hatched arrow in the middle of the schematic shows the first choice for focus. Experimental photographs help determine the optimal focal point, easy with digital SLR cameras.

The illustration in Figure 6.10 suggests using a shorter focal length; however, too short a focal length can cause distortion problems. Recall that the 55 mm lens is the closest the digital camera gets to what the human eye sees. Establishing photographs should represent as much as possible of what investigators see. If the photographer uses a wide-angle lens to capture more of the scene, the resulting photographs can appear "off." That is, it may not be a best representation of what investigators saw. There are circumstances, however, where the photographer needs to use a wide-angle lens to get the entire scene into the photograph. In these instances, be wary of focal lengths <24 mm and should ensure that the midrange photographs are taken using a 55 mm lens so that distortion is minimized.

6.5.3.2 Midrange Photographs

After taking establishing photographs, the next step is to "get closer" to the evidence photographically so that the relative position of the evidence in a specific area of the scene is clearer. For example, the establishing shot may show a knife lying some distance from the outstretched right arm of the deceased. It is critical to pinpoint the knife's position perfectly, which may require more than a single photograph encompassing multiple perspectives: taken from the feet of the deceased, from the outstretched right arm, looking from the knife to the outstretched arm, from the left and right sides of the deceased, from the head of the deceased, from all doorways (if they not too far away), and so on. In this way, the knife's position relative to the doorway, to the deceased, and to other rooms will be preserved—archived.

A bloodstain pattern on a wall should be captured in midrange photographs, and the entire pattern captured. A procedure for accomplishing this is described in Chapter 15.

Establishing photographs tell an observer that the bloodstain pattern is present, but the midrange shot captures the size and shape of the entire pattern—evidence marker and scales in place. Subsequent close-up photographs detail specific droplets of interest: directionality, size, those having included air bubbles, pieces of tissue, and so on. Bloodstain patterns should *never* be photographed using a flash, especially using the camera's pop-up flash, because the flash will washout stain detail. Bounce flash can be appropriate, however.

Generally, scales are not necessary for midrange photographs. There are exceptions, though, such as bloodstain patterns. Sometimes, midrange photographs of an entire bloodstain pattern are not possible because of its size. In these instances, sectoring is a way to capture segments of the pattern, which are then spliced together to form an entire pattern.

A single bloodstain pattern at a scene should not present an archiving problem, but multiple bloodstain patterns should be labeled sequentially. That is, each pattern should have a specific designation different from other tagged evidence. Thus, if most of the evidence at the scene is tagged as, say, items 1–99, the bloodstain patterns could be tagged using alphabet markers A–Z. Another term used is "roadmapping" (attributed to Toby Wolson, Miami Dade County Crime Laboratory, p. 161, [12] (see Chapter 14)). Scales should be present in all bloodstain pattern photographs.

6.5.3.3 *Close-Up Photographs*

Evidence details that have criminalistic or investigative value—knife length and width—must be preserved photographically. An important category of evidence that should be included is impression or pattern evidence: fingerprints, footwear impressions, tire tracks, tool marks, and so on. The first photograph is taken without scales and the second with scales. The scales chosen must also be appropriate: A fingerprint requires millimeter scales while a knife on the floor does not require as much detail and can be photographed using an inch rule. All close-ups should be shot using a tripod because any movement will blur or obliterate critical structural detail.

Students often question which items to photograph in close-up views. A working rule of thumb is any evidence that will be removed from the scene that has direct comparative value. This includes weapons, bullet fragments, bullet impact marks, shell casing, impression evidence, fingerprints, and so on. Close-up photographs do not have a DOF issue, which means the photographer is free to open the shutter and concentrate on focus and filling the frame of the viewfinder with the image of the evidence.

Normally close-up photographs do not have a DOF because they represent evidence on planar surfaces. There are instances, however, where surfaces are curved, for example, fingerprints on door knobs. In these instances, the selection of the proper *f*/stop is important.

6.5.4 Illumination

The foregoing sections included a discussion of exposure, the process of determining the "proper" amount of light that hits the digital sensor. Another topic deals with not the amount of light but the relative position and type of light entering the camera. In other words, the location of the light source relative to the position of light before it enters the camera. The type of light refers to something other than white light: IR, UV, or light from an ALS.

An example is the photography of impression evidence, a common category of physical evidence that has texture and surface topology. Photographing texture (topology), especially something subtle, such as a fingerprint or a dry residue footwear impression, can be tricky and requires an oblique light source. Using an oblique light source, per se, may not be appropriate unless the correct angle of the light entering the camera is determined, typically empirically.

For photographers, light is either controlled or uncontrolled. In a controlled setting, the photographer controls the type, the amount, and location of the light entering the camera, which can be accomplished by using flash, slaves, or a technique called painting by light. An uncontrolled environment uses primarily ambient light, which the photographer must make work. Figure 6.11 shows examples of how to control light sources for the direct lighting of evidence. It shows three different methods for obtaining direct lighting. The scene circumstances determine the specific positioning of the light source. Impression evidence—evidence having texture insufficient for casting—usually requires oblique lighting: A 45° or 10° light source is used for 3D textured impressions, such as footwear or tire track impressions in mud.

Figure 6.12 shows where to place the light source depending on the depth of the impression. Impressions that have a shallow texture—fingerprints and dry residue footwear impressions (see the example on the right in Figure 6.12)—require a near-floor-level light source. For deeper impressions (see the example on the left in Figure 6.12), less of an oblique light source usually suffices. The optimal position of the light source can be variable and will be determined by the scene circumstances.

A clear example of footprints is shown in Figure 6.13 [13].

Even a rocket scientist can see the dramatic effect that changing the angle had on the quality of the resulting photographs. Without question, the 10° oblique lighting gave the best result. Students typically fail to experiment with illumination angles to determine the correct one. Usually, they try to make the best of a situation using either ambient lighting or oblique lighting with a flashlight or other light sources near the floor.

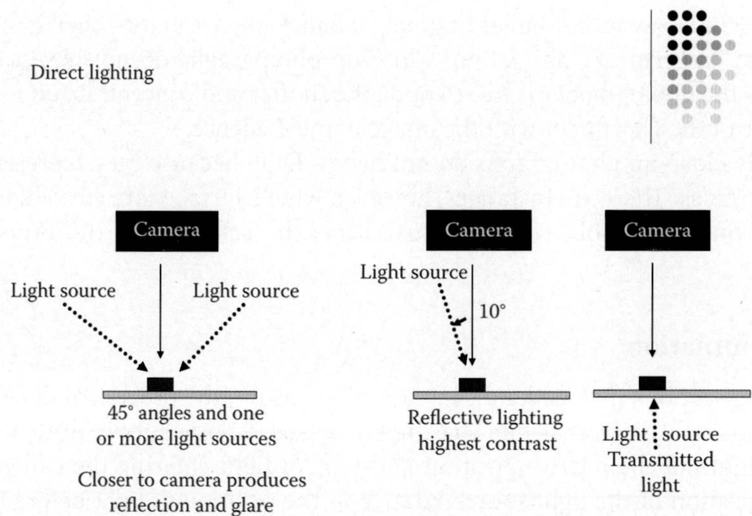

Figure 6.11 Controlled lighting of evidence.

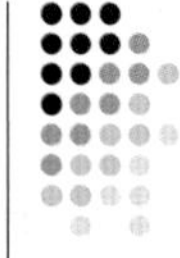

Low angle light for impression evidence:
Wet and dry residue footwear prints, tool marks, fingerprints

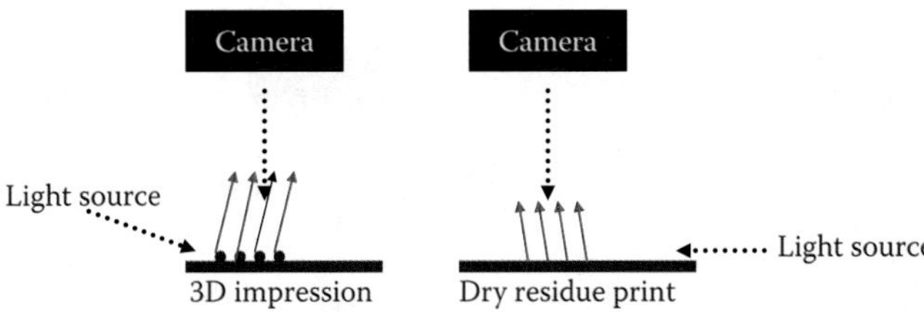

Wet and dry residue footwear prints, tool marks, fingerprints

Figure 6.12 Oblique lighting of impression evidence.

Clearly, the winner of the footwear impression photo contest is the one who takes the time to ascertain the most appropriate angle from which to obtain the most impression detail.

Sometimes it is necessary to soften the light by bouncing it from a reflected source—paper, glass, the ceiling, and so on—to the object being photographed. Figure 6.14 illustrates how to accomplish this, understanding that these are meant to be guides and do not reflect all possible variations.

The ingenuity and experience of the photographer will ultimately determine whether the photography is successful.

Photography of impression
Evidence

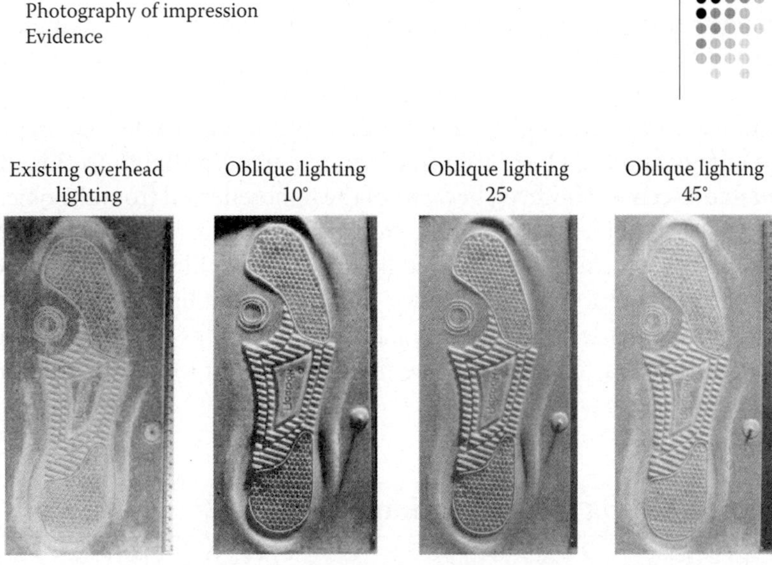

Figure 6.13 Three-dimensional footwear impressions highlighted using light at different angles. (From W. J. Bodziak. 2000. *Footwear Impression Evidence. Detection, Recovery and Examination*, 2nd edn. Boca Raton, FL: CRC Press, pp. 47–48. With permission.)

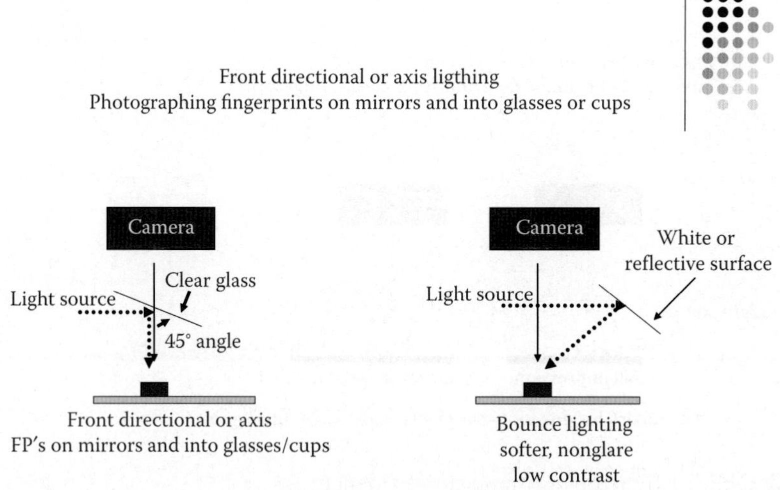

Figure 6.14 Fingerprint photography using bounced (reflected) light.

6.5.5 Filters

Filters are useful to darken, make warmer (or cooler), or eliminate glare in photographs. The first commercial filters were made by Frederick Wratten and C. E. Mees, whose company was the forerunner of Eastman Kodak. Their filters had numbers associated with each, and these have become the standard notation and labeling for optical filters [14]. Filters exist for most photographic applications: Some specifically block or pass visible, UV (1A-2C), or IR (87C or 89B) light and some darken a photograph a specific number of stops (85N3, 85N6, and 85N9). Other manufactures make special lines of filters—FujiFilm and MaxMax—for specific UV or IR photography [15]. Most filters have limited utility. However, some are important depending on the subject photographed. For example, polarizing filters are used to filter out glare.

Other filters are used in conjunction with ALSs. Specific wavelengths of light interact with matter in basic ways: The light is absorbed, transmitted, or reflected. Sometimes, the light absorbs energy and then loses it in the form of a photon (light). In this instance, the light is called fluorescence. However, because of the light reflected from the object, the fluorescence may not be visible to the naked eye or the camera. That is, the reflected light masks the fluorescence. Losing the reflected light means blocking it so that it never makes it to the observer (camera and/or person). This is accomplished using barrier filters. Figure 6.15 shows the process. The orange barrier filter blocks the reflected light (green) from entering the camera (or the eye). The fluorescence (pink) enters the camera and is "seen" by the digital sensor.

6.6 Forensic-Specific Considerations

6.6.1 Camera Positions

Camera positioning is critical because criminalists in the forensic laboratory must make comparisons to exemplars (known standards) against the photographs taken at the crime

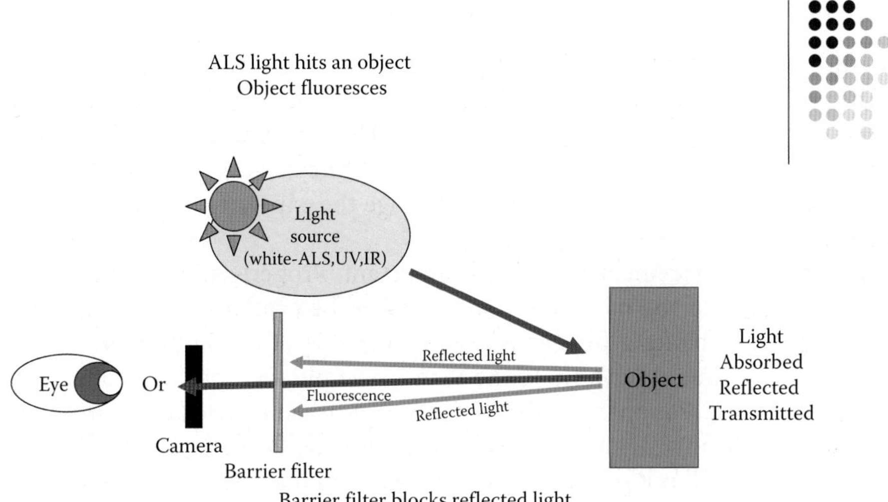

Figure 6.15 Interaction of light with matter.

scene. If the scene photograph is distorted or not perpendicular and horizontal to the plane in which the evidence lies, direct comparisons may be compromised. An inviolate rule is that all photographs must be taken parallel (horizontal) to the plane and the lens must be perpendicular (vertical) to the evidence. Figure 6.16 illustrates how to position the camera relative to the evidence. The dotted lines show the perpendicular (vertical) and the horizontal (parallel) aspects. If the "cross" is not parallel to the plane of the evidence, the resulting photograph will have minimal or conditional forensic value, even if scales are present.

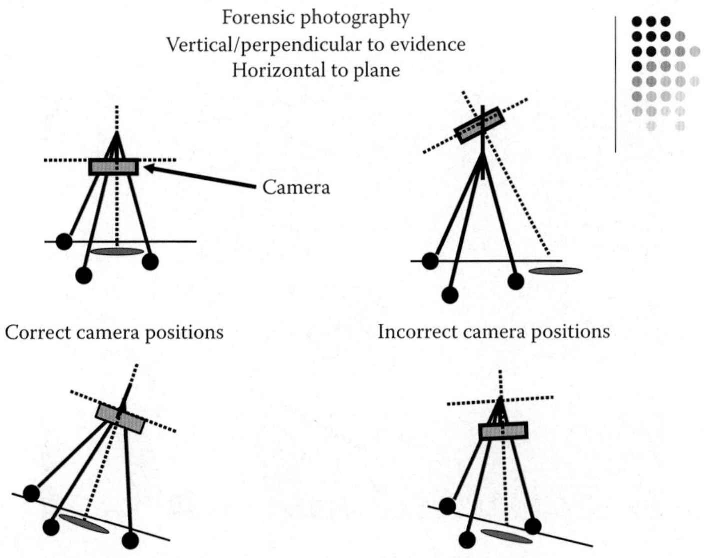

Figure 6.16 Positioning the camera relative to evidence.

6.6.2 Scales

All close-up and some midrange photographs must have scales in at least one photograph. The problem with scales is that the exposure sometimes changes after placing the scale near the evidence. Students often complain that their photographs are darker with scales than without. The reason is that the scale (white scales) reflects additional light into the camera, which forces the camera to change the exposure by reducing the size of the aperture.

Additionally, the placement of scales is important. Properly aligning the scales along the width and length of the most important sides of the evidence is critical. This means placing a single scale along a fingerprint or on one side of the knife is not forensically proper. Both scales should have the same detail. The photograph of a bullet through a windshield in Figure 6.17 is an example. Students were asked in an exam to critique it. One response said that the investigator used two different scale formats. Although not esthetically appealing, this will not preclude a criminalist from making accurate measurements. The answer to the question concerns the positioning of the scales. In this photograph, the scales were positioned incorrectly, not along the length and width of the bullet hole. The black lines illustrate how the scales should be positioned.

6.7 Photography of Common Scene Scenarios

All crime scene investigations follow a roadmap or menu of activities. The challenge is to follow a precise schedule without undermining the intellectual thought process. Chapter 3 discusses how these critical processes fit together and how and why logic is an integral and unifying part of that process. Photography is but one piece, a part, of the investigative puzzle. This means that forensic photography as a critical archiving medium must always take place logically and fit into the investigation without hindering its flow.

As discussed, establishing photography is one of the first activities on the agenda. This is as it should be, but this, too, must be done logically and based on the team leader's investigative philosophy. So, while establishing photography of the scene comes first, there is

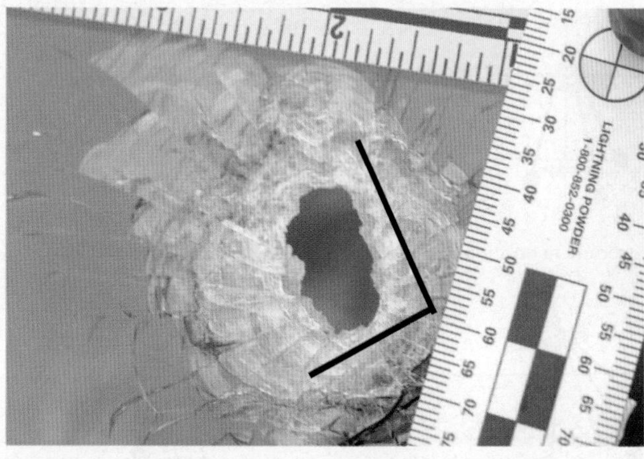

Figure 6.17 Bullet hole in windshield and incorrect placement of scales. (Photograph by Robert C. Shaler.)

logic with respect to the specific location where it begins and the sequence of the process. Generally, photography should begin where most of the activity took place. Since this is also where the crime scene team will begin its investigative efforts and where the photographer and team will spend most of their time, scheduling will be critical. If one part of the process happens out of phase, such as photography, the investigation will be inefficient and the team may miss critical evidence. For example, photographing the body is certainly important, but it should be done properly and at the proper time, which will be dictated by how the investigation moves forward and the medical examiner's schedule.

Because of how the "Scene Processing Cascade" was presented, readers of Chapter 3 might incorrectly conclude that all crime scenes are handled in the same manner. That would be an incorrect assumption. Each crime scene is unique, and while that discussion was partly philosophical, it left the responsibility of the scene management squarely up to the team leader, with the caveat that the investigation should be a logical and systematic process based on the scientific method. However, it makes sense that certain crime categories have evidence types in common. It also makes sense that students who are learning or honing their investigative craft should be aware of the array of evidence categories present in certain crime types, at least minimally, from an archiving perspective.

If logic is the guiding principle of scene investigations, and of archiving for this discussion, then defining scene types with respect to archiving might seem at odds with the philosophy of this text. However, taking into consideration crime types is important because certain ones, such as, vehicular accidents, homicides, sexual assaults, burglaries, hit-and-run, suicide, arson, and bombings, have specific recurring attributes. That said, there is always the consideration of logic and how it relates to what must be photographed at a particular scene type. And although the following suggestions should be taken seriously, there is the understanding that each scene is unique and therefore dictates the specific parameters required in order to archive it properly. Students should study these lists to familiarize themselves with the common characteristics and the differences among them. Hopefully, these will guide novice photographers so that they can successfully archive new scene situations.

6.7.1 Vehicular Accidents

Vehicular accidents are complicated, almost always outdoors, and often occur in high-traffic areas. Importantly, archiving these scenes is as much a public service as an insurance issue because the trauma and the possibility of criminal as well as civil law suits loom large. As with all crime scene photography, the forensic archivist must strive for objectivity and thoroughness. As mentioned, this discussion is not an in-depth study of accident scene photography, but simply a list of accident scene subjects that, if present, should be captured [16]. Certainly, evidence may exist that is not in the list.

In addition to capturing these macroscene elements—vehicles, vehicle impact points, blood, debris, skid marks, and so on—it is important to portray those intangible but important characteristics endemic to accident scenes: the sightlines of the divers and witnesses and obstructions that might have hindered those sightlines. Traffic controls and the relative location of signals, yield and stop signs that might have or should have been observed by the drivers, are also important. All photographs should be taken at drivers' eye level, if at all possible. For example, if one of the vehicles is a Honda Accord, the photographer must determine the sightline of that driver and then photographically portray this to the impact point. This does not mean simply kneeling down to a height that the photographer "believes" represents the drive's sitting height in the vehicle and thus his/her sightline. It means taking measurements so that the height of the sightline is as accurate as possible, and the measurements should be recorded in an appropriate log. The following factors should be considered:

- How the weight of the driver may have lowered the vehicle and how that could have affected the sightline
- The slope of the roadway and how that may have affected the driver
- Obstacles in the sightline, such as trees, signs, or other vehicles

If the drivers are not present because of injuries or death, all measurements will be estimates made on the fly. Information and sizes can be obtained from the medical examiner. Regardless, the exact heights at which the photographs were taken must be recorded, and, if estimates are needed, these must be recorded as well. If needed, more accurate measurements can be made at a later time. Since these scenes are usually outdoor incidents, accidents can occur because of factors outside the control of the driver; for instance, glare from sunlight, darkness, and bad weather can cause vision problems. Capturing this information is critical. Sun glare may have temporarily blinded a driver from seeing a traffic light, stop sign, or another vehicle. The photographer must capture this, if possible. This means working quickly because time changes the perspective and location of the sun. It might mean returning to the scene when the proper conditions are present. This, of course, is an elusive target and extremely difficult to duplicate precisely. Still, it is important to make an attempt and presenting a jury with an example of how the glare affected the driver's vision can be important. Table 6.5 is meant as a guide for photographing vehicular accident scenes.

6.7.2 Homicide Scenes

Homicides translate to dead bodies, which are an aspect of the macroscene. They are also scenes unto themselves. They have critical evidence that can eventually help close the investigation or provide critical probative evidence. They also tend to be a focal point. A dead body is not necessarily a major source of fragile evidence requiring immediate attention, and it does not need to be removed from the scene immediately. It may, in fact, not be where most of the scene activity took place. In fact, indoor homicide scenes often display signs of activity that carries across several rooms. The forensic archivist must capture this activity in a continuum from photo to photo (and/or video) as though the filming took place while the crime was happening. While impossible, philosophically that is the goal: "Miss nothing."

Philosophy often gets pushed aside in favor of what is practical. In fact, the true-grit scene investigation—fingerprinting, enhancements, trajectories, evidence collection, and so on—cannot begin until establishing photography is concluded, which is why the place to begin photographing (and sketching) is where most of the activity took place (struggle, bloodstains, etc.).

Many researchers believe the body is the most important part of the scene. Certainly, it is a vivid, visible, and visceral reminder of what happened, but this notion is far from correct. The medical examiner/coroner needs to conduct an investigation concerning the

Table 6.5 Guidelines for Photographing Vehicular Accident Scenes

Subject of Photograph	Reason for the Photograph
Drivers' viewpoint	What the driver saw
Point of impact	Where hit took place in relation to other aspects of the scene
Traffic control devices	Their location is important to know
Skid marks	Movement before and after the impact: speed, acceleration/ deacceleration
Roadway condition	Aspects of the road that could have had an impact on the accident
Roadway	Roadway environment: slope, potholes, defects, debris from impact location, position of vehicles
Instructions	Obstructions that would have hindered drivers' or witnesses' view of accident
Biological evidence	Blood, hair, flesh, or other biological evidence on the ground or on the vehicles' underside, tires, windshield, and so on
Tire tracks	Location and duration of tire tracks
Footprints	Location of shoeprints of drivers, passengers, and witnesses, if available
Impression prints in vehicle paint	Close-up photographs to document possible paint transfer and fabric impressions
Trace evidence	Fabric, glass, trace evidence on ground or imbedded in the vehicles
Defects in vehicles	Damage and noticeable defects, such as sagging springs to suggest instability. Aspects of vehicles not working—turn signals, headlights, and so on
Debris	Location of debris from the collision—glass, plastic, metal, trace evidence
Roadside	Environment at accident site as well as leading to and from the collision point
Interior photographs of vehicles	Positioning of blood, speedometer reading, positioning of seats, position of shifting levers, footprints on pedals, and so on
Establishing shots of vehicles	VIN numbers, license plates, overview of front, back, and sides of vehicles

Source: Adapted from L. S. Miller. 2006. *Police Photography*, 5th edn. Cincinnati, OH: Anderson Publishing, pp. 135–168.

circumstances surrounding the death, and the scene is a part of that investigation. But the medical examiner also wants to transport the body to the morgue as soon as possible. Candidly, though, autopsies in large metropolitan areas do not often begin until the next day unless the case is special for any number of reasons. Routine cases do not warrant that much attention. So waiting before moving and transporting the body is not a big deal. It is more important to conduct the investigation logically, systematically, and completely, which means photographing the body is only one part of the archiving process.

Eventually, the body becomes the photographer's focal point, even though the medical examiner and detectives have been likely hovering over it for some time. At this point, the photographer should use a specific set of procedures to document the entire body and its immediate environment properly. A serious consideration of the DOF is important, and shooting for the maxim DOF using an *f*/number of 11–32 is not unreasonable. The top part of Table 6.6 (I: Body and Surroundings) shows how to photograph the body and why.

Table 6.6 Guidelines for Photographing the Body at Homicide Scenes

	Reasons for the Photograph
I: Body and Surroundings	
Establishing overhead view	Capture surrounding area from an aerial view. The shot should be as vertical as possible.
Midrange photographs of body taken clockwise—head to feet, right arm and side, feet to head, left arm and side. A tripod may not be necessary.	Perspective of body's surrounding. Typically midrange shots.
Close-up views—head, hands, feet, clothing, wounds, bite marks, and so on. Tripod may be necessary	Documents the detail of the body.
Weapon-specific photographs	Capture bullet holes in furniture, walls, or other defects—knife marks, and so on.
Mark the position of the body with markers. It is not necessary to outline the entire body with chalk, just location of head, hands, and feet.	Knowing the precise location of the body helps if investigators must return to the scene. Photographs of markers of head, hands, and feet show their relationship to the scene.
ALS photography of the body	To visualize the biological evidence (semen, saliva, etc.) and fibers. Important at the scene to show relative location in relation to position of the body.
II: Ancillary Archiving	
Establishing photographs of the scene exterior, typically from a distance (e.g., from 75 to 100 ft.). Shots of the front of the house and driveway. Move clockwise. Depending on weather conditions, may be the final photographs. Include landscaping and impression evidence. Aerial photographs may be necessary. On-line services may be able to provide these.	Establishes the exterior boundaries of the scene location. It might be helpful in establishing egress and/or entry routes, possibly in retrospect.
Photograph looking away from the scene	Perspective of the area surrounding the scene from the scene's viewpoint.
All rooms that have activity.	Areas where evidence is likely.
All areas that do not have activity.	Unknown when nonactive areas of the indoor scene may provide important evidence.
Establishing, midrange, and close-up photographs of areas where fingerprints are found or where they might be.	Provide a visual perspective of perpetrator movement through the scene.
All impression evidence should be photographed.	Comparison with exemplars from suspects.

Source: Adapted from L. S. Miller. 2006. *Police Photography*, 5th edn. Cincinnati, OH: Anderson Publishing, pp. 135–168.

Homicide scenes have other important considerations. Importantly, though, no archiving activity should occur out of sequence (see Chapter 3). When an investigation goes on tangents, evidence can be easily missed, and there is the real chance of botching the investigation. The lower part of Table 6.6 (II: Ancillary Archiving) offers several suggestions with respect to winding down the photographic aspect of the investigation. These must be photographed at the proper time during the investigation. Generally, establishing photography occurs before midrange and that before close-up photography.

6.7.3 Nonhomicide Sexual Assaults

Sexual assault/battery is an important crime category that, too, has a common thread of evidence. Although usually violent, these crimes are different in that a sexual assault survivor may be able to relate details having important investigative value. From the forensic photographer's perspective, details of the attack location or locations may be critical in documenting the allegation. If the survivor was abducted from the street or on a jogging path in the woods, archiving the physical attributes of those locations is critical: macroscene elements, such as footprints, tire tracks, ripped clothing, and so on, photographed *in situ* to avoid confusion with respect to its location. Thus, for the forensic photogapher, the survivor can be a personal video camera of the attack. The details of what happened and where is key to locating probative evidence. A sexual assault nurse examiner (SANE) usually performs the physical examination, collects physical evidence from the survivor, and conducts the interview, sometimes in the presence of the investigating detective. This interview is critical for the crime scene team leader and the team's photographer.

These cases can take place inside a residence, inside vehicles, outdoors, or any place where a woman can be attacked. As suggested above, this might be along a jogger's path in the woods. New York City's jewel, Central Park, for example, has the unfortunate distinction of being the location of many sexual assaults. Sometimes, the subsequent scene investigation takes place after the SANE nurse's interview. It may be that the vehicle described by the sexual assault survivor may not be recovered quickly or ever.

Luckily for the investigators, unless there is blood present, semen, saliva, and trace evidence are not readily visible, especially on light surfaces, and there is good chance that critical biological evidence will remain at the location where the assault took place. The archivist has two responsibilities:

- Capture the location of the scene—as with any scene, such as a burglary (many sexual assaults begin as burglaries) or a homicide (many homicides are sexually motivated)
- Archive the location of biological evidence

Appropriate archiving of biological evidence requires photography using an ALS because this is the best way to visualize the semen, saliva, and urine. The photographer should have a series of barrier filters (e.g., orange, yellow, and red) that fit onto the lens. In combination with the ALS at 450 nm (the CSS setting on the MiniScope™ 400), semen, saliva, and urine will fluoresce. The orange filter blocks reflected light and allows the fluorescence into the camera.

Correctly capturing these scene details supports the survivor's allegation of where the attack occurred and provides her with a scientific ally in the courtroom. If the attack took place in a vehicle, finding semen and/or saliva on the seat and archiving it can be a critical piece of evidence. Not all investigators and even forensic scientists will agree. Their position is that DNA analysis is more important because it identifies the person who left the semen. In instances such as finding the attacker's semen on the survivor's bed sheet on her bed, this is certainly true. But in the example where the attack took place in the vehicle of the accused is conceptually different. Here, finding the attacker's semen in the back seat of his car is not necessarily probative evidence that he raped the survivor. However, if the survivor describes the vehicle and tells the jury that the attack took place in the back seat, the photographs of fluorescing semen on the seat in that location is strong support of her

Table 6.7 Guidelines for Nonhomicide Sexual Assault Scenes

Sexual Assault	Reason for Photograph
Normal scene photography including entrance and egress points. Complete interior and exterior establishing shots such as those used in homicide investigations.	• Establishing photography is a standard operating procedure for all scene photography, regardless of scene type. • Entrance and egress points are important to document because possibly their location can support or refute the allegation.
ALS photography of the scene	This is important so that the location of biological evidence and fiber evidence can be visualized. The location of this evidence is important in verifying and supporting the victim's statements.

Source: Adapted from L. S. Miller. 2006. *Police Photography*, 5th edn. Cincinnati, OH: Anderson Publishing, pp. 135–168.

allegation. Her testimony, the on-scene photographs of the fluorescing semen, and the laboratory determination that the semen is the defendant's should be enough to convict the defendant. If the semen stain is mixed with the survivor's vaginal secretions (vaginal epithelial cell DNA), this, too, supports her allegation that the attack took place in the back seat of the defendant's car, and it should seal the conviction.

A common strategy in the DNA era is that the sex was consensual. However, testimony from the SANE nurse concerning a survivor's injuries should circumvent suggestions to that effect. Table 6.7 gives guidelines for archiving nonhomicide sexual assault scenes.

6.7.4 Suicides

The medical examiner/coroner is responsible for reporting the manner of death to the local health authorities and must classify the death into one of five categories: homicide, suicide, accident, medical intervention, and undetermined. For law enforcement, the medical examiner's report is important because the determination that a suspicious death is a suicide closes the case for the police. Such a determination cannot legally be made by the police or the crime scene investigators, although each plays a part in the investigation.

Certainly, though, the crime scene unit, specifically the team leader, should never approach a death investigation with the preconceived notion that it was a suicide, accident, or homicide. The team leader might short circuit the investigation in a suicidal death, but only after the investigation has run its proper course. This means treating all deaths as though they were homicides. This is the only way in which suspicious deaths investigations will receive a proper and comprehensive investigation, which includes archiving.

For gunshot suicides, photographing the body is incredibly important, as it is for all death investigations. Here, photography of the entrance and exit wounds—if visible to the photographer—shows them in relation to the position of the body and the final location of the weapon. Many suicide gunshots occur at close range, which means that the presence of GSR, stippling, and fouling should be captured using establishing, midrange, and close-up photographs, ideally *in situ*, so that their relationship to the position of the body is preserved. A gunshot wound to the chest may suggest a homicide, but suicide—at least in the early stages of the investigation—should not be ruled out. In these instances, the clothing of the deceased will likely be bloody, but the investigator needs to know whether GSR is under the blood. IR photography could help. The IR light goes through the blood to the underlying garment (or skin). The GSR particles absorb IR light, which means they are darker than the blood. If the garment does not absorb IR light, it will be possible for the camera to "see" the GSR, which can be photographed.

Figure 6.18 shows an IR photograph of GSR on a black T-shirt. The GSR particles are seen as black dots on a light surface. Under blood, the GSR is seen as dark spots on a lighter surface even though blood absorbs the IR light in the region of the electromagnetic spectrum. The black T-shirt does not absorb the IR light, so whatever absorbs the IR light under the blood is also visible. The LCD viewer on the digital IR camera allows the photographer to determine this at the scene.

Suicides are difficult. They can be bloody, as much as the most violent homicide: Knife, bullet wounds and hanging are common. For these, the team leader and the photographer should never assume the manner of death is a suicide, even if it is abundantly apparent and the scene screams "suicide." These cases have aspects that should not be ignored and must be archived: ligature marks on all sides of the neck, knots associated with a noose, injuries on hands, location of bruising, and so on.

In the absence of a suicide note, suicide cases are even more difficult to investigate. Even so, its presence, per se, should not automatically suggest a self-inflicted death. When the note is present, archiving its location and the writing on it is important. The deceased's body should also be treated like any other death investigation (see the discussion on homicide cases in Section 6.7.2). The point is a suicide can appear like a homicide and neither the amount of blood nor its location should suggest one manner of death or the other until the investigation is completed and all evidence and metadata are available. If the medical examiner rules the death a suicide, proper archiving will be critical because the family will need to be convinced, and there may be insurance and other legal issues to deal with in the future. The guidelines in Table 6.6 for photographing homicide scenes apply equally to suicide scenes.

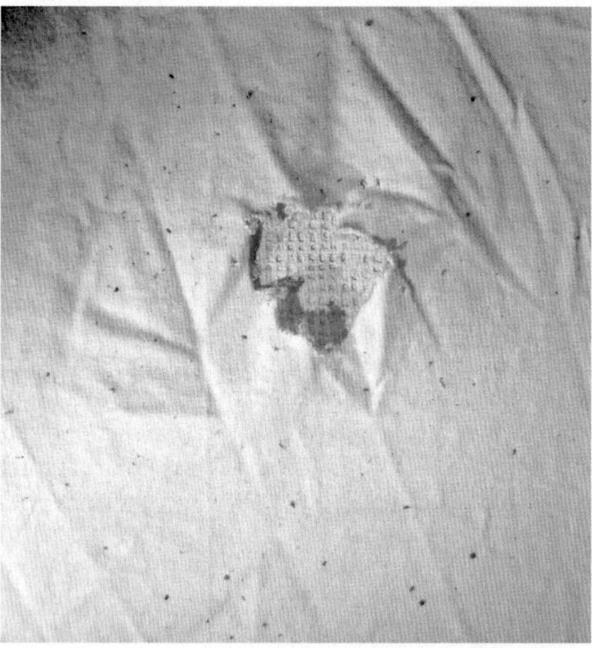

Figure 6.18 Infrared Photograph of gunshot residue (GSR) under blood on black T-shirt. (Photograph by Ralph R. Ristenbatt III. With permission.)

6.7.5 Hit-and-Run Cases

Like most vehicular accidents, hit-and-run cases typically occur outside, and should be treated photographically in the same way (see Table 6.5). Unlike vehicular accidents, hit-and-run cases run the gamut from vehicular homicide, involuntary manslaughter, to leaving the scene of an accident at the scene. The basic difference between a hit-and-run case and a vehicular accident case is that the latter often involves two vehicles while the former involves a vehicle that is missing after having fled the scene. The successful solution to the case is proving that a specific vehicle had been at the scene, which means archiving and collecting evidence at the scene, on the victim (if the victim is a person), and/or on another stuck vehicle.

One aspect of this proof is photographic. Table 6.5 for vehicular accidents is also appropriate for these cases. Documenting the driver's and victim's sightline, point of impact, debris field, and biological evidence photographically is critical. Microscene evidence can be the critical parameter that leads to a conviction. Such evidence can include blood and tissue, paint and paint chips, fabric impressions, glass, and plastic. Documenting the location and photographically recording this evidence is critical, as is other possible forensic characteristics of the scene—tire tracks, shoeprints, roadway surface, and so on. If the hit-and-run case involves a pedestrian who dies at the scene, the guidelines in Table 6.6 apply.

6.7.6 Fatal Accidents: Body inside the Vehicle

Like hit-and-run cases, accidents in which fatalities occur are similar to vehicular accidents discussed above, and the guidelines in Tables 6.5 and 6.6 are appropriate for these scenes. To be successful, scene scientists/investigators and forensic photographers should never take a case at face value, that is, assume a case is what it appears to be. Fatal accidents are no exceptions. The identification of the driver of the vehicle may be in question. The position of the body may be staged. The photographic record, subsequent DNA analysis, detective work, and criminalistics will tie the case together. The science applied should spell out the particulars of the case.

From the forensic photographer's perspective, then, blood and other bodily fluids should be captured photographically. As in sexual assault cases, using ALS may be helpful in locating and then photographing saliva and bloodstains. The interior of the vehicle in these cases can be a particularly important source of probative evidence because this is where the participants of the crime (if it was a crime) were located.

Sometimes pinpointing who was driving can be critical because discrepancies occur from witness descriptions and/or descriptions by the person(s) who survived the accident. Those who participated in the scene or even witnesses may lie to investigators. Finding DNA evidence (blood, saliva, etc.) can help, but capturing the location where the DNA was collected photographically may be critical as is the location of blood spatter patterns, which an expert may need to interpret at a future time. Released airbags may also have surface biological evidence—saliva and/or blood—and their location can also help pinpoint who was sitting where.

6.7.7 Burglary: Breaking and Entering

The role of the forensic photographer in these cases is to provide visual evidence that a particular individual was the person who committed the crime. Thus, establishing followed by midrange and close-up photographs are critical. Certainly, the characteristics of the case will dictate the photographic process.

For example, burglars often leave behind personal items, such as tools, latex gloves, ski masks, cigarette butts, semen, saliva, feces, and urine. These can be critical elements needed to identify who committed the crime because they might have DNA present. Fingerprints from the latex gloves are important because they may have the wearer's DNA. The DNA in these cases is critical because, in addition to identifying the specific individual in the extant crime, it can link an individual to other burglaries or even more violent crimes, such as sexual assaults and homicides.

Impression evidence, such as tool marks and shoeprints, is another important class of evidence that might be present. This evidence can be compared to a tool or a shoe found in the possession of a suspect. Proper archiving of these impressions photographically is a skill the forensic photographer must master. Not only are the establishing and midrange photographs important to show their location at the scene, but also the criminalist in the crime laboratory needs close-up photographs with scales to make proper comparisons.

6.7.8 Fire Scenes: Arson

Fire photography and videography are critically important. Ideally, the forensic photographer will be at the scene as soon as possible after its discovery. These scenes are difficult, tedious, dangerous, and complex. There may be dead bodies as an accidental consequence or the direct result of a murder. The forensic photographer's role begins while the fire is burning and continues long after it is out, as the fire marshal sifts through the fire debris to uncover the fire burn patterns.

Many consider fire investigations a combination of art and science, an opinion not shared in this text. Fire scenes must be considered and treated like any crime scene, and all crime scene investigations are scientific endeavors. When art becomes a part of the process, it is a mistake. Perhaps a better word for "art" in this context is the term "experience." The National Fire Protection Association (NFPA) considers fire investigations a crime scene that, if properly done, requires the use of the scientific method [17]. Regardless of the terminology employed, the goal of a fire investigation is to first establish the origin(s) and then the cause (p. 313, [12]). The proper investigation of the origin and cause of the fire ideally begins while the fire is burning. Tables 6.8A and B show examples of what should be captured photographically with the understanding that a fire scene is actually a crime in progress, and that capturing the fire photographically while it burns and until it is out is archiving a living historical account of that crime. Other photographic considerations are discussed in Chapter 22.

6.8 Special Photographic Situations

The earlier sections discussed the basic functions of the camera—exposure, DOF, and so on—as they relate to forensic photography. The forensic archivist regularly encounters challenging circumstances, some of which can be anticipated, others not so easily. Those that can be predicted, however, are important enough to require some discussion.

Table 6.8A Guidelines for Photographing Fire Scenes while Burning

The Burning Fire Scene	Reason for Photograph
Establishing exterior shots of the fire—external meter necessary for digital photography, RAW files critical	External meter captures correct incident light. Use RAW files to obtain the proper white balance (is impossible with JPEG files).
Photograph all sides of the burning building while burning	• Fires flow upward and outward from a source in a three-dimensional pattern. Establishing shots capture this movement. • Establishing shots may capture fire flow changing direction if a new fuel source is encountered or if fire reaches an obstruction. • May capture flashover—fire is not suppressed in a confined space, reaches 1100°F, and ignitable items burn. Items below hot gas layer and not in direct contact with flame ignite. Help propagate the fire. • Document color of flames—indicate type of material burning. • Individuals in the crowd or standing alone watching the fire.

Source: Adapted from L. S. Miller. 2006. *Police Photography*, 5th edn. Cincinnati, OH: Anderson Publishing, pp. 135–168.

6.8.1 Night and Low-Light Scenes

Exposure is critical, and if incorrect, the photograph may be too dark or too light and can lose or minimize its forensic utility. Indoors and outdoors, exposure can be problematic for many reasons. At night or in dark situations, exposure poses more of a problem because the light the camera needs to record an image is either minimal or not available. If the ISO and aperture/shutter combinations do not compensate for the diminished light, an artificial source or an extended exposure time is necessary.

Table 6.8B Guidelines for Photographing Fire Scenes after Suppression Efforts

After the Fire Is Out	Reason for Photograph
Establishing exterior shots	• Identify fire-flow patterns to correlate with those taken while the fire was burning. Elevated views help locate roof involvement. • Difficult as many tracks and damage related to fire fighting efforts may obliterate traces of the perpetrator(s). Identify entrance/egress points of possible arsonists. Discarded items used to start the fire, tire tracks of nonofficial vehicles, and so on.
Establishing interior shots of the fire. External meter is necessary.	Purpose is same for any scene where the fire and fire suppression activities are archived. Indicates possible location of fire patterns and preserves damage and position of bodies or missing items.
Midrange interior shots	• Document char, smoke, and soot patterns to understand development of the fire flow. Damage patterns on furniture: charring, soot, melting, and the location of vertical and low-burn patterns. • Document immediate surroundings of evidence of a criminal nature, such as bodies and accelerant patterns pointed out by the fire marshal.
Close-up interior shots	Document fire patterns or signs indicating natural, accidental, or deliberately set fire.

Source: Adapted from L. S. Miller. 2006. *Police Photography*, 5th edn. Cincinnati, OH: Anderson Publishing, pp. 135–168.

With respect to artificial light sources, this means using a form of flash: pop-up flash that comes with the camera, an external flash attached to the "hot shoe" on the camera, slaves, floodlights, or other special techniques, such as painting with light or light fill.

The flash unit on top of the camera should *never* be used to photograph evidence directly except in extraordinary situations. The reason is simple—washout. The direct flash of the camera's on-board flash can be too bright and can washout details of the evidence or obliterate it entirely. For most digital photography—not film photography—at crime scenes, flash should be a secondary consideration, not the first choice of light source, unless the scene is so dark that extra light is necessary. That is not to imply that flash photography has no forensic value. It does in specific situations.

Flash has value when the evidence and the background on which it lies are essentially the same color, that is, when there is too little contrast. Impression evidence is an example (see the explanation in Section 6.8.2).

6.8.1.1 *Painting with Light*

Painting with light is a technique for illuminating large outdoor scenes. The photographer sets the camera on a tripod to stabilize it, opens the shutter to "bulb (B)," and keeps it open while moving a flash unit around the area photographed. A long synchronization cord is necessary that allows the attached flash to illuminate up to 150 ft. Generally, the following sequence will suffice [18]:

- Mount the camera on a tripod; up to 500 ft. can be captured.
- Set the camera shutter to "B" (bulb setting) and the *f*/stop to a midsetting, such as *f*/8 to *f*/16.
- Remove extraneous light from the scene.
- Trip the camera shutter to open the shutter.
- Fire flash at farthest point from the camera and repeat at various locations, changing flash angle and moving back toward the camera.
- Retrip the shutter to finish the photography.

6.8.1.2 *Slaves*

Slaves are noncamera-attached flash units that trigger when another flash goes off. Using slaves is similar to painting with light except that the photographer places individual flash units in strategically located positions at the crime scene. When the on-board flash of the camera goes off, the light triggers the slaves to flash simultaneously. In small areas at indoor scenes and small outdoor scenes, this technique may be preferable to the painting-with-light technique.

An example of using slaves to illuminate a completely dark patio is shown in Figure 6.19. Here, four slaves were positioned appropriately and triggered by the on-camera flash.

6.8.2 Impression Evidence Photography

Impression evidence photography is all about creating contrast between the surface on which the impression lies and the texture of the impression. Although impression evidence is discussed in detail in Chapters 11 and 12, a discussion of archiving impression evidence is appropriate here. Generally, this requires the same technique as that used to locate

Figure 6.19 Photography of impression evidence. (Photograph by Ralph Ristenbatt III. With permission.)

the impression evidence at crime scenes—oblique lighting. While shoeprint impression evidence is the focus of this discussion, the principles apply to all impression evidence: the positioning of the light dictates how well the texture of the evidence will appear in the photograph. And that in turn determines how well the forensic scientist can match the scene imprint to a standard taken from a suspect.

The concept of establishing and midrange photography relative to the location of impression evidence in the scene is still relevant but will not be covered in this discussion. However, close-up photography is critical, and impression evidence photography offers its own set of challenges. As with all close-up forensic photography, photographs should be taken with and without scales and they should capture the length and width of the entire impression.

Capturing the impression's detail is an experimental procedure, which means that there will be a trial-and-error period to determine the appropriate angle at which to hold the light source. The rule of thumb is that an attachable flash should be held at an angle of 10°. It may well be that the specific situation requires a different angle to obtain acceptable results. Before ALSs were readily available, flash was the recommended light source for impression evidence photography. Now, however, the different wavelength settings of the ALS, including white light, give equally good, if not better results. Also, the different wavelengths can be used to help enhance the texture and can give better results than white light.

Bodziak [13] recommends a minimum of four photographs of each impression: three photographs with scales with the flash held at the experimentally determined optimum angles of 90°, 180°, and 270° around the impression ensure that shadows from the tripod's legs do not interfere; a fourth photograph is taken without scales. Figure 6.20 illustrates the positioning of the tripod and the light source. The small tripod diagram on the left of Figure 6.20 illustrates the vertical positioning of the light source—approximately 45°. The circle diagram to the right illustrates the positioning (broken arrows) of the light source in

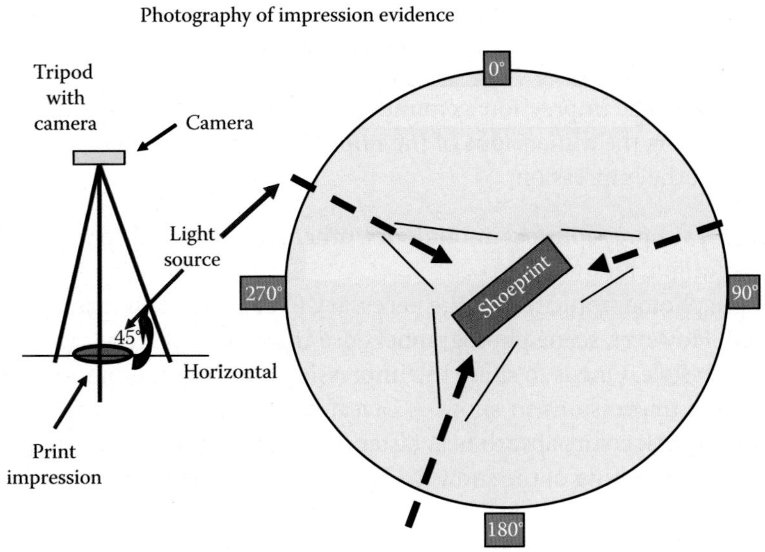

Figure 6.20 Dark patio illuminated with slaves. (Adapted from Bodziak, W. J. 2000. *Footwear Impression Evidence. Detection, Recovery and Examination,* 2nd edn. Boca Raton, FL: CRC Press.)

100° increments around the impression. In order to capture the entire impression, it might be necessary to move the light source around the circle.

The idea is to capture the texture photographically, and capturing it properly might require photographs from other angles. Flash is recommended, but, as flash can create shadows, the scale should always be placed along the long and short edges of the impression.

Outdoor impression evidence photography can be difficult because sunlight can create shadows that obliterate details. Hilderbrand [19] recommends putting something in the path of the sunlight to create a shadow over the entire impression and then use flash to capture the detail. If the impression is deep in, say, mud, the light source may have to be held higher. The photographer will need to experiment to find the correct angle for the light source. Digital cameras give the photographer the option of seeing the results of the photograph immediately, so that experimenting with different light source angles and locations make determining the best conditions relatively easy and quick. If there is significant glare, a UV filter or polarizing lens covers may be necessary.

For two-dimensional (2D) impressions, the flash or ALS should be held as close to the surface as possible so that the light can reflect off of whatever topography is present. The principle is the same as for deeper impressions, the difference between 2D and 3D impressions being only the depth of the impression.

For shallow impressions—dust prints, fingerprints, and tool marks—the same number of photographs are necessary as for 3D impressions. In both situations, an externally attached flash held at various angles can capture the appropriate detail. For example, the photograph of dust prints shown in Figure 6.13 in Section 6.5.4 illustrates the point. The worst exposure of the group of four photographs was taken using overhead, ambient lighting [17]. The best forensic photograph, the one with the most details for comparison, came from using a light source held at 10° from the vertical.

For 3D impressions, photography is particularly important as a backup to casting, and the following aspects of the impression must be captured:

- An overview of the impression as found
- Scales capturing the dimensions of the impressions on two sides
- The detail of the impression

Since most 3D impressions occur outdoors, other concerns also come into play, such as temperature, sunlight, and weather.

Much of the photographic technique necessary to capture 3D impressions has already been discussed. However, scene photographers use tricks to capture as much detail photographically as possible. One is to spray the impression with gray automotive primer paint, especially true for impressions in snow. A caveat concerns the dark color of the sprayed impression. Since dark colors absorb heat faster than lighter colors, sprayed impressions in sunlight may hasten melting of the snow in the impression. The team must work as quickly as possible.

6.8.3 Close-Up Photography

The principles discussed above apply equally to evidence items photographed close-up. The forensic relevance of close-up photographs is twofold: (1) establish the measurements of the item and (2) preserve the critical detail of the evidence as examined. Several commonly occurring types of evidence require close-up photographs. These include weapons (knives, guns, etc.) at the scene or received in the laboratory, fingerprints (developed latent prints and patent prints), other impression evidence (footwear impressions, cartridge cases, etc.), and blood. Some of the guiding principles discussed above, such as DOF, may not necessarily apply in close-up photography, which makes close-up photography easier than that used at the crime scene. The reason is the variables are fewer, although there are challenges. The following sections discuss those aspects of photography that the close-up photographer must consider.

6.8.3.1 Image in the Viewfinder

The image of the photograph in the viewfinder must take up as much of the viewing area as possible. Figures 6.21 and 6.22 illustrate the point. Figure 6.21 shows an example of a close-up photograph of an Amido black-developed bloody fingerprint on a hammer. This is typical of the close-up photographs taken by students. The problem is that the camera was too far from the print. The fingerprint in Figure 6.22 is a cropped image of Figure 6.21. Although the cropped photograph captures the appropriate image, cropping is not the appropriate way to convert a badly thought-out photographic procedure into an acceptable one. The original photograph should have had the entire image in the viewfinder before taking the photograph. Something like the photograph in Figure 6.22 should fill the camera's LCD.

6.8.3.2 The Close-Up Lens

An appropriate lens is critical. Close-up lenses are called macrolenses that typically have a minimum *f*/number between 1.4 and 3.5. A typical close-up lens is the Nikkor 60 mm *f*/1.4 macrolens. The smaller the *f*/number, the faster the lens. This means the photographer can work under minimal lighting conditions. Also, fast lenses mean that flash photography might not be necessary. Although zoom lenses are not recommended for close-up photography, especially those considered "kit lenses," an acceptable example of

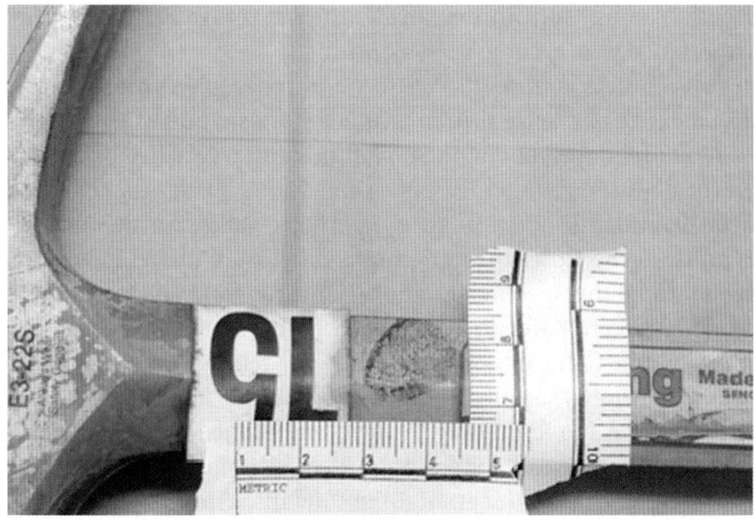

Figure 6.21 Close-up photograph of Amido black-enhanced bloody fingerprint on hammer. (Photograph by Robert C. Shaler.)

an appropriate zoom lens is the Sigma 24–70 *f*/2.8 macrozoom. If a dedicated macrolens is not available, a way to use zoom lenses for close-up work is to focus on the item at the usual 55 mm setting and then zoom into the image until it fills the viewfinder. A tripod is essential to eliminate camera shake. See Section 6.5.

6.8.3.3 *Illumination*

Illumination for close-up photography of objects must be even and must not produce glare or shadows. This means using light sources in creative ways. At the scene, available lighting and/or alternate lighting often proves the most important deterrent to obtaining the perfect forensic photograph. Capturing the evidence *in situ* is the photographer's greatest challenge because the item cannot be moved to a more convenient location until

Figure 6.22 Viewfinder-filled image of Figure 6.21.

the on-scene work is completed. This means taking advantage of whatever the scene offers while using experience to overcome the obstacles.

Although flash is discouraged for on-scene photography except in special circumstances, it can be extremely helpful in creating a glare/shadow-free environment. Using attached but not mounted (i.e., not on the top of the camera) flash held at various distances or angles from the object, or bouncing light from various objects (paper, ceiling, etc.) onto the object can be helpful. The key words are experience and experimentation. There are no set guidelines for on-scene close-up photography other than knowing how to use the camera and understanding the specific situation (lighting/glare/shadows) under which the photograph must be taken. After that, it is the photographer's experience and ability to create great photographs that captures the forensicaly relevant photographs.

In-laboratory lighting is usually not an issue because laboratories have copy stands with lights and other ways to illuminate the evidence evenly. Again, flash is generally discouraged because of the potential for washout. However, flash or other means of creating external lighting can be helpful. It can highlight details, especially in capturing detail on evidence in shadows.

6.8.3.4 Depth of Field

DOF is usually shallow, which means a wide open aperture setting to the minimum *f*/number permitted by the lens. A curved surface requires careful consideration of the DOF.

6.8.3.5 Focus

The most important reason for taking close-up photographs is to capture the minute details of the evidence for comparison. This means that close-up focus in the photographs must be "tack sharp." From a digital photography perspective, "tack-sharp" means the photograph in the viewfinder must be in focus to the maximum level the camera can zoom in on the image in the viewfinder.

Capturing focal detail to this extent means anchoring the camera to eliminate camera shake. Anyone who has attempted to hold a camera steady while taking close-up photographs understands how difficult this can be. Certainly fast lenses help. At the scene, anchoring the camera means using a tripod. In the laboratory, this means using a tripod, a copy stand, or other means of steadying the camera.

One way to help focus is to use an electronic shutter-triggering mechanism. Most modern camera manufacturers offer ways to trip the shutter without touching the camera. Another method is to shut off the antishake mechanism. On a tripod, the antishake system is not necessary, and, if it is active, it will shake the camera very slightly causing blur.

6.8.3.6 Scales

Scales and their position are critical and must be included in close-up photographs. As mentioned earlier, close-up photographs are taken with and without scales.

References

1. *Merriam–Webster Online Dictionary*. Archive. Available at: http://www.merriam-webster.com/dictionary/archive (accessed July 15, 2011).

2. *PC Magazine* online. Active archiving. Available at: http://www.pcmag.com/encyclopedia_term/0,2542,t=active+archiving&i=37447,00.asp# (accessed March 20, 2009).
3. Available at: http://www.digital-slr-guide.com/what-is-a-digital-slr.html (accessed April 1, 2009).
4. Available at: http://www.digital-slr-guide.com/crop-factor.html (accessed November 1, 2010).
5. H. L. Blitzer and J. Jacobia. 2002. Chapter 4: Storing and archiving images. In: *Forensic Digital Imaging and Photography*. San Diego, CA: Academic Press, pp. 54–60.
6. S. Kelby. 2006. Chapter 1: Pro tips for getting really sharp photos. In: *The Digital Photography Book*, Vol. 1. Berkeley, CA: Peachpit Press, p. 1.
7. B. Peterson. 2004. *Understanding Exposure*, Revised Edition. New York, NY: Amphoto Books, pp. 32–33.
8. D. R. Redsicker. 2001. *The Practical Methodology of Forensic Photography*, 2nd edn. Boca Raton, FL: CRC Press, p. 266.
9. S. Kelby. 2006. Chapter 8: Taking advantage of digital like a pro. In: *The Digital Photography Book*, Vol. 1. Berkeley, CA: Peachpit Press, pp. 155.
10. S. Weiss. 2009. Macrophotography. *Evidence Technology Magazine*, 7(6):14–17.
11. *The Nikon Guide to Digital Photography with the D40 Digital Camera*, pp. 45, 49. Available at: http://nikonusa.com/pdf/manuals/noprint/D40_noprint.pdf.
12. R. M. Gardner. 2005. *Practical Crime Scene Processing and Investigation*. Boca Raton, FL: CRC Press, pp. 140, 161, 313.
13. W. J. Bodziak. 2000. *Footwear Impression Evidence. Detection, Recovery and Examination*, 2nd edn. Boca Raton, FL: CRC Press, pp. 47–48.
14. Wratten filters. Available at: http://en.wikipedia.org/wiki/Wratten_number (accessed April 22, 2009).
15. XNite filters. Available at: http://maxmax.com/aXNiteFilters.htm (accessed April 22, 2009).
16. L. S. Miller. 2006. *Police Photography*, 5th edn. Cincinnati, OH: Anderson Publishing, pp. 135–168.
17. National Fire Protection Association. 2008. Chapter 4: Basic methodology. In: *NFPA 921 Guide for Fire and Explosion Investigations*. Quincy, MA: NFPA, pp. 921–16.
18. H. C. Lee, T. Palmbach, and M. T. Miller. 2001. *Henry Lee's Handbook of Crime Scene Investigation*. San Diego, CA: Academic Press, pp. 94–96.
19. D. S. Hilderbrand. 1999. Chapter VIII: Recovery through photography. In: *Footwear, The Missed Evidence—A Field Guide to the Collection and Preservation of Forensic Footwear Impression Evidence*. Wildomar, CA: Staggs Publishing, pp. 46–47.

Workshop 1: Photography—Camera Basics

W1.1 Introduction

The key to successful forensic photography is intimate familiarity with the modern digital SLR camera. Digital photography has become the *de facto* standard for archiving the scene. The reasons are obvious: color film and developing are no longer readily available and digital photography gives archivists the opportunity to "experiment" in order to obtain the perfect exposure and forensic perspective. Before beginning this workshop, readers should review Chapter 6. SLR cameras are necessary for quality forensic photography. The reason is that interchanging lenses is the key to capturing the perfect perspective offered by the scene. The following assumes that the student is using a Nikon D40 or better camera. Other cameras are certainly appropriate and, although the location of specific functions on the camera can differ, all modern cameras have at least those functions considered for this introduction to the camera.

W1.2 Required Tools

- Camera: Digital (12 megapixel minimum)
- Lenses:
    - Wide angle (*f*/2.8 24–70) or other
    - Telephoto (*f*/2.8 80–200) or other
    - Close-up (*f*/2.8 60 mm) or other
- Detachable flash
- Tripod with ball head
- Memory card of 8–32 gigabytes

W1.3 Camera Basics

The following are the essential functions for successful forensic photography. These are the basics, but cameras can have many sophisticated functions that can increase the quality of the photographs.

W1.3.1 File Formats

Most SLR cameras offer choices for storing photographs. Some cameras give choices: JPEG, RAW (NEF for Nikons), and TIFF (tif). For most forensic photography, the RAW + JPEG setting is the best. This gives the photographer the ability to quickly review the photograph as a JPEG and to save it as a RAW, noncompressed file. The importance of saving the photograph in a file that is not compressed (RAW) is that compression (JPEG files) leads to automatic loss of information. The disadvantage is that the camera chooses what information to exclude from the file. In the RAW mode, no information is lost.

W1.3.2 Camera Function Dials and Menu Options

- Menu: Most digital cameras have menus that can access the same functions as the dials or buttons on the camera. The menus allow access to these same functions as well as to others (e.g., file formats) that are not included as dials or buttons on the camera body.
- On–off switch (self-explanatory).
- A: In the aperture (*f*/number) priority mode, the photographer sets the aperture (*f*/number) and the camera sets the shutter speed. The smaller the *f*/number, the larger the opening.
- S: In the shutter priority mode, the photographer sets the shutter speed (how long the aperture stays open) and the camera sets the aperture.
- M: In the manual mode, the photographer sets both the aperture and the shutter speed.
- P: In the program mode, the camera chooses what it believes is the correct exposure for the current lighting conditions. This is sometimes a good place to start, and the photographer can individually adjust the aperture and shutter speed.
- Auto: In this point-and-shoot mode, the camera decides on the exposure by setting the aperture, shutter speed, and the ISO setting. It is not recommended to use

"auto" for forensic purposes. In this setting, some cameras do not allow the photographer to adjust other camera settings.
- ISO: This digital sensor sensitivity setting can be used to take photographs in dim light. The higher the ISO, the more sensitive the digital sensor. In "auto," the ISO is set by the camera and cannot be adjusted by the photographer.
- WB: Digital cameras must be told how to interpret white balance. The camera does this by offering a menu of choices that reflect common photographic shooting situations. These menus can be simple or complex. Generally, they include settings for
  - Auto
  - Custom
  - Flash
  - Shade
  - Cloudy
  - Direct sunlight
  - Incandescent lighting
  - Fluorescent lighting
- Format: This setting, accessed through the menu, allows the photographer to format (erase) the memory card. It is important that all photographs are downloaded to a hard drive immediately after photography is completed. After downloading, the memory card can be formatted or ideally stored.
- Metering: This setting allows the photographer to choose how the camera is to meter light. Choices can include among others matrix, spot, and averaging. These choices are usually accessed by using the menu, but, on some cameras, they are available as a dial or button on the camera body.

W1.4 Exercise 1

For the following exercises, use a lens set between 50 and 60 mm. This is the setting that most approximates the human eye.

W1.4.1 Aperture Priority

This is the most important setting for the forensic photographer because it is how the photographer selects the perspective of the resulting photograph. The aperture is also considered the DOF selector, that is, "what is in focus." The larger the *f*/number, the smaller the opening and the greater the DOF.

In this exercise, the relative importance of the aperture will be demonstrated by taking photographs at different aperture (*f*/number) settings.

W1.4.1.1 Procedure

- Select a location that allows your field of view to have several objects close up and others in the distance. This is easily done outdoors. If indoors, choose a hallway that is well lit. Choose the WB from the menu or the dial so that it reflects the type of light available (incandescent light bulbs or fluorescent lighting).
- In Table W1.1, list the items/objects in your field of view, beginning with the closest and ending with the item furthest away.
- Stand approximately 5–8 ft. from the first object (entry "1." in Table W1.1).

Table W1.1 Objects in Field of View

Object in Field of View	Approximate Distance from Photographer
1.	
2.	
3.	
4.	
5.	

- Set the camera on "auto" and take a picture. Record the aperture and shutter speed chosen by the camera.
- Set the camera on "A," aperture priority, at the lowest *f*/number the camera will allow; this is determined by the lens; for example, if the lens is rated at *f*/2.8, the lowest *f*/number the camera will allow is an "A" setting of 2.8; if the lens is rated at *f*/4.0, the lowest *f*/number available will be 4.
- Take photographs at the *f*/numbers listed in Table W1.2. If the camera does not allow the *f*/2.8 setting, there is nothing to fill in.
- Circle the aperture/shutter speed combination that gave the greatest DOF.
- Circle the aperture/shutter speed combination that gave the shallowest DOF.
- Compare the two photographs with the one taken with the camera set on "auto."

W1.4.1.2 Questions

- In 500 words or less, explain the differences between the photograph taken on "auto" with those taken at maximum and shallowest DOF.
- Using the results from Exercise 1, in 500 words or less, discuss the concept of DOF. To illustrate your points, include examples (photographs) that were obtained. Use Chapter 6 as a guide.
- In 500 words or less, discuss aperture priority with respect to how *f*/numbers affect exposure. Use examples from Exercise 1.
- In the list of aperture settings in Table W1.2, which of the following would be examples of one full stop?
    - A: *f*/8.0 to *f*/11.0
    - B: *f*/22 to *f*/16
    - C: *f*/2.8 to *f*/8.0
    - D: None of the above

Table W1.2 Aperture Priority Exercise

Aperture Setting	Shutter Speed (Set by Camera)	List the Objects in Table W1.1 That Are in Focus	Describe Quality of Photograph (Over/Under Exposed, etc.)
2.8			
4.0			
5.6			
8.0			
11.0			
16.0			
22.0			

W1.4.2 Shutter Speed

W1.4.2.1 Procedure

- Set the camera on "S."
- Take a series of photographs of the objects in Table W1.1 using the shutter peeds listed in Table W1.3.
- Fill in the information in Table W1.3.

W1.4.2.2 Questions

- In 500 words or less, describe the effect shutter speed has on DOF, if any. Use examples from your data to illustrate the discussion.
- From Table W1.3, which of the following is known as moving a full stop?
  - A: Shutter speed of 100th to 400th
  - B: Shutter speed of 40th to 80th
  - C: Shutter speed of 60th to 100th
  - D: None of the above
- If you chose "None of the above" as your answer, explain why.
- If you chose one of the top 3 (A, B, C) as your answer, explain why.

W1.4.3 Manual Priority

W1.4.3.1 Procedure

- Set the WB and ISO on "auto."
- Set the camera on "A" and choose the *f*/stop (*f*/number) that gave the greatest DOF as listed in Table W1.2.
- Set the camera on "M" and set the shutter speed corresponding to the aperture that you selected above (i.e., the shutter speed that gave the greatest DOF as listed in Table W1.2).
- Keeping the aperture constant, take a series of photographs using shutter speeds that increase by one-third of a stop toward faster shutter speeds than the one selected from Table W1.1.
- Keeping the aperture constant, take a second series of photographs using shutter speeds one-third of a stop slower than the one selected from Table W1.3.
- Fill in Table W1.4.
- Choose the best photograph.

Table W1.3 Shutter Speed Priority Exercise

Shutter Speed (s)	Aperture (Set by Camera)	List the Objects in Table W1.1 That Are in Focus	Describe Quality of Photograph (Over/Underexposed, etc.)
10th			
20th			
40th			
100th			
200th			
400th			
800th			

Table W1.4 Manual Priority Exercise

Manual Priority Shutter Speed (s)	Aperture (Set by Photographer—Should Be the Same for Each Entry)	Describe Quality of Photograph (Over/Underexposed, etc.)	Place an "X" beside the Best Photograph
Shutter speed from Table W1.1	Aperture selected from Table W1.1		

W1.4.3.2 Questions

- Does the best photograph have the same shutter speed as the one you selected from Table W1.1 (Yes or No)?
- In 500 words or less, explain why?
- In 500 words or less, explain why the manual "M" setting on the camera gives more or less control of the photographic outcome than when choosing "A," "S," or "auto."

W1.5 Dark Environment Photography

W1.5.1 ISO

ISO refers to the sensitivity of the digital sensor, which means that in darkened environments, increasing the sensitivity makes it possible to obtain photographs in dark places.

W1.5.1.1 Procedure

- Darken a room sufficiently so that there is very little light entering. The room should not be so dark that you can't see anything.
- Set the camera to aperture priority and select *f*/5.6.
- Set the ISO to "auto."
- Put the camera on a tripod and take a photograph. Describe the photograph in Table W1.5.
- Using Table W1.5 as a guide, take photographs at the ISO settings listed.
- Fill in Table W1.5 after each photograph.

If all of the photographs appear too dark, reset the aperture to *f*/4.0 and retake the photographs. If the photographs are too light, reset the aperture to *f*/11 and retake the photographs. Describe the photographs in Table W1.6.

Table W1.5 ISO Exercise

ISO	Aperture (Set by Photographer)	Shutter Speed (Set by Camera)	Describe Quality of Photograph (Over/Underexposed, etc.)	Place an "X" beside the Best Photograph
"AUTO"	*f*/7.3			
100	*f*/7.3			
200	*f*/7.3			
400	*f*/7.3			
800	*f*/7.3			
1600	*f*/7.3			

Table W1.6 Painting with Light and Slaves Exercise

Shutter	Aperture (Set by Photographer)	Describe Quality of Photograph (Off-Camera Flash)	Describe Quality of Photograph (Slaves)
Bulb	Wide open (smallest *f*/stop allowed)		
Bulb	*f*/7.3		
Bulb	*f*/7.3		
Bulb	*f*/7.3		
Bulb	*f*/7.3		
Bulb	*f*/7.3		

W1.5.1.2 Questions

- Circle the photograph that gave the best result for aperture, ISO, and shutter speed. Does the photograph have sufficient DOF? If so, explain why. If not, explain why.
- If the DOF was too shallow, what would you do to deepen it?
- If all the photographs taken (at different ISOs) using an aperture of *f*/4.0 were too dark, what would you do to lighten them (assume *f*/4.0 is as low as the camera would allow)?

W1.5.2 Painting with Light or Using Slaves

At dark scenes where it is necessary to lighten areas with intense shadows, a technique called painting with light is sometimes useful. In this exercise, you will need a second person using an off-camera flash. On a tripod, the shutter is open. A second person takes a flash tethered to the camera (with a long cord) and begins triggering the flash manually to illuminate areas in shadow.

Another approach is to place slaves in strategic places. The flash from the camera will trigger the slaves to fire simultaneously to illuminate the area.

W1.5.2.1 Procedure

- A dark street, alley, or patio can be used for this exercise. Set the camera on a tripod at a strategic location. Attach an off-camera flash unit and set the camera on bulb.
- Open the shutter.
- A second person (or the photographer) can walk to darkened areas and trigger the off-camera flash manually. After all the areas have been illuminated, shut the shutter.
- Repeat the exercise using slaves.
- Fill in Table W1.6.

W1.5.2.2 Questions

- Which technique gave the best results for the area you were photographing?
- In your opinion, which technique is the easiest to use and which gives the best and most consistent illumination in most circumstances?
- In 500 words or less, explain why.

W1.6 Close-Up Photography

In close-up photography, there are three inviolate rules: (1) the image being photographed must take up the entire viewfinder on the back of the camera; (2) scales of appropriate dimensions must be used; and (3) photographs with and without scales must be taken.

Table W1.7 Close-Up Photography Exercise

Photographs	First Shutter Speed	Second Shutter Speed	ISO	Describe Quality of Photograph
Without Scales				
1. First shutter speed				
2. Final shutter speed				
With Scales				
1. First shutter speed				
2. Final shutter speed				

W1.6.1 Procedure

- Place a quarter on the floor.
- Set the camera on aperture priority and set the aperture to the lowest *f*/stop (*f*/number) the camera will allow; for close-up photographs, DOF is not a concern.
- Put the camera on a tripod and position it so that it is directly over the quarter and the quarter fills the viewfinder.
- Take the photograph. Examine the photograph for focus and exposure (lighting).
- If the photograph is too dark, reset the camera to manual priority "M" and set the shutter speed to allow in more light.
- Take the photograph and re-examine the result. Repeat the procedure until you have the perfect exposure. Record the *f*/stop, shutter speed, and ISO in Table W1.7.
- Repeat the exercise using scales vertically and horizontally along two sides of the quarter.

In those instances where an ALS is used to highlight fingerprints dusted with fluorescent powder or super-glued fingerprints stained with fluorescent stains or powder, the procedure of obtaining the close-up photograph is essentially the same. The difference is that a barrier filter is placed over the lens so that the fluorescence reaches the digital sensor without being overwhelmed by reflected light. The photographic principles remain the same; the process for obtaining the perfect photograph does not change.

W1.6.2 Questions

- In 1000 words or less, explain why you made the changes you did to obtain the perfect close-up photograph of the quarter.
- If there are differences in the camera settings between the photographs taken with and without scales, explain what they are and why they occurred.

The Paper Trail
Case Files, Worksheets, Notes, and Sketches

7

7.1 Introduction: General Considerations

Chapter 6 discussed forensic archiving of a scene as a multiplex of processes encompassing more than simply taking photographs. This is true. Archiving is a complex endeavor that often begins with videography followed by photography and sketching. And while the title of this chapter is "The Paper Trail," this is actually a misnomer because the archive can include numerous technologies including 3D imaging. In fact, archiving encompasses the entire work product of the crime scene unit including all media used to record the scene activity. Much of this information is in a paper format, hence the title, but in the not-too-distant future the archive will increasingly be electronic. Regardless of the format, it must be protected and archived in a case file. The following discussion considers those activities that protect the integrity of the investigation, each an integral aspect of the archiving process.

7.2 Case Files

A case file can be defined as

> The location, virtual or otherwise, where the investigative record is maintained.

Sometimes referred to as a case jacket, the case file contains the paperwork (worksheets, notes, photographs, sketches, etc.), and it is the heart and soul of the investigation. It is the official record of the investigation and the location of investigators' reports, sketches, worksheets, written notes, audio and/or photographic CDs, printed photographs, investigative leads, witness statements, and so on. It is where investigators new to a case can review the case history of what was done in the original investigation.

From the definition above, it is clear that the case file can be paper and/or electronic. It can reside in a file cabinet, cardboard boxes in the basement of the police station, or on a backed-up hard drive. Regardless, the files must be secure. If they are originally in paper format, they should be converted to an electronic one that is noncorruptible. Electronic case files must be backed-up and the original files protected from hackers.

Pages in the case file are numbered sequentially. For example, if there are 52 pages, the first page of 52 would be either 1 of 52 or 1/52. New additions to the case file are added sequentially. A page added out of sequence is given a number indicating it was put into the case file at a later time and placed at that location. For example, corrections to page 135 should be inserted after page 135, and labeled as 135A. New pages are added sequentially at the end of the case file.

7.2.1 Worksheets

Worksheets fall into four basic categories: forms, audio, handwritten notes, and sketches. They can be anything relevant to the investigation that a scientist/investigator fills out, prepares, or records. These include investigative notes or thoughts and anything digitally recorded or typed into a computer. They include draft and final sketches. All worksheets must be maintained in the case file.

7.2.1.1 Forms

In many sections of this text, "named" scene activities are discussed. An example is scene searches which, if performed rote and blindly, can compromise the scientific approach. Forms are similar because they are a class of crutches, but they represent critical records. Filling them out is an important activity designed to ensure that nothing significant is either forgotten or lost. Each investigative agency has its own form structure, which is not important, because all forms require similar, if not identical, information. Some agencies have detailed forms and others not so much. Commonly, the forms used include chain of custody, scene response, photographic, and measurement logs, quality assurance forms, and so on. Where these exist, they must be filled out completely, including case numbers, the initials of the person filling out the form, and other specified information.

If the form has multiple pages, each page should be filled out and numbered sequentially in a format that indicates the page number and the total number of pages.

Examples of forms used in the Penn State University crime scene investigation course are shown in Text Boxes 7.1 through 7.9. The scene response log in Text Box 7.1 is a record of individuals who were at the scene. It documents who they were, their contact information, when they arrived, and when they left. If the team responds to the scene more than once, the team leader or designated person fills, out a separate form each day the team is at the scene. The form also captures critical weather information, for example, raining, sunny, temperature, and so on.

Text Box 7.1 Scene Response Log

<table>
<tr><td colspan="2">PSU Case No.</td><td>Date</td><td>Scene Arrival Time</td><td>Scene Departure Time</td></tr>
<tr><td colspan="3" rowspan="2">Scene Address/Location</td><td>Scene (Indoor/ Outdoor)</td><td>Scene Secured (Yes/No)</td></tr>
<tr><td colspan="2">Weather Conditions (if applicable)</td></tr>
<tr><td colspan="5">PERSONNEL AT SCENE</td></tr>
<tr><td>Personnel (Full Name and Rank) Contact Information</td><td>Shield No.</td><td>Agency</td><td>Arrival Time</td><td>Departure Time</td></tr>
<tr><td></td><td></td><td></td><td></td><td></td></tr>
<tr><td></td><td></td><td></td><td></td><td></td></tr>
<tr><td></td><td></td><td></td><td></td><td></td></tr>
<tr><td></td><td></td><td></td><td></td><td></td></tr>
<tr><td></td><td></td><td></td><td></td><td></td></tr>
<tr><td></td><td></td><td></td><td></td><td></td></tr>
</table>

Text Box 7.2 Chain of Custody and Evidence Transfer Logs

Chain of Custody Log			
PSU Case No.	**Victim Name(s):**	**Criminalist(s):**	
Item ID	**Description**		
Evidence Transfer Log—Signatures			
Item ID	**Received From (Include Shield No.)**	**Received By (Include Shield No.)**	**Date**

Text Box 7.2 documents the control of evidence. The chain of custody (sometimes known as the chain of evidence or the chain) form in Text Box 7.2 is an important document because it represents the history of a piece of evidence. It is critical to ensure that the evidence history is never lost. It documents the evidence from the time it is packaged (and where it was found) at the crime scene to its transfer to labs, property rooms, courts, to when it is eventually destroyed. The team leader must ensure that each item of evidence collected has a documented signature history. This signature represents its transit history, which must remain intact until it is eventually destroyed. It does not matter whether it goes to the police property clerk's office and remains there forever or whether it has a transfer history from the scene to the crime laboratory to the court and back to the property clerk's office. This is the history of the movement of the evidence within the criminal justice system; it must remain intact. A break in that history—known as a break in the chain—compromises the integrity of the evidence and leaves it at risk of not being admissible in a court of law.

The chain of custody form has two parts as shown in Text Box 7.2. The top part captures the item number and description of each item collected at the scene for that specific form. The bottom part shows the transfer of evidence (with signatures and/or initials) of those involved in the transfer, ensuring the important signature history of the movement from the time it was collected at the scene to when it is disposed of at some future date.

The forms in Text Boxes 7.3 and 7.4 ought to be used by all scene investigators. They document how impression evidence is treated at the scene. The form in Text Box 7.3 is for fingerprints and that in Text Box 7.4 is for nonfingerprint impression evidence, such as footwear or tire track impressions, tool marks, bite marks, and so on. Each captures

Text Box 7.3 Latent Fingerprint Processing Log

Name: Sgt Harvey Wallbanger		Date: 8/15/11		Time: 10:10 p.m.
Item No.	**Object Printed/Method**	**Location**	**Gathered by**	**Photo by/Method**
65	Door knob/black powder	Entrance to house	Sgt Wallbanger	Millicent Way/ Close-up
		Living room	Sgt Wallbanger	None

Note: All places and objects examined for latent prints should be in the log. Negative attempts will not have an Item Number.

important information: the item number, the object on which the print (impression) was found, the method used to visualize it (unless it was a patent print), the location of the object at the scene, the person who collected the print (impression), the method of how it was collected (tape lifted, gel lifted, etc.), the person who photographed the print, and the method used to photograph it (digital SLR, ALS, etc.). In the example shown in Text Box 7.3, Sgt Harvey Wallbanger successfully dusted a fingerprint on a doorknob, which was photographed by Millicent Way. He unsuccessfully attempted to develop a print on a window in the living room.

Text Box 7.4 documents the collection of other types of impression evidence. In the example in Text Box 7.4, a fictitious Det. Robert Wishburn collected a 2D footwear impression in the living room using an electrostatic lifter. Millicent Way photographed the original impression.

Text Box 7.4 General Impression Evidence Processing Log

	Name: Det. Robert Wishburn		Date: 8/15/11	Time: 11:31 p.m.
Item No.	**Impression Category/Method**	**Location**	**Gathered by**	**Photo by/Type**
104	Two-dimensional footwear impression/electrostatic lift	Floor in living room	Det. Wishburn	Millicent Way/ Close-up

Note: All places and objects examined for latent prints should be in the log. Negative attempts will not have an Item No.

7.2.1.2 *Mistakes*

Filling out forms, whether by hand or digitally, is done by humans, so mistakes occur and are expected. Corrections of mistakes on all forensic documents have a specific format: Run a single line through the mistake and then write the correct information above the mistake. Place initials and the date of the correction next to or above the correction (many texts advocate simply using initials, but this is a mistake). Never obliterate or white-out a mistake. If the date is not included, there is no way of knowing when the mistake was identified and corrected.

Students are generally sloppy when it comes to preparing case files. They fail, at first, to understand the need for such precision, and the tedium of the paperwork slowly grinds them down to the point where they begin making the mistakes. Harsh grading has a way of changing that, but, in the real world, grading is not an option. The team leader's responsibility is to ensure that the details on the forms are not overlooked and that all forms are filled out completely.

7.3 Sketches

Gardner [1] suggests that sketching the crime scene involves two separate actions: one artistic, although most crime scene sketches are hardly artistic, beginning as a rough drawing done at the scene, and the second analytical, which pinpoints the relative location of the elements of the scene. He considers the latter analytical because it requires taking measurements of the boundaries and the elements at the scene, a process similar to mapping. Although no true analysis is involved, for the purposes of this discussion, Gardner's [1] concept of forensic sketching can be adapted and defined as

> A marriage of drawing and making measurements of crime scene elements, the final rendering of which is a perspective that renders the scene understandable to the lay public and provides information to investigators.

Typically, sketching occurs twice. Rough sketches (drafts) are done contemporaneously with the scene investigation and are discoverable as evidence for admission in a legal proceeding. A final sketch, that is, a final rendering, is a cleaned-up version of the rough sketch; it, too, is discoverable. Although sketches are visible products of the investigative process, other work also falls into the category of forensic archiving because, like sketching, it represents the work product of the crime scene team and thus is a part of the permanent investigative record. The complete work product of the scene investigation, including paperwork, becomes a part of the investigation's case file.

So, where does sketching fall into the investigative sequence? As the discussion this text continually points out, there is a logical thought process that should happen before any physical activity. Historically, before there was photography, there was sketching, and it remains an essential skill. Sketches are important because they lay out the scene in a way that neither photographs nor video can. They provide an overview and the precise and/or relative location of evidence. An initial rough sketch is made at the scene which is converted to a final sketch prepared off-site. Both the draft and final sketches are part of the case file. Sketching is among the first activities at the scene, and it occurs contemporaneously with photographing and searching for and protecting the fragile evidence. Where to begin the sketch (e.g., which room to sketch first) is a decision the team leader makes. It is his/her responsibility to make certain that the entire scene including each critical item, such as furniture, blood trails, footprints, tire tracks, blood spatter, bodies, weapons, and so on, is captured without interrupting the investigative process. Delaying the scene investigation to wait for sketchers is certainly not time efficient.

Determining how to sketch important information depends on the investigator's and/or team leader's perceived importance of each item of evidence. This does not imply that items are left out of the sketch. It simply means that there are items that require precise placement and others that do not. As summarized in Figure 7.1, sketches are important for several reasons and have multiple purposes. They provide an overview of the scene and the relative relationship of evidence. They complement photo and video archiving by clarifying confusing details. They enhance investigators' recall of the scene details when time comes to testify in court or to review cold cases. They help to orient the scene layout to scientists/investigators and attorneys, the judge and the jury, and they clarify the relationships of evidence at the scene and relational information seen in videos or photographs.

The nuts and bolts of preparing a scene sketch most effectively involve two people working together. This makes the rough sketching easier and faster: the measure and one draws and records the information. The final sketch made from the rough draft should include the following information.

- Address—place of the sketch
- Date and time
- Temperature/weather conditions—sunny, cloudy, raining, and so on
- Cardinal coordinate (N/S) indicators
- Name of sketcher(s)—individuals who did the sketch
- Case number
- Notation whether sketch is rough or final
- Legend to capture information in the sketch

There are various ways to make a sketch. One of the early methods was to use graph paper for both the final and rough sketches. The detail in the final sketch can use templates

Purpose of the sketch

- Overview of scene and relative relationships of evidence
- Complements photography and videography
- Ties elements of a scene together
- Eliminates extraneous or confusing details seen in photos and videos.
- Depicts appearance of scene
- Not meant to be an architectural drawing

Why are sketches important?

- Memory
  - Helps investigators recall details
- Clarifies relationships of objects at scene?
  - Prosecutors/attorneys/juries

What does it become?

- Permanent record in the case file

Figure 7.1 The purpose and importance of sketches.

Text Box 7.5 Sketch Worksheet

PSU Case No. 1-008	**Date: 8/15/11**	**Criminalist/ Investigator:**
Rough Draft: Y (X) N	**Scale: 1 in.= 1 ft.**	**Emily Born**

available for forensic supplies. Computer programs and 3D imaging systems can speed the final sketch after measurement data are entered: 3D imaging systems take thousands of measurements in 360° using IR lasers to measure the scene. These measurements are turned into 3D drawings using dedicated software. The problem with these systems is that they are slow and can restrict movement in the scene in areas being imaged. CAD programs, some of which have been adapted for crime scene work,[*] can convert rough measurements into final polished sketches. An example of a sketch worksheet is shown in Text Box 7.5. In the example, the sketch is a rough draft made at the scene. The date and the scale are on the worksheet so that these are not forgotten. It is not necessary to have standard worksheets such as this, but having them makes the case file neater and appear more professional.

7.3.1 Indoor Sketch Types

Over the years, investigators have devised various ways to sketch a scene. Many of these have names, termed "named" sketches in this text. The most common ones are discussed in the following sections.

7.3.1.1 Plan Sketch

This is an overview, bird's-eye view, or floor plan of the scene. This is the simplest scene sketch for a jury to understand and is essentially required for all crime scenes. Its simplicity lies in the fact that it gives an accurate overview of the scene and the relative location of evidence observed. The rough plan sketch is made at the scene and is not drawn to scale. The final sketch is prepared at a later time and must be drawn to scale. A partial plan sketch can be made of the individual components of the scene, such as walls with bullet holes or

[*] The crime zone and the crash zone.

Text Box 7.6 Students Plan Sketch of Outdoor Scene. (Used with permission from Lauren Rothwell.)

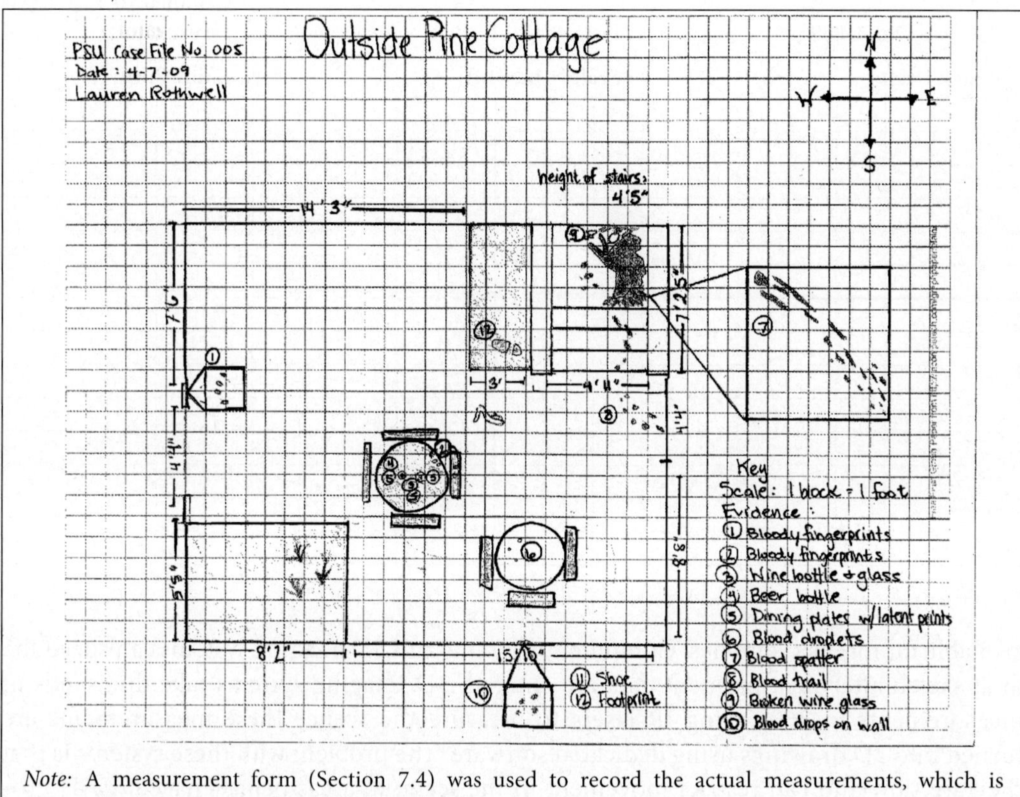

Note: A measurement form (Section 7.4) was used to record the actual measurements, which is why they are not included in the sketch.

bloodstain patterns, because they are not typically considered part of the floor plan. An example of a student's plan sketch for an outdoor scene is shown in Text Box 7.6.

The sketch in this example has interesting details, but it has problems too. First, the detail of the area—landscaping—around the house where the crime took place is out of proportion with respect to the house. The legend explaining the meaning of the various icons is an important addition, but its construction is poor.

Another example of a student's plan sketch is shown in Figure 7.2. The sketch is appropriate in most aspects. The appropriate information is recorded, the scene shows the important items of evidence, and the legend is appropriate for what was observed and recorded. Since this is a final sketch, the lines should not have been drawn freehand.

7.3.1.2 Cross-Projection or Exploded Sketch

A cross-projection sketch is essentially a flattened view of the scene, much like a box with its sides, top, and bottom pressed into a single plane. These sketches are useful for scenes where the walls and ceilings have important probative evidence such as bloodstain patterns, bullet defects, and so on. They are appropriate for rooms but not for an entire building. Figure 7.3 shows a cross-projection sketch. The schematic shows the ceiling, walls, and floor flattened to show where on these surfaces evidence was located.

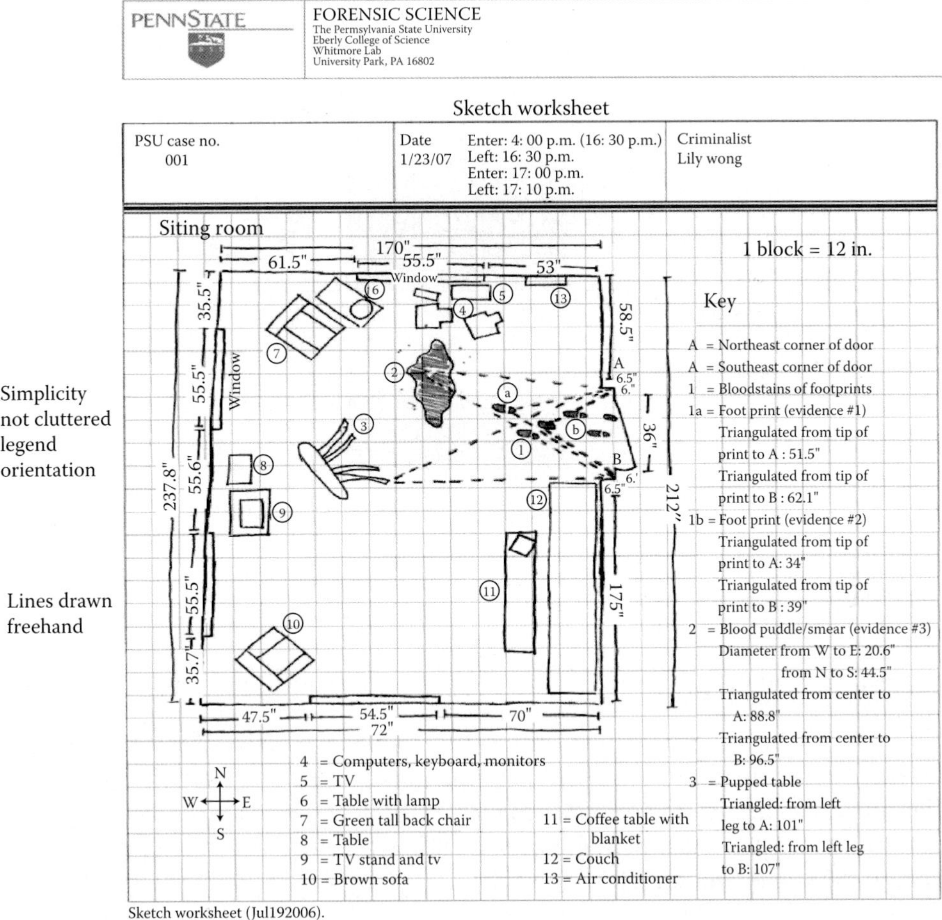

Figure 7.2 Student's indoor plan sketch. Used with permission from Lily Wong.

The sketch in Figure 7.3 is oversimplified as an example of a cross-projection sketch. The measurements taken at the scene are maintained in a separate measurement log and, understandably, are not used in the sketch to keep it simple.

7.3.1.3 *Elevation Sketch*

An elevation sketch documents a side-view of one part of a scene, such as a wall or a ceiling with bloodstain spatter or bullet holes. The measurements should be included in the sketch to indicate the exact location and, in the case of a bloodstain pattern, its size. An elevation sketch might also show the position of bullet defects.

7.3.1.4 *Perspective Sketch: 3D Rendering of a Scene*

A perspective sketch depicts the 3D aspects of the scene. This type of sketch requires either artistic skills if done freehand or specialized 3D software. These sketches are becoming more popular as software programs become more readily available, and are the favorites of students who have access to these programs on college campuses.

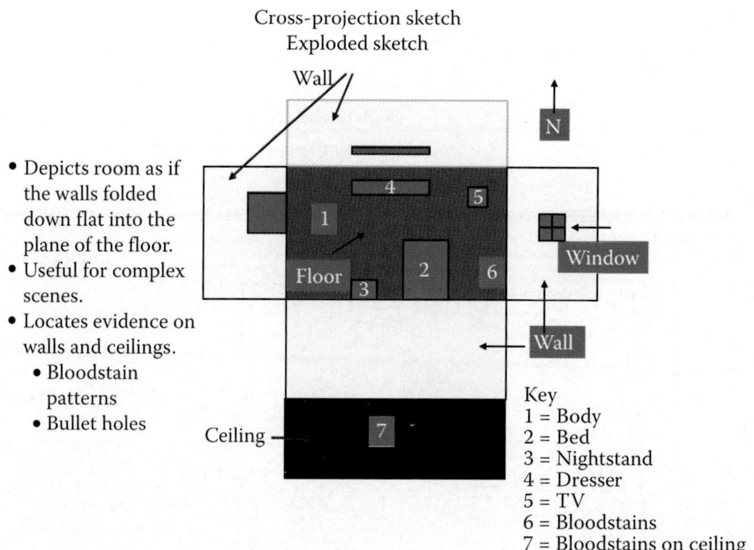

Figure 7.3 Cross-projection sketch.

7.3.2 Outdoor Sketches

Outdoor sketches are essentially plan sketches, typically overviews of the area designated as the crime scene. These can be sketches of fields, parking lots, paths in the woods, and so on. They illustrate the location of evidence such as the debris field and body locations after, say, an airliner crashes. Examples will be shown later in the discussion of measuring the evidence at the scene, Section 7.4.

7.4 Measuring the Scene

Determining the dimensions of the scene and pinpointing evidence is a critical aspect of sketching. It is commonly accomplished using tape measures, IR laser 3D imaging instrumentation, or rolling devices that "click-off" measurements as one rolls a wheel along the perimeter of a large area. Regardless of how the measuring is accomplished, they must be precise enough to allow a scene scientist/investigator to return to the scene at a later date and, using the recorded measurements and photographs, understand the placement of evidence in its original location. Measurements are also critical for reinvestigating the scene when the case turns cold.

This brings up the principle of significant figures versus accuracy and the question of what is adequate. So, if one measures the length of a room using a tape measure and finds one wall to be 15 ft. 3½ in., does it matter that someone else measures it to be 15 ft. 3¼ in.? Absolutely not! Measurement error occurs as a result of humans making measurements manually. And it is not worth the scene scientist's/investigator's time to measure a wall three times in order to obtain an average and associated error bars. Once is enough, and the single measurement is the one that should be used.

There seems to be an ongoing discussion of whether to use cloth or steel measuring tapes. The fact is, given the preciseness required for scene measurements either should suffice as long as one type is used at each scene. For laser measurements, where the measurements can be in decimals, such as 15 ft. 3.45 in., the number can be rounded to 15 ft. 3.5 in. or 15 ft. 3½ in.

The specific method used to make measurements to pinpoint evidence and other items, such as furniture, is really a matter of common sense. The most accurate and also the most tedious measuring method is triangulation. Mostly, it is overkill. Such preciseness should be reserved for measuring critically probative evidence, such as a weapon lying on the floor. Other items at the scene, such as furniture against the wall, do not need to be fixed so precisely, except to note their location relative to a fixed object at the scene, such as a corner along the wall. The size of the piece of furniture fixes its location.

Measuring outdoor scenes uses the same principles as those described below for fixing the location of evidence indoors. The main difference can be the size of the scene. The tools needed to measure indoor and outdoor scenes are listed below.

- Indoor
  - Measuring tape (metal is preferred but not essential)
  - Compass to designate N/S
  - Pencil—it is okay to erase on a rough sketch
  - Gridded grid paper
  - Measurement logs
- Outdoor
  - Measuring tape—long lengths, measuring wheel, laser measuring devices
  - Compass to designate cardinal coordinates
  - Gridded paper
  - Compass rose (usually for large unencumbered areas)
  - Measurement logs
  - Pencil

7.4.1 Locating Objects

Locating objects at the scene (indoor scenes) is typically done using two measuring methods and variations of these. Deciding which method to use is a matter of understanding how a method works and using logic to make that decision. The two methods are triangulation and baseline.

7.4.1.1 Triangulation

Triangulation, the most precise method for placing an item of evidence, is accomplished by measuring the object relative to two fixed, immovable points at the scene. Figure 7.4 illustrates the method.

As shown in Figure 7.4, the "X" is a knife and "Y" is a cigarette butt at the scene. Points "A" and "B" are corners at opposite ends of a wall and the distance between them measured. These are the fixed points used in the triangulation method. The distances from "X" and "Y" to both "A" and "B" fix these items at the scene. The data must be collected and maintained in a separate log. Text Box 7.7 shows an example of a triangulation log that would be filled out contemporaneously while making the measurements. The illustration is for a bloody knife lying between the sofa and a chair in the living room. The measurements were

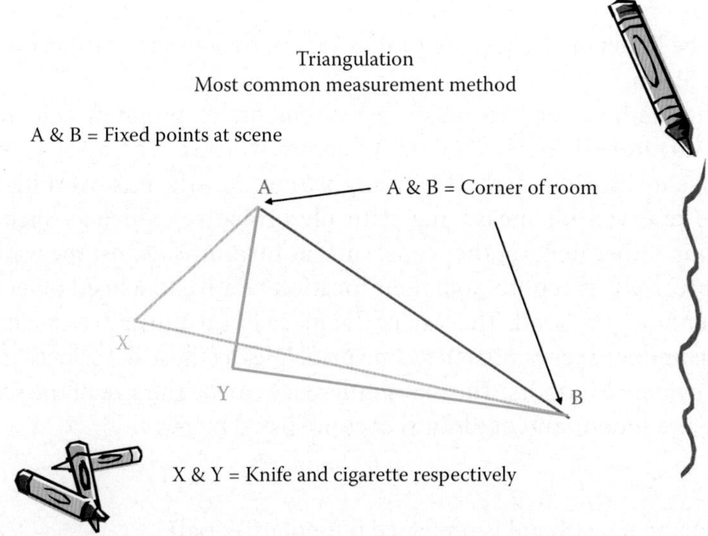

Figure 7.4 Triangulation method.

made from two fixed locations in the living room: the southwest corner and the doorjamb leading into the kitchen.

7.4.1.2 Baseline Method

In the baseline method, an object/evidence (furniture, etc.) is located relative to a perpendicular drop to a line, which is real, such as a wall. An example is shown in Figure 7.5. The

Text Box 7.7 Triangulation Measurement Log

PSU Case No. 1-008	Victim Name(s): UNK Sketchers Names: Emily Way and Steven Wang		Measurement Location: 155 Western Pl, State College, PA Date: 8/15/11	
Item No.	**Description of Item Measured**	**Distance to Fixed Location 1**	**Distance to Fixed Location 2**	**Remarks**
32	Bloody knife	32 in./corner of doorjamb to kitchen	18 in./southwest corner of living room	Knife lying between sofa and chair in living room

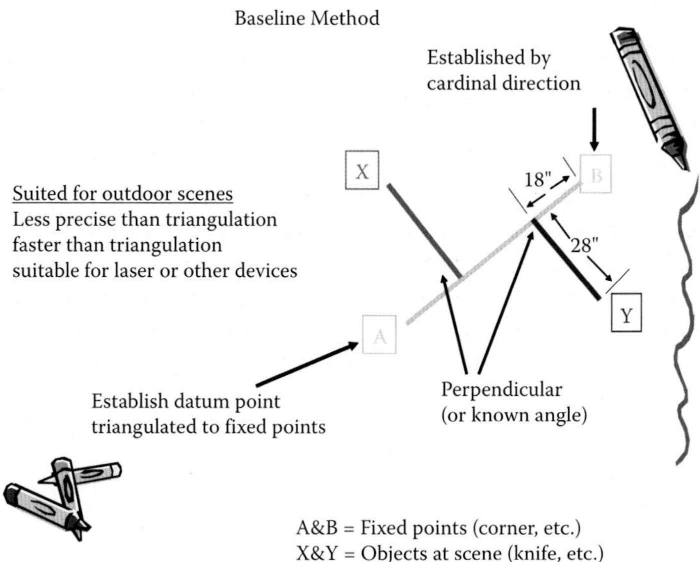

Figure 7.5 Baseline method.

distance from point "B" (18 in.) to where the perpendicular falls on the line between "A" and "B" (which can be determined by a cardinal direction) and the distance from that point to the evidence (28 in.) fixes the location of that evidence. An example of a baseline measurement log form is shown in Text Box 7.8.

This is a generic measurement form log because it is equally applicable to the traditional baseline method or its variations. Like the triangulation measurement log in Text Box 7.7, it can be used as a legend or table of measurements instead of putting them into an already cluttered sketch. In the example in Text Box 7.8, the bloody baseball bat was measured as 48 in. along the southwest wall from the doorjamb and 14 in. off the perpendicular to the baseball bat.

Text Box 7.8 Baseline Measurement Log

PSU Case No. 1-008	**Victim Name(s): Unknown Sketchers Names: Millicent Way and Steven Wang**		**Measurement Location: 155 Western Pl, State College, PA Date: 8/15/11**		
Item No.	**Description of Item Measured**	**Distance along Baseline/ Location**	**Distance off Baseline/ Location**	**Direction From Baseline to Item**	**Remarks**
40	Bloody baseball bat	48 in. from door kitchen doorjamb along southwest wall	14 in./southwest wall	90°	None

A variation, the modified baseline method, uses angles from a fixed object instead of the perpendicular, as shown in Figure 7.6. Here, instead of using the perpendicular, the angle from the evidence to the reference line is measured as is the distance from to the evidence to the line. The line between "A" and "B" helps to fix the evidence in place.

Another variation of the modified baseline method is known as the polar coordinate method. This uses a virtual line fixed by cardinal directions: north (N), south (S), east (E), or west (W). The initial fixed point can be a GPS location or it can be a fixed object. A virtual baseline fixes the location of evidence in conjunction with triangulation or baseline measurements made to items of evidence. So, whether the measurement runs from the object to be measured to a virtual or real line (e.g., a wall) or whether it is 90° or some other angle does not matter. The object is fixed at the scene. The major attributes of this method are listed below:

- Evidence scattered over open areas
    - Airline crashes
    - Bombing scenes
- Needs a direct line of sight—cannot be hindered
    - Woods or other objects
- Uses surveying techniques
    - Total station or other 3D imaging systems
    - GPS coordinates
    - Laser or IR measuring devices
- Start at single datum point
    - GPS
    - Triangulation to fixed point

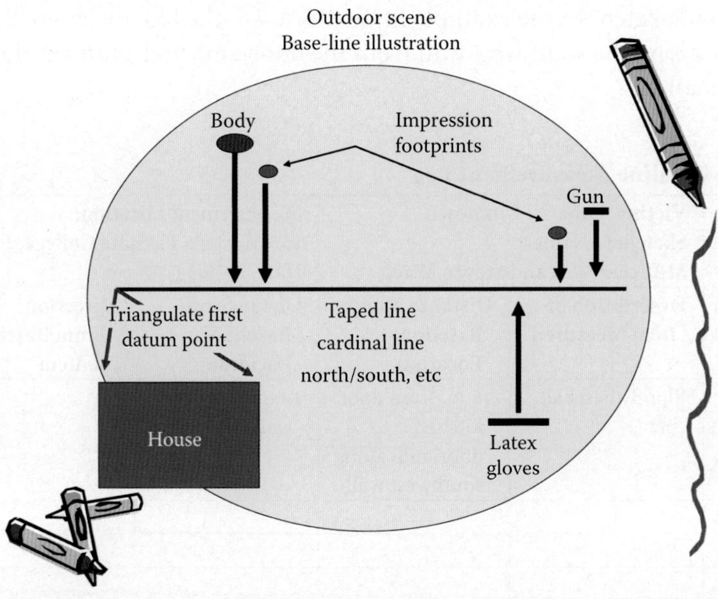

Figure 7.6 Modified baseline measurement method. (Adapted from R. M. Gardner. 2005. *Practical Crime Scene Processing and Investigation*. Boca Raton, FL: CRC Press, pp. 163–202. With permission.)

7.4.2 Photogrammetry

Photogrammetry is a technique for converting photographs into a 3D rendition of the scene [2,3]. Specialized software [4] is necessary from which items at the scene, such as evidence cones, natural formations, vehicles, and so on, are referenced to different photographic views of the same area. Common items in each photograph are referenced and tied together electronically. One caveat is that at least one measurement must be known. After referencing, the data are converted into a CAD format and loaded into a CAD program that renders the scene in a 3D format.

7.4.3 Outdoor Scene Measurements

Outdoor scene measurements are best accomplished by combining the polar coordinate method with triangulation and/or the baseline methods of measurement. An issue with outdoor scenes concerns finding fixed points of reference because they are not always readily apparent or available.

In Figures 7.7 and 7.8, the first fixed point is made by triangulating a point in the scene from a house. Subsequent measurements of evidence at the scene are made from a virtual line (actually a tape measure laid on the ground) through the scene, where the direction of the line (tape measure) is a cardinal designation: N, S, E, or W. Measurements off that line (tape measure) can be made using either triangulation (Figure 7.4) or the baseline method (Figure 7.5) or combinations of triangulation and baseline methods. Figures 7.7 and 7.8 illustrate the baseline and triangulation methods used to measure outdoor scenes, respectively. Figure 7.9 illustrates the use of the compass rose or azimuth board for measuring evidence.

In Figure 7.7, the items of evidence were measured using a baseline method. The steps for accomplishing this follow:

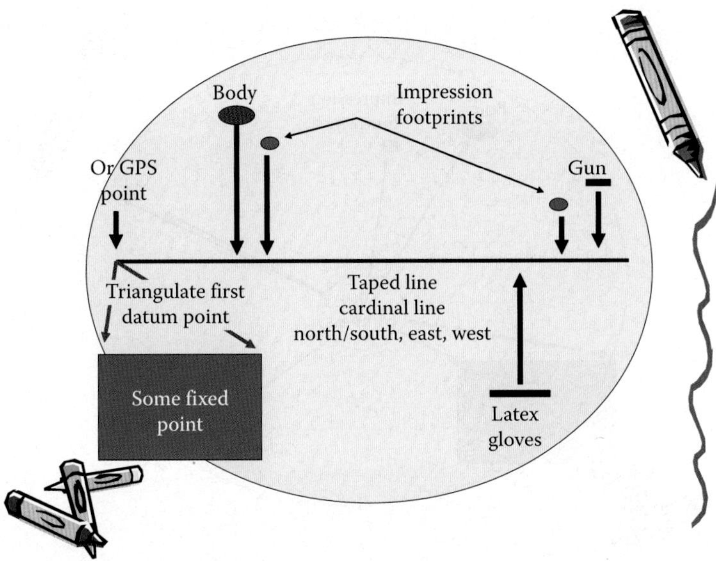

Figure 7.7 Baseline method of measuring an outdoor scene. (Adapted from R. M. Gardner. 2005. *Practical Crime Scene Processing and Investigation*. Boca Raton, FL: CRC Press, pp. 163–202. With permission.)

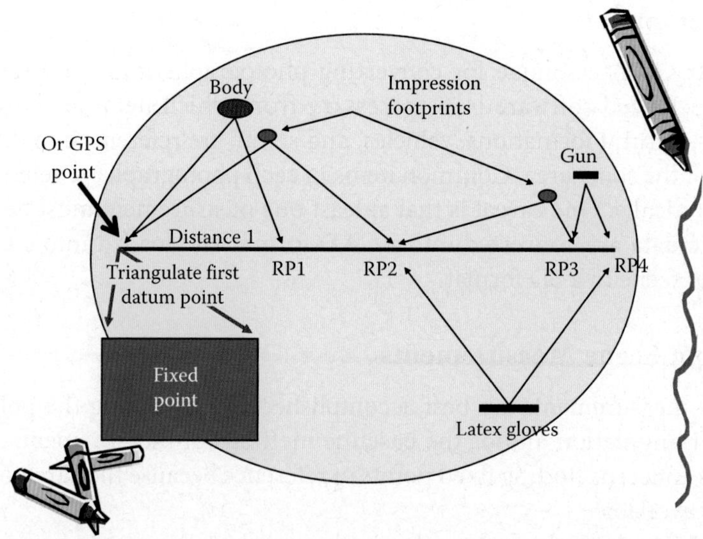

Figure 7.8 Triangulation method of measuring an outdoor scene. (Adapted from R. M. Gardner. 2005. *Practical Crime Scene Processing and Investigation*. Boca Raton, FL: CRC Press, pp. 163–202. With permission.)

- Determine the first fixed point (triangulation from another fixed point or GPS coordinate).
- Run a line through the scene (tape measure) along a polar coordinate (cardinal direction: N, S, E, or W).
- Drop a perpendicular from an item of evidence to the line running though the scene.
- Measure this distance.

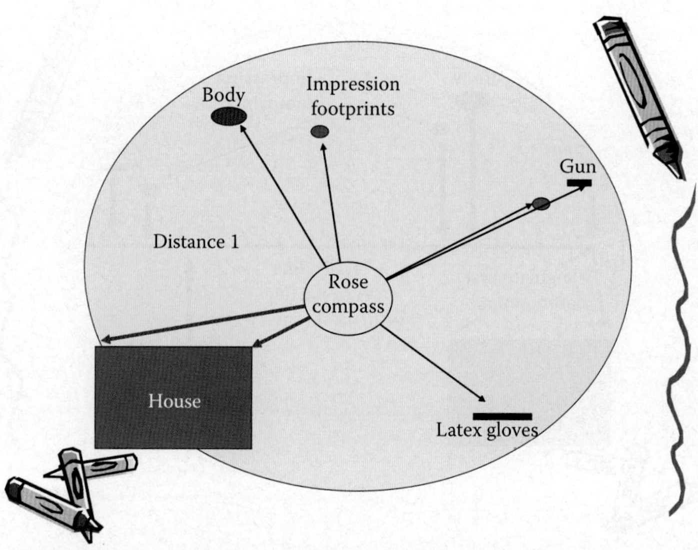

Figure 7.9 Using the azimuth board (compass rose) to measure an outdoor scene. (Adapted from R. M. Gardner. 2005. *Practical Crime Scene Processing and Investigation*. Boca Raton, FL: CRC Press, pp. 163–202.)

- Measure the distance from the fixed point to the perpendicular drop point.
- Repeat this sequence for all items of evidence.

A similar sequence is used to triangulate evidence at an outdoor scene (Figure 7.8). Instead of dropping a perpendicular to the line running through the scene, two reference points (RP1 and RP2) are chosen along the line. The distance from the fixed point to each reference point is measured and recorded in a log. The distance from each reference point to each item of evidence at the scene is measured.

The compass rose or azimuth board is an alternative method for measuring an outdoor scene. An example illustrating how to use the compass rose is shown in Figure 7.9. The compass rose is useful for large open areas, but it can also be used for more closed areas, depending on the area. A procedure follows:

- Fix the board to the ground by staking the center hole with an appropriate dowel and the four corner holes.
- Triangulate the middle hole and one corner hole to two fixed objects at the scene (or GPS coordinates if appropriate fixed objects are not available) so that the compass can be returned to its original location at some future date.
- Run a line (tape measure) from the center hole (secured by an appropriate stake) to each item of evidence.
- Measure the distance from the compass to the item of evidence and record the distance (inches) in a log. Also record the degree the tape passes over. Since the compass rose is marked in degrees (0°–360°), the precise location of each item of evidence is fixed as "X" number of inches (feet) at "Y" degrees from the center of the compass rose.

A photo of students investigating a wooded scene is shown in Figure 7.10. The student crime scene teams were faced with searching the scene for evidence of a serial killer. After completing the search and marking evidence, the students measured the scene. They chose the compass rose because it gave them a fixed reference point at the scene. In choosing the compass rose, they subsequently realized that they had a problem: Trees and bushes at the scene interfered with the straight line measurements. They solved the problem by using the compass rose in two different locations after bisecting the area.

The azimuth (compass rose) measurement log (Text Box 7.9) shows the data collected by the students, which they used to obtain the angles and distances from the compass to each item of evidence. The log also shows the item numbers, the description of each item identified, and the measurements taken.

The scene sketch in Text Box 7.10 shows the student's sketch of the scene. Notice the two locations of the compass rose that were independently fixed at the scene.

7.5 Securing the Archive

Once obtained, archives must be made secure. In a world of hackers and identity thieves, a great deal of thought must go into how to secure a scene's records. Security measures fall into various categories based on the format of the records, for example, paper, digital, photographic, video, and so on. For electronic records, the guidelines used for protecting health information (PHI) should be appropriate [4].

Figure 7.10 Wooded scene. (Photograph by Robert C. Shaler.)

Text Box 7.9 Azimuth (Compass Rose) Measurement Log. (Used with permission from Amanda "Max" Yerkey, Matthew Irick, Leighanne Alger and Emily Dreibelbis.)

PENNSTATE

FORENSIC SCIENCE
The Pennsylvania State University
Eberly College of Science
Whitmore Lab
University Park, PA 16802

Compass Rose Measurement Log

PSU CASE NO.	VICTIM NAME(S)	MEASUREMENT LOCATION
7	SKETCHERS NAMES: EMILY, MAX, MATT, LEIGH	OUTDOOR SCENE DATE: 4/13/10

Item No.	Description of Item Measured	Distance	Angle	Remarks
	FP 1	37'5"	63	
	FP 2	58'9"	265	
G	Black Bag	37'1"	63	
18	Shell Casing	42'	84	
59	Skull	23'8"	4	
68	Skull	27'3"	344	
28	Bag	29'7"	325	
94	Head	35'5"	296	
I	Paper Bag	35'2"	290	

Text Box 7.10 Sketch of Scene Showing Positions of Two Azimuth Compass Locations. (Used with permission from Frank Santoriello.)

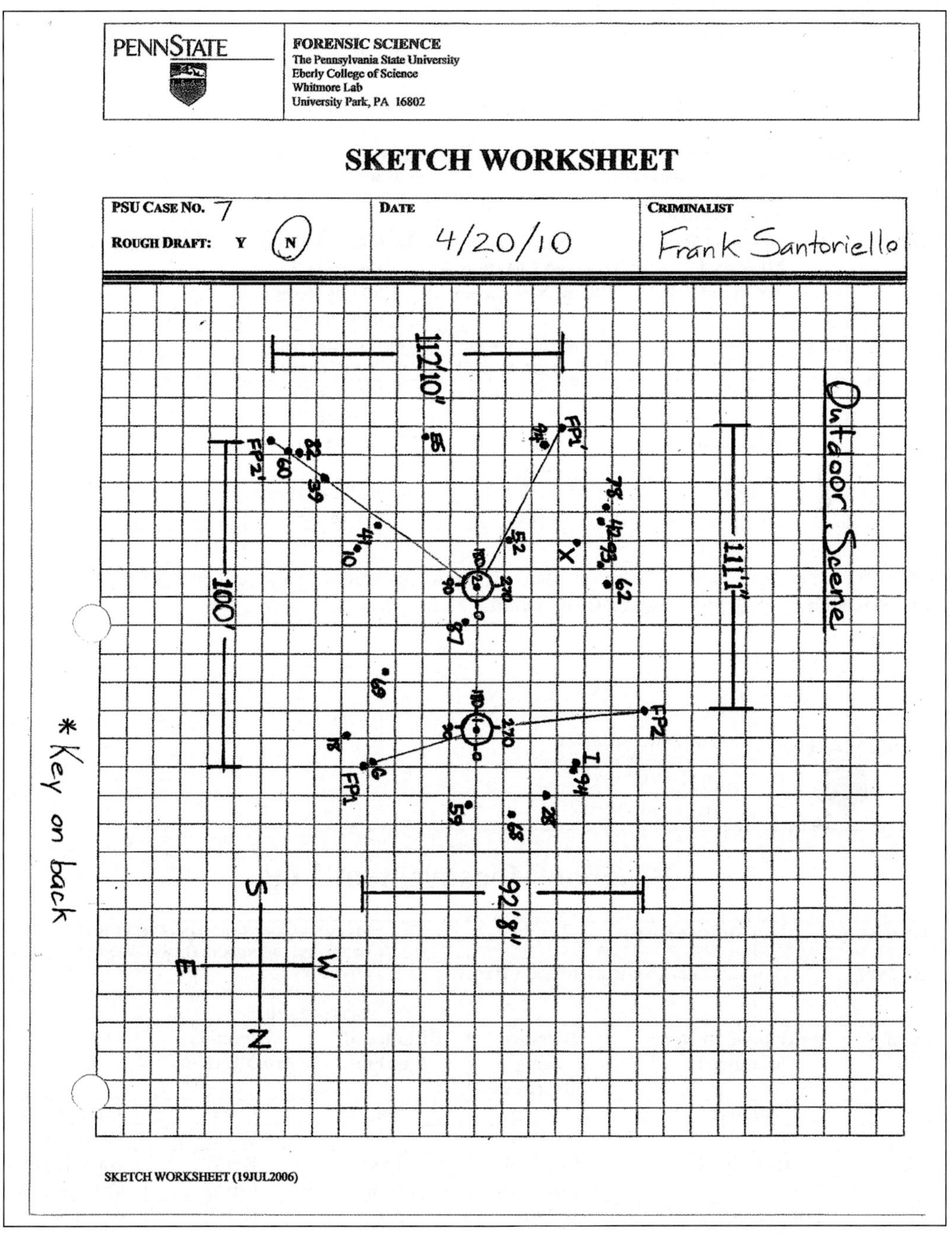

PENNSTATE

FORENSIC SCIENCE
The Pennsylvania State University
Eberly College of Science
Whitmore Lab
University Park, PA 16802

SKETCH WORKSHEET

PSU CASE NO. 7	DATE	CRIMINALIST
ROUGH DRAFT: Y (N)	4/20/10	Frank Santoriello

SKETCH WORKSHEET (19JUL2006)

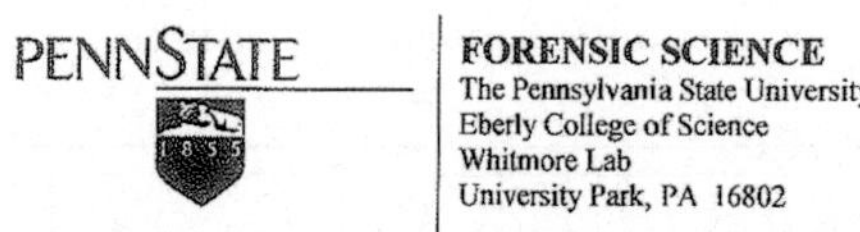

Triangulation Measurement Log

PSU CASE NO.	VICTIM NAME(S)	MEASUREMENT LOCATION
7	MRS. ROTHLESBERGER SKETCHERS NAMES: EMILY AND ALICA	UPSTAIR BEDROOM DATE: 4/14/10

Item No.	Description of Item Measured	Distance To Fixed Location 1	Distance to Fixed Location 2	Remarks
	TV Stand	5'8" to NW corner	2'8" left closet door jamb	
	Crib	2'9" to NE corner	11" to East wall	
	Shelf	3'9" right, E wall	9'6" SW corner	
	Bed	1'11" to SW corner	7'11" left door jamb	
	Night Stand	2'1" to left door jamb	5'7" to SW corner	
92	Boot	1'3" Back to SE corner	10'8.5" Front to SW corner	

Figure 7.11 Example of triangulation measurement log of indoor scene. Used with permission from Emily Dreibelbis and Alicia Zimmerman.

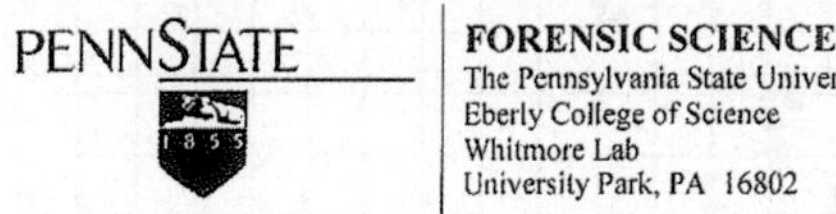

Baseline Measurement Log

PSU CASE NO.	VICTIM NAME(S)	MEASUREMENT LOCATION GREAT ROOM UPSTAIRS (LIVING AND GAME) – SPRUCE COTTAGE
PSU 2B 07	SKETCHERS NAMES: KIMBERLY DAVEY	DATE: 4/13/10

Item No.	Description of Item Measured	Distance along Baseline	Distance off Baseline	Direction From Baseline	Remarks
A	Dresser	13ft 1in	5in	E→W	Back Right
		18ft 7in	0	E→W	Back Left
B	Red Couch	19ft 7.5in	1ft 9in	E→W	Back Right
		19ft 7.5in	4ft 1in	E→W	Front Right
D	Green Chair	29ft	5ft	E→W	Front Right
		31ft 5in	6ft 6in	E→W	Back Left
E	End Table	28ft 4in	9ft 8in	E→W	Front Right
		27ft 1in	12ft	E→W	Back Left

Figure 7.12 Example of baseline measurement log of indoor scene. Used with permission from Kimberly Davey.

References

1. R. M. Gardner. 2005. Chapter 7: Crime scene sketching and mapping. In: *Practical Crime Scene Processing and Investigation*. Boca Raton, FL: CRC Press, pp. 163–202.
2. D. Templeton. 2008. November–December, 6(6).
3. *iWitness*. Close range photogrammetry. The premier close range photogrammetry software for accident reconstruction. Available at: http://www.iwitnessphoto.com/ (accessed January 19, 2011).
4. Federal Register, Department of Health and Human Services. Forty-five CFR Parts 160, 162 and 164, Health Insurance Reform: Security Rule; Final Rule, Part II, February 20, 2003.

Workshop 2: Sketching the Scene

W2.1 Introduction

Before photography became the preferred tool for archiving a scene, investigators used sketches, which is still an essential skill. Sketches are important because they lay out the scene in a way that neither photographs nor videos can. They give investigators and others a general overview and the precise and/or relative location of evidence.

An initial rough sketch is done at the scene and then a final sketch is prepared at another location. Both the draft and final sketches become part of the case file. Sketching is one of the initial activities of an investigation and is contemporaneous with photographing and protecting the fragile evidence. Sketches should include the measurements of each critical item including furniture, blood trails, footprints, tire tracks, blood spatter, bodies, weapons, and so on. Determining which measurement method to use depends on the importance of an item as perceived by the sketcher. The most tedious method, triangulation, and is not typically used for general scene items such as furniture, because preciseness of these items are not critical to the investigation. Furniture against the wall does not need to be fixed except to note its location relative to a fixed corner along the wall. The size of the piece of furniture fixes its location. But triangulation is necessary for critical items such as a weapon on the floor or the location of bloodstains.

Outdoor scenes use the same principles as those described below for general sketching and fixing the location of evidence. The main difference is the size of the scene.

W2.2 Required Tools

A sketcher needs certain tools to complete the job correctly. Mostly, these are materials that anyone using common sense would think of. Generally, a scene must be measured, which means having the appropriate tools at hand. If the scene is small, a 200-ft. measuring tape is overkill. But an outdoor scene that includes an open field would probably need a tool that measures continually. Recording the orientation of the scene would require a compass. Certainly, a mechanism for sketching is necessary. Whether this is done manually or using a computer is a sketcher's preference. The following sections consider the tools needed for sketching manually.

W2.2.1 Indoor Tools

The following list includes materials that would be needed to sketch items to obtain all of the information at a scene

- Measuring tape (metal is preferred but not essential)
- Compass to designate N/S
- Pencil—it is okay to erase on a rough sketch
- Colored pencils to identify easily blood, etc.
- Sketch pad—grid paper
- Clipboard

W2.2.2 Outdoor Tools

- Measuring tape—long lengths, measuring wheel, laser measuring devices
- Compass to designate cardinal coordinates
- Sketch pad—grid paper
- Compass rose (for large unencumbered areas)
- Clipboard
- Pencil

W2.3 General Methods for Measuring the Scene

Locating objects at the scene (indoor scenes) is typically done in two ways by using variations of the following methods.

W2.3.1 Triangulation

Triangulation is the most precise method for fixing the location of an object, whether indoor or outdoor. This is accomplished by measuring two fixed and immovable points at the scene. Figure 7.4 illustrates the method. The reader should review this information before doing the exercises in this workshop.

W2.3.2 The Baseline Method

In the baseline method, an object or evidence (e.g., furniture, etc.) is located off of the perpendicular drop to a wall. A variation, the modified baseline method, uses angles from a fixed object instead of from the perpendicular. A third variation uses the cardinal directions (N, S, E, W) off of a fixed or virtual line. Again, the reader should review the baseline method of fixing objects at a scene before doing the exercises in this workshop.

The modified baseline method is shown in Figure 7.5, where the items, the broken wine glass, X, is fixed off of either a fixed or virtual line established using cardinal coordinates. This example shows the line fixed from the corner of a wall. A line from the wine glass to the fixed line is determined by the distance to the line and the angle at which it hits the line.

W2.4 Indoor Scene Measurements

Measuring indoor scenes is straightforward using triangulation or the baseline methods. The perimeter of each area is measured and the locations of windows, doors, radiators, stairways, and so on are fixed precisely. Furniture and other items commonly found at the scene are also fixed using a variation of the baseline method. Other items, such as knocked-over furniture, items of obvious evidence, bloodstains, and so on, are fixed using triangulation. Weapons, bloodstains, and pattern evidence are fixed using triangulation.

W2.5 Outdoor Scene Measurements

Outdoor scenes are sometimes more difficult because true fixed points may not be readily apparent. In the illustration in Figure 7.4, a house becomes the fixed point and then measurements are made from a line through the scene created by using cardinal coordinates. Measurements off that line can be made using either the triangulation or baseline methods or combinations of both. The reader should review Chapter 7 before doing the exercises in this workshop.

The procedure for using the compass rose is also discussed in Chapter 7. In short, the compass is attached to the ground and then triangulated from GPS or fixed points to fix its location close to the center of the scene. As the compass is marked in degrees (0°–360°), each item of evidence is marked as "X" number of inches at "Y" degrees from the center of the compass rose. This is illustrated in Figure 7.9.

W2.6 Instructor Demonstration

The techniques of the baseline and triangulation methods for locating objects at a scene are demonstrated here. Also, the use of the appropriate forms is demonstrated. The compass rose and its application in outdoor scenes is also explained. An outdoor scene is appropriate because the instruction takes into consideration the measuring methods (triangulation, baseline) and their use of cardinal coordinates, GPS, and the compass rose.

W2.7 Exercises

W2.7.1 An Outdoor Scene

Instructors will take students to a mock outdoor scene, which can be an open field, a wooded area, or both. Students must conduct an outdoor search to find the evidence, pinpoint their locations, and then sketch the search area. The method they use is their choice, which will be determined by the scene circumstances. The sketch will be a map of the scene, which they will do by determining the location of the evidence using one of the three methods described above. When finished and all the evidence has been located and mapped, the students will repeat the exercise in order demonstrate precision in measuring and mapping. They pinpoint the location of the originally found evidence as though returning to the scene for a second time?

W2.7.2 An Indoor Scene

After completing the outdoor scene, each crime scene team will measure two adjacent rooms in a house. The rooms will have had evidence placed at various locations, some not having easy access. At the same time, members of the team will simultaneously photograph the mock scene. The exercise challenges students who must design a sketching strategy that does not interfere with other archiving processes such as photography and/or videography.

W2.7.2.1 Procedure

- Make the rough sketch using the sketch worksheet (Table W2.1) or graph paper.
- Convert each rough sketch into a final sketch. It is okay to use a computer to generate the final sketch. The final sketch should be on graph paper.

Table W2.1 Sketch Worksheet

PSU Case No.			Date	
Rough Draft:	Y	N	Address:	Criminalist(s)

- Use a pencil to make the rough sketch. It is okay to erase on the rough sketch.
- Do not hand-draw lines in the final sketch and use pen and ink.
- Use colored pencils to fill in bloody footwear tracks, blood, greenery (bushes, etc.), and so on.
- Fill in all the information requested on the sketch forms.
- Include N/S designations in the sketch.
- Include weather conditions in the sketch.
- Record measurements into the triangulation log (Table W2.2), the baseline measurement log, (Table W2.3), or the compass rose log (Table W2.4).

Table W2.2 Example of Triangulation Measurement Log

PSU Case No.	**Victim Name(s)**		**Measurement Location**		
	Sketchers Names:		**Date:** **Address:**		
Item No.	**Description of Item Measured**	**From Item**	**To Fixed Location**	**Distance**	**Remarks**
1	Revolver	On Floor	NW Corner	85"	Moved Table
	Revolver	On Floor	SW Corner	65"	—

Table W2.3 Example of Baseline Measurement Log

PSU Case No.	**Victim Name(s)** **Sketchers Names:**			**Measurement Location** **Date:** **Address:**	
Item No.	Description of Item Measured	Distance along Baseline	Distance off Baseline	Direction Angle From Baseline	Remarks
2	Chair	45¾"	36½"	Perpendicular	Front rt leg
	Chair	18½"	18½"	Perpendicular	Left rear leg

Table W2.4 Compass Rose/Azimuth Board Measurement Log

Compass Rose/Azimuth Board Log				
PSU Case No.	**Victim Name(s)** **Sketchers Names:**		**Measurement Location** **Date:** **Address:**	
Item No.	**Description of Item Measured**	**Distance (Inches) from Board to Item**	**Angle from Board to Item**	**Remarks**
1	Bone	239 in.	248 degrees	On surface

W2.8 Questions

- Why is it necessary to sketch the scene?
- In 500 words or less, explain the significance of the compass rose for outdoor scenes.
- If an item of evidence, a bloody knife, is seen under a piece of furniture, it must be part of the sketch. How would you include it in your sketch? Circle the correct answer.
- Move the furniture and then sketch the item .
- Take the item out from under the furniture and indicate on the sketch that the item had been removed.
- Wait until photography has been completed. Then move the furniture and sketch the item in place.
- It really doesn't matter how you do it.
- I have a better way to do it. See my written statement below.

Videography
The Forensic Documentary

8

8.1 Introduction

Modern video cameras, camcorders, even digital single lens reflex (SLR) cameras have progressed dramatically in recent years, a process that will continue. As of this writing, digital camcorders record in high definition (HD), and depending on the camera, the resulting screen resolution can be 720 or 1080, the highest resolution available on televisions. Even relatively inexpensive camcorders record in 1080 HD and can deliver 14 megapixel still photographs. Modern digital camcorders are affordable and readily available, so there is no excuse for a police agency or crime scene unit not to have video capability, even as part of the functionality of a contemporary digital SLR camera. This mixed-capability digital recording/photography in the same camera can change how the forensic archivist works.

Now that video capabilities are so widely available, one might consider replacing photography with video as the premiere scene-archiving tool. That would be a mistake. Video, per se, does provide the same detail as still digital photography, which still does not offer the resolution of 35 mm photography except in extremely expensive cameras. As photography was for sketching, video is for photography and sketching; Video is complementary for photography and sketching. However, as video technology moves forward, its use at crime scenes will increasingly add more completeness to the archiving process. For now, though, it is not a standalone tool.

8.1.1 The Forensic Value of Crime Scene Video

Video gives a view of the scene not duplicated by still photography or sketching. Too, it does not provide the same clarity of detail as photography or the bird's eye view of the scene sketch. So, its value is that it offers a visual perspective that other archiving methods do not and cannot. In essence, the video is the immediate complement to the walk-through that the first officer takes with the team leader when the scene responsibility changes hands. In the video walk-through, investigators "see" the scene through the eyes of the videographer as the camera, moves from place to place, capturing an overview of each. In an indoor scene, the videographer moves from room to room in sequence, capturing everything, zooming in on items that could become evidence, for example, footwear impressions, blood trails, bodies, and so on. In outdoor scenes, the videographer must move slowly from an entrance point determined from found evidence and then move logically into the scene.

Video is a mechanism for gaining an immediate appreciation and "feel" for the scene that cannot be captured by still photography. Thus video should be the first step in archiving a crime scene because it provides that important "feel" for the scene. Video works because it is also closer to how we view the world, which makes it a natural viewing medium compared with the staccato and static nature of photographs or the detached overview in

Table 8.1 Reasons for Crime Scene Video

Objective	Reason
Unbiased documentation	Present objective facts, conditions, and sequence of events
Visual proof of the crime	Of a fire or other crime
Testimony	Use the video as demonstrative evidence for the jury
Refresh memory	Long delays between the crime and the courtroom can change or dull scene details

a sketch. Video gives an immediate understanding of how evidence relates to the crime. Sketch and photographs reinforce what video presents.

8.1.1.1 Objective of the Video

There are four reasons for taking video of a crime scene other than as a complement to still photography and sketching. Generally, these are presented in Table 8.1 [1].

8.1.2 Crime Scene Video Is a Documentary

The video process is deceptively simple; point the camera, turn it on, and, moving it slowly from side to side, proceed through the scene in a logical sequence. Actually, the video of the crime scene is not that easy. As for all archiving, the role of the videographer is the same as any forensic archivist; capture the scene in an as original state as possible. The responsibility of the forensic videographer, like the forensic photographer, is not to consider the scene as a work of art but more as a response to what the scene is saying. The scene dictates the process and the resulting video. The forensic videographer is not making a movie in the Hollywood scene, but instead a documentary of the crime. In this context, the crime scene video informs its viewers about a topic or an issue, which in this instance is the scene of the crime. Like any endeavor that is worthwhile and done correctly, making a crime scene documentary is difficult and tedious.

The crime scene documentary should be thought out carefully, such that the area of the scene must tell its story, the essence of which the forensic videographer must capture completely. In a sense, the scene videographer has it easier than the Hollywood videographer because the crime scene is not a matter of determining which perspective is the most interesting or visually appealing. The forensic videographer should be concerned only with how the scene presents the evidence of the crime, which is why the walk-through process of making the video is important. The video starts at the beginning, for example, the entrance to the scene and progresses through the scene without stopping and finishes at an egress point or another logical finishing point. Thus the documentary takes the view from the entrance to the scene, through the scene, and out at the egress point. If the egress point is the same as the entrance point, the video must capture that as well. Certainly, actual entrance/egress points, hidden evidence, and so on, is unknown at that time, but the video must capture everything that is known.

8.1.3 Basic Video Terminology

Before discussions on the process of videoing the crime scene, it is important to briefly define some terminology employed in the video world. The information in Table 8.2 was adapted from [2].

Table 8.2 Video Terminology

Terminology	Definition
NTSC: National Television System Committee	Camcorders produced in the United States, Japan, Central and South America, and some parts of Asia. In NSTC, 30 frames are transmitted each second. Individual picture frame has 525 individual scan lines.
PAL: Phase Alternating Line	System used in the UK, Australia, and New Zealand. In PAL, 25 frames are transmitted each second. Individual picture frame has 625 individual scan lines.
CODEC: COmpressor-DECompressor	A program that encodes and decodes video. When shooting, a CODEC program compresses the video to make it fit on your camcorder's memory system. Putting camcorder video on the Internet or a DVD requires another CODEC to compress video to smaller file size suitable for the Web or a DVD.
MiniDV:	The small tape used to record digital video (DV). Currently gives best video picture quality to record standard definition video (SD) and high definition (HD) known as HDV.
HDV	High Definition Video recorded to tape.
HDD	Hard Disk Drive where video is compressed and recorded using CODEC.
Flash Drive	Solid-state drive records video.
AVCHD: Advanced Video Codec High Definition	New video recording system replacing MPEG2 as the used in the latest tapeless camcorders. Can record SD and HD. Uses an MPEG4 CODEC, also known as H.264
FLV: Flash Video	Web standard and most compatible video type with all PC and Mac users. Used by video share sites on the Web, for example, YouTube. Gives best compatibility, file size, and video quality.
	MOV is Apple's version of FLV. WMV is Microsoft's version of FLV. Neither MOV nor WMV offers the compatibility of FLV.
SWF	Scaled down version of FLV. Not suitable for Web video.
AVI	Oldest video format. Huge files that are not compressed. Editing software on computers use AVI files to give highest quality before compressing.
CCD: Charge-Coupled Devices	Imaging system used by some camcorders. More expensive camcorders use 3CCDs, each taking separate measurements of red, green, and blue light.
Streaming Video	Video is "streamed" in real time using special hosting and software.
Progressive Download	Video being downloaded from source while watching. 99% of video on Web, for example, YouTube.
Video Resolution	1. Number of distinct pixels in each dimension that can be displayed. 2. NTSC standard = 720 × 48, 3. PAL = 720 × 576, 4. HD: 720p = 720 × 489: 1080p = 1920 × 1080.
HD Aspect Ratio	16:9 (widescreen)
NSTC and PAL Aspect Ratio	4:3

8.1.4 Essential Video Camera Features

All cameras have certain built-in features, some more than others. For forensic videography, the usual features are necessary as are others [1,3]. These include the following:

- Appropriate carrying cases with padded interior
- Mechanism to prevent water/moisture from getting into the camera

- Play/record/fast-forward/rewind/playback
- Three-way power (indoor AC adaptor/outdoor battery pack/vehicle battery cord)
  - Store battery packs in cool, dry place
  - Ensure battery packs are fully charged
  - Protect from cold temperatures
- Locking record button to prevent accidental recording
- Power Zoom and close up (macro)
- Automatic and manual focusing
- Automatic iris to maintain light for proper picture brightness and contrast
- Automatic white balance for continuous automatic adjustment for optimum color balance
- Pause mechanism
- Audio and microphone
- Hard disk drive (HDD) and flash drive capability
- Time/date stamp
- Lighting capability—separate attachments necessary for extremely low light and light mounting for on-camera light [2]
- 3CCDs
- Low light recording
- Single frame recording
- Greater than 12 mega pixel single (still) photography capability

8.1.5 Requirements of a Forensic Videographer

The credentials of someone who does forensic videography are important to producing a high quality forensic video. First, the videographer must understand the basic elements of forensic videography. Second, the videographer should be an experienced crime scene investigator. This is critical because only someone with this experience is capable of understanding the relationship of the scene to the evidence it presents. This is, in essence, why video is so important and why someone who does not have this experience is not a proper person to record the scene documentary. Third, the videographer must have hands-on experience producing high quality video.

8.1.5.1 Camera Movement Terminology

Understanding video terminology is important because this is the language videographers use to communicate. Table 8.3 gives general definitions for terms used with respect to movement. The camera movements above are essential to any video, and forensic videography is no exception.

Table 8.3 Camera Movement Terminology

Terminology	Interpretation
Zoom	Move the camera closer toward or farther away from your subject
Pan	Rotate the camera horizontally from side to side
Tilt	Rotate the camera up and down
Dolly	Move the camera forward or backward
Truck	Move the camera to the left or to the right

8.2 Basic Forensic Videography: The Scene Video

The experienced videographer who is also a scene scientist/investigator is in the best position to produce high quality scene documentary video. As with all documentary filming, research is the key to producing a quality product. From a crime scene perspective, the essential research means becoming familiar with the scene. The following is a suggested checklist of activity that should take place, in sequence, before starting to record the Scene Video.

- Walk through the scene with the team leader to gain an understanding of the scene geometry.
- Map the scene layout and determine the video sequence, for example, where to begin and where to end.
- In a second walk-through, assess video- and camera-specific challenges, for example, lighting, scene obstacles, weather issues, white balance, ISO settings, and so on.
- Discuss with the team leader what the video should include. The discussion should include entrance/egress points, important potential evidence, indoor/outdoor considerations, video perspectives, and so on.

The Scene Video is the video equivalent of the walk-through taken by the team leader and the first officer. It is a continuous process, ideally without interruption from beginning to end. Along the way, each area of the scene is captured on video. As videoing continues, the videographer slowly walks through the scene capturing as much as possible. An example of the process is shown in the mock scene depicted in Figure 8.1. The entrance to this area of the scene is to the right. While the video is running, the videographer stops, for example, at positions 1–4 in the diagram, and pans right, left, up, and down in order to record whatever investigative information is visible at that perspective. At position 4 in the diagram, red arrows illustrate the different video perspectives that should be captured at each position. At position 2, the knife lying next to the chair becomes visible and must be recorded. For

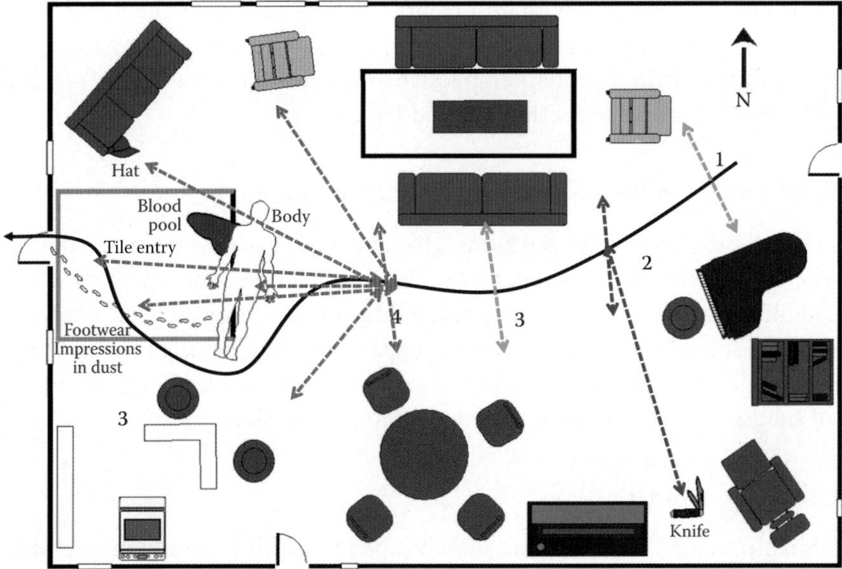

Figure 8.1 The scene video: the video process.

each item of evidence seen, a close-up—zoom—is necessary: the knife, the blood pool, the body, the hat, and the footwear impressions in dust. The Scene Video process in Figure 8.1 should not be confused with the topic video discussed in Section 8.3.

It is inappropriate for an inexperienced person to video a crime scene. Even for experienced videographers, the crime scene presents serious challenges. The reader should review Chapter 6 with respect to archivist to determine what is important to capture. In essence, the scene video is active archiving. There are video-specific considerations to which the videographer must adhere.

8.2.1 Camera Speed and Position

Remember the torture of watching home videos taken by the typical amateur home photographer? The camera movements are torture: jerky, nausea-induced panning, and roller coaster ride-like zooming. For the forensic world, the secret to video basics, even for the home videographer, is to slow down and obey the speed limit. When panning, the speed limit should be 8–10 s/quarter turn or slower. What does that mean? If you stand facing an object, say a bloody knife lying in one corner of the room, and you want to show its relationship to a body lying on the opposite side of the room, position yourself so that the camera forms a triangle midway (or close to it) between the knife and the body. Since the body is the most visible object at homicide scenes, capture its location first and then, while counting off seconds in your head, slowly pan from the body to the knife. The angle is $<180^\circ$ which means panning from the body to the knife shot should take no fewer than 16–20 s.

8.2.2 Camera Distances and Angles

In the artistic arena, camera distances and angles make the video more interesting. In a forensic documentary, camera distances and angles are dictated by the scene. For example, capturing a knife partly hidden under a sofa is important, but capturing it from a single perspective is not the correct way to archive its location. Consider the knife from various perspectives, most importantly from the question of how and why it ended up where it is. Then, film the knife from various perspectives in order for a viewer to see it from the location(s) from its origin. See Section 8.3 and Figure 8.2.

8.2.3 Establishing Video Shows the Backdrop of the Scene

In Figure 8.1, the various video positions give the viewer an overview of the scene seen through the eyes of the scene perspective. This perspective is accomplished using wide angle or establishing video. Establishing video differs its photographic partner since it captures more of the scene because of its panning capability. Establishing photography requires overlapping single, still shots to capture the same information and even then, it is simply an array of snapshots without the feel of the video perspective.

8.2.4 Close-Up Detail

After establishing video, the forensic videographer should take advantage of the zoom and macro characteristics of the camera lens. In Figure 8.1, each position (1–4 in the diagram) represents an establishing video showing the relationship of the items of

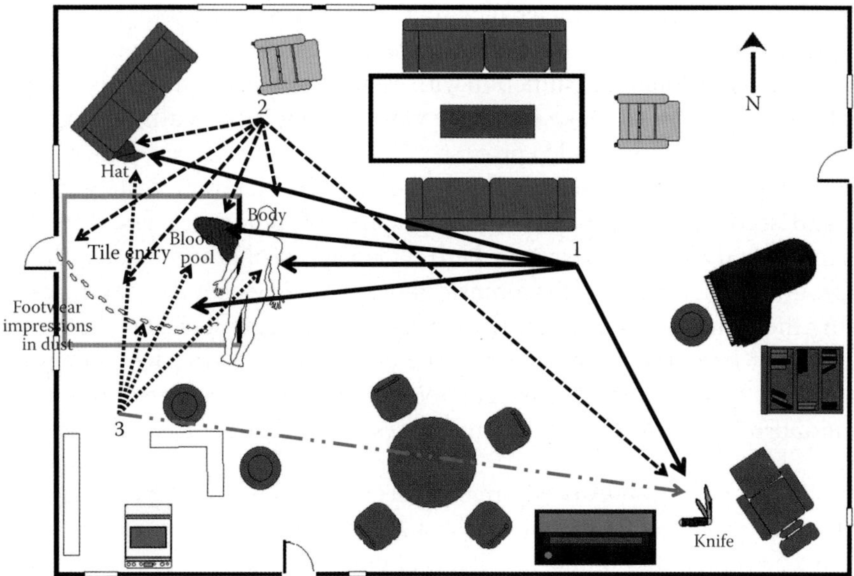

Figure 8.2 The topic video: capturing specific detail.

evidence captured in the video. Shooting from those same positions, the videographer would video a close up of each item in order to obtain a detailed view, as illustrated by the arrows in Figure 8.1. After obtaining the detail, the video would slowly zoom back to the original video position. The zoom-out to the original position must be done slowly, important because it reinforces the relationship among the different items of evidence. It also repeats the camera perspective in reverse.

In Figure 8.1, each position should have a series of video zoom shots, for example, like the arrows in position 4, with each representing a close-up shot of an item of evidence. The zoom speed is also important because it allows the viewer to observe items in the video that the videographer might not have considered important. Slow zoom is essential because it allows a more detail of the surrounding area captured by the video.

8.3 The Forensic Topic Video and Forensic Photography

In Chapter 7, a great deal of space was devoted to the establishing, midrange and close-up photographs of evidence. From that discussion, the student might have the impression that video and photography are completely separate technologies, which they are, but they are merging. The merging of technologies presents alternatives or an expansion to the traditional way of thinking about archiving scenes. The traditional paradigm says that video precedes still photography because the scene video captures the essence of the team leader's walk through the scene. There is, of course, no suggestion to discontinue that practice. What could and perhaps should change is how the forensic archivist utilizes the merged technology in the same camera.

Assume that the scene walk-through video (the scene video) is complete. Now, the forensic photographer is going to archive the scene photographically. In this scenario, the first series of photographs taken would be establishing shots. There is no reason why this paradigm cannot be tweaked somewhat by combining video and photographic activities to produce a topic video. In order not to confuse the scene walk-through video (scene video), we consider the video done in conjunction with establishing photography as a "topic video." Figure 8.1 illustrates how to make the scene video, which is the walk-through video, and Figure 8.2 illustrates the topic video process.

The new paradigm has the scene being videoed twice, first immediately after the walk-through and secondarily during the photographic archiving process. The topic video captures individual parts of the scene where evidence is visible and records the area individually from the perspective of the forensic photographer, who is also taking establishing shots using the same camera. Since the scene video videographer and the forensic photographer might be different members of the crime scene team, they will perceive the scene differently and possibly identify different points of interest. For an indoor homicide scene, one approach of this dual archiving process might proceed as follows:

- Establishing photography of the area (a part of a scene) using photography
- Video the area from different establishing perspectives (Figure 8.2) and then zooming in and out on important items of potential evidence
- Midrange photography of these items of potential evidence
- Close-up photography of items when necessary

The entire archived record of the area will have a set of digital photographs augmented by two videos taken by different team members, one the scene video and the other the topic video. While somewhat redundant, the overall archived product of the scene will present a better and more complete record of the scene.

The position(s) of the camera for capturing topic videos is critical. Consider the same mock scene in Figure 8.1 but illustrated differently in Figure 8.2. The knife is across the room lying on the floor near a reclining chair. The forensic photographer/videographer has to capture each item of evidence as it relates to other evidentiary items in the area and how they relate to the scene. Figure 8.2 shows three different positions (1, 2, and 3 on the diagram) a forensic photographer/videographer might take to capture this evidence at this scene. The arrows from the videographer's position to each item of evidence illustrate the perspectives the video will capture. It is obvious that each position offers a different perspective and each alone is insufficient to adequately capture the detail necessary to adequately show how they relate.

8.4 The Prescene Checklist

The equipment necessary to properly capture the scene is rapidly becoming more affordable. And, as mentioned, several digital cameras have HD video capability and several camcorders have digital photographic capabilities. Before leaving to work on a scene, the digital equipment manager, for example, the forensic videographer/photographer must ensure that the items of the following checklist have been done:

- Batteries are fully charged.
- Sufficient memory to record several hours of video either on the HDD and/or flash drives. This might mean having a portable hard drive and/or additional memory cards available for downloading.

- Lighting equipment is available and appropriate (for example, light stands and so on) and is working and that spare bulbs are available.
- Video title generator and "shake free" operation. If a title generator is not available, then save approximately 15 s at the beginning of the tape for the addition of a title card with any pertinent information to the beginning of the crime scene tape. Alternatively, the title could be done at the scene using a prepared title card.

8.5 On-Scene Fundamentals

Once the video camera begins recording, do not stop until taping is complete. If the camera has a pause feature, it is alright to use that. As mentioned, the key to videotaping is slow camera movement. Normally, videoing is not ideal for viewing detail because videographers tend to pan past objects too quickly. Slow panning is necessary and each area should be panned twice in order to prevent unnecessary rewinding of the tape for viewers.

Begin taping with a general overview of the scene and surrounding area. Wide angle and close-ups are necessary to demonstrate the layout of the evidence and its relationship and relevance to the scene. For indoor scenes, the video can show how various areas, for example, rooms, are laid out in relation to each other and how they can be accessed. This complements the sketch because the video shows the real-life obstacles, and so on, that the sketch does not. After taping is complete, leave about 15 s of blank tape to prevent the crime scene tape from running into anything previously recorded.

Transfer the tape to a high quality master tape. Remove the recording tabs from the master tape after transferring the crime scene tape and store the latter in a safe place. The original tape is the official record of the videoed scene. As such it is the evidence. Copies made from the master tape are not considered original evidence and might not be admissible in court.

References

1. D. R. Redsicker. 2001. Chapter 3 Video for fire/crime scenes. In *The Practical Methodology of Forensic Photography*. 2nd Edition. CRC Press, pp. 75–104.
2. Web Video for Dummies. Video Terminology. Available at http://www.webvideofordummies.com/videoterminology.html, Accessed December 14, 2010.
3. HRW. Using the Video Camera. Available at http://go.hrw.com/resources/go_ss/teacher99/toolkit/TOOLKT23.pdf, Accessed December 14, 2010.

tape

Impression Evidence: Patterns of Identity

Fingerprints I
The Intellectual Ingredients

9

Mark Twain's 1883 memoir, *Life on the Mississippi*, described how a murderer was identified by fingerprints. In a later book, *Pudd'n Head Wilson*—1893, he described a dramatic court trial that included fingerprint identification.

9.1 Introduction

This chapter is an introduction to finding fingerprints and developing them on-scene. A similar approach applies equally to developing prints in the laboratory, where procedures are performed under more controlled conditions. The purpose is to introduce students to the philosophy of fingerprint development, specifically to introduce the concept of adopting a reasoned, intellectual, and logical approach for finding and enhancing prints. The next chapter introduces and discusses specific print-developing techniques including when and where they should be used.

On June 24, 1895, Mark Twain was interviewed by a reporter from the *Elmira Advertiser* concerning a bloody hand print found at the scene of a murder. The quote is from the *Dallas Morning News* of July 2, 1895:

> "Elmira, N.Y., June 23.—Mark Twain was found at Quarry farm today, where he is resting quietly preparatory to taking his lecture tour around the world. He was asked what he thought of the hand-print found at the Henry house and what similarity it bore to the bloody hand mystery solved by Pudd'n-Head Wilson.
>
> "He said he had not read the latest phases of the Henry murder, but when shown the account in a newspaper of finding a bloody handprint on the basement door he said: "They seem to be in doubt as to which of the two made that hand-print, the assassin or the murdered man. I should think that would be easy to determine. They have a man under arrest whom they suspect, as I understand it, and I should think they could easily get a hand-print from him and compare it with the bloody hand-print and then determine whether he made it or not. There is nothing in this case that you or I can suggest that would not suggest itself to anybody's mind. Thus far that hand-print has not a value, because it is not determinable whose it is. You don't know whether it is valuable until you know that it is not the hand of the dead man. If it is the hand of a survivor it can have some value.
>
> "If it is clear that hand-print, so the marking of the ball of the thumb, for instance, is distinct and can be followed, there can be a print taken from that and then enlarged by a pantographer ten or twenty times, so that there is no mistaking these lines, because they are clearly defined. Then unquestionably they can take as many thumb marks corresponding with those until they find the man that left that hand-print there. That is sure. When a thumb mark is magnified the difference in the lines can be easily detected between ten or twenty thumbs—that is, you can find as many innocent people as you please in that way, but there is only one guilty. There is only one thumb in the world that will correspond with the print that that man left there. When they have found the man who made that thumb print they will know him sure without any question at all, and there will be no need of an expert to determine whose hand made the print.

> "When you have got that far you have not arrived at any goal yet. It will be pretty strong evidence, but there is a suggestion that there could have been several persons there and you want to know who it was that killed the man. But whether he is guilty or not you won't know. It if were known that there were no persons present but the assassin and the victim you know you have got the assassin. It is well worth while to follow that clew if they can find that the dead man did not leave that print there. If that body is not decomposed it will be an easy matter to find out whether he made the hand-print or not. If he did not, that narrows the murder down considerably. I do not say that the bloody hand-print can convict anybody, but it can help. It will be remembered that in 'Pudd'n-Head Wilson' it was proved the bloody finger prints on the dagger were not left there by the accused person in court, but were made by a person in court, but not accused [1]."

Twain demonstrated not only more than a superficial understanding of fingerprints and how to match them to an individual, but also an understanding of the value of physical evidence: that jumping to conclusions about the probative value of evidence may not be correct. In fact, he was among the first to write about fingerprints and their value in solving crimes, seen in his 1883 memoir *Life on the Mississippi.*

As Twain understood, fingerprints are fairly ubiquitous. Although in *Pudd'n Head Wilson* he used a bloody hand print as a twist in the story, it was an example of a class of prints found at scenes, patent prints, that is visible. In addition to patent prints, fingerprints are manifested at scenes in other ways: latent prints that are invisible to the naked eye and plastic prints, a form of patent print imbedded into a malleable substance such as chewing gum or wet soap. A problem for on-scene investigation is locating probative, latent prints. Although patent prints should be obvious, rendering them useful still requires a well-considered strategy with respect to applying the appropriate science.

Enhancing prints at the scene or in the print laboratory is deceptively easy. The term "deceptively" refers to on-line and other published recipes, commercial vendors, workshops, and on-the-job training. The workshops (info-shops) "teach" techniques in a pseudoscientific forum. The result is that attendees and students leave with a false sense of confidence; they believe they know everything there is to know about using that technique at scenes, even though they have little or no understanding of the underlying science or its limitations. Additionally, commercial manufacturers sell premade kits, sometimes with instructions, to anyone willing to buy them. Thus, there is no barrier to the curious investigator to using them at scenes without rigorously validating the technique. Finally, the Internet offers advice, suggestions, and procedures from self-professed current and ex-practitioners who "share" their expertise to anyone who cares to spend the time to read. Here, too, no barrier exists precluding anyone from using those techniques at a scene.

Fingerprints are fragile, and the techniques used to visualize them can easily damage friction ridge detail. For example, powder dusting is commonly employed, but a heavy or a not-so-gentle technique can affect the quality of the resulting print, as can over dusting [2]. The responsibility of the team leader and/or laboratory scientist is to preserve the original print detail as it was left at the scene. Thus, using new or novel techniques without employing a scientific approach, understanding the underlying science, doing an in-depth validation, and being blind proficiency tested is risky. The result of forging ahead without appropriate knowledge, training, validation, and proficiency testing enhances the possibility of destroying the evidence.

9.2 A Reasoned, Scientific Approach

Fingerprint development has a long history, an evolution if you will, in scientific terms. Scientists and investigators have spent decades devising methods to develop and enhance fingerprints at scenes and in latent print laboratories. The target of these investigations, the components of the print residue, has been the subject of scientific inquiry, its purpose being to develop methods that give greater resolution and increased sensitivity. The result has culminated in a menu of methods.

For the practicing scene scientist/investigator, new methods can appear complex. They are increasingly made to take advantage of sophisticated chemical, immunological, physical, and imaging technologies, so it is no wonder that students and scene scientists/investigators perhaps prefer dusting and its variations for developing prints on certain surfaces. Certainly dusting has a long history in fingerprint development [3–5]. It is easy and the results are nearly instantaneous understandably. Investigators prefer methods with which they are comfortable. And it could be one reason why they might be reluctant to embrace new technology. This plus unfamiliarity with new techniques, skepticism concerning how well they perform versus those in their comfort zone, and insecurity about the underlying science might be other reasons. Also, the newer techniques are more complex and increasingly require more rigorously controlled conditions.

9.2.1 On-Scene Printing: Menu-Driven versus Logic-Based Approaches

Like crime scene searches, the current fingerprint paradigm is a menu-driven approach designed for nonscientists to know when to employ methods in order to minimize the errors. Certainly this approach has merits born from a wealth of experience and success. In fact, if this paradigm had not been successful, the number of criminals apprehended and successfully prosecuted would be incrementally less impressive. Success certainly speaks loudly, but there is an important flip side to that coin.

Should there have been more successes? Could more criminals have been apprehended? Yes! And, were all the probative prints that could have been found and developed actually developed? The answer, certainly, is no! How many prints at those crimes were treated improperly, how many unsuccessful attempts were there versus those that were successful, and how many unsuccessful ones should have been successful? These questions, of course, have no answers because the data does not exist. Although fingerprint development methods are mostly laboratory-based, many have on-scene applications.

Certainly, there are reasons, good and bad, for developing/enhancing prints in the field, and whether this is the best course of action depends on several factors: the dynamics of the investigation, the location of the prints, the surface on which the prints lie, and so on. The decision to process prints on-scene, however, should be determined by scene-related constraints even though the natural tendency is to develop as many at the scene as possible. But the reasons for processing on-scene make sense only in the context of the investigation. The overriding concern should be the value of the information if development attempts at the scene are unsuccessful. In other words, is it critical for developing to be done at the scene or should the evidence be collected and packaged and taken to the laboratory? Will the delay impair the timeline of the investigation?

Certainly, there is always the item that cannot be taken easily to the laboratory; a doorjamb or a window that was the entry point to the scene. And then, there is the necessity to find and develop prints where the perpetrator likely touched. The decision process is illustrated in Figure 9.1. At an outdoor crime scene, it might be better to collect and package all transferrable printable evidence and take it to the laboratory, especially if the weather is deteriorating and protecting the evidence at the scene is impossible.

Another consideration is time. All scenes have time constraints, some more than others. But if processing the scene quickly is critical, for whatever reason, then regardless of the logic for developing prints on-scene, transportable, fingerprint evidence should go to the laboratory. Dusting a doorjamb for prints is easy and fast, but prints on other surfaces can present special problems, and if possible these should be handled in the laboratory.

Once the decision is made to process prints on-scene, a cascade of decisions logically follows: surface, resources, environment, age of the print, amount and quality of print residue present, knowledge, experience, technology, and technology limitations are among the most important. Most investigators lean toward dusting, believing this to be the best, easiest, and quickest way to obtain results. For a given circumstance, that may, in fact, be true. But dusting blindly is wrong. In fact, no print development should occur without properly considering the nuances of the scene. The diagram in Figure 9.2 illustrates the considerations that should promulgate decisions. The list above can be placed into one of three classes: the scene, the tools, and logic.

9.2.1.1 The Scene

The scene presents scene scientists/investigators with their first set of considerations including the surface on which prints lie, the environment at the scene, and the age of the print (length of time) it was in that environment. Each is discussed below.

9.2.1.2 Surface Characteristics

The current print-processing paradigm considers surface as the most critical first consideration in developing latent fingerprints, a reasonable approach. An example concerns how a particular surface is protected. Is it painted, and if so, is the paint matte, semigloss,

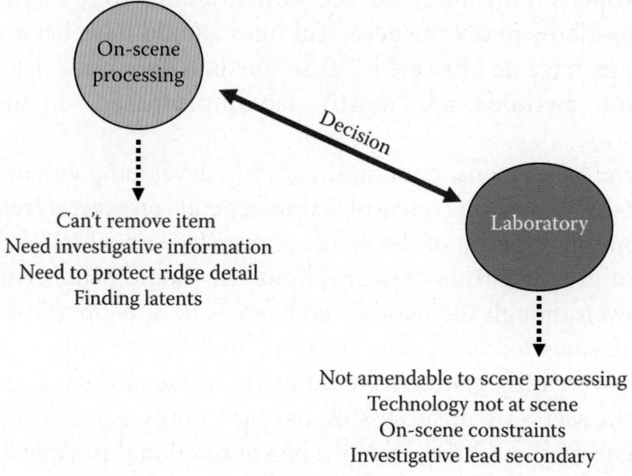

Figure 9.1 On-scene or laboratory processing.

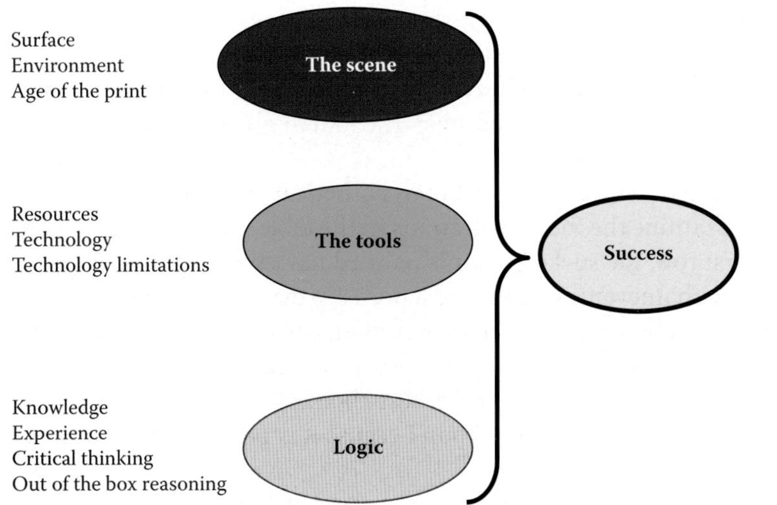

Figure 9.2 Fingerprint development strategy.

gloss, or is it one of the newer finishes with texture? Does the paint have additives such as antimildew chemicals and how do these affect print processing? Is the surface itself smooth or textured, and if textured, how much depth is there?

Porosity is another consideration. Is the surface paint porous, nonporous, or semiporous? How will a highly porous surface affect print development? Another consideration is color; is it dark, light, or somewhere in-between? What development methods are applicable if it is a dark color? The final decision is technology. Which is best suited to give successful results: physical, chemical, imaging, or topology acquisition? What resources are needed?

Table 9.1 illustrates a logical approach for developing fingerprints on a doorjamb. The doorjamb surface has four different possible surface treatments. Each row represents different sets of decisions: texture, porosity, and developing techniques (columns 2–4, respectively). To simplify and illustrate the process, the table considers only surface issues, which is only the first step in determining how to best find, develop, and preserve fingerprints at the scene. Photography, lifting, and preservation each requires a separate set of decisions.

Table 9.1 Logic of a Fingerprint Development Strategy

Color/Paint	Texture	Porosity	Developing Alternatives
Navy/semigloss	Slight texture and uneven surfaces	Nonporous	Powders, superglue fuming, wet chemistry, chemical imaging, SPR, powder suspensions. Topology acquisition.
White paint—matt	Slight texture and uneven surfaces	Nonporous, semiporous	Powders, superglue fuming, wet chemistry, chemical imaging, SPR, powder suspensions. Topology acquisition.
Bare wood	Grained texture and uneven surfaces	Porous	Powders, Ninhydrin, DFO, powder suspensions, magnetic powder, chemical imaging.

Note: DFO, 1,8-diazafluren-9-one; SPR, small particle reagent.

Consider the first column, which shows different ways in which a surface can be protected: painted or not? The second column shows textures for each of the surface types: smooth, lightly textured, more heavily textured? The third shows the porosity for each surface: porous, nonporous, semiporous? The fourth gives alternatives for how to develop the prints on that particular surface.

Each row illustrates a different set of hypothetical characteristics to illustrate the decision process. Examine the four illustrations in the table under the first column title. Left to right in the first row, the surface color is painted navy blue with a semigloss paint. It has a slight texture with uneven surfaces, and a porosity that is either nonporous or semiporous. The last column offers print development alternatives. As expected, print development redundancies show up—dusting, superglue fuming, and so on—and they show up in three of the four examples. But are these the best choices? What other choices are there? Bare wood is the oddball surface in the group because it is porous, which means possibly a different set of development choices.

This is a doorjamb, so deciding whether to develop prints on-scene is a no decision because it will likely not be cut out and taken to the latent print laboratory. Still, there are decisions to make. And before deciding on a specific method, serious thought should go into trying to ascertain what the final results will be with each technique in this specific circumstance.

9.2.1.3 Environmental Conditions and the Age of the Print

The environment and the length of time a print is exposed to that environment affects decisions concerning a development strategy. No one questions that heat, humidity, pollution, UV radiation, dust, and time affect the print quality. It is important to understand why and how the environment plays a critical role in the integrity of the fingerprint residue because it can dictate which method has the best chance of success. If it is hot and humid and the surface is one of those discussed above, dusting or superglue fuming may have the best chance of success. If the temperature is moderate, 50°F, and the humidity is between 20% and 90%, the same may be true. If it is winter and the humidity is low and the house overheated, the print could be dry (dehydrated print residue) and unresponsive to traditional dusting or even superglue fuming. The scene scientist/investigator must realize this is a possibility. Studies designed to explore the superglue fuming reaction in eccrine prints has shown that lactate in the residue is the initiator of the superglue fuming reaction. In fact if lactate is gone, whether because of excess heat (>50°C) or from UV radiation, superglue fuming will not work [6].

9.2.1.4 The Tools

After considering the scene, the environment, and the age of the print, the next decision concerns the tools necessary to do the job properly. This decision balances what can be done at the scene against the tools available. In other words, if the tools available in the laboratory will give superior developed prints, should we attempt to develop them on-scene using a technique that could give less than optimum results, but results nevertheless? Normally, laboratory work is done in a more controlled environment, which should lead to better results. This decision is also about resources. A general rule of thumb: never sacrifice quality for expediency without a top notch reason.

9.2.1.5 Resources

Success may well depend on available resources. If the crime scene unit can only dust, alternative strategies are nearly nonexistent. If the unit can only dust at the scene but has additional capabilities at the latent print laboratory, such as superglue fuming or other chemical methods, there is at least an alternative. If the laboratory resources are more expansive, the prognosis is for a better chance of success and a better quality result.

9.2.1.6 Technology and Its Limitations

Technology is slowly but surely taking control of the scientific aspect of crime scene investigations. This raises the issue of who should be applying it at scenes. All technology has limitations that must be understood. However, scene investigators learn how to use the technology much like actors learn how to act—method acting—but most have little understanding of the science underlying the technology. This means that there is little understanding of when the science will be successful and when it will not. That said this does not imply that most applications of science in the field are unsuccessful. They have been successful because they are mostly employed in routine situations for which the technology has been developed. However, circumstances crop up where applying a particular technique may not work as planned, if at all. Such failure might not be understood by the investigator, and when that happens failures are bound to follow. The inclination is to blame failure on the quality of the print rather than on an inappropriately applied technology.

In the doorjamb scenario above, superglue fuming of the navy-colored doorjamb might seem like an appropriate method. The result will be an off-white print against a dark blue background. Not a bad choice. But how does someone superglue fume a doorjamb? One approach might be to use a fuming wand or a dome, two similar techniques. Generally, blindly fuming with a wand or a dome is fundamentally a nonscientific exercise. First, wand fuming is not controlled properly; cyanoacrylate vapors are concentrated unevenly across the print. Second, the wands and/or domes do not control the humidity, which varies widely from day-to-day, season-to-season, and location in the country. The result is a print that can be simultaneously over and underdeveloped or not developed at all.

After fuming, the developed print is visualized, which is an enhancement process that becomes a choice among doing nothing except photography, dusting, or staining using a fluorescent dye (a recent fluorescent fuming method using the dome has been introduced). Fluorescent methods are inherently more sensitive but they too have their problems. Dusting is certainly safer because if the fumed print is on a semiporous surface, it might absorb the fluorescent stain creating a fluorescent background that competes with the print's fluorescence. In lieu of fuming, an alternative is dusting with a fluorescent, white, or aluminum flake powder. They will contrast well with the navy blue paint. However, black dusting powder might be a better choice because the fumed print is already off-white on a dark (navy) background, so dusting with a black powder would contrast with the color of the polycyanoacrylate-developed print. An alternative to superglue fuming, might be to employ lanthanide chemistry which stains the oils in the residue to give a fluorescent print. This, too, might be a good choice if the surface circumstances are appropriate. But if the background reacts with or absorbs the lanthanide reagents, there is, again, a risk that background fluorescence will compete with that of the developed print.

The examples above reinforce the idea that these decisions are not easy and that an unthinking selection of a print development technique can lead to problems and failure. The goal is to capture the print as it was left at the scene. If it was pristine at the scene, then it should be pristine after developing. If it was partial with some smudging, then that same detail should be reflected in the developed print.

Table 9.2 lists other factors to consider when developing prints. Each column represents what must be done. The categories across the top represent possible action items. For example, in the Photography column, the investigator must decide whether fingerprint photography takes place at the scene or in the laboratory or both and whether establishing, midrange, or close-up (ideally all three) shots are necessary. Certainly, the camera settings should guarantee that the captured image representing the print close-up image has sufficient forensic detail (focus and size). Photographic decisions, especially in digital single lens reflex (SLR) photography, are forgiving because experimenting is part of the process. However, lifting is an unforgiving process and a poor lift is inexcusable. There are few second chances.

9.2.1.7 Logic

This refers to the intellectual ingredients necessary to locate fingerprints leading to an eventual successful development and lift. This is as much an intellectual exercise as it is physical, and having the best technology does not guarantee the success. Also, in addition to knowing how to use the technology, the scene scientist/investigator must know where and when to employ it. Successfully finding probative prints involves a myriad of skills, the most important being logic, experience and, of course, knowledge. Scene logic is a soup of essential skills, some innate, others born from knowledge and experience. Understanding the scene environment and the nature of the crime gives experience, critical thinking, and thinking out-of-the-box a reasoned approach to an effective strategy. This is the only formula for success.

Table 9.2 Additional Factors in Developing Prints

Developing Prints	Photography	Lifting	Transporting
Scene/laboratory decision	Determined by decision to develop at the scene or in the laboratory	Determined by decision to develop at the scene or in the laboratory	Lifting/packaging/ preservation techniques
Surface, color, experience, resources, environment, age DFO (1,8-diazafluren-9-one)	Photographic: establishing, midrange, close-up, filters	Not relevant	Not relevant
Porous Surface	Decision of which photos to take (establishing/ midrange/close-up): Choices include exposure (*f*/stop, shutter speed, ISO, metering, white balance)	Print protection	Packaging
Superglue fuming, amino acid chemistry, lipid chemistry, imaging, heating		Tape, gel, gelatin lifter, casting, superglue fuming	
Nonporous Surface		Lift card/contrast	
Superglue fuming, solid-state acquisition, corrosion chemistry, powder dusting, imaging, fluorescent, or nonfluorescent techniques	Other decisions: contrast, fluorescent techniques, and so on		

9.2.1.8 Knowledge of the Science

Simply knowing how to investigate crime scenes, employing critical thinking and using logic is not enough to guarantee success in the field. The missing ingredients are knowing which techniques are available for developing fingerprints and understanding how they work in specific circumstances. Knowing and understanding the dynamics of crime scene investigation are additional ingredients for understanding how evidence "talks" and why this translates into knowing the likely location of evidence, for example, fingerprints. An open window at a burglary scene should attract attention and although it may or may not have been how the burglar got into the scene or left it, the mere fact it is there warrants investigation. Maybe it was already open, but other evidence such as footprints in the dirt outside the window or the dry residue prints on the floor under the window might raise its importance up a notch. Areas at the scene where a struggle took place may lead to fingerprints on objects or on the floor. Other telltale signs might lead to places or objects a perpetrator touched: A weapon on the floor, a smashed lamp, a knife, a fork, drinking vessels, doorjambs and windows at entrance and egress points, and so on.

9.2.1.9 Experience

Suffice to say that experienced scene scientists/investigators are better at developing and finding prints than a novice or a student. The subject above gives examples. Experience also rules when it comes to employing science and using technology. Understanding the science—experience with it—is critical.

9.2.1.10 Critical Thinking

This is the process of assessing and digesting the information the scene presents and then distilling it so that the probative evidence pops out and speaks. The language is one that criminalists and experienced investigators understand.

- An open window may or may not be related, and if the former, developed fingerprints (why develop them in the first place?) on the windowsill are irrelevant.
- The area of a struggle will say that someone fell onto the floor and that there might be usable prints.
- Bloodstains on the floor in the kitchen might be significant.
- Eating utensils might have prints that can be important.
- Bloodstains in the kitchen might be irrelevant, if they occurred because the deceased suffered a lacerated a finger while chopping onions—check the body for recent finger wounds (the medical examiner might decide this is a defensive wound).
- A partially chopped onion on the cutting board, some of it mixed with a drop of blood, and a bloody knife lying on the floor should scream "No relevance."
- A bloodstain out of context from other blood at the scene should also scream: "Perp injured." Certainly the blood itself is a critical piece of evidence, but it is likely not the only evidence in that area.

9.2.1.11 Out-of-the-Box Reasoning

This is different from critical thinking, albeit an extension of it. Few individuals process information like this because it is a process of thinking critically and then translating that into an investigative strategy leading directly to the most probative evidence. It is also a process of marrying seemingly unrelated information and developing a hypothesis of what happened. The illustration of the "lone, out-of-place" bloodstain is an example. In Chapter 1, a bloody palm print led to the successful prosecution of a murder even though experienced crime scene investigators ignored it because they failed to understand how it related to the overall context of the crime. Such thinking involves more than experience. It is, in fact, a mind that works on a different level, one that creates order from chaos. These individuals "see" evidentiary links and how they fit together. Others use their experience to approximate it. It is a gift.

References

1. Available at: http://www.twainquotes.com/interviews/FingerprintInterview.html, Accessed November 4, 2010.
2. J. D. James, 1991. Anthony pounds and Brian Wilshire, obliteration of latent prints. *J. Forensic Sci.* 36(5):1386.
3. R. D. Olsen, 1978. Chapter V—Latent fingerprint powder techniques. In *Scott's Fingerprint Mechanics*. Charles C. Thomas, Springfield, IL, pp. 209–240.
4. H. C. Lee and R. E. Gaensslen, 2001. Chapter 4—Methods of latent fingerprint development. In *Advances in Fingerprint Technology*, 2nd Edition. Eds. H. C. Lee and R. E. Gaensslen. Boca Raton, FL: CRC Press, pp. 108–113.
5. C. Champod, C. Lennard, P. Margot, and M. Stoilovic, 2004. Chapter 4—Fingerprint detection techniques. In *Fingerprints and Other Ridge Skin Impressions*. Boca Raton, FL: CRC Press, pp. 136–138.
6. G. DePaoli, S. A. Lewis Sr., E. L. Schuette, L. A Lewis, R. M. Connaster, and T. Farkas, 2010. Photo- and thermal-degradation studies of select eccrine fingerprint constituents. *J. Forensic Sci.* 55(4):962–969.

Fingerprints II
On-Scene Considerations

10

The Koala has fingerprints that are so similar to the human fingerprint that it is almost impossible to tell them apart because of the pattern, shape and size of the ridges [1].

10.1 Introduction

Fingerprints occur in three forms: latent (invisible), patent (visible), and impression or plastic, a subcategory of patent prints because the ridge detail impressed into a malleable material is visible. Champod et al. [2] categorize these as positive, negative, and indented, respectively. Once thought to be useless and without probative value, smudged prints, a subcategory of latent and patent prints, have little or no discernable friction ridge detail for comparative purposes. As science increasingly discovers better and more sophisticated tools to analyze fingerprints, smudged prints (e.g., DNA extracted from smudged prints) may play an increasingly important role as investigative tools.

Figure 10.1 illustrates broadly the types of fingerprints found at scenes of crimes and what must be done in order to develop them. This can involve physical techniques as simple as powder dusting or chemical treatment as complex as superglue fuming or lanthanide chemistry. It might also simply require using a special light source that causes the fingerprint residue to fluorescence; an example is an argon or Hd:YAG laser [3] or an ALS.

A patent print may require nothing more than photography followed by using a method to lift the print. On the other hand, a partial print might require a well-thought-out strategy for enhancing that which is visible and that which is latent. If the evidence is transportable, other techniques are available in the laboratory where the conditions are controlled better. If the print is plastic, that is, impressed into a soft surface, the scene scientist/investigator might decide to cast it using a silicone-based material. The resulting cast can be enhanced in the laboratory. The foregoing was purposely broad as a way to emphasize that the print types that populate scenes can unleash a myriad of development of choices, many of which can be confusing to a student or a novice investigator.

Career crime scene investigators have their personal routines for developing fingerprints. Brown [4] has written that photography of patent and plastic prints is sufficient to capture the detail necessary to make comparisons:

> Of the three types of fingerprints, visible fingerprints can be photographed directly, and impression fingerprints can usually be photographed under special lighting conditions. It is only the invisible latent fingerprints that are difficult to photograph. They must first be made visible.

However, following Brown's [4] advice could lead to failure to adequately capture potentially probative evidence. Patent prints are unique. They exist because of contamination from an exogenous source, such as blood, oils, cosmetics, and so on. Using photography as the sole means of archiving these prints captures only that which is

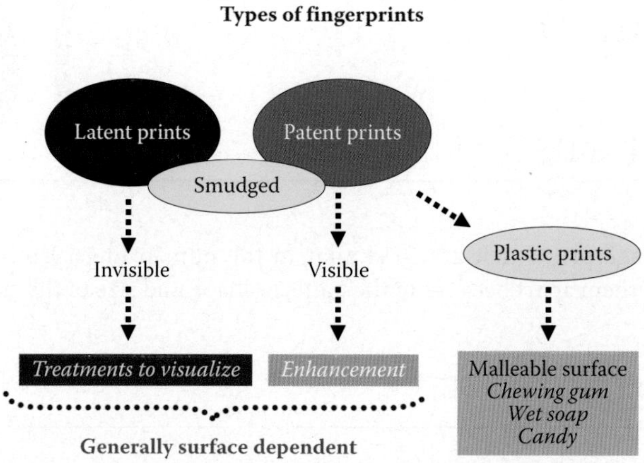

Types of fingerprints

Latent prints
Patent prints
Smudged
Invisible
Visible
Plastic prints
Treatments to visualize
Enhancement
Malleable surface
Chewing gum
Wet soap
Candy
Generally surface dependent

Figure 10.1 Categories of fingerprints at crime scenes. (Adapted from Bandey, H. L. and Hardy, T. 2006. The Powders Process Study 3: Evaluation of fingerprint powders on textured surfaces and U-PVC. *HOSDB Fingerprint and Footwear Forensics Newsletter*, Publication No. 67/08.)

visible and can miss that which is latent. It is critical to understand that patent prints might also have a latent part. Enhancing these should include a well-thought-out strategy designed to enhance all potential ridges that are present in the deposited fingerprint. An example of the thought process required will be discussed in the section about patent prints (Section 10.8).

Understanding how to develop fingerprints at the scene or in the laboratory requires an understanding not of how fingerprints form in the uterus but of the chemistry of the fingerprint residue left at the scene. This means understanding the origin of the fingerprint residue.

10.2 The Glandular Origin of Fingerprints

Fingerprints at scenes of crimes result from someone touching a surface and leaving a residue. The chemical components of that residue are a mixture of secretions from sweat glands present in the skin as well as from exogenous contaminants—blood, oils, cosmetics, and so on. Although this seems rather simple because the components of glandular secretions are known, the fact is that it is complicated. The glands necessary to form the fingerprint residue are not all present on the friction ridge skin of the hands or feet, and the fingerprint residue at the scene may also be contaminated by exogenous sources, that is, substances not manufactured by the body.

Generally, fingerprint residue contains primarily water soluble and/or insoluble substances. The glands secreting directly onto the friction ridge skin are sweat glands or sudiferous glands, of which there are two types: apocrine and merocrine (relating to or produced by glands that make secretions without cell damage or disintegration). Both have myoepithelial cells that lie between the gland cells and the underlying basal lamina. These cells contract, that is, squeeze, causing discharges on the surface. These are the secretions found on the skin [5].

Sweat glands play specific roles in the body. The "apocrine glands" are scent glands and respond to emotional stress. They begin functioning at puberty and produce moisture during emotional experiences such as when someone is upset, frightened, or experiences pain. They are also active when a person is sexually stimulated. In adults, the apocrine glands are most numerous in the armpits (axillae), groin associated with hair follicles and in the regions around the nipples (areoles). Historically, secretions from these glands have not been forensically important, especially with respect to locating latent fingerprints at the crime scene. They are viscous and cloudy and potentially acted on by bacteria to produce a noticeable odor [6]. It is unfortunate that these secretions have not found a routine forensic utility because their location suggests a potential forensic role in sexual assault investigations.

The primary merocrine glands on the skin, the eccrine sweat glands, are present throughout the body and are more numerous than apocrine glands. The approximately three million eccrine glands in an adult are most numerous on the palms and soles—approximately 3000 glands/in. Their densities range from 60/cm^2 on the thigh to 350/cm^2 on the forehead [7]. They appear as coiled structures lying deep within the second dermal layer of the skin, the dermis. The coil runs up through the upper dermal layer, the epidermis, and empties onto the skin surface, specifically the epidermal ridges of the friction ridge skin. They are not associated with hair follicles. The coiled portion of the gland is closed at its deep end and is lined with sweat-producing cells that respond to elevated body temperature due to environmental heat or physical exercise and produce profuse sweating on hot days or when a person is physically stressed. The moisture is also noticeable on the palms and soles when someone is emotionally stressed. These secretions include several substances that have forensic value with respect to fingerprint development.

Another gland that contributes to fingerprint residue is the sebaceous gland, also known as a holocrine gland (secretions derived from the substance of the gland itself). The secretions come from the oily substances of broken cells, sebaceous cells, which produce globules of a fatty material that accumulate inside the cell causing them to swell and burst. The resulting mixture of fatty material and cellular debris on the skin is called "sebum," and is found on all areas of the skin except the friction ridge skin. Sebum is most prominent on the forehead and areas where there is hair.

The secretions of the eccrine, holocrine, and sebaceous glands form the fingerprint residue left at the crime scene. Unlike eccrine glands, sebaceous glands are not found on the friction ridge detail skin—palms of the hands, soles of the feet, fingertips, toes—but are found on other regions of the body with higher concentrations on the head, neck hair, and so on. The apocrine glands do not secrete as much material as the other two, and, though they are located on all areas of the body, they are most prominently associated with hair follicles in the groin. Importantly, sebaceous and apocrine glands are associated with hair follicles but eccrine glands are not.

Sebaceous secretions become a component of fingerprint residue when an individual touches regions of the skin where these glands are plentiful, such as the head, cheeks, and forehead. The eccrine glands are located on all regions of the body but are particularly plentiful on the friction ridge skin—palms of the hands and soles of the feet. By definition, they will always contribute to the fingerprint residue. From a practical perspective, apocrine secretions contribute to the print residue only if someone touches the groin area.

For the investigator, the following discussion may seem academic and not particularly relevant to how one successfully locates fingerprints at the crime scene. In order to properly and successfully develop fingerprints at the scene or in the laboratory, the scene scientist/investigator must understand the chemistry of the fingerprint residue and how and why it interacts or reacts with various surfaces and its immediate environment.

As mentioned, fingerprint residue contains two broad categories of chemicals: those that are soluble in water and those that are not. The water-soluble substances arise primarily from eccrine glands found on the friction ridge skin. The water-insoluble substances come primarily from the sebaceous glands found on skin populated by hair follicles. A third gland, the apocrine gland also secretes substances that may be a component of the fingerprint residue, but, mostly, these secretions are in lesser amounts and traditionally are not considered forensically important. The subject of the chemical components of fingerprints has been discussed in-depth by several authors; the primary most recent works include those by Champod et al. [1] and Ramotowski [8], and earlier by Knowles [9].

The schematic in Figure 10.2 illustrates the origin of the endogenous fingerprint residue and why it contains a mixture of each of the body's major secretory glands. The contributory substances shown represent the primary classes of substances of interest. Students and novice investigators should not lose sight of the fact that the diagram is a snapshot of the complex nature of the residue mixture present. In fact, each gland secretes many more substances.

As illustrated, each gland can contribute to the overall chemistry of residue. The relative contribution of each depends on the habits, stress level, and physical exertion of the person leaving the print. If someone continually runs his/her fingers through the scalp or habitually touches the face or forehead, his/her prints should have an abundance of sebaceous

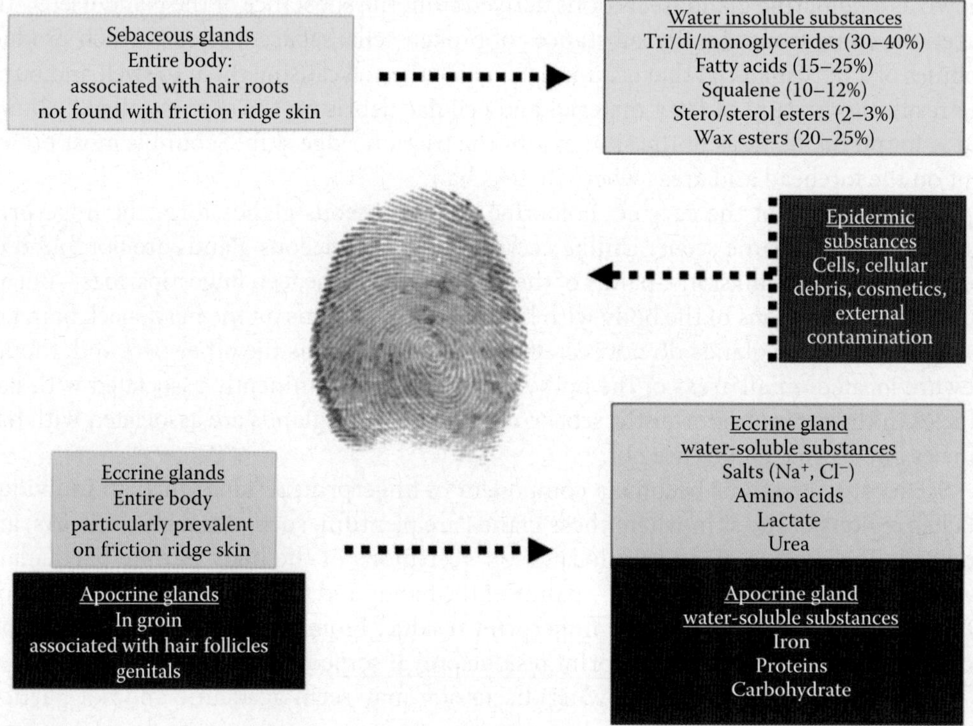

Figure 10.2 Origin of fingerprint residue.

secretions. If s/he is fastidious and is continually washing, the prints might be cleaner, that is, they should have a relatively smaller amount of sebaceous oils. If, during a sexual assault, the assailant touches their or the victim's groin region and then subsequently touches something at the scene, say, a knife, the residue on the handle of the knife should have an elevated level of apocrine secretions.

From at least an academic perspective, it should be possible to determine the relative proportions of secretions that each gland contributes to the fingerprint by measuring the concentration of sebaceous, eccrine, and apocrine-specific substances. For example, delta 6 fatty acids have a sebaceous origin and lactate is one of the prominent constituents of eccrine secretions. Determining their ratio might provide information with respect to the relative contribution of each gland to the fingerprint. From an investigative perspective, with respect to developing useable prints, knowing the relative glandular contribution to fingerprint residue might allow a more precise development at the scene, although this is unlikely. More likely this would occur in the latent print laboratory. Certainly, at the scene, this will not be known *a priori*, and testing could ruin the print detail.

Wargacki et al. [10] believe that fingerprints consist of only 5% sebaceous secretions, which leads them to conclude that eccrine secretions comprise the bulk of the print residue. They speculate that eccrine secretions—lactate—initiate the superglue fuming print development reaction (discussed below) using the heat and humidity (H&H) method and that aged and otherwise-compromised latent fingerprints can be recovered using acetic acid or ammonia vapors [10].

10.3 Finding Fingerprints at Scenes: General Considerations

Latent and patent fingerprints can be anywhere and everywhere. The problem is locating those that are latent and then developing them. Transportable evidence that might have fingerprints can be taken to the latent print laboratory. Some prints will need to be developed at the scene (see Chapter 9).

Figure 10.3 offers suggestions where fingerprints might be at scenes. Certainly, it is a waste of time to memorize the list because the most important of these is one's imagination to the extent that one becomes the burglar (perpetrator). This is when a search for probative prints pays off. Essentially, this search is an intellectual exercise (see Chapter 9). The thought process might go something like this: "What would I touch if I were the scumbag who did this?"

Individual scene types (e.g., burglaries, homicides, sexual assaults, and so on) are not discussed per se, except to arson scenes which are considered more with respect to how heat affects the stability of fingerprint residue.

10.4 Fingerprint Development Strategies

Experienced investigators recognize that surface type dictates their approach toward developing fingerprints at the scene and in the laboratory. They apply techniques that work the best on certain surface types. General considerations of surface effects have been discussed in Chapter 9, and a logic-based decision process was suggested as a way to determine the most effective approach for developing fingerprints.

The Scene Is the Ultimate Guide

- Point of entry
  - Broken entry
    - Prints (including shoe prints)
      - Lock
      - Immediate surrounds
  - Window
    - Pieces of broken glass
      - May have blood
      - May have been tossed aside to conceal entry
    - Windowsill window jam
    - Tables used to support weight
    - Floor where burglar
- Trace the path
  - Where eaten/drink
    - Glass and china are good targets of prints
    - Can discard gloves
  - Light switches
  - Circuit breakers/fuses/light bulbs loosened
  - Areas where gloves were a hindrance
  - Toilet-flush lever
- Tools left behind
  - Flashlight batteries
  - Latex gloves
- General surfaces
- Fabrics
- Use your imagination …
- BE THE BURGLAR

Figure 10.3 Finding fingerprints at the scene.

Interestingly, most texts ignore "thought" as an integral part of the development strategy. They incorrectly assume that menu-driven approaches based almost entirely on whether the surface is porous, semiporous, or nonporous are sufficient. Some authors of crime scene investigation texts barely treat the subject. For instance, Lee et al. [11] write,

> Physical methods are used for any dry, non-porous surfaces like glass or plastic. (p. 137)

For dry and wet surfaces, they write,

> Chemical processing methods for latent fingerprints can be used on dry and wet surfaces. (p. 138)

And, for latent prints on porous surfaces, they caution,

> Latent prints on porous surfaces are visualized by the use of chemical methods. Because of the nature of the surface and the fact that the friction ridge secretions are dissolved into the surface, the chemical method chosen for visualization must react with the secretions and not the surface. (p.139)

Fisher [12] considers surfaces not as distinct topics but as broad entry-level discussions related to specific developing techniques. Gardner [13] goes into more detail than either Lee et al. [11] or Fisher [12], considering surfaces and the characteristics of porous surfaces, nonporous smooth and rough surfaces, and special surfaces. Fish et al. [14] discuss surfaces much like Fisher [12] but add a reference chart of techniques published by the Chesapeake Bay Division of the International Association of Identification (IAI) to guide investigators. They do not explain, however, how to use the techniques or the caveats involved with each [14]. The Chesapeake Bay Division of the IAI Website [15] lists reagents for use on various surface types: porous, nonporous, glass, plastic, wet, postcyanoacrylate, metal, adhesive tape, glossy paper, cartridge cases, raw wood, post-ninhydrin, and UV-induced. The Website has links to the specific techniques. Each method considers the pitfalls, formulations for the techniques they propose and safety concerns. It also offers a cascade for applying the method [15]. Fingerprint texts by Champod et al. [1] and Lee and Gaensslen [16] discuss surfaces in detail as well as techniques compatible with them. The most comprehensive compilation of development techniques is published by the British Home Office (Home Office Scientific Development Branch—HOSDB), whose manual titled *Manual of Fingerprint Development Techniques* covers fingerprint development techniques and surfaces for which they are compatible [17]. The manual presents workable schematics—cascades—for applying various techniques in sequence. It also gives safety considerations and reagent formulations. The manual considers surfaces in the context of the most compatible fingerprint techniques for that surface, and it presents charts outlining a sequential approach to print development, including primary, special, and secondary routes of analyses.

For students and novice investigators, choosing a development method for a specific application can be confounding, especially if significant resources are available. The following discussion considers the techniques student beginners should understand. They should also practice in a workshop/laboratory setting to gain hands-on aspects experience. Then they should use the methods in mock scene situations before moving on to more complicated and real-world applications.

10.4.1 Porous Surfaces

Paper evidence is important because successful fingerprint searches can pinpoint terrorist activities and forgeries and/or provide investigative information in major crime investigations. The end result can be a critical vehicle leading to a successful prosecution. Paper is usually defined as a porous surface and is usually treated as such for developing latent prints. However, there are caveats to this approach.

Because they absorb fingerprint residue, porous surfaces are treated differently from nonporous ones. Papers absorb fingerprint residue to varying degrees and amounts, which is determined by the paper's absorption characteristics as well as other absorption effectors such as humidity, temperature, and the environment. For this reason, porous surfaces can be classified into groups based on how quickly they absorb print residue.

Some papers are considered "hard" and often have a glossy sheen. They typically do not absorb fingerprint residue readily or quickly. An example is a glitzy magazine cover, where the choice of a particular fingerprint development method may be different from that for a high-absorptive paper in which residue penetrates easily and quickly.

10.4.1.1 Fingerprint Penetration into the Surface Matrix

Champod et al. [1] discuss the absorption of fingerprint residue into the porous matrix over time. Figure 10.4, adapted from their text, illustrates their thoughts with respect to the relative penetration of the various components of the fingerprint residue into the surface matrix.

Almog et al. [18] also examined porous surfaces and considered the depth and shape of the fingerprint residue penetrating porous material. Their study consisted of 15 types of paper using fluorescence microscopy of amino acids in the fingerprint residue. Their goal was to understand how residue penetration varied with porosity, smoothness, and density compared with the quality of the developed prints. Expectedly, penetration varied considerably from paper to paper according to the following progression (least to most): brown wrapping paper, smooth copier paper, the inner side of an envelope, writing paper, copier,

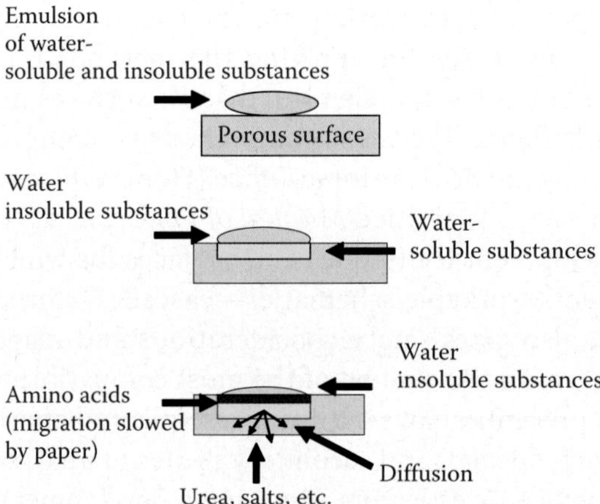

Figure 10.4 Aging of latent prints on porous surfaces. (Adapted from Champod, C., Lennard, C., Margot, P., and Stoilovic, M. 2004. *Fingerprints and Other Ridge Skin Impressions*. International Forensic Science and Investigation Series. Boca Raton, FL: CRC Press, p. 110. With permission.)

the outer side of an envelope, cotton paper, and postcard board. They discovered an inverse relationship between penetration and the smoothness of the paper and a direct relationship with porosity. With respect to quality, they obtained the best quality when the print residue penetrated the porous matrix to a depth of between 40 and 60 μm. Very shallow and very deep penetrations correlated with poorer quality prints. It is important to remember that they were looking at only the amino acids and water-soluble substances and not at the oily sebaceous secretions of the residue.

The study by Almog et al. [18] is nonetheless important because it changes how one approaches developing latent prints on porous surfaces. It divides porous surfaces into two broad categories, and the techniques used to develop prints on each are different. Those applied to smooth, nonporous surfaces are also appropriate for papers that have a low print residue penetration. Those that foster deeper penetration require a development strategy for developing the eccrine print components, for example, amino acids.

10.4.1.2 Fingerprint Development Cascades for Porous Surfaces

A fingerprinting cascade is a sequence of fingerprint development techniques performed such that each subsequent application of a technique makes visible additional latent prints. Texts on fingerprinting [1,16] and at least one crime scene text [13] as well as companies that sell reagents to law enforcement discuss and/or recommend sequential development strategies or cascades for developing fingerprints. These cascades are menu-driven, and their value lies in the fact that their developers have already considered the effect each step has on subsequent development techniques. Thus, the first step of the sequence, say, iodine fuming of a piece of paper, should not adversely affect the next step, such as treating the paper with ninhydrin. If a method does not permit follow-on testing, then the cascade stops.

Although menu-driven, with beginning and ending sequences, a cascade does not necessarily require carrying it to completion. If the first or second step gives high-quality prints and there is reason to believe other prints are not present, there may be no need to continue, and it can be stopped. In other words, the scene scientist/investigator uses logic, experience, and an understanding of the science and its limitations to decide when to stop the cascade. This is not guesswork, but a well-thought-out decision. Importantly, each step in the cascade must be documented photographically before proceeding to the next step in order to protect what has been developed.

Why discuss the cascade concept before introducing individual development techniques? The reason is to illustrate, for students at least, that each development technique must be thoroughly analyzed. For example, before using, say, lanthanide chemistry to develop a print on a wall, the scene scientist/investigator must understand its limitation (see Chapter 9).

Figure 10.5 shows a development cascade for porous surfaces; the format but not the specific content of the cascade was adapted from the text by Champod et al. [1]. The cascade considers porous surfaces in general. It does not take into consideration the work done by Almog et al. [18].

One can interpret the cascade in Figure 10.5 as follows. If the surface on which the print lies is dry, there are choices with respect to how to proceed. Step one is to use "optical detection," that is, attempt to detect the latent prints using a light source such as a flashlight or a laser or an alternate light source. Step two offers several choices.

- Path 1 uses lanthanide chemistry to develop the print; if this is the choice, the cascade stops and the fingerprints developed are fluorescent and visualized as "luminescence."
- Path 2 involves visualizing fingerprints using either 1,8-diazafluoren-9-one (DFO) or indanedione. This is followed by ninhydrin and a visual observation or "absorption mode" of the prints developed. Treatment of the ninhydrin prints with zinc or cadmium salts results in "luminescence." A final treatment could involve physical developer.
- Path 3 deviates from Path 2 by using a newer technique, "nano-gold deposition," after ninhydrin instead of treatment with zinc or cadmium salts. After the nano-gold deposition, the prints are treated with physical developer.

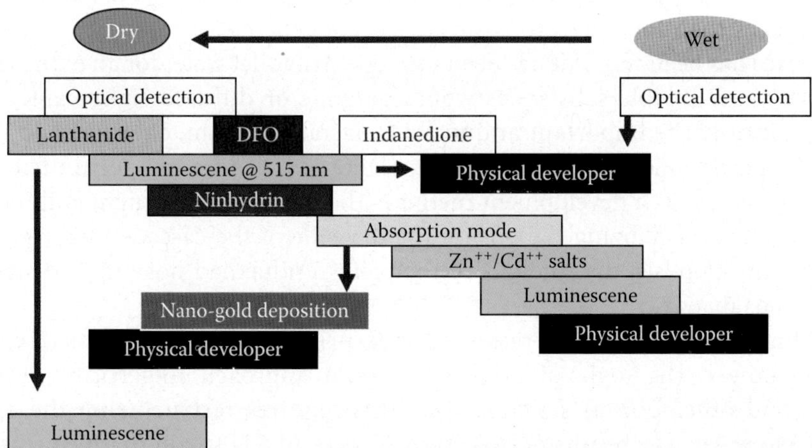

Figure 10.5 Suggested print development cascade for porous surfaces. (Adapted from Champod, C., Lennard, C., Margot, P., and Stoilovic, M. 2004. *Fingerprints and Other Ridge Skin Impressions*. International Forensic Science and Investigation Series. Boca Raton, FL: CRC Press, pp. 135, 148,155,159,163, 172 and 173.)

The cascade is a roadmap of possibilities, and the specific path used is determined by a number of factors. If the surface is wet, the approach would be to dry the matrix on which the prints are to be developed. The reason is that there are more choices for print development when the surface is dry than when it is wet. If this is impossible, there is only one path to follow: Optical observation followed by a physical developer.

For students, cascades can be confusing. Cascades are typically similar but not necessarily identical, as one scene scientist/investigator may disagree with specific techniques or their sequence in a particular cascade. This means that a particular cascade is not set in stone and can be changed; this might not be a function of correct or incorrect techniques but of individuals with different opinions on how to attack specific problems. For example, a seasoned examiner will recognize that information is omitted from the cascade above—iodine fuming. This is an older technique and not used as much (if at all) as it was in the past. But it remains a viable alternative for developing fingerprints on sensitive documents. A cascade can also change as new technology appears, such as the introduction of nanogold deposition in the example above.

Gardner [13] recommends an on-scene testing cascade for paper and suggests the following reagent sequence: DFO, ninhydrin, and silver nitrate (see discussion in Reference [13], pp. 229–234). Like the iodine-fuming method mentioned above, many modern latent print examiners do not recommend silver nitrate applications because it is not as sensitive a development method as some of the more recently developed techniques. That does not imply that it is useless, however. It detects the chloride ion, which is a prevalent chemical species in all fingerprints.

In one cascade, as discussed by Lee and Gaensslen [16], which is mislabeled, there is the suggestion that iodine fuming is an alternative. They correctly warn that fixing iodine fumed prints with 7,8-benzoflavone stops the cascade. However, if iodine fuming is not stopped, DFO is a logical next step: iodine fuming, DFO, laser excitation, ninhydrin, zinc chloride, laser excitation again, and, finally, silver nitrate. They also suggest physical developer is an alternative to the zinc/silver nitrate path (see discussion in Reference [16], pp. 154–160).

As suggested above, drying might be advantageous because there are more techniques for dry surfaces than for wet porous surfaces. This depends, of course, on how long the porous surface has been wet. If it has been immersed in toilet water for an extended period, most of the water-soluble substances would be gone or diffused significantly from the matrix, specifically the important amino acids, lactate, sodium, chloride, and urea. This means a cascade designed for porous surfaces (DFO or 1,2-indanedione, ninhydrin, and so on) would be useless as a development method. The oils, however, might still remain, and methods based on visualizing the oils on the dry side of the cascade might give fruitful results. This presupposes that the oils of the print residue had not diffused significantly into the porous matrix.

The Almog study—the penetration of fingerprint residue into the matrix of porous surfaces—changed the logic of how one should approach fingerprint development on papers and other porous surfaces [18]. This requires restructuring the cascade in Figure 10.5 to reflect the results of that study. Figure 10.6 is an alternative print development technique that takes into consideration the work done by Almog et al. [18], which makes more sense than the cascade in Figure 10.5. The cascade in Figure 10.6 gives print developers a better chance of success if they are attempting to develop prints on porous surfaces.

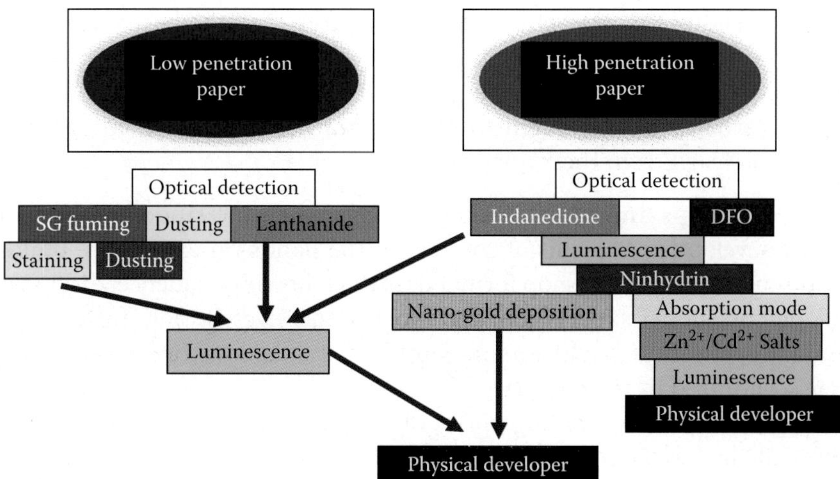

Figure 10.6 Alternative print development cascade for porous surfaces considering penetration into substrate.

Cascades can be confusing, and they might leave students and novice investigators scratching their heads wondering where to begin. In truth, cascades are relatively simple because they present the names and relative position that each technique occupies in the process. Knowing where each technique begins and what it might replace is part of the learning process. To that end, the following is an example of how to teach students to use cascades.

- Classroom discussion presents forensic theory, logic, and the chemistry of each step in the cascade. The discussion includes limitations of each technique and examples in real-life or mock scenes of how to perform the method.
- Workshops include demonstrations and hands-on practice with each technique individually and in a cascades.
- Challenging exercises marry the didactic and the practical.
- Mock crime scenes present challenging fingerprint situations in order to solidify what has been learned. These present situations that were not discussed in the classroom or in the workshops.

Students slowly absorb what they need to know in order to apply each technique and understand why it occupies a particular position in the cascade and how to think through applying it in the field.

Since the education of forensic scientists and crime scene investigators often follows different paths, one in the laboratory and the other in the field, it is necessary to conduct in-depth training for print development on porous and nonporous surfaces. Students need to appreciate what they are doing and why. They must understand what happens in the field and how that relates to laboratory testing.

10.4.1.2.1 Classroom Discussion The classroom discussion/lecture gives instructors the opportunity to discuss—teach—the science behind each development technique and its limitations. This is also the time to discuss when each might not be successful.

Still, experience shows that didactic instruction leaves even the best students confused about when and how to apply a specific technique, except powder dusting, in a given circumstance. This means that learning must continue in a hands-on environment because this is when students begin to understand how and when to apply the techniques. They also learn from their mistakes.

10.4.1.2.2 Workshops and Mock Scenes This is when the students begin to understand how to develop latent prints at the scene. The hands-on experience builds on the classroom discussion. The workshop format uses the following sequence: discussion, demonstration, practice under supervision, and mock scene investigation. Instructors discuss each technique again individually and in depth. After a demonstration, students practice while being scrutinized by instructors.

Workshop discussion covers fingerprint development cascades both from a historical perspective—the historical development of the techniques—and from a logical approach: why cascades exist, why techniques have a particular place in the cascade, and their limitations and use in the field.

At the end of the workshop, students have a "feel" for how these techniques evolved historically and how to apply them to develop latent prints. Through guided exercises, they learn that some surfaces might be resistant to print development. That is, they learn this by failing to develop prints on some surfaces under certain environmental conditions. Slowly, they understand which technique develops which components of the fingerprint residue and why.

10.4.2 Nonporous Surfaces

At most crime scenes nonporous surfaces are the most abundant, which makes them important candidates for developing latent fingerprints at crimes scenes. It is no wonder, then, that a great deal of effort has been put into researching new methods for developing fingerprints. The result is a dizzying array of techniques, the choice, of which can be confusing for students, novice investigators, and even experienced scene investigators. The following discussion covers the most important techniques applied to nonporous surfaces and the rationale for using them.

Before discussing how to obtain prints from nonporous surfaces, it is important that students and scene scientists/investigators understand what happens to prints on nonporous surfaces. The first consideration is what happens as the print ages. Figure 10.7 illustrates the aging process for nonporous surfaces [1].

As Figure 10.7 shows, the fingerprint residue slowly dehydrates over time, a process that is quick or slow depending on the surface characteristics and the environment to which the print is exposed. As the print ages, the emulsion that defines the print residue eventually dries leaving only a relatively nonreactive chemical species. Other effects, such as oxidation, pollution, and so on, that can affect the fingerprint residue and subsequent development of the prints are not shown in Figure 10.7.

The print residue is an emulsion that is normally stabilized by the glycerides present; however, when the emulsion dries, its aqueous phase is no longer present, which changes the chemical environment of the print residue. The residue is still present but it is no longer an emulsion. It is possible to rehydrate the emulsion using acetic acid or ammonia vapors [10,19]. Figure 10.8 summarizes what happens to the print emulsion as it dries.

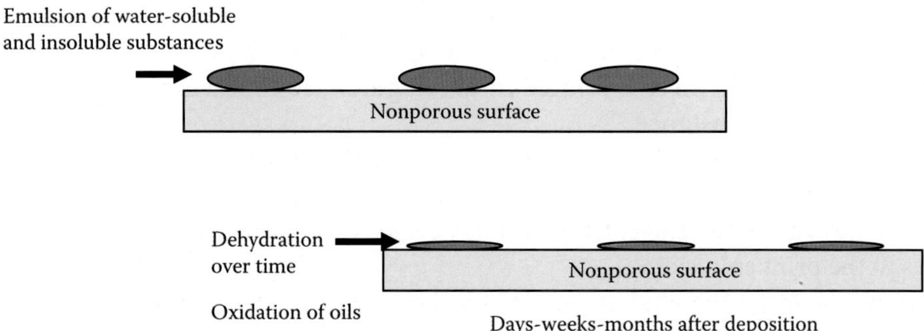

Figure 10.7 Aging of latent fingerprints on nonporous surfaces. (Adapted from *ODEC*, Animal fingerprints, http://www.odec.ca/projects/2004/fren4j0/public_html/animal_fingerprints.htm, accessed January 25, 2011. With permission.)

10.4.2.1 Powder Dusting

Scene detectives have used dusting powders to develop fingerprints since the nineteenth century, a trend that continues unabated. A recent study in Great Britain showed that approximately 50% of their on-scene fingerprint identifications came from dusted fingerprints [20]. Powders are the most ubiquitous technique for developing prints on non-porous and selected porous surfaces, and their widespread use should not come as a surprise as they are the staple of crime scene investigators. The thought of a crime scene detective dusting prints evokes the image of a black powder-laden brush swishing back and forth, bespectacled eyes leaning through a suspended black dust cloud to see ridge detail as it slowly emerges through the haze. The image is false, of course, but experience shows that the aftermath of processed crime scenes sometimes appears as though a black tornado has swept though the scene as walls, tables, and so on, have changed to black and gray.

Since the early days of black-only powder, a growing list of dusting powders has been available from commercial suppliers, complicating the selection process. Most powders are designed to solve surface-related problems such as texture, porosity, color, cleanliness, and so on. Luckily, the vast array of choices can be grouped into a relatively small number of categories depending on their chemical composition and particle size or

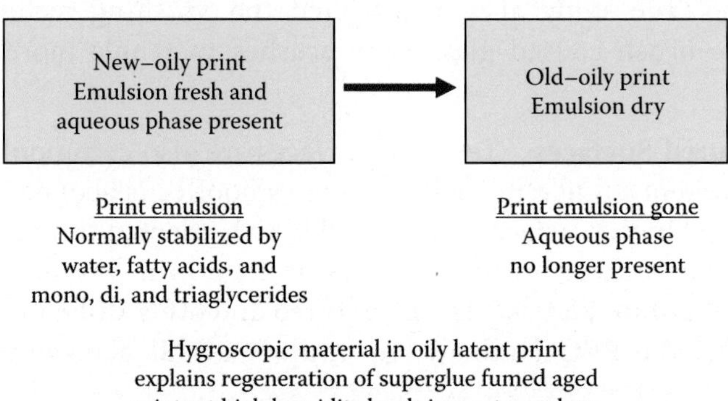

Figure 10.8 Effects of drying print emulsion.

shape. Each category has a specific formulation and characteristics that affect its interaction with the fingerprint residue, the surface, and thus its ultimate visibility. Unfortunately, though, there is limited in-depth guidance concerning which powder to use in a specific circumstance.

Many factors influence the success of powder dusting, some of which are not under the control of the scene scientist/investigator. These include the nature and condition of the surface, the clarity of the ridge detail and its age. All affect how well a particular powder adheres to the print emulsion.

Another factor is the equipment. Again, there is a plethora of powders and powder brushes from which to choose, and the reason why an examiner chooses one over the other is usually based on experience with a particular product, the nature of the surface, word of mouth, and preferences of a crime scene unit. Often the choice is not based on a rigorous evaluation of specific powder/brush combinations used for a specific application. Studies by the HOSDB addressed this issue. The work resulted in three publications, which are summarized in the following sections [21–23].

10.4.2.1.1 Fingerprint Brushes and Smooth Surfaces In the first study, the HOSDB evaluated brushes that British investigators used with aluminum powders on smooth surfaces. Although a large number of brushes are available, they generally fall into two major classes: "zephyr"- and "artist"-style fiber mountings [21]. Zephyr-style mountings are generally made for man-made brush fibers where the fibers are cut straight, long, and attached to a handle. The head of a fiber bundle in the "mop" or "artist"-style mounts is rounded. Selecting the correct brush is important because, if dusting is done incorrectly or with a heavy hand, the ridge detail can be obscured or destroyed [22].

The British study used aluminum flake powder for prints aged 24 h to 7 days on a range of surfaces commonly found at scenes: glass, unplasticized polyvinyl chloride (u-PVC), uncleaned and cleaned gloss-painted wood, and painted automotive metal. The results showed that unstarched glass fiber brushes were superior to squirrel, polyester, and nylon feather brushes, whether the brush was zephyr- or artist-mounted. However, slightly damp, greasy, or sticky surfaces had problems. Other problems occurred if the brush was used too vigorously because of the tendency of brush fibers to tangle. The recommendation for these surfaces: the squirrel zephyr type and the tapered polyester (Tetra washable) are good alternatives because they were found to be less prone to tangling. The study also investigated the brushing technique and found that spinning the brush caused glass fiber brushes to tangle more easily, which is undesirable.

10.4.2.1.2 Textured Surfaces Textured surfaces are also commonly encountered at scenes and they present a different challenge from smooth surfaces because powder particles can be trapped in the surface crevices. Table 10.1, adapted from the text by Bandey and Hardy [23], shows three broad categories of fingerprint powder that the HOSDB researched with regard to their success on textured and other difficult surfaces. The surfaces studied included u-PVC, laminated furniture, matt kitchen worktops, and old and worn wood.

Whether the British experience reflects the experience of American scene investigators is open to question, but their study is the only objective evaluation available. What

Table 10.1 Powder Success on Textured and Difficult Surfaces

Powders for Textured and Difficult Surfaces	Powder Characteristics	Results of Study: On-Scene Application
Flake powders: Metallic flake	Metallic flakes lie on surface of ridges; print appears reflective; ridge detail appears continuous.	
Aluminum		Most efficient on glass but works as well as alternatives on other smooth surfaces.
Brass		(Bronze or Gold) Performs similarly to aluminum but should be used only on smooth silver surfaces where aluminum would have low contrast.
Magenta flake		Can be an alternative to black magnetic for dark, textured surfaces.
Black powders: Granular carbon particles with other powders added to change the color to jet black, gray, or other colors	Ridge detail can be heavier around sweat pores giving a "granular" appearance.	Black granular: To be used on some smooth surfaces only
Magnetic powders: Variations in color based on the addition of other powders	Two forms: 1. Single-component powder: Magnetic particles act as the developing powder. 2. Two-component system: Magnetic particles act as a carrier for nonmagnetic powder.	Black magnetic powders are most effective on textured and u-PVC surfaces. Other magnetic powders (gray, silver, and so on) are not effective and are less sensitive. White magnetic powders are less sensitive but are effective on dark surfaces.

is clear is that two powders reflect the choice of scene investigators: aluminum flake and black granular powder, the latter a popular choice with American investigators. However, other choices are available from commercial forensic supply sources, a list that includes metallic powders, black, gray (dual), fluorescent, magnetic, bichromatic, powder formulations, and so on. With so many choices, students and novice investigators expectedly may have a difficult time choosing which technique to use and when. To that end, the results of the HOSDB research are summarized below.

- Aluminum flake powder should be used wherever possible and applied with a glass fiber brush.
- Zephyr-style squirrel and tapered polyester brushes should be used on surfaces where glass fiber brushes might tangle or clog because of surface contamination—dampness, grease, or oil.
- Glass evidence should be dusted with aluminum powder unless there is the possibility of contamination and tangling of the glass fiber brush.
- Black or jet-black magnetic powders should be used on textured surfaces.
- Black or jet-black magnetic powders should be used on u-PVC surfaces.
- All surfaces may respond better to chemical treatment, and this should be considered before embarking on a fruitless strategy.

10.5 Fingerprints and DNA

The HOSDB study also considered the effect powder dusting could have on the ability to obtain usable DNA profiles. The following summarizes the findings:

- Lifting fingerprints using traditional lifting methods—tape and gels—does not quantitatively capture the DNA. After lifting, the area should be swabbed to collect the remaining cellular material present. The HOSDB study reported obtaining partial DNA profiles using low copy number techniques from both the lift and the swabs taken from the lifted area.
- There is little possibility of contaminating a fingerprint's DNA with that of another as using the same brush. To avoid the issue, use clean brushes and fresh powder between dusting.
- Magnetic powder dusting reduces the chance of contaminating a fingerprint's DNA with that of another. Do not mix used and fresh dusting powder by releasing the used powder into the original reservoir.
- Fluorescent powders, although not usually recommended, can be used to maximize an investigator's ability to locate fingerprints having DNA evidence.

Spear [24] published work concerning how various latent fingerprint developing reagents affected the ability of forensic DNA laboratories to obtain useable DNA and categorized the work of the California Criminalistics Institute which summarized the work of other researchers [24]. With a few exceptions and with some variable results, the data showed that fingerprint development methods can be expected to yield useable DNA from bloodstains and bloody fingerprints. One exception was sticky-side powder which did not give useable polymerase chain reaction (PCR)-based DNA typing results. Some results, though, were variable, which appeared to be researcher-dependent. Sometimes the development method gave useable DNA results. Sometimes the results were listed as "use with care," which meant ". . . if the biological stain is not marginal, this process will probably be OK" (p. 3). Methods falling into this category involved the use of UV light, physical developer, ninhydrin with a secondary metallic salt, DFO, Amido black, diaminobenzidine (DAB), cyanoacrylate fuming with rhodamine, or luminol [24].

10.5.1 Superglue (Cyanoacrylate) Fuming

Another widely used technique at scenes as well as in the laboratory takes advantage of the fact that superglue fumes (cyanoacrylate monomer) react with components in the fingerprint residue to form polycyanoacrylate polymer along the ridges. The result is a residue that is nearly invisible on light surfaces and off-white on dark surfaces.

According to German [25], a latent print examiner with the U.S. Army Criminal Investigation Laboratory (USACIL) appropriated the technique from the Japanese National Police Agency in 1979. From a scene and case perspective, superglue fuming at the scene has its advantages.

- The fuming process protects fingerprints, which reduces the risk of damage during transport to the laboratory.
- The polycyanoacrylate entombs the DNA present.

- On-scene fuming is appropriate for objects that cannot be transported to the laboratory.
- On-scene fuming is possible and recommended for objects that will be damaged during transport to the laboratory.
- On-scene fuming can be used to obtain on-scene investigatory information.

There are disadvantages as well.

- On-scene fuming is typically done in an uncontrolled environment, which can be detrimental to quality of the developed print.
- Most on-scene cyanoacrylate fuming involves the H&H fuming process, leaving the possibility of overdevelopment.
- Because of the ease of the technique, there is little consideration of an appropriate strategy for using on-scene superglue fuming development.

10.5.1.1 Chemistry of the Cyanoacrylate Reaction

The chemical mechanism of the cyanoacrylate (superglue) polymerization reaction is well known and understood. Understanding the reaction is important because knowing when and how to use it, based on how the environment or the surface might affect the quality of the fingerprint residue, can lead to success, failure, or weak or partial success. The reaction is an attack by a Lewis base on the terminal carbon of the cyanoacrylate monomer. As that carbon carries a strong electropositive charge because of the electronegative properties of the monomer's cyanide and ester groups, it is vulnerable to attack by a pair of electrons, characteristic of Lewis bases. Depending on the attacking agent, the reaction often happens quickly and at room temperature. This can be easily demonstrated by dropping a drop of superglue into a small amount of water or ethanol. The result is a cloudy solution that quickly grows as the monomer polymerizes to form the white polycyanoacrylate polymer. The reaction (set up the same way by adding superglue to dye powders) also proceeds extremely quickly with most of the dyes used in fingerprint superglue staining: basic yellow 40, rhodamine 6G, and so on.

Figure 10.9 illustrates the cyanoacrylate polymerization reaction mechanism when catalyzed by catalytic species of hydroxide ion (sodium hydroxide—NaOH) or

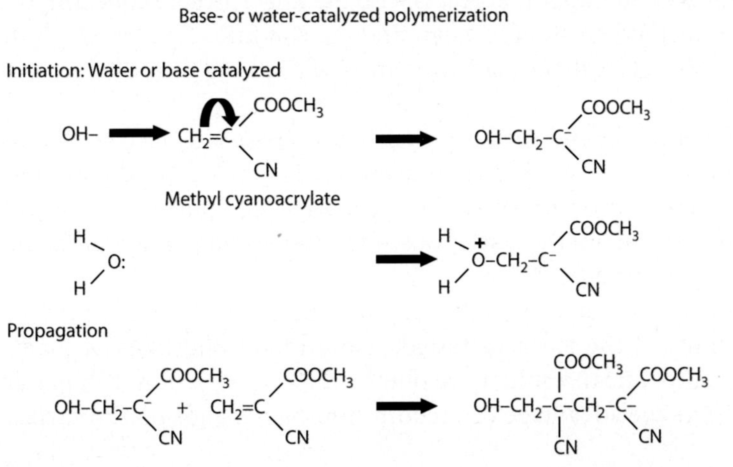

Base- or water-catalyzed polymerization
Initiation: Water or base catalyzed
OH– → CH_2=C(COOCH$_3$)(CN) → OH–CH_2–C$^-$(COOCH$_3$)(CN)
Methyl cyanoacrylate
H_2O: → H_2O$^+$–CH_2–C$^-$(COOCH$_3$)(CN)
Propagation
OH–CH_2–C$^-$(COOCH$_3$)(CN) + CH_2=C(COOCH$_3$)(CN) → OH–CH_2–C(COOCH$_3$)(CN)–CH_2–C$^-$(COOCH$_3$)(CN)

Figure 10.9 Mechanism of the superglue fuming reaction.

Table 10.2 Vacuum and Heat and Humidity Fuming Methods Compared

Surface	Vacuum	Heat and Humidity	Equal Development
Aluminum foil	70	9	20
Acetate	19	56	26
Ziploc® bag	52	6	43
Glad® bag100	100	0	0
Garbage bag	31	19	50
Garbage bag	87	2	41
White plastic bag	56	20	24
Black plastic bag	87	6	7
Cigarette packaging	96	4	0

Source: From J. E. Watkin, et al. 1994. *Journal of Forensic Identification,* 44(5):545–557. With permission.

water. Importantly, the reaction occurs with other forensically important chemicals having the appropriate structure. Examples include rhodamine 6G, basic yellow 40, 8-hydroxyquinoline, methanol, ethanol, and so on.* As the fingerprint residue is an emulsion in which water is present, there is the possibility that this is the attacking species. However, there are other attacking species in print residue that can polymerize superglue as well, including fatty acids, amino acids, and lactate. Most crime scene investigators believe that water vapor is necessary for superglue polymerization. The water vapor used in the superglue reaction probably keeps the aqueous phase of the emulsion saturated, but it is most likely the water in the emulsion that creates the environment for other reactive species to initiate the reaction; that the superglue reaction can occur in the absence of water vapor—vacuum superglue fuming—argues against water vapor as the prime initiator.

10.5.1.2 Superglue Fuming Methods

Superglue fuming falls into two basic categories: H&H and vacuum, and variations of these. Most fuming in the laboratory or at the crime scene uses the H&H method because of the widespread belief that water is required for the polymerization reaction. Each method creates a cyanoacrylate vapor that reacts with the fingerprint residue. Importantly, the way in which each method creates the vapor and the conditions under which the polymerization reactions take place differ markedly, and the resulting fumed fingerprints have different characteristics.

Such differences should send a signal that there is a legitimate decision concerning which method to use in specific circumstances, instead of blindly forging ahead with a method that is familiar or for which the appropriate equipment is readily available. As an example, Table 10.2 shows the results of a side-by-side comparison of the two methods for a selected group of surfaces [26].

Table 10.2 shows that vacuum fuming produces better-quality prints than the H&H method for most of the surfaces tested, using their conditions of print development. Similar but not identical results were obtained using a vacuum cabinet and a humidity chamber [27]. As the advantage of vacuum fuming depends on the surface, an on-scene

* Robert C. Shaler. Unpublished results.

(or laboratory) decision must be made to determine which method to use in a given circumstance. For example, as seen in Table 10.2, Ziploc® bags, garbage bags, and white plastic bags fared almost equally with either technique, a slight edge for vacuum fuming. However, Glad® bags were 100% better when using vacuum fuming while acetate surfaces responded better to H&H fuming; the other study [27] had almost the opposite results with Glad® bags. Aluminum foil fared better using vacuum fuming, but neither study found fuming ideal for aluminum foil. The bottom line is that it is not an all or nothing decision. The discrepancies between the two studies suggest that more research is needed. These also suggest that on-scene fuming requires careful thought before forging ahead. They also highlight the absolute need to rigorously validate fuming methods.

From a practical on-scene perspective, Table 10.2 (an in-house validation or list) can be a guide. If the evidence in question is on the list, choosing the best method is simple. For example, if the evidence is an acetate surface, then H&H is the choice, and on-scene fuming might be a viable choice. On the other hand, if the item is a cigarette package, vacuum fuming is the clear and better choice, which might not typically be an on-scene procedure. Ideally, the cigarette package should be photographed, adequately protected, packaged, and carefully transported to the laboratory. On-scene superglue fuming of the cigarette package using H&H conditions under the guise of protecting the print for transit may well end up ruining or compromising it as evidence. Therefore, choosing the most appropriate method for on-scene applications should be a decision process based on known scientific data instead of blindly using one technique over another.

A problem is that scene scientists/investigators may not know the chemistry of specific surfaces or be familiar with the surfaces listed in Table 10.2. This is probably the norm. The prudent approach is to take everything that can be transported to the laboratory for analysis. For those items that must be fingerprinted at the scene, some thought should go into which method would produce the best results.

The HOSDB invested in on-scene fuming chambers after researching the H&H versus vacuum issue, deciding to control the atmosphere at 80% ± 2% relative humidity to ensure proper on-scene fuming using the H&H method. Humidity above 80% produced overdeveloped prints [28]. More recent work suggests that using a single humidity cutoff might not be appropriate and that the temperature of the evidence related to the specific heat capacity is a factor in superglue development of prints on nonporous surfaces [29]. This presents a problem for the following on-scene fuming development methods.

- The superglue wand (Cyanowand™*) is essentially a heating element that vaporizes cyanoacrylate monomer into the air. The examiner aims the fumes at the area to be developed and allows them to react with the latent print. In these situations, no fingerprint control (to know when the reaction is complete) is possible and there is no mechanism to control the humidity.
- The FumaDome™† is the same technique except that the wand is encased within a plastic dome, which corrals the fumes and controls their distribution more effectively and evenly. Although a fingerprint control can be placed inside the dome, it is usually not easily included because of the system's architecture. Again,

* http://www.securityandsafetysupply.com/news/lp-29.htm (accessed November 5, 2010).
† http://www.executiveforensics.com/fuma-domepress.pdf (accessed November 5, 2010).

there is no mechanism to control the humidity, although it would be simple enough to include one.

- Homemade plastic tents that surround evidence at the scene are held in place with tape. Superglue fumes are produced from a cotton ball that has been saturated with a solution of sodium bicarbonate and then dried. A few drops of superglue placed on the cotton ball initiates the reaction to release the cyanoacrylate monomer, which occurs from the interaction of the superglue with the sodium bicarbonate and cotton. A fingerprint placed on the plastic is the development control. Here, too, there is no attempt to control the humidity.
- Commercial or homemade variations are usually enclosures containing separate hot plates for water and superglue. The evidence is placed into the tank and the heat from the hot plates vaporizes the superglue. The reaction is monitored by a print placed on the container wall or on a fingerprint card placed inside the container.

The problem with these methods is control. The fuming environment is completely uncontrolled. H&H fuming requires, optimally, 80% relative humidity, which these methods fail to take into consideration. Certainly, the FumaDome™, homemade containers, and commercially available plastic tents can be retrofitted to measure and control the humidity. With respect to knowing when fuming is complete, the standard practice is to place a fingerprint inside the fuming environment. When that print develops, presumably so has the evidence. There is no doubt that using a standard fingerprint as a control is the correct scientific approach. However, using just any control, such as placing a fingerprint onto plastic or fingerprint card, is not practicing science correctly. Certainly, failure to include a control is not practicing science. Equally important is the control itself. For example, a black fingerprint card or a print placed inside a plastic tent is not an appropriate control for developing prints on a brass doorknob. The only proper control for a brass doorknob is a piece of brass. Applying a method to fume prints without using a control or using an inappropriate control, such as with a fuming wand or dome, is inexcusable.

10.5.1.2.1 H&H Cyanoacrylate Fuming As discussed, the H&H method uses heat instead of vacuum to volatilize the cyanoacrylate monomer. Importantly, cyanoacrylate is a cyanide compound, which means that there is the possibility of producing cyanide gas if the monomer (cyanoacrylate) breaks from overheating. To prevent this overheating, the temperature used to volatilize the monomer should not go above 120°C.

Although H&H fuming is a popular on-scene technique, it seems there are as many variations of the process as there are people using it, which results in scientific on-scene chaos. To illustrate, in a conversation with highly experienced crime scene detectives, a popular variation was not to use an external water source. The ambient relative humidity was thought to be sufficient. The justification was simply that "fingerprints are obtained." These detectives were from New Jersey and New York, where the humidity typically lies in an appropriate range for superglue fuming, especially in the summer. However, these same detectives used the technique in the winter when the relative humidity can be much lower. Most researchers believe that the humidity should be at least 65%, with the optimum about 80%. These detectives defended their choice saying that they were able to develop prints most of the time. As mentioned, the HOSDB standardized the on-scene development by using fuming chambers set at 80% relative humidity [28].

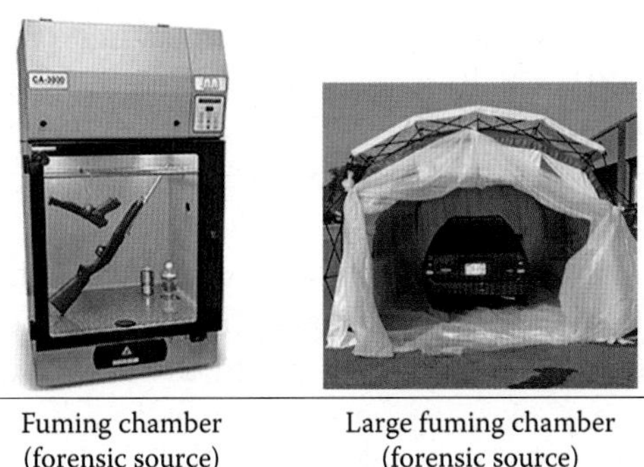

Fuming chamber (forensic source) | Large fuming chamber (forensic source)

Figure 10.10 Commercially available superglue fuming mechanisms.

Because the fuming process is forgiving, it is easy to delude oneself into thinking that, if results are obtained, it does not matter how the test was conducted. Such reasoning is certainly nonscientific and borders on incompetence. Just because a method is simple to use and inexpensive to set up does not mean that the appropriate scientific procedures and controls should be ignored.

As mentioned, the equipment and supplies required for cyanoacrylate fuming are simple: superglue, an aluminum pan or foil, and two heat sources (light bulb or coffee warmer or a coffee hot plate to volatilize the cyanoacrylate; another hot plate to vaporize water). Place these in a fuming chamber—a fish tank with a cover—and you have a superglue fuming chamber. The chamber itself can be as simple as a cardboard box or something more elaborate and commercially available. According to German [25], a cardboard box the size of a breadbox or a fish tank (". . . only if you enjoy cleaning off glass with lots of elbow grease periodically") will create fingerprints. Other variations include an upside-down garbage can or even a file cabinet drawer.

Commercially available fuming chambers and devices taken from manufacturer's Websites are shown in Figure 10.10. The top left of this figure shows a large fuming chamber that holds large items. The top right shows an on-scene fuming wand that works without an exogenous water source, where the superglue is heated by a butane torch. A similar device is the FumaDome (bottom photograph). It also uses a butane flame to heat the cyanoacrylate but contains the fumes inside the dome. The commercial suppliers are listed under each item. Even large tents have been used to develop fingerprints on large objects such as vehicles.

German [25] describes an on-scene homemade system that would make Rube Goldberg* proud. A typical procedure for cyanoacrylate fuming is described below:

- Inside a cardboard box and in one corner place a coffee warmer and a cup of hot water or coffee (a second coffee warmer can be used to heat the water). *There is no provision to monitor the humidity or to control it.*
- In an aluminum tray, place several drops of superglue—enough to cover a nickel.
- Place the evidence inside the box, arranging the evidence for maximum exposure—cans leaning against the corners of the box, baggies hung by paper clips, and so on.

* Reuben Lucius Goldberg (July 4, 1883–December 7, 1970) was a Jewish American cartoonist, sculptor, author, engineer, and inventor. Goldberg is best known for a series of popular cartoons he created depicting complex devices that perform simple tasks in indirect, convoluted ways—now known as Rube Goldberg machines" [30].

- On another piece of aluminum, place a sebaceous fingerprint (rub a finger against the side of the nose) that will be a control. When this fingerprint develops, the process can be considered complete.
- Place the superglue on the coffee warmer.
- Close the box.
- After 10 min, turn off the heat, open the box, and check the control print. If the control print has developed, the process is finished. If the control print has not turned a little white, add more superglue to the aluminum tray and fume for another 10 min.
- Submit the evidence to the laboratory regardless of whether visible fumed prints are present.

Several drops of cyanoacrylate are placed into an aluminum pan (or aluminum foil configured into an appropriate shape) and the heat source turned on. Water is placed in another aluminum pan and heated. Most suppliers recommend using 1 oz dropping bottles for dispensing the superglue. Inexpensive commercial systems are available that are clear, plastic "tents" that fit over a frame. The evidence is placed or hung inside the "tent" and the fuming process proceeds as described above. The value of these "see-through" systems is that they allow the investigator to know when control fingerprints are finished. This is important because over fuming is easy.

10.5.1.2.2 Vacuum Cyanoacrylate Fuming Vacuum cyanoacrylate fuming requires a vacuum of approximately 1 μTorr. Commercial systems are available, but homemade systems made from vacuum chambers and vacuum pumps available from scientific supply houses work just as well for small evidentiary items; they are easier to set up and can be easily transported to the scene.

Necessary equipment includes a vacuum pump, a vacuum chamber, and an aluminum tray to hold the cyanoacrylate. Interestingly, no external source of water is necessary for vacuum cyanoacrylate fuming because the fuming reaction takes place in near-zero relative humidity; this suggests that exogenous water vapor is not necessary to obtain fumed prints. On-scene vacuum fuming can be done on smooth, flat surfaces, but is difficult on textured surfaces because creating a sufficient vacuum seal is problematic, though not impossible. The evidence must fit inside the vacuum chamber, and only a few systems exist that can handle large items. Vacuum systems for rifles, for example, are available commercially.

The procedure for vacuum fuming follows:

- Place the evidence and a control print into the vacuum chamber.
- Turn on the vacuum and monitor the pressure until it reaches 25 in.Hg.
- Turn off the vacuum and monitor the development of the fingerprint (if using a clear vacuum chamber) on the control print (or appropriate control surface). A flashlight helps to see the developing print.

One of the advantages of vacuum fuming is that it is not necessary to turn plastic bags inside out, as it is with H&H fuming because the fumes penetrate inside the bags.

10.5.1.2.3 Visualizing Cyanoacrylate Fumed Fingerprints Regardless of the fuming technique, visualizing the fumed print requires a second process that typically includes either powder dusting or staining the fumed print with a fluorescent dye. Another system has recently been developed which involves a vapor fluorescent dye, CN-Yellow™* that reacts with the polycyanoacrylate after the fuming process is complete.

10.5.1.2.3.1 Powder Dusting Cyanoacrylate Fumed Prints The choice of dusting powder for fumed prints depends on the color of the underlying surface. The beauty of this system is that on-scene fuming is a way of protecting the print while transporting it to the latent print laboratory, where a decision concerning its development is made and visualizing is done in a controlled laboratory environment.

There are instances, however, when on-scene development is the only option, such as on surfaces that cannot be transported to the laboratory. Dusting a fumed print is no different from routine print dusting for any surface. The only difference is that the location of the print is already known. Lifting is also done in the same way, and the dusted, fumed print is lifted using tape and transferred to a fingerprint card. Because the cyanoacrylate fumed print has a rigid structure, the print can be redusted and lifted numerous times. A sequence for developing cyanoacrylate fumed prints follows:

- Photograph the cyanoacrylate fumed print using oblique lighting.
- Dust the print using a powder that contrasts well with the surface. The choices include black powder, black magnetic powder, white magnetic powder, and fluorescent powder.
- Take a close-up photograph of the dusted print. If fluorescent powder is used, an ALS should be used to photograph the print.
- Lift the print using tape or a gel lifter.
- Examine the quality of the lifted print. If the dusting is not acceptable, redust the print. If over dusted, relift the print.

10.5.1.2.3.2 Staining Cyanoacrylate Fumed Prints Another way to visualize cyanoacrylate fumed prints is to stain them using a fluorescent dye. The process is simple and many dye choices are available commercially or can be made in the laboratory. Some of these include ardrox, rhodamine 6G, and basic yellow 40. Mixtures of these are also available to observe prints on multicolored, nonporous surfaces.

On-scene staining of fumed prints without thinking through the process can ruin the evidence, if the surface absorbs the dye. If so, the background fluorescence can mask or reduce the contrast of the print's fluorescence. The following is a step-wise process for fluorescent staining fumed prints:

- Photograph the unstained cyanoacrylate fumed print using oblique lighting.
- Stain a small area of the surface that is fingerprint-free for 3 min (longer than the time for staining the fingerprint).
- Wash the area with water and then examine using an ALS to ensure that the surface does not take up the stain.

* "CN-Yellow™ is photo-luminescent cyanoacrylate. This CN-Yellow™/dye blend is specific to print residue. Developed prints can be observed almost immediately in many cases. CN-Yellow™ is cured into a proprietary, steel wool cartridge with an indefinite shelf life. It is dispersed using a butane torch with a flameless burner for easy use in field or lab. The amount of CN-Yellow™ in each cartridge is pre-measured, reducing the risk of over development. CN-Yellow™ developed prints are visualized with a wide spectrum, UV to 515nm, but are optimized at 450nm. The highly luminescent, stable prints can often be seen from 12 to 20ʹ away" [31].

- If the surface does not absorb the dye (i.e., fluorescence is not observed), soak the cyanoacrylate fumed print with the dye and allow it to sit in contact with the dye for 2 min.
- Wash the stained print with water and let dry.
- Using the ALS, find the wavelength that gives the best contrast between the print's fluorescence and the surface.
- Photograph the stained fingerprint under the ALS at a wavelength that maximizes the signal and not background fluorescence.

An alternative to using liquid fluorescent dyes for staining is to use a vaporized dye (CN-Yellow™). The dye is volatilized in a heat chamber, such as the Lumi-Dome™*. The dye interacts with the polymerized cyanoacrylate on the fingerprint ridges creating fluorescent print.

10.5.1.2.3.3 Cyanoacrylate Fume Safety On-scene safety is always an important consideration, especially when using chemicals or creating chemical reactions. Superglue fumes are caustic but otherwise not dangerous. In fact, superglue is used to "suture" internal wounds during surgery. Still, caution is necessary, and wearing fume masks, gloves, and protective outer clothing should be mandatory. Ideally, fuming should be done in a fume hood in a well-ventilated space. At the scene, this might not be possible, though collapsible, portable fume hoods are available. If safety cannot be guaranteed, on-scene fuming should be one of the last activities at the scene.

10.5.1.2.3.4 Packaging, Protecting, and Storage of Cyanoacrylate Fumed Evidence After developing fumed fingerprints, protecting them during transport is necessary. Although the cyanoacrylate polymerization process is more or less entombing, the fumed print is still fragile. This means fumed prints must be immobilized sufficiently well to guard against contact with surfaces during transit, a precaution to be taken whether or not prints are fumed. Superglue fumed prints should be placed inside a container and anchored so that the fumed print does not come into contact with the packaging. They should be immobile.

10.6 Lifting Developed Prints

10.6.1 Powder Lifts

After developing and photographing prints, the next step is lifting, so that they can be examined by latent print examiners. The process, like many on-scene manipulations, is deceptively easy, and there is skill involved. The most important skill is to be able to use thought to obtain a successful lift. The considerations are discussed in the following sections.

10.6.1.1 Surface

Obviously prints are found on all surface types, and once developed they remain on that surface. After photography, the next step is lifting. Just as deciding which method is appropriate for developing the prints, critical thought is essential for determining the best method for lifting the print. One is the surface texture. The photographs in Figure 10.11a and b illustrate the point. Figure 10.11a shows a photograph of a room with a light-pink

* http://www.executiveforensics.com/systems.htm (accessed November 5, 2010).

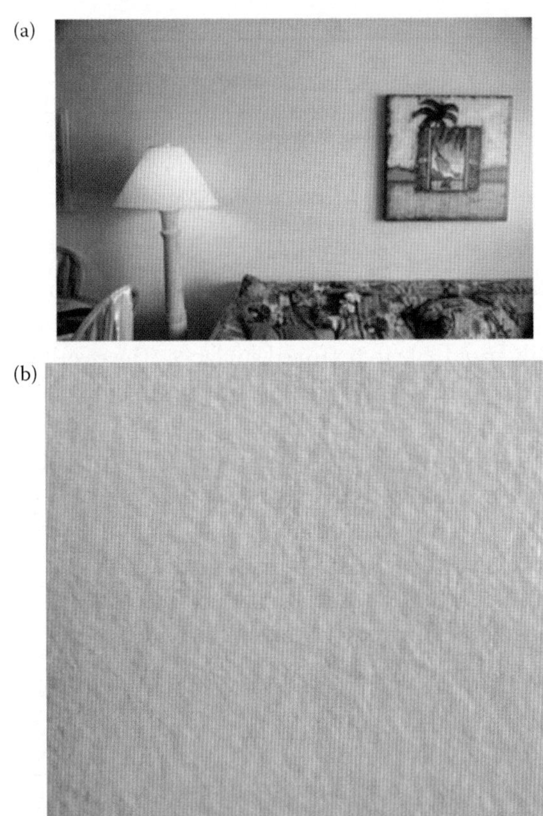

Figure 10.11 (a) Wall in room. (b) Texture of wall in Figure 10.11a.

painted wall, a seemingly ideal place to dust for prints. The second photograph, Figure 10.11b, is a close-up of the wall. Notice that the texture is a series of hills and valleys that can affect the quality of the lift depending on the technique used.

Regardless of the situation, logic should control the approach/strategy for developing fingerprints on all surfaces. These methods are considered in the following sections.

10.6.1.1.1 Tape Lifting On perfectly flat, smooth surfaces, tape lifting is the fastest and easiest method for lifting dusted prints. Interestingly, the tape-lifting process does not always lift the entire dusted print, leaving some of the print detail behind, including some of the DNA.* Suppose tape was used to lift prints shown on the surfaces shown in Figure 10.11b. When the lifted print is transferred to a fingerprint card and examined, gaps might be visible in the friction ridge detail.

This means that tape lifting was not the correct method to use. The end product could be the inability of the latent print examiner to adequately compare the print. The reason this happens is illustrated in Figure 10.12. The undulating line (green) represents the wall, the black dots are the print ridges dusted with black powder and the blue line is the lifting tape. The assumption is that the print penetrates part way into the depth (depending on

* Jennifer Nabozny. Unpublished results. Penn State Forensic Science Program. Research as partial fulfillment for professional masters in forensic science.

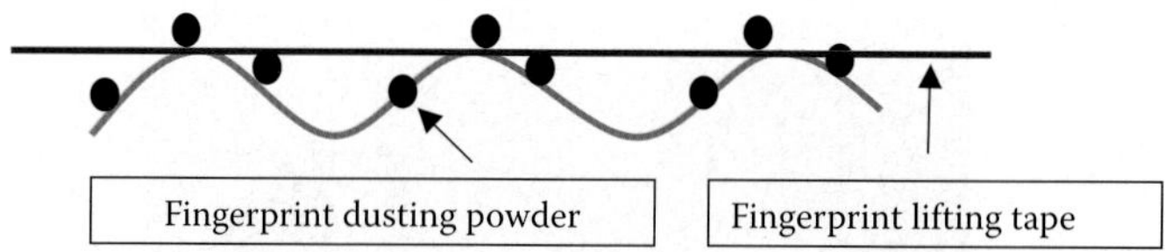

Figure 10.12 Effect of texture on tape-lifted powder-dusted print.

pressure applied) of the textured surface. The dusted ridges also extend partway into the recesses of the texture. When lifting, the tape does not extend into the texture because it is fairly rigid and not easily moldable to textured surfaces. The result is a partially lifted print, where the only dust (print) that was lifted was where the tape came into contact with the powder on the higher surfaces.

After lifting, the print is placed on a fingerprint lift card. The choice of card is determined by the color of the dusting powder, such as:

- Black dusting powder for a white fingerprint lift card
- White dusting or fluorescent powder for a black lift card
- Gold or aluminum flake powder for a black lift card

10.6.1.1.2 Mikrosil™ Casting Mikrosil™ and other brands of silicone casting materials work well with dusted prints on textured surfaces. The pliable silicone, in Figure 10.13 (purple), conforms to the texture of the surface and engulfs the dust-developed print. When the silicone hardens and is removed, its adhesive forces (stickiness) entrap the dust on the print ridges and lift it intact. The lifted mold can be fixed to a fingerprint card to preserve it. Preparing the silicone casting material is a simple matter of following the directions from the manufacturer.

10.6.1.1.3 Gel Lifters (Gellifters) Gel lifters are commercially available in the form of rubber or acetate-backed flexible gelatin (Chapter 11, Section 11.5.1.2). With respect to malleability, gel lifters are between tape and silicone. They have enough "give" and stickiness to capture ridge detail in the examples shown above but not if the texture runs too deep. Gel lifters are black, white, and clear, so if the choice is to use a gel lifter, the one to use is determined by the color of the dusting powder that should contrast well with the color of the gel lifter surface. The color can follow the same sequence as the color of the fingerprint lift card in the discussion above.

10.6.1.1.4 Tex-Lifts Tex-lifts are liquid glues that are painted over the developed print. Because it is a liquid, it can capture ridge detail on slightly textured surfaces. The Tex-lift liquid is a light blue color that dries clear, so the color of the powder is unimportant, as long

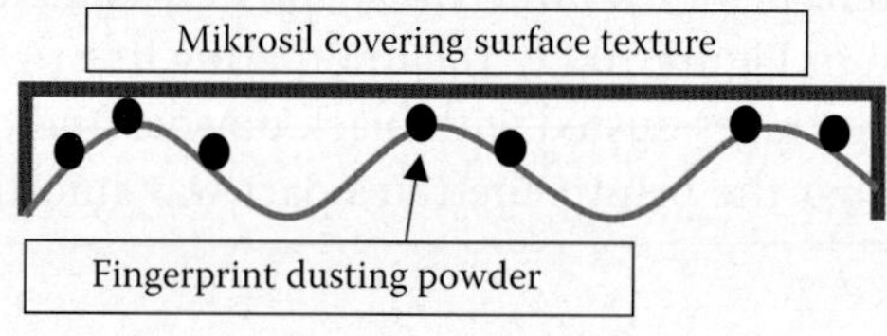

Figure 10.13 Mikrosil entrapment of dusted print.

as it contrasts with the surface. After the Tex-lift dries, the captured print is lifted with lifting tape (or gel lifter) and placed on a fingerprint lift card of an appropriate color.

10.6.1.1.5 Cyanoacrylate Fumed Prints As discussed, cyanoacrylate fumed prints are different because the fuming process develops the print. They sometimes need further treatment to make them visible. Generally, there are two choices: powder dusting and fluorescent staining; the procedures have been discussed previously. Fumed and dusted prints are easily lifted using tape, a process that can be repeated without damaging the polycyanoacrylate entrapped print. Also, the surface is not as critical because the fumed print forms a crust that sits on top of the fingerprint residue. If the prints on the surface shown in Figure 10.11b had been developed with superglue fumes, lifting the prints with tape should easily recover the print detail instead of a partial print obtained after tape lifting the nonsuperglue fumed and dusted the print. One caveat: The DNA and the print residue remain entombed by the polycyanoacrylate polymer. Lifting the fumed and dusted print does not lift the DNA.

10.7 Fingerprints on Adhesive Tapes

From an investigative perspective, tapes are important because they are routinely used to seal boxes, letters, and packaging. They are also used to restrain people and thus constitute an important class of evidence. Adhesive tape is a special category of nonporous evidence because it presents two distinct surfaces, each having unique development issues.

Anyone who has handled adhesive tapes knows that it is easy for fingers to stick to the sticky side of the tape, resulting in a print impression transferred to the tape. Simultaneously, a latent print might be deposited onto the smooth side of the tape. Even when criminals use latex gloves, handling adhesive tapes presents a problem because the stickiness makes handling the tape clumsy, and the result is often torn gloves or no attempt to use gloves at all. Finding fingerprints on adhesive tapes is a worthwhile endeavor. In fact, the on-scene thought process should be that prints are present on both the smooth and the sticky sides of tapes.

Historically, developing fingerprints on the sticky side of tapes has presented problems. Traditional dusting powder does not work because it sticks to the adhesive and masks prints that might be present. To overcome this, scientists and investigators have established a variety of methods for developing adhesive-side prints.

A problem with developing prints on the sticky side of tapes results from the chemistry of the adhesives, which affects subsequent print development. There can also be physical issues concerning collecting tapes and rendering them ready for print development. A rule of thumb should be that the print is collected, preserved, and taken to the laboratory for development, especially if the tape is stuck to itself. However, there might be rare instances when this is impossible, and unsticking the tape and developing the prints at the scene is necessary.

10.7.1 Removing Tape from Its Substrate

Because the two surfaces of adhesive tapes have such different properties, a reliable strategy is needed for preserving the print evidence on both sides of the tape. An immediate problem often is how to remove the tape from the surface on which it sticks without ruining the prints. Several methods have been proposed: physical means, cooling, solvents, and freezing.

10.7.1.1 Physical Processes

This refers to physically removing the tape from the surface to which it sticks by pulling or teasing. The premise is that this is the easiest and fastest method and causes the least damage to the underlying prints. The process is tedious and there is always the possibility of distorting the tape, which can alter underlying prints, especially if the two surfaces—tape and surface in contact—are tightly bound by the adhesive. Simply pulling the tape from a surface is not recommended without a good reason.

10.7.1.2 Cooling

Many jurisdictions recommend cooling adhesive tapes as a way to unstick them from surfaces or to unstick them from themselves. Recommendations include freezing using liquid nitrogen or a microcircuit freezing spray (see Section 10.7.1.3). The goal is to cool the tapes below the adhesive's critical "glass transition temperature." One way to accomplish this is with liquid nitrogen. Another might be to use dry ice. When sufficiently cooled, the adhesive solidifies so that it can be *gently and slowly* pulled from the surface or from the sticky side of an adhering adhesive. Essentially the frozen adhesive "fractures" from the surface to which it is bound [32].

10.7.1.3 Freezer Spray

Using a freezer spray is tantamount to freezing. Made for the electronics industry, these sprays replace liquid nitrogen for separating adhesives from various surfaces except from other adhesives. The temperature of the sprays is about −65°F, so precautions are necessary, such as wearing appropriate personal protective equipment (PPE) including gloves, face mask, protective clothing, and so on.

A procedure for using a freezer spray for separating adhesives from surfaces is described below:

- Use the freezer spray on localized and very small areas of the tape.
- As the freezer spray can freeze skin, it is imperative that the user wear thermal gloves.
- Do not use the freezer spray to remove adhesive from paper, cardboard, or adhesives adhering to adhesives.
- Using a freezer spray is the method of choice for removing adhesive tapes from plastic bags and other plastic material.
- Superglue fuming is appropriate for prints on the smooth side of tapes, and should be used before working on the adhesive side. The reason is that the fingerprints on the smooth side will be destroyed during cooling because of the condensation that forms. Superglue fuming can develop prints on both the smooth and the adhesive side of tapes. After the smooth-side prints develop and are lifted, freezer spray is appropriate.

10.7.1.4 Solvents

Hydrocarbon-based solvents have been recommended for adhesives stuck to other adhesives. One such commercially available solvent is UnDo™. The process is slow and tedious, and only tiny amounts of solvent should be used because too much will dissolve the adhesive and ruin prints. Students typically have little success.

Disengagement of adhesives from adhesives using solvents should be done carefully. This is an alternative method for disengaging adhesives from paper and cardboard and for separating adhesives from adhesives.

10.7.2 Packaging and Protecting Adhesive Tapes

The three factors of concern with regard to packaging and protecting adhesive tapes are

- Protecting prints on both sides of the tape during transit to the laboratory.
- Protecting prints on the adhesive side of the tape while processing the smooth side.
- Packaging the tape to prevent the inadvertent contamination or obliteration of the prints.

An effective method for protecting and storing the adhesive side is to place a silicone release paper over the adhesive side. It has a smooth, low, easily removed adhesion surface that will not disturb the adhesive. Just as fingerprints can be transferred to the adhesive side, they can also transfer onto the silicone paper. Gloves must be worn while working with adhesive tapes and silicone release paper.

Tapes should be stored in high-quality cardboard or plastic boxes, and care must be taken to prevent the adhesive side of the tape from coming into contact with the box surfaces. The tape is placed adhesive side down onto the silicone release paper. The protected tape is transferred to the storage box and fixed in place inside the box. More than one strand of adhesive tape can be fixed to the silicone release paper and that can be put into the storage box. Each tape must be labeled properly.

10.7.3 Developing Fingerprints on the Adhesive Side of Tapes

Several techniques are available for developing prints on the sticky side of tapes. These include using commercially available reagents such as small particle reagent (SPR), black-and-white WetWop, sticky-side powder, TapeGlo™, Gentian violet, iron oxide powder-based suspension among others. With the exception of TapeGlo and Gentian violet, each is a powder-based suspension in a dilute detergent solution. TapeGlo is a fluorescent dye and Gentian violet (basic yellow 3) is a solution that stains fats. Importantly, none of these products develop prints on all adhesives all of the time, which is a problem for deciding which of these to use. The answer lies in knowing or being able to discern the chemistry of individual adhesives.

Chemically, the adhesives of tapes differ, which is why powder suspensions and chemical formulation development techniques work with one type of tape and not another. Generally, tape adhesives are categorized as either rubber- or acrylic-based. Masking tape represents a third category, which can have either type of adhesive. It is its porosity, however, that creates problems for print development.

Knowing the specific formulation of the adhesive on tapes is important because it presents development problems for on-scene print and in-laboratory print development. Knowing which type of adhesive is present is an important first step in the development process, because if the incorrect technique is used, ruining prints is a distinct possibility. One way to ascertain which adhesive is present is to use infrared spectroscopy, which is not practical at the scene. A spot test is useful, however. It can easily and quickly identify the correct procedural direction [32]. The spot test technique for differentiating between acrylic- and rubber-based adhesives is described below. The procedure for administering the spot test is discussed in Section 10.7.3.3.

10.7.3.1 Rubber-Based Adhesives

Most tapes have rubber-based adhesives and, while they come in different colors and sizes, they should be receptive to dye and powder suspension development methods. These adhesives should also respond to cyanoacrylate fuming followed by fluorescent dye staining, which also works on the smooth side of the tape. The decision process includes ascertaining whether to develop prints at the scene and, if so, which method to use. The specific method depends on the scene circumstances, the chemistry of the adhesive or the evidence itself, and an individual's comfort zone using a particular development technique. The color of the tape is also important. If the decision is to attempt to develop prints, powder suspensions are a common choice.

10.7.3.1.1 Powder Suspensions Two powder suspensions, black and white, are recommended for developing fingerprints on rubber-based adhesives. Two different formulations are available: carbon-based (available commercially) and iron oxide-based (prepared in-house) suspensions.

10.7.3.1.1.1 Formulation of Iron Oxide Powder Suspension

- 20 g Iron (black powder suspension—Fe_3O_4 or 10 g titanium dioxide (rutile form—white powder suspension).
- While stirring, 20 mL stock detergent solution is added (500 mL Photoflo (Kodak) stirred into 500 mL distilled water—stored indefinitely). This produces a very thick solution that can be painted onto the adhesive side of the tape.

10.7.3.1.1.2 Procedure for Using Powder Suspensions on the Sticky Side of Adhesive Tapes

- Conduct a spot test first to determine adhesive type (see Section 10.7.3.3).
- Cut tape (if possible) into workable lengths of <2 ft. using a zigzag cut.
- Apply powder suspension using a soft animal hair brush.
- Leave suspension in place on tape for up to 30 s—do not allow it to dry.
- Wash tape with tap water.
- Dry the tape at room temperature.
- If the developed fingerprints are faint or lacking ridge detail, it is possible to repeat the process.
- Photograph the developed fingerprints.

10.7.3.1.1.3 Interferences and Precautions Developing prints using powder suspensions does not destroy the DNA present in the print, which means obtaining DNA profiles should be possible. However, other forensic examinations may be compromised, such as handwriting, ink, indented impression, fiber, hair, and paint analysis.

10.7.3.1.1.4 Safety Precautions There are no known hazards with powder suspensions. Scene scientists/investigators should wear lab coats, nonporous gloves, and eye protection. If the chemical or suspension is swallowed, medical attention must be sought. If splashed into the eyes or onto the skin, washing with cold, running water is advised. If soreness or other symptoms persist, medical attention must be sought. Solid chemicals on the skin should be brushed off and then washed under cold, running water. Fingerprint development should be done in a well-ventilated area, preferably in a down-draft or chemical fume hood.

- Iron oxide is harmful.
- Titanium dioxide is harmful.
- Carbon-based suspensions are not harmful.

10.7.3.2 Acrylic-Based Adhesives

Although few tapes fall into this category, they are physically indistinguishable from rubber-based adhesives. The spot test described in Section 10.7.3.3 is an important first step in deciding which technique to apply. A dot of a powder suspension applied to an acrylic-based adhesive cannot be washed from the adhesive, leaving a heavy, black background that will mask prints. A preferred method for developing fingerprints on acrylic-based adhesives is the nonphenolic version of Gentian violet (basic yellow 3) [32].

10.7.3.2.1 Basic Violet 3 Basic violet 3 is a dye that stains the fatty components of sebaceous secretions but not acrylic-based adhesives. The result is an intense purple color of the print ridges.

10.7.3.2.1.1 Formulation

- Concentrated dye solution: 5 g of basic violet 3 is weighed and 250 mL ethanol is stirred until dissolved.
- While stirring, 1 mL of dye solution is added to 25 mL stock detergent solution.
- 10 g Aerosol OT—sodium dioctyl sulfosuccinate (CAS No.: 577–11)7—is added to 1 L distilled water and stirred for 12 h)
- If an obvious gold film forms after adding stock detergent, the solution is discarded and the concentrated dye solution remade.

10.7.3.2.1.2 Procedure

- Pour working dye solution into clean glass dish (Petri dish).
- Draw adhesive tape through the solution two to three times.
- Check for fingerprint development. Repeat the step if weak development is seen. Fingerprint development will not be visible on dark surfaces. Discard working solution after use.
- Rinse tape under running, cold tap water until excess dye is gone. Float cellulose-based tapes on the surface to prevent curling.
- Photograph developed fingerprints.
- For dark surfaces, the fingerprints must be transferred. Before transferring, fluorescence examination may pinpoint the presence of developed fingerprints.

10.7.3.2.1.3 Interferences and Precautions The developed fingerprints are still amenable to DNA analysis, but may interfere with handwriting, ink, indented impression, fiber, hair, and paint analyses.

10.7.3.2.1.4 Safety Precautions There are no known hazards provided normal precautions are observed. Lab coats, nonporous gloves, and eye protection are mandatory. If skin or eye contact occurs, it is essential to wash with cold, running water. If soreness or other symptoms persist, medical attention must be sought. If the solid chemical gets on the skin, it should be brushed off and then the area washed under cold, running water. Fingerprint development should be done in a well-ventilated area, especially in a down-draft or chemical fume hood.

- Aerosol is harmful and an irritant.
- Ethanol is flammable and harmful.
- Basic violet 3 is toxic and an irritant. It is also a suspected carcinogen, mutagen, and toxic for reproduction.

10.7.3.3 Spot Testing Adhesives [32]

The following procedure can be used to differentiate between rubber-based and acrylic-based adhesives on the sticky side of tapes.

- Apply a toothpick-sized but clear spot of black or white powder suspension to a section of the tape that is less likely to have been handled.
- Wash the spot and only that area of the tape with tap water until the excess powder is gone.
- If powder remains on the spot, the adhesive is *probably* acrylic-based and prints should be developed using an aqueous version of basic violet 3 (Gentian violet).
- If the tape is see-through after washing the test spot, it is probably a rubber-based adhesive and prints should be developed using powder suspensions.

10.8 Patent Prints

As mentioned, patent prints can have a latent component that must be considered in the strategy to develop the entire print. A class was presented with a problem to develop a partial bloody fingerprint on a concrete block painted with a white, glossy paint. They were also told that only the middle part of the print (approximately one-third of the ridge detail was visible) was in blood. The students were to assume that the visible ridges were in blood and had to devise a strategy for developing and archiving the entire print. After some coaxing, they realized that the print might have two parts: patent and latent. As Champod et al. [1] point out, "Fingermarks in blood are a common example . . ." (p. 105).

The students also had to consider whether the latent part of the print might also be in blood visibly below the detection limits of the human eye; it is well known that the human eye does not easily perceive low concentrations of blood, so it would not be unusual for an investigator to "miss" details if that happened to be the situation. The students' opinions were split into two strategies.

10.8.1 Strategy One

The first strategy developed by the majority of the class is outlined below:

- Dust the sebaceous secretions to develop the latent part of the print.
- Photograph the dusted print.

- Lift the dusted print using either tape or a gel lifter.
- Stain the patent part of the print using acid violet 17 or acid black 1 (Amido black) for blood proteins.

10.8.2 Strategy Two

A minority of the students decided the following was the best approach for developing the entire print:

- Fix the proteins in the patent part of the print using 5-sulfosalicylic acid.
- Stain the blood proteins using acid violet 17 or aqueous-based acid black 1. Note that using aqueous-based staining solutions runs the risk of washing away DNA present. Using organic-based staining solutions runs the risk of dissolving fingerprint emulsion that would preclude subsequent dusting.
- Photograph the developed patent print.
- Dust the print to visualize the oils in the latent part of the print.
- Lift the print using tape or gel lifter.

After some discussion, the students had to decide which strategy was the most logical: to dust the sebaceous secretions, if any, first or to develop the patent, bloody part of the print first. Each side presented their reasoning for what they thought might happen at each step in the development process. Figure 10.14 illustrates the student's first strategic approach—to develop sebaceous secretions first.

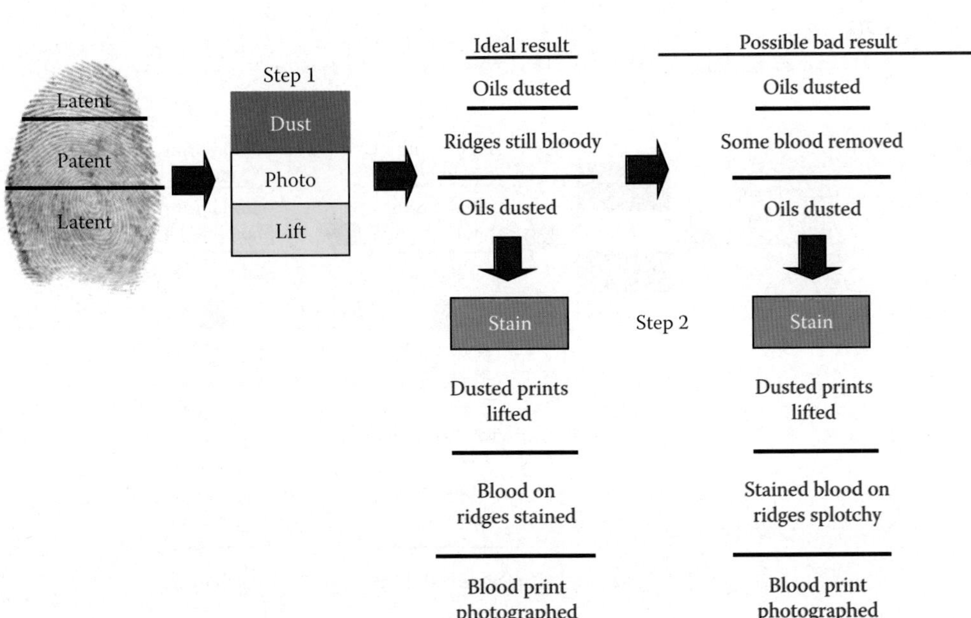

Figure 10.14 Student's first strategic approach and consequences.

Students thought dusting would preserve the sebaceous, oily ridge details while not affecting the bloody portion of the print. They thought that the next step should be to stain and thus enhance the visibility of the blood proteins, which they would then photograph. Their reasoning was that, if sebaceous oils were dusted, the dusted print would be lifted before staining the blood proteins. The ideal result is shown in Figure 10.14 under the column labeled "Ideal result."

When asked whether they thought that lifting the dusted portion before staining might also lift some of the blood, the students confessed that they had not considered the possibility. If that happened, protein staining might reveal blood-stained ridges having a splotchy or interrupted appearance; certainly not an ideal result. They realized that their approach might work if most of the latent parts of the print were actually bloody and dusting first revealed no ridge detail. This sequence is illustrated in Figure 10.14 under the label "Possible bad result."

The second strategy was to develop the bloody part of the fingerprint using an aqueous-based protein stain. They thought that by staining the blood proteins using an aqueous process they would not destroy the sebaceous oils in the latent areas of the print. This strategy and possible results are shown in Figure 10.15. The "Possible bad results" column illustrates what might also happen: splotchy dusting after staining and lifting of stained parts of print.

The point of the exercise was for the students to consider all possible outcomes, realistic or not, before embarking on a strategy. A well-reasoned procedure minimizes mistakes and prevents obliteration of evidence. The discussion in Chapter 9 touched on factors that should be included in an overall strategy: color, surface, texture, environment, and so on. An aspect not considered in that discussion was the print residue itself.

Students typically learn these lessons the hard way, after ruining several prints. Usually, they develop the blood and forget that part of the print detail in blood was visible but part

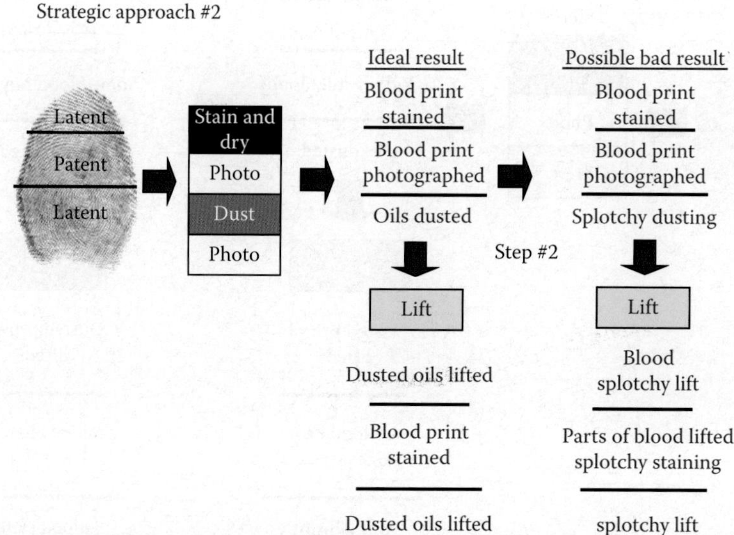

Figure 10.15 Student's second strategic approach and consequences. (Photograph by Robert C. Shaler.)

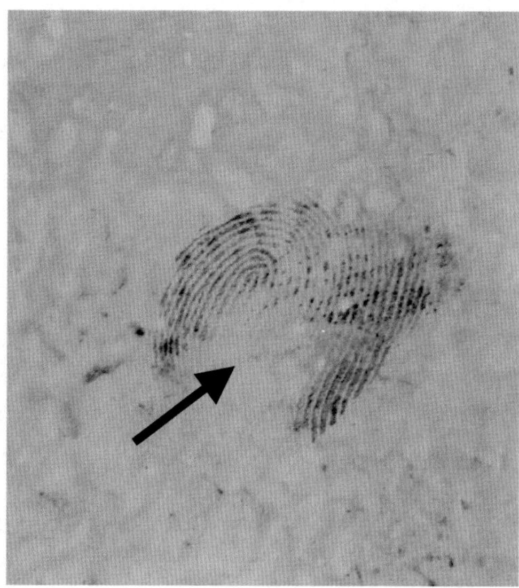

Figure 10.16 Coomassie blue–stained bloody fingerprint.

of the print in blood was invisible. An example is shown in the photograph in Figure 10.16. The bloody part of the print was stained using Coomassie blue.* It was obvious that the print had more blood on the ridges after staining than before. This cannot be known *a priori*, but it should be expected.

After staining, more of the print was visible, that is, areas not having visible blood and thus latent to the eye were also stained. The student thought her work was finished. However, she had other options, which she should have considered but did not. A quick glance at the stained print is revealing: unstained areas of the print (arrow) remain unstained. Are there sebaceous print residues in those areas that should have been developed or at least considered as part of the print development strategy?

Had the student dusted the print first, ridge detail uncontaminated with blood might have been developed. Had the student dusted the print after staining, the oils could still capture the dust and reveal additional detail. However, DNA might not be present.

10.9 Impression Evidence in Blood

Although this chapter concerns fingerprints, it is important for students to realize that fingerprints in blood are common occurrences at crime scenes. It is also true that impression evidence other than fingerprints can occur in blood. Importantly, the techniques to enhance blood are same whether the evidence is a bloody footwear impression or a fingerprint. Thus, developing a strategy, as in the case of fingerprints, to obtain all impression

* ". . . the name of two similar triphenylmethane dyes that were developed for use in the textile industry but are now commonly used for staining proteins in analytical biochemistry. Coomassie Brilliant Blue G-250 differs from Coomassie Brilliant Blue R-250 by the addition of two methyl groups. The name 'Coomassie' is a registered trademark of Imperial Chemical Industries" [33].

details in blood applies equally to footwear and tire track impressions and, in some circumstances, to fabric impressions. The unifying factor is the need to enhance the entire blood impression and capture it photographically, or to lift it. Luckily, research has been fairly extensive. As with fingerprint evidence, surface types are the first to be taken into consideration in a reasoned approach.

10.9.1 Blood as Multitasking Evidence

Students should never forget the multitasking aspect of blood as evidence. Blood prints represent a particularly important and relevant class of physical evidence. However, it is critical to consider blood evidence as more than just a way to identify someone.

Thus, knowing the composition of biological fluids, blood in particular, and their significance from a forensic perspective is a valuable discussion. As shown in Figure 10.17, blood is a tissue composed fundamentally of two parts: cells and plasma. The cellular component comprises about 45% of the total and the plasma 55%. On average, an adult male has approximately 5 pints of blood, and the liquid part, the plasma, contains biochemicals, organic and inorganic chemicals, and water. The cellular component consists of red blood cells, platelets, and white blood cells. Although somewhat academic, the forensically relevant components of blood are illustrated schematically so that scene analysts can see the components and the fraction of blood from which each comes. Knowing from where a specific component comes is important because it can dictate a specific course of action for a particular analytical scheme.

Translating Figure 10.17 into its forensic context takes into consideration more than simply developing ridge or footwear print detail or swabbing to grab cells for DNA analysis. This does not imply that friction ridge detail, footwear detail, and DNA are unimportant. They are, even critically so, but it is also important to understand that other forensically relevant information is potentially available. So, simply enhancing the print at a scene and then photographing it could be doing the investigation a disservice. Blood prints should always be collected and transported to the crime laboratory for further analysis, if possible.

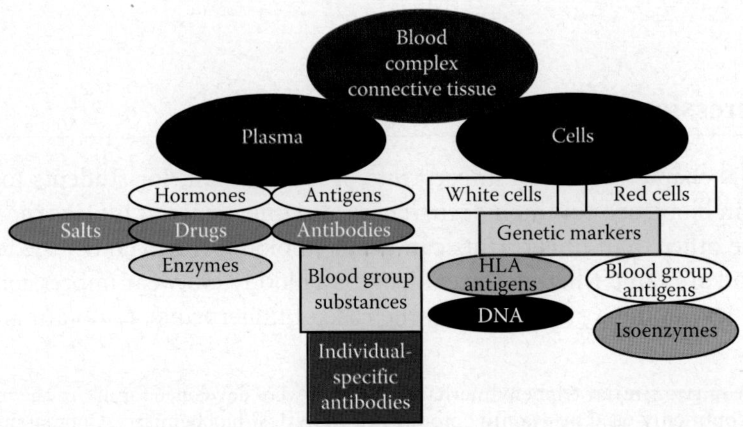

Figure 10.17 Forensically speaking, what is blood?

There should be some consideration about blood in terms of how to capture all the information at the scene. And the thought process should look at blood (semen, saliva, urine, and so on) in the very broad context of the insoluble components in water—the cells—and those that are soluble (proteins, salts, hormones, drugs, and so on). One particular cell, the red blood cell (erythrocyte), holds an honored place in forensic investigations because it contains a protein, hemoglobin, which is forensically important not just because it has a red color.

Hemoglobin is the oxygen-carrying protein, which when combined with oxygen gives blood its red color. It is also why we can breathe the oxygen in the air. It is composed of two moieties: heme and a protein, globin. For this discussion, heme is the forensically important part of the molecule because it carries iron in the form of iron porphyrin. As a group of molecules, porphyrins are heterocyclic, that is, they are ringed compounds containing carbon and other atoms. Structurally, they contain one pyrroline and three pyrrole chemical groups connected by methane bridges (=CH–). Importantly, porphyrins complex with metals (heme and chlorophyll are examples) and are highly conjugated (multiple double bonds), which is why they are colored. In fact, the word porphyrin comes from the Greek meaning purple.*

When complexed with iron, the structure is known as heme, and it forms the basis of a class of tests called catalytic tests that have been in continuous use since the mid-1800s to detect dried and/or occult blood.

Although a significant body of scientific literature exists concerning the forensic application of catalytic tests, an in-depth discussion is beyond the scope of this chapter. Suffice to say that for over 150 years scientists have been searching for a way to specifically detect the presence of human blood using a single, simple chemically based test. Mostly, these efforts have failed. But many of the tests survive and form today what are called presumptive tests. These catalytic tests are highly sensitive and, when positive, provide an investigator a reasonable probability that blood is present. The results of these tests, in some cases, are highly colored or give off light, that is, they luminescence. The reaction of these chemicals with the ferric iron in heme with peroxide is known as an oxidation–reduction reaction (redox reaction).

Fortunately, detecting blood and staining blood at the crime scene is a tool in the scene investigator's repertoire. The following discussion is concerned with enhancing bloody fingerprints using chemicals that either react with heme in an oxidation–reduction reaction (catalytic tests) or stain the proteins in the blood. The chemistry of detecting blood using catalytic tests is discussed in Chapter 13. Table 10.3 compares heme-reacting chemicals (diaminobenzine, leucocrystal violet, and luminol). Each was considered for its ability to enhance blood at the scene. In a separate study, tests were conducted on various surfaces: porous, semiporous, and nonporous [35]. The results show that the presumptive chemical tests, the catalytic tests, are not the best choice for developing bloodstain impressions at crime scenes [35]. This is true whether the bloody impression is a fingerprint, footwear impression, or tire track impression.

* "Any of various compounds with a macrocyclic structure that consists essentially of four pyrrole rings joined by four =CH– groups; especially : one (as chlorophyll or hemoglobin) containing a central metal atom and usually exhibiting biological activity. Origin of porphyin from Greek porphyra purple. First known use: 1910" [34].

Table 10.3 Comparison of Blood Staining Reagents

Staining Reagent	Reacting Species	Porous	Semiporous	Nonporous
Diaminobenzine	Heme	+2	+2	+1
Leuco crystal violet	Heme	+2	+2	—
Luminol	Heme	+1	+1	—
Acid violet 19+	Heme	+2	+2	+1
Fluorescein	Amino groups	+1	+1	—
1,8-Diazafluoren-9-one	Amino groups	+4	+2	—
Lucifer yellow VS	Amino groups	—	—	+4
Ninhydrin	Amino groups	+3	+2	—
SYPRO	Amino groups	+3	+2	+2
Acid black 1 (WEAA)	Protein	+4	+3	+3
Acid violet 17	Protein	+4	+3	+3
Acid yellow 7	Protein	—	—	+4

Source: Adapted from Sears V. G. and Prizeman, T. M., *Journal of Forensic Identification*, 50(5), 470–480, 2000.

Other blood constituents such as amino acids are used to develop fingerprints from porous surfaces. They are also the building blocks of proteins and are part of a group of molecules having amino groups as part of their molecular structure. These amines are classified as primary, secondary, and tertiary ($-NH_2$, NHR, NR_2, respectively, where "R" is a functional group such as methyl). In the blood, the most commonly occurring are the α-amino acids and proteins, the latter being amides with terminal amino groups still present.

A number of chemicals react with amino groups to form either colored or fluorescent products (e.g., ninhydrin, DFO, 1,2-indanedione), which are traditionally considered amino acid reactive chemicals used to develop fingerprints on porous surfaces. However, they also react with the proteins in blood to produce the same color as they do with fingerprints. For ninhydrin, this would be Ruhemann's purple; for DFO, fluorescein; and 1,2-indanedione, the reaction product is fluorescent. Another amino group reactive chemical is Lucifer yellow S, which, although no longer available, also forms a fluorescent product.

How does an investigator choose which reagent is the best to develop impression prints in blood? Table 10.3 is a summary of tests adapted from research conducted by the HOSDB in Great Britain. They analyzed combinations of absorbing and fluorescent dyes, such as Crowles double stain (a combination of acid blue 83 and acid red 71), brilliant sulfaflavine, and benzoxanthene yellow, which they used in double and triple stain solutions [36]. The results were clear-cut for enhancing bloody fingerprints [37].

Thus, there are choices for enhancing bloody impression evidence at a crime scene. The traditional and trusted technique is to use one of the two formulations (methanol-based or aqueous-based) for Amido black, also known as acid black 1. Sears et al. [35–37] devised a third formulation that, in their hands, gave better results: For porous surfaces, three dyes were superior. Acid black 1 and acid violet 17 gave colored products. In another study, acid yellow 7 gave a fluorescent product after lifting with a white gel lifter,* which was particularly effective on nonfluorescing dark surfaces. On nonporous surfaces, acid black 1, acid

* http://www.usa.bvda.com/ (accessed December 20, 2010).

violet 17, and acid yellow 7 were, again, the best reagents. DFO turned out to be a good reagent for porous surfaces [35–37], which is not unexpected because it is commonly used for developing fingerprints on paper. One would expect 1,2-indanedione to work well, but this was not tested. The only caveat for using any of these reagents concerns background staining, which must be known and determined before testing potentially probative evidence. The following are the formulations for the bloodstain developing reagents discussed above.

10.9.1.1 HOSDB Formulation for Acid Black 1, Acid Violet 17, and Acid Yellow 7

HOSDB developed the following water/ethanol/acetic acid formulation for common blood staining solutions.

- 1 g dye
- 250 mL ethanol
- 50 mL acetic acid
- 700 mL water
- The destaining solution contains only the solvents

The FBI advocates three protein staining methods, each having a protein fixative imbedded in the solution. Two use Amido black (naphthol blue black—acid black 1), one methanol-based, the other aqueous, and the third uses DAB [37].

10.9.1.2 FBI Formulation for Acid Black 1

Methanol formulas:

- 2 g Amido black and 100 mL glacial acetic acid
- 900 mL methanol
- The destaining solution does not contain the dye

Aqueous formulas:

- 20 g 5-sulfosalicylic acid in 500 mL distilled water.
- 3 g Amido black and 3 g sodium carbonate.
- 50 mL formic acid and 50 mL glacial acetic.
- Kodak Photo-Flo 600diluted to 1 L with distilled water. The solution should stand for several days before use.

DAB procedures:

- Using solution A (fixative): 20 g 5-sulfosalicyclic acid plus 1 L distilled water
- Using solution B (buffer): 100 mL 1 M phosphate buffer (pH 7.4)
- Using solution C (DAB) 1 g 3,3′-diaminobenzidine tetrahydrochloride
- 100 mL distilled water
- Using solution D (developer) 1 mL 30% hydrogen peroxide, 180 mL solution B, 20 mL solution C

10.9.1.3 General Protein Fixing Procedure

The following is a general procedure for fixing proteins in blood before staining.

- Ensure that proper safety precautions are followed.
- Fix proteins in the thicker bloodstains for approximately 5 min (2–3 min for weaker stains). This ensures that the DAB solution does not dissolve the proteins. If not properly fixed, the stain will smear the impression.

10.9.1.3.1 Choices for Fixing Blood in Impression Prints There are choices for fixing bloodstains at the crime scene. The best choice is 5-sulfosalicylic acid dehydrate. Methanol is given as a choice because it is often a component of staining/fixing blood-staining solutions.

10.9.1.3.1.1 Methanol Methanol is a poison, flammable, and can soften or dissolve (ruin) some surfaces, for example, paints, varnishes, and some plastics. This means that the surface must be pretested to ensure that the solvent will not adversely affect it before using it to fix bloodstains. Additionally, it may not denature heavily bloodstained impressions completely unless the fixing time is extended.

10.9.1.3.1.2 5-Sulfosalicylic Acid Dihydrate Sulfosalicylic acid denatures proteins and is easier and safer to use than methanol. A recommended fixing solution would be a 2% solution: 20 g 5-sulfosalicyclic acid dihydrate dissolved in 1000 mL distilled water. The stain should be soaked with the fixing solution using one of the following methods depending on the surface and orientation of the impression.

10.9.1.4 General Procedure for Staining Blood Impressions

- Immersion or dipping: Immerse or dip the impression or object into a fixative solution and allow it to sit for an appropriate amount of time, depending on the thickness of the blood.
- Spraying: Spray the bloodstained impression. This is a messy method that is useful for bloody fingerprints on vertical surfaces.
- Covering or tissue method: In the covering or tissue method, place a paper/tissue over the impression and pour the fixative solution over the tissue, allowing it to remain in contact with the bloodstained impression for an appropriate time—3–5 min.
- Imbedded gel overlay*: After fixing, another method for staining on weak stains uses gel lifters (BVDA or homemade gels) impregnated with the dye.
  - Float the gel side of a white gel lifter on the staining solution in a tray for approximately 3 min.
  - Lightly blot the excess stain from the lifter.
  - Carefully place the gel lifter over the stain and hold it in place for 2–3 min. Use a fingerprint roller to ensure a snug fit between the gel and the impression.
  - Lift the gel from the print.
  - Pour a small amount of destain solution over the stained impression and allow it to soak for a 2–3 min.

* Robert C. Shaler. Unpublished results.

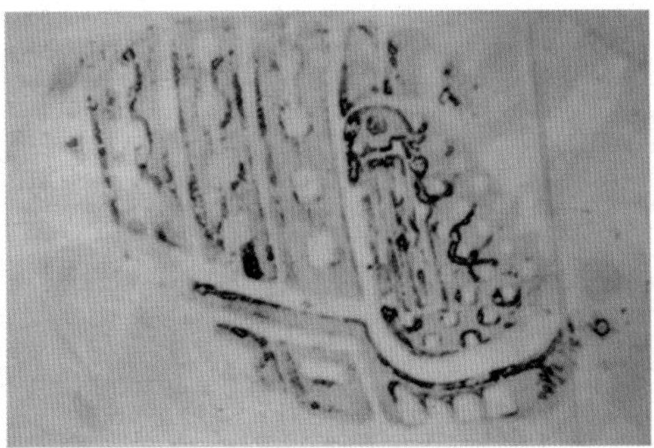

Figure 10.18 Acid violet 17–stained bloody footprint using gel immersion procedure. (Photograph by Robert C. Shaler.)

- Carefully blot the destain solution from the impression and allow it to dry.
- Photograph the stained prints.
- Place a white gel lifter over the stained impression and use a fingerprint roller to ensure a snug fit between the gel and the stained impression.
- Allow the gel to remain in place for approximately 30 min.
- Lift the gel and protect the lifted impression with the acetate covering that came with the lifter. An example of a bloody footwear impression stained as described above and then lifted with a white gel lifter is shown in Figure 10.18.

10.9.1.5 General Procedure for On-Scene Blood Print Staining

- Stain blood proteins using one of the procedures above. Staining can vary from approximately 30 s to 1 min (FBI methanol method [38]) or 3–5 min (FBI aqueous Amido method [38]).
- Rinse the excess stain from the impression and dry. Staining can be repeated until the sensitivity is satisfactory. As with all staining methods, be careful that the background is not heavily stained.
- Destain the background using the destaining solution.
- Photograph the stained impression.
- Lift the stained impression with a white gel lifter.

Figure 10.19 shows an acid violet 17–stained blood print on an outdoor fence post enhanced by a student using the tissue overlay technique.

10.10 Fingerprints and Heat: Fire Scenes

Arsonists and terrorists handle accelerants, explosives, and incendiary devices. At the scene, these are considered fire and explosion debris. Incendiary devices, such as Molotov cocktails, are examples of debris on which fingerprints might be present. A perception is that the fire and/or explosive environment destroys conventional evidence such as fingerprints. This is apparently not true, although the literature on the persistence of fingerprints at arson scenes and on incendiary devices is scanty and often anecdotal.

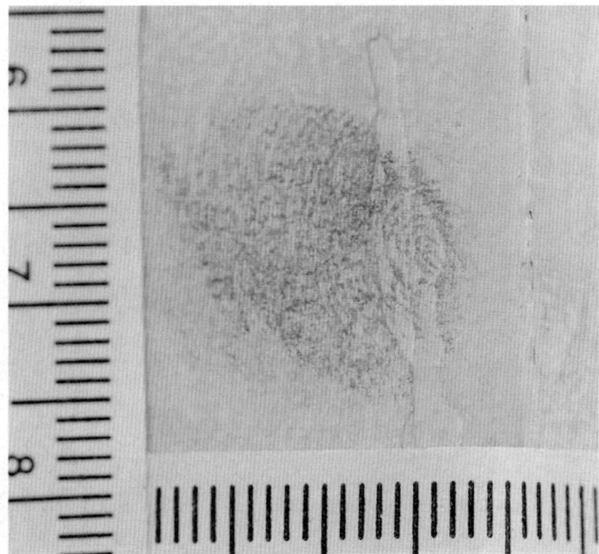

Figure 10.19 Acid violet 17–stained fingerprint using tissue overlay technique. (Photograph by Robert C. Shaler.)

Harper [39] showed that fingerprints can persist at temperatures up to 200°C, especially if carbon (soot) covers them. In experiments, fires were purposely set with the containers of a kerosene/gasoline mixture used to start the fire and then left inside the burning building. After extinguishing the fire using ordinary efforts, these containers were recovered. Attempts to locate fingerprints on those items a few feet from the point of origin were unsuccessful. However, rooms adjacent to the point of origin that received extensive heat and smoke gave identifiable prints. Nonporous objects in or close to the point of origin rarely gave identifiable prints. In one instance, a light fixture gave prints in soot that had become fixed onto the surface [40]. Tyranski and Petraco [41] reported an interaction of gasoline with the container that resulted in a plastic print. Just as it is likely that useable fingerprints can be found at arson scenes, the same is true for incendiary devices, although the body of literature is even scantier [41].

So, while it is possible to uncover prints at arson scenes, there is the question of how much heat this fragile evidence can withstand. Some studies have been designed to address this topic.

10.10.1 Effect of Heat on Fingerprints

Several studies suggest that fingerprints can withstand the temperatures measured at arson scenes. Studies by Harper [39] and Shelef et al. [42] and work of the HOSDB [43] suggest that fingerprints can withstand temperatures of at least 300°C. Additionally, the recovery of useful marks on articles covered by heavy soot deposits suggests that these might withstand temperatures up to 700°C or more.

Another issue is that of how much heat fingerprints in blood can withstand. From HOSDB laboratory experiments, it is safe to say that blood prints survive heat up to approximately 200°C [43]. Developing blood prints exposed to this much heat is a problem because none of the standard protein-staining methods or presumptive blood tests work; catalytic tests fail at temperatures below 150°C. Fortunately, blood forms a protective layer on the surface before flaking off which means that the surface oxidation between the ridge detail (blood-covered ridges) and those nonprotected areas (the grooves) is different. Thus, processes sensitive to surface conditions (e.g., vacuum metal deposition) will develop prints where blood prints have been exposed to temperatures as high as 900°C [43].

10.10.2 Locating Fingerprints at Arson Scenes

As it is possible to retrieve prints from arson scenes and from incendiary devices or their fragments, finding them should be a priority of arson and explosive scene investigators. Knowing where to look is a problem because items of potential evidence may be soot covered. One consideration is temperature. Scene scientists/investigators should attempt to gauge the hottest points and then confine collecting evidence in areas where temperatures did not rise above 300°C.

Another consideration relates to fire suppression. Water is not usually detrimental to the oils in fingerprint residue because they are insoluble. However, if the temperature of the fire is high enough to destroy the organic components of exposed residue, only inorganic salts will remain, which are soluble in water. Fire suppression efforts may dissolve these salts and efforts to develop prints will be futile.

A caveat might be some metallic surfaces. There is the possibility that the print residue may act as a barrier or resist against oxidation so that the unprotected metal might etch [44]. Additionally, since soot can protect fingerprints, soot-covered, potentially probative evidence should always be considered as potential evidence. Soot causes problems in the laboratory because scientists must remove the soot without destroying the prints.

Table 10.4 Techniques for Print Development of Heat-Exposed Prints

Fingerprint Development Method	Use and Limitations
Visualization	All items should be examined visually because heat and soot affect prints in various ways. Soot may preferentially deposit on oily surfaces. Heat may develop ridge detail on paper. Residue can bake on metallic surfaces.
Black powder suspension	Best for nonporous surfaces <200°C
Black magnetic powder	Not useful >200°C
Small particle reagent	Less useful than powder suspensions
Superglue fuming + basic yellow 40	Good up to 500°C on nonporous surfaces
Vacuum metal deposition	Laboratory technique but appropriate up to 900°C. Water or dried water spots can interfere.
1,8-Diazafluoren-9-one	Performs poorly when paper has been wet
Ninhydrin	See 1,8-diazafluoren-9-one
Physical developer	Develops prints on charred paper in laboratory environment
Infrared imaging	Useful for areas where charring and soot deposit are in the viewfinder of the infrared camera. Use lens filter >715 nm—RG850 filter.
Blood protein stains	Good up to 200°C
Heme-specific stains	Stops working >150°C

10.10.3 On-Scene Activity

The success of finding useable fingerprints requires knowledge of the literature, where investigators reported success, and research results that have answered questions concerning the effects of temperature, accelerant, and so on. Generally, scene scientists/investigators should consider the following [43], given today's technology.

- Fingerprints exposed to <300°C may be retrievable.
- Items of potentially probative evidence protected from direct exposure to heat and smoke may have retrievable fingerprints.
- Less soot covering fingerprints is better because the soot cover must be removed in the laboratory. The presence of heavy soot deposits, however, does not mean removal techniques will not be successful.
- Dry evidence has a better chance of providing probative fingerprint detail than wet evidence.
- Where fingerprint residue has dried from the heat, rehumidification may be successful, but the possibility of destroying the ridge detail is a concern.

According to the HOSDB, Table 10.4 reflects lessons learned from anecdotal work and systematic research with respect to what is known about how well traditional development techniques work on retrieving prints from arson evidence [43].

References

1. *ODEC.* Animal fingerprints. Available at: http://www.odec.ca/projects/2004/fren4j0/public_html/animal_fingerprints.htm (accessed January 25, 2011).
2. C. Champod, C. Lennard, P. Margot, and M. Stoilovic. 2004. Chapter 4: Fingerprint detection techniques. In: *Fingerprints and Other Ridge Skin Impressions.* International Forensic Science and Investigation Series. Boca Raton, FL: CRC Press, pp. 105–179.
3. Home Office Scientific Development Branch. 2006. Operational performance of Nd:YAG green (532 nm) laser. *HOSDB Fingerprint Development and Imaging Newsletter*, Publication No. 34/06.
4. E. W. Brown. The Cyanoacrylate Fuming Method. Available at: http://www.ccs.neu.edu/home/feneric/cyanoacrylate.html (accessed January 28, 09).
5. *Wikipedia.* Sweat gland. Available at: http:/en.wikipedia.org/wiki/Sweat_glands (accessed January 30, 2009).
6. P. M. Quinton. 1983. Sweating and its disorders. *Annual Review of Medicine*, 34:429–452.
7. W. Montagna and P. F. Parakkal (eds). 1974. *The Structure of Skin*, 3rd edn. New York, NY: Academic Press.
8. R. S. Ramotowski. 2001. Composition of latent print residue. In: H. C. Lee and R. E. Gaensslen (eds), *Advances in Fingerprint Technology*, 2nd edn. Boca Raton, FL: CRC Press, pp. 63–104.
9. A. M. Knowles. 1978. Aspects of physicochemical methods for the detection of latent fingerprints. *Journal of Physics E: Scientific Instruments*, 11:713–721.
10. S. P. Wargacki, L. A. Lewis, and M. D. Dadmum. 2008. Enhancing the quality of aged latent fingerprints developed by superglue fuming: Loss and replenishment of initiator. *Journal of Forensic Sciences*, 53(5):1138–1144.
11. H. C. Lee, T. Palmbach, and M. T. Miller. 2005. *Henry Lee's Crime Scene Handbook.* San Diego, CA: Academic Press, pp. 137–139.

12. B. A. J. Fisher. 2004. *Techniques of Crime Scene Investigation*, 7th edn. Boca Raton, FL: CRC Press, pp. 93–115.
13. R. M. Gardner. 2005. *Practical Crime Scene Processing and Investigation*. Boca Raton, FL: CRC Press, pp. 228–247.
14. J. T. Fish, L. S. Miller, and M. C. Braswell. 2007. *Crime Scene Investigation*. Newark, NJ: Matthew Bender & Company, Inc., pp. 83–94.
15. Chesapeake Bay Division of the International Association of Identification. Available at: http://www .cbdiai.org/Reagents/main.html (accessed November 4, 2010).
16. H. C. Lee and R. E. Gaensslen (eds). 2001. *Advances in Fingerprint Technology*, 2nd edn. Boca Raton, FL: CRC Press, Chapters 4–7, pp. 106–271.
17. Police Scientific Development Branch (PSDB). 2004 [1998]. In: T. Kent (ed.), *Manual of Fingerprint Development Techniques,* 2nd edn revision. Sandridge: British Home Office, PSDB.
18. A. Joseph, M. Azoury, Y. Elmaliah, L Berenstein, and A. Zaban. 2004. Fingerprints' third dimension: The depth and shape of fingerprints penetration into paper—Cross section examination by fluorescence microscopy. *Journal of Forensic Sciences*, 49(5):1–5.
19. D. T. Burns, J. K. Brown, and K. K. Harvey. 1998. Base-activated latent prints with a cyanoacrylate monomer. A quantitative study using Fourier-transform infrared spectroscopy. *Analytica Chimica Acta*, 362(2–3):171–176.
20. H. L. Bandey. 2006. The Powders Process Study 2: Evaluation of fingerprint powders on smooth surfaces. *HOSDB Fingerprint Development and Imaging Newsletter: Special Edition*, Publication No. 08/06.
21. H. L. Bandey. 2004. The Powders Process Study 1: Evaluation of fingerprint brushes for use with aluminum powder. *HOSDB Fingerprint Development and Imaging Newsletter: Special Edition*, Publication No. 54/04.
22. J. D. James, A. Pounds, and B. Wilshire. 1991. Obliteration of latent fingerprints. *Journal of Forensic Sciences*, 36(5):1376–1386.
23. H. L. Bandey and T. Hardy. 2006. The Powders Process Study 3: Evaluation of fingerprint powders on textured surfaces and U-PVC. *HOSDB Fingerprint and Footwear Forensics Newsletter*, Publication No. 67/08.
24. T. F. Spear, N. Khoshkebari, J. Clark, and M. Murphy. Summary of the impact of fingerprint reagents on the ability to obtain typing results using PCR-based DNA methods or conventional typing methods. California: California Criminalistics Institute. Available at www.CACNews.org/training/fingerprint_effects_DNA.pdf (accessed July 25, 2011).
25. E. German. Cyanoacrylate (superglue) fuming tips. Available at: http://www.onin.com/fp/cyanoho.html (accessed October 7, 2009).
26. J. E. Watkin, D. A. Wilkinson, A. H. Misner, and A. B. Yamashita. 1994. Cyanoacrylate fuming of latent prints: Vacuum versus heat/humidity. *Journal of Forensic Identification*, 44(5):545–557.
27. C. W. Bessman, E. N. Robert, J. L. Shelley, C. Terrance, and R. Herrman. 2005. Comparison of cyanoacrylate fuming in a vacuum cabinet to a humidity fuming chamber. *Journal of Forensic Identification*, 55(1):10–27.
28. H. L. Bandey and T. Kent. 2003. Superglue treatment of crime scenes. HOSDB Publication No. 30/03.
29. D. Weaver, A. Wheeler, G. Pokharel, M. A. Hines, S. Farmer, and J. Basher. Final report: Specific heat capacity thermal function fingerprint development process. Available at: http://www.executiveforensics.com/files/final%20report%204.28.pdf (accessed November 5, 2010).
30. *Wikipedia*. Rube Goldberg. Available at: http://en.wikipedia.org/wiki/Rube_Goldberg (accessed November 5, 2010).
31. Arrowhead Forensics. Available at: http://www.crime-scene.com/store/A-CNYP-1.shtml (accessed November 5, 2010).

32. Police Scientific Development Branch. 2006. Additional fingerprint development techniques for adhesive tapes. *HOSDB Fingerprint and Imaging Newsletter*, Publication No. 23/06.
33. *Wikipedia*. Coomassie Brilliant Blue. Available at: http://en.wikipedia.org/wiki/Coomassie_Brilliant_Blue (accessed February 22, 2011).
34. *Merriam-Webster Online Dictionary*. Porphyrin. Available at: http://www.merriam-webster.com/dictionary/porphyrin (accessed January 26, 2011).
35. V. G. Sears and T. M. Prizeman. 2000. Enhancement of fingerprints in blood—Part 1. The optimization of Amido black. *Journal of Forensic Identification*, 50(5):470–480.
36. V. G. Sears, C. P. G. Butcher, and T. M. Prizeman. 2001. Enhancements of fingerprints in blood—Part 2. Protein dyes. *Journal of Forensic Identification*, 51(1):28–38.
37. V. G. Sears, C. P. G. Butcher, and L. A. Fitzgerald. 2005. Enhancements of fingerprints in blood—Part 3. Reactive techniques, acid yellow 7, and process sequences. *Journal of Forensic Identification*, 55(6):741–763.
38. U.S. Department of Justice Federal Bureau of Investigation, Laboratory Division. 2000. *Processing Guide for Developing Latent Prints*. Washington, DC: U.S. Department of Justice.
39. W. W. Harper. 1938. Latent fingerprints at high temperatures. *Journal of Criminal Law, Criminology, and Police Science*, 39:580–583.
40. M. A. Spawn. 1994. Effects of fire on fingerprint evidence. *Fingerprint World*, 20(76):45–76.
41. W. Tyranski and N. Petraco. 1981. An interesting arson case involving a plastic. *Fingerprint Identification News*, June:9.
42. R. Shelef, A. Levy, I. Rhima, S. Tsaroom, and R. Elkayam. 1996. Development of latent fingerprints from incendiary bottles. *Journal of Forensic Identification*, 45(5):557–569.
43. S. M. Bleay, G. Bradshaw, and J. E. Moore. 2006. *HOSDB Fingerprint Development and Imaging Newsletter*, Publication No. 26/06.
44. A. A. Cantu, D. A. Leben, R. S. Ramotowski, J. Kopera, and J. R. Sinuns. 1998. Use of acidified hydrogen peroxide to remove excess gun blue from gun blue-treated cartridge cases and to develop latent prints on untreated cartridge cases. *Journal of Forensic Sciences*, 43:294–298.

Workshop 3: Fingerprints on Nonporous Surfaces—Dusting Powders

When dusting for prints always wear a dust mask and gloves.

W3.1 Inked and Rolled Prints

Exemplars are collected by inking and rolling prints onto 10-digit fingerprint cards. More often, police departments collect fingerprints digitally. This workshop does not include collecting inked, rolled, or digital prints.

W3.2 Developing Fingerprints at the Scene Using Dusting Powders

Dusting is a common method for locating latent prints on *nonporous surfaces* at the crime scene. Some nonporous surfaces, such as glitzy magazine covers, have "hard" surfaces. Sometimes powder dusting reveals prints, though glitzy magazine covers might require a dusting powder other than black. The most common powders are black and gray, the latter also known as dual. Which to use is usually a matter of preference learned through experience. Dual powders have the advantage in that they can be effective when used on surfaces having background colors. Black powders have better contrast on lighter surfaces. Dual powder works well on light and dark surfaces, appearing dark gray on the light surfaces and silvery on dark surfaces.

The aim of this exercise is to learn to care for dusting brushes and powders. These will be used on a variety of nonporous surfaces because those are the most amenable to dusting powders.

The technique of powder dusting is a little like a gently sifting powder onto the print surface. The dusting motion is circular accomplished by moving the brush over the surface without touching or barely touching it. The movement can be first clockwise and then counterclockwise. The purpose of moving the brush in two directions is to be certain that both sides of the print ridges come into contact with the powder. A gentle touch is important. Too harsh a technique can distort the ridge detail and can even ruin it, and applying too much powder can over dust the print and cause distortion.

W3.3 Fingerprint Residue

Refer to Chapter 9 for a discussion on fingerprint residue.

W3.3.1 General Guidelines for Print Development

The following list of guidelines is for students and inexperienced investigators who are learning to dust for fingerprints. Dusting is a slow, controlled technique where swirling a fingerprint brush using a back-and-forth motion coats both sides of the ridges. The secret is to use as small an amount of powder as possible.

- Less powder is better for all powders but especially for fluorescent powders.
- Never touch the surface with the dusting brush.
- Never put the brush in the original powder source. Always use a separate reservoir, such as a small amount of powder onto a piece of paper or into a separate container.
- Always remove (twirl "stick" end of the brush rapidly between the palms of both hands) excess powder from a brush before dusting.
- Never put new powder on a "used" brush. Always check to see if there is sufficient powder for dusting first.
- Never lay a brush onto a flat surface as this will flatten the bristles. Lean it against a container so that the bristles remain suspended.
- Dedicate a brush for a specific powder: Brushes should never be used for more than one powder type.
- Practice patience. Harsh or otherwise rough treatment of the print or the dusting surface is not a proper dusting technique and can cause problems, such as over dusting and smudging of the ridge detail.

W3.3.2 Powders Available

Over the years, dusting has evolved to the point where many powder formulations are available commercially. Table W3.1 shows a short list of dusting powders available. For this workshop, powders can be categorized as direct powders, fluorescent powders, magnetic powders, and multipurpose powders.

Table W3.1 Dusting Powders Available

Direct Powders	Fluorescent Powders	Magnetic Powders	Multipurpose
Black	Red	Black magnetic	Bichromatic
Dual contrast	Yellow	Dual magnetic	PrintGlo™
	Green	Fluorescent magnetic	

W3.3.3 Demonstration

An instructor will demonstrate the proper technique for visualizing latent fingerprints from nonporous surfaces using a powder from each category in Table W3.1. The instruction will include:

- Use of a respirator mask
- Proper handling of the powder reservoir
- Preparing an operational powder source
- Proper handling of new and used brushes
- Proper dusting techniques
- Filling in the information onto fingerprint lift cards
- Lifting prints using tape to fingerprint card, gel lifters, and Mikrosil™ casts. See Section 10.11.6
- Over dusting
- Challenges of over dusting and possible correction technique
- Magnifying lens to examine print quality
- Use of the ALS for visualizing fluorescent powders
- Photography of dusted fingerprints and fluorescent fingerprints using tripods and the ALS

W3.3.4 Exercise 1: Dusting Nonporous Surfaces

Choose several nonporous objects, for example, plastic plates, plastic bags, and so on, and place your own fingerprints on them in several places after running your fingers over your forehead or cheek with your fingers. Choose one powder from each of the categories in TableW3.1.

- Practice developing your own fingerprints on these surfaces.
- Show the developed prints to an instructor.
- Repeat the exercise until an instructor is satisfied with the quality of the developed print.
- For powders in the multipurpose column, fill in Table W3.2.

Table W3.2 Exercise I: Nonporous Surfaces

Powder Used	Description of the Visible and ALS Results

Table W3.3 Exercise 2: Fill-In Table

Object at Scene	Yes or No/Powder Choice/ALS Wavelength/Goggle	Object at Scene	Yes or No/Powder Choice/ALS Wavelength/Goggle
Turned over chair (Raw wood chair)		Table next to window (varnished wood)	
Outside front door knob (brass)		Floor next to body (dark tile)	
Inside front door knob (brass)		Patent prints next to body (blood)	
Windowsill (white paint)		*People* Magazine on the floor next to the body	

W3.3.5 Exercise 2: Finding and Lifting Latent Fingerprints in a Mock Scene

- Envision the following scene: You are responsible for finding and developing fingerprints at a crime scene. When you enter the scene, you see a body lying in the middle of the floor in a pool of blood. There are obvious patent prints in blood near the body. Several chairs are turned over and a window is open. A footwear impression is in mud under the window. Bloody footprints lead away from the body toward the front door.
- Place a Y (yes) or N (no) next to the item in Table W3.3 that you believe should be fingerprinted. If you place a (Y), choose the most appropriate powder (BLK, MagBLK, and so on) that is the *best* choice for developing the fingerprints on that object. If a fluorescent powder is your choice, place the wavelength (Y = yellow, O = orange, R = red, and N = nothing) and goggles you would need to see the developed print.

W3.4 Fingerprints on Wet Surfaces

Latent fingerprints on wet, nonporous surfaces present special problems because using dusting powders directly will become a mess and the prints will be ruined. There are two approaches. The first is to dry the object and then treat it using traditional dusting or other techniques. If it is absolutely necessary to develop the prints at the scene, there are ways in which this can be accomplished. A common method uses the "small particle reagent" (SPR), which is a weak detergent solution of a microcrystalline molybdenum dioxide.

W3.4.1 Demonstration

The demonstration includes the following:

- Preparation of SPR reagent
- Use of black and white on wet objects
- Lifting developed prints

W3.4.1.1 SPR Procedure

- Remove the plate from the water.
- Dry the plate.
- Depending on the color (dark or light), spray the plate in the SPR area of the print development room in Spruce Cottage—allow the SPR to run over the evidence, but do not spray the place where you believe prints might be located.

- Allow the SPR-sprayed plate to stand for approximately one minute and then rinse the plate by spraying *gently* with water—do not spray directly onto visualized prints.
- Dry the developed print.
- Lift the print with lifting tape and transfer to a fingerprint card.

W3.4.1.2 Alternative SPR Procedure

- Dry the evidence.
- Superglue fume or dust the print with fluorescent or other powder.

W3.4.1.3 Alternative Formulations for Wet Surfaces

- Sticky-side powder.
- WetWop™ (black or white formulations) are also available.

W3.4.2 Exercise 3: Latent Prints on Wet Surfaces

- Fingerprints have been placed on variously colored plates in a sink filled with water. Choose one plate. Develop the fingerprints on the plate using SPR.
- Examine the print for quality using a magnifying lens.
- Show your developed print to an instructor.
- Photograph the print. Show the photograph to an instructor.

W3.5 Prints on the Sticky Side of Adhesive Tapes

Fingerprints occur on both sides of adhesive tapes. Depending on the chemistry of the adhesive, certain powders can be effective for developing prints. A number of reagents, some of which are powder-based, have been successfully used to develop prints on the sticky side of adhesive tapes. Unfortunately, experience shows that not all of these are applicable to all tapes, due to the adhesive materials on the tape.

W3.5.1 Sticky-Side Fingerprint Developing Reagents

Powder and nonpowder formulations have been devised for the sticky side of adhesive tapes.

- TapeGlo™-fluorescent visualized using UV light
- Sticky-side powder
- Gentian violet (crystal violet also known as basic violet 3)—not a powder
- SPR
- WetWop™

W3.5.2 Spot Testing the Sticky-Side Chemistry

Before attempting to develop prints on the sticky side of an adhesive, perform a spot test to see which development technique is most appropriate. The choices for developing the prints with powder are carbon-based or iron oxide-based powder suspensions or a chemical technique using a nonphenolic version of basic violet 3 (Gentian violet). TapeGlo™ is a fluorescent visualizing agent.

W3.5.2.1 Spot Test Procedure

- Apply a toothpick-sized but clear spot of black or white powder suspension to a section of the tape that is less likely to have been handled.
- Wash the spot and only that area of the tape with tap water until the excess powder is gone.

- If powder remains on the spot, the adhesive is *probably* acrylic-based and should be developed using an aqueous version of basic violet 3 (Gentian violet).
- If the tape is visible after washing the test spot, the tape is probably a rubber-based adhesive and can be developed using powder suspensions.
- If the tape is still heavily stained, the adhesive is probably an acrylic adhesive.

W3.5.3 Exercise 4: Finding Prints on the Sticky Side of Adhesive Tape

W3.5.3.1 Demonstration An instructor will demonstrate the following techniques:

- Choosing an appropriate development method by spot-testing adhesives
- Use carbon-based and iron-based reagents for rubber-based adhesives
- Use basic violet 3 for acrylic-based adhesives
- Use TapeGlo™

W3.5.3.2 Developing Fingerprints on Adhesive Tapes Fingerprints have been placed on various adhesive tapes. Choose three tapes and develop fingerprints using an appropriate technique. Fill in Table W3.4.

W3.6 Lifting Fingerprints

There a number of ways to lift powder-dusted prints. The oldest and most common method is to use clear or opaque tape to transfer the dusted print to a fingerprint card. The sticky side of the tape lifts the powder, which is then transferred to a "print lift card." The specific card will depend on the background. If black or dual dusting powders are used to develop the print, a white lift card is used. If fluorescent powder or white powder is used, a black lift card might give more contrast. The technique is easy but requires practice. The following is a list of choices. Generally, the choice depends on the surface and the background color.

- Tape lift: For nonporous, smooth surfaces
- Photography: Before lifting
- Casting with Mikrosil™: For uneven surfaces
- Tex-lift gel: For nonporous, uneven surfaces
- Gelatin lifters (Gellifters): For nonporous, uneven surfaces

W3.6.1 Tape-Lifting Procedure

The following guidelines are important:

- After tearing the tape, fold back a corner onto itself so that the next person who uses the tape does not have to invent a way to unstick it.

Table W3.4 Exercise 4: Fill-In Table

Tape	Result of Spot Test	Technique	Quality of Print
1			
2			
3			
4			
5			

- Carefully cover the dusted print so that air bubbles do not form under the tape.
- Slowly remove the tape and "stuck" print from the surface.
- Place the lifted print onto the print lift card carefully and slowly. Do not allow bubbles to form under the tape.

W3.6.2 Exercise 5: Lifting Dusted Fingerprints

Several fingerprints have been placed on nonporous objects. Develop the prints and then lift to an appropriate print lift card. Be sure to fill out the information on the back of the card. Show the lifted print to an instructor.

W3.7 Fluorescent Powders

Fluorescent powders are treated much like conventional dusting powders except *much less* powder is required to develop the prints. The reason is that fluorescence is much more sensitive than visual methods. Typically, fluorescent powders are used when the backgrounds are multicolored where dusting powders are not as easily seen. Dedicated brushes are used for fluorescent powders.

Choose two from the following list of fluorescent powders that are available:

- Black emerald
- Black euby powder
- PrintGlo™
- Magnetic fluorescent powder
- Dual fluorescent powder
- Bichromatic powder

W3.7.1 Demonstration

An instructor will demonstrate the following techniques:

- Dusting procedure using fluorescent powders
- Visualizing fluorescent powders using the ALS
- Selection of goggle type with ALS
- Lifting fluorescent developed prints
- Transferring lift to fingerprint card

W3.7.2 Exercise 6

Choose a magazine with a multicolored, hard finish, a newspaper (use different kinds of newspaper), and a red plastic cup.

- Place your fingerprints on each item and then develop these using the fluorescent powders of your choice.
- Photograph the developed prints.
- Lift the prints using the most appropriate lifting method and transfer to an appropriate fingerprint lift card.
- Show the lifted print and the photograph to an instructor.

W3.8 Mikrosil™ Casting—Tex-Lift—Gellifters

Silicone-based casting materials are manufactured so that fine detail can be captured. Most Mikrosil™ applications involve casting fine detail impression evidence, such as tool marks, but it can also be used to lift dusted fingerprints on uneven surfaces. Gel-based procedures have also been developed. Two of these are available: Tex-lift and rubber-backed gelatin lifters.

W3.8.1 Demonstration for Lifting Black and Dual-Dusted Fingerprints

An instructor will demonstrate how to prepare Mikrosil™ casting material using the following methods:

- Using a solid surface that is disposable, make a line of the white Mikrosil™ (large tube) approximately 2 in. long. Beside this, run a line of hardener (small tube).
- Using the wooden spatulas provided, mix the two for approximately 1 min, ensuring that they are completely mixed.
- Spoon the Mikrosil™ mixture over the dusted print and spread into a thin film—not lumpy or thick—and allow it to cure or harden for approximately 15 min. When it is fully cured—not sticky to the touch—it is ready to be transferred to a fingerprint card.

An instructor will demonstrate how to lift prints using Tex-lift and Gellifters using the following procedures:

- Spread a small amount of Tex-lift onto the print using a spatula.
- Allow the gel to dry—this can take some time.
- Lift the print using lifting tape and adhere to a fingerprint card.

W3.8.2 Exercise 8: Lifting Prints Using Gels and Mikrosil™ Casts

Prepare several side-by-side black powder/dual powder-dusted prints on highly textured surfaces. Lift the prints using Mikrosil™ and a white gel lifter (cut to size). After removing the lifts, compare the quality of the two and photograph them side by side. Fill in Table W3.5. Repeat the process using Tex-lift.

W3.9 Prints on Skin: Demonstration

Obtaining fingerprints from human skin is a process that is typically unsuccessful. However, successful results have been reported. Additionally, it should be possible to obtain

Table W3.5 Exercise 8: Fill-In Table

Lifting Method	Surface Texture (Smooth, Rough, Highly Textured)	Results Describe Quality of Lift	Rank Rank the methods 1–5 (1 = The Worst)
Mikrosil Cast			
Gellifter			
TexLift			

DNA from human skin that has been handled by another person, especially after a violent attack. One method that has shown some success is known as the "Adding Machine Paper Technique," developed by the FBI's Evidence Response Team units. The secret of the method is to absorb the oils from the latent print onto highly absorbent and porous paper, and adding machine paper seems to be an ideal medium.

- Roll the paper on the area of the body. Apply gentle pressure.
- Mark the tape with a pencil or pen to document the anatomical position of the tape (left palm side of the wrist, and so on).
- Fix the tape—skin contact side up—inside a container.
- Dust the print using light strokes of a magnetic brush and fine fingerprint powder (MoonGlo or Midnight Blue, DJOES, Inc., Ocoee, FL).

W3.10 Finding Prints at the Scene: Demonstration

Locating prints at the scene is sometimes a trial-and-error process. However, locating them is a systematic, and logical process (see Chapter 9). Examples of prime places to search include entry and egress points, areas where obvious activity has taken place, and objects that have been moved. Since latent prints, by definition, are invisible, techniques that can help locate them include:

- Reflected ultraviolet light (RUVIS)
- ALS
- Oblique lighting using a flashlight or the white light of an ALS, especially on mirrors, glass, and other hard surfaces

After finding the print, if successful, developing them is next. As discussed in Chapter 9, consider alternative visualizing approaches before lunging into a half-thought-out approach. Searching for prints using oblique lighting from a flashlight sometimes works. RUVIS is another approach. The issue is that, even though the first approach is unsuccessful, it does not mean that another approach will not succeed. Perseverance is the operative word. Developing prints requires a careful strategy. The following should be studied and considered carefully before embarking on a specific development strategy.

- Surface: The surface may dictate the development method—porous or nonporous?
- *Porous surface*: Absorb the components of the print.
  - The general age of the print is a consideration.
  - If the print is relatively fresh—say hours and the surface is "hard"—dusting might be one choice.
  - Superglue fuming is another consideration followed by dusting or staining.
  - Traditionally, the approach for porous surfaces will be a cascade. See Chapter 10. Ideally this is done in the laboratory, which means collecting and packaging the evidence.
- Heat and humidity can dictate the approach to take.
- *Nonporous surface*: Does not absorb the print residue.
- *Semiporous surface*: Absorb print residue slowly.

- Development of prints is dependent on the environmental conditions. A hot environment increases the absorption rate. Oily materials in the print will be absorbed into the surface matrix.
- Environmental conditions: Is it cold or hot, humid or dry? A hot environment will dry out oily prints. A humid environment tends to prolong prints. Prints in a humid and arid environment require rehydration, such as using a steam iron containing vinegar.

W3.10.1 Reflected Ultraviolet Light

RUVIS is a method used for locating fingerprints at scenes. Like most methods, it is not always successful. In this approach, reflected UV light is used at 254 nm. This light is harmful to the eyes and can burn the retina. The RUVIS can also be used to locate footprints at a scene.

Goggles must be used with this or any alternative light source. The drawback to the RUVIS is that it is cumbersome, slow, and tedious.

W3.10.2 Alternate Light Source

Sometimes the crime scene search (CSS) or other wavelength settings on the ALS highlight latent prints at scenes. Also, the white light, while bright, is used obliquely to find prints.

W3.10.3 Oblique Lighting

Using a flashlight held at an oblique angle (also the white light setting on the ALS) can help locate latent prints at scenes. This is particularly effective on glass and dark surfaces.

Workshop 4: Fingerprints on Nonporous (Continued) and Porous Surfaces

W4.1 Nonporous Surfaces (Continued)

W4.1.1 Super Glue Fuming and Enhancement: Background

Always wear a chemical respirator when working with chemicals.

Read the references of the history of superglue fuming in your text. It is important to note that superglue development of fingerprints has assumed an important, almost revered, place in the crime scene investigation lexicon. Its importance is not just that it is a convenient way to develop latent prints on nonporous surfaces but it also *protects* the prints by covering them under a polymer of polycyanoacrylate. Cyanoacrylate-developed latent prints are off-white and must be developed by powder dusting, observation with oblique lighting, RUVIS, or fluorescent staining. Cyanoacrylate-developed prints have value after development because:

- They are protected from destruction during transport to the laboratory.
- They can be used as a first step in a sequential developmental cascade.
- They trap cellular, for example, DNA, material that can be subsequently recovered.

Jurisdictions have varying procedures for developing cyanoacrylate prints at the scene. The aim of this workshop is to learn the basic methods. This is not to say that the chemical processing of the prints cannot be carried out at the scene. It can, but care must be taken and an understanding of how the development process affects the surface. Keep in mind that some items cannot be transported to the laboratory and must be developed, photographed, and/or enhanced at the scene. If so, determine how best to develop the cyanoacrylate-developed latent prints. There are several choices.

- Dusting with powder: This process can be repeated many times because the polycyanoacrylate is stable. Use black, dual, or fluorescent powders—with or without magnetic powders.
- Stain with fluorescent dyes or use lanthanide chemistry to stain the lipids trapped by the superglue.
- Photograph the developed prints using RUVIS and then enhance as above.

Recent work to understand how the superglue fuming process works has been published. It is clear that an initiation process occurs as a nucleophilic attack. The chemicals that initiate are varied and typically attack the C = C moiety in the cyanoacrylate molecule. Chemicals include carboxylic acids, free fatty acids, amino acids, lactate, and, possibly, the pyruvate in fingerprints. Water trapped within the print emulsion is also a factor. It is likely that the attack occurs from the water in sebaceous/eccrine emulsions. Another possibility is that the water in print emulsions offers an environment for other species to initiate the attack. Other weak bases such as ethanol and methanol can also initiate the reaction.

W4.1.1.1 Exercise 1: Superglue Fuming

- Purposes
  - To discuss appropriate safety procedures when using the glue fuming chamber
  - How to use the RUVIS for observing cyanoacrylate-developed prints
  - How to stain cyanoacrylate-developed prints
  - How to dust (and redust) cyanoacrylate-developed prints
  - How to lift dusted cyanoacrylate-developed prints
- Supplies/reagents
  - Microscope slides
  - Basic yellow 40
  - Black dusting powders
  - Fluorescent dusting powders
  - Rhodamine 6G
- Equipment
  - Adjustable heater
  - RUVIS
  - Respirator masks, goggles, gloves, and lab coats
- Procedure—work in groups of two or three
  - Wash your hands using soap and then dry your hands with alcohol—this is how to prepare "clean" eccrine prints. Do not touch other parts of your body.
  - Wait approximately 3 min then place a fingerprint three times (next to each other and successively) on each of three microscope slides.
  - Repeat using three fresh microscope slides using the same finger after wiping your forehead and/or cheek.
  - Turn on the heat source in the fuming tent and allow it to come to temperature for several minutes.

- Place an aluminum tray containing water on another heat source and measure the humidity until it comes to between 60% and 70%.
- Place a fingerprint (after rubbing your forehead) on a black fingerprint lift card. Place the six microscope slides on a stand and the standard print in the fuming chamber.
- Fume the prints until the standard print on the lift card just begins to develop—do not overdevelop.
- Remove the fumed prints.

W4.1.1.2 Exercise 2: Fluorescent Staining Superglue-Developed Prints

- Procedures
- Place one of the clean print slides and one of the oily print slides in the basic yellow 40 slide holder and allow it to stain for 2 min.
  - Repeat with another slide by placing it in the rhodamine 6G slide holder.
- Remove the slides and wash them in running water. *Note*: Be careful to keep the water from running directly on the stained prints.
- Allow the prints to dry.
- Observe the prints in a darkened room using the ALS.

W4.1.1.3 Exercise 3: Dusting Superglue-Developed Prints

- Procedures
  - Dust the third fumed microscope slide with black powder or magnetic fluorescent powder. *Do not overdust* the prints.
  - Lift the black powder dusted prints as you would any dusted fingerprint and transfer to a white print lift card.
  - Observe the fluorescent prints using the ALS—300–400 nm. Before using the ALS, be certain to wear clear goggles.
  - Lift the print using tape and transfer to a black pint lift card.

W4.1.1.4 Exercise 4: Vacuum Superglue Fuming Super glue fumes can also be obtained under a vacuum. The cyanoacrylate fumed prints obtained are more translucent and resistant to overdevelopment, which is unlike H&H fumed prints. Directions for using the vacuum system are posted next to the apparatus.

- Put "clean prints" onto microscope slides as described above.
- Put oily prints onto clean microscope slides as described above.
- Following the directions next to the vacuum apparatus, fume the prints for 10–15 min.
- Enhance the prints by dusting with black powder and by staining with basic yellow.
- Compare these cyanoacrylate-enhanced prints with those obtained using the H&H method.

W4.1.2 Prints on Metallic Surfaces: Corrosion Analysis

There has been a lot of interest in developing prints on metallic surfaces, such as weapons, cartridge cases, and so on. Mostly, these techniques are not successful. Traditional techniques do not always work well. One recent technique took advantage of the corrosive effect of the salts in fingerprints on the surface of metallic objects. The success of this method depends on the metal and its reduction potential.

- Procedures
    - Place a sebaceous fingerprint onto a piece of brass.
    - Hold the metal under a flame.
    - When the fingerprint develops, the reaction is finished.

W4.2 Porous Surfaces

Porous surfaces offer unique challenges to fingerprint examiners because the print diffuses into the matrix. The components of the print remain the same, but the techniques used to develop them change. Typically and historically, this process meant iodine development of the oils followed by ninhydrin development of the amino acids and proteins in the prints. The problem with this approach is that the iodine reaction is not particularly sensitive and disappears rapidly over time, although it is useful for fuming sensitive documents. Ninhydrin works well to develop prints but it too deteriorates over time.

Although ninhydrin is a viable approach for fingerprint development, other techniques have gained in popularity with the increase in knowledge of the chemical composition of fingerprints and as other chemicals have shown increased sensitivity. Researchers worked to increase the sensitivity of the ninhydrin reaction, developing ninhydrin analogs, specifically ones having fluorescent properties. These newer chemicals have been incorporated into a cascade development scheme that is better suited to finding prints on porous surfaces.

The first of these approaches was to combine ninhydrin-developed prints (Ruhemann's purple) with zinc or cadmium metal ions. At low temperatures, these complexes fluoresce. This treatment follows ninhydrin development, not before because the zinc or cadmium reacts with Ruhemann's purple. Another chemical, DFO, has increased sensitivity, meaning it locates prints that ninhydrin does not. Typically, DFO treatment occurs before ninhydrin, so that following DFO with ninydrin has become an accepted print development procedure. Another chemical, 1,2-indanedione, was found to react better and faster with amino acids than DFO and hence can replace DFO as a development agent. In fact, it may also obviate the need to use ninhydrin.

These chemicals, however, do not develop the oils in porous substrate latent prints. The prints developed sometimes appear spotty due to pores on the ridges where the secretions accumulate.

A typical cascade might include the following: iodine, DFO, (or 1,2-indanedione) ninhydrin, physical developer. Iodine-developed prints can be enhanced by adding starch followed by steam, which leads to dark blue-black prints. Using a physical developer is another technique where silver ions are reduced to metallic silver with the resultant formation of dark prints.

W4.2.1 Exercise 1: Iodine Fuming

Iodine vapors combine with the oils in fingerprints to give a nonpermanent record of prints on paper and other substrates. A humid atmosphere is important for developing latent prints using iodine. The developed prints disappear fairly quickly, so it is important to photograph the results. Once located, the prints can be enhanced with ninhydrin (see Section 10.12.2.2).

- Procedures
    - Place oily fingerprints on white paper.

- Follow the directions on the iodine fuming device to develop prints on the paper.
- Dust the prints with powdered starch.
- Use a steam iron (without acetic acid) to just moisten the prints. Observe the color that forms.

W4.2.2 Exercise 2: Ninhydrin-Developed fingerprints

The aim of this exercise is to learn to develop fingerprints on paper using ninhydrin. Ninhydrin is a chemical that combines with the amino acids and proteins in fingerprints in the presence of heat and humidity to form a complex called Ruhemann's purple. Prints on paper are dipped into a bath of 0.5% ninhydrin in a solvent (acetic acid, HFE7100, ethyl acetate, methanol). The paper is allowed to dry and then a steam iron is passed over the paper. The prints develop as reddish-purple fingerprints.

- Procedures
  - Place fresh oily prints on white paper such that the prints cover four quadrants.
  - Cut the paper into fourths.
  - Using a magnetic duster, dust one of the fourths using black magnetic powder—set the dusted print aside.
    - Dip the paper into an organic solvent without ninhydrin (use the ninhydrin solvent) and allow it to dry.
    - Develop the dried paper with ninhydrin as described below.
  - On another fourth, dip the paper into a solution of ninhydrin and develop as described below.
    - Set the paper aside for superglue fuming.
      - After fuming, dust the paper with black magnetic powder.
  - Dip two other fourths of the paper into an organic solvent.
    - Dust one of the fourths using magnetic black powder.
    - Superglue fume the other.
  - Be prepared to discuss the results.
- Ninhydrin development
  - Dip the paper into a solution of ninhydrin—completely saturate the paper.
    - A tray containing 100 mL of ninhydrin will work fine.
    - Alternatively, spray or brush the ninhydrin onto the paper.
  - Allow the paper to dry.
  - Place the paper onto a heated plate and allow the steam of an iron (containing dilute acetic acid—approximately 5%) to pass over the paper. Continue heating and steaming until all prints stop developing. Do not overdevelop the prints.
  - Alternatively, place the dried paper onto a flat surface and pass a hot steam iron over the paper until the prints develop. This method is typically faster. Prints can also be developed using a clothing press set at 120°C or hotter.

W4.2.3 Exercise 3: DFO-Developed Prints

DFO reacts with the amino acids and proteins in fingerprints to produce a fluorescent print that is visualized with the ALS. Scientists should be aware of the chemical reactions that take place and how the ninhydrin, DFO, and 1,2-indanedione reactions differ.

- Procedures
  - Place prints onto a piece of white paper.
  - Spray the paper with (or dip into) a solution of DFO.
  - Allow the paper to dry.
  - Place the paper onto a hot plate for approximately 10–30 min—monitor the development of the prints using the ALS.
  - Photograph the developed prints.
  - Follow this development with the ninhydrin procedure described above.
  - Photograph the ninhydrin-developed prints.

W4.2.4 Exercise 4: 1,2-Indanedione-Developed Prints

Indanedione reacts with the amino acids and proteins in fingerprints to produce a fluorescent print that is visualized with the ALS.

- Procedures
  - Place prints onto a piece of white paper.
  - Spray the paper with the indanedione solution in the fume hood and allow the paper to dry.
  - Place the paper onto a dry hot plate and cover the paper with a transparent plate.
  - Monitor the development of the fingerprints using an ALS at 535 nm—the hand-held ALS works well for this purpose (use the AC instead of the battery).
  - After print development, develop additional prints using the procedure for ninhydrin. This is the first two steps of the print development cascade discussed in Chapter 10.

W4.2.5 Exercise 5: Heat-Developed Prints

Although this method has not found a home in practice, it has created research designed to utilize heat to develop latent prints. This method, which works on porous and presumably other surfaces, involves heating the prints at approximately 200°C for 10–20 s. After 10 s the prints should show weak fluorescence at a wavelength of about 505 nm, visualized using a 450 nm filter (goggles). On further heating, the print turns a darker gray and should be visible to the naked eye.

- Procedures
  - Place prints onto white paper.
  - Place the paper into an oven at 300°C.
  - After 20 s, remove the paper and view the prints that have developed.

W4.2.6 Exercise 6: Lanthanide-Developed Prints

Many lanthanide elements in the periodic chart form fluorescent coordination complexes. One of these, Europium, has been used to develop fluorescent prints on both porous and nonporous surfaces using a procedure similar to that using SPR. The surface is sprayed carefully with reagent 1 and then allowed to dry. Once dry, the surface is sprayed again with reagent 2 and again allowed to dry. The developed prints are visualized under UV light. If there is significant background, the surface can be washed with water, which can quench the background fluorescence. The caveat to using this procedure is that if the background absorbs the reagent and fluoresces, it can mask the fluorescence of the developed print.

W4.3 Questions

- In 1000 words or less, discuss the importance of cascades for the development of latent fingerprints on a piece of cardboard.
- Consider the following surfaces. Which would work with superglue fuming, which with ninhydrin, and which with black magnetic powder dusting?
  - Aluminum
  - Plastic
  - Xerox paper
  - Painted wall
- In 500 words or less, explain why you chose the response you did for each of the three development methods (superglue fuming, ninhydrin, black magnetic powder dusting).

Pattern Evidence I
Footwear Impressions

11

"But one false statement was made by Barrymore at the inquest. He said that there were no traces upon the ground round the body. He did not observe any. But I did—some little distance off, but fresh and clear."

"Footprints?"

"Footprints."

"A man's or a woman's?"

Dr. Mortimer looked strangely at us for an instant, and his voice sank almost to a whisper as he answered:

"Mr. Holmes, they were the footprints of a gigantic hound!" (p. 352) [1]

11.1 Introduction

With the exception of fingerprints, impression or pattern evidence, as a class of physical evidence, may be the most overlooked in investigations. The reasons vary, but much has to do with training and the failure to apply logic when searching the scene. The team leader is responsible for the investigation and must dictate the team's strategy, which includes when and where to search for or consider that impression evidence is present. Figure 11.1 shows several reasons why impression evidence may be overlooked or ignored.

Although impression evidence comprises a large diverse group, it is almost axiomatic that at least one category will be present at most scenes. Generally, the most prevalent are fingerprints, footwear and tire impressions, and tool marks. Bite marks, lip prints, and ear prints comprise another category but occur much less frequently. Tool mark impressions comprise several subcategories that include bullet impressions, cartridge case impressions, and marks made by other tools such as screw drivers, saws, and so on. Figure 11.2 illustrates the various categories of impression evidence.

Because of the diversity of impression evidence, this chapter and Chapter 12 focus on the commonly occurring examples from the crime scene perspective: footwear and tire impressions respectively. Fingerprints were discussed in Chapters 9 and 10.

11.2 General Characteristics of Impression Evidence

Generally, impressions occur when a patterned object, for example, the sole of a shoe or the ridges of a finger, interacts with a surface leaving an impression either on the surface or indented. As the following illustration shows, impressions can be either 2D or 3D. Patterns lying on the surface—2D patterns—are classified as latent (invisible) or patent (visible). Examples are fingerprints, footwear impressions, and tire track impressions, among others. Dust impressions are usually classified or defined as 2D impressions, but in reality they

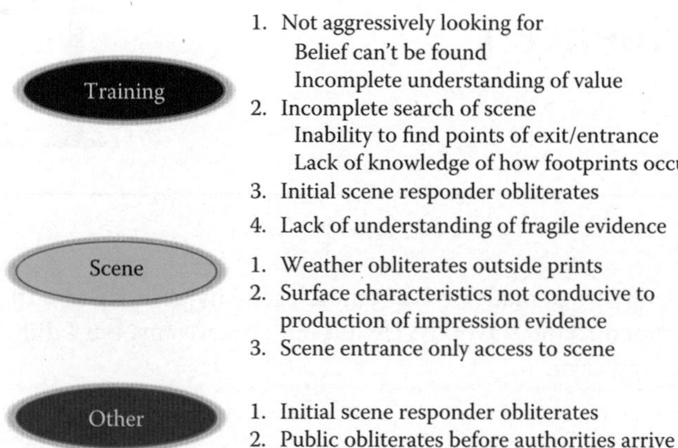

Figure 11.1 Why impression evidence is overlooked.

are 3D impressions because they have depth and surface topology, albeit shallow. This is illustrated in Figure 11.3 [2].

Impressions that occur when an object impresses its pattern into a softer surface, such as when someone steps into wet mud and leaves a footwear impression, are 3D impressions. Neil Armstrong's famous footwear impression on the moon is an example of a 3D impression (see Figure 11.4) [3]. Another example is when someone transfers ridge detail from a finger by handling a soft surface, such as wet soap (as in Figure 11.5), putty, or chewing gum. These are classified as plastic prints.

11.3 Footwear Impressions (Marks)

11.3.1 Is Footwear Evidence Important?

The forensic value of evidence refers to its future use to help ascertain the truth of alleged facts of an incident to either inculpate* or exculpate† suspects. Footwear impression

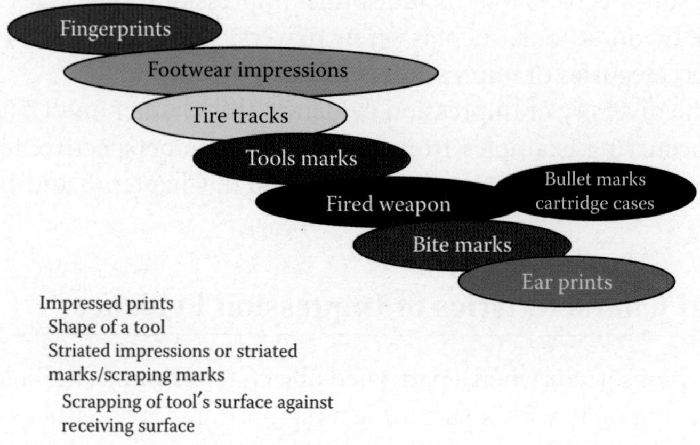

Figure 11.2 Categories of impression evidence.

* "Incriminate" [4].
† "To clear from alleged fault or guilt" [5].

General classes of impression prints

2D–impression/dry and wet residue prints

Imprints or impressions
- Residue print is a more apt term
- "Impression" is commonly used term
- Transfer of residue surface to an object to a receiving surface
  - Hard surface impressions
  - Soil on a shoe sole to a floor

3D–Indented/compressed prints

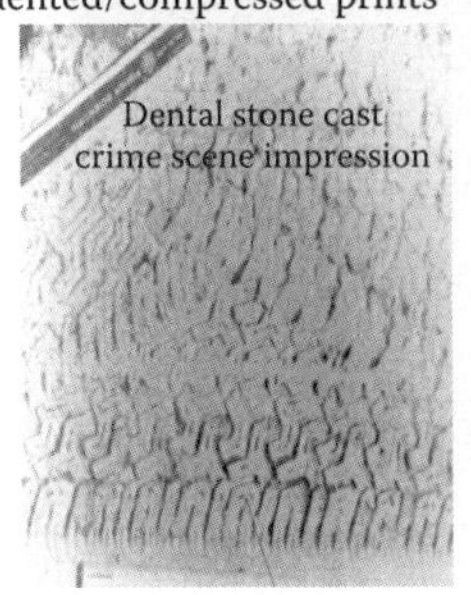

Impressed prints or compression marks
Impressed into softer surfaces
- Footwear impressions in soil
- Tool mark in wood
- Dental impression on skin

Figure 11.3 Classifying impression evidence. (Top photograph by Robert C. Shaler. Bottom photograph from L. Nause, *Forensic Tire Impression Identification,* Ottawa: Canadian Police Research Centre, 2001, pp. 34, 80. With permission.)

evidence is a category collectively called associative evidence. That is, it helps investigators (police and prosecutors), juries, and the trier of fact because it supports the contention that someone may have been (or not) at a crime scene. Although taken alone, associative evidence should not be determinative of guilt, but it can help circumstantially toward that end. Thus, linking footwear impression to an individual shoe can be critical evidence that a prosecutor can introduce at trial. It may also be helpful for investigators to understand the veracity of a witness or a suspect's statements.

Figure 11.4 Neil Armstrong's footwear impression print on the moon. (Available at http://www.nasa.gov/audience/forstudents/k-4/home/F_Apollo_11.html, accessed September 7, 2009.)

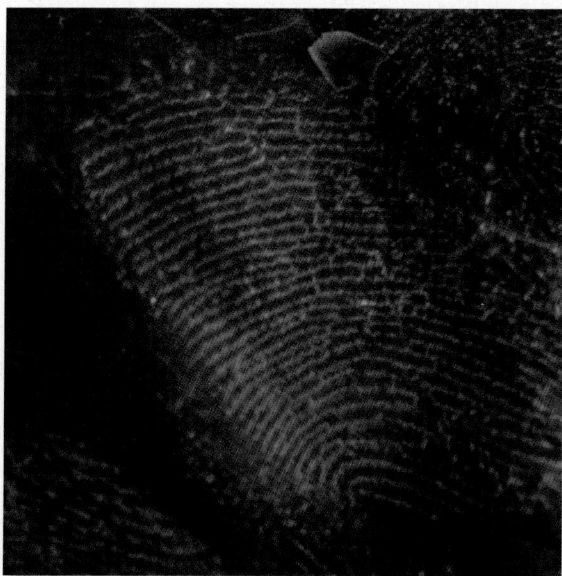

Figure 11.5 Impression print in soap developed by a Penn State forensic science student using fluorescent powder. (Photograph by Robert Shaler.)

Locating footwear evidence at the crime scene is not easy, but logic can point where to search. On might ask, if finding footwear evidence is not easy and if it has only associative value, why spend the time? The most obvious reason is that footwear impression evidence can *help* identify a shoe that left the impression. This is important because it places someone at the scene, which is incriminating if there is no good reason for the person being there. Scene footwear impressions have been compared successfully with impressions made from shoes taken from suspects, and forensic experts have testified that scene impressions and exemplar impressions were made by a specific shoe. Such testimony can be case defining. This is why taking the time and making the effort to locate, photograph, and lift footwear (and tire track) impression evidence is crucial.

How valid are footwear and tire track matches? A recent report by the National Research Council of the National Academy of Sciences (sometimes also referred to as the NAS report) suggests that pattern (impression) evidence interpretations should have a better-defined statistical basis [6]. The report says that additional research is necessary in order to determine the underlying scientific basis of pattern evidence comparisons. Certainly, practitioners do not universally agree that a statistical basis is necessary for making forensically valid comparisons. The NAS report does not say or imply that footwear comparisons are not valid nor does it specifically say that comparisons have no forensic value.

As Figure 11.6 shows, there are three main reasons for actively pursuing footwear impressions: links to other crimes, the possibility of identifying a minimum number of perpetrators, and the possibility of uncovering additional probative evidence. In this regard, databases of footwear sole patterns exist through which investigators can identify a sole's manufacturer,* thus providing important investigative information. Also, these

* SoleMate—Database maintained by Foster + Freeman LTD, http://www.fosterfreeman.com/products/shoeprints/solemate/solemate.html (accessed September 7, 2009).

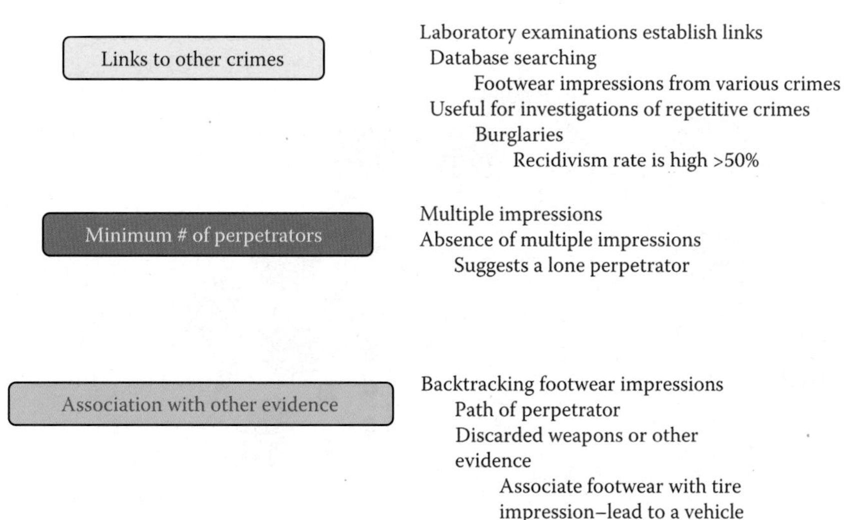

Figure 11.6 The value of impression evidence.

databases can compare patterns with those found at other scenes in order to identify whether this type of shoe pattern has been seen at other crimes.

Identifying *unknown* footwear impressions, for example, not the victim's shoe, at a scene has investigative importance because it tells investigators how many people might have been involved in the crime. For example, if there were three unknown impressions, it might suggest that there were a minimum of three people involved in the crime. If there was only one unknown impression, it might suggest a lone perpetrator. The operative phrase is "minimum number," as other perpetrators may not have left impressions or were not found. Unknown footwear impressions might have come from innocent people who belonged at the scene for whatever reason. These will not be known during the investigation unless there is a mechanism at the scene to compare the class characteristics of shoes from people who belonged at the scene.

Examine Figure 11.7, the crime scene diagram. Instead of a single burglar, suppose two were partners in the crime. If the two burglars entered at different points, the footprints at "Entry point 1" and those at "Entry point 2" would be expected to be different. If both impressions differed from those of the shoes of the deceased, would there be sufficient reason to suspect that *at least* two perpetrators committed the crime? The actual number would not be known, of course, because other participants may not have left impressions or were not discovered. Even if the footprints had the same sole pattern (class characteristics) and they were both entering the house, this also suggests that at least two people were involved. A remote possibility is that the same person entered the house at two locations on separate occasions. Close examination of the size of the impressions might dispel that argument.

These are important investigative leads because they are determined on-the-spot during the investigation. Consider passive archiving of the scene. If the scene scientists/investigators were just photographing, collecting, and packaging evidence without making these critical comparisons, the investigative information would have to wait until the fingerprints and/or footwear impressions were compared by latent print examiners and the footwear impressions were examined in the laboratory. Typically, the laboratory examinations would not be conducted until exemplar impressions were available, which means a suspect

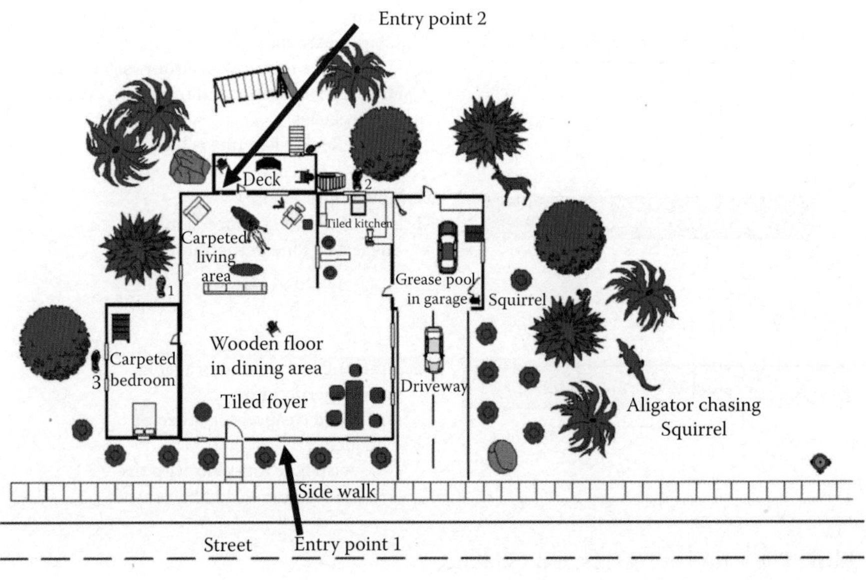

Figure 11.7 Hypothetical burglary scene.

would likely be in custody. The on-scene investigative information can help the investigation at an earlier stage and possibly accelerate it.

Finally, following the unknown footwear impressions through the scene can lead to probative evidence: the egress point or movement during the commission of the crime. It might lead to fingerprints, discarded evidence, ski masks, burglary tools, etc. Importantly, footwear impressions can provide important on-the-spot investigative information. Hopefully, it will stimulate possibilities for locating impressions at the scene. Table 11.1 lists additional information that might help the investigative process.

11.3.2 Classifying Footwear Impressions

Footwear impressions are classified into three categories:

- *Visible*: Those that occur after someone steps into a foreign substance and then transfers the substance to a clean surface. Depending upon the background

Table 11.1 What Can Footwear Evidence Tell You?

- Impressions at scene can be incriminating
  - Shows person was at the scene
    - Likely participated in the crime
  - Someone who has no business being there
- Impressions can be from innocent people who had reason to be at the scene
- Rebut or confirm suspect and/or witness statements
  - Often admit presence
    - Location of impressions may refute what suspect says
    - Location of impressions may confirm witness statements

color, a visible print may be a simple impression made from the dust on the sole of the shoe.

- *Plastic*: Those that occur when someone steps into a malleable (soft) surface and leaves a 3D impression. Typically, this could be an impression in mud or cement.
- *Latent*: Those that are invisible to the naked eye and typically require an aided eye to render them visible.

Scene scientists/investigators should expect impression evidence to be at the scene. They can use the logic in the following mental checklist.

- What is the likelihood that probative impressions are at this scene?
- Where would they most likely occur?
- In what form would they be: wet or dry residue, plastic, latent, visible?
- What is the most appropriate strategy to visualize them?
- What is the most appropriate strategy to enhance them?

11.3.3 Scene Investigation versus Laboratory Processes

Enhancing footwear impressions brings up the subject of what happens in the field versus what happens in the forensic laboratory. Certainly, it is not be the scene scientist/investigator's responsibility to compare scene-collected impression evidence with exemplars taken from suspects or to testify to these comparisons. Such comparisons are in the domain of the laboratory criminalist. However, it is the scene scientist/investigator's job to ensure that the laboratory criminalist receives impression evidence of sufficient quality to make these comparisons. For students and investigators, it is important to understand the specific roles that the scene scientist/investigator and the laboratory have in locating, collecting, preserving, and enhancing impression evidence. Figure 11.8 illustrates this point.

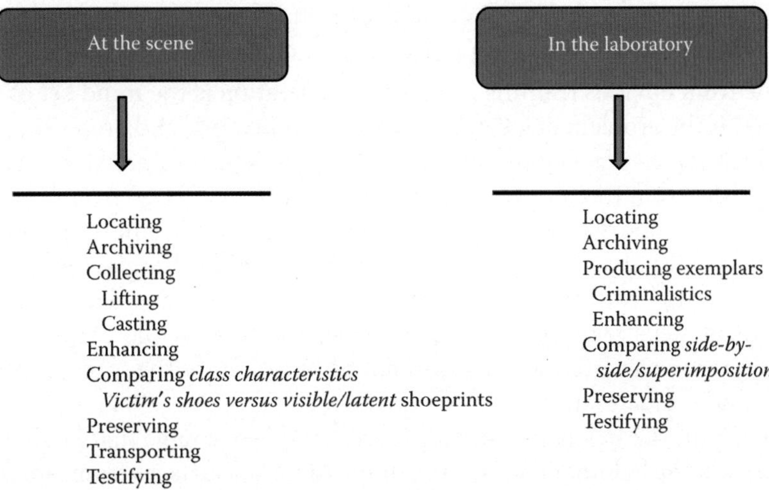

Figure 11.8 The scene investigator versus the laboratory analysis.

The responsibilities of the scene scientist/investigator are listed on the left side of Figure 11.8 and the laboratory investigator's on the right. A quick analysis reveals that the two lists have several categories in common. Although this seems to suggest an overlap in responsibility—for example, each list shows "Comparing"—the fact is that it is not. The differences are in the details; the laboratory criminalist's job requires much more rigor and, though both make comparisons, only the laboratory criminalist can testify to the "match" based on individualizing characteristics. The scene scientist/investigator uses class characteristics at the scene to ascertain how many different patterns might be present. If the scene pattern is unknown, it might have been made by the perpetrator, which requires further, more rigorous forensic scrutiny by the laboratory criminalist. Other similarities in the two lists include archiving, enhancing, and testifying. Like the example for comparisons, each involves a different level of rigor.

Enhancing footwear impressions at the scene requires discussion because it can involve the application of science—chemistry. The purpose, of course, is to enhance or improve the visibility of the scene impression. The problem is that applying chemistry and other scientific techniques at the scene, unless there is no other choice, is risky because there is always the possibility of ruining the impression. In fact, a rule of thumb is to shun on-scene chemistry or other science unless it is absolutely necessary; the impression cannot be transported to the laboratory. The reason is logically simple. Unlike the crime laboratory, the scene is an uncontrolled environment. The laboratory is a controlled environment, and the criminalist can assess the specific characteristics of the surface and consider the chemical components of the impression before embarking on an enhancement strategy. At the scene, such in-depth assessments are nearly impossible.

11.3.4 Likelihood That Footwear Impressions Are Present

Before embarking on a search for footwear impressions, the team leader should discuss with the team where footwear impressions might be present. Just as all crimes have biological evidence (see Chapter 13), there is always a reasonable chance that footwear impressions are present. Though this may seem intuitive, apparently it is not. As the title to Hilderbrand's book states, "The Missed Evidence" [7].

In the introduction, we discussed the question of why footwear impressions are overlooked. Aside from obvious training issues, a consideration is the mind-set of the investigator. Another is the problem of locating, archiving, collecting, and preserving impression evidence, which means understanding the surfaces on which impressions are found and whether a transfer from the shoe to that surface was likely.

For example, if a burglar enters a house through a window and steps onto a carpet, what is the probability that the dirt residue from the sole of the burglar's shoe will leave an impression? Entering from the outside defines the type of residue that should be on the shoe. Subsequent steps transfer that residue from the shoe to the carpet. Whether the resulting impression has forensic value will not be known until the scene scientist/investigator finds it and evaluates it.

Examine Figure 4.7 in Chapter 4. This is an example of a table that might be used as a guide to ascertain the likelihood of finding impressions on surfaces from either wet or dry footwear (see pp. 17–20 in Reference [8]). If the burglar's shoes are dry, an impression in dust is likely (first line in Bodziak's chart—Figure 4.8). However, if it had been raining and

Table 11.2 Finding Footwear Impressions at the Scene

Where Are 2D Footprints at the Scene?
Most Found on Floor Surfaces
Magazines/newspapers, etc.
Title floors
Dust prints on carpets
Shoe prints on doors—kicked-in doors
Finding Requires Careful Inspection of the Scene
Impression evidence is a category of fragile evidence.
One of the first scence activities is to locate.

the burglar's feet are wet (not muddy), it is unlikely the impression was transferred, or that the impression would be found.

11.3.5 Finding Footwear Evidence at the Scene

Not surprisingly, most footwear impressions are found on floors. Probative impressions, those having evidentiary value, will likely be where the perpetrator entered or exited the premises, and tiled or hardwood foyer entries or linoleum tile are prime candidates for places to search. Footwear evidence should also be expected in areas of activity or at entrance and egress points. The list in Table 11.2 is not all inclusive but is provided to give examples of possible locations where impression evidence might be found, with the understanding that each scene has its own peculiarities and that finding impression evidence requires an intimate relationship between the scene scientist/investigator and the scene.

The crime scene diagram in Figure 11.7 is an instructional example of how to think about locating footwear impressions.* Entry Point 1 (at the bottom middle of the diagram) is where a burglar entered the house. After breaking the window, s/he stepped onto the tiled foyer. Should footwear impressions be there?

Figure 4.7 does not specify what to expect from a tiled foyer, but logic does. It tells us that tile is a hard, nonporous surface, which should be a likely place for footwear impressions. These could be either dry (dust) or wet residue prints depending on the weather. Logic also tells us that these prints might be visible if the tile is a contrasting color to the impressions or that the impressions might be difficult to see if the color of the tile is similar to the color of dust.

As the burglar moved through the house toward where the body was found, the residue on the shoes would gradually diminish and, after stepping on the carpet, the remaining residue would be gone after only a few steps. Examining the entry point outside the residence, where the burglar stood before climbing through the window, might reveal additional impressions. If the area had been wet and the area under the window muddy, the footwear impression might be impressed in the mud, which means the patterned sole might be visible. Photography and casting would preserve it. Another consideration has to do with another type of evidence—glass. If the burglar stepped onto broken glass, shards might be imbedded in the sole or just scratched or nicked it, creating what some might consider a unique pattern.

* Diagram created using Scene PD4 Software, http://www.trancite.com/pro_spd.php.

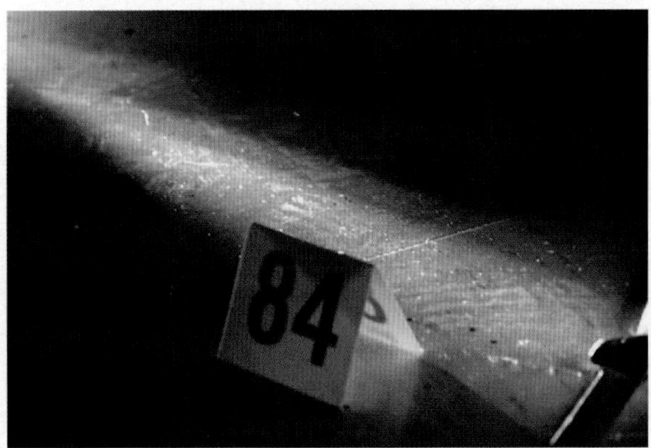

Figure 11.9 Photograph of oblique light enhanced two-dimensional footwear impressions. (Photograph by Robert C. Shaler.)

If the burglar had entered through "Entry point 2" (top of the diagram), logic suggests that footwear impressions should be on the outside deck leading into the carpeted living area. Entering the house means stepping onto the carpet, and, according to Bodziak's chart (Figure 4.8 in Chapter 4), dry residue prints should be visible. If the prints are not readily apparent, logic says to use an aide, for example, oblique light (flashlight or ALS), to visualize them (see Figure 11.9). Once seen, the next step would be to ascertain their probative forensic value.

If a sequence of patterned prints suggest a single person walking, another piece of information might be helpful, which is not completely diagnostic. This is something often referred to as gait or walking pattern (see discussions by Hilderbrand [7], pp. 7–8, and Cassidy [9], pp. 113–119) and refers to a person's stride. The walking pattern can be determined from a series of footwear impressions. This information can be informative although not necessarily diagnostic of how the person actually walks. Remember, the scene is a place of stress for everyone, and a person's stride made during the commission of a crime may or may not reflect that person's normal way of walking. Nevertheless, if sufficient pattern detail is present, that is, several identifiable steps, the walking pattern should be documented photographically with scales and appropriate measurements.

11.3.6 Common Footwear Transfers

Scene scientists/investigators should be aware, minimally at least, of the most common types of footwear transfers. These can include

- Dirt and/or dust
- Wet grass
- Grease, oil, wax, or furniture polish
- Blood or other fluids

Dirt or dust on the shoe may have come from outside the crime scene where a perpetrator stood waiting until it was the correct time to enter. Since footwear (and tire track) impressions are commonly found in dirt and/or dust, it is important that the scene scientist/investigator examine the components of soil and dust in the area of the crime, for example, whether it is muddy, sandy, dusty, and so on.

A perpetrator may have stepped onto a grassy lawn that was wet from dew or rain and then onto a paved sidewalk before entering the scene. After entering the scene, an impression may result from stepping onto a freshly waxed floor or onto a piece of furniture while climbing through a window. The fact is that impressions can be found on almost any surface: kicked-in doors, vegetation, snow, and tiled or carpeted floors. Impressions in blood can or other liquids that spill during the commission of a crime can help trace a perpetrator's movements. The scene scientist/investigator who is "one" with the scene should be able to find the more difficult impression transfers.

11.3.7 Enhancing Footwear Impressions: Understanding the Composition of Dust and Soil

Dust is a general name for solid particles with diameters <500 μm. It comes from the atmosphere from a variety of sources including: soil dust lifted up by wind, pollution, volcanic eruptions, animals, and people. Dust found in the human environment, for example, homes, offices, and so on, contains human skin cells, bacteria, plant pollen, human and animal hairs, feathers, textile fibers, paper fibers, minerals from outdoor soil, and other materials, all from the local habitat [10].

The quantity and composition of house dust varies greatly with seasonal and environmental factors such as the surroundings, exchange of outside air, age of the house, building materials and their condition, and the quantity of furniture and carpets, as well as their state of preservation. It also depends on the ventilation, heating/cooling systems, and habits of those living in the house. House dust consists of inorganic (minerals) and organic matter, their relative proportions varying considerably. Dust from homes with animals (have pets) consist nearly completely of organic material. In a study of 318 house samples, the proportion of organic matter ranged between <5% and >95%. A survey of homes in New Zealand showed that the organic content of house dust in 11 homes ranged between 25.7% and 56.5%, and floor dust from 7 Danish offices had an organic fraction of 33% [9].

The current paradigm for enhancing dust impressions at crime scenes, other than photography, is one-dimensional, typically using a chemical test to visualize the mineral content of the dust. Nause (see p. 34 in Reference [2]) lists reagents that can be used in specific circumstances.

- Dust or dirt
  - Ammonium or potassium thiocyanate: Since dust and/or dirt usually contain iron in varying amounts, test a small part of the impression for the presence of iron. If iron is present, carefully spraying the reagent onto the impression should result in a darker color—reddish brown. Before spraying ascertain whether the surface reacts with the reagent. If it does, the test will ruin the impression.
  - 8-Hydroxyquinoline: Spraying with 8-hydroxyquinoline gives a fluorescent reaction with iron, aluminum, and magnesium under UV light. The resulting yellow-white fluorescence must be photographed immediately. Testing the background surface before spraying is critical as is testing a small part of the impression to see whether the reagent reacts with the dust/dirt present. It is possible that the background will fluoresce and the impression print does not. The result will be a reverse fluorescent impression.

- Oil or fats
  - Iodine fuming*: Iodine fuming followed by development with 7,8-benzophenone gives a blue/purple color. Test a small part of the impression and the surface to see whether the iodine is reacting. The test is not a chemical reaction that takes place but more of an incorporation of the iodine into the matrix of the oil/fat.
    - Another way to visualize iodine infused impression is to dust it with cornstarch and then hold a steam iron over the impression. The iodine will react with the starch to form a dark blue color (see p. 34 in Reference [2]).
- Salt
  - NaCl/$AgNO_3$/AgCl: In the winter, tires traveling over roads salted with sodium chloride (NaCl) will have the salt on the tread. This will be transferred to a surface over which the vehicle travels. Spraying the impression with silver nitrate ($AgNO_3$) will form silver chloride (AgCl) in those areas of the impression containing the chloride ion. Shining a UV light or allowing sunlight to bake the impression will convert the AgCl to metallic silver (Ag), which appears dark gray or black (see p. 34 in Reference [2]).

Certainly, the chemical approach is reasonable, but knowing the chemical composition of the dust/soil that comprises the impression *a priori* before blindly attempting to visualize one of the metallic ions present would help. It is possible to sample a small portion of the dust using metal ion test kits available from forensic supply houses.

11.4 2D Impression Evidence

The large class of 2D impression evidence encompasses a broad range of impressions including dust prints—tire and footwear—fingerprints, lip prints, and so on, each resulting from the transfer of something from the original impression to a receiving surface. The material transferred need not only be dust. In fact, it can be anything: Coca Cola™, motor oil, dust, mud, dust aqueous slurry that dries, lipstick, and so on. The first order of business is finding the evidence, which is not always easy because it can be invisible or nearly so to the naked eye. Overcoming human deficiency is simply a matter of using our most valuable asset, intelligence (i.e., knowing where to look), and combining that with appropriate technological tools: ALS, RUVIS, or other technology. Traces of 2D impressions are found most anywhere and their number and variation are quite large. The examples that follow only illustrate the point:

- Wet and dry (dust) residue prints on hard surfaces
- Wet and dry residue prints on soft surfaces (carpeting, clothing, furniture, etc.)
- Impressions made from nondust contaminants on the sole of the shoe (e.g., motor oil, beverages, blood, etc.)
- Wet impressions on concrete, bricks, and so on

The point is that impression evidence is likely present at scenes simply because people are involved.

* Robert C. Shaler. Unpublished results.

11.4.1 Finding 2D Footwear Impressions at the Scene

There are two classes of latent or near-latent 2D footwear prints at crime scenes: dry residue (dust) and wet residue prints (dust or mud).

- A dry shoe deposits dust onto an appropriate surface; this is an example of the fracture of evidence as defined by the principle of divisible matter.
- A wet shoe deposits a dust (or mud) slurry onto the surface.

These 2D impression prints become visible (patent) when the dust or mud (or another substance, e.g., blood, oil, etc.) transfers to a surface having a contrasting color, such as when tan-colored dust transfers to a dark, tiled surface. The discussion above with respect to "knowing" where to find the evidence is still appropriate, and it is an integral part of locating footwear evidence at the scene. However, knowing where footwear evidence might be is only one part of a multifaceted puzzle. Another is how to make the impression visible and then how to archive and preserve it. If the print is latent or nearly latent, using a light source is a common way to highlight the impression. Although various methods have been used, the following section discusses the most common.

11.4.1.1 Using Light to Locate Impression Evidence

- *Flashlight*: A flashlight held at an oblique angle. The light reflects off of the raised ridges of the impression and goes to the eye (or camera). Since footwear impressions constitute a class of fragile evidence, the impression should be marked with an evidence marker to avoid its inadvertent destruction. The principle is illustrated in Figure 6.13 (Chapter 6). An example is shown in in Figure 11.9.
- *Mirror*: Another method is to use the flashlight held obliquely to the floor with the light beam pointed obliquely in the direction of a mirror. The impressions visible in the mirror should be marked as evidence. Figure 11.10 illustrates the technique and the photograph on the right shows what is seen in the mirror [11].

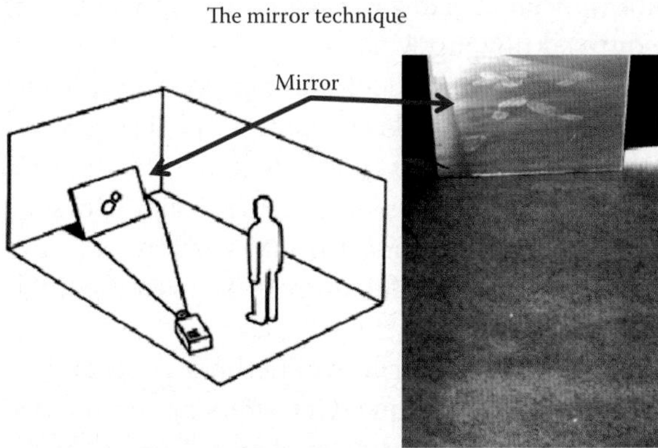

Figure 11.10 Mirror technique for enhancing 2D footwear impressions. (Adapted from Evident Crime Scene Technologies, BVDA gel lifter mirror technique, http://www.evidentcrimescene.com/cata/cast/mirrortech.html, accessed October 5, 2010.)

- *RUVIS*: A third method uses reflected UV light in a hand-held instrument called the RUVIS. The principle is the same as discussed above except that the reflected light is 254 nm UV light that reflects into the RUVIS. The image in the viewfinder is seen as a light (or dark) image over a green background.
- *ALS*: Similar to the first two, the ALS light set on white or other wavelengths effectively highlights dry or wet residue impressions. An advantage of the ALS is that different wavelengths can be effective at "subtracting out" the background, which can increase the contrast of the print to the surface.
- *Short-wave UV light*: A fourth method uses short-wave UV light, much like one uses a flashlight. This technique is appropriate for substrates that fluoresce under UV light. The impression appears dark on a brightly fluorescent background. Generally, a high-intensity UV light is necessary.
- *Natural light*: Sometimes natural light hitting a floor at the appropriate angle can highlight impressions present. While not equivalent to a comprehensive search, seeing footwear impressions in this way should signal an investigator that a search is necessary and to mark them so they are not inadvertently destroyed during the scene investigation.

Using oblique lighting, whether from a flashlight, an ALS, or a UV light is a common way to "see" dust prints on a hard surface, for example, a tile foyer, linoleum, or wood floor, and so on. Once seen, however, the problem is identifying the kind of print, because this determines how it should be lifted and transferred to the crime laboratory. Commonly, this means determining whether the impression is a dry (dust) or wet residue print. That is, was it made from a dry or wet shoe? Determining this dictates how the print will be treated in subsequent analysis.

11.5 Dry Residue Impressions

Determining whether footwear prints are dry or wet residue impressions defines to some extent downstream analysis because dry residue (dust) prints follow a different path than those made by wet impressions. Certainly, if the impression has significant detail, preserving it is of paramount importance. However, ascertaining whether the print is formed by dry or wet residue requires knowing what to do. Before "touching" the impression, it is imperative to archive it. Though not difficult, proper photographic technique for footwear impressions is not a trivial task. The goal is to capture the impression detail that is present.

After photography, the first consideration is whether the impression was made from a dust-covered or a wet shoe. Many consider this a reasonable first step. Certainly, this is not necessarily strictly true, but the conventional wisdom is to use a simple method to determine the difference: attempt the lift using an electrostatic lifter.

Actually, there are two complementary methods for lifting dry residue prints. Electrostatic lifting is an easy, nondestructive method. A second method is to use a gel lifter, which is also an easy, fast technique. Gel lifters are extremely versatile and can be applied to capture many types of impression evidence. The "sticky" gel lifter will lift most, if not all, of the print. However, if surrounding dust is present, that would be lifted as well. One must consider what to do if either or both methods fail. Other than photography, is there a fall-back plan to preserve the print?

Before blindly using the electrostatic lifter, it is wise to first consider whether an electrostatic lift will be effective. In this regard, scene-related concerns should reveal the best method to use. These include the amount of dust on the surrounding surface which might mask the impression detail of the print, the texture of the surface with respect to whether it is too deep to put a charge on the dust, and finally the thickness and porosity of the surface [12].

11.5.1 Science of Lifting Dry and Wet Residue Prints

The dust/mud particles on a substrate will transfer to a lifting material (electrostatic lifter and gel lifter) if the sum of the forces applied on them, chemical and physical, are greater than the forces holding the dust to the substrate. In other works, whether to use electrostatic or adhesive (sticky) methods to lift a dust print is decided by determining which method can best overcome the forces holding the print on the surface [12].

11.5.1.1 Electrostatic Lifting

Electrostatic lifters and gel lifters work by two different mechanisms. In the former, a metallic-backed black Mylar® film* is electrically charged by a DC power source. This creates a charge imbalance between the film and the surface. When this happens, the film is attracted to the surface on which the dust impression lies only if the surface resists electric flow and is charged positively. If the distance between the surfaces (opposite charges) is close enough, the film and the surface are attracted to each other. There are situations where the distance is too great.

Electrostatic charge is defined by Coulomb's law,† which says that too large a distance between the film and the surface can diminish the charge imbalance and thus the static electricity between them. So, if the surface on which the impression lies is highly textured, that is, rough, the attractive forces will be diminished and the impression might not lift. This happens because the ability of the electrostatic method to lift prints depends on the charge on the film (metallic sheet), which is determined by the power source used to create the electrostatic charge, and the strength of the opposite charge on the surface on which the impression lies. The strength of the charge is inversely dependent on the distance between the film and the surface. On a porous surface, for example, a carpet, the metallic film will not bind well to the surface because of the distance between the opposite charges. Figure 11.11 illustrates this process.

The advantage of electrostatic lifting is the detail that can be preserved on the film. What if the impression does not lift? Is that proof that the impression was formed from a wet shoe? Maybe not. In addition to texture and porosity of the surface, there can be another consideration—that of humidity.

Humidity has been studied with regard to a similar technique using an electrostatic detection apparatus (ESDA) for the detection of indented writing. Studies show there is a broad range of acceptable humidity, but when the relative humidity rises above 98% at room temperature the quality of the print drops. At cold temperatures, lower humidity also causes a decrease in the quality of the highlighted indented printing [14]. While the ESDA technique is not identical to electrostatic lifting, the principle is, and one

* Mylar® is a registered trademark of Dupont Teijin films.

† Coulomb's law: "a statement in physics: the force of attraction or repulsion acting along a straight line between two electric charges is directly proportional to the product of the charges and inversely to the square of the distance between them" [13].

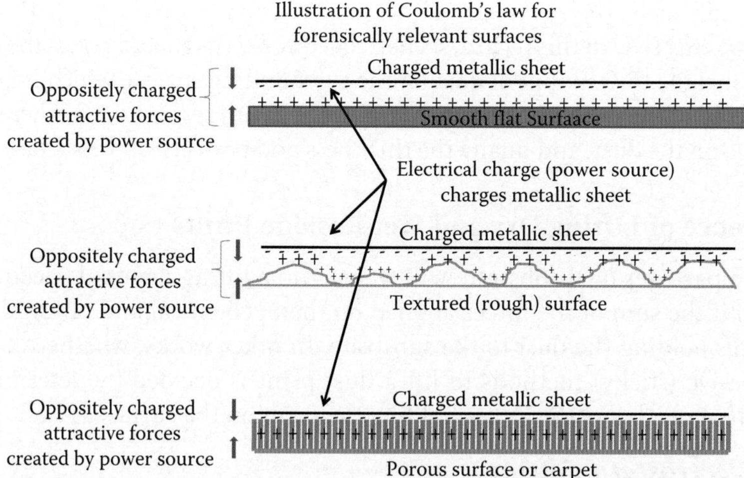

Figure 11.11 Electrostatic lifting on smooth, textured, and porous surfaces.

might expect similar deterioration of the quality of lifted impressions using an electrostatic lifter. Generally, though, using electrostatic lifters under normal conditions of temperature and humidity should give good results. What happens if the relative humidity is extremely low? The ESDA process *requires* humidity, which opens the possibility that the absence or near absence of humidity may also affect the quality of electrostatic lifts.

The electrostatic lifting process using commercially available equipment is straightforward, and homemade devices are simple to make; a stun gun can be used.* A general procedure for using an electrostatic lifter is given below:

- Place the black side of a foil-backed Mylar film, cut to just larger than the size of the impression, over the impression.
- Place a grounding plate 1–2 in. from the long side of the impression.
- Place the high-voltage contacts in contact with the grounding plate and the foil side of the Mylar film.
- Turn on the voltage; this creates a static charge on the dust particles causing the Mylar film to be "sucked" onto the surface.
- Roll out air bubbles with a fingerprint roller.
- Turn off the lifter.
- Carefully lift the print and examine using oblique lighting from a flashlight.
- Photograph the lifted print using scales. An example is shown in Figure 11.12.
- Place the lifted print in a high-quality cardboard box (shaped like a pizza box) and tape it to the bottom.
- Do not allow the lifted print to come into contact with plastic, as that will discharge the electrostatic charge on the Mylar and release the impression.

* See Gizmos and Gadgets website: http://www.csigizmos.com/products/dustlifting/stungun.html (accessed September 15, 2009).

Figure 11.12 Electrostatic lift of dust print from linoleum tile floor. (Photograph by Robert C. Shaler. Image converted to black and white in Photoshop CS3.)

Electrostatically lifted prints are quite fragile. Keeping the impression away from anything that can discharge the film will destroy the print, but physical contact with anything, such as brushing against the print, also removes or obscures detail. Storage creates longevity problems as well. The metallic-backed Mylar film has a residual charge that attracts excess dust. Additionally, the film gradually loses its charge, which means the impression will be lost over time; thus, the only way to preserve lifted impressions is photographically.

Impressions lifted from paper can be subjected to chemical analysis. These should be taken to the crime laboratory, where chemical procedures might reveal more impression in detail and the analysis will be conducted in a controlled laboratory environment.

Storing lifts in flat cardboard boxes preserves them more effectively than other suggested methods such as rolling and storing them in tubes. A problem with flat storage is that dust is attracted to the surface because of a retained residual static charge. The dust problem can be exacerbated by storing the lifts open to air or in low-grade cardboard. Even if stored in a high-quality cardboard box, the residual charge will eventually dissipate resulting in the complete loss of the impression. Storage conditions are also important. High humidity increases the rate of residual charge degradation, thus storage with a desiccant such as silica gel should be taped to the inside of the box. It is recommended that the lifts are stored such that the humidity does not exceed 50% [15].

11.5.1.2 Gelatin Lifters/Gel Lifters (Gellifters)

The other technique for lifting dust print impressions is to transfer the impression to a sticky surface such as a gel lifter. As shown in Table 11.3, these are effective multitasking tools for investigators. They are gelatin-based and available in different forms: rubber-backed (black, white, or clear) and acetate-backed.* Table 11.3 shows the types of gel lifters, their characteristics, and how each might be used to collect and/or enhance the evidence [16].

* See BVDA website: http://www.bvda.com/EN/index.html (accessed November 18, 2010).

Table 11.3 Gel Lifter Types

Gel Lifter Type	Characteristics	Possible Uses

Black	The black color reflects light from illumination source. Light not reflected is absorbed. Traces picked up by the Gellifter reflect the light giving high contrast between the lifted material and the gelatin layer.	• Footwear impression lifts
		• Fingerprint lifts developed with
		  • Powders
		  • Superglue
		  • SPR
		• Fingerprints on some adhesive sides
		• Postmortem fingerprinting
		• Fingerprints on latex gloves

White	Gelatin layer reported to absorb blood and dyes from stained impressions. White has a low fluorescence, which gives sufficient contrast to observe fluorescent dusted fingerprints and footwear impressions and blood impressions with acid yellow 7 or Hungarian red.	• Fingerprints in traces of blood • Fingerprints in staining solutions • Muddy shoeprints on nonporous surfaces stained with safranine O
Clear	The transparent gel lifters have a clear polyester backing.	• Fingerprints developed using powders to yield positive print • Exemplar footwear impressions

Source: Adapted from BVDA, Gellifters brochure, http://www.bvda.com/EN/download/Gellifter_brochure.pdf, accessed January 26, 2011.

The science of gel lifting dust from a surface is a different from that used in the electrostatic process. Gel lifters have a sticky (not a glue-like) porous surface. During lifting, the gel lifter is pressed onto the surface holding the impression. Its porous gelatin surface penetrates into the pores of the impression-held surface and the dust particles stick to it. When the gel lifter is removed, the dust remains on the lifter as the adhesive characteristics of the gel lifter overcome the forces holding the dust to its original surface. These are termed adhesion forces.* Lifting (binding) occurs when the gel lifter (adhesive) and the dust (adherent) have similar solubility characteristics. That is, strong adhesion bonds form when the two surfaces spontaneously "wet" each other.

Because of the "wetting" characteristic of gel lifters, they are capable of lifting dry as well as wet residue impressions unlike electrostatic lifters. For preservation purposes, both methods have the same function. However, since gel lifters also lift wet residue impressions, they are not a reliable method for differentiating between the two types of impressions. Certainly, this should not be an important issue because the purpose in lifting impressions is to preserve them for comparison purposes.

In addition to the scientific differences between how the two lifting methods work, gel lifters are significantly more expensive than electrostatic lifters (except for the initial cost for the lifter and lifting Mylar). Also, gel lifters pick up surrounding contaminating material such as dust or other particles, which can mask the lifted impression. It is possible to remove excess interfering and contaminating substances from gel lifters with repeated lifting of the gel surface using an adhesive lifter [18]. For dry residue prints, the light tan color of the impression is nicely off-set by the black color of the gel lifter. Like electrostatic lifters, gel lifters can lift impressions from hard surfaces, paper, carpeting, clothing, etc. They are particularly useful on vertical surfaces.

* Adhesion: "an attraction or repulsion between the molecules of unlike substances in contact" [17].

A recent study by Weisner et al. [12] comparing electrostatic lifting with gel lifting showed that gel lifters were superior for some surfaces, electrostatic for others, and for some there were no differences. Gel lifters gave better results on corrugated cardboard, flannel cloth, towel, brown paper, Mazonite, wet residue prints, and nonflat porous surfaces. Electrostatic lifting gave better results on plaster board and dusty floors. The two techniques gave essentially the same results on plastic sheets, white paper, and linoleum. The study recommended using electrostatic lifting first and gel lifters second because using electrostatic lifting second gave poorer results [12].

Storing gel lifts in uncovered boxes works well, but generally it is recommended that only high-grade cardboard boxes be used because the lower-grade boxes tend to shed fibers onto the lifted image. Also, breathable boxes keep condensation from forming on the lifts. Finally, removing the acetate sheet that comes with the lifter removes some of the image, which is why storing gel lifts without the acetate sheet is recommended. Generally, store gel lifts in the same way as electrostatic lifts: in a high-grade cardboard box without the acetate cover. There is the possibility that an over-dusted or densely dusted impression can benefit from repeated removal of the acetate cover because this tends to remove some of the excess dust and render the lifted impression sharper (see pp. 59–97 in Reference [8]).

11.6 Wet Residue Impressions

Wet residue impressions occur when the slurry on the sole of a wet or damp shoe transfers material to a receiving surface and then dries. The resulting dried impression is called a wet residue impression (or mark) and more or less is "fixed" to the surface. Generally, attempts to lift the dried slurry using an electrostatic lifter fail, which is why the electrostatic lifter is a good way to determine whether an impression was made from a wet or dry shoe. If the impression lifts, it likely originated from a dry shoe, and it should be protected and preserved as described above. If it does not lift, the impression should be treated as though it came from a wet shoe. The decision process is illustrated in the Figure 11.13. Understand that differentiating between dry and wet impressions pertains only to impressions in dust and/or mud. Impressions made with other materials, for example, grease, oil, blood, and so on, cannot be lifted with an electrostatic lifter, and perhaps neither with a gel lifter.

11.6.1 Enhancing Wet Residue Impressions

The following on-scene checklist is a guide for the scene scientist/investigator, who ultimately has the responsibility for preserving impressions with as much detail as possible. Developing or enhancing wet residue impressions follows a specific path, the ultimate success of which requires an understanding of the science underlying the technique, its limitations, and the surface chemistry on which the impression lies. Before embarking on a development technique, scene scientists/investigators should weigh carefully the pros and cons of on-scene enhancement. Generally, several techniques are available that can help.

- Dusting with black magnetic powder followed by photography and lifting using a white gel lifter
- Painting with powder suspensions, for example, WetWop™ or iron oxide in a dilute Photoflo™ solution

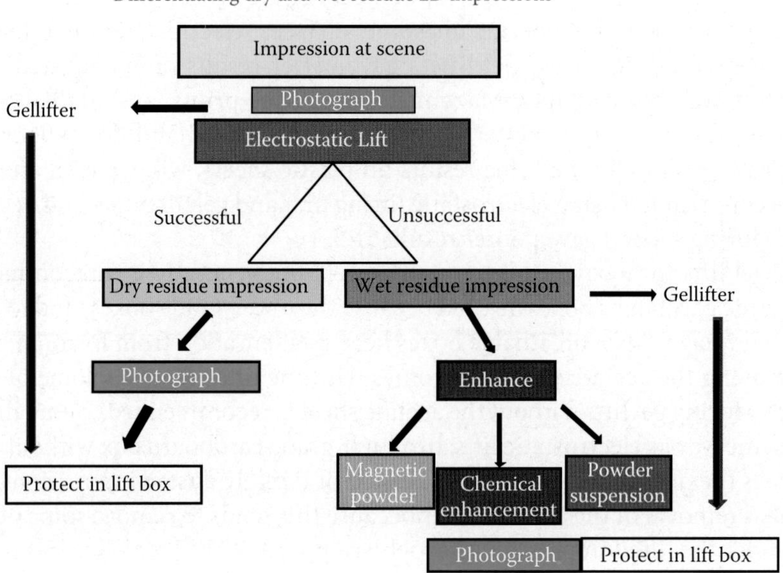

Figure 11.13 Decision tree for differentiating dry from wet residue impression evidence.

- Iodine fuming followed by development with 7,8-benzophenone
- Superglue fuming followed by basic yellow 40 (or other fluorescent dye) staining
- Gel lifting

These techniques are suggestions only. Table 11.4 gives more detailed information and considers a wider range of contaminated footwear impressions.

11.7 Visible (Patent) Impressions: Contaminating Substances

Enhancing footwear impression at the scene requires an understanding of the chemistry and physical properties of the impression. Although many may argue that on-scene chemistry is potentially harmful to the evidence—no argument here—it is a strategy the scene scientist/investigator should at least consider because considering all alternatives—chemical and/or physical—leads to the best approach from an evidence preservation perspective. The HOSDB in Great Britain studied how different contaminating substances on footwear impressions react with fingerprint enhancement methods [15]. Their purpose was to ascertain the most effective method for enhancing impressions at the scene. A partial rendering of the results are shown in Table 11.4. In addition, columns were added to include electrostatic and gel lifts.

Table 11.4 lists the soft drinks Sprite and Diet Coke, for example. Inspection of the results suggests that most methods would not be suitable for enhancing or lifting impressions made with these methods. However, several techniques might be useful. Interestingly, Sprite impressions responded much better than Diet Coke impressions to several methods including magnetic powder, black powder, and powder suspensions. Diet Coke reacted relatively poorly with most attempts including magnetic powder and powder suspensions. It is tempting to speculate that the sugar in Sprite gives it an enhancement advantage over

Table 11.4 Comparison of Two-Dimensional Residue Impression Enhancement Techniques

	Static Lift[a]	Gel Lift[b]	VMD	SG/ BY40	Mag Black	Aluminum	Black Powder	Powder Suspension[c]
Soil—Clay	— -	+	+ +	— -	— -	— -	+ +	+ +
Soil—Loam	+	+	+ +	— -	— -	— -	— -	+ ++ +
Soil—Chalk	+ ++	+ ++	+ +	— -	— -	— -	+ +	+ +
Grass stain	— -	+	+ +	— -	— -	— -	+ +	+ ++ +
Engine oil	— -	+ +	+ ++ +	+ ++ +	+ ++ +	+ +	— -	+ +
WD40	— -	+ +	+ +	+ ++ +	+ ++ +	+ ++ +	+ ++ +	+ +
Baby oil	— -	+ +	+ +	+ ++ +	+ ++ +	+ +	+ +	— -
Kitchen fat	— -	+ +	+ ++ +	+ ++ +	+ ++ +	+ ++ +	+ ++ +	+ ++ +
Diesel fuel	— -	+ +	+ +	+ ++	+ +	+ +	+ +	— -
Detergent	— -	+ +	+ ++ +	+ ++ +	+ ++ +	+ ++ +	+ ++ +	+ ++ +
Dish soap	— -	+ +	+ +	+ ++ +	+ ++ +	+ ++ +	+ ++ +	+ +
Sprite	— -	+ +	+ +	+ +	+ +	+ +	+ ++ +	+ ++ +
Diet Coke	— -	+ +	+ +	+ +	— -	— -	+ +	+ +
Milk	— -	+ +	+ ++ +	+ ++ +	+ ++ +	+ +	+ ++ +	+ ++ +
Beer	— -	+ +	+ +	+ +	+ +	— -	— -	+ ++ +
Cider	— -	+ +	+ +	+ +	+ +	+ +	+ +	+ ++ +
Dusty shoeprint	+ ++ +	+ ++ +	+ ++ +	— -	— -	— -	— -	— -

Source: Adapted from Home Office Scientific Development Branch (HOSDB), *HOSDB Fingerprint and Footwear Forensics Newsletter*, Publication No. 24/08, 2008.

Notes: Static Lift, electrostatic lifter; Gel Lift, gel lifter; VMD, vacuum metal deposition; SG/BY40, superglue fuming followed by basic yellow 40; Mag Black, black magnetic powder; Aluminum, aluminum flake powder.

[a,b] Expected result.

[c] Powder suspensions typically contain powder, detergent, and water. Generally, iron oxide-based formulations are more effective than carbon-based ones such as in WetWop™.

Diet Coke because of its stickiness. Thus, at the scene, it might be helpful for the scene scientist/investigator to test a small uninformative area of an impression for sugar or check if the impression is "tacky" before embarking on an enhancement strategy. For others, several might be appropriate. Deciding which depends on the specific circumstance (e.g., surface).

We know that soil contains iron and other metals. Although not shown in Table 11.4, there are various ways to enhance footwear impressions chemically. It is well known that ammonium thiocyanate reacts with iron and 8-hydroxyquinoline with iron and other metals and that if these metals are present, solutions of these chemicals can enhance footwear impressions (see p. 34 in Reference [2]). The best and most logical approach toward applying chemical methods is to use them in the laboratory instead of at the scene. However, the circumstances at some scenes might require that impressions are enhanced at the scene.

Impressions have a variety of chemical species present, each of which has a chemistry that is potentially exploitable to produce a colored or fluorescent product. The enhanced impression is photographed and transferred, if possible, to the forensic laboratory. The list in Table 11.5 illustrates chemical methods that can be used either in the laboratory or at the scene to enhance wet (and dry) residue impressions.

Table 11.5 Chemical Methods for Enhancing Footwear/Tire Track Impressions

Technique	Analyte Tested	Procedure	Result Expected
Ammonium or potassium thiocyanate	Iron (Fe)	Spray	Red-brown
8-Hydroxyquinoline	Fe, Ca, Al, others	Spray	Fluorescence under UV light
1,8-Diazafluoren-9-one	Amino acids/proteins	Treat gel-lifted surface at 95°C	Fluorescence at 515–535 nm
Safranine O	Oils	Treat gel-lifted surface	Fluorescence at 535 nm
Iodine	Oils	Fume in humidity followed by a benzophenone soak	Blue/purple
pH of impression	$CaCO_3$	Spray or soak	Blue
Superglue fuming	Nucleophilic species	Fume after humidifying impression	Dust- or stain-developed impression

Choosing one method versus another depends on the following:

- Chemistry of the recipient surface
- Chemistry of the impression
- Preservation technique

The chemistry of the surface is critical to the successful enhancement of the impression. If, for example, the impression lies on a linoleum floor and the only chemical tool available at the scene is 8-hydroxyquinoline, a reaction of the surface with the reagent is always a possibility. The surface fluorescence will mask the fluorescence of the impression rendering it useless as evidence. Always check the surface to ensure that it does not react with the reagent.

The chemistry of the impression is also critical. Before treating any impression, determine whether the components in the impression are going to react with the reagent and give the expected color or fluorescence.

11.8 Preserving Enhanced Footwear Impressions

After enhancing, the scene scientist/investigator is faced with to preserving the impression. Certainly, the first line of attack is photography. In fact, photographic archiving should occur before enhancing. Assuming that the initial photography and enhancement are completed, preserving the impression for the laboratory criminalist is critical. For wet residue and contaminated visible prints, one method is to use gel lifters.

A general method for using gel lifters is given below:

- Determine the specific gel lifter color that gives the best contrast between the impression and the lifter. If the impression is wet residue mud, then a black gel lifter would give the best contrast. If the impression had been dusted with black magnetic or iron oxide powder suspension, a white gel lifter may offer the best contrast. An example of a black magnetic powder-dusted wet impression is shown in Figure 11.14.
- Choose a gel lifter that completely covers the impression.
- Remove the acetate backing from the gel lifter.

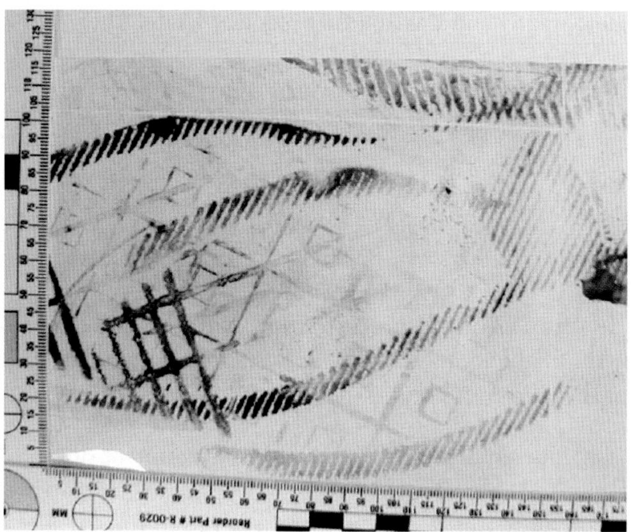

Figure 11.14 Impression dusted with black magnetic powder and lifted using a white gel lifter. (Photography by Robert C. Shaler.)

- Ascertain the proper orientation of the impression.
- Carefully lay the gel lifter over the impression, beginning at one end and gently lowering the lifter onto the impression until it is completely covered.
- Using a fingerprint roller, roll the top surface of the lifter to ensure a snug fit between the impression and the surface to eliminate air bubbles.
- Allow the impression to remain in contact for at least a minute—this will be increased depending on the impression (blood prints take more time). If the impression was developed chemically, the lifter may remain in contact for several minutes.
- Remove the impression and, using oblique light, photograph the transferred impression. At this point, whatever impression remains on the surface may be treated chemically to see if additional detail is present.
- Place the lifted impression in a high-quality cardboard box. Do not replace the acetate cover.

A procedure for protecting and preserving electrostatic lifts was discussed in Section 11.5.1.1. Chemically treated impressions are usually archived photographically. If an unenhanced impression can be transported to the laboratory, it must be preserved so that the impression will not be destroyed. Treating it like an electrostatic lift would not be a mistake. Place the lift into a high-quality cardboard box and anchor it so that it does not move inside the box. If the impression is on paper, the paper should be taped to the box. Transfer the protected lift to the forensic laboratory.

11.9 3D Impression Evidence

As mentioned above, impression evidence at scenes can have 3D characteristics, that is, a surface topography. This discussion focuses on footwear marks impressed into a soft receiving surface, where the impression is a clear 3D pattern. For forensic purposes, 3D

Table 11.6 How Photography and Casting Complement Each Other

Photography	Casting
Shows impression as found at the scene	Direct mold of the original impression
Condition and detail	Reproduces microscopic characteristics
Can give best reproduction from coarse surfaces	Gives reproduction of sides of outsoles not reproduced in photographs
A backup for casting	Backup for photography

impressions have depth in addition to length and width and are most commonly found outdoors in soft or malleable receiving surfaces such as soil, sand, or snow. The quality, that is, the detail of these impressions, varies with

- The receiving surface's malleability, texture, and composition
- The detail present in the source origin
- The mode by which the impression was transferred to the surface
- The effects of weather: temperature, rain, and snow

The scene scientist/investigator has no control over how the impression is generated or its clarity. S/he inherits the impression at the scene and has the responsibility to capture its detail as completely and as clearly as possible. Normally, this involves two activities: (i) photography and (ii) casting. Bodziak [8] defines casting as

> The filling of a three-dimensional footwear impression with a material that will acquire and retain the characteristics that were left in that impression by the footwear. (p. 476)

Importantly, each archiving technique complements the other, as shown in Table 11.6. The choice between photography and casting is not an either/or decision. Both are critical and both must be carried out to properly archive the impressions.

Deciding what to cast may be obvious most, but not all, of the time. Figure 11.15 illustrates those on-scene situations where casting is important.

When casting impression evidence, take extreme care must to preserve the maximum detail of the impression. Generally, unless the impression is on a sloped surface, it is not necessary to build a barrier. However, using a barrier is a good idea because it helps contain the wet (slurry) casting material. After creating the casting slurry in water, it must be poured into the impression. This is a critical step because, if it is done sloppily, the resulting

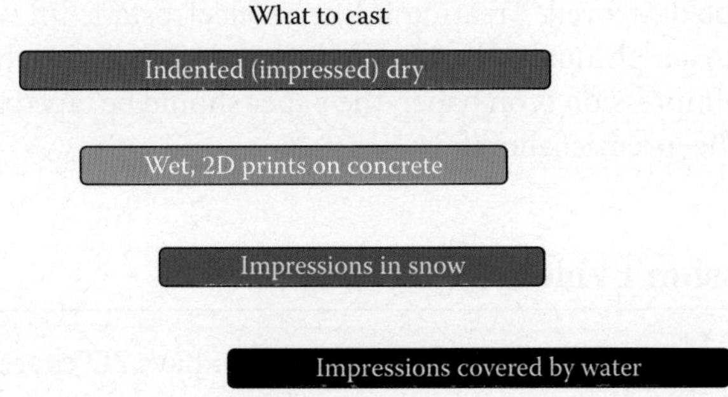

Figure 11.15 Impressions that must be cast.

cast can be ruined or at least its detail compromised for future comparison with an exemplar from a known pair of shoes (or tires).

Indented (impressed) dry impressions are the most obvious. These are typically footprints or tire tracks in mud. Wet 2D prints on concrete are not as obvious, but they are amenable to casting. The expression "Haste makes waste" is appropriate. In these instances, the waste refers to losing the evidence as the impression loses detail because of a combination of the cement absorbing the water and evaporation. Although casting 2D impressions on concrete is covered in Table 11.7, the technique is important enough to discuss. The procedure follows:

- Photograph the impression quickly.
- Dust the impression with magnetic powder (use a contrasting powder).
- Cast the impression using dental stone. Lifting the cast without damaging it can be troublesome. Some place a leading edge of plastic or other material around the edges. Sometimes this works, sometimes it does not. The problem is the hardened cast can become "glued" to the casting surface.

Impressions in snow can be cast but because of the problem of melting snow, photography using a contrasting material, such as automotive primer, is a critical first step. Casting in water is easy and straightforward. The process is illustrated in Table 11.8.

11.9.1 Photographic Archiving of 3D Impression Evidence

Certainly the first step in archiving an impression is to capture it photographically. A method for photographing impression evidence was discussed in Chapter 6. The difference between 2D and 3D photographic archiving reflects the contrast available in the impression, essentially a reflection of the media on or in which the impression lies. Table 11.7 is a guide to help formulate a strategy for developing both 2D and 3D impressions.

In the column "Enhancement Method," the techniques for creating the appropriate contrast for photographic archiving are presented. For example, in the row labeled "Snow," the recommended procedure is to use automotive gray primer paint as a method for creating sufficient contrast so that photography can capture the impression's detail. (Shield the sun as the darker paint absorbs heat and will melt the impression.) This would be followed by a "snow print wax" spray (or powder). The snow print wax spray creates a thin wax layer covering the impression. Hopefully, the wax stabilizes the impression sufficiently to allow casting. Thus, the approach for snow would be a sequence beginning with photography of the native impression, spray painting to create sufficient contrast for photography, using the snow print wax, and finally casting. Notice, too that archiving involves photography whereas preservation involves photography and/or casting. The final cast should always be photographed. Table 11.7 lists various surfaces, the type or category of the impression present, an appropriate archiving method, choices of enhancement methods, and methods for preserving the evidence (see pp. 61–62 in Reference [7]).

11.9.2 Casting to Preserve 3D Impression Evidence

Casting 3D impressions is not a choice but a requirement. All crime scene units should have casting material (dental stone, water, and mixing supplies) in their mobile crime scene

Table 11.7 Guidelines for Archiving, Enhancing, and Preserving Impression Evidence

Impression and Surface	Category of Impression	Archiving Method	Enhancement Method	Preservation Method
Wet soil or mud (*fine consistency*)	3D	Photograph	1. Dust with black/fluorescent or bicolor magnetic powder	Casting using dental stone
Concrete	2D	Photograph quickly	1. Quickly dust with black/fluorescent or bicolor magnetic powder	1. Rephotograph 2. Cast using dental stone
In dry soil (*hard-packed or loose; consistency coarse to powder-fine*)	3D	Photograph	1. Stabilize with hair spray or lacquer 2. Spray with automotive primer paint of appropriate contrasting color	1. Rephotograph 2. Cast using dental stone
Sand (*variable texture—retains small amount of impression detail*)	3D	Photograph	1. Stabilize with spray paint (black) or snow print wax or snow print powder 2. Spray with automotive primer paint	1. Rephotograph 2. Cast using dental stone
Snow (*temperature affects impression detail*)	3D	Photograph	1. Stabilize with automotive primer paint (gray) and/or snow print wax or snow print powder 2. Spray with automotive primer paint	1. Rephotograph 2. Cast using dental stone or jade stone
Dry residue—dust on hard surfaces (*high detail on hard surfaces*)	2D	Photograph	1. Lift using electrostatic or gelatin lifter 2. Chemical enhancement	1. Rephotograph 2. Preserve as per Section 11.5.1.1
Wet residue—dust or mud on hard surfaces (*high-detail impressions*)	2D	Photograph	1. Cannot be lifted using electrostatic lifters; can be lifted using gelatin lifter 2. Dust with magnetic powder (dual color or black) 3. Treat for the presence of iron or other metals 4. Cyanoacrylate fume followed by powder dusting or fluorescent staining (surface dependant)	1. Rephotograph 2. Lift with gel lifter 3. Preserve as per Section 11.5.1.2
Dust—fabrics (*carpet, upholstery—detailed impressions within the fabric nap or on the surface*)	2D	Photograph	1. If dust—lift as above	1. Rephotograph 2. Cast using jade stone 3. Lift with gel lifter
Blood (*can produce high-detail impressions*)	2D	Photograph	1. Light surfaces—stain with acid violet 17 2. Dark surfaces—stain with basic yellow 7 or 1,8-diazafluoren-9-one	1. Rephotograph 2. Lift using gelatin lifter

Source: Adapted from D. S., Hilderbrand, *Footwear, The Missed Evidence—A Field Guide to the Collection and Preservation of Forensic Footwear Impression Evidence*, Staggs Publishing, Wildomar, CA, 1999, pp. 61–62.

Table 11.8 Casting Underwater Impressions

- Drain or remove excess water—not absolutely necessary
  - Pipette or syringe
  - Carefully absorb with paper towel
  - Pour casting material as usual
- If water can't be removed
  - Frame the impression
  - Sift dry casting powder gently into water above the impression
  - Allow powder to fall to bottom of the impression
  - Sift until 1" of powder covers the area
  - Allow powder to saturate the water
  - Make a dental stone slurry and add the framed area
    - Slurry settles into the water and into impression
  - Cover entire impression
  - Allow to set for at least 1 h

unit. Though the process is simple, obtaining a successful and useful impression requires forethought and a strategy depending on the weather, the type of casting material, and the surface holding the impression. The goal, of course, is to capture the essence of the impression so that criminalists can make valid comparisons with known shoe impressions. Before discussing casting in specific circumstances, understanding the casting material is important.

Most commercial forensic suppliers offer forensic-quality casting material. Generally, the material is dental stone, but experience shows that, though these produce useable 3D casts, some perform better than others. Essentially, all casting material is a form of gypsum, considered plasters made from calcium sulfate dihydrate ($CaSO_4 \cdot (2H_2O)$). The difference between plaster and dental stone is the degree to which each is heated. The general sequence is [19]

$$CaSO_4\ (2H_2O)\ (\text{Plaster}) \xrightarrow{\Delta} CaSO_4\ \left(1\tfrac{1}{2}\,H_2O\right)(\text{Stone}) \tag{11.1}$$

Proper casting requires knowledge about the consistency and the strength of the casting material. Consistency refers to the ratio of the quantity of water needed per weight of powder used to make the cast. A consistency of "50" means that there are 50 parts of water per 100 parts of powder. The consistency determines the density, hardness, and strength of the resulting cast. It also dictates the drying time of the cast; the more water, the longer it takes for the cast to "set."

The strength of a cast is referred to as its dry compressive strength (measured in psi—pounds per square inch), which reflects how the cast (water and powder) is mixed. Generally, mixing by hand does not produce a cast with as much strength as one mixed in a commercial mixer. Also, manufacturers recommend adding powder—sifted—into the water. Scene scientists/investigators often use preweighed dental stone powder (typically in plastic bags) to which they add water, the reverse of manufacturers' recommendations. So, the on-scene procedures used by law enforcement are probably not the optimum method with respect to the final strength of the dental stone. But success speaks for itself.

For on-scene processing, the dental stone should meet minimal strength requirements of about 8000 psi. Plaster of paris has a psi of about 5000, which means, though it has been used successfully as a casting agent, the casts it produced did not have the optimum strength and they chipped easily. Today's dental stone has a psi ranging as high 15,000, making it ideal as a casting medium for 3D impressions.

The general procedure for making a cast follows.

11.9.2.1 Materials Required

- *Dental stone powder*: Generally, 2–3 lbs of dental stone will cover most footwear impressions: 3 lbs (1365 g) is better, especially when casting on a slope. Forensic-quality dental stone is available in 3 lb premeasured plastic bags.
  - There are three common methods for using dental stone in the field: the bucket method, where dental stone is added to water and allowed to settle; the zippable plastic bag method, where water is added to preweighed dental stone in a plastic bag and massaged for 1–2 min to mix the water; and the bottle method, where water is added to dental stone in a plastic bottle and then shaken for approximately 40 s. Recent research suggests that the bottle method produces casts of a higher quality than the plastic bag method without the effort involved in the bucket method, which produces casts of the best quality [20].
- *Adding water*: The amount of water is a critical factor for obtaining strong, high-quality impressions. For field work, store sufficient water in a separate zippable plastic bag or bottle for 3 lbs (1865 g) of dental stone. The exact amount of water necessary can be calculated, but in practice this will be determined by the consistency of the dental stone and the weather. If it is cold, a little less water will aid hardening. If the temperature is below freezing, the water should be prepared as a 5% potassium sulfate solution because it accelerates the setting of the mold by lowering the freezing point. Generally, a rule of thumb is between 280 and 350 mL (no more than 1½ cups) for each 2+ (2.2 lbs or 1 kg) lbs of dental stone [19] or between 400 and 480 mL for 3 lbs of dental stone.
  - *Bucket method*: Add dental stone to water in a rubber casting bucket (available from forensic supply houses) and allow it to settle to the bottom. Then, mix the slurry together until it is ready to be poured into the impression.
  - *Bottle method*: Add water to dental stone weighed into a bottle and shake for approximately 40 s.
  - *Zippable plastic bag method*: Add the water to the dental stone in the plastic bag and massage the bag for 1–2 min.
- *Casting frame or mold*: On flat surfaces, dental stone does not require a barrier. Casting on a slope may require a barrier to keep the dental stone slurry from running out of the impression. Generally, the casting frame is recommended because it results in a better thickness of the cast.
- *Bucket or rubber mixing bowl*: If the plastic bag method is not used, the dental stone should be mixed in a mixing container.
- *Broad stick or spoon*: For mixing the dental stone.
- *A wooden baffle*: This is used to temper the flow of dental stone to the impression. A hand will also serve this purpose.

11.9.2.2 *Preparing the Impression*

- *Debris in the impression*: Do not remove debris from the interior of the impression that was clearly made at the time the impression was made. Loose leaves or twigs lying *on top of* the impression can be removed.
- *Release agents*: In the past, release agents—hair spray, dirt hardener, shellac, etc.—were used to prevent soil or other surface material from sticking to the cast. These are not necessary with dental stone.
- *Dental stone*: Mixing the dental stone using the zippable plastic bag method is a simple matter of pouring water into the powder and then gently mixing the powder by hand until there is an even distribution of the powder and water. The slurry is ready to pour when it has a viscosity of thick cream or pancake batter. Remember, the hardening process begins as soon as the powder and the water mix together. It should also be remembered that hardening is an exothermic reaction, which means it gives off heat.

11.9.2.3 *General Casting Procedure*

- *Pouring*: When the slurry attains the appropriate viscosity, open the bag and very carefully pour the mixture gently into the impression, moving from one end to the other in a continuous motion. See the illustration in Figure 11.16.
- *Watering out*: This is the term for what happens when water from the dental stone forms on top of the hardening mold. This occurs when the ratio of water:powder is not correct or was not mixed long enough. Dental stone requires 18.6 parts water to 100 parts powder in order for the mold to form. Water above this amount is excess and must be removed by evaporation. If not removed, it will usually move to the surface ("watering out").

General casting procedure

Pouring Procedure

- Release agent
  - Lightly mist above impression with hair spray
  - A controversial procedure
  - Keeps integrity of the detail intact
  - Can also use commercial hardening products
    - Dirt hardener
  - Talc powder seems to work as well as anything
- Use "baffle" about 2" above imprint and tipped at shallow angle
  - Paper covered clipboard
  - Or strong cardboard
- Pour casting material onto baffle and allow uniform flow onto imprint
  - Avoid irregularities or "waves" in plaster
- Allow first pour to become firm
  - Prepare second batch–if necessary
  - After hardening scratch identifying information into surface with dowel or knife

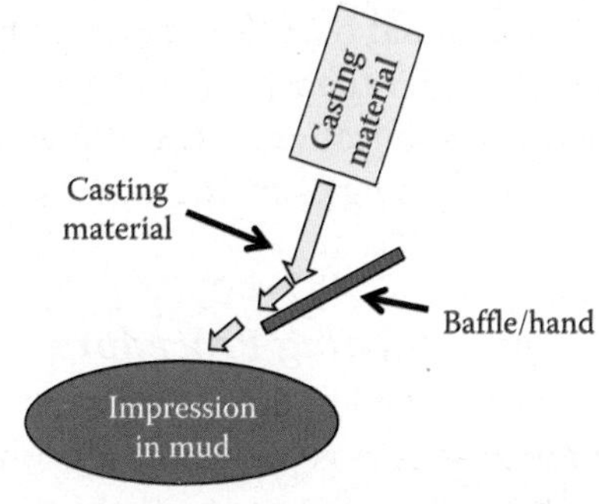

Figure 11.16 Procedure for casting three-dimensional impressions.

- *Curing*: Usually, the strength of the cast increases over time and will not be as hard 1 h after hardening as when cured overnight. When completely cured, it will "ping" or "ring" when snipped with a finger.
- *Marking*: When the cast is hard enough—still warm and hard—but not completely cured, scratch the cast with initials, the date, and the time into the surface of the mold.

11.9.2.4 Lifting the Cast

- *Losing the gloss*: As the cast hardens, the surface will gradually change from a high gloss to a dull finish. When this happens—30 min or longer depending on weather—the cast can be lifted carefully from the impression.
- *Lifting*: Try to get your fingers of both hands underneath the long edge of the cast. Then gently lift the cast toward the other edge.
- *Cleaning*: Do not clean the cast until it has cured. The dirt adhering to the cast can be valuable in soil comparisons. Any dirt adhering to the cast should be preserved in a nonplastic container. Small boxes are ideal. A complete cleaning can be done by immersing the cast in a saturated solution of potassium sulfate.
- *Drying*: The cast should dry for 24–48 h before cleaning.

11.9.3 Special Circumstances

11.9.3.1 Casting in Snow

Casting footwear and tire track impressions in snow is possible. To be successful, however, there are specific precautions. First, one must ensure that the snow has a good solid impression. Second, use a casting material that does not dilute the snow. Third, ensure that sunlight does not hit the impression. Fourth, contrasting detail should be captured by first spray painting the impression before casting.

Photography is the first step to archiving an impression. The problem with snow is that there is little contrast because of the color of snow and impression detail. One way to increase the contrast is to spray the impression with automotive gray primer paint. Another is to use the snow print wax spray [21] or snow print powder. The spray is an aerosol wax that forms a wax mold over the impression. Since it is bright red (see Figure 11.17), it also creates contrast. After the wax mold has solidified—three applications with approximately 2–5 min between applications—the impression is cast with dental stone as described above. Snow Print Powder works in the same way except that the power is sprinkled into the impression.

11.9.3.2 Snow Casting Procedure

- Spray the impression lightly with the snow print wax at an angle in order to highlight the raised areas of the impression. Do not cover the entire area of the impression. This is the best time to photograph the sprayed impression.
- Do not hold the spray too close to the impression because the blast from the aerosol can damage the impression's detail.
- The red (or other colored sprays) attract heat, so it is important to shield the impression from the sun.

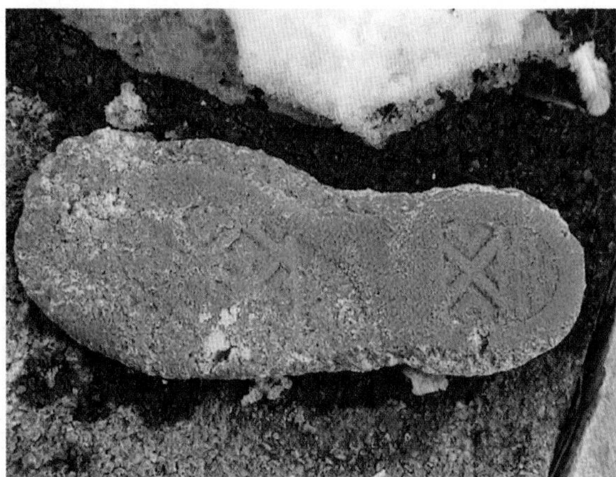

Figure 11.17 Photograph of snow print wax lifted impression in snow. (Photograph by Robert C. Shaler.)

- Spray the impression with two or three more applications, ensuring that the entire impression is covered in wax. A properly sprayed impression will not reveal much detail when viewed from above.
- Allow the wax mold to dry for approximately 5–10 min. Shield impression from the sun.
- Prepare dental stone slurry. When it reaches the usual consistency signifying it is ready to be poured into the impression, allow it to incubate a little longer so that when it hits the snow print wax covering the impression, the heat will have dissipated somewhat, which should protect the waxed impression.
- When the cast is still hardening, scratch initials, the date, and the time into the cast.
- Allow the impression to sit for approximately 60 min before lifting.
- After lifting, immediately photograph the cast.

Snow print casts are fragile, and the wax molding is easily destroyed. Importantly, The cast should be kept away from sunlight. If melting occurs, cast detail will be lost. Technology and casting materials change over time, exemplified by the progression from plaster of paris casts—fragile and required forms and supporting "sticks" to hold them together—to dental stone that is harder and easier to cast and use. It is certain that better and more convenient products will be available in the future. The future may well be the use of imaging techniques followed by 3D printing to a plastic mold.

References

1. A. C. Doyle, 1902. *The Hound of the Baskervilles*, Chapter 2, In: The Original Illustrated Sherlock Holmes. Castle Books Secaucus, NJ, 1980, p. 352.
2. L. Nause. 2001. *Forensic Tire Impression Identification*. Ottawa: Canadian Police Research Centre, pp. 34, 80.
3. NASA. 2004. Apollo 11—First footprint on the moon. Available at: http://www.nasa.gov/audience/forstudents/k-4/home/F_Apollo_11.html, accessed September 7, 2009.

4. *Merriam-Webster Online Dictionary*. Inculpate. Available at: http://www.merriam-webster.com/dictionary/inculpate (accessed November 10, 2010).
5. *Merriam-Webster Online Dictionary*. Exculpate. Available at: http://www.merriam-webster.com/dictionary/exculpate?show = 0&t = 1289418588 (accessed November 10, 2010).
6. Committee on Identifying the Needs of the Forensic Science Community, Committee on Science, Technology and Law Policy and Global Affairs, Committee on Applied and Theoretical Statistics, Division on Engineering and Physical Sciences, National Research Council of the National Academies. 2009. Chapter 5: Descriptions of some forensic science disciplines. *Strengthening Forensic Science in the United States: A Path Forward*. Washington, DC: National Academies Press, pp. 145–150.
7. D. S. Hilderbrand. 1999. *Footwear, The Missed Evidence—A Field Guide to the Collection and Preservation of Forensic Footwear Impression Evidence*. Wildomar, CA: Staggs Publishing.
8. W. J. Bodziak. 2000. *Footwear Impression Evidence—Detection, Recovery, and Examination*. Boca Raton, FL: CRC Press, p. 476.
9. M. J. Cassidy. 1995. *Footwear Identification*. Salem, OR: Lightning Powder Company, pp. 113–119.
10. *Wikipedia*. Dust. Available at: http://en.wikipedia.org/wiki/Dust (accessed April 18, 2010).
11. Evident Crime Scene Technologies. BVDA gellifter mirror technique. Available at: http://www.evidentcrimescene.com/cata/cast/mirrortech.html (accessed October 5, 2010).
12. S. Wiesner, T. Tsach, C. Belser, and Y. Shor. 2011. A comparative research of two lifting methods: Electrostatic lifter gelatin lifter. *Journal of Forensic Sciences* 56(S1):S58–S62.
13. *Merriam-Webster Online Dictionary*. Coloumb's Law. Available at: http://www.merriam-webster.com/dictionary/coulomb%27s + law?show = 0&t = 1295790698 (accessed January 23, 2011).
14. M. L. Pearse and J. S. Brennan, 1996. Importance of absolute humidity in the operation of the electrostatic detection apparatus. *Forensic Science International* 83:121–131.
15. Home Office Scientific Development Branch (HOSDB). 2008. Fingerprint processes for footwear mark enhancement. *HOSDB Fingerprint and Footwear Forensics Newsletter*, Publication No. 24/08.
16. BVDA. Gellifters brochure. Available at: http://www.bvda.com/EN/download/Gellifter_brochure.pdf (accessed January 26, 2011).
17. *Online Free Dictionary* (*Physics/General Physics*). Adhesion. Available at: http://www.thefreedictionary.com/adhesion (accessed January 23, 2011).
18. Y. Shor, T. Tsach, and S. Wiesner, 2005. Removing interfering contaminations from gel lifters. *Journal of Forensic Sciences* 50(6):1–8.
19. A. Cohen, S. Wiesner, A. Grafit, and Y. Shor, 2011. A new method for casting three-dimensional shoeprints and tire marks with dental stone. *Journal of Forensic Sciences* 56(S1):S210–S213.
20. K. Carlsson. 1982. A new method for securing impressions in snow. *Crime Laboratory Digest* (December):1–4.
21. S. M. Ojena, 1984. A new improved technique for casting impressions in snow. *Journal of Forensic Sciences* 29(1):322–325.

Pattern Evidence II
Vehicle-Involved Scenes

12

A person dies in a car accident every 12 minutes and each year car crashes kill 40,000 people [1].

12.1 Introduction

This chapter is meant to serve as an overview of vehicle-related scenes from the perspective of tire track impression evidence, its importance, and some scene parameters that crime scene units should consider when investigating vehicle-involved crimes. This chapter is not an all-inclusive field guide. For that, the reader should consider texts devoted to tire track impression evidence [2,3]. A number of on-scene topics have or will be discussed in other chapters, but vehicle scenes involve scene circumstances that are not found in other scenes.

12.2 Vehicle-Involved Scenes

Vehicle-involved scenes run the gamut of scene types: homicides, sexual assaults, burglaries, drive-by shootings, terrorist events, and so on. Thus, identifying a vehicle used in connection with a crime or an incident should be a critical part of the on-scene investigation. Vehicles are also involved in shooting incidents, but this is discussed later in Chapter 21.

In a typical homicide investigation, scene scientists/investigators should consider carefully the possibility that specific categories of physical evidence related to the crime are present. Hit-and-run crimes, whether vehicle–vehicle, vehicle–person, vehicle–other object, involve vehicles that leave the scene. In these crimes, damage to the vehicles (and the victim) creates the physical evidence needed to prove that a suspect vehicle was at the scene; this evidence should be collectible either as packaged evidence or in the form of photographs and measurements. An article from the *New York Daily News* is an example [4]:

> The victim (name omitted), 47, stepped out of her stalled car and was getting help from a passing good Samaritan when another car suddenly roared down Tartee St, police said. As that black 2000 Mazda tired to squeeze between the two parked vehicles, it ran over the victim, crushing the woman under its wheels, police said. "The car was fling. I mean, really flying," said a witness (name withheld) who was in the car directly behind the suspect's vehicle. "That women flew, she have had a chance. One second she as just there and the next minute she's dead in the road." The victim's hat and shoes were blown off by the impact, witnesses said. She died instantly. (p. 12)

The suspect and his vehicle were found. The New York City Police Department (NYPD) crime scene unit had the responsibility of investigating the car to prove it was the vehicle that struck the victim.

Hit-and-run cases are not the only vehicle-involved crimes. The kidnapping of a child, for example, involves a vehicle for transport and, although it is absolutely critical to find physical evidence that the child had been inside the car, the reality is that such evidence may not be present or may have been removed. The task, then, is to find physical evidence from other sources. Certainly the vehicle had been at the abduction location, and finding evidence to prove that it had been there is an example of critically important associative evidence. It may be the only evidence available linking the suspect to the crime scene.

Each vehicle involved in a crime has a factual history relating to how the vehicle was involved. The scene scientist/investigator's job is to sort through these facts and proceed logically and carefully, using intellectual and scientific tools at his/her disposable to find the appropriate and correct probative evidence. The abducted child case is such an example. No evidence was inside the suspect vehicle to prove the child had been there. This forces the scene scientist/investigator to consider other, perhaps indirect, avenues to move the investigation forward. Certainly, the abductor and his vehicle had been at the scene and hopefully left evidence of that. The original investigation should include a thorough investigation not just of the inside from where the child had been taken but also of the outside where the vehicle might have been parked. Hopefully, physical evidence of the vehicle being there had been collected and the scene archived properly. An example of important physical evidence vehicles leave behind is tire track impressions.

12.2.1 Tire Track Impression Evidence: Evidence Often Overlooked

Although the discussion in Chapter 11 dealt with locating, enhancing, photographing, and archiving *footwear* impression evidence, much of that discussion is applicable to tire track evidence as well. Like footwear impressions, tire track evidence is classified as 2D or 3D. And, also, like footwear impressions, tire tracks are commonly dust- or otherwise-contaminated 2D impressions or indented impressions, in a soft surface. Again, like footwear evidence, the physical characteristics needed for meaningful criminalistic-quality comparisons are categorized as class or individualizing, the former providing information about the tread design and the latter physical deformities embedded in the tread of the tire from daily usage.

Enhancing tire track evidence involves many of the same principles as applicable to footwear evidence and includes photography and chemical enhancements. Importantly, photography is not only a method to archive the impression but also to enhance it. Chemical treatments attempt to take advantage of the inherent chemical signature of the impression—minerals, such as iron and aluminum, and so on, organics, or bio-materials—to more clearly visualize the impression. The chemical enhancements are essentially the same as those used to enhance the footwear evidence.

If the forensic analysis of tire track and footwear impression evidence is so similar, why discuss tire track evidence as a separate category? Why not just read the previous chapter? The answer lies in the differences in the forensic information they provide. Each provides evidence of either the individual (shoe impressions) or the vehicle (tire impressions) being at the scene, the latter suggesting the vehicle was *used* in the crime. Tire track impressions are different because they can provide investigative information about the vehicle whereas sneaker prints, for example, do not really narrow the field of suspects for investigators. Understand that the forensic information available from tire track impressions provides information toward identifying the vehicle and not the person. Once known, the owner of the vehicle can be identified, although the owner is not necessarily the person who had been driving. Still, it is an investigative lead.

12.2.1.1 Why Conduct a Comprehensive Forensic On-Scene Investigation of Tire Track Evidence?

The reason is simple: to identify the vehicle used during the commission of a crime. There is more to tire track analysis [3,4] at the crime scene than students might suspect. Although hinted at above, it is important to quickly discuss why tire track evidence has forensic value. It is certainly possible that the vehicle used during the commission of the crime will not be present at the scene. Thus, it is critical that on-scene scientists/investigators identify and collect/document all of the physical evidence present that can be used to identify that vehicle once it is found. Competent on-scene work is the only mechanism for obtaining this information. It should be pointed out that all of the physical evidence present may not be there in all vehicle-involved scene investigations. Regardless, the information should be looked for. The list in Table 12.1 gives suggestions for what to look for during the investigation (see pp. 57–72 in Reference [3]).

Determining how the vehicle was maneuvered is directly related to identifying the appropriate tire tracks and then studying them carefully to ascertain whether the vehicle was, for example, driven to a particular point, stopped, and turned around. If the tire track impressions are readily apparent, specific characteristics of the vehicle can also be determined: stance, track width, turning radius, tread wear, vehicle mechanical problems, and so on. The on-scene investigation is the only place to find these vehicular characteristics (see pp. 57–72 in Reference [3]).

Identifying the front-and-back tires is important and, if possible, the number of occupants, the latter might be a matter of finding different sets of footprints. The age of the vehicle—old or new—can be related to the number of different tires (different treads) at the scene. A vehicle with four different tires might be older than one having all tires of the same tread design.

Table 12.1 Helpful Information in Vehicle-Involved Investigations

- How vehicle was maneuvered?
- What are the vehicle's characteristics?
  - Stance
  - Track measurements
    - Wheelbase
  - Tread wear indicators
  - Wear bars
  - Indicators of vehicle age
- How many vehicles and how many occupants were present?
- Were objects loaded or unloaded into/from the vehicle?
- Who was driving the vehicle?
  - DNA from inside the vehicle or from fingerprints on the vehicle
- What was the direction of travel
- What is the relationship of impressions at scene to arrangement of tires on suspect vehicle
- What is the position of front of the vehicle?
  - Impressions by front and rear tires
- Which impressions must be archived?
  - Which track locations are most appropriate to archive?
- What other relevant evidence is present?
  - Footwear Impressions
  - Fluid spills

Why is it important to know which tire impressions come from the front-and-rear tires? The reason is that the information from these impressions can help pinpoint important physical characteristics of the vehicle. For example, if the vehicle was moving out of, say, a dirt parking lot, the turning diameter might be determined. Knowing the leading edge of front-and-back tires can lead to measuring the wheelbase and the track width, both characteristics of vehicles. If there are multiple tracks, identifying those coming from the suspect's vehicle is important.

The direction the vehicle was moving can be determined from the on-scene investigation by closely examining the tire tracks and then using known factors and/or common sense to show the direction of travel. The following incomplete list gives suggestions of how to use scene evidence to determine the correct direction (see p. 13 in Reference [3]):

- The dirt/debris/gravel kicked up by spinning wheels indicates spinning tires
- Striations by sidewall in a furrow (in mud or snow) show which direction the tire was rolling
- Tracks pinpoint where the vehicle stopped and backed up to change the direction
- Overlapping front-and-rear tire tracks can provide directional information
- Tracks help determine whether the vehicle was coming to or leaving the scene
- Flattened grass or small plants indicate the direction
- Tire tread patterns have directional indicators
- Tires lift damp soil or snow slightly in direction of travel
- Tires deposit transferred material in direction of travel
- Mud, dirty water, or fluids are splashed or thrown on other surfaces—vertical or horizontal—in the direction of travel

Other information from impression evidence can be present as well. Finding and documenting footwear impressions give an estimate of the minimum number of people involved in the crime as well as provide 2D or 3D footwear impression evidence.

Finally, conclusively identifying the specific vehicle requires a detailed scientific analysis to compare the scene evidence against the tire tread of a suspect vehicle. While identifying the specific vehicle requires recovering it and making direct comparisons, the scene scientist/investigator and laboratory analyst have recourses that can narrow the search among the possible universe of vehicles. Still, until the suspect vehicle is located and impounded, scene scientists/investigators must be certain to completely archive, collect, and preserve all tire track evidences.

12.2.2 On-Scene Considerations

Cutting corners in any investigation is not an option because no one contemporaneously at the scene knows whether a seemingly unimportant piece of what might have not been considered as evidence suddenly plays a prominent role in the investigation. Thus, scene scientists/investigators should work as though anything at scenes has potentially probative value. This presents problems for vehicle-involved scenes because there is the misperception that tire track impressions have little forensic or investigative value. Certainly, the general principles applied to all scenes holds good for vehicle-involved scenes too; management, archiving, searching, and so on are the essential ingredients of vehicular scene investigations. See also Chapter 21.

12.2.2.1 *Management*

Management of the scene should follow the guidelines presented in Chapter 3. While these principles are inviolate, there are unique characteristics of vehicle-involved scenes. Specifically, these involve identifying, archiving, characterizing, and preserving the physical evidence.

12.2.2.2 *Archiving*

The process of archiving (photographing, sketching, video, 3D-imaging) tire track impressions and other vehicle-involved scene evidence is much like that for footwear impression evidence, as discussed in Chapter 11.

12.2.2.2.1 Photographs Each photograph must tell the story the scene offers. That is, establishing or overview shots must completely illustrate the relationship of the tire track impressions to the overall scene. If the crime involves the burglary of a convenience store, for example, the photos of tire tracks in the parking lot must show them in relation to the front of the store as well as to the street. The midrange photos must illustrate properly how the tire track impressions relate to other evidence nearby, such as footwear impressions, if present, and their relationship to the tire track impressions must be absolutely unambiguous. Scales should show distances involved and these should be included in the photographs (taken with and without scales). If evidence markers are take used, the initial photographs without the markers in place and then, again, with the markers in place. Table 12.2 is a guide to photography of tire track impressions.

Each photographic series must have specific information, and each photograph must have its specific identifying information. Much of what is required is the same for all forensic photographs (Chapter 6), but tire track impression photographs need additional information as shown in the following list (see p. 14 in Reference [3]):

- Case number
- Location
- Photographer's name
- Date
- Time
- Scales used in the plane of impression
- Tire position marked on vehicle—right front, and so on

Table 12.2 Photography of Tire Track Impressions

Photos Must Include Markers to Identify Tire Position on Vehicle
• Establishing or overview photographs   • Tell the story and relationship of how the tire tracks relate to the overall scene. Photos with and without evidence markers in place.
• Midrange   • Tell the story of how the tire track evidence relate to each other and to nearby objects. Photos with evidence markers are important to establish evidence-to-evidence relationships.
• Close-ups   • These include at least 24" of all four impressions, appropriately identify which tire, for example, right front and so on, being photographed. Photos with and without scales must be included.

- Arrow pointing to front of vehicle—establishes inside and outside edge of impression
- Impression number—first, second, third, fourth, or more impressions recorded
- North/south directions

12.2.2.2.2 Sketches: Vehicle-Critical Measurements Generally, vehicle sketches should conform to the principles discussed in Chapter 7. As with all sketches, the vehicle sketch must be complete and sufficiently detailed to permit a determination of specific vehicle characteristics; this is dependent on the amount and detail of the tire track impressions present. This implies that the specific vehicle-related information, for example, wheelbase, stance, and so on, be included on the sketch or over several sketches, which means making the effort to obtain these critical measurements from relevant impressions. Sketches should document the presence of scene-related as well as nonscene-related impressions. This means that all the tire track impressions found in the dirt where, for instance, someone had been abducted must be included in the sketch. On that sketch, the evidence impressions should be highlighted (see p. 45 in Reference [2]).

12.2.2.3 On-Scene Information

The following considers some of the on-scene information that should be obtained, if possible, that can lead to identifying specific characteristics of an unknown vehicle. These measurements are taken from tire track impressions at the scene.

12.2.2.3.1 Wheelbase The wheelbase of the vehicle is defined as the distance between the leading edge of the front-and-rear tires. Figure 12.1 illustrates how to determine the wheelbase from tire track impressions at the scene [3].

12.2.2.3.2 Front-and-Rear Track Widths The front and rear track widths are defined as the distance between the middle of the leading edge of the front-and-back tires, respectively. Figure 12.2 also illustrates how to determine the front-and-rear track widths from tire track evidence at the scene [3]. Mechanical issues with a vehicle can affect how these impressions appear. Among others, one is camber, which is the "tilt" of the tires as they rest on the ground. Figure 12.2 shows the differences between normal and abnormal camber, which can be positive or negative, each signifying improper alignment or worn front-end

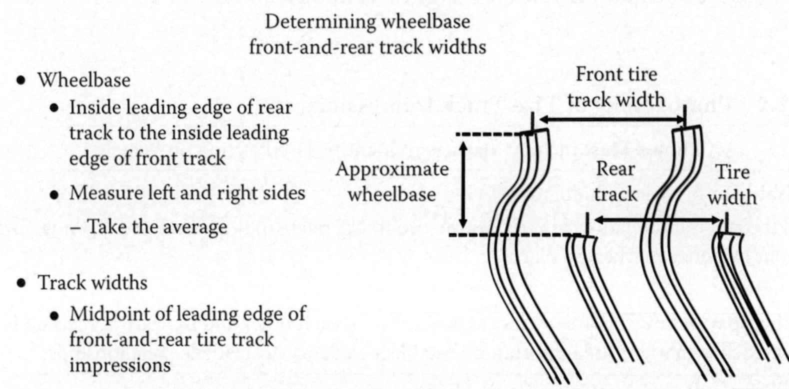

Figure 12.1 Wheelbase determination. (Adapted from L. Nause. 2001. *Forensic Tire Impression Identification*. Ottawa: Canadian Police Research Centre. With permission.)

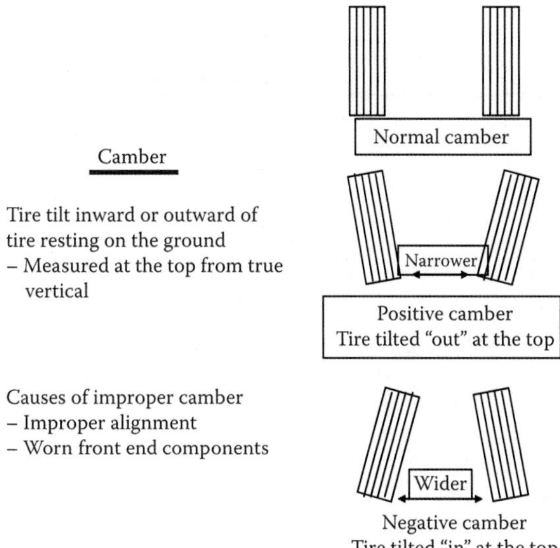

Figure 12.2 Factors affecting track width: Camber. (Adapted from L. Nause. 2001. *Forensic Tire Impression Identification*. Ottawa: Canadian Police Research Centre. With permission from Royal Canadian Mounted Police.)

parts of the vehicle. Positive camber is defined as the tires tilted further apart, "out," at the top. Negative camber is defined as the tires tilted closer, "in," at the top, each with respect to what the camber is supposed to be (see p. 68 in Reference [2]).

12.2.2.3.3 Turning Diameter The turning diameter is defined as the diameter of the circle made when the vehicle is driven in a circle. It, too, can be determined from the measurements taken of the impressions at the scene. Figure 12.3 illustrates the process. Importantly, not all tire impression evidence will have sufficient information to make these measurements. Diagrammatically, it seems that a significant amount of a turning impression is necessary to calculate the turning diameter. This is not necessarily true, however it does punctuate the importance of preserving the impression during the investigation. The measurements are made at the scene, although, theoretically, they could be made from 3D imaging equipment at the scene or in the laboratory from aerial photographs taken above the impression, if a known size marker is available. Calculations should be done by laboratory personnel.

Calculations can be made using the following procedures (see p. 69 in Reference [3]):

- Select segment of the front tire reflecting sharpest portion of turn.
- Make an imaginary line between two points of track arc (A–AA) (Figure 13.5).
  - Measure the distance from the outer margin to the outer margin (A to AA).
- Bisect A–AA and then draw line B–C at right angles to A–AA and extend to arc point B. Line F is the distance between C and AA.
- Draw another line C–D between the bisected point and the inside of the rear tire track arc point D.
- Measure the distance from C to B—that is, line E.
- Calculate diameter according to Equation 12.1 [2, p. 70] or 12.2 [3, p. 69].

$$\text{Diameter} = (\text{Line } F^2/8 \times \text{Line } E + E/2) \text{ [3, p. 69].} \tag{12.1}$$

$$\text{Diameter} = (\text{Line } F^2/\text{Line } E) + \text{Line } E \text{ [2, p. 70].} \tag{12.2}$$

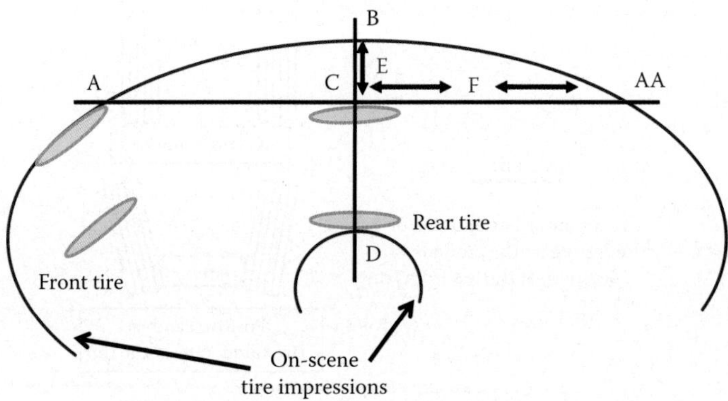

Figure 12.3 Calculating the turning diameter. (Adapted from P. McDonald. 1993. *Tire Imprint Evidence*. Boca Raton, FL: CRC Press, p. 70; L. Nause. 2001. *Forensic Tire Impression Identification*. Ottawa: Canadian Police Research Centre, p. 69. Used with permission from the Royal Canadian Mounted Police.)

12.2.2.3.4 Tread Design Width (Arc Width) The tread design width is defined as the measurement from one edge of the design to the other. These measurements can only be made at the scene and from the actual impression. This information can help investigators identify an unknown impression (see pp. 69–71 in Reference [3]).

12.2.2.3.5 Tread Depth (Skid Depth) The tread depth is defined as the depth of an impression based on the manufacturer's nonskid design of the tread. In new tires, these can range from 11/32 to 12/32 of an inch, although mud and snow tires are deeper and will be as much as between 14/32 and 16/32 of an inch. These measurements can help eliminate suspect vehicles. For example, if the tread depth measured at the scene is 8/32, and a suspected car is 12/32, the suspected car could not have been involved in the crime (see p. 70 in Reference [3]).

Performing these measurements at the scene is a simple matter of using a scale calibrated in 1/32 of an inch (or a 15 mm forensic scale). The scale should be lowered into the impression and the depth read from the scale. Castings made from the impression can also be used to determine the tread depth. The procedures for determining tread depth is shown below:

- *Equipment*
  - Tread depth gauge (measures in 1/32) or 15 mm ruler
  - Newer tires: 11/32 to 16/32 in.
  - Maximum depths suggest newer tires
  - Wear bars are set at 2/32
  - Wear patterns appear as solid bar in the tire impression
- *Procedures*
  - Estimate height of groove in scene impression
  - Set depth gauge on impression groove
  - Carefully lower gauge into impression and read depth from the scale
  - Alternatively, measure depth from cast in dental stone

12.2.2.3.6 Tire Circumference: Suspect Vehicle If the tire track impression is long enough, it might be possible to approximate the tire's rolling circumference by finding an accidental-repeated characteristic, such as a gouge or cut, along the imprint. The distance between these repeated marks is the rolling tire circumference (see pp. 82–109 in Reference [2] and pp. 69–71 in Reference [3]). When repeated it represents one full revolution of the tire. This is important because comparing apples to apples is the only way to obtain correct data. That is, the same measurement made at the crime scene will be from, say, gouge to gouge as seen in the impression. This measurement will not be the same as one taken by wrapping the measuring tape around the tire, which will be larger because the scene impression is flat but the actual tire has a curved arc (see p. 71 in Reference [3]).

12.2.3 Impressions Other than Dirt

Like the sole of shoes, 2D impressions of tire tracks are visible because of contaminants adhering to the tread, dirt, and dust being the most common. Other contaminants can also create impressions: water, grease (oil), or blood. Each will leave a visible impression and each can be enhanced, although the enhancement method will differ depending on the contaminant. Tables 11.3 and 11.5 can are guides for how to enhance the impressions. Obviously there is a variety of choices and scene scientist/investigators must staine to make the proper decision. Archiving the impression photographically is the first step followed by a serious consideration of the enhancement choices and the variables offered by the scene: surface material, the chemistry of the impression material (dirt, oil, blood, and so on), and the chemistry of the enhancement method.

References

1. Edgar Snyder and Associates. Car accident statistics. Available at: http://www.edgarsnyder.com/car-accident/resources/statistics.html.
2. P. McDonald. 1993. *Tire Imprint Evidence*. Boca Raton, FL: CRC Press.
3. L. Nause. 2001. *Forensic Tire Impression Identification*. Ottawa: Canadian Police Research Centre.
4. K. Nocera and J. Lemire. 2010. Killed in tragic hit-run. *New York Daily News*, July 11, p. 12.

Workshop 5: Pattern Evidence

W5.1 2D and 3D Footwear Impressions

W5.1.1 Exercise 1: Casting Footprint and Tire Track Impressions Using Dental Stone

The aim of this exercise is to introduce evidence casting using dental stone. Although casting is relatively simple, there are some precautions. It would be wise to review Chapter 11 at this time.

- A mold may be necessary if the impression print is on an angle or sloped surface.
- While carefully pouring the casting solution into the impression, do not pour the slurry directly onto the impression.
- Do not wait too long to pour the casting slurry.

- As the slurry dries, scratch your initials, date, and time (and case number, if known) into the hardening casting material.
- If an impression print is wet or is covered with water, the print is still salvageable.
- Impressions in snow are salvageable.
- Cold weather slows the hardening process.
- Hot weather speeds the hardening process.
- Snow is not a detriment to casting a useable 3D impression.

W5.1.1.1 Casting Here, we will cast a footprint in mud and/or dust and/or snow. Additionally, we will cast a wet print on cement. Follow the formulas in Chapter 11. Generally, 3 lbs of dental stone and three cups of water in separate bottles or separate plastic bags should suffice (prepare two).

- Procedures for casting footwear/tire impressions found in mud or dust
  - Photograph the impression. Sometimes spraying gray primer paint into the impression enhances detail and makes photography easier.
  - *If necessary*, place a mold around the footprint, leaving an inch or two between the top of the impressed print and the edge. For tire tracks, cast approximately 24 in., if possible. This will require more dental stone, 4–5 lbs.
  1. Remove twigs and other debris that might have fallen into the print impression and might be obscuring the print detail.
  2. Carefully spray hair spray into the impression print, ensuring that the detail is not disturbed. Allow the sprayed impression to dry. This is not always necessary.
  3. Prepare the dental stone slurry. Slowly add 2 lbs of dental stone powder (commercially available) into two cups of water (have backup dental stone and water handy). Continually mix—not creating bubbles—until the slurry has the consistency of pancake batter. Be prepared to prepare a second slurry if the first is not sufficient to create a mold of appropriate strength.
  4. Carefully pour the slurry into the impression print, *not* directly onto the impression. Pouring at an angle and using a ladle, deflect the slurry gently into the impression, guiding it onto the impression.
  5. Before the mold hardens, scratch the case number (if known), your initials, date, and time into the back of the mold.
  6. Once the cast is hard, remove it from the impression print, lifting it carefully to ensure that it does not crack or break.
  7. Photograph the mold with its adhering dirt. Leave the dirt in place for approximately 24 h and then scrape the adhering dirt into a container that can be sealed.
  8. Show the final cast to an instructor for grading.
- Procedures for casting footwear/tire impressions found in snow
  - Create a mold of the snow using SnowPrint™ Wax, a commercially available product that you carefully spray into the impression.
  - After spraying the wax into the impression, allow it to dry (harden) 2–5 min.
  - Repeat the process twice more, for a total of three applications of the wax.

  - Very carefully, pour the dental stone slurry (prepared according the instructions in Chapter 11) into the mold as described above.
  - As the slurry solidifies, it becomes warm, which tends to melt the snow. Therefore, pour the slurry into the impression at the last possible moment.
  - When the cast begins to harden, scratch your initials, the time, date, and the case number (if known) into the cast.
  - After it hardens sufficiently to lift, show it to an instructor for grading.
- Procedures for casting water-filled impressions of footwear/tire imprints: If the impression is filled with water, it presents unique problems. Instead of pouring a slurry of dental stone into the impression, sift dry dental stone powder into the impression until it takes up all of the water. Then pour a slurry of the dental stone (prepared as described above) onto the casting powder that is in the impression.
  - Find or create an impression print that is filled with water or add water to a dry impression print.
  - Follow the procedure above.
  - After lifting the cast, show it to an instructor for grading.
- Procedures for casting wet prints on cement: If the impression is on concrete and is wet, it can be dusted using a magnetic dusting powder and then cast using dental stone.
  - Prepare a wet footprint on cement.
  - Dust the print with black magnetic powder. Photograph the dusted print with and without scales in place.
  - Cast the print using dental stone.
  - Lift the print and photograph.
  - Show the lifted cast and the photograph to an instructor for grading.

W5.2 Locating Dry (Dust) Residue Prints

Dust prints are among the most fragile evidence types because they are difficult to see with the unaided eye. They are also rarely collected because they are secondary in the thought process of investigators and are easily destroyed. They are not usually thought of in the initial aspects of the investigation and are commonly overlooked and/or destroyed at scenes. These impressions should be expected at the entrance and exit areas; so walking in these areas when entering a scene must be done carefully. Therefore, finding dry residue prints before they become obliterated is an important and potentially critical aspect of scene investigation. These prints are also considered a class of evidence—fragile evidence. This is why finding dust prints and marking their locations must be one of the first activities of crime scene investigation. In this exercise, we will use various light sources to locate dry (dust) prints.

There are several ways to locate dust prints at a scene. Typically, these involve oblique lighting using a flashlight or an ALS, either singly or sequentially. Additionally, simultaneously using the light source with a mirror helps find prints that can be missed using either the flashlight or the ALS singly.

Another tool that is helpful in finding prints is the reflected UV light. An equipment that uses reflected UV light is the RUVIS.

W5.2.1 Exercise 2a: Finding Dry and Wet Residue Prints Indoors

The goal is to find as many dry and wet impression prints as possible for both comparative purposes in the laboratory and to ascertain the number of people at the scene.

- Tools
  - Mirror
  - Light sources
  - ALS
  - Flashlights
  - RUVIS
- Procedures
  - Darken the room in any way you can. Use tarps of Spruce in the basement to cover the windows and doorways, if necessary.
  - Standing at each of the central points and corners of the room shine a flashlight across the room while holding the light source near or on the floor. Observe the pattern of latent dust prints in the room.
    - Mark the prints that are located using evidence markers.
  - Repeat the procedures in the same room using a mirror held near the floor at an angle so that dry residue prints are visible in the mirror.
    - Place the mirror at various spots around the room.
    - Using either a flashlight or the "white" light of the ALS, shine the light at an oblique angle toward the mirror.
    - The reflection of the floor in the mirror will highlight dry and wet residue footprints.
    - Mark the footprints with evidence markers.
  - Repeat the procedures with the ALS at various settings.
  - Use the RUVIS.
    - Observe the footprints located using the RUVIS.
    - Decide which of the found prints have the most discernible information to use for comparative purposes.
    - See if the RUVIS locates additional prints.
  - Compare the number of prints found by the different methods.
  - Fill in Tables W5.1, W5.2, and W5.3
  - Show the tables to an instructor for grading.

Table W5.1 Exercise 2a: Linoleum Fill-In Table

Method Used	Put an 'X' against the Method that Gave the Best Results
Flashlight—Oblique Light	
ALS White Light—Oblique Light	
Mirror—Flashlight	
Mirror—ALS White Light	
RUVIS	

Table W5.2 Exercise 2a: Newspaper Fill-In Table

Method Used	Number of Prints Located
Flashlight—Oblique Light	
ALS White Light—Oblique Light	
Mirror—Flashlight	
Mirror—ALS White Light	
RUVIS	

Table W5.3 Exercise 2a: Cardboard Fill-In Table

Method Used	Number of Prints Located
Flashlight—Oblique Light	
ALS White Light—Oblique Light	
Mirror—Flashlight	
Mirror—ALS White Light	
RUVIS	

W5.2.2 Exercise 2b: Finding Dust Prints Outdoors

Dry residue prints outdoors are typically thought of as tire tracks at crime scenes, although footprints can be located on porches, stairs, and so on. The same procedures are used for outdoor prints as for those indoors. The technique for finding dry residue prints outdoors is demonstrated here.

W5.3 Lifting Wet and Dry Residue Dust Prints

W5.3.1 Dry Residue Prints

Considered fragile evidence, dry residue prints are essentially impression prints in dust. These form from the residue left behind as someone walks into a scene from the outdoors. These prints can be seen using oblique lighting or reflected in a mirror.

Lifting dry residue prints is an easy, though exacting, process. These prints are fragile and are easily destroyed, so extreme care is required. Importantly, shoeprints may be found not only on the floor but also on any object that is on the floor, which is why objects on the floor, although moveable, may offer important physical evidence in the form of shoeprints. There are typically two lifting procedures for dry "dust" residue prints. One is to use a commercial gel lifter, the same kind used for lifting dusted fingerprints from uneven surfaces. Mostly, black gel lifters are used as the black background provides sufficient contrast with the lighter-colored impression print. Gel lifters can be used to lift prints on carpets and other fabrics, although the lifter will attract fibers that can partially mask the lifted print. Sometimes, the interfering fibers can be removed by carefully "lifting" them with subsequent layers of fingerprint tape. The second method is to use an electrostatic lifter. This is a high-voltage, low-amperage device that creates an electrostatic charge on a black plastic sheet that has metallic foil on the upper surface. The electrostatic charge on the Mylar film attracts the dust, retaining the original pattern. It is important to understand that wet residue prints will not be lifted by an electrostatic lifter.

W5.3.1.1 Gel Lift (Gellifters) Gel lifters are rubber-backed, flexible, gelatin-based lifting material. Commercially, they are black, white, and transparent, which gives them flexibility in creating an appropriate contrasting background. They are typically used to lift powder-dusted fingerprints and dry residue dust prints. It is also possible to make gelatin lifters using 12% gelatin, 44% glycerol, and 1% lampblack and allowing it to dry on an appropriate background.

- General procedures for using gel lifters
  - Commercial lifter: remove the clear backing from the lifter.
  - Press the lifter onto the impressed evidence—eliminate air bubbles.
  - The manufacturer recommends the lifter remain in contact with the impression evidence (footprint) for approximately 10 min.
  - After lifting, photograph the print.
  - Preserve the print by replacing the clear cover. For long-term storage, do not replace the acetate clear cover.
  - High pressure on the lifter enhances its ability to lift prints. However, the pressure must be evenly distributed.
- Procedures for using a gel lifter to lift a dry residue dust print
  - Photograph the dry residue print before enhancement. When photographing the print, follow the following procedures.
    - Determine the angle that gives the best view of the dust print.
    - Maintain the camera at the proper angle (vertical or horizontal) to the print, photograph the dust print. Move the light source to the three recommended positions and take a photo at each position (Chapter 11).
    - Lift the print using the gel lifter.
    - Compare the photograph with the lifted print.
    - Show the photograph and the gel lift to an instructor for grading.

W5.3.1.2 Electrostatic Lift An electric current is passed through a specially prepared foil-backed, black Mylar film that creates an electrostatic charge to the surface. The electrostatic charges lift the dust to the black side of the Mylar film.

- Procedures for using an electrostatic lifter
  - Cut a piece of foil-backed black Mylar so that it is just larger than the dust print to be lifted. Ensure that there is no excess Mylar.
  - Place the Mylar, black side toward the impression print, over the print.
  - Position the electrostatic device so that one contact rests on the Mylar foil and the other as a ground. Do not place the device more than 1–2 in. away from the foil
  - Turn on the current to the lowest position and then gradually increase the current.
  - As the Mylar adheres (flatten) to the floor surface, gently brush it smooth using a foam paddle (foam paint brush).
  - After the Mylar adheres to the floor surface, turn off the current and gently lift it. Turn it over to observe the print.
  - Photograph the print.
  - Using a flashlight at an oblique angle will visualize the print easily.
    - Store and preserve the lifted print by carefully placing it into a high quality cardboard box.

- Alternatively, the print can be transferred to a gel lifter.
- Prepare two side-by-side dust prints. Lift one with the gel lifter and a second using the electrostatic lifter. Place the two lifts side by side and compare them. Which is the better lift?
- Photograph the lifts side by side.
- Show the photographs and the lifts to the instructor for grading.

W5.3.2 Wet Residue Prints

Wet prints are impression prints made from wet and/or muddy feet. These prints cannot be lifted using an electrostatic lifer but can be lifted using a gel lifter. Sometimes, enhancing wet residue prints is necessary. This can be accomplished in several ways.

W5.3.2.1 Enhancing Wet Residue Prints

W5.3.2.1.1 Magnetic Dusting Powder

- Procedures
  - Test a small portion of the residue print with the dusting powder to determine whether the print will attract dusting powder.
  - If the print does not accept dusting powder, stop the process.
  - If the dusting powder enhances the print, continue dusting until the print is visible.
  - Transfer the print to a white gel lifter.

W5.3.2.1.2 Cyanoacrylate Fuming Superglue fuming of wet residue impression prints is not always successful. Experience has shown that some wet residue impression prints have sufficient water vapor occluded in the print to sustain superglue fuming. Whether to superglue fume or lift the print is a decision made at the crime scene. A procedure that has been successful in the author's hands follows:

- Tools
  - Box to cover impression.
    - Two heat sources.
    - Superglue.
    - Water (or steam iron).
- Procedures
  - Cover the impression with a cardboard or plastic box (one end capable of being opened enough for a steam iron to deliver the steam to the impression). Alternately, use a hot plate and a small tray of heated water placed inside the box. Allow the steam to build inside the box for several seconds. Do not allow the background surface to become wet. (The wet surface will initiate cyanoacrylate polymerization and cause interference with the fumed impression.)
    - Stop humidifying when the relative humidity reaches 80%. If the relative humidity is high (80%), rehydration is not necessary.
    - Do not remove the water source.
  - Place an aluminum tray containing superglue on the heat source.
  - Allow the fuming to continue for several minutes—10–30 min.
  - Turn off the heat source.
  - Check the glued print with the RUVIS or by using oblique lighting with a flashlight or an ALS.

- The fumed impression can be enhanced by dusting with black or fluorescent magnetic powder or by staining with a fluorescent dye, such as basic yellow 40.
- If staining, check for background fluorescence by washing a part of the substrate with basic yellow 40 followed by a water wash.
- Check with the ALS for background fluorescence.
- If the background fluoresces, do not process the glued print with basic yellow 40.
- Dust the print with powder.

W5.3.2.1.3 Chemical Enhancement

- Procedures using 8-hydorxyquinoline
  - Have photographic equipment set up to take fluorescent photographs.
  - Prepare fresh solution of 8-hydorxyquinoline or purchase commercially and check the reagent with a swab impregnated with soil. If the soil contains iron, the swab will fluoresce under UV light. If fluorescence is not present, do not test the print for iron.
  - Test a nonresidue portion of the substrate (floor, etc.). If the swab fluoresces, do not use 8-hydorxyquinoline to enhance the impression. If the swab does not fluoresce, enhance the impression with 8-hydorxyquinoline.
  - If iron is present and the floor does not give fluorescence, gently spray the surface with the reagent. Monitor the progress using a UV light source.
  - Photograph the result immediately.
- Procedures using ammonium thiocyanate
  - Prepare a fresh solution of ammonium thiocyanate or purchase commercially.
  - Check impression and the floor as described for 8-hydorxyquinoline above. A rust-like color is an indication that iron is present. If the color does not appear, do not test the print for iron and try another approach.
  - If iron is present, gently spray the impression. The color should appear almost immediately.
  - After spraying, photograph the result.
  - Lift the sprayed impression onto a white gel lifter.
- Procedures using ammonium pyrrolidine carbamate
  - Proceed as for ammonium thiocyanate above. If iron is present, the color of the impression will be black or dark gray.

W5.3.2.1.4 Wet Footprints on Concrete Wet footprints on concrete are 2D prints. However, there are references that suggest these can be cast using dental stone. Alternatively, these can be dusted using a magnetic dusting powder and photographed.

- Procedures
  - Use black magnetic dusting powder. Traditional dusting procedure deposits dust in the crevices of the concrete, which reduces the contrast between the background and the dusted print.
  - Time is of the essence because the wet print will be absorbed by the concrete and quickly dry due to evaporation.
  - Photograph the impression before and after dusting. It is critical that the photograph be taken quickly.
  - Dust the print using a highly contrasting magnetic powder. For most types of cement, this will be black magnetic powder.
  - Remove excess powder using the magnet.

W5.3.2.2 Exercise 3: Enhancing Wet Residue Prints The aim of this exercise is to create wet impression prints on linoleum, and then enhance the prints using dusting powder, followed by superglue fuming, and by dye staining.

- Procedures
  - Moisten the soles of your shoes with a damp mop.
  - Step onto a floor coated with dirt and then walk a few steps into an adjoining room.
  - Allow the prints to dry. On separate prints:
    - Dust with black magnetic dusting powder.
    - Dust with normal black dusting powder.
    - Dust with magnetic fluorescent powder.
  - Photograph the dusted prints with and without an ALS (for the fluorescence magnetic dusting powder).
  - Show the dusted prints and photographs to an instructor for grading.
  - Lift the black powder dusted prints using a white gel lifter.
  - Lift the magnetic fluorescent powder prints using a black gel lifter.
  - Set up a superglue scene fuming chamber as described above.
  - Superglue fume a set of wet residue prints.
    - Check the relative humidity. If it is below 80%, use a steam iron or heat source and water in a tray to rehydrate the print for a few seconds. When the relative humidity inside the box reaches 80%, turn off the heat source and allow the print to absorb the water vapor for a few minutes. Check the humidity.
    - Ensure that the background is dry.
  - Place 20 drops of super glue onto another heat source and super glue the impression for 20–30 min. Keep water vapor inside the box to maintain the relative humidity at or near 80%.
  - After fuming, turn off the heat to the water and the superglue to keep the fumes from dissipating into the room.
  - Using oblique lighting, inspect the impression to see if supergluing was successful (look for an off-white residue on the impression).
  - Dust one half of the superglued impression using black magnetic powder.
  - Lift the powder using a white gel lifter, photograph and show to an instructor for grading.
  - On the other half of the superglued impression:
    - Test the floor with the stain (basic yellow 40 purchased commercially) for background fluorescence.
    - If none is present, spray the impression with basic yellow 40 fluorescent dye.
    - Allow to sit for approximately 2 min and rinse with water.
    - Blow the excess water off the impression using a heat gun.
    - Dry the print and observe fluorescence using the UV light setting on the ALS.
    - Photograph and show to an instructor for grading.

W5.4 Tire Impression Evidence

W5.4.1 Recording Known Tire Impressions

It is recommended that the reader review Chapter 12 at this point. Tire impressions can have important investigative information. They can identify the number of vehicles at the scene, the direction of travel, the approximate time that the vehicles were there, as well as other information. For these reasons and others, recording tire impressions of suspect vehicles is critically important. There are several ways of recording tire impressions. First, it is important that the tire be on the suspect vehicle. Second, the impression must be made so that it is not distorted in any way. There are three common ways to record tire impressions: the petroleum jelly (Vaseline®) and magna black powder brush method on art paper, the inking method on art board, and inking followed by a transparent acetate strip method. As an exercise, the petroleum jelly method illustrates how to record known tire impressions. The other methods are similar and are not considered for this discussion.

W5.4.1.1 The Petroleum Jelly (Vaseline®) Method

- Procedures
  - Locate the wear bars (tread wear indicators) that run laterally across the tread. Mark their location on the sidewall of the tire.
  - Lightly grease the tread with petroleum jelly. Take care not to put too much on the tire so that accidental marks and sipes are not obliterated by the petroleum jelly.
  - Place 1/4 in. art board on the ground in front of the tire and tape the boards together.
  - Number the art board (1–4) in order, beginning where the tire first runs over the art board.
  - Record critical tire information about the tire on the art board.
  - Record the date and initials of investigators doing the experiment.
  - Stop pushing the car just before the ungreased part of the tire is about to run over the art board. Record the location of wear bars on the art board as the tire records that part of the impression onto the art board.
  - Lightly grease the ungreased part of the tire and continue pushing the car until this area is recoded on the art board.
  - Carefully remove the art board. Do not rub the petroleum jelly areas together. Place a piece of acetate over the art board to protect it.
  - Using black magnetic powder, dust the greased tire impression.
  - Photograph the dusted impression.
  - Show the dusted impression and the photographs to an instructor for grading.

W5.4.1.2 Exercise 4: Recording Tire Impressions The aim of this exercise is to learn how to record tire's impression from a suspect vehicle. Follow the procedure in 12.3.4.1.1 to record and dust the impression from a vehicle. Photographs the dusted impression and show to an instructor.

W5.4.2 Determining Wheelbase from Tire Impressions

In addition to the important aspect of archiving tire track impressions, seven measurements can be made at the scene of impressions at the scene. Most important are those that can be used to identify a suspect vehicle involved in the crime. These are

- Wheelbase
- Front-and-rear track width
- Turning diameter
- Tread design width (arc width)

- Tread depth (skid depth)
- Tire circumference

For this workshop, only the wheelbase and front-and-rear track widths will be determined from tire track impressions. See Chapter 12 Sections 12.2.2.3.2 to 12.2.2.3.6 for discussion on the other four characteristics of tire track impressions.

W5.4.2.1 Wheelbase The wheelbase is the distance between the front-and-rear axles of the vehicle. To determine the wheelbase, a break in the flow, such as when a car reverses direction, of the tire impressions is necessary to ascertain the leading edges of the front-and-rear tires. Measurements should be taken from both sides.

- Procedures
  - If the tire impression is pointing straight ahead—no turn, measure from the leading edge of the front tire to the leading edge of the rear tire, as shown in the Figure W5.1.
  - If the wheels are turned, measure from the outside and inside. The side opposite the direction of the turn will be larger. Take the average of the two measurements.

W5.4.2.2 Front-and-Rear Track Widths Use the diagram in Figure W5.2 as a guide to measuring front-and-rear track widths.

- Procedures
  - For the front track width of vehicle, measure (inches) from the midpoint of the left front tire impression to the midpoint of the right front tire impression.
  - For the rear track width of vehicle, measure (inches) from the midpoint of the left rear tire impression to the midpoint of the right-rear tire impression.
  - If the leading edges of the tire impressions are curved, use the following procedures to approximate the distance.
  - Locate the leading edge of the front-and-rear tires and draw a line just touching the midpoint of the curved edge and parallel to what would be the straight edge of the tire impression if it was not curved.

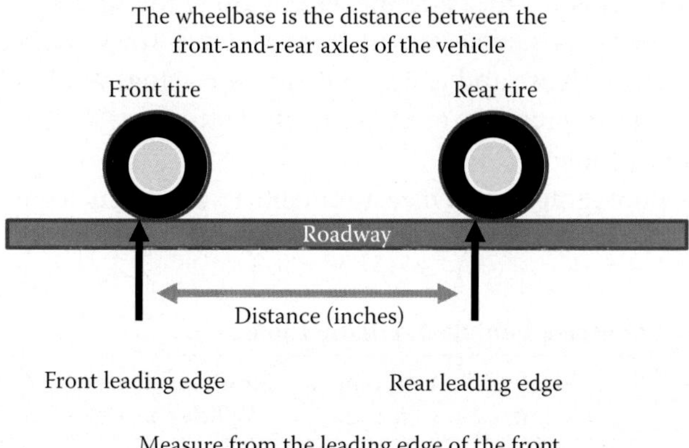

Figure W5.1 Measuring wheelbase from impressions at the scene.

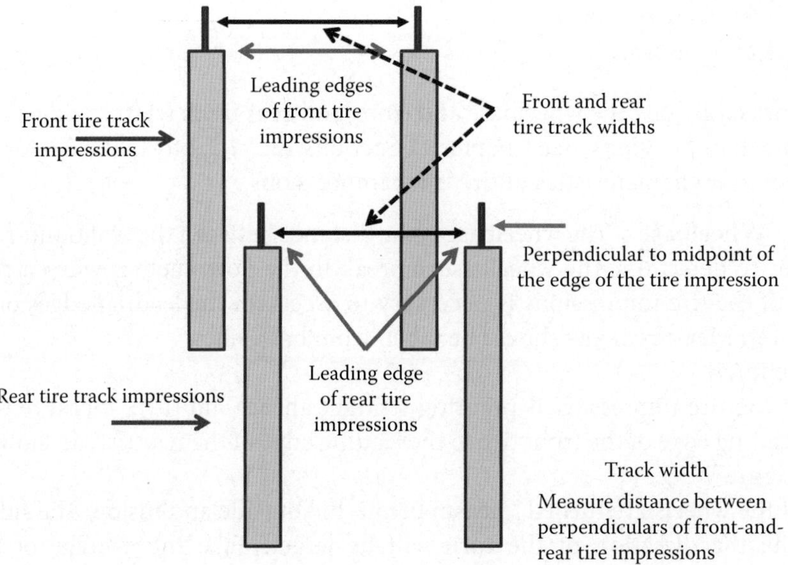

Figure W5.2 Measuring the track width from impressions at the scene.

- Project a perpendicular from the midpoint of the parallel line for each tire impression.
- Measure the distance between the perpendicular lines for both the front-and-rear tire impressions.

W5.4.2.3 Exercise 4: Measuring Wheelbase and Track Width The aim of this exercise is to measure wheelbase and track width. Here, drive a car over a dusty area and then into a parking lot. Stop the vehicle and then back up while turning the wheel. This will create front and rear tire track impressions on the pavement.

- Procedures
  - Photograph the impressions as though archiving them as part of a crime scene.
  - From the impressions, measure the wheelbase of the vehicle.
  - From the impressions, measure the front and rear track widths.
  - Measure the wheelbase and track widths of the actual vehicle.
  - Compare your impression measurements with those taken from the actual vehicle. Fill in Table W5.4
  - Show your photographs and measurements to an instructor for grading.

Table W5.4 Exercise Vehicle 4: Fill-In Table

Vehicle	Measurement from Impressions (Inches)	Measurement from Vehicle (Inches)	% Difference (Inches)
Wheelbase			
Front track width			
Rear track width			

W5.5 Questions

- In 1000 words or less, describe how electrostatic lifters and gel lifters work and why electrostatic lifters are not the superior lifting method for dry residue impressions.
- Explain why a dry residue print and the floor on which it rests must be tested with 8-hydorxyquinoline before spraying the print for the presence of iron.
- Explain why it is necessary to obtain a petroleum jelly imprint of a suspect's vehicle.

The Biological Crime Scene

IV

The Biological Crime Scene
It's Not Just about DNA

13

When asked what his gut feeling was concerning the guilt of a particular suspect, an NYPD detective said, "I don't have gut feelings anymore. I wait for DNA."*

13.1 Introduction

Consider the totality of the evidence at a crime scene. A mental checklist might include footwear impression evidence, bloodstains, bullets, and so on. All are important, but scene investigators often fail to find one or more, simply assuming that it was not present. This is not unusual and it is expected. For example, ballistics evidence is not expected and should not be present if the crime did not involve a shooting. Failing to locate biological evidence, however, has a different "feel" because of the lofty importance DNA evidence enjoys. Such importance is given to DNA because it can identify someone to the exclusion of everyone in the world. This is why crime scene investigators and scientists often focus on finding biological evidence, so much so that their rallying cry might well be, "Find DNA and you've got your perp." This works because DNA profiles from biological evidence collected at the crime scene are uploaded into an FBI-maintained database—CODIS (the Combined DNA Indexing System). Once in the system, scene profiles can be matched to other crime scenes, convicted felons, arrestees, or to identify the missing persons. It should not come as a surprise that DNA is so coveted from investigational and legal perspectives. There are scenes, however, where investigators fail to find biological evidence. The fact is they missed it.

It is probably safe to say that every crime scene involving people probably had biological evidence present, which means that scene investigators have been missing biological evidence for a long time. This statement will cause investigators to bristle, but before dismissing the idea as academic folly, consider it from this perspective: Anyone entering a room brings along something of themselves. When they leave the room, they leave something behind. Certainly, whatever is left behind might be difficult or even impossible to find.

Consider this example. An investigator enters a scene and finds a young male body lying on the floor. The deceased has no head hair and a large contusion on the side of his head. There is no obvious bloodstain spatter such as from the impact blow. In fact, there is no apparent active bleeding, only a trickle of blood from the deceased's head, no blood droplets on the floor, and no sign of a struggle. Outside the back door and lying on the pavement is an old, broken brick with rough edges. The location is not particularly unusual and would not raise suspicion that it is the murder weapon. In fact, picking up the brick and casually examining it reveals nothing except, perhaps, some dirt: certainly no hair and no obvious blood or skin. But this is, indeed, the murder weapon, and biological evidence is present. In fact, by definition, biological evidence must be present. Many scene

* Conversation with the author.

investigators will fail to collect the brick, and others might, just to be safe. Both may well believe the brick holds no evidentiary value. The forensic scientist in the laboratory could have a different opinion because it is possible to find shed skin cells lodged in the crevices of the brick. Certainly, this is not an on-scene procedure, but the message is that biological evidence is always present. Unfortunately, we do not yet have the technology to detect all of its traces at the scene.

13.1.1 Categories of Biological Evidence

The most commonly occurring examples of biological evidence usually come from humans and animals because people are usually the victim or the perpetrator of a crime, and, since people have pets, their biological material is also be present. Table 13.1 lists examples of forensically important biological evidence, some of which is commonly or not so commonly encountered.

In the "Common Examples" list, some examples of forensically important biological evidence, such as blood, occur more often than others. Others, such as fingerprint residue or sloughed-off cells, also occur commonly, but investigators usually do not consider them common examples of biological evidence; the former is not thought of as biological evidence and the latter is not usually visible. The reason is that the value of fingerprint residue is thought of in terms of its friction ridge detail. Fingerprints contain biological substances, some of which has current or potential forensic value: fatty acids, proteins, and cells (DNA). Thinking of fingerprint residue differently may pave the way for it to become more valuable as an example of biological evidence.

What about sloughed-off cells? No one questions the premise that cellular material is an example of biological evidence because it is a source of DNA. So, when a perpetrator holds a weapon or picks up an object with an uncovered hand, cellular material transfers from the hand to the object. In fact, increasingly modern forensic DNA analysis involves what has become known as "touch evidence." This is why scene investigators

Table 13.1 Forensically Important Biological Substances

Common Examples
Blood–Human and Animal
Semen
Saliva
Urine
Feces
Vomit
Hair
Fingerprint residue
Sloughed off cells
The Not So Common Examples
Bacteria
Plant material
Pollen
Viruses

and scientists must consider all evidence from a biological perspective, even if it is invisible to the naked eye. They must think of evidence differently and consider that biological evidence lurks on unlikely sources. Even the most commonly occurring biological evidence must be considered from the perspective of its location at the scene, its pattern, and its donor.

13.1.2 Searching for Biological Evidence

Arguably the team's most important responsibility, given the critical importance of DNA, is to find and collect anything biological. This is a deceptively easy task; however, because it is everywhere, the most probative of it may represent only a small fraction of the totality of the biological spectrum present. In a very real sense, biological evidence is a critical element of the macroscene—bloodstain patterns, droplets, and so on—and/or the microscene—pollen, bacteria, and so on. With the possible exception of biocrimes (see Chapter 15), the most probative biological evidence comes from people: those who live where the crime occurred, visitors where the crime took place but who had nothing to do with the event, public officials who investigate the scene, and the criminal who commits the crime. The challenge is to find that which is important within the milieu of all that is present. This is a huge challenge, and successful searching requires all of one's senses, thinking creatively, and a hefty dose of common sense. Luck helps, too.

The successful search for biological evidence, any evidence for that matter, requires special attributes and diligence. Acquiring the appropriate expertise is not a matter of attending a workshop that teaches one how to use an ALS to locate semen or saliva, how to apply presumptive chemical tests at a scene to classify an unknown stain, or to use immunochromatographic cards to confirm the results of presumptive tests. As Figure 13.1 illustrates, the mission uses "The cognitive tools." Cognitive activities are necessary to make the scene investigation successful; these are listed under the title, "The cognitive tools."

The first line under the title, "Your brain" and those that follow, except for "The evidence analysis cascade," indicate cognitive activities that are self-obvious. Certainly, without the appropriate scientific education, experience, brains that think creatively and skeptically, understanding the underlying science behind the technology, and being aware of and knowing how and when to apply it, the scene investigation is poised for disaster. The arrows

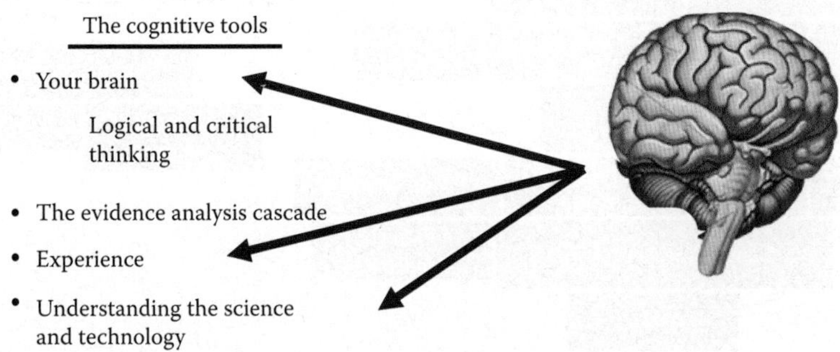

Figure 13.1 The scene investigator's cognitive tools.

pointing from the brain cartoon (in Figure 13.1) to each of these cognitive activities emphasize the need for our best asset, our brain, in ensuring the scene investigation is successful.

The evidence analysis cascade (EAC) in Figure 13.2 refers to the analytical sequence used in the crime laboratory to analyze the biological evidence. It is, however, a sequence with which crime scene scientists/investigators should be familiar. The EAC is important because it highlights commonality between what is done in the laboratory and what is done in the field. From a biological perspective, this is critical because using an incorrect approach to locate, collect, and preserve biological evidence can compromise the laboratory's ability to isolate and obtain, say, DNA. The EAC shows the common types of physical evidence (yellow boxes in Figure 13.2) found at the scene that is taken to the laboratory.

The left side of the cascade refers to biological evidence. Interestingly, several steps of the EAC have common laboratory and scene equivalents (red boxes in Figure 13.2). The crime laboratory-only categories are in the blue boxes. Those common categories include but are not limited to the following:

- Observation
- Presumptive testing
- Confirmatory testing
- Pattern analysis

Whether done at the scene or in the laboratory, the first stage of any analysis is observation, usually a gross visual inspection, highlighting the evidence using various illumination techniques. The laboratory scientist usually follows the gross inspection using a more rigorous examination, which is not typically something the scene scientist/investigator will do because it is either outside his/her expertise or is not appropriate. However, with the coming of hand-held digital microscopes and magnifying lenses, a form of microscopy might be useful at the scene.

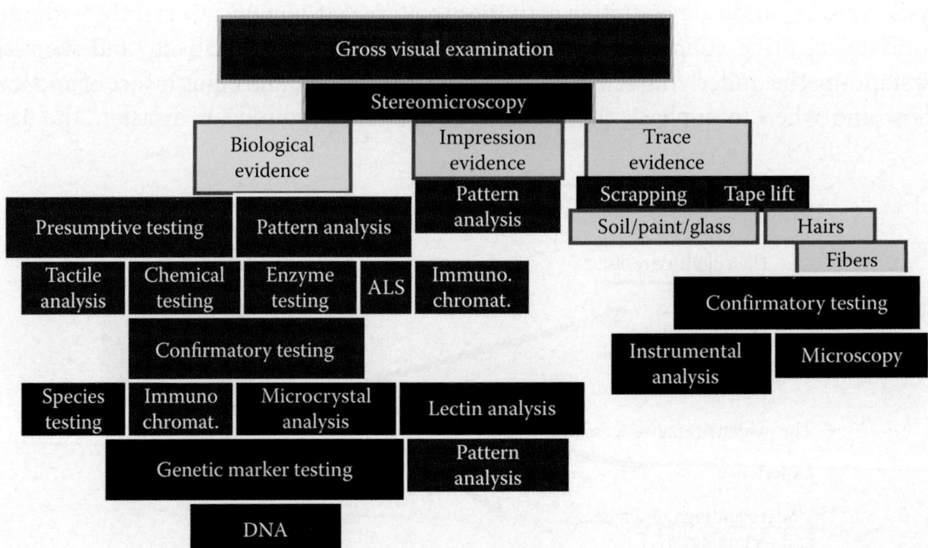

Figure 13.2 The evidence analysis cascade.

The next topic is presumptive testing. If blood, semen, or saliva is suspected, a series of presumptive tests can help the scene scientist believe an unknown stain has a biological origin. In-laboratory presumptive tests have typically included touching, chemical testing, enzyme testing, ALS examination, and/or immunological testing. The on-scene version of these tests is essentially the same. The next step in the analytical scheme is confirmatory testing, which would mean using immunochromatographic cards to confirm human blood [1], semen [2], or saliva [3] at the scene. Other confirmatory tests for blood, such as ouchterlony, cross-over electrophoresis, and so on, are laboratory-based and are not applicable for on-scene testing. Laboratory testing of appropriate biological samples typically concludes with DNA analysis.

Laboratory and on-scene testing may require a form of pattern analysis and matching. The on-scene and laboratory examinations are similar, but the former differs substantially from the laboratory-based pattern interpretations. For example, bloodstain patterns are best interpreted at the scene because of the importance of viewing them in the context of what took place. This is, in fact, critical.

The laboratory may receive clothing or weapons with bloodstain patterns that must be interpreted, but these interpretations take place outside of the context of the scene environment, though that context cannot be ignored. The message: Crime scene scientists/investigators use many of the same techniques as those used by criminalists in the laboratory. This is why it is important that scene scientists/investigators understand the science behind the testing and the logic of the EAC as an analytical progression.

13.2 Locating Biological Evidence at the Scene

As listed in Table 13.2, our eye is a critical tool for finding biological evidence. Our natural instinct is to think of blood because it is usually visible. But other kinds of biological evidence become visible when technology rescues the eye. "Touch" is an older technique that was used before ALSs were available. This was a common technique of gently running a gloved or ungloved (an earlier time) hand over the evidence, such as a bed sheet, to find, say, dried semen by its "crusty" feel. The "feel" test was easier in the days when latex or nylon gloves were not worn. The same "feel" still exists, but is muted because of the gloves.

High-intensity light sources have replaced touch for locating latent biological stains. The historical sequence started with UV lights followed by lasers and then ALSs; the latter make locating biological evidence easier and faster, especially for semen, saliva, urine, and blood. For years, before light sources were commonplace, scene scientists/investigators

Table 13.2 Locating Biological Evidence at the Scene

The eye
Touch
High intensity and alternate light sources
Chemical tests
Enzymatic tests
Immunological tests
Your brain

used chemical tests to determine whether reddish stains might be blood. In the 1950s, they used enzymatic tests (acid phosphatase—AP—test) to determine whether a crusty stain might be semen. More recently, scene-forward immunological tests have entered the forensic arena to confirm whether a stain is human blood, semen, or even saliva. Regardless of the technology, the most important tool the scene scientist possesses is the brain. The reason is our brain marries our cognitive activity with technology. It is the best tool for finding biological evidence.

Early scene investigators had few tools and limited technology with which to find biological evidence, which is why they relied on their brains, their experience, and knowledge of crime types. The question then, how can one's knowledge of crime types help? Consider homicides, where one expects to find blood. But finding semen at a homicide scene depends on whether the crime was sexually motivated. Finding semen at sexual assault scenes, however, is an expectation as are bite marks and blood. Until DNA evidence became so important, solving burglaries was largely limited to finding the burglar's fingerprints or other physical evidence, such as footwear impressions, coupled with good detective work. If biological evidence was present, such as blood left by the burglar who cut himself, the perpetrator could not be identified because immunological and biochemical genetic testing—ABO blood group and enzyme polymorphism testing—was not powerful enough. DNA analysis changed that, making it a critical focus of property crime investigations [4]. The discussion that follows focuses on the most common examples of biological evidence, how to find them at the scene, and how to preserve them as evidence for subsequent analysis.

13.3 Commonly Occurring Biological Evidence

13.3.1 Blood

Unquestionably, blood is the most commonly occurring biological evidence. It is found in the most important crime types: homicides, sexual assaults, burglary, assault, and so on. The discussion on blood in Chapter 10 contains Figure 10.17, Forensically speaking: what is blood. The discussion considered blood and the forensically critical information available from it. It would be appropriate to review that discussion before continuing.

The EAC discussed earlier shows the techniques that have been used successfully to find and/or confirm the presence of biological evidence: tactile analysis, chemical testing, enzyme testing, an ALS, and immunochromatographic cards. Historically, tactile analysis and enzyme testing have not played an important role in finding blood at the scene. In modern investigations for blood, the eye, chemical testing, the ALS [5], and immunochromatographic cards form the investigator's arsenal for locating and/or presumptively testing and/or confirming the presence of human blood at the crime scene.

13.3.1.1 On-Scene Testing for Blood

The term "presumptive testing" refers to a test result that helps an investigator decide whether a particular stain *might* have investigative value. A presumptive test, then, is a "maybe" test, one where a positive result means that the stain *might* be blood. These are not confirmation tests. Other tests are necessary to confirm whether biological material is present. As for blood, presumptive tests are available for any forensically important biological materials. The following section considers the presumptive tests.

13.3.1.2 The Unaided Human Eye

The oldest presumptive test is the human eye. The lay person or student may think that since blood is red, it is easy to see. Or is it? Actually, dried blood can be red, brown, yellow, green, or black, and understanding the conditions under which these transitions occur is important. The eye, too, is not a stand-alone instrument because it is connected to the brain. So, when we look at something red at the crime scene, our brain is interpreting the color and then determining (presumptively) that the red substance is blood. Thus we are actually evaluating it in the context of our experience, and that is what is being tested. Like eyewitness testimony, however, our experiences are not infallible or applicable to all situations, and certainly it is not the most reliable indicator of the ground truth. For an experienced scene investigator, observing something red having the appearance of blood spatter means that it "looks like" blood. It does not mean that it is blood. The investigator's experience is important, but his/her certainty that something is what one thinks it is does not make it so. The human eye, then, is not a confirmatory test, but coupling those observational skills with experience certainly narrows the range of possibilities. Examining evidence with the unaided eye is a good first approach, but technology enhances the likelihood of finding blood.

13.3.1.3 The Aided Human Eye: ALSs

Light enhances an investigator's ability to "see" evidence where it normally would be invisible. Oblique lighting is an example of how light helps find impression evidence (see Chapter 11). Although the flashlight remains an important on-scene tool, recent developments in light technology—lasers and ALSs—have produced portable, high-intensity instruments with tunable wavelengths that can highlight some categories of evidence better. The most useful of these is the ALS, which has proven to be a versatile resource for scene investigators because it enhances the ability of the human eye to "see." The molecules that comprise the evidence absorb specific wavelengths of light. When this happens, the evidence appears dark. If the molecules lose energy, they might be seen as light—fluorescence. This happens because an ALS has a tunable wavelengths that offer the scene scientist choices depending on the scene situation. Tunable wavelengths are typically not available on a normal flashlight.

With blood, the ALS has minimal use because no wavelength in the visible spectrum causes blood to fluoresce. However, there are "tricks" the scene scientist can use, depending on the surface on which the blood lies. For example, the 415 nm setting on the ALS makes blood appear darker on light backgrounds [5], thus enhancing the apparent visibility. This occurs because dried blood absorbs light at 415 nm, which is why it appears darker instead of reddish or reddish brown. The increase in contrast between the blood and the surface forces the eye into a more favorable region of the electromagnetic spectrum. On a dark surface, the 415 nm setting is not appropriate because making the blood appear darker is counterproductive. Figure 13.3 illustrates the point.

Blood on dark surfaces is difficult to see and is easily missed, which forces scene scientists/investigators to choose the alternate methods. The first and easiest is to subtract out the background by using different wavelengths (colors) on the ALS. If successful, the blood

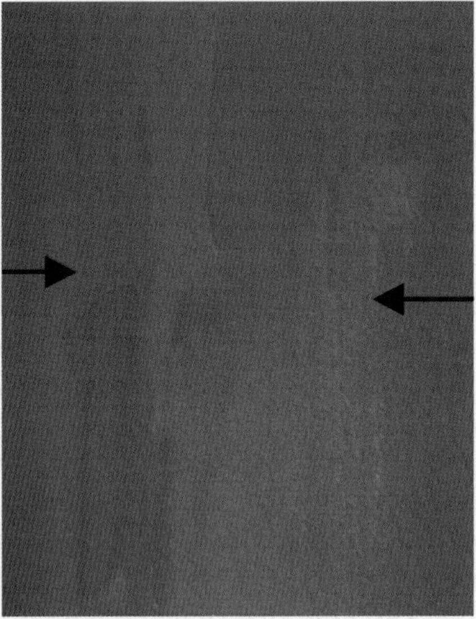

Figure 13.3 Using the alternate light source to identify the blood.

will usually appear dark against a lighter background. An example could be dried blood on a red wall. Here, the contrast between the blood and the wall is minimal. The CSS setting on the CrimeScope™ 400 (blue-green) on the ALS can lighten the background (light blue) without affecting the darker color of the blood. The result will be dark blood spots on a light blue background.

Reddish or dark foodstuff stains can be confused with blood, so differentiating these from blood prevents the crime laboratory from having to analyze the superfluous and irrelevant evidence. Such differentiation is easily accomplished using the ALS: Blood absorbs light at 415 nm and will not fluoresce under long-wave UV light (300–400 nm settings on an ALS). Tomato-based foods may or may not absorb light at 415 nm (usually less so than blood) but usually give a blue-white fluorescence and a yellow or yellow-orange fluorescence under long-wave UV light. Figure 13.3 is an example of blood and ketchup smeared on an orange wall, allowed to dry, then photographed under long-wave UV light from an ALS, and observed using clear goggles. The stain on the left—left arrow—is a bloodstain and the stain on the right—right arrow—is a ketchup stain. The blood absorbs the light, which is why it appears darker. The ketchup has a blue-white fluorescence.

On dark, shiny surfaces, such as shiny magazine covers, the ALS helps little in subtracting out the background. In these instances, however, oblique lighting using the white-light setting on the ALS or a simple flashlight is useful. Table 13.3 gives examples of ALS wavelengths and how they can be used to highlight/locate biological evidence at the scene. The right column lists what goggles to use.

13.3.1.4 IR Cameras: Combining Searching and Photography

Fortunately for scene investigators blood absorbs light in the IR region, which makes it appear dark, much like it absorbs light at 415 nm. In certain situations, this can be useful to help visualize blood on dark backgrounds or, sometimes, on dark, shiny surfaces as well.

Table 13.3 Wavelengths of Alternate Light Source to Locate Biological Material

Wavelength (nm)	Principal Use	Viewing Goggles
White light	• General scene scanning • Fingerprints on shiny surfaces • Blood on dark shiny surfaces	Clear
Long wavelength UV: 300–400	• Hair, fiber, fluorescent material—powders • Body fluids/bruises/bite marks/tomato-based foodstuff • Other food stains	Clear or yellow
415	• Darkens bloodstains • Can darken tomato-based food stains	Clear
450	• Body fluids (semen/saliva/urine)—fluorescent materials • Powders/teeth/bones	Orange
465	• Fluorescent materials/powders • Body fluids	Orange
485	As for 465 nm	Orange
525/570	• 1,8-Diazafluoren-9-one • Superglue prints	Red

In the past, using IR light was a delayed process because developing IR film was necessary. This made on-scene useless because it took time before the investigators knew whether the IR light had "found" blood. Usually, IR photography was used as a vehicle to highlight blood patterns on dark surfaces where it was known that blood was present and was not an on-scene tool for finding difficult-to-see bloodstains. Digital cameras changed that the digital IR camera and the ALS have become valuable on-scene partners as tools to help locate dried blood on difficult surfaces. The reason is that digital cameras have characteristics different from those of film cameras simply because the LCD viewers in the former allow scene scientists/investigators to "see" the blood *in situ* without having to take a photograph. Now, there is an instantaneous peek at what is present on a dark surface that does not absorb light in the IR region. In essence, the camera expands an investigator's sight range into the real-time near IR, making the digital IR camera an indispensible tool for on-scene investigations when the ALS is of little or no help. Importantly, too, the LCD IR image can be photographed and included as an archiving tool.

The IR-highlighted stain can be tested with presumptive chemicals or tested using immunochromatographic cards to ascertain whether it is blood or human blood, respectively. Figure 13.4 shows a photograph of the LCD viewer of an IR camera (Fuji 9000S converted IR mode) of bloodstains on a red carpet. The stains on the carpet were invisible to the naked eye and to the settings on the ALS—the ALS could not effectively subtract out the background to visualize the blood. The stains, however, were visible in the LCD on the IR camera.

Unfortunately, all dark or reddish surfaces are not amenable to the digital IR technique. In order for the IR principle to work, the surface must not absorb light in the IR region. If it does, both the blood and the surface will appear dark. It is simple enough to find whether the surface absorbs light. Simply turn on the digital IR camera and look through the LCD viewer. If the surface appears dark, it absorbs light in the IR region. If it appears whitish, it does not, and blood should be visible if it is present.

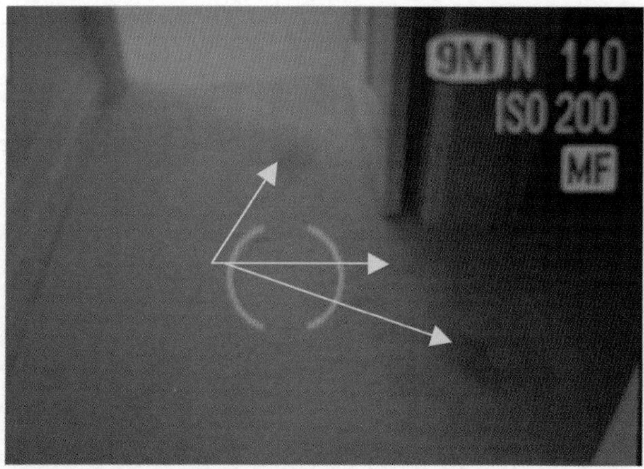

Figure 13.4 Photograph of liquid crystal display of infrared digital camera.

13.3.1.5 Chemical Presumptive Testing

Chemical tests that react with blood were developed in the mid-nineteenth century. Their importance was to give investigators a method of determining whether an unknown stain might be blood by narrowing the range of possible substances. A positive chemical test means that there is approximately a 95% chance that the unknown stain is or contains blood. This is important because many reddish or dark stains at a crime scene are not blood. A simple example is a stain made from the spray of a shaken Coca Cola™ can on a dark wall. Each of these chemical tests works on the same principle.

The chemicals used to identify a stain as blood can be divided into two categories: those that produce colors and those that produce luminescence [6,7]. The former include a range of dyes that turn color in the presence of hemoglobin, a protein component of blood, and peroxide—hydrogen peroxide is a most commonly used peroxide. Vast arrays of these reagents are available commercially. The most common include: phenolphthalein (KM reagents), leucocrystal violet (LCV), TMB, orthotoluidine, orthotolidine, and leucomalachite green, among others.

The second category includes chemicals react with hemoglobin and peroxide but instead of turning color, they luminesce, known as chemiluminescence. This group includes luminol, the chemiluminescence of which has been extensively investigated [8–10] and has been used primarily at crime scenes where clean-up is suspected. Luminol and fluorescein have enjoyed a long forensic history, but BlueStar™ is a recently available formulation for which claims of greater and longer luminescent intensity exist. Although it might seem as though BlueStar™ is a new reagent, it is apparently an optimized and reformulated version of luminol. Claims are that BlueStar™ is superior to luminol for crime scene work for several reasons. One important reason is that its luminescence can be seen in dim instead of dark areas [11]. BlueStar™ comes in two formulations, one for on-scene use and the other for training. Since the reagent is expensive, the training formulation is a less expensive version but its manufacturers warn it will destroy the DNA. The more expensive, non-training version of BlueStar™ designed for on-scene use supposedly does not destroy the DNA. Certainly the luminescence produced can be dramatic as shown in Figures 13.5 and 13.6. The sink in the photograph had been washed with water as had the red wall. Blood was not visible before students began working on the scene.

Figure 13.5 Bluestar enhancement of washed bloodstains. (Photograph by Robert C. Shaler.)

Figure 13.6 Bluestar developed bloodstains on red wall. (Photograph by Robert C. Shaler.)

These chemicals work on the same principle. Called catalytic tests, they have been around for over 100 years. The general reaction is shown in Figure 13.7.

The heme moiety of hemoglobin (the red protein in blood) reacts with and cleaves hydrogen peroxide producing an oxygen free radical—step 1 in Figure 13.7. The free radical reacts with a dye (the reduced version) in step 2, oxidizing it to produce a color. The color formed depends on the chemical properties of the dye, with colors ranging from pink to intense green. Figure 13.8 illustrates the process for one of the more common blood presumptive catalytic reagents—the KM reagent [12]. The step-wise process described is for absorbing blood onto a moistened sterile cotton swab. The subsequent steps to administer the test are common for all presumptive tests except for luminol and BlueStar™, which produce a luminescent product instead of a colored one.

For the luminescence-producing reagents, the room must be darkened and the blood fixed (so that it does not dissolve) by spraying with a 2% solution of 5-sulfosalicylic acid. During a long photographic exposure, the area is sprayed with luminol or BlueStar™. The luminescence will fade, so it is critical to document the reaction photographically (Figures 13.5 and 13.6), and not merely to record in field notes that a positive luminol (BlueStar™) reaction was obtained. There are two important photographic requirements: (i) the scene details (e.g., furniture, chairs, carpets, etc.) should be visible in the

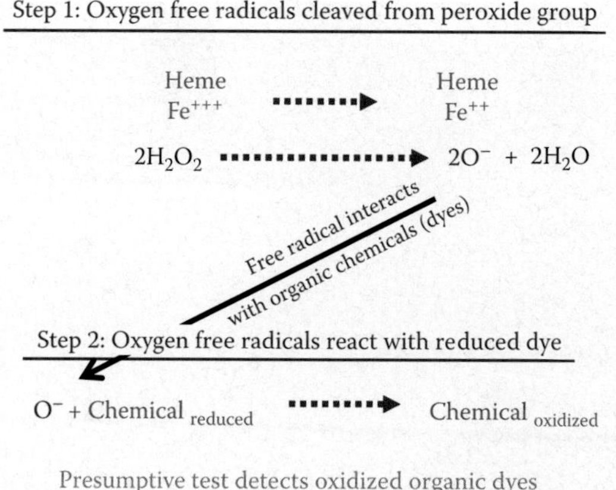

Figure 13.7 General reaction of blood presumptive chemical tests.

photograph and (ii) the luminescence should overlay the scene so that the scene details are visible. Examples are shown in Figures 13.5 and 13.6 in the context of the room (red wall) and on the sink in the bathroom. The general steps for this are listed below:

- Darken the room (if using luminol or dim the room for BlueStar™) or area as much as possible. Even with BlueStar™, the darker the better. Sometimes covering windows, door areas, exit lights, etc. with black plastic bags will suffice.
- Spray the suspect area with 2% 5-sulfosalicylic acid and allow it to dry.
- Set the camera on a tripod, set the aperture to "bulb," turn off lights, and photograph the area using a 2 min exposure. Check that photograph is not overexposed. If overexposed, adjust the shutter speed and retake the photograph.
- If the exposure is adequate (i.e., scene detail is visible in the photograph), trip the shutter and spray the area with BlueStar™. Allow luminescence to develop. When fluorescence begins to fade, spray the area again. Continue this process for the entire 2 min. Then trip the shutter and observe the photograph.

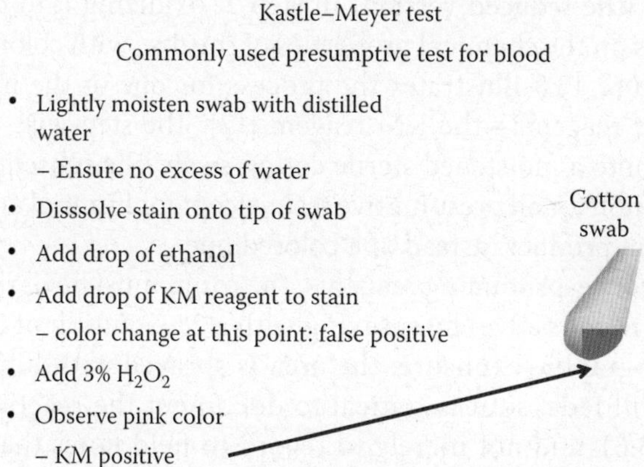

Figure 13.8 Kastle–Meyer reaction with dried blood.

False positive luminescence is possible with luminol and BlueStar™, usually with metals and bleach. Since bleach is used to clean blood, the bleach-cleaned areas give an initial luminescence that fades quickly. The same is true for certain metals, for example, copper pipes, and so on. Presumptive blood testing reagents are useful because they provide immediate investigative information. Substances that have peroxidase activity, such as horseradish, also give a false positive.

The choice of which to use and when is important. For example, consider the scene in which an informant says that a particular individual had been murdered 3 years earlier. Certainly, finding the blood visually or even with an ALS might be fruitless. It might even be that the entire scene had been remodeled or repainted. After an exhaustive but unsuccessful search for visible blood, the team leader might discuss the following with the team:

- Should the team spray using BlueStar™ and, if so, can the team darken the room sufficiently?
- Should the team use a reagent that forms a color, such as leucocrystal violet? [13]
- If the investigation is based on an informant's information that the room had, for example, been painted to hide blood, the team must consider the possibility of finding the blood "under" the paint and discuss how to accomplish that. One consideration is spraying with BlueStar™.

13.3.1.6 Lateral Flow Immunochromatography

Lateral flow immunochromatography is a rapid technique for identifying small amounts of specific molecules. Its forensic application has been largely used to identify the forensically important biological substances—blood, semen, saliva, and urine. The specific tests can be conducted at the scene; however, unlike the presumptive chemical testing reagents discussed above, they must be purchased commercially, which raises the cost per test significantly. Unlike presumptive tests, they specifically identify unknown stains as human blood (some cards cross-react with ferret blood), semen, or saliva (salivary amylase).

Although these tests come in the form of testing kits, they, too, must pass quality tests for sensitivity and specificity. See Chapter 23. The same set of cotton swabs prepared for blood quality control testing will suffice—a separate set of cotton swabs should each be prepared for human semen and saliva. A tabular record, such as Table 23.1, should be maintained with other quality records. A forensic validation of immunochromatographic cards has been published [14].

A problem with immunochromatographic cards (rapid stain identification—RSID™—cards), especially those from Abacus Diagnostics and OTEB, is that they suffer from what is known as the "hook effect" [15]. This happens when testing overly concentrated samples of human blood (RSID™ cards do not demonstrate a hook effect). The result is a negtive test, even if human blood is present. If the scene scientist is not aware and does not understand this anomaly and fails to test an appropriately small or diluted samples, an incorrect and potentially a misinterpretation result. When the hook effect occurs, the sample must be diluted and rerun. The quickness, ease of operation, specificity, and sensitivity of immunochromatographic cards makes it tempting to avoid the traditional chemical tests entirely. If cost was not an issue, this might be the best choice because these tests confirm the presence of human blood in a single test. Importantly, the used immunocard and/or the extract used to run the test can be submitted to the laboratory for DNA analysis, which would save the laboratory time in selecting certain scene stains from submitted crime scene samples for DNA analysis* [16], although laboratories prefer to extract the samples in-house. The stain extract used for the cards at the scene should also be saved because the DNA can be analyzed.

Cost aside, for many scenes using the immunochromatographic cards exclusively is probably a mistake, if all blood tested turns out to be nonhuman. A negative test typically means that human blood is not present; false negatives with highly concentrated blood extracts can be obtained. One exception is the blood test by RSID™, which has no hook effect [17]. A true negative occurs when there is insufficient human blood present; all tests have limits of sensitivity. Of the immunocards available, the Abacus Diagnostics card for blood is the more sensitive; the HemaTrace™ card detects lower amounts of blood than the RSID™ card. Scene practitioners should be aware of the difference among products and should test the cards for sensitivity and specificity as part of the validation aspect of a comprehensive quality assurance program. See Chapter 23.

13.3.1.7 Collecting and Packaging Blood Evidence

The mechanism used to collect and preserve blood evidence is critical. If done incorrectly, the result can compromise or destroy the evidence. There are seven invariant rules: that apply generally to all classes of biological evidence.

- Always wear protective clothing—face masks, gloves, proper outer wear, and shoe/boot covers.
- Dry all blood evidence. If that is not possible, transport it to the forensic laboratory as soon as possible, ensuring that it does not come into contact with other evidence.
- Never package blood evidence in plastic. Always use paper.
- Package each item of evidence individually. Never mix items.
- Never allow adjacent bloodstains (even if dry) to come into contact with other stains on the same or other items of evidence.
- Store all biological evidence in a cool dark place, if possible. This means keeping the evidence away from sunlight and heat, such as in a police car or crime scene unit vehicle on a hot day, while processing the scene.
- Collect the entire sample, if possible. This may not be possible because of the size or fixed location of an object. If this is not possible, cut the entire stain from the larger item and document the location photographically. If necessary, collect evidence on lightly moistened swabs.

Following these rules ensures that blood evidence—biological evidence generally—is collected and preserved properly.

Blood evidence comes in forms and can occur in patterns that have important interpretative information. Collecting it properly depends on the form it takes: pools, droplets, trail swipes, castoff, weapons, furniture, and clothing. If possible, the entire bloody object should be collected and packaged. This gives the laboratory the opportunity to decide

* Reena Roy and Tam Ho, personal communication. Forensic Science Program. Pennsylvania State University, 2011.

which stains are important. If that decision is made at the scene, there is the real possibility that important evidence might be lost. For example, if a grouping of dried blood stains on a piece of furniture has more than one individual's blood present and if the investigator chooses only one of several stains to collect, the second person's blood might never be analyzed, which can compromise the scene analysis, an understanding of the ground truth of what happened, and thus the reconstruction of the events.

If the blood evidence is wet, say, a droplet lying on a tile foyer, the following steps should be followed:

- Determine the length time it takes to dry (carefully monitor how long it takes to dry).
- Collect the dried material by scrapping into an appropriate collection vehicle—a druggist fold bindle or coin or glassine envelope.
- Record the temperature, humidity, and the conditions where the stain was located (windy, sunlight, shade, etc.).

If the stain is large, such as a wet pool, the following steps should be followed:

- Absorb a small amount of the stain onto a cotton swab.
- Place it into a small swab box (a small rectangular box with holes near one end like those used to dry vaginal swabs in sexual assault cases)
- Allow it to dry.

If the evidence is a blood trail, the following steps should be followed:

- Determine the direction of travel.
- Photograph the diagnostic droplets to preserve the information.
- Collect representative droplets from the beginning, middle, and end of the trail by swabbing them onto a moistened cotton swab or scrapping them into separate envelopes.
- Package them separately. A stepwise process for swabbing is shown below:
  - Lightly moisten swab and shake off excess.
  - Dissolve bloodstain onto tip of swab, keeping sample as concentrated as possible.
  - Dry swab appropriately, ideally in swab drying box.
- Package dried swab (wet swab cannot be dried immediately) in swab box.

Dried blood found on clothing should be packaged by folding the garment around brown or white wrapping paper, ensuring that individual stains on the garment do not come into contact with other stains. After folding the evidence, the entire garment should be placed in a separate paper evidence bag and labeled appropriately.

13.3.2 Semen

The second most prominent class of biological evidence found at scenes is semen. Generally, modern scene scientists/investigators locate semen using an ALS on the CSS setting or using another appropriate wavelength. Typically, scene scientist/investigators wears orange goggles using blue light at approximately 450 nm, but the wavelength is what dictates whether to use orange or another color of goggles, if any. For some wavelengths, for example, 415 nm, only clear goggles are necessary.

All investigators knows what semen is, but few have a complete understanding of its biological origin or its forensic potential. The male ejaculate is a liquid that contains cells, the origin of which is mostly the seminal vesicles—approximately 46–80%, with the prostate gland producing between 13% and 33%; the remainder comes from the testicles, epididymus, and the bulbourethral and urethral glands. Forensic investigators also know that semen plays an important role in identifying the assailants in sexually motivated crimes because of the DNA present in the spermatozoa. Like blood, semen has a much broader forensic potential than simply a source of DNA. Students and novice investigators should understand how broad this potential can be. Figure 13.9 illustrates this.

Like blood, semen has cellular and liquid (plasma) fractions. Each potentially can play an important forensic role. For example, the liquid portion, seminal plasma, contains the same soluble components found in blood, and same forensic information is potentially available. For example, metabolites of illicit and therapeutic drugs are present which are identifiable in dried semen or from semen from the vaginal swabs of a rape survivor. If the DNA profile from the spermatozoa cannot be matched to a previously incarcerated felon in CODIS, it has little investigative value. However, learning that the semen has an illicit drug profile may provide an investigative lead. Likewise, a smoker has nicotine metabolites, which gives personal information about the assailant.

Like blood analysis, semen analysis has evolved in parallel with advances in science. Since 1677 when Johan Ham showed Anton von Leeuwenhoek spermatozoa in the microscope* in 1677, identifying semen microscopically has become forensic gold standard. Forensic laboratory scientists, though, work with dried stains, so a microscopic analysis, while necessary, is time consuming. In the early part of the twentieth century, much of the semen identification in rape cases was done in hospital laboratories, which received a vaginal lavage as part of the clinical examination of the sexual assault survivor. Generally, hospital laboratories performed two tests: a sperm mobility test and a

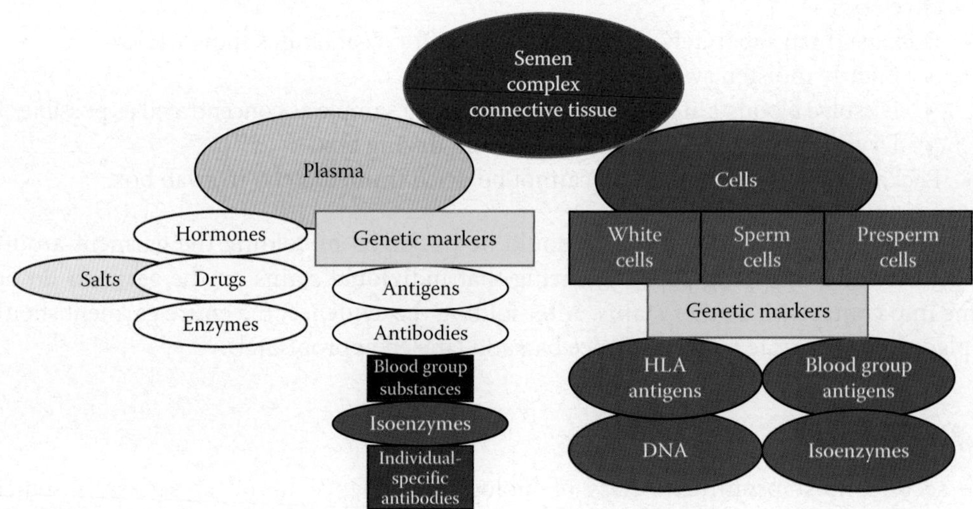

Figure 13.9 Forensically speaking, what is semen?

* E.G. Ruestow, 1983. Images and Ideas: Leeuwenhoek and his perception of spermatozoa. *History of Biology*, 16(2):185–224.

quantitative AP or prostatic acid phosphatase (PAP) analysis, the latter popular in the 1940s, 1950s, and 1960s as a way to show that semen was present in the vaginal vault. The analysis of AP (PAP) gained popularity because semen has high concentrations [18,19]. Hospital laboratories quantified the amount of AP present. If the level was above a certain cut-off, the interpretation was that semen was present, diagnostic of sexual penetration.

Forensic laboratories went in a different analytical direction. They typically received dried vaginal swabs from the police instead of a vaginal lavage, which made determining the level of AP difficult. So, they used the AP test differently. They added a small amount of the AP reagent to a small cutting of the dried stain and measured the time it took for the test reagent to turn color. If the color change was rapid, <30 s, usually almost instantaneously unless the sample was very old, the laboratory had evidence that the dried stain might contain semen. In essence, the AP test was used as a presumptive indication that semen might be present. They confirmed the presence of semen microscopically by observing spermatozoa. The purpose of this discussion is to show that forensic scientists have historically used a sequence of tests to identify semen in dried stains, culminating in identifying the vehicle of conception, spermatozoa. This analytical sequence changed in the 1970s with the discovery of a semen-specific protein known as p30 by forensic scientists [20,21] and prostate-specific antigen (PSA) by clinical scientists [22].

For on-scene applications, there has historically neither been the time nor the resources to perform microscopic or immunological analyses for spermatozoa. In fact, that is not the job of scene investigators. They are responsible for finding the evidence and transporting it to a forensic laboratory for analysis. In the 1950s and 1960s, the "crusty feel" of dried semen was a quick check for the presence of semen. At that time, laboratory scientists used this same tactile "test" because it was fast and could be easily performed on evidence where semen might logically be expected, such as bed sheets. Another on-scene technique was the first true ALS, the black light also known as Wood's light [23]. Short-wave UV light caused semen to fluoresce, and it worked well for semen stains on light, unwashed, as well as dark fabric. It did not work on light, detergent-washed fabric because detergents in the fabric interfered with the luminescence of the semen.

The same AP test as used in the forensic laboratory to presumptively identify semen was adapted for scene use. The test was used essentially like the chemical tests for blood. Interpreting it was much the same, too, and was based on the time it took to produce a specific color. It was and still is a presumptive test. A schematic of the components of the AP test is shown in Figure 13.10.

13.3.2.1 Performing the AP Test on Fresh Semen Stains

13.3.2.2 Quality Assurance and Control Testing

On the day of use, a known semen stain (positive control) and a negative reagent control (distilled water) are tested to ensure the reagents meet minimum standards. General guidelines for ensuring the quality of testing reagents are discussed in Section 13.6. All quality results must be archived. If controls fail, it is poor practice to continue using the reagent until the problem has been resolved or new reagents that meet minimum standards are prepared. If the results of the test are positive, a substrate control (if available)

- Sodium alpha-naphthyl phosphate
  - Molecule split by AP
  - Frees the naphthyl group
- Fast blue–*ortho dianisidine*
  - Combines with naphthyl group
- Produces bright pink to a dark blue/purple color

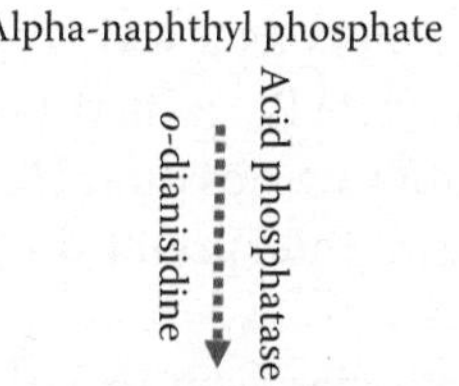

Figure 13.10 Acid phosphatase (AP) test for semen.

must also be tested, unless the stain is on a cotton swab. The test results must be maintained in the case file.

- *AP test procedure*
  - Lightly moisten sterile swab with distilled water and press or gently rub it against the suspected stain.
  - Add one to two drops of sodium *a*-naphthyl AP solution.
  - Add one to two drops of *o*-dianisidine dye solution.
  - The development of a blue/purple color within 10–15 s is indicative of AP levels consistent with semen.
  - For samples giving inconclusive result (longer color development times), semen must be confirmed microscopically or by showing the presence of p30.
- Interpretation of results
  - Positive reaction: Blue/purple color within 10–15 s.
  - Negative reaction: No color development, slight/slow color development.
  - Inconclusive reaction: Slow moderate to strong color development longer than 15 s and not longer than 30 s.

There are variations on how to run the AP test.

- One is to dab the unknown stain with a cotton swab moistened with the reagent and wait for the color to change on the evidence or the moistened swab. This is not a preferred method.
- A preferable method is to moisten the swab with water, dissolve a small amount of the unknown stain onto the swab, and then test the swab with the AP reagent. A rapid color change from colorless to dark blue to purple is a positive test.
- Another, but not recommended, variation is to moisten the unknown stain directly with the reagent by dropping microdroplets from a micropipette directly onto the stain. Again, a rapid color change is diagnostic of a positive test.
- Another variation is to screen large areas to locate invisible semen stains, a technique called AP screening. A piece of filter paper is moistened with water and then rubbed over larger areas of, say, a bed sheet sectioned into a grid. A positive AP test result on the filter paper is an indication that semen is present in that grid area. The AP screening method is not popular since the introduction of high-powered ALSs,

which highlight semen and other biological fluids better and faster without the use of chemicals.

Confirmatory tests were not available for on-scene dried semen testing until recently. The immunochromatographic cards described for blood are also available for on-scene testing to identify the presence of semen proteins, p30 (also known as PSA, manufactured by Abacus Diagnostics) [24], and semenogelin manufactured by RSID™ [25]. The proper use of the cards can quickly identify human semen at the scene. The AP test, which is still useful, does not identify human semen or even semen. It is a presumptive test. Immunochromatographic cards are expensive, which means the relatively inexpensive AP test, which requires fresh reagents, can screen unknown stains quicker and cheaper. The ALS is superior because, except for the initial expense, it covers a larger area and requires no testing reagents. Replacement bulbs are expensive.

13.3.2.3 Establishing a Rationale for Searching for Semen

A rationale or decision tree should be in place for locating biological evidence at a scene. Certainly, the first line of attack is logic, which leads to where semen might be. At obviously sexually motivated crimes, searching for semen takes place in the most logical places: beds, sofas, car seats, and so on. However, there are nonsexually motivated scenes where a perpetrator might masturbate, urinate, or defecate. In fact, burglary scenes have a higher incidence of semen than one might expect. For whatever reason, perhaps after fondling a female's undergarments or jewelry, burglars masturbate, inadvertently leaving their biological signature. So searching for semen should not be confined to the obvious crime type and should not be a one-step, check-the-bedroom-only endeavor.

There is still the question of how an investigator should search for semen evidence. The easiest and probably the best method is using the ALS, a first line of attack. Even when using the ALS, there should be a rationale, a written procedure, for deciding which ALS positive stains to test further and how and which to collect for the laboratory. There should be a tabular record of which wavelengths to use and photographs of what to expect. These should be prepared and maintained by the investigating unit. The ALS is the first avenue of analysis, but it should never be forgotten that the ALS is useful for locating not only semen but also other biological evidence, such as saliva, urine, and trace evidence. The following is a list of alternative ways to use the ALS to locate semen.

- Use the ALS to locate possible semen, saliva, or urine stains and allow the laboratory to decide which to test further. This is by far the safest approach because it leaves the choice of subsequent DNA analysis to the laboratory. Mark and photograph stains the ALS highlights.
- Use the ALS to locate possible probative stains and then use the AP test to determine which might be semen. The laboratory would likely retest the stain with the ALS and the AP test and then perform DNA analysis, if warranted. Procedures for using the ALS, the AP (discussed above) test, and immunochromatographic cards for semen testing are presented in Workshop 8.
- Use the ALS followed by an immunochromatographic test. (The AP test is not used.) The more definitive/confirmatory immunological test is performed. A positive test

shows the stain analyzed is semen, which alerts the laboratory that subsequent analysis is warranted. However, a negative immunochromatographic card test suggests the ALS-highlighted stain is not semen. The card might be in error, however, due to the hook effect. A second test for AP might be positive. If only the ALS is used at the scene, the laboratory will retest the stain to confirm the presence of semen. False negative results for the AP and the immunochromatographic card tests can occur with old stains that have been environmentally compromised for extended periods of time. In such cases, the negative test may be simply a matter of the stain being so insoluble that insufficient material was dissolved for the test to be positive.

When ALS highlights something that could have a biological origin, the area should be marked by either circling the area or highlighting the location with a marker or an arrow sticker. This shows where the positive presumptive test result was obtained. It does not mean that this is the only stain present or that it might be semen. *It simply means that someone observed something using an ALS and that it might require further analysis.* The investigator's initials and date should also be affixed to or marked on the evidence. The location should be archived photographically so that the laboratory knows exactly which stain on the evidence gave a positive ALS. There should be no guesswork for laboratory scientists.

Figure 13.11 shows an example of an old stain taken of a young girl's slip using an ALS. The slip was taken from the body of a young girl who had been attacked, raped, and murdered over 40 years before the ALS analysis. The areas in yellow and marked with letters and numbers (A1, A2, etc.) are luminescent areas highlighted by the ALS. These were semen stains. The AP test, evaluated using most established standards, was negative—it took a long time for the reagent to show a very weak purple color. This was expected because the stains

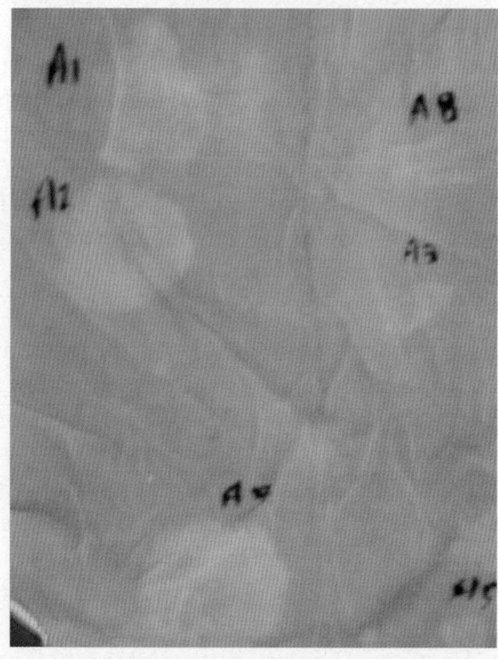

Figure 13.11 Alternate light source highlight of semen on slip. (Photograph by Ralph Ristenbatt III.)

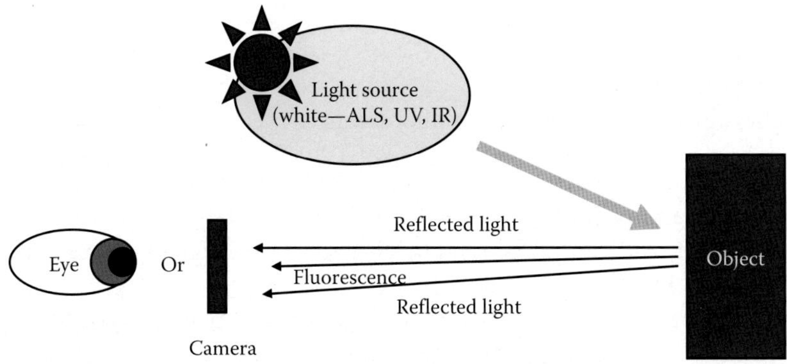

Figure 13.12 Reflected light interferes with fluorescence produced by alternate light interacting with object.

had been stored improperly for over 40 years. The only tests giving positive results were the ALS and an immunological test for PSA (p30). Dissolving the stain to give the positive anti-p30 test result required dissolving the stain for an extended period of time. However, if the test had been done at the scene using an immunochromatographic card, the test result would likely have been positive. Subsequent DNA testing using low copy number (LCN) techniques gave a full short tandem repeat (STR) profile and identified the murderer over 40 years later. Standard STR testing gave only a partial DNA profile.

The primary steps necessary to use an ALS to locate biological fluids on garments are listed below.

- Examine the evidence using the 450 nm wavelength of the ALS (the CSS and other wavelength settings on the MiniScope™ 400 can highlight semen or other fluorescing biological substances—some without using goggles; however, the preferred method is to use the 450 nm setting and barrier filters or goggles). The two schematics in Figures 13.12 and 13.13 illustrate the process. When light of an appropriate wavelength impacts on a surface containing semen, well-known phenomena can occur.

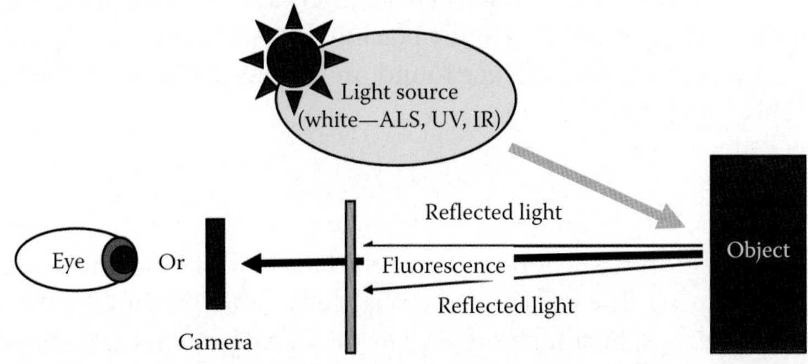

Figure 13.13 Barrier filter blocks reflected light.

- Light is absorbed.
- Light is transmitted.
- Light is reflected.
- Light is given off in the form of fluorescence.

If the incident light causes fluorescence, the reflected light and the fluorescent light travel to the camera and/or the investigator's eye. Unfortunately, the fluorescence is masked by the reflected light, and cannot be seen by either the investigator or the camera. This is illustrated in Figure 13.12.

However, if a barrier filter—in this instance an orange plate or goggles—is placed in the path of mixed reflected and fluorescence lights, the former is absorbed (blocked) by the barrier filter. The fluorescence, however, is not and passes through the filter to the camera (or the eye), which records the light. The barrier filter (orange for finding semen) is illustrated in Figure 13.13.

Technology on the horizon may have dramatic effects on how scene investigations proceed suggests that on-scene DNA analysis may be possible [26]. When or if this becomes a reality, the dynamics of the crime scene investigations will change dramatically because DNA profiles produced at the scene can be uploaded directly into a local, searchable DNA profile database. The subsequent investigative result may identify the perpetrator or provide links to one or more crimes. This rapid, investigative information can be critical for solving the crimes. Simply knowing how many different bloodstains or semen stains there are on a bed sheet can alter and speed the investigative process by providing information quicker. There are also serious possible repercussions, however. The major issues include: Who does the work and how will the scientific integrity and quality be controlled?

13.3.2.4 Collecting and Packaging Semen Evidence

The invariant rules discussed for collecting and packaging blood evidence (Section 13.3.1.7) hold equally for semen evidence. The packaging guidelines are also the same. Generally, semen evidence at the scene is dry. If not, it should be air dried. It is typically found on tissue paper, clothing, towels, bed sheets, pillows, blankets, furniture, as droplets on the floor, or on the skin of a deceased individual or live survivor. Collecting it can be done by taking the entire dried stain or by swabbing it onto a lightly moistened sterile cotton-tipped swab designed for semen evidence. The swabs can be dried at the scene using a drying device designed for drying swabs at the scene or by placing the swab into a cardboard holder [27]. Guidelines for collecting semen evidence found on various surfaces whether liquid or dry are shown in Table 13.4 [28].

13.3.3 Saliva

Saliva is another biological tissue found at crime scenes. Like blood and semen, it also has two parts: liquid and cells. The cells are epithelial cells that contain DNA. The liquid part is composed of salts, drugs, hormones, as well as dissolved proteins and enzymes different from those present in semen and blood. Figure 13.14 illustrates this.

From a forensic perspective, the most important constituent of saliva, other than DNA, is the enzyme alpha amylase, which is important for ascertaining whether an unknown stain might be saliva. Before the prevalent use of the ALS to locate biological evidence,

Table 13.4 Collecting Semen Evidence at the Scene

Semen at the Scene	Procedure
Semen and seminal stains/liquid semen evidence found at a scene (e.g., droplets on floor)	Archive all semen evidence: notes, photography, videotape, and sketching.
	Depending on surface, collect in syringe or disposable pipette. Transfer to clean, sterile tube. Label tube with the case and item number, date, time, location, and name of the collector. Keep refrigerated and submit to laboratory as soon as possible.
	Or: Absorb liquid semen onto clean cotton cloth. Air dry, package, seal, and label appropriately.
Seminal stains on movable objects (e.g., panties, clothing, bed sheets, pillows, etc.)	Collect as is. If stain is wet, air dry thoroughly. Package items separately in a clean paper container. Refrigerate packaged items if possible. Submit to laboratory as soon as possible.
Seminal stains on large objects that can be cut (e.g., furniture, carpet, etc.)	Cut stain from items document, and package as above. Use disposable scalpel, new blade, or scissors to cut stained area. Place each cutting in separate piece of clean paper. Make druggist fold to secure evidence. Place the druggist fold into paper container, seal, and label.
Seminal stains on immovable, nonabsorbent surfaces (e.g., floors, counters, and metal surfaces)	Document stain. Use disposable scalpel or new blade to scrape stain onto clean paper, and fold the paper into a druggist fold container. Place druggist into own paper container, seal, and label properly.

finding saliva at crime scenes was mostly luck because it was often associated with semen in a sexual assault or associated with a bite mark. Historically, identifying a dried saliva stain meant identifying the salivary component in the largest concentration, the enzyme alpha amylase (AMY). The problem is that, like AP, amylase occurs in most forensically important tissues: AMY 1 is found in blood and saliva and AMY 2 is found in blood, pancreas, and vaginal secretions [28,29].

The diagnostic characteristic of saliva, like AP in semen, is the amount of the amylase present and its genetic origin. The human body produces two different amylases: AMY 1

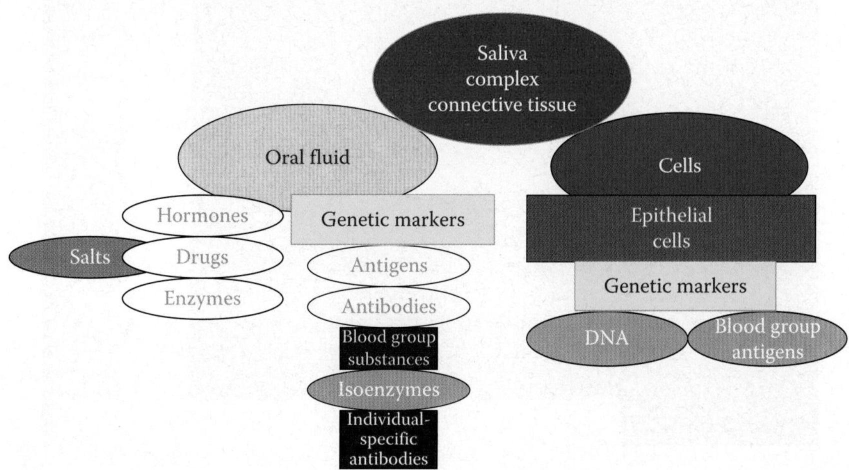

Figure 13.14 Forensically speaking, what is saliva?

and AMY 2, each a separate gene product, the former occurring in saliva. Thus, identifying AMY 1 serves as a presumptive test for the presence of saliva. The on-scene location of saliva has typically not been a target of investigators. One reason is that robust, easily employed techniques for identifying AMY 1 have not been available. This has changed somewhat, however, because the higher-powered ALSs cause saliva to fluoresce, although weakly. Once a fluorescent area is located, presumptive tests for amylase can show that saliva might be present. On dark surfaces or garments, it is sometimes possible to visualize the saliva stain using oblique lighting from either an ALS or a flashlight. Figure 13.15 illustrates this with an ALS white light held obliquely to highlight a bite impression on a Navy Pea Coat. The light color is dried salvia. Notice the teeth impressions in the fabric (white arrows). Although this might be something a laboratory should do, it can also be an on-scene activity.

There are three methods for presumptively identifying saliva: the Phadebas test, the starch–iodine diffusion test, and immunochromatographic cards. Whether to use these tests at scenes is a decision that requires careful consideration. The Phadebas test is commercially available in a simple, scene-forward format [30]. The starch–iodine diffusion test requires the scene scientist/investigator prepare the reagents at the scene, which is inconvenient and time consuming and likely not worth the effort. The immunochromatographic cards for alpha amylase, similar to those for blood and semen, are commercially available and can determine whether an unknown stain contains alpha amylase (AMY 1). The question, however, is whether on-scene work is important, for the specific investigation. Even though saliva can be identified, at least presumptively using immunochromatographic cards, there is always the decision whether to use them at the scene or protect the evidence for testing at the laboratory. An example of the RSID™ immunochromatographic card to identify the alpha amylase is shown in Figure 13.16. In this test, the researchers analyzed ferret saliva and human saliva. They obtained a negative test with ferret saliva proving that there is no cross-reaction as there is with blood using the human blood immunocard manufactured by Abacus Diagnostics.

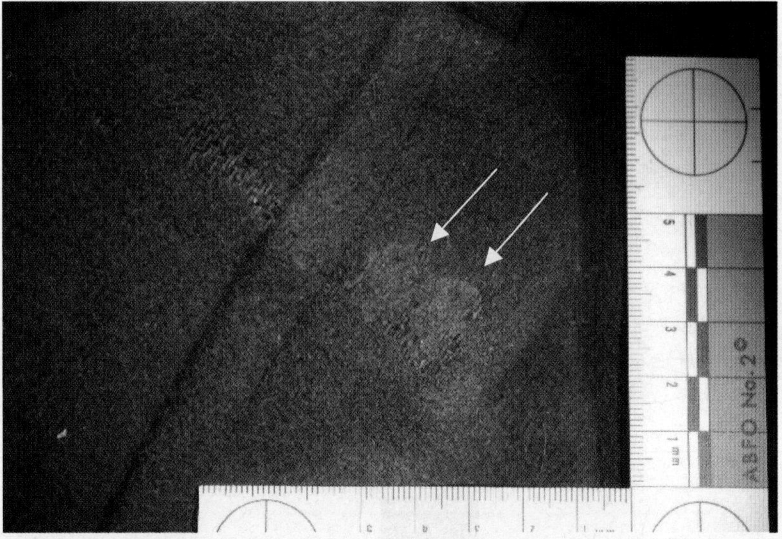

Figure 13.15 Alternate light source highlighting dried saliva on a Navy Pea Coat. (Photograph by Ralph Ristenbatt III.)

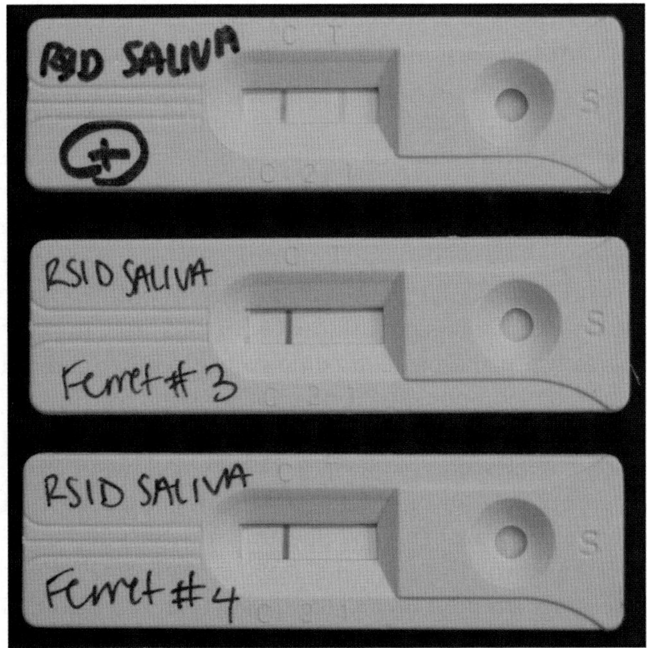

Figure 13.16 Rapid stain identification chromatographic card for saliva.

Like with on-scene semen testing, the scene scientist/investigator should have a rationale for on-scene saliva testing versus simply collecting the evidence and submitting it to the laboratory. In fact, the real question should be: Is on-scene saliva testing ever necessary? Certainly, there might be instances where the presence of saliva can have scene-specific reconstructive value. For example, if the ALS fluorescent positive area on a victim's shirt or blouse is saliva, its location and pattern may suggest it came from an assailant instead of the victim. Such testing can be important for the investigation if it provides immediate investigative information that cannot wait. The team leader makes that decision. Finding a fluorescent stain on the wall, for instance, might have investigative and/or reconstructive value, if the stain is saliva and it tells the investigator, based on the stain's pattern, that someone pressed a face against the wall. Perhaps it was the assailant's. If the investigators perceive that there is no immediate obvious value to the stain, it might never be collected, which would be a mistake. The primary question remains, however: How important is finding saliva in the overall investigative mission? Sometimes that question cannot be answered until later in the investigation. In other words, it is a mistake to forego collecting any biological evidence.

13.3.3.1 Collecting and Packaging Saliva Evidence

Collecting and packaging saliva evidence is exactly the same as for semen evidence (see Section 13.3.2.4 and Table 13.4).

13.3.4 Urine

Urine is another important biological fluid that occurs at crime scenes, and it is not uncommon for a perpetrator to urinate at the scene, either on the floor or in a toilet. Generally, finding it is not a problem because of its characteristic odor. Once dried, however, it fluoresces weakly under the ALS or under the UV light, giving various colors. An immunochromatographic card has been developed to identify the urine at the scene. The test works well with urine stains on fabric but is less sensitive with blood and urine mixed stains. Until the RSID™-urine immunochromatographic card, there were no reliable on-scene test techniques for identifying the urine, even presumptively, except for odor, so there was no chance of ruining the evidence before transmitting it to a forensic laboratory. Perpetrators do use toilets, so it is important to collect the contents of toilets, if there is a suggestion that urine is present. Since urine contains cellular material, the forensic laboratory needs to have a sufficient cellular DNA to obtain a DNA profile. Outdoor scenes should be searched thoroughly because it is not unheard of to find urine in snow.

Like semen and saliva, urine has two components: cellular and liquid, as shown in Figure 13.17. Urine also has components having potential forensic utility.

The component in the highest concentration in urine is urea. Unfortunately, there is no easy way of testing for it at the scene, but there is an enzymatic assay available to laboratory scientists, probably to be replaced by the RSID™-urine immunochromatographic card. The assay uses a commercially available enzyme, urease, which decomposes urea into carbon dioxide and ammonia, which is easily detectable in a pH assay. The chemical reaction for the enzymatic decomposition of urea using urease is shown below. One way to detect the ammonia is using a pH indicator because ammonia is strongly basic, as shown in the enzymatic reaction

$$\text{Urea} + H_2O \rightarrow CO_2 + 2NH_3 \tag{13.1}$$

13.3.4.1 Collecting and Packaging Urine Evidence

Collecting and packaging urine depends on how it manifests itself at the scene. If removed from the toilet, there will be a substantial volume to collect and package. If toilet contents are collected, it should be transported immediately to the forensic laboratory. This is often impossible, however, given the constraints of an investigation. The problem is that the urethral epithelial cells should not remain in the urine's wet, acidic environment for extended periods [31]. The reason is that it has a deleterious effect on the DNA. If the urine contents cannot be transported immediately, the urine contents should be frozen as soon as possible or at least put on ice. Finding ice at convenience stores is not difficult or expensive. It then is the laboratory's job to determine how to extract the DNA.

If the urine is wet and in a puddle, say, on the floor, it can be collected in a container, such as described in Table 13.4 for liquid semen, and treated as discussed above or, alternatively,

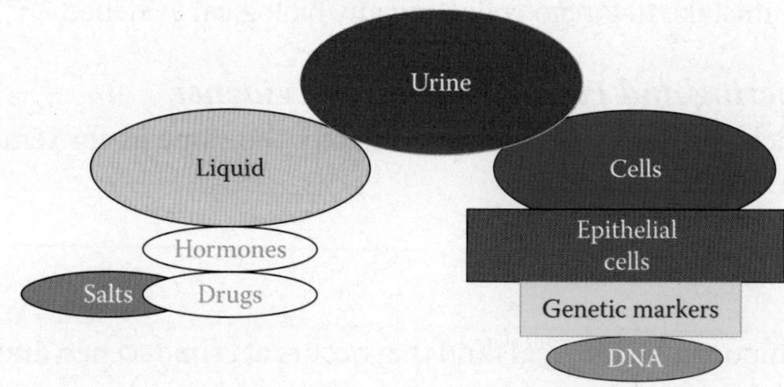

Figure 13.17 Forensically speaking, what is urine?

absorbed onto an absorbent material, such as a sponge, a towel or filter, or bench paper, and allowed to dry. Once dry, the DNA will be more stable than if the urine remains wet. Sometimes urine is found on clothing that is either wet or already dry. If wet or damp, dry the evidence as soon as possible, preferably at the scene. Again, once dry, the DNA should be relatively stable, certainly for several hours until it can be taken to the forensic laboratory.

13.3.5 Feces

Human metabolism results in a waste product known as feces, which has been found at scenes of crimes, often in piles. Perpetrators defecate at scenes, so searching for their feces at the scene is an endeavor with important identifying implications. Locating it is not usually difficult, as its odor and/or characteristic appearance are fairly diagnostic, overwhelming, and quite obvious. There are instances, however, where dried brown swipes may be present that do not have the characteristic fecal odor, as drying mutes it. The easiest way to determine whether a dried brown stain is feces is to swab a small amount onto a wet cotton swab and then smell it. Once feces are redissolved, the offensive odor is unmistakable.

13.3.5.1 Collecting and Packaging Feces Evidence

Collecting and packaging wet feces is a simple matter of scooping it up, placing it into a casserole-like dish, and sealing it. If the evidence cannot be transported to the laboratory immediately, it should be frozen or at least put on ice. Keeping the feces cold is important because it has a host of destructive enzymes that can destroy cellular material, including the DNA.

Feces can have important forensic value. Like its biological cousins its components have potential investigative information, the most important being DNA. There are other forensically important considerations as well. As a by-product of digestion, it has foodstuffs that might help identify a meal the perpetrator ate or ingested drugs.

13.3.6 Vomit

Although not one of the more commonly occurring types of biological evidence, it is certainly found at scenes of crimes. Vomit can be important for the same reasons that feces are important: it contains cellular material that has DNA and it has foodstuffs that can tell something about the immediate eating habits of the person who vomited. Finding vomit at scenes is usually not difficult, again, because the odor is so distinctive. Dried vomit stains have an odor, and, like feces, dissolving a small amount in water and boiling releases the odor. There are tests for rennin, an enzyme in vomit, the presence of which can give more confidence that an unknown stain is vomit, but the odor test is sufficient for investigative purposes. The laboratory will do the appropriate tests, which will most likely be to extract the DNA.

13.3.6.1 Collecting and Packaging Vomit Evidence

The rule for collecting, packaging, and preserving vomit is the same as for feces and urine evidence. Like urine and feces, the acidic environment of vomit can be detrimental to the integrity of DNA, so collecting it and either drying it or freezing it as soon as possible is critical.

13.3.7 Hair

Although biological in origin, hair is almost ubiquitous. Nevertheless, finding probative hair evidence can be crucial in the final adjudication of a case. The recent NAS report [32] determined that hair comparisons should be done in conjunction with mitochondrial DNA (mtDNA) analysis . Although there has been concern with respect to the reliability of microscopic hair comparisons [(see p. 161 in Reference [32]), hair still has forensic value. Basically, it is a biological material and a pipeline to what we eat. That is, what we eat and metabolize is in the hair. If we ingest drugs, the drugs and/or their metabolites will be in the hair and the location of the drugs in the hair shaft is an indication of the time since the drug ingestion [33].

Hair grows from hair follicles, which means DNA is present. Although the hair has both nuclear and mtDNA, the former is found mostly in the hair root and only tiny amounts are present in the shaft. The shaft, however, is an ample source of mtDNA. Unfortunately, mtDNA is not sufficiently unique to provide the investigation with a unique identification.

Understanding the structure of hair and how that can help determine which type of DNA testing is appropriate is important. It is also important to understand the meaning of hair found at the scene. Hair clutched in the hand of a dead victim suggests hair had been pulled from an assailant during a struggle. Although collecting this hair is the responsibility of the medical examiner, ensure that the hair is collected and preserved for DNA analysis. This is the responsibility of the crime scene team leader, who must capture the hair clump photographically.

The discussion in this chapter, however, is concerned with locating hair, collecting it, and ensuring that it gets to the forensic laboratory for analysis. With respect to locating hair, the discussion of trace evidence and the microscene is relevant (Chapter 17).

Finding probative hair evidence requires logic and the appropriate use of technology and collection techniques. Certainly, a flashlight is appropriate as is the ALS. The technique is to highlight the hair by holding the light source at an oblique angle and to search those locations that make the most sense. An example is a homicide scene, and depending on how the homicide occurred, the body of the deceased and/or its immediate vicinity should have the hair of the assailant present, if a struggle took place in that area. If the combatants fell onto furniture, that too would be a logical place to search for probative hair evidence.

13.3.7.1 Collecting and Packaging Hair Evidence

There are three common methods used to collect hair evidence. These methods will be discussed more fully in Chapter 17. The methods generally used are listed below:

- The hunt and peck (picking) method using tweezers to lift hair and placing it into an appropriate container (envelope)
- Taping, that is, lifting the hair onto the sticky side of tape
- Vacuuming

13.3.8 Fingerprint/Skin Residue

Crime scene investigators do not usually categorize fingerprint residue as a type of biological evidence. The reason is that the uniqueness of the friction ridge detail present on fingers, palms, and the soles of the feet had always been more important. That was before

DNA. Even with the advent of automated identification systems, its promise has not been what investigators had hoped because of the relatively low percentage of useable fingerprints at scenes. This might be more the fault of how prints are deposited but also in some measure of how investigators look for and lift latent prints. This could change. Fingerprints contain biological material in two forms: the emulsion and the cellular content of the finger's epithelial cells. When a print is left on a surface, a certain amount of cellular material remains with the print residue. The number of epithelial cells deposited depends on factors that include:

- Time since last hand washing
- Tendency of the individual to shed cells, such as whether the individual is a shedder
- Mechanism by which the print was deposited, that is, whether it was rubbed onto the surface or gently placed

Each cell has approximately 6 pg of nuclear DNA in its nucleus. Though it is possible to obtain a DNA profile from a single cell, a form of forensic DNA testing called LCN testing usually requires approximately 22–25 pg (approximately four cells) of template DNA per amplification to obtain a useable profile. This is not a lot of cells, but preliminary experiments suggest that perhaps a maximum of 20% of useable fingerprints have sufficient DNA to obtain a nuclear DNA profile. Interestingly, mtDNA is present in the cells in the fingerprint emulsion, and even a single cell has a better chance of giving an mtDNA profile because each cell has multiple copies of mtDNA, whereas there is only one copy of nuclear DNA.

Importantly, too, skin residue can be transferred to a surface. Consider the burglar who is looking into a prospective residence and places his head against the window in order to better see. The forehead is a particularly good source of cellular material, and the residue on the window should be a decent source of DNA. A bare arm swiped across a wall or onto a table after someone falls onto it can also be a source of skin residue and hence DNA. Logically, understanding how the crime took place is crucial for determining whether skin residue will be an important source of biological evidence and thus play a critical role in the investigation.

13.3.8.1 Collecting and Packaging Skin Residue

For prints with useable friction ridge detail, the procedures currently used to collect fingerprints should be amenable to collecting a print's adhering cellular content. Quantitative amounts of DNA are not collected by the traditional fingerprint collection methods: print lifting tape, casting with silicone-casting material such as Mikrosil™ or with rubber-backed gel lifters.* Studies show that swabbing lifts the cells and that DNA profiles can be obtained from the swabs. For smudged fingerprints and other skin prints, finding them is the first issue. Generally, powder dusting or an ALS might be the best way to find these prints. Once located, the print can be swabbed and preserved by placing the swab into a swab collection box of the type used for collecting the vaginal swabs in rape cases. The boxed swab should be placed in a larger paper container. As for any biological evidence, no plastic containers should be used.

* Jennifer Nabozny and Robert C. Shaler. Unpublished results. Forensic Science Program. Pennsylvania State University, 2011.

13.3.9 Sloughed-Off Cells

This is an elusive category of biological evidence for which no on-scene technology yet exists, so one might consider it impossible to find. But this is most likely the most prevalent category of physical evidence, bar none, because it is occurs where there are people. So, what are sloughed-off cells? Generally, this refers to continually shed cells. A term that illustrates the point, even if not completely accurate, is dandruff. Everyone sheds cells, and in the heat of a struggle, more cells should be shed than normal. If located and collected, these cells could be an important source of DNA.

13.3.9.1 Collecting and Packaging Sloughed-Off Cell Evidence

How would we find sloughed-off cells at the scene? Although no dedicated research exists, the following are possible choices:

- Use the taping technique for collecting trace evidence. It will "lift" sloughed-off cells from most any surface. It is impractical, however, to tape the entire surface of the crime scene, but logic should lead to the appropriate areas.
- Use fingerprint lift tape. Preliminary work suggests that this is an inefficient method for collecting DNA from fingerprint residue.* Swabbing the print residue remaining after lifting will capture the print residue and the cellular material left behind.
- Use a gel lifter to lift the fingerprint. Preliminary work suggests that gel lifters are not an efficient way to lift cellular material (DNA) from fingerprints. As with fingerprint lift tape, swabbing after gel lifting captures the DNA left behind.
- For smudged prints, swabbing is the preferred method.

13.4 Not-as-Common Biological Evidence

13.4.1 Bacteria/Spores/Viruses

In a world concerned with weapons of mass destruction, this is a particularly relevant topic. After the 2001 attacks on the World Trade Center and the Pentagon, packages containing Anthrax spores were sent in the U.S. mail to Florida, New Jersey, and New York. The possibility of finding a suspicious white powder containing biological material (spores) at crime scenes is apparently real, which presents an insidious threat. The danger exists not only for those conducting the investigation but also the outside world, if the material is not handled properly. For investigators, there is only one way to deal with suspicious powders (see Chapter 16):

- All obviously suspicious powders should be left alone.
- The scene should be sealed.
- Anyone at the scene should be quarantined.
- A Hazmat crew should be contacted.

While the thought of an obviously suspicious powder is particularly frightening, all white (or colored) powders are not suspicious or of biological origin. A murder scene where obvious drug activity is present may have powders that are clandestinely prepared drugs.

* Jennifer Nabozny and Robert C. Shaler. Unpublished results. Forensic Science Program. Pennsylvania State University, 2011.

Certainly, these are dangerous, but they can be tested presumptively at the scene for possible drug content. The team leader and the scene scientist/investigator should decide how to handle the situation based on what the scene offers. For example, a triple homicide where there are lines of white powder on a dining room table suggests cocaine. Another scene that has strange-looking laboratory equipment may suggest something more sinister.

13.4.2 Plant Material

This category of evidence, in truth, is very common. In the introduction above, four categories of not-so-commonly occurring biological evidence were presented: bacteria, plant material, pollen, and viruses. In truth, each of these is extremely common. Utilizing them for forensic applications is not so common, however.

Plant material has DNA, so a plant DNA profile can be determined in much the same way as human DNA. Collecting and packaging plant material is done like any biological evidence. Finding probative plant material is the problem. Sometimes plant material can be found associated with tire tracks or shoeprints. These can be lifted with a gel lifter because they will stick to the sticky side of the gel lifter. It is important to examine all tracks for the presence of plant material. If present, collect it carefully as possible using tweezers and putt it into an appropriate container—a coin or glassing envelope—and then label appropriately.

Pollen is a source of plant material that will be on all surfaces. It is small and hard to detect. In some seasons, it is easy to see, as the pollen grains are seemingly everywhere. These will have little evidentiary value as everything will have these present. Pollen is useful as evidence when it is found associated with something at the scene that had been collected for another purpose—a shirt from the deceased where pollen grains were transferred during the commission of a crime, the sole of a shoe from someone who came from another country and brought the pollen with him/her.

Those who study pollen from a forensic perspective are called forensic palynologists. Pollen reveals where a person or object has been because specific regions/locations of the world have a distinctive collection of pollen species. It can even reveal the season when a particular object picked up the pollen.*

There are no standardized methods for collecting the pollen at the scene. However, the techniques used by investigators in the Anthrax investigation should be considered (Chapter 16). Taping techniques used to collect trace evidence should also be successful.

13.5 Condom Evidence

In an age filled with the fear of contracting diseases such as AIDS and sexually transmitted diseases, individuals often practice safe sex using condoms. Even sexual assault assailants wear them, probably not from the fear of contracting a disease but more likely to avoid leaving DNA evidence. When this happens, the value of the semen evidence and the

* Forensic Palynology: "Forensic palynology is the study of pollen and powdered minerals, their identification, and where and when they occur, to ascertain that a body or other object was in a certain place at a certain time. Palynology is the study of pollen, spores, and other microscopic plant bodies such as dinoflagellates (marine algal cysts). Pollen carries the male sex cells of flowering plants and plants that produce cones (e.g., pine trees). Spores are asexual reproductive bodies of ferns, mosses, and fungi" [34].

victim's vaginal secretions or saliva on the assailant's penis are lost to the investigation. While the important DNA may be gone, condoms leave trace evidence that can still help the investigation.

The construction material of basic condoms can be a variety of natural and synthetic materials, each manufacturer having its propriety formulas, even among its own brands. Examples include lamb membranes, polyurethane plastic, and latex rubber—the largest percent of condoms sold. Condoms leave trace evidence in the form of particulates, lubricants, and spermicide. Particulates are finely powdered corn or potato starch, powdered lycopodium, silica, and talc. Lubricants are important because they provide lubrication, which rapists need because it helps the process [35]. Condoms lubricants are classified as either wet or dry and have an oily consistency; dry lubricants are water-insoluble and wet ones are either water-based or water-soluble. Differences occur within dry lubricants because of varying viscosity grades used by manufacturers. These silicon-based oils are easily recovered and analyzed. Wet lubricants contain polyethylene glycol or a gel similar to vaginal lubricants. Criminalists can associate specific formulations with particular condom brands. Lubricated condoms may also contain the spermicide nonoxynol-9, which can be recovered. By analyzing each trace present in sexual assault evidence, the criminalist can construct a profile of a condom by identifying the particulates, the lubricant, and spermicide present from other evidence found at the scene or collected at the hospital.

Certainly, condom trace evidence does not have the perpetrator identification capability of a DNA profile, but it can substantiate a victim's allegation that a sexual assault took place by proving evidence of penetration and thus of the crime. It can also help identify a serial rapist by linking common condom types. For these reasons, finding, packaging, and preserving the condom trace evidence at sexual assault scenes is an important endeavor.

13.5.1 Collecting and Packaging Condom Evidence

Finding a condom at a sexual assault scene can be important evidence that can link a suspect to the scene and thus the crime. The DNA profile from the material collected from the condom should provide a DNA profile of not only the suspect but also the victim (vaginal DNA), which places the suspect in direct contact with the victim. There is little more convincing evidence. The following is a list of guidelines for collecting and packaging the condom evidence.

- Wear powder-free gloves to protect against bloodborne pathogen infection and to avoid leaving particulates similar to those used by some condom brands.
- Package condom evidence in a breathable box or envelope. If possible, dry wet semen before packaging.
- Package investigator's evidence collecting gloves separately and submit them with the evidence so that the forensic laboratory can verify that the gloves did not leave behind any particulates.
- Locate any used condom and foil packaging. DNA from the victim on the outside proves that the condom was used with the victim and seminal fluid from the assailant on the inside will be the best evidence against a suspect.
- Save empty condom packets for fingerprint analysis.

- Wipe the inside of the condom package with a clean cotton swab that will become the standard for comparison with traces recovered from the victim and the suspect. The inside of an empty condom package should not contain fingerprints but might contain lubricant, spermicide, and particulate residues.

13.6 Quality Assurance at the Scene

As a consequence of the NAS report, accreditation of forensic units is a growing concern (see pp. 195–200 in Reference [32]). A trademark of accreditation is the unit's quality assurance program, which ensures that its work product meets minimum quality standards.

Establishing a quality assurance program for all aspects of the team's work product is essential, for an indepth discussion of quality programs, see Chapter 23.

References

1. M. N. Hockmeister, B. Budowle, R. Sparkes, O. Rudin, C. Gehrig, M. Thali, et al. 1999. Validation studies of an immunochromatographic 1-step test for the forensic identification of human blood. *Journal of Forensic Sciences*, 44(3):597–602.
2. I. Sato, K. Kojima, T. Yamasaki, K. Yoshida, M. Yoshiike, S. Takano, et al. 2004. Rapid detection of semenogelin by one-step immunochromatographic assay for semen identification. *Journal of Immunological Methods*, 287(1–2):137–145.
3. J. B. Old, B. A. Schweers, P. W. Boonlayangoor, and K. A. Reich. 2009. Developmental validation of RSID-saliva: A lateral flow immunochromatographic test strip for the forensic detection of saliva. *Journal of Forensic Sciences*, 54(4):866–873.
4. E. Zedlewski and M. B. Murphy. 2006. DNA analysis for "minor" crimes: A major benefit for law enforcement. *NIJ Journal*, January (253). Available at: nij.gov/journals/253/dna_analysis.html.
5. M. Stoilovic. 1991. Detection of semen and blood stains using Polilight as a light source. *Forensic Science International*, 51(2):289–296.
6. E. Johnston, C. E. Ames, K. E. Dagnall, J. Foster, and B. E. Daniel. 2008. Comparison of presumptive blood test kits including Hexagon. *Journal of Forensic Sciences*, 53(3):687–689.
7. S. S. Tobe, N. Watson, and N. N. Daeid. 2007. Evaluation of six presumptive tests for blood: Their specificity, sensitivity, and effect on high molecular weight DNA. *Journal of Forensic Sciences*, 52(1):102–109.
8. T. Nieman. 1989. Detection based on solution-phase chemiluminescence systems. In: J. W. Birks (ed.), *Chemiluminescence and Photochemical Reaction Detection in Chromatography.* New York, NY: VCH Publishers, pp. 99–123.
9. T. I. Quickenden and P. D. Cooper. 2001. Increasing the specificity of the forensic luminol test for blood. *Luminescence*, 16:251–253.
10. W. Specht. 1937. Die chemiluminesenz des hamins, ein hilfsmittel zur affindung und erkennung forensisch wichturger blutspuren. *Angewandte Chemie*, 50:155–157.
11. L. Dilbeck. 2006. Use of Bluestar forensic in lieu of luminol at crime scenes. *Journal of Forensic Identification*, 56(5):706–720.
12. R. S. Higaki and W. M. S. Philip. 1976. A study of the sensitivity and specificity of phenolphthalein as an indicator test for blood. *Canadian Society Forensic Science Journal*, 9(3):97–102.
13. W. Bodziak. *European Meeting for Shoe Print and Tool Mark Examiners, Helsinki, Finland*, May 8–11, 1995. Available at: http://www.bvda.com/EN/prdctinf/LCV_Bodziak.html (accessed February 4, 2011).

14. RSID-Blood. Available at: http://www.ifi-test.com/pdf/RSID-Blood_Poster.pdf (accessed May 2009).
15. A. W. Butch. 2000. Dilution protocols for detection of hook effects/prozone phenomenon. *Clinical Chemistry*, 46:1719–1720.
16. N.A. 2010. Developmental validation of a novel lateral flow strip for the rapid identification of human blood. Rapid Stain Identification-blood, RSID-Blood™. Available at: http://www.ifi-test.com/pdf/BloodValid.pdf (accessed February 4, 2011).
17. G. F. Sensabaugh. 1978. The quantitative AP test. A statistical analysis of endogenous and postcoital AP in the vagina. *Journal of Forensic Sciences*, 23(4):833–843.
18. A. B. Gutman and E. B. Gutman. 1941. Quantitative relations of a prostatic component (acid phosphatase) of human seminal fluid. *Endocrinology*, 28:115..
19. S. S. Kind. 1957. The use of the acid phosphatase test in searching for seminal stains. *Journal of Criminal Law, Criminology, and Police Science*, 47:597.
20. H. C. B. Graves, George F. Sensabaugh, and E. T. Blake. 1985. Postcoital detection of a male-specific semen protein—Application to the investigation of rape. *New England Journal of Medicine*, 312:338–343.
21. G. F. Sensabaugh. 1978. The isolation and characterization of a semen-specific protein from human seminal plasma: A potential new marker for semen identification. *Journal of Forensic Sciences*, 23:106–115.
22. M. C. Wang, L. A. Valenzuela, G. P. Murphy, and T. M. Chu. 1976. Purification of a human prostate specific antigen. *Investigative Urology*, 17:159–163.
23. R. W. Woods. 1919. Communications secretes au Moyen de Rayons Lumineux. *Journal de Physique (Theoretical and Applied)*, 9:77.
24. Abacus Diagnostics. Semen identification test. Available at: http://www.abacusdiagnostics.com/semen.htm (accessed February 5, 2011).
25. IFI Independent Forensics. RSID™-semen. Available at: http://www.ifi-test.com/rsid_semen.php (accessed February 5, 2011).
26. R. Radtkey, L. Feng, M. Muralhidar, M. Duhon, D. Canter, D. DiPierro, S. Fallon, E. Tu, K. McElfresh, M. Nerenberg, and R. Sosnowski. 2000. Rapid, high fidelity analysis of simple sequence repeats on an electronically active DNA microchip. *Nucleic Acids Research*, 28(7):E17.
27. Sirchie website. EZ-dry swab box kit. Available at: http://store.sirchie.com/EZ-DRY-Swab-Box-Kit-P1687.aspx (accessed February 5, 2011).
28. A. Horii, M. Emi, N. Tomita, T. Nishide, M. Ogawa, T. Mori, and K. Matsubara.1987. Primary structure of human pancreatic alpha-amylase gene: Its comparison with human salivary alpha-amylase gene. *Gene*, 60(1):57–64.
29. D. L. Gumucio, K. Wiebauer, R. M. Caldwell, L. C. Samuelson, and M. H. Meisler. 1988. Concerted evolution of human amylase genes. *Molecular and Cellular Biology*, 8(3):1197–1205.
30. Phadebas website. Available at: http://www.phadebasamylasetest.com/applications/forensic;jsessionid = 29714F000D3F85643F5ACA4D0BE33A9D (accessed February 4, 2011).
31. V. Castella, N. Dimo-Simonin, C. Brandt-Casadevall, N. Robinson, M. Saugy, F. Taroni, and P. Mangin. 2006. Forensic identification of urine samples: A comparison between nuclear and mitochondrial DNA markers. *International Journal of Legal Medicine*, 120(2):67–72.
32. Committee on Identifying the Needs of the Forensic Science Community, Committee on Science, Technology and Law Policy and Global Affairs, Committee on Applied and Theoretical Statistics, Division on Engineering and Physical Sciences, National Research Council of the National Academies. 2009. *Strengthening Forensic Science in the United States: A Path Forward.* Washington, DC: The National Academies Press, p. 161, 195–200.
33. R. Martz, B. Donnelly, D. Fetterolf, L. Lasswell, G. W. Hine, and W. L. Hearn. 1991. The use of hair analysis to document a cocaine overdose before death. *Journal of Analytical Toxicology*, 15:279–281.

34. *Wikipedia*. Forensic palynology. Available at: http://en.wikipedia.org/wiki/Pollen#Forensic_palynology (accessed June 2, 2009).
35. R. D. Blackledge and L. R. Cabiness. 1983. Examination for petroleum based lubricants in evidence from rapes and sodomies. *Journal of Forensic. Sciences,* 28:451–462.

Workshop 6: Biological Fluids at the Scene—Blood

W6.1 Introduction: Identifying Blood at the Scene

The purpose of this workshop is to expand on the concept of blood at crime scenes in order to enhance one's ability to choose the probative evidence at the scene. There are essentially three ways to recognize blood at the scene of a crime:

- Visual examination
  - Unaided eye
  - Aided eye
- Chemical testing
- Immunological testing

W6.2 Visual Examination

The fallacy is that blood is always a reddish color. Nothing could be further from the truth. A second fallacy is that it is always visible to the unaided eye. This, too, is not completely true. There is no such thing as invisible blood, but the fact is that blood may be present in such dilute or small amounts that the eye cannot perceive its presence. The reason is that this is the region of the electromagnetic spectrum where the human eye is least sensitive. In situations where someone attempts to clean the scene, the blood may be extremely dilute and barely, if at all, visible to the naked eye. Although clean-up is rarely successful, the end result is crime scene that "appears" clean.

W6.2.1 Exercise 1: Using the ALS to Locate Blood

Always wear goggles when using the ALS.

The ALS is the first tool used to determine whether something might be blood. Blood absorbs light at 415 and 455 nm on the ALS. Because it absorbs light at these wavelengths, it appears black or dark on a light surface. On different colored or dark surfaces, the ALS may have minimal value in locating the blood. Here, the ALS may prove valuable because the color of the background may be effectively minimized by selecting appropriate wavelengths, which might increase the contrast between the background and the bloodstains. One value of the ALS is its ability to help the investigator differentiate among various substances that appear like blood but are not.

W6.2.1.1 Procedure

- Several "red" or "reddish" substances have been put on walls.
- Use the ALS (wearing clear goggles, tune the ALS to 415, 455 nm, CSS and 300–400 nm, respectively) to highlight the stains.
- After each wavelength, photograph the results.

Table W6.1 Using Light to Differentiate between Bloodstains and Tomato-Based Food Stains

Substance	415 nm	455 nm	CSS	300–400 nm
1				
2				
3				
4				
5				
6				
7				

- Record your results in Table W6.1. For example, if the substances fluoresces indicate that and the color of the fluorescence.
- Show your photographs and tabulated results to an instructor for grading.

W6.3 Chemical Testing

Always wear protective and appropriate facial masks and goggles when working with chemicals.

Unlike most physical evidence identified at the crime scene, biological evidence is truly multitasking because it has the potential of providing multiple and disparate pieces of investigative information.

- The simple fact that biological evidence might contain DNA means it has the potential of specifically identifying who left the evidence at the scene. The information is not available immediately, though; so as an immediate investigative tool, it minimal value. Because it does not provide the crime scene investigator with information that can help during the scene investigation.
- The location of biological evidence at the scene, such as a bloodstain spatter patterns, can help pinpoint the sequence of events of the crime.
- By identifying how long a particular stain has been at the scene, the investigator can estimate how long the scene has been there, which might differ from the postmortem interval (PMI) determined during the autopsy.

W6.3.1 Exercise 2: Presumptive Identification of Blood at the Scene

In the presence of peroxide, the heme moiety in blood (hemoglobin) reacts with organic dyes to produce a colored or luminescent product.

W6.3.1.1 KM Reagent

W6.3.1.1.1 Preparation of KM Reagent

Materials required

Phenolphthalein: 2 g
Sodium hydroxide or potassium hydroxide: 20 g
Distilled water: 100 ml
3% Hydrogen peroxide (in a dropper bottle)

Reflux the first three ingredients with 20 g of zinc until solution becomes colorless (2–3 h). Store this stock solution in a dark bottle under refrigeration with some added zinc to keep it in the reduced form. (Consult with safety officer for the disposal of zinc.)

W6.3.1.1.2 KM Procedure: Two-Stage Method The working solution is the stock solution or a 1:5 dilution of the stock solution in ethanol. An essential aspect of the test is to use controls: positive control (bloodstain) and negative control (unstained material).

- Swab, scrape, or cut a piece of a suspected bloodstain.
- Apply one or two drops of phenolphthalein solution.
- Add a similar amount of 3% hydrogen peroxide to the sampling.
- Record the time it takes to form a pink color.

W6.3.1.1.3 KM Procedure: Three-Stage Method

- The working solution is the stock solution or a 1:5 dilution of the stock solution in distilled water.
- Swab, scrape, or cut a piece of a suspected bloodstain.
- Using a moist filter paper or cotton-tipped swab, press against the stain to dissolve a small amount onto the tip of the swab.
- Apply in sequence: one or two drops of ethanol (or methanol), a drop of phenolphthalein, and finally a drop of 3% hydrogen peroxide to the swab.
- Record the time it takes to form a color.

W6.3.1.1.4 KM Test Interpretation A rapidly developing bright pink color indicates a positive test. Do not allow the test to continue beyond 30 s. Color will develop without the presence of blood on standing [1].

W6.3.1.2 TMB Reagent

W6.3.1.2.1 Preparation of TMB Reagent

Materials required

TMB: 2 g
Glacial acetic acid: 100 mL

Or

TMB: 0.06 g
Absolute ethanol: 30 mL
3% Hydrogen peroxide

W6.3.1.2.2 TMB Procedure

- Swab, scrape, or cut a piece of suspected bloodstain
- Apply one drop of TMB solution
- Add a drop of hydrogen peroxide to the sampling
- Record the time it takes to form a color

W6.3.1.2.3 TMB Test Interpretation A rapidly developing blue-green color—30s—indicates a positive test. The color will develop in the absence of blood on standing [2].

W6.3.1.3 Luminol

W6.3.1.3.1 Preparation of Luminol (3-aminophthalhydrazide)

Materials to prepare solution A

Luminol: 1.0 g
Sodium carbonate: 50 g
Distilled water: 500 mL
Materials to prepare solution B

Sodium perborate: 7.0 g
Distilled water: 500 mL

Working solution for luminol is solution A + solution B: This must be used immediately.

W6.3.1.3.2 Luminol Procedure

- Prespraying with a solution of 2% sulfosalicylic acid will fix the stain and prevent dissolution and subsequent running.
- Allow the area to dry.
- Setup the camera and tripod.
- Darken the room.
- Take a test photograph at an exposure of 2 min using the "Bulb" setting on the camera. Adjust aperture and exposure time so that approximately 2 min is used to record the luminal.
- Spray reagent working solution over suspected bloodstain in complete darkness.

W6.3.1.3.3 Luminol Test Interpretation The reagent luminesces in the presence of bloodstains. Flashes of light indicate a false positive reaction. The test will give a false positive with certain metals—copper is an example [3].

W6.3.1.4 BlueStar™

BlueStar™ is an optimized formulation of luminol. It comes in tablet form. Two tablets are dissolved in approximately 8 oz. of water. The luminescence observed lasts longer and is more intense than for most luminol formulations.

W6.3.2 Exercise 3: Finding "Invisible" Bloodstains at the Scene: BlueStar™

The purpose of this exercise is for students to learn how to use BlueStar™ to locate dried blood at crime scenes and to photograph the results. The preparation of the BlueStar™ reagent is simply a matter of completely dissolving two tablets in 8 oz. of water. The reagent should be used immediately.

W6.3.2.1 Procedure

- Prespray the area using 2% 5-sulfosalicylic acid. This fixes the blood. (Bloodstains can also be stabilized by spraying with either methanol (poison) or a 2% 5-sulfosalicylic acid solution—recommended.)
- After fixing the bloodstain, darken the room.
- Photograph the area using the "Bulb" function on the camera and the flash (if necessary).
- This might require several test photographs (prepare to hold the shutter open for 2 min) to obtain an adequate overlay of the luminescing blood.
- With the lens still open, spray the BlueStar™ on the area under investigations.
- Allow the lens to stay open for approximately 2 min while spraying to keep the luminescence active. Do not spray the BlueStar™ on an area that was not previously fixed.
- Spray an area that is suspected of having been previously cleaned of blood.
- Photograph the luminescence.
- Show the photograph to an instructor for grading.

W6.4 Immunological Testing: Identifying Human Blood at the Scene

Newer tests for identifying blood, semen, and saliva have been developed using lateral flow immunochromatography. These tests use antibodies made specifically against proteins found in forensically relevant fluids: blood, semen, and saliva. These tests are only commercially available in kits in a card or cassette format. Two of the kits for blood are ABA HemaTrace and RSID™-Blood cards. One advantage these kits have over the chemical reagents for detecting blood is that they will identify human blood (one kit has a false positive result with ferret blood). See Workshop V-I.

W6.4.1 Exercise 4: Identifying Human Blood

The purpose of this exercise is to demonstrate how to identify human blood using test kit immunochromatography cards. After a demonstration, students will work in pairs to identify human bloodstains having varying amounts of blood.

W6.4.1.1 Procedure

- Three stains containing 5 µL of human blood of different dilutions (1/10, 1/100, 1/1000) are provided on clean cotton swabs.
- Following the directions in the kits, dissolve the entire amount of blood in the solution provided in the kit.
- Follow the directions in the kits and add the solution to the cassette.
- After the appropriate time suggested by the kits' directions, examine the card.
- Fill out Table W6.2
- Photograph the results.
- Show the photographs and the filled-out table to an instructor for grading.

W6.5 Nonblood Evidence at the Scene: Detecting Sugars Using HemaStix™ Strips

W6.5.1 HemaStix™ Strips

HemaStix™ strips have a pad impregnated with TMB. Although these strips give a positive test with blood, the reaction is a single step, which means there is a heightened possibility of obtaining a false positive test result.

W6.5.2 Sugar-Containing Stains

Scenes of crimes have different types of stains that can often be mistaken for blood. One of these occurs from spilled or sprayed soda pop, such as Coke or Pepsi. These stains can be presumptively identified using Benedict's reaction, which is for reducing the sugars. Sugar stains will not react with chemical tests for blood or with immunochromatographic cards.

Table W6.2 Immunochromatography: Exercise 4 Fill-In Table

Sample Number	Lines Observed 1: strong or weak 2: both strong 3: one strong and one weak	Interpretation (Human Blood: Y/N)
1		
2		
3		

References

1. R. S. Higaki and W. M. S. Philip. 1976. A study of the sensitivity and specificity of phenolphthalein as an indicator test for blood. *Canadian Society of Forensic Science Journal*, 9(3):97–102.
2. D. Garner, 1976. An evaluation of tetramethylbenzidine as a presumptive test for blood. *Journal of Forensic Sciences*, 21(4):816–821.
3. L. T. Lytle and D. G Hedgecock. 1978. Chemiluminescence in the visualization of forensic bloodstains. *Journal of Forensic Sciences*, 23(3):550–562.

Workshop 7: Drying Time of Blood

W7.1 Introduction

Temperature, air flow, and humidity affect the time it takes for blood to dry. Knowing how long blood has been at a scene can help determine when the crime took place.

W7.2 Exercise 1: Drying Time of Blood Droplets

In this exercise, we will examine how temperature and humidity affect the drying time of blood. Additionally, we will examine how pools of blood dry.

W7.2.1 Procedure

- Working in pairs and using a Pasteur pipette, drop single blood droplets onto several different nonporous surfaces (outlined below).
- Place one into each of the following.
  - Chamber of known humidity and temperature
  - A refrigerator
  - Outside in the sun
    Record the humidity and temperature.
  - Outside in the shade
  - Inside on a windowsill in the sun
  - Inside on a windowsill in the shade
- Record the time each drop is placed.
- Examine each droplet as it dries.
- Record the time the droplet is completely dry.
- Fill out Table W7.1

Table W7.1 Drying Time of Blood Droplets Exercise 1 Fill-In Table

Starting Time	Time of Edge Crust Formation	Time When Droplet Is Dry	Calculate Drying Time
Humidity chamber			
Refrigerator			
Outside in sun			
Outside in shade			
Inside on windowsill in sun			
Inside on windowsill in shade			

Table W7.2 Drying Time of Blood Pool Exercise 2 Fill-In Table

Starting Time	Time of Edge Crust Formation	Time of Top Surface to Form Crust	Time of Undersurface to Dry	Calculate Complete Drying Time
Blood pool on carpet				
Blood pool on linoleum				

W7.3 Exercise 2: Drying Time of a Blood Pool

The purpose of this exercise is to illustrate how long it takes for large quantities of blood to dry.

W7.3.1 Procedure

- Pour 1 L of blood from a beaker onto two surfaces.
  - Thick-pile plush carpet
  - Linoleum floor
- Repeat the drying experiment above and fill in Table W7.2
- Record the time it takes to form the stages in the drying process.

Workshop 8: Locating Semen and Saliva at the Scene

W8.1 Introduction

Semen is a particularly important piece of evidence. As the male ejaculatory fluid, it is linked to sexual activity. It also has DNA present which means that there is the distinct possibility that the semen donor can be identified unequivocally. If the semen results from criminal activity, its presence is all that more important. Luckily for investigators, commercially available ALSs can easily highlight semen at the scene. No longer do investigators need to use the tactile method of finding "crusty" stains on bed sheets, perform AP mapping techniques, or use UV light. Saliva, too, is a biological fluid that is often associated with sexual assault crimes and also with other violent crimes. Typically, it is found in the laboratory associated with sexual assault evidence. It is also important evidence in biting incidents.

W8.2 Exercise 1: Using the ALS to Find Semen at Crime Scenes

Forensically important substances will fluoresce to varying degrees under the ALS at various wavelengths. The CSS setting on the MiniScope™ is the best setting for finding semen. The most commonly occurring use is to locate semen and salvia at the scene. The instructor will demonstrate how to use the ALS to locate dried semen stains.

Each pair of students will be given swatches of white-and-black T-shirt material containing semen stains diluted to 1,000,000 times.

- Procedures
  - Set the ALS on the CSS setting (if using the MiniScope™) or on 450 nm if using another ALS.
  - Put on orange goggles.

Table W8.1 Dilutions of Semen

Dilution of Semen	CSS Setting	415 nm	300–400 nm	535 nm
Neat				
1/100				
1/1000				
1/10,000				
1/100,000				
1/1,000,000				

- Darken the room.
- Use the ALS to examine the semen stains using the CSS setting (450 nm), 415, 300–400, and 535 nm wavelengths.
- Fill in Table W8.1 for the white-and-black T-shirt material.
- Photograph the ALS highlighted stains.
- Show the photographs to an instructor for grading.

In addition to the ALS, immunochromatographic cards have been manufactured to permit the identification of semen and saliva (Chapter 13). These cards work in the same way as the cards for identifying the human blood (Workshop 6) and are not demonstrated in this workshop.

W8.3 Exercise 2: Using the ALS to Find Saliva at Crime Scenes

Saliva can be found at scenes for various reasons. A sneeze or a cough produces a salivary aerosol. Additionally, an injury to the mouth can produce a salivary aerosol possibly mixed with blood. It is possible to identify the presence of salivary components in a two ways, the ALS is the most commonly used at scenes. Usually, saliva has a weaker fluoresce than as semen. Vaginal secretions also fluoresce under the ALS CSS setting.

The instructor will demonstrate how to locate semen, saliva, and vaginal secretions on a bed sheet using the ALS.

- Procedure
- Each pair of students will be given swatches of white and dark bed sheet material containing saliva stains diluted to 1,000,000 times. Follow the same procedure as for semen stains in Exercise 1 (Section W8.2.2). Fill out Table W8.2
- Circle the point at which you can no longer detect the saliva on the white-and-dark bed sheet at each of the wavelengths used.

Table W8.2 Dilutions of Saliva

Dilution of Saliva	CSS Setting	415 nm	300–400 nm	535 nm
Neat				
1/100				
1/1000				
1/10,000				
1/100,000				
1/1,000,000				

W8.4 Questions

- In 1000 words or less, explain the difference in sensitivity of the ALS with respect to locating semen versus saliva on fabric material at crime scenes.
- In 1000 words or less, discuss case types (homicide, burglary, etc.) in which you might expect to find saliva at a crime scene. Include in this discussion the specific locations where you would look. Do not limit yourself to the bedroom and bedding fabric. You might also consider mixtures with other body fluids.

Introduction to Bloodstain Pattern Analysis
The Basics

14

14.1 Introduction

The purpose of this chapter is not to create bloodstain pattern analysis (BPA) experts but, instead, to introduce students and novice scene scientists/investigators to the topic. Hopefully, using this as a base, they should recognize critical patterns when they encounter them and document them properly so that the potential value of the evidence is not lost. The take-home lesson of this chapter is that the most inexperienced student or novice scene scientist/investigator should realize that no bloodstain pattern should be overlooked or go unarchived photographically and possibly videographically. Sketching is not a satisfactory method to archive bloodstain patterns except to show where they are and to record their breadth and width (see Chapter 15).

Like glass, blood evidence can provide investigators with a range of investigative information. Data gathered from blood evidence were discussed in Chapter 13 and some are considered below:

- Origin/source of blood at the scene (i.e., whose blood?)
- Distance from a target
- Direction of travel
- Energy of impact
- Handedness
- Relative position and movement of victim and assailant
- Minimum number of blows
- Sequence of events

Each of the above is a topic worth considering in depth, and its forensic value should be understood by students and scene scientists/investigators. Chapter 13 discusses what some consider the most important reason for finding, collecting, and preserving blood evidence at the scene—DNA. It can determine the presence of someone, to the exclusion of everyone else. For this reason, blood and the patterns it forms—blood evidence—must never be overlooked or considered lightly during an investigation. Knowing whose blood made a particular pattern is important. Understanding how the pattern formed can also provide a critical piece of investigative information. Learning whose blood was where at the scene takes time, but BPA can be done on the spot. For examining and analyzing the blood evidence, the following two factors should be considered: (i) whose blood it is, and (ii) the circumstances of blood deposition.

The latter category—the circumstances of blood deposition—consumes the remainder of this chapter simply because bloodstain patterns can be more valuable for the investigation or to the medical examiner than knowing whose blood it is. Sometimes, there is no doubt about whose blood it is, simply by understanding the pattern and its location. Other than the first in the list of eight reasons, the others refer to more esoteric questions concerning how and why the blood ended up where it was.

Like the scene investigation itself, BPA at the scene is deceptively easy. So, before considering the topic in more detail, it might be helpful to present, arguably, the historical presence and growth of BPA into the criminal justice system and specifically law enforcement in the United States. This is a different discussion from the traditional historical account, where each investigator's contribution to the field is considered in some depth. The traditional historical account has been considered by others [1,2].

14.2 Historical Perspectives: BPA in the United States

The premise of bloodstain pattern analysts (agencies)* is that when blood leaves the human body or a blood-covered object, it produces interpretable patterns. Bloodstains patterns occur in multiple scene types, and investigators expect to find them at scenes of violent crimes and suicides. Interpreting these patterns reliably depends on the training and experience of the individual analyst. While not a new discipline, much like crime scene investigation in general, BPA has attracted individuals having diverse educational and professional backgrounds. Such diversity seems shocking for a discipline supposedly having a basis in science [4]. Shouldn't science be practiced by scientists? The NAS report [5] questions the scientific basis of pattern evidence, including BPA, because conclusions are seemingly based more on experience than on scientific principle, even if the underlying basis of the conclusions is science-based.

Much of forensics—as defined in Chapter 1—is an amalgamation or partnership of forensic scientists and law enforcement professionals participating cooperatively in the American criminal justice system: one is the scientist and the other the investigator. Crime scene investigation is likely the largest subdiscipline of forensics, where science is practiced mostly by nonscientists and scientists, each often performing the same function. Certainly, BPA belongs in that paradigm. This explains why lay investigators, who also perform science at the scene, quickly adopted BPA as an investigative purview.† Criminalists who participate in scene investigations also embraced BPA. It might be interesting to trace how such a diverse group of professionals became so entrenched in the BPA arena.

Arguably, this began in the United States at the University of California Berkley with the work of Dr. Paul Kirk, a biochemist and respected forensic scientist. Dr. Kirk was hired to investigate the 1950s murder of Dr. Sam Sheppard's wife. Sheppard was arrested and convicted of the crime. He claimed that an intruder entered his house and murdered his wife. Dr. Kirk went to the scene, and wrote a brief concerning what he considered evidence of someone else at the scene [7]. A book written by Sheppard's son, Sam Reese Sheppard, and attorney Cynthia Cooper, *Mockery of Justice: The True Story of the Sam Sheppard Murder Case* [8], produced DNA evidence suggesting that Kirk's interpretation was correct. Kirk's work in the case has become a legendary example of BPA. Interestingly, Kirk's work went seemingly unnoticed by police officials and crime scene investigators for some reason.

* Agency: ". . . an individual, a law enforcement department, a private company, or a government or private laboratory . . . that provides BPA as one of its functions" [3].

† Purview: "the range or limit of authority, competence, responsibility, concern, or intention" [6].

Perhaps, law enforcement did not agree with his interpretations. Perhaps, it considered his work esoteric and beyond the skills of lay professionals.

The next important work in this area was a booklet by Herbert MacDonell and L. Bialousz, *Flight Characteristics and Bloodstain Patterns of Human Blood* [9]. MacDonell's experiments and those he borrowed from other investigators—for example, the work of Balthazard et al. in 1939 [10]—caught the attention of law enforcement. MacDonell offered workshops designed to train law enforcement officers how to interpret bloodstain patterns, the result being a proliferation of individuals working on BPA cases throughout the world. Importantly, the simplicity of these workshops spawned a cadre* of self-styled experts who offered workshops and published books and articles. Criminalists were also attracted to the discipline, much like they are to crime scene investigation.

MacDonell's workshops and those that followed presented BPA in an easy-to-follow, format, which was and continues to be nonrigorous. Initially, there were no written examinations or other traditional-grading mechanisms, which meant failing was not likely. In a sense, these workshops were like modern infomercials. Everyone who completed the workshop received a certificate of attendance, giving many a sense of expertise. By requiring not much more other than completing a week-long course, attendees left with the feeling that BPA was simple enough to practice.

Recognizing the need for a formal organization around which the growing hoard of BPA analysts could communicate, MacDonell was instrumental in establishing the International Association of Bloodstain Pattern Analysts (IABPA), founded in 1983 [12]. On-going workshops and a growing membership in the IABPA resulted in the continued proliferation of lay investigators, many having dubious scientific and/or investigative credentials, who performed BPA in casework for both sides of the adversarial system. Their opinion testimony has played a critical role in determining the innocence or guilt.

The books, newsletters, and articles until recently have been geared to a law enforcement audience. These are uncomplicated. They use easy to understand, with nonscientific terminology. Some of the more recent publications are more scientific in nature, as shown in a recent IABPA newsletter [13].

The International Association of Investigators (IAI) initially considered BPA a part of its crime scene certification. At the time of this writing, the IAI made BPA its discipline and is now certifying individuals who meet its requirements. Although the 2009 NAS report [5] questions the scientific basis of BPA, practitioners dispute this, and Scientific Working Group on Bloodstain Pattern Analysis (SWGSTAIN) put together an extensive bibliography of relevant articles to counter possible legal challenges to BPA [14]. Even before the NAS report was published, however, Laber et al. [15] working in the Minnesota crime laboratory who have been active in bloodstain pattern research and education wrote that BPA is a scientific endeavor. The following quote was taken from the introduction and conclusion of their article, which preempted the NAS report. They warned BPA analysts to move quickly to strengthen the discipline. Concerning the dynamics of how blood patterns form, they wrote [15]:

> Relatively little however, has been documented about the dynamics of the blood transfer event. . .. BPA is a discipline that has relied heavily on the experience of the witness . . . *closer*

* Cadre: "a nucleus or core group especially of trained personnel able to assume control and to train others; *broadly*: a group of people having some unifying relationship" [11].

> *scrutiny of the methods used in BPA will highlight the relative lack of underpinning scientific research and validation studies.* (pp. 4, 11) [Emphasis added.]

As the number of cases involving BPA and the number of analysts increased, it became clear that standards were needed. In 2002, the FBI began sponsoring a professional group devoted to BPA, the SWGSTAIN, whose mission is

> ... to serve as a professional forum in which BPA practitioners and practitioners from related fields can discuss and evaluate methods, techniques, protocols, quality assurance, education, and research relating to BPA [16,17].

SWGSTAIN began formulating guidelines for practicing BPA. The logical place to begin was to standardize BPA terminology [18] in order to create a mechanism for communicating and to eliminate the confusing terminology from individuals who had published works on their own in the absence of a standard. Interestingly, the SWGSTAIN final version was not published until after publication of the NAS report in 2009. Before SWGSTAIN published its terminology, authors recognized how complicated BPA patterns could be and began using their own. A few examples will suffice to illustrate the point: Bevel and Gardner [1] use a classification system where the main categories are the Spatter Family, the Non-Spatter Family, and Complex Patterns; James et al. [19] include the categories of Passive, Spatter, and Altered; and Wonder [20] provides a flow diagram to assist in classifying the bloodstain patterns, where the main categories are spatter groups, spatters not a criteria, and composites. For now, SWGSTAIN's terminology is a welcome attempt at standardization. Importantly, it offers a terminological playing field from which BPA analysts and novices can communicate.

Table 14.1 has been adapted from the terminology listed on the SWGSTAIN Web site [18]. No photographs are associated with the table, but some examples are in the text and the Internet also has examples. Some are for the IABPA terminology [21]. The same Web site also lists the new SWGSTAIN terminology [22]. Laber et al. [15] filmed blood patterns as they formed (see also the MFRC Web site [23]).

14.3 Scientific Basis of BPA

If BPA has a basis in science, then testimony at trial should be admitted into evidence as long as the testifying expert analyst meets appropriate standards and has the appropriate credentials. So, what criteria should a competent BPA analyst meet? The BPA expert should understand the physics and mathematics relating to BPA, gained through education and experimentation with blood while applying the principles of the relevant scientific disciplines: biochemistry, fluid mechanics (dynamics), physics, chemistry, ballistics, and mathematics. These disciplines form the scientific basis of BPA, and their principles must explain why blood forms the patterns it does. If they cannot, then BPA does not have a basis in science and must be considered under the arts.

As the NAS report implies, someone's life depends on the reliability on the opinion of someone whose sole basis for that opinion is experience. This does not imply that BPA has no scientific basis or that the opinions rendered in court are incorrect. The scientific basis, although probably solid, must be proven: SWGSTAIN provides references designed to document the scientific basis of BPA [14]. The following discussion is designed as an overview of the disciplines relevant to BPA.

Table 14.1 2009 Recommended SWGSTAIN BPA Terminology

Terminology	Definition
Accompanying drop	A small blood drop produced as a by-product of drop formation.
Angle of impact	The acute angle (alpha), relative to the plane of a target, at which a blood drop strikes the target.
Altered stain	A bloodstain with characteristics that indicate a physical change has occurred.
Area of convergence	The area containing the intersections generated by lines drawn through the long axes of individual stains that indicates in two dimensions the location of the blood source.
Area of origin	The three-dimensional location from which spatter originated.
Backspatter pattern	A bloodstain pattern resulting from blood drops that traveled in the opposite direction of the external force applied; associated with an entrance wound created by a projectile.
Blood clot	A gelatinous mass formed by a complex mechanism involving red blood cells, fibrinogen, platelets, and other clotting factors.
Bloodstain	A deposit of blood on a surface.
Bloodstain pattern	A grouping or distribution of bloodstains that indicates through regular or repetitive form, order, or arrangement the manner in which the pattern was deposited.
Bubble ring	An outline within a bloodstain resulting from air in the blood.
Cast-off pattern	A bloodstain pattern resulting from blood drops released from an object due to its motion.
Cessation cast-off pattern	A bloodstain pattern resulting from blood drops released from an object due to its rapid deceleration.
Directionality	The characteristic of a bloodstain that indicates the direction blood was moving at the time of deposition.
Directional angle	The angle (gamma) between the long axis of a spatter stain and a defined reference line on the target.
Drip pattern	A bloodstain pattern resulting from a liquid that dripped into another liquid, at least one of which was blood.
Drip stain	A bloodstain resulting from a falling drop that formed due to gravity.
Drip trail	A bloodstain pattern resulting from the movement of a source of drip stains between two points.
Edge characteristic	A physical feature of the periphery of a bloodstain.
Expiration pattern	A bloodstain pattern resulting from blood forced by airflow out of the nose, mouth, or a wound.
Flow pattern	A bloodstain pattern resulting from the movement of a volume of blood on a surface due to gravity or movement of the target.
Forward spatter pattern	A bloodstain pattern resulting from blood drops that traveled in the same direction as the impact force.
Impact pattern	A bloodstain pattern resulting from an object striking liquid blood.
Insect stain	A bloodstain resulting from insect activity.
Mist pattern	A bloodstain pattern resulting from blood reduced to a spray of microdrops as a result of the force applied.
Parent stain	A bloodstain from which a satellite stain originated.
Perimeter stain	An altered stain that consists of the peripheral characteristics of the original stain.
Pool	A bloodstain resulting from an accumulation of liquid blood on a surface.

continued

Table 14.1 (Continued) 2009 Recommended SWGSTAIN BPA Terminology

Projected pattern	A bloodstain pattern resulting from the ejection of a volume of blood under pressure.
Satellite stain	A smaller bloodstain that originated during the formation of the parent stain as a result of blood impacting a surface.
Saturation stain	A bloodstain resulting from the accumulation of liquid blood in an absorbent material.
Serum stain	The stain resulting from the liquid portion of blood (serum) that separates during coagulation.
Spatter Stain	A bloodstain resulting from a blood drop dispersed through the air due to an external force applied to a source of liquid blood.
Splash pattern	A bloodstain pattern resulting from a volume of liquid blood that falls or spills onto a surface.
Swipe pattern	A bloodstain pattern resulting from the transfer of blood from a blood-bearing surface onto another surface, with characteristics that indicate relative motion between the two surfaces.
Target	A surface onto which blood has been deposited.
Transfer stain	A bloodstain resulting from contact between a blood-bearing surface and another surface.
Void	An absence of blood in an otherwise continuous bloodstain or bloodstain pattern.
Wipe pattern	An altered bloodstain pattern resulting from an object moving through a preexisting wet bloodstain.

Source: Adapted from FBI, Scientific Working Group on Bloodstain Pattern Analysis: Recommended terminology. *Forensic Science Communications*, 11(2), 2009. http://www2.fbi.gov/hq/lab/fsc/backissu/april2009/standards/2009_04_standards01.htm.

14.3.1 Biochemistry

To address the topic properly, one must understand the nature of blood, which requires knowledge of biochemistry and physics. As described in Chapter 13, blood is a tissue, a liquid/solid suspension of plasma and cells. The liquid fraction (plasma) is a water-based, complex mixture of dissolved proteins, salts, and other molecules. The solid fraction contains a variety of cell types. Thus, blood is classified as a viscoelastic* [24] non-Newtonian fluid† [25]. And understanding what happens to it after it leaves the human body, whether acted upon by a force or just passively dripping from an object, requires more than empirically observing how bloodstains form in a workshop setting or in the field.

* Viscoelastic: "having appreciable and conjoint viscous and elastic properties" [24].

† Non-Newtonian: "fluid whose flow properties differ in any way from those of Newtonian fluids. Most commonly the viscosity of non-Newtonian fluids is not independent of shear rate or shear rate history. However, there are some non-Newtonian fluids with shear-independent viscosity, that nonetheless exhibit normal stress-differences or other non-Newtonian behavior. Many salt solutions and molten polymers are non-Newtonian fluids, as are many commonly found substances such as ketchup, custard, toothpaste, starch suspensions, paint, blood, and shampoo. In a Newtonian fluid, the relation between the shear stress and the shear rate is linear, passing through the origin, the constant of proportionality being the coefficient of viscosity. In a non-Newtonian fluid, the relation between the shear stress and the shear rate is different, and can even be time-dependent. Therefore, a constant coefficient of viscosity cannot be defined" [25].

14.3.2 Physics

The laws of physics apply to blood droplets in flight. Fortunately, physics is a well-studied and documented discipline, and the direct application to blood droplet formation and its flight characteristics should be understood. The problem for BPA is that these considerations have been taken for granted and, aside from empirical studies in workshop settings, too few publications exist documenting that blood flight conforms to these laws. Certainly, one would expect that it does. The following sections examine briefly physics-related disciplines relevant to blood droplet movement.

14.3.2.1 Surface Tension

Blood plasma is composed of macromolecules, namely proteins and carbohydrates, and water and other dissolved salts and molecules. Its physical properties—viscosity and surface tension—are mainly determined by the dissolved macromolecules in the plasma. Surface tension* forces blood droplets (or any liquid) to maintain its integral structure, retain its shape, until acted on by a force greater than the force of surface tension. An external force creates blood spatter and thus the patterns observed at crime scenes. In the strictest sense, how the force is applied and its strength, determines the visual appearance of the resulting pattern.

14.3.2.2 Fluid Mechanics (Dynamics)

Fluid mechanics is the study of fluids (liquids, gases, and plasmas) and the forces that act on them.† Thus, its laws define blood in motion after being acted on by a force. Fluid mechanics, either fluid statics (fluids at rest) or fluid kinetics (fluids in motion), is a branch of continuum mechanics, which considers matter (including blood) as models in a continuum rather than as discrete atoms. Using fluid dynamic computations to describe blood in motion, for example, bloodstains formed from impact spatter, is particularly relevant. Typically, these computations fall into the purview of scientists who practice computational fluid dynamics.‡ The bottom line is that every drop of blood (or perhaps pattern of blood) at the crime scene can and perhaps should be described mathematically. Some publications exist, but a comprehensive study has not been done systematically.

14.3.2.3 Trajectory Analysis (Ballistics)

When a blood droplet leaves the human body under a force, it forms an arc, a path described mathematically. The droplet represents a projectile and its path is its trajectory. Much like

* Surface tension: "the attractive force exerted upon the surface molecules of a liquid by the molecules beneath that tends to draw the surface molecules into the bulk of the liquid and makes the liquid assume the shape having the least surface area" [26].

† Fluid mechanics: "a branch of mechanics dealing with the properties of liquids and gases" [27]. According to Wikipedia, "*Fluid mechanics* is the study of fluids and the forces on them. (Fluids include liquids, gases, and plasmas.) Fluid mechanics can be divided into fluid kinematics, the study of fluid motion, and fluid dynamics, the study of the effect of forces on fluid motion, which can further be divided into fluid statics, the study of fluids at rest, and fluid kinetics, the study of fluids in motion" [28].

‡ Computational fluid dynamics (CFD): "branch of fluid mechanics that uses numerical methods and algorithms to solve and analyze the problems that involve fluid flows" [29].

a bullet, the shape of the arc a blood droplet takes to its terminus depends on gravity, wind currents, temperature, humidity, and friction. In the absence of these external influences, the arc described by the blood droplet's path would be a parabola defined by a uniform, homogeneous gravitational force field. In the real world, such a singular effect is nonexistent. Air resistance (friction), drag, and nonuniform gravitational forces exert their influence on the path. So, in the real world, the path the droplet takes is not a true parabola, its trajectory reflecting the influences of drag and gravity.

*14.3.2.4 Gravitation (Gravity)**

Gravity is one of the four fundamental interactions of nature (which include strong and weak interactions, electromagnetism, and gravitation), where objects having mass attract one another [31]. Described by the general theory of relativity, it is a consequence of the curvature of space time that governs the motion of inertial objects and causes dispersed matter to coalesce, such as when the earth and other planets formed after the Big Bang. It is also the force that causes objects to fall to the ground when dropped. It keeps the planets in their orbits around the sun and the moon around the earth. Gravity's influence on blood droplets was mentioned earlier as affecting a droplet's trajectory (path) because it defines the path an object (blood droplet) takes (nongravitational influences such as drag not considered) until it finds its terminus. Thus, gravity is responsible for the natural consequence of fluid flow. Its influence is starkly apparent in the visual pattern of spattered blood at scenes as well as its pooling and flow.

14.3.2.5 Terminal Velocity

One area of study of BPA concerns the concept of terminal velocity, also a concept of fluid dynamics. A blood droplet reaches its terminal velocity (settling velocity) when its acceleration due to the downward force of gravity equals the upward force of drag. When a blood droplet's speed is constant, drag equals the droplet's weight, and its acceleration is zero. For bloodstains falling from identical heights and having a constant weight (volume), their terminal velocities will be identical. Similarly, when a blood droplet reaches its terminal velocity, the resulting stain, say on a hard flat surface, will have a constant diameter, regardless of the height from which it falls. Generally, terminal velocity occurs at approximately 20 ft., but empirical experiments (in student workshops at Penn State) show that bloodstain diameters change very little after falling approximately 7 ft. (see p. 21 in Reference [2]). This is illustrated in Figure 14.1, taken from the work by James and Eckert [2]. The cardboard, onto which the droplets fell, although smooth, had texture as evidenced by the formation of spines coming off of the parent drop and satellite droplets surrounding the parent drop. The scalloping edge characteristics of the droplets are also indicative of a textured surface.

* Gravity: "the gravitational attraction of the mass of the earth, the moon, or a planet for bodies at or near its surface *(2)* : a fundamental physical force that is responsible for interactions which occur because of mass between particles, between aggregations of matter (as stars and planets), and between particles (as photons) and aggregations of matter, that is 10^{-39} times the strength of the strong force, and that extends over infinite distances but is dominant over macroscopic distances especially between aggregations of matter—called also *gravitation, gravitational force*" [30].

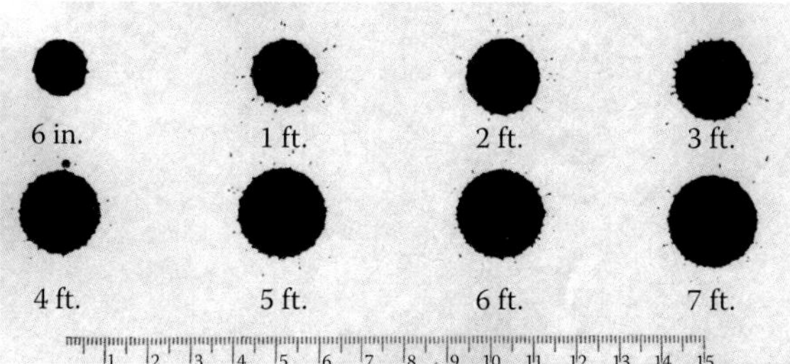

Single drops of blood falling onto smooth cardboard from various heights. Little change in diameter beyond 7 ft.

Figure 14.1 Height versus droplet stain diameter. (From S. H. James and W. G. Eckert. 1999. *Interpretation of Bloodstain Evidence at Crime Scenes*, 2nd edn. New York, NY: CRC Press. With permission.)

14.3.2.6 Centripetal Force

When wet blood is cast off a moving object (a weapon, hands, etc.), only one force is at work, centripetal force.* This is a force directed toward the center of the path of the moving object. When the adhesive forces holding the blood onto the object are greater than the centripetal force, the blood will fly off the object tangentially in a straight line. The resulting impact site is a direct link to the location of the object at the precise moment the blood left the object. The centripetal force should not be confused with centrifugal force,† which is a perceived force that does not exist. Blood cast off a weapon is an example of centripetal force (see Section 14.4.2.7.5).

14.4 Fundamental Principles of BPA

Empirical work has identified areas of BPA that many consider fundamental. These include the direction of movement of a bloodstain and the angle of impact, that is, the angle at which blood droplets strike a surface. Other fundamental characteristics affecting resulting bloodstain include shape, volume, and so on.

14.4.1 Blood Droplets and Surface Tension: Shape of a Falling Droplet

Foundational research by Pizzola et al. [34,35] helped define the property of blood in motion by documenting widely held beliefs about how blood droplet patterns form. Their work confirmed that the principle of fluid dynamics does apply to blood droplets in motion. This had been suspected but not proven. They demonstrated how surface tension affects falling droplets, as illustrated in Figure 14.2.

* Centripetal force: "the force that is necessary to keep an object moving in a curved path and that is directed inward toward the center of rotation <a string on the end of which a stone is whirled about exerts *centripetal force* on the stone>" [32].

† Centrifugal force: "the apparent force that is felt by an object moving in a curved path that acts outwardly away from the center of rotation" [33].

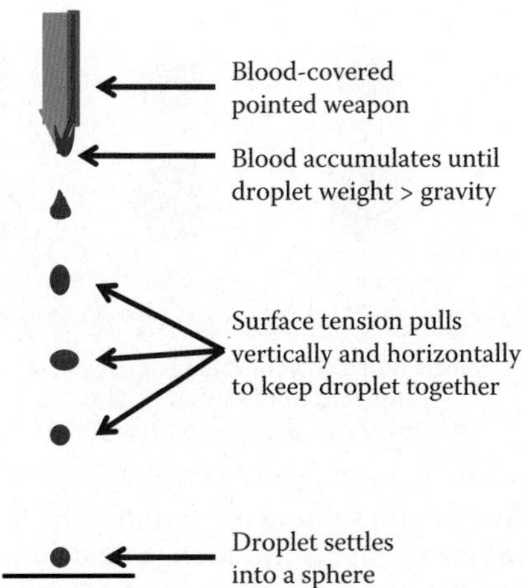

Figure 14.2 Effect of surface tension on the shape of blood droplets.

When blood drips from an object, whether passively or actively (bleeding wound), it accumulates at the leading edge of the object until so much is there that its weight overcomes the force of gravity. Then, the droplet leaves the surface and begins to fall and accelerates until it reaches its terminal velocity. At first, its shape is flattened (top photograph in the sequence in Figure 14.2). The surface tension pulls vertically and horizontally to keep the droplet together, eventually resulting in a spherical shape.

14.4.2 Defining the Direction of Blood Travel

14.4.2.1 Shape of Blood Droplets after Striking Surfaces

Eckert [36] illustrated what bloodstains should look like after striking a sloped surface (falling directly downward at 90°)—top left of Figure 14.3—it forms a circle, and, depending on the texture of the surface (smooth, textured, dusty, etc.), its edge characteristics exhibit varying amounts and intensity of scalloping. As the impact angle becomes more and more acute, the stain elongates, eventually forming a tail—bottom right of Figure 14.3, which points toward the direction the blood droplet was traveling. The tail is an easy way to determine the direction in which the blood droplets are moving. In Eckert's [36] experiment, blood droplets were dropped onto a hard surface and then photographed. Most BPA workshops have students work through a set of experiments that empirically demonstrate the shape blood takes as it hits surfaces at various angles. Students are asked to perform the experiment and to calculate the angle of impact (Workshop A).

14.4.2.2 Dynamics of Blood-Striking-Angled Surfaces

Pizzola et al. [34,35] showed what happens to blood when it strikes an angled surface. The snapshots from their video clearly demonstrate the process of droplet touch expansion and tail formation. Their work is shown in Figure 14.4.

14.4.2.3 Blood or Drip Trails

According to the SWGSTAIN terminology [18], a drip trail is, "A bloodstain pattern resulting from the movement of a source of drip stains between two points." When blood drips

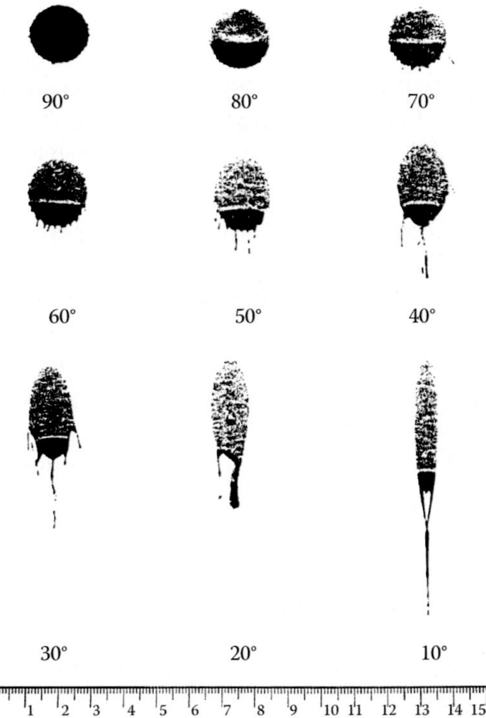

Figure 14.3 Shape of blood after striking surfaces at various angles. (From S. H. James and W. G. Eckert, *Interpretation of Bloodstain Evidence at Crime Scenes*, 2nd edn., New York: CRC Press, 1999. With permission.)

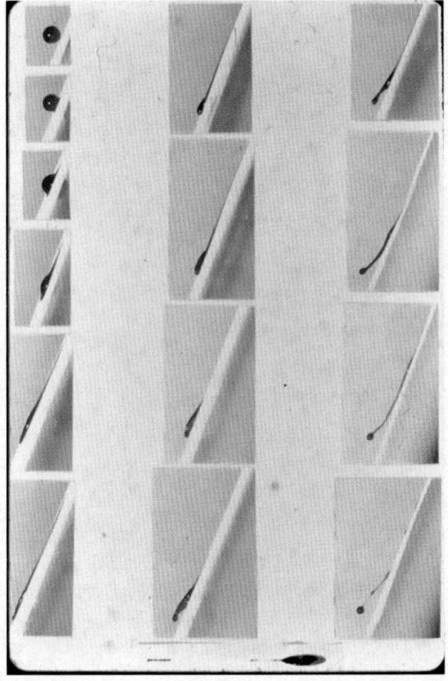

Figure 14.4 Snapshots from high-speed video of blood droplet hitting angled surface. (From P. A. Pizzola, S. Roth, and P. R. Deforest, *Journal of Forensic Sciences*, 31(1):50–64, 1986. With permission.)

from an object in motion, the resulting droplet shapes can range from nearly circular (falling nearly perpendicular to the surface) to elongated (hitting the surface at an angle) depending on the speed of the travel. If the droplets form elongated stains, determining the direction of travel is a simple matter of seeing which direction the stain points (see Section 14.4.2.1). However, for blood dripping from slowly moving objects, such as from someone walking with a bleeding wound, the droplets can be nearly circular and mimic droplets falling vertically from a height. An example of a drip trail is shown in Figure 14.5. Arrows show three droplets in the trail.

Determining the direction of these stains depends on closely examining edge characteristics, and this very much depends on the texture of the interacting surface—that is, how smooth it is. Generally, the edge characteristics of droplets in motion point in the direction in which the droplet is traveling, which in most circumstances would be the direction in which the person is moving. Depending on the texture of the interacting surface, the leading edge (the edge in the direction of travel) will be more or less uneven. On extremely smooth surfaces, the edge characteristics of the droplet are minimal or nearly nonexistent. On textured surfaces, edge characteristics are rough, that is, they exhibit scalloping and could have spines or satellite stains. When the edge characteristics are prominent, they are diagnostic of the direction in which someone who was bleeding, for example, was moving.

Relying on a single droplet in a drip trail to determine the direction of movement is a mistake, however, and can lead to misinterpretation or confusion. Figure 14.6 is an example of a droplet stain from a bleeding hand of someone who was walking. It has, at first glance, the appropriate diagnostic edge characteristics: scalloping on the left, suggesting it originated from someone moving from right to left. On closer inspection, however, edge

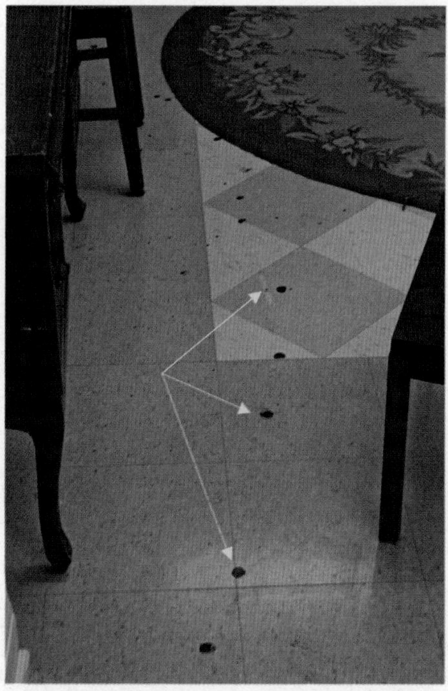

Figure 14.5 Drip trail. (Photograph by Robert C. Shaler.)

Figure 14.6 Blood droplet in blood drip trail. (Photograph by Robert C. Shaler.)

scalloping is also present on the right edge—in the lighter area of the droplet in Figure 14.6. Interpretation of such edge characteristics can be confusing because the blood concentrated on the left side of the droplet suggesting that it lies on a floor slanting left. In truth, the floor is horizontal, and the lighter clear area resulted from the aqueous droplet being repelled by wax on a freshly waxed floor. Closer inspection of the light area on the right side of the droplet shows scalloping and small satellite stains, the latter suggesting movement from left to right. This is the correct interpretation. Interpreting the droplet as moving from right to left would have been incorrect. If other stains in the trail were equally confusing, the logical interpretation should be inconclusive.

On highly textured surfaces, such as a wooden porch, scalloping, spines, and satellite stains are common, and determining the direction of travel is relatively straightforward. But even under these circumstances, using a single stain to determine the direction of travel is prone to error. For example, if a droplet hits a particularly rough area, it could result in edge characteristics on all sides of the droplet stain. Again, choosing several stains is the proper technique for determining the direction of travel of a blood trail.

14.4.2.4 Shape and Size of Bloodstains

The shape of bloodstains is dependent not only on the angle at which it impacts the surface, but also on the characteristics of the surface it impacts: texture, absorptive properties, and thickness. Figure 14.7 shows blood droplet stains on T-shirt material (top photograph) and on a thick, absorptive cotton towel (bottom photograph). Generally, the rougher the surface the greater its texture and the more disrupted the resulting droplet stain will appear. In the upper stain, on T-shirt material, the edge of the stain is irregular, spines are apparent, as are satellite droplets, all misshapen due to the texture of the material. The bottom stain is a droplet of the same volume and dropped from the same height as that on the T-shirt material. This is a highly absorptive, thick cotton towel, and the shape of the droplet stain is decidedly different from that on the T-shirt material.

The diameter of a droplet stain depends not only on the volume of the droplet, but also on the absorptive properties of the surface. If the surface absorbs liquids readily and is thick enough, the appearance of the stain tends to be compact, reflecting the ability of the surface to absorb the blood quickly and deeply into its matrix (the lower photograph in Figure 14.7). By contrast, if the surface is highly absorbent but thin, the resulting stain spreads out quickly because the fabric wicks the blood away from the impact site (the top

- Shape v. target surface
  - Texture (rough or smooth)
    - Affects shape of droplet
    - Collisions with surfaces that are not flat
- Size
  - Distance fallen
    - Little change in diameter beyond 8 ft.
  - Absorptivity/porosity
    - More absorptive, better spreading of droplet into surface
  - Thickness
    - Thick, absorptive surface pulls droplet into matrix and keeps from spreading

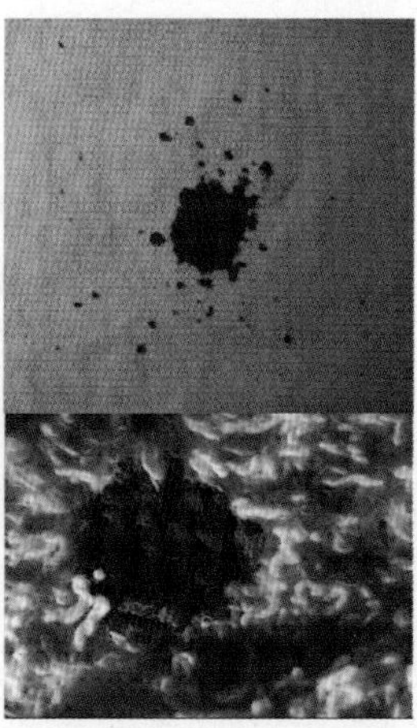

Figure 14.7 Effect of surface absorption on shape and size of bloodstains. (Photograph by Robert C. Shaler.)

photograph in Figure 14.7). The edge of the stain in the bottom photograph is irregular, but there are no spines or satellites. Presumably, the absorptivity of the towel interrupted the ability of the textured surface to overcome the surface tension by quickly absorbing the droplet into the towel's matrix.

Figure 14.8 illustrates how the texture of the surface affects the appearance of the resulting stain, minus the absorptive effect discussed above. All four photographs are of blood droplets dropping onto a nonporous surface. The top two photographs illustrate how sandpaper grit (roughness)—400 (smoother) and 150 (rougher)—affects the appearance of the resulting stain. The general rule of thumb is that the rougher the surface, the more disrupted the resulting stain. The 150 grit sandpaper is rougher and disrupts the droplet

Single droplets falling onto various surfaces

Figure 14.8 Effect of surface texture on the shape of bloodstains. (Photographs by Robert C. Shaler.)

more than one falling onto a piece of the smoother, 400 grit sandpaper. In each case, the same volume of blood fell from the same height. Each droplet stain has spines and satellite stains are apparent (left arrow). The stain on the 400 grit sandpaper clearly shows its scalloped edge while the stain on the 150 grit sandpaper is so badly disrupted that the scallops are not visible.

The lower left photograph in Figure 14.8 shows a stain produced from a droplet impacting a piece of wood. The surface texture of the wood disrupts the droplet as much as the 150 grit sandpaper (upper right). The lower right photograph shows what happens to a droplet falling onto the hooked side of Velcro, the blood being wicked along the hooks (right and left) giving an unusual stain with elongated spines. Satellite stains are also visible (right arrows).

14.4.2.5 Perimeter Stain: Ghosting or Skeletonization

When a blood droplet hits a surface or is transferred to it after wiping against it, the blood is still wet. Over time it will dry. The drying process moves from the outside toward the inside. This happens because the outside edges of the droplet are shallower and lose their water quicker than the middle of the droplet which is thicker. The solid fraction of the blood dries as a crust. Therefore, as the stain dries, its edges dry quicker. If someone or something brushes across the drying droplet, the edges form an outline of the original droplet (see arrows in Figure 14.9).

14.4.2.6 Calculating the Angle of Impact

Understanding the mechanism of why blood forms elongated stains as the angle at which it strikes becomes increasingly small is critical in understanding how to determine the angle at which the blood impacted with the surface. As mentioned, Pizzola et al. [34,35] Figure 14.4 demonstrated photographically how elongated patterns form. Though BPA analysts had been calculating impact angles for decades before their work was published, they confirmed and validated BPA analysts' use of trigonometric functions.

Figure 14.10 is adapted from MacDonell and Bialousz's [37] geometric model for calculating the impact angle. When a blood droplet hits a surface it forms a right triangle (illustrated in Figure 14.10), whose angle *A* can be calculated using trigonometric

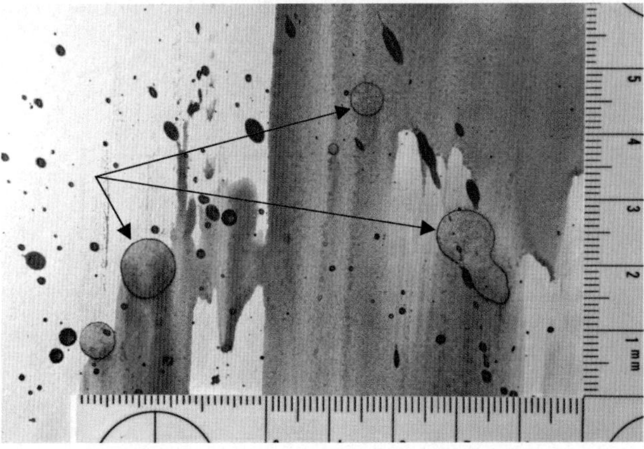

Figure 14.9 Ghosting or skeletonization.

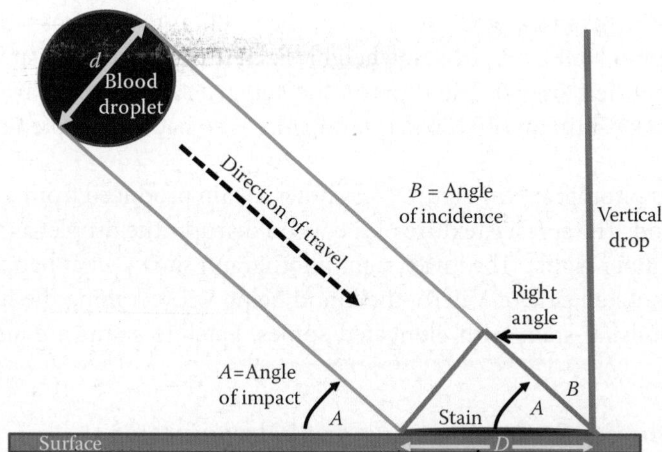

Figure 14.10 Droplet size versus stain size. (Adapted from H. L. MacDonell and L. Bialousz. 1973. *Laboratory Manual on the Geometric Interpretation of Human Bloodstain Evidence*. Corning, NY: Laboratory of Forensic Science.)

functions. The step-by-step procedure for measuring a stain prior to making the calculation is listed below:

- Approximate the outline of a stain as shown in Figure 14.11—red oval. Do not include the stain's tail in the approximation.
- Measure the length (L) and the width (W) from the stain. Calculate the fraction by dividing the width by the length (W/L) (Figure 14.11).
- Calculate the impact angle by calculating the arc sine ($\sin^{-1}$) of the fraction (W/L). A fraction of 0.5 represents a 30° angle.

Significant error is built into calculating the impact angle, which arises from measurement error, error in selecting an appropriate stain (the more elongated the stain, the less the error; the more circular the stain, the greater the error), and surface characteristics that distort the stain by differential absorption or other surface characteristics. Error rates can

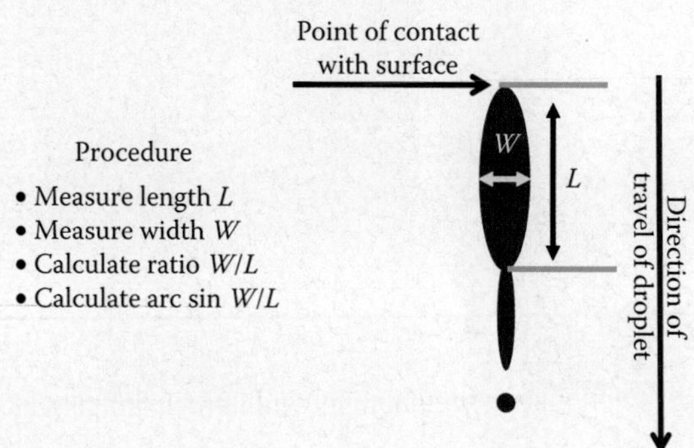

Figure 14.11 Calculating the angle of impact.

be quite high and can range from 1%–2% to over 20%, with an average of approximately 5%. Recent publications [38,39] have targeted errors in calculating impact angles using more rigorous mathematical methods.

14.4.2.7 Determining the Origin of an Impact

Knowing how to determine the angle of impact, the angle at which a blood droplet struck a surface, is the first step in determining the point of convergence of a number of blood droplets that originated from a single source.

14.4.2.7.1 Point of Convergence or Back Projection in Two Dimensions The point of convergence represents the 2D location of an impact, such as what happens in blunt force trauma when someone is beaten with an object or a fist. Importantly, for blood to be spattered, it must be present, which means that a first impact produced blood. The back projection approach is helpful in determining a possible minimum number of blows or impacts. Multiple points of convergence suggest multiple blows. This is also a mechanism for selecting the proper bloodstains from within a bloodstain impact spatter pattern to use in determining the 3D area of impact.

The procedure outlined in Figure 14.12 lists the steps necessary to determine the 2D point of impact. After determining the direction of travel (blood points in the direction in which it was moving), back project a line through the axis of the blood droplet stain. Repeat this procedure for several droplets (as many as 20 per impact pattern). The point (or general area) where they meet is the 2D point of convergence. This represents

- The 2D point of impact of at least one impact.
- The point of impact of more than one impact, if the multiple impacts had the same precise spatial location.

14.4.2.7.2 Area of Origin in Three Dimensions The spatial location of an impact that caused impact spatter pattern can be important in piecing together a possible sequence of events. Essentially, this is the third dimension of the 2D back projection shown above. If

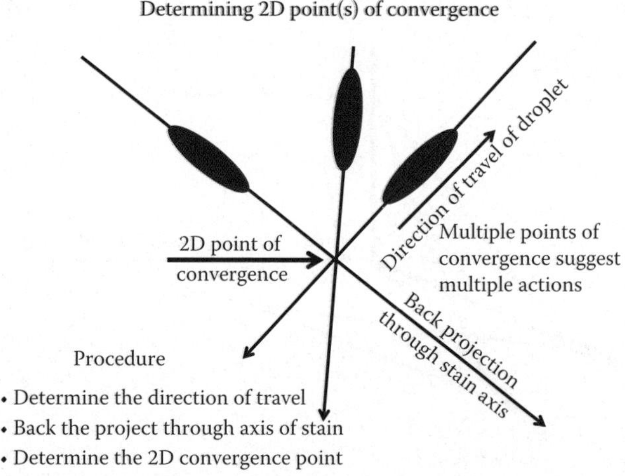

Figure 14.12 Back projection method for point of convergence.

the point of convergence can be determined, it is a simple matter of converting that into a 3D image using 3D imaging techniques, such as 3D scene imaging systems, CAD programs or software specifically designed for the application. It can also be approximated at the scene using what is known as the string method, manually or by lasers. Alternatively, the spatial area (point) can be calculated using a combined manual/trigonometric method. The steps for that process are listed below.

14.4.2.7.3 The Tangent Method

- Use the stains as in the 2D back projection method discussed above. Back project the stains to the point of convergence—Step 1 in Figure 14.13 was illustrated in Figure 14.12.
- Measure the width (W) and the length (L) of two droplet stains.
- Calculate the impact angle by taking the arc sine of the width divided by the length of the bloodstain.
- Measure the distance from the point where the blood droplet hit the surface to the point of convergence.
- The height of the area of impact (Z) is calculated using the tangent function, as shown in Figure 14.13.

14.4.2.7.4 The String Method The string method mentioned above is a manual procedure for approximating the area of origin resulting from an impact. Generally, several appropriate stains are selected (10–20 stains) from within a bloodstain pattern; sometimes determining the best stains can be identified using the 2D back projection process. An example of the string method is shown in Figure 14.14. In the example, impact spatter was created to recreate a stomping death, and a blood-soaked mock head was stomped several times. The back projection method was used to identify the appropriate stains (dark pencil lines drawn through the axes of several bloodstains are visible). Next, the impact angles were measured and anchored at those angles. The area of impact is where the strings more

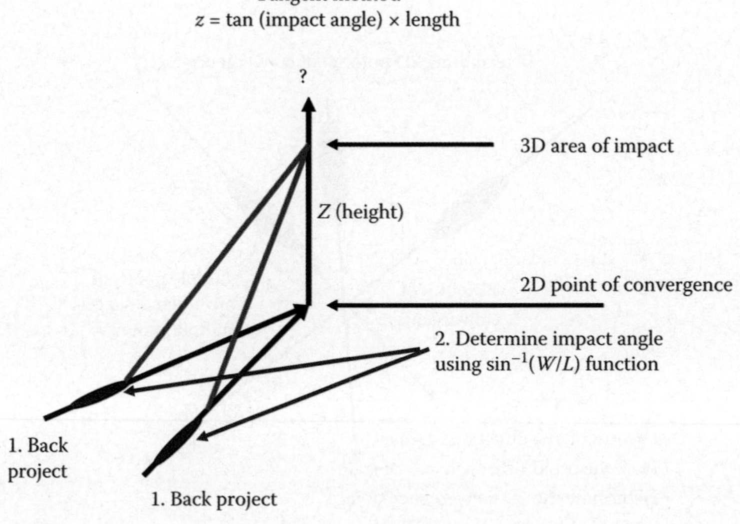

Figure 14.13 Tangent method to determine area of origin.

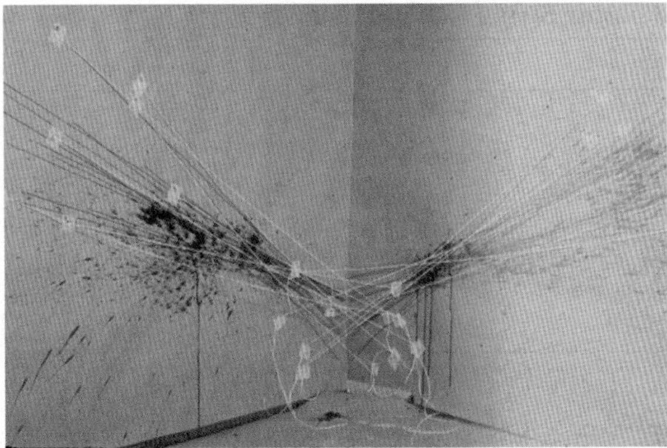

Figure 14.14 An example of the string method.

or less converge. The imprecision of the area determined is related to multiple stomping actions, many of which were not in the same precise location of the mock head but not thus far removed so as to create multiple impact areas.

Appropriate stains have the following specific characteristics:

- They should be traveling linearly, which means they still posses most of the energy imparted to them during the impact. The easiest way of determining which stains are appropriate is to identify them from a back projection 2D analysis. As the stains lose energy, they begin to arc and fall, and are of no use to the analyst trying to determine the spatial origin of an impact.
- Stains should be as elongated as possible, given the complexities of the pattern analyzed. Measuring these stains is less prone to error than circular stains.

14.4.2.7.4.1 Step-by-Step Procedure of the String Method

- Depending on the quality of the pattern, choose as many as 20-elongated stains that were traveling linearly from the impact point before striking the surface. Number each stain sequentially and tape that number to the wall (surface) next to the stain. Record the information in a log.
- Calculate the impact angle for each stain (arc sine width/length). Record the angle in a log and onto the piece of tape placed next to the stain on the impact surface.
- Tape the end of a long piece of string at the precise point where the blood droplet hit the surface.
- Ensuring the tape holding the string is secure and using a zero-edge protractor, track the string through the center of the stain's axis along the protractor at the calculated impact angle. Pull the string taut and attach it to the surface, the floor or other object. Re-check the measurements and the determined stain trajectory (the string) to ensure the angle of the droplet impact an angle is correct. Repeat the process for as many an 20 stains in the pattern. If the pattern is from a single event, if the appropriate stains were selected, if the measurements were determined correctly, and if the string was run at the correct angle, the strings should converge in an area in space that approximates the area of the impact. If the area of convergence seems too large, the process might not have been performed correctly. Table 14.2 gives troubleshooting suggestions.

Table 14.2 Troubleshooting String Method Problems

Reason	Correction Method
Poor stain selection	Re-examine the impact pattern and the stains selected.
Incorrect stain measurement	Repeat measurements to ensure measurement accuracy.
Incorrect angle using the zero-edge protractor	If angles were calculated correctly (above), check the protractor positioning. If placed correctly, recheck string positioning.
Multiple impacts occurring in the same general spatial location	Use 2D back projections to determine whether multiple impacts occurred. If so, use the 2D method to choose stains from each impact and make overlapping 3D area of impact determinations.

14.4.2.7.5 Cast Off When blood leaves a blood-covered object, it can either drip passively or be propelled from it. In the forensic circumstance, blood leaves a blood-covered object when the centripetal force acting on it overcomes the adhesive forces holding the blood onto the object (Figure 14.15). This is true whether the blood cast from the object occurs while the bloody object is being swung or if it comes to an abrupt halt (cessation cast off) Figure 14.16.

If blood is on a bloody knife and the knife is swung in an arc, blood will be propelled (cast off) in a path that is tangentially straight from that point and travel until it hits/impacts a surface. If blood hits the surface while still traveling in the straight line, the shape it takes will represent the angle of the impact. Therefore, trigonometric functions can be used to calculate its impact angle and also backtrack to the spatial location of when it left the bloody object.

More than one droplet will usually leave the bloody object as it moves through its path, the preponderance of which will form a pattern characteristic of the surface of bloody object. These characteristics are listed below:

- Surface area of the object facing the impact surface: Thus, if the bloody object is a hand and the hand is sideways (edgewise) to the impact surface, say a wall, the cast-off pattern formed represents that surface of the hand facing the impact. In this instance, it will be a broad line of individual droplets. As the hand moves

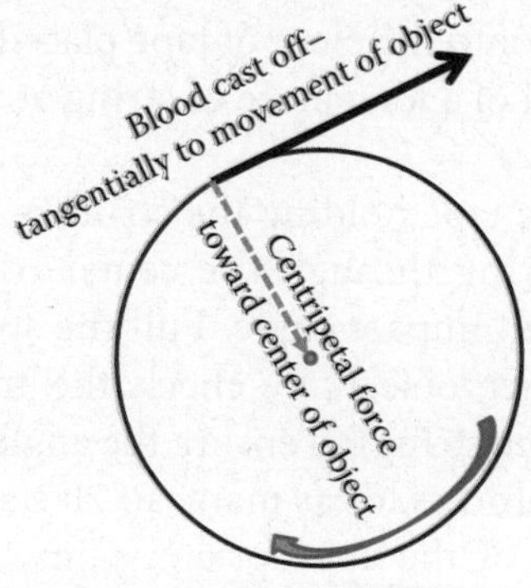

Figure 14.15 Centripetal force and cast-off.

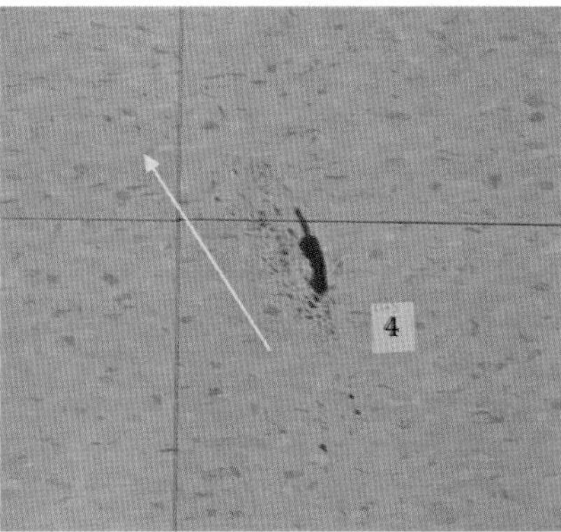

Figure 14.16 Cessation cast-off. (Photograph by Robert C. Shaler.)

through its arc, the hand will change its position and, perhaps, individual fingers will now face the wall. As this happens, the cast-off pattern will broaden and might, at its end, show the cast-off pattern from individual fingers.

- The breadth of the cast-off pattern: This reflects the blood-covered surface area of the surface facing the impact site. Thus, a knife blade (edge) will often give a single line of cast-off staining, while a baseball bat can give a broader cast-off pattern. If the knife's flat side of the blade is facing the impact surface, the breadth of the cast-off pattern will reflect the width of the knife blade, although not its actual dimensions.

A unique type of cast-off occurs when a bloody object comes to a rapid halt. This can occur when a blood-covered weapon strikes a wall, a person, or some other object. Figure 14.16 shows an example of a bloody knife falling to the floor. The yellow arrow shows the direction of the movement of the object as it hit the floor.

14.4.2.7.6 Bubble Stains Bubble stains form when air is present in the droplet. An example is shown in Figure 14.17. The arrows point to the air bubbles in the stain. These are expected in blood expectorated from the lungs or from the mouth.

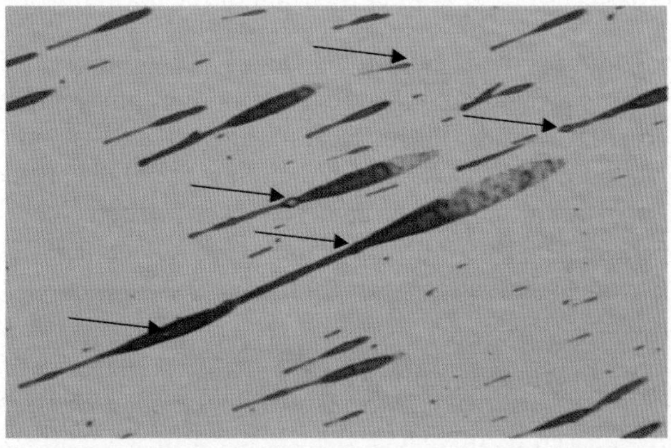

Figure 14.17 Expectorated blood: Air pockets in stain. (Photograph by Robert C. Shaler.)

14.5 Archiving Bloodstain Patterns

The process of archiving evidence was discussed previously in Chapters 6, 7, and 8, and those principles still apply. However, scene investigators are not BPA analysts, but they need to understand and recognize those principles and then follow the guidelines below to properly preserve the evidence. The best way to learn how to recognize important bloodstain patterns is to study bloodstain patterns and the underlying scientific principles relevant to BPA, take an approved BPA workshop, gain on-scene experience, and by experimentation. Even the student and novice scene scientist/investigator can learn to recognize the patterns that should be archived. Examples of bloodstains patterns are posted on the Internet and are described in texts [1,2,19,20].

The BPA analyst, student, or novice scene scientist/investigator should approach each bloodstain pattern analytically, hopefully applying reasoning presented throughout this text. The first step is to examine the bloodstain pattern carefully to ascertain its overall characteristics. The next step is to try to answer the following questions:

- How much area does the pattern encompass?
- Is the pattern a composite of multiple patterns?
- How might this pattern have occurred?

Next, the investigator begins the archiving process. A checklist in Table 14.3 can be used as a guide.

Figure 14.18 shows a midrange shot of a bed and the wall behind the bed taken at a scene before scales were in place. The stains on the bed, those on the wall behind the bed, and those on the floor next to the bed were important. Not shown in the photograph are the cast-off stains: on the ceiling above the bed, on the wall to the left of the bed, and on the wall opposite the bed.

Visually, there are multiple superimposed patterns that must be captured for a meaningful archive. The photograph can be broken down into its most visually apparent components (others are also present):

- Multiple impact spatters
- Large swipe/wipe pattern on the wall behind the bed leading from just above the bed and flowing downward toward the floor
- Smaller swipe patterns on the wall to the right of the main impact spatter

Close-up photographs provide additional detail, for example, misting, and so on. Capturing these patterns properly requires several photographs beginning with an establishing shot (not shown), the midrange of each staining area (this photograph is only one of several necessary), followed by close-ups of the relevant details present in various areas of the overall pattern. The initial photographs are taken without scales, which should be repeated with scales pasted on the wall. This is important to detail and preserve the overall size of the pattern as well as subpatterns within the whole.

14.6 Bloodstain Artifacts: Selected Examples

Experienced investigators know that when they arrive at the scene it is no longer virginal. That is, it must be considered a scene that is not as it was when the crime took place. This

Table 14.3 BPA Archiving Guidelines

Checklist	Reason
Determine the total area the pattern covers by examining adjoining walls, floors, and ceiling.	Ensures that subsequent archiving will not miss important areas of the pattern
Measure perimeter of each area of pattern staining. Record measurements in appropriate log.	Archives entire pattern without scales which can cover droplets from adjoining or overlapping patterns
Bloodstain patterns should be photographed first in the raw, without scales, so that subsequent analysis is not hindered by their presence.	
Cordon off each pattern using adhesive measuring tape ruled in inches or by snapping a powdered stains. Include the entire pattern—width and length. Photograph the pattern with the scales in place using forensically appropriate photos: establishing, midrange and close-ups, if appropriate. If not possible to capture its entirety, grid the area and photograph each grid separately.	Scales ensure that the size (width and length) of a pattern is captured Gridding is a least preferred method, but is useful to capture the detail in extremely large patterns
Video record the pattern using a digital camera having video capability (or use a dedicated video camera). Capture each area of the pattern. Show relationship of each to the whole. Capture areas adjacent to the pattern (e.g., walls, floor, and ceiling). Use close ups where appropriate.	Gives the BPA analyst the overall perspective of the pattern
Photograph each area of the pattern having special characteristics. • Radial impact spatter can have value in determining the spatial area of the impact. If analysis is not done at scene, capture individual droplets (numbered sequentially and taped to the surface) for length/width measurements for stain pattern analysis software. • Impact pattern with imbedded mist pattern—capture the latter, measuring overall size and that of representative droplets. • Complex pattern with multiple overlapping characteristics (multiple impact patterns and/or multiple cast-off patterns or is an impact pattern containing cessation cast off). Capture subpatterns separately showing relationship to overall pattern.	Alerts the BPA analyst with regard to pattern complexity or to the fact that the information within the pattern might have additional interpretative data

Figure 14.18 Midrange photograph of bloodstains at scene. (Photograph by Robert C. Shaler.)

is true for many reasons, some of which were discussed in Chapter 4 under the topic of evidence dynamics (Section 4.4). Blood evidence is not exempt from the ravages of evidence dynamics. Examples of things that can happen range from clean-up activity to officials responding to the scene to emergency medical personnel trying to save lives and even common weather complications. Another common concern is artifacts, which can occur from people who work on the scene to insects who dine or traipse through the scene. The following illustrates how insect activity can affect blood stain patterns at the scene.

14.6.1 Insect Activity

It is well known by experienced BPA analysts that insects can leave artifactual marks in blood at the scene. Forensic entomologist Jason H. Byrd wrote [40],

> Insects can also affect the interpretation of blood spatter pattern analysis. Roaches simply walking through pooled and splattered blood will produce tracking that may not be readily recognizable to the untrained observer. Specks of blood in unique and unusual areas (such as on ceilings) may mislead crime scene technicians unless they are aware of the appearance of blood contaminated roach tracks. Similarly, flies and fleas may also track through pooled and spattered blood. However, flies will also feed on the blood and then pass the partially digested blood in its feces, which are known as "flyspecks." Flies will also regurgitate and possibly drop a blood droplet on a remote surface, which may serve to confuse bloodstain analysis. Fleas feeding on the living pass a large amount of undigested blood (used as the larval food source) on many household surfaces. If a crime occurs in a heavily infected apartment, fecal drops already present would serve to confuse analysts as those droplets would test positive for human blood. Therefore it is important to recognize and properly document the natural artifacts that may occur from the presence, feeding, and defecation of roaches, flies, and fleas.

14.6.1.1 Flies

Contamination and artifacts from insects dining on dried or wet blood at the scene should be anticipated by the BPA analyst, and scene scientists/investigators should understand that such activity is common. Figure 14.19 shows an example of a bloodstain pattern from fly activity. Artifactual staining can confuse BPA analysts but that from flies should not have.

The shapes and sizes of the individual stains are characteristic of the patterns that form, and these have been described comprehensively by Suhra et al. [41]. An overview of their results is presented in Table 14.4.

14.6.1.2 Cockroaches

Cockroaches also feast on blood at the scene. And like flies, they leave telltale marks of their activity that can be misinterpreted. An illustration is shown in Figure 14.20.

14.6.2 On-Scene Activity

Figure 14.21a and b illustrate how crime scene unit activity can affect bloodstains. Note the wall next to the deceased and the bag in the corner behind the deceased. Figure 14.21a shows the bloodstain patterns before the crime scene arrived at the scene and began working. Figure 14.21b shows the bloodstain artifacts after the unit had completed processing the scene but before the body had been removed. Both figures illustrate the importance

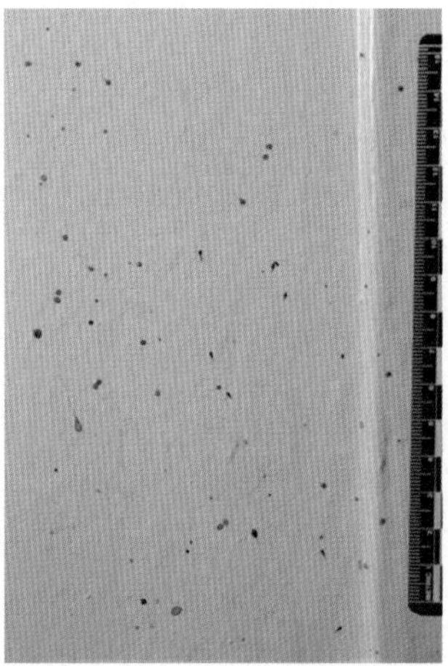

Figure 14.19 Fly artifact bloodstains on wall. (Photograph by Ralph R. Ristenbatt III. With permission.)

Table 14.4 Overview of Fly Bloodstain Characteristics

Type	Characteristics	Size (mm)
Fecal	Symmetrical and asymmetrical round spots having three levels of pigmentation: creamy, brownish, and dark.	0.5–4
Vomit/regurgitation	Craters from sucking activity are surrounded by raised edges having a dark perimeter. The surface is irregular and reflective.	1–2
Trailing (swiping due to defecation)	Distinguished by two segments, a body and a tail, appearing sperm-like, tear-shaped, or snake-like.	4.8–9.2

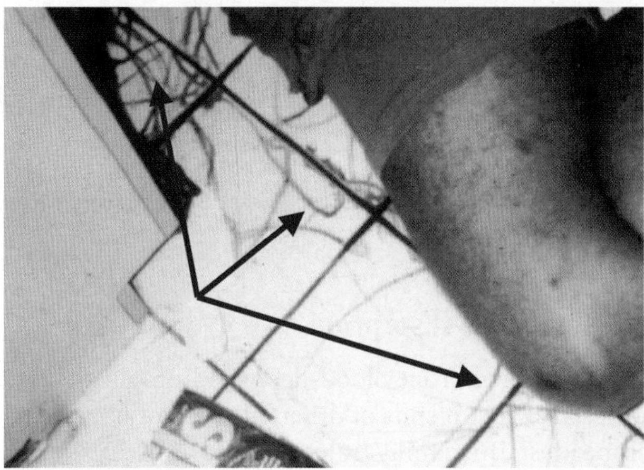

Figure 14.20 Cockroach bloodstain patterns. (Photograph by Ralph R. Ristenbatt III. With permission.)

of on-scene archiving before actively working on the scene or removing the evidence. The bloodstain artifacts on the wall in Figure 14.21b were created by the crime scene unit after removing the evidence from the corner—seen in Figure 14.21a. The perspective shown in each figure is slightly different, which is why some of the detail in Figure 14.21a is missing in Figure 14.21b.

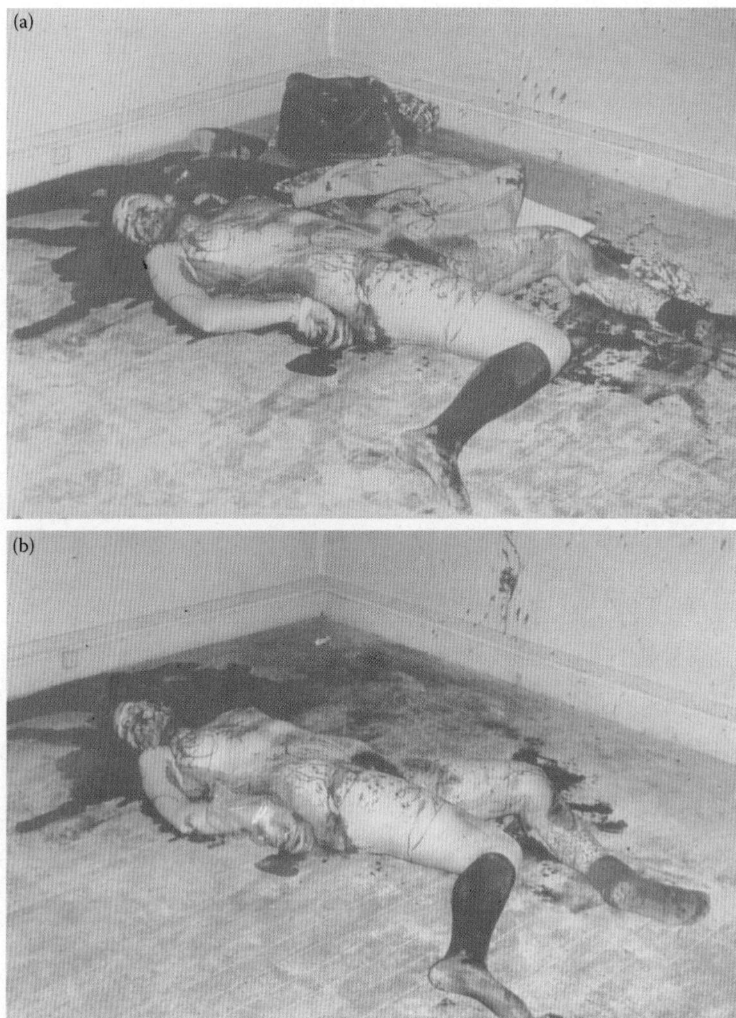

Figure 14.21 (a) Bloodstain patterns at scene. (b) Bloodstain artifacts introduced by investigators. (Photograph by Robert C. Shaler.)

14.6.3 Fabrics: Differential Absorption

Interpreting bloodstain patterns from blood deposited on garments can pose problems because modern fabrics are often blends of different types of fibers, each of which has different absorptive properties. This is illustrated in Figure 14.22. Note how the blood was wicked horizontally (yellow arrow).

14.7 Becoming a BPA Analyst

The organizations associated with BPA, SWGSTAIN, and the IABPA recommend specific training courses of instruction for investigators who desire to be BPA analysts. The IAI offers a certificate program and SWIGSTAIN has recommended quality assurance guidelines for agencies performing BPA analysts.

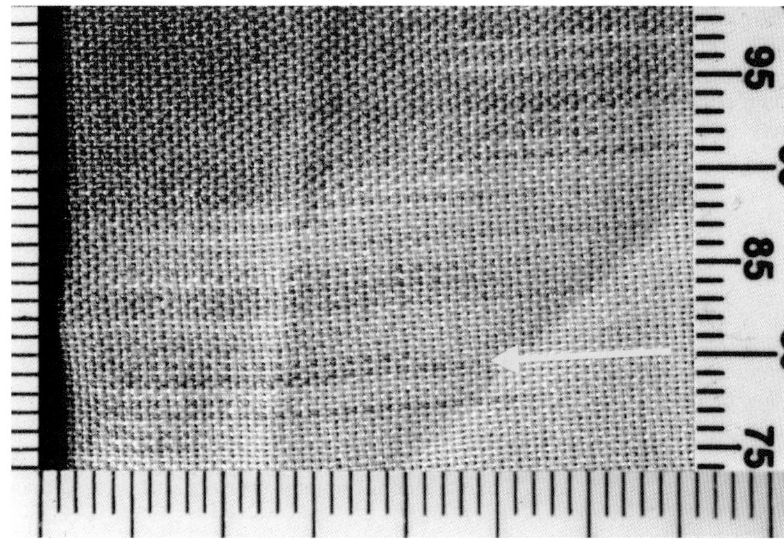

Figure 14.22 Bloodstain artifact pattern in fabric. (Photograph by Ralph R. Ristenbatt III. With permission.)

14.7.1 SWGSTAIN-Recommended Guidelines for Training

SWGSTAIN recommended pretraining (skills, knowledge, abilities) educational requirements for an individual currently in or entering into a BPA training program and the minimum training requirements for trainees before practicing as a BPA analyst. SWGSTAIN also requires a mentorship, whose responsibility it is to evaluate the trainee's progress toward completing the required education and training objectives stated in the BPA analyst curriculum. Table 14.5 was adapted from the SWGSTAIN guidelines published by the IABPA in March 2008 [42].

14.7.2 BPA Certification

The IAI offers a program to certify BPA analysts. The program consists of 40 h in an approved workshop that provides theory, study, and practice including [42]:

- Flight characteristics and stain patterns.
- Examination and identification of bloodstain evidence.
- Documentation of blood stains and patterns.
- Oral and/or visual presentation of physical activity of blood droplets illustrating blood as fluid being acted upon by motion or force. Past research, treatise, or other reference materials for the student.
- Laboratory exercises that document bloodstains and standards by previous research. Exercises must include—but not be limited to those listed in Table 14.6.

Other categories of the certification program include the preparation of a laboratory manual with a glossary of approved terms that describes the exercises performed and observations made. Other topics of the course of instruction include knowledge of the preservation and adequate documentation of BPA evidence.

Table 14.5 Summary of SWGSTAIN Guidelines for BPA Training

Category	Description
Minimum training requirements for BPA trainees	
Education	Bachelor's degree in field of study related to BPA from accredited college or university. Associate's degree or equivalent in a field of study related to BPA from accredited college or university and 2 years of job-related experience. High school diploma or equivalent and 4 years of job-related, but not limited to, experience as crime scene technician, criminalist, homicide/criminal investigator.
Required minimum objectives through accepted training methods specific to BPA training	1. Demonstrate an understanding of health and safety issues associated with BPA. 2. Demonstrate an awareness of bloodborne pathogens and other related health hazards. 3. Demonstrate an awareness of biohazard safety equipment and procedures. 4. Demonstrate knowledge of the history of BPA. 5. Demonstrate an understanding of the scientific principles as they relate to BPA. 6. Demonstrate an understanding of the scientific method and its application to BPA experimentation, to include a. Problem identification b. Hypothesis c. Experimentation/data collection d. Data analysis e. Theory/conclusions 7. Demonstrate an understanding of the principles of physics as they relate to BPA, to include a. Physical laws of motion b. Surface tension c. Viscosity d. Gravity e. Air resistance f. Velocity 8. Demonstrate an understanding of bloodstain pattern principles and their application to BPA. 9. Demonstrate an understanding of blood components and related human anatomy and physiology. 10. Demonstrate an understanding of the effects of target surface characteristics on the resulting bloodstain patterns. 11. Demonstrate an understanding of the effect of environmental factors on the formation and/or drying time of bloodstain patterns, to include a. Air flow b. Humidity c. Temperature d. Substrate characteristics e. Animal/insect activity 12. Demonstrate an understanding of the characteristics of blood in motion, to include a. Drop formation b. Oscillation

Table 14.5 (Continued) Summary of SWGSTAIN Guidelines for BPA Training

Category	Description
	c. Flight paths d. Accompanying drop e. Wave cast off f. Distribution of stains g. Kinetic energy 13. Demonstrate an understanding of health and safety issues associated with BPA. 14. Demonstrate an awareness of bloodborne pathogens and other related health hazards. 15. Demonstrate an understanding of the mathematical principles that relate to BPA, to include knowledge of the methods used to measure the bloodstains and bloodstain patterns. These include a. Methods for the measurement of individual bloodstains. b. Trigonometric functions as they relate to BPA. c. Methods for origin determination. 16. Demonstrate an understanding of how the physical appearance of bloodstain patterns (size, shape, distribution, and location) relates to the mechanism by which they were created. 17. Demonstrate the ability to identify the bloodstain patterns. 18. Demonstrate acceptable documentation methods of bloodstain pattern evidence, including documentation techniques specific to BPA, to include a. Photography b. Sketching c. Note-taking 19. Demonstrate an understanding of the methodologies for the preservation and collection of bloodstain pattern evidence that allow for future examination(s). 20. Demonstrate an understanding of bloodletting injuries, their locations, and their potential effects on the bloodstain pattern(s). 21. Demonstrate an understanding of searching, chemical testing, and enhancement techniques as they pertain to bloodstains. 22. Demonstrate an understanding of the limitations of BPA. 23. Demonstrate the ability to apply BPA to assist in the reconstruction of a bloodletting event(s). 24. Demonstrate the ability to communicate findings, conclusions, and opinions by written and/or verbal methods.
Mentorship	Document and participate in a mentorship program. This training should include, but is not limited to, the evaluation of the required objectives, the review of completed casework, supervised BPA scene and laboratory work, and the observation of expert testimony.
Competency testing	Participate in and successfully complete a competency test prior to performing independent analysis and rendering expert opinion. Competency testing may be administered incrementally and/or cumulatively to allow the trainee to conduct some of the analyses independently.
Continuing education	A minimum of 8 h of training related to BPA should be completed annually. This may include, but is not limited to, attending professional conferences, seminars, and/or workshops.

continued

Table 14.5 (Continued) Summary of SWGSTAIN Guidelines for BPA Training

Category	Description
	Membership to a professional organization(s) related to BPA is recommended.
Minimum requirements for BPA mentor	1. A mentor must be an active practitioner in the field of BPA and should have a minimum of 3 years of casework experience as a qualified BPA analyst. 2. A mentor should have fulfilled all previously stated requirements for a BPA analyst.

Entrance to the program includes 3 years of practice in BPA, an approved 40 h BPA course, an approved 40 h course in photography, and 240 h of instruction in fields of study relating to BPA, such as crime scene investigation, evidence recovery, blood detection techniques, medicolegal death investigation, and forensic science and technology. The IAI provides a reading list, and the written examination includes the following topics:

- BPA terminology
- Documentation, photography, illustration, and sketching of bloodstains and bloodstain patterns
- Wound pathology
- Investigative procedures
- Crime scene processing
- History of BPA
- BPA theory and logic
- Mathematics (basic understanding pertaining to discipline applications)
- Stain and stain pattern recognition (characteristics and visual recognition)

The IAI certification program [43] seems rigorous, but it lacks the scientific rigor necessary to ensure that BPA analysts completely understand the scientific basis of how and why patterns form at crime scenes. As of this writing, the IAI specifies no requirement that BPA analysts have a degree in science or at least college level courses in the discipline forming the scientific foundation of BPA (Section 14.3).

Table 14.6 Laboratory Exercises for BPA Certification

Category
Falling blood
Surface considerations
Blood in motion
Increased blood volumes
Flow patterns (horizontal/vertical)
Projected bloodstains and patterns
Forceful impact spatter patterns
Transfer stains and impression patterns
Other topics—not required

Table 14.7 Quality Assurance Guidelines for BPA

Standard	Description
Personnel and qualifications	The agency must have written specifications defining the minimum education, training, and experience required of an individual in order to perform BPA as per the SWGSTAIN education and training documents.
Standard operating procedures: The agency must have written and approved standard operating procedures regarding BPA.	Items that should be included are 3.1. Title 3.2. Scope 3.3. Equipment, materials, and reagents 3.4. Procedures 3.5. Report generation, review, and approval 3.6. Calculations 3.7. Limitations 3.8. Safety 3.9. References 3.10. Standard operating procedure approval
Case files	The agency must have written procedures for the content and maintenance of BPA case files.
Assessments	The agency should have in place a documented program of ongoing skill assessment of the bloodstain pattern analyst. a. It is recommended that each bloodstain pattern analyst participate in case reanalysis or proficiency testing annually. b. It is recommended that the agency have a documented program that annually assesses the testimony of each bloodstain pattern analyst.
Corrective action	The agency should establish written procedures to be followed for corrective actions addressing such issues as administrative, analytical, interpretive, or skill-assessment errors.
Safety	The agency should maintain a documented health and safety program. This should include health and safety practices consistent with standards for the occupational exposure to bloodborne pathogens and occupational exposure to hazardous chemicals used in BPA.
Facilities	The agency must have a documented program that ensures that the facility is secured from unauthorized access and maintained in a condition that minimizes the risk of contamination of evidence.
Evidence control	The agency must have a documented evidence control system to ensure the integrity of physical evidence.
Equipment and reagents	The agency should have a documented program to monitor the maintenance and calibration of equipment and/or instrumentation that affect(s) the accuracy and validity of the BPA. The agency should have in place documented procedures for testing the reagents used in casework to ensure their functionality.

14.8 Quality Assurance Guidelines for BPA

The recommended quality assurance program for BPA analysts resembles most reasonable quality assurance programs in forensic science, for example, the American Society of Crime Laboratory Directors/Laboratory Accreditation Board (ASCLD/LAB) Legacy Program. The purpose of a comprehensive quality assurance program is to ensure that the users of the service provided receive a quality product. This begins with management and goes to on-scene testing and collecting, packaging, and preserving the evidence. Table 14.7 lists these guidelines as adapted from the list described in the IABPA March 2008 newsletter [42].

References

1. T. Bevel and R. M. Gardner. 2002. *Bloodstain Pattern Analysis: With an Introduction to Crime Scene Reconstruction*, 2nd edn. Boca Raton, FL: CRC Press.
2. S. H. James and W. G. Eckert. 1999. *Interpretation of Bloodstain Evidence at Crime Scenes*, 2nd edn. New York, NY: CRC Press.
3. FBI. 2008. Scientific Working Group on Bloodstain Pattern Analysis (SWGSTAIN): Guidelines for a quality assurance program in bloodstain analysis. *Forensic Science Communications*, 10(1). Available at: http://www.fbi.gov/about-us/lab/forensic-science-communications/fsc/jan2008/standards/2008_01_standards02.htm.
4. R. M. Gardner and T. Griffin. 2010. Foundations for the discipline of bloodstain pattern analysis: A response to the report by the National Academy of Sciences. *Journal of Forensic Identification*, 60(4):477–494.
5. The Committee on Identifying the Needs of the Forensic Science Community, Committee on Science, Technology and Law Policy and Global Affairs, Committee on Applied and Theoretical Statistics, Division on Engineering and Physical Sciences, National Research Council of the National Academies. 2009. *Strengthening Forensic Science in the United States: A Path Forward.* Washington, DC: National Academies Press, pp. 127–191.
6. *Merriam-Webster Online Dictionary. Purview.* Available at: http://www.merriam-webster.com/dictionary/purview (accessed August 29, 2010).
7. State of Ohio v. Samuel H. Sheppard. 1955. In *Kirk, P.L. 1955*, Court of Common Pleas, Criminal Branch, No. 64571, p. 1.
8. C. Cooper and S.R. Sheppard. 1995. *Mockery of Justice: The True Story of the Sam Sheppard Murder Case.* Boston, MA: Northeastern University Press, pp. 5–13.
9. H. L. MacDonell and L. Bialousz, 1971. *Flight Characteristics and Bloodstain Patterns of Human Blood.* Washington, DC: Law Enforcement Assistance Administration.
10. V. Balthazard, R. Piédeliévre, H. Desoille, and L. Dérobert. 1939. Etude des gouttes de sang projete. In: *Annual Medecine Legale Criminol.* Paris, France: 22nd Congress of Forensic Medicine, pp. 265–323.
11. *Merriam-Webster Online Dictionary.* Cadre. Available at: http://www.merriam-webster.com/dictionary/cadre (accessed August 29, 2010).
12. IABPA Web site. Available at: http://www.iabpa.org/SWGSTAINReferenceListbyGroupApril2009.pdf (accessed February 7, 2011).
13. B. Yamashita. 2009. Physics and mathematics in bloodstain pattern analysis. Third European IABPA. *IABPA News*, 25(4):21. Available at: http://www.iabpa.org/December2009news.pdf (accessed July 24, 2011).
14. SWGSTAIN Research Subcommittee. 2009. Bibliography project. Available at: http://www.iabpa.org/SWGSTAINReferenceListbyGroupApril2009.pdf (accessed February 5, 2011).

15. T. L. Laber, B. P. Epstein, and M. C. Taylor. 2008. High speed digital video analysis of bloodstain pattern formation from common bloodletting mechanisms. MFRC Project No. 06-S-02. *IABPA News*, p. 9. Available at: http://www.iabpa.org/June2008final.pdf (accessed July 24, 2011).
16. Scientific Working Group on Bloodstain Pattern Analysis (SWGSTAIN) Web site. SWGSTAIN bylaws. Available at: http://www.swgstain.org/about-swgstain (accessed February 5, 2011).
17. National Criminal Justice Reference Service. Available at: http://www.ncjrs.gov/app/publications/abstract.aspx?ID=240512(accessed July 24, 2011).
18. FBI. 2009. Scientific Working Group on Bloodstain Pattern Analysis: Recommended terminology. *Forensic Science Communications*, 11(2). Available at: http://www2.fbi.gov/hq/lab/fsc/backissu/april2009/standards/2009_04_standards01.htm.
19. S. H. James, P. Kish, and P. Sutton. 2005. *Principles of Bloodstain Pattern Analysis: Theory and Practice*. New York, NY: CRC Press.
20. A. Wonder. 2007. *Bloodstain Pattern Evidence: Objective Approaches and Case Applications*. San Diego, CA: Elsevier Academic Press.
21. HemoSpat. Bloodstain pattern analysis terminology—IABPA. Available at: http://hemospat.com/terminology/ (accessed July 24, 2011).
22. HemoSpat. Bloodstain pattern analysis terminology—SWGSTAIN. Available at: http://hemospat.com/terminology/?org=SWGSTAIN (accessed July 24, 2011).
23. The Ames Laboratory, Department of Energy, Midwest Forensic Resource Center. Bloodstain formation videos. Available at: http://www.ameslab.gov/mfrc (accessed February 5, 2011).
24. *Merriam-Webster Online Dictionary*. Viscoelastic. Available at: http://www.merriam-webster.com/dictionary/viscoelastic (accessed February 6, 2011).
25. *Wikipedia*. Non-Newtonian. Available at: http://en.wikipedia.org/wiki/Non-Newtonian_fluid (accessed February 6, 2011).
26. *Merriam-Webster Online Dictionary*. Surface tension. Available at: http://www.merriam-webster.com/dictionary/surface%20tension (accessed February 6, 2011).
27. *Merriam-Webster Online Dictionary*. Fluid mechanics. Available at: http://www.merriam-webster.com/dictionary/fluid%20mechanics (accessed February 6, 2011).
28. *Wikipedia*. Fluid mechanics. Available at: http://en.wikipedia.org/wiki/Fluid_mechanics (accessed February 6, 2011).
29. *Wikipedia*. Computational fluid dynamics. Available at: http://en.wikipedia.org/wiki/Computational_fluid_dynamics (accessed July 24, 2011).
30. *Merriam-Webster Online Dictionary*. Gravity. Available at: http://www.merriam-webster.com/dictionary/gravity (accessed February 6, 2011).
31. P. Davies. 1986. *The Forces of Nature*, 2nd edn. Cambridge: Cambridge University Press.
32. *Merriam-Webster Online Dictionary*. Centripetal force. Available at: http://www.merriam-webster.com/dictionary/centripetal%20force (accessed September 6, 2010).
33. *Merriam-Webster Online Dictionary*. Centrifugal force. Available at: http://www.merriam-webster.com/dictionary/centrifugal+force?show=0&t=1283792070 (accessed September 6, 2010).
34. P. A. Pizzola, S. Roth, and P. R. Deforest. 1986. Blood droplet dynamics: I. *Journal of Forensic Sciences*, 31(1):36–49.
35. P. A. Pizzola, S. Roth, and P. R. Deforest. 1986. Blood droplet dynamics: II. *Journal of Forensic Sciences*, 31(1):50–64.
36. W. G. Eckert. 1992. *Introduction to Forensic Sciences*. New York, NY: Elsevier, p. 171.
37. H. L. MacDonell and L. Bialousz. 1973. *Laboratory Manual on the Geometric Interpretation of Human Bloodstain Evidence*. Corning, NY: Laboratory of Forensic Science.
38. W. Rowe. 2006. Errors in determining the point of origin of bloodstains. *Forensic Science International*, 161:47–51.
39. C. Willis, A. K. Piranian, J. R. Donaggio, R. Barnett, and W. Rowe, 2001. Errors in the estimation of the distance of fall and angles of impact blood drops. *Forensic Science International*, 123:1–4.

40. J. H. Byrd. Forensic entomology: Insects in legal investigations. Available at: http://www.forensicentomology.com/definition.htm (accessed September 13, 2010).
41. R. M. Zuha, M. Supriyani, and B. Omar. 2008. Fly artifact documentation of *Chrysomya megacephala* (Fabricius) (Diptera: Calliphoridae)—A forensically important blowfly species in Malaysia. *Tropical Biomedicine*, 25(1):17–22.
42. International Association of Bloodstain Pattern Analysts. 2008. Standards and guidelines. Scientific Working Group on Bloodstain Pattern Analysis: Guidelines for the minimum educational and training requirements for bloodstain pattern analysts. *IABPA News*, 24(1):15–21. Available at: http://www.iabpa.org/March%202008%20News.pdf.
43. International Association for Identification (IAI). Bloodstain pattern examiner certification requirements. Available at: http://www.theiai.org/certifications/bloodstain/requirements.php (accessed August 31, 2010).

Workshop 9: BPA—The Basics

W9.1 Introduction: Patterns in Blood

The purpose of this workshop is to expand the concept of blood at the crime scene. The reader is referred to Chapter 14. When blood leaves the body and deposits onto a surface or a bloody object comes into contact with another object or surface, a pattern is produced. Sometimes, it is possible to interpret that pattern by BPA in order to identify its source (of the pattern). The success of these interpretations depends on the experience and imagination of the investigator in recognizing and making the associations with other aspects of the crime scene or in associating the bloodstain patterns with objects or injuries incurred by live or deceased individuals.

W9.2 Falling Blood Droplets

Blood dropping onto a surface leaves a distinct pattern depending on movement and/or angularity. For example, a vertical drop of blood leaves a circular pattern. The surface on which the droplet falls also affects the shape and size of the resulting pattern. A droplet flying in the air will subsequently land on a surface and depending on the angle it strikes that surface might leave an elongated-shaped pattern. A blood dropping from a blood-covered object or from an open wound can give information concerning the direction of travel of the injured person.

W9.2.1 Exercise 1: Vertically Dropping Blood

W9.2.1.1 Procedure For this exercise, work in pairs or teams of three. Using a Pasteur pipette, drop individual droplets of blood vertically onto various surfaces.

- *Flat smooth surfaces*: Linoleum floor
  - The diameter of a blood droplet approaches a maximum after reaching approximately 7–8 ft. Test this assumption by dropping blood from a squeeze dropping bottle from distances of: 6 in., and 1, 2, 3, 4, 5, 7, and 8 ft.
  - Measure the diameter of the resulting fallen droplet.
  - Graph the droplet diameter versus height.
  - Show the graph to an instructor for grading.

- *Textured surfaces*: Fabric. The surface texture can affect the final shape of a droplet. Generally, the rougher the surface, the more distorted the spherical aspect of the droplet. From several heights (1, 5, and 7 ft.), drop single droplets on to various surfaces:
  - Raw wood
  - Paper towel
  - T-shirt material
  - Bath towel material
  - 100, 150, and 400 grit sandpaper
  - Fuzzy and hooked sides of Velcro
- *Blood falling onto blood*: Blood falling onto blood produces easily recognizable patterns that are sometimes misinterpreted. Working in teams or pairs, repeat step 2 above by dripping 200 drops of blood from a squeeze dropping bottle onto itself from heights of 1, 5, and 7 ft.
  - Measure the diameter of the resulting patterns.
    - Repeat the experiment with the blood pool forming 1 ft. from a wall.
  - Measure the height of blood spatter on the wall.
    - Repeat the experiment but place a chair 1 ft. from the dropping blood.
  - Examine the pattern for the presence of void areas.
  - Measure the height of staining on the chair.
- *Satellite Spatter*
  - Examine the droplets onto the various surfaces in step 2 above.
  - Fill in Table W9.1 and show it to an instructor for grading.
- *Ghosting/skeletonization*: Ghosting occurs when a blood droplet is partially dry and something wipes across it leaving an outline of the stain's perimeter as dried blood.
  - Make several droplets onto linoleum or other nonporous surface and allow them to dry for periods of time: 1, 5, and 30 min.
  - Wipe across each droplet at the specified time.
  - Record what you observe in Table W9.2
  - Show the table to an instructor for grading.

Table W9.1 Effect of Surface Texture on Size and Shape of Bloodstain

Surface	Extent of Satellite Formation (None, Few, Many)	Effect of Surface on Droplet Size
Raw wood		
Paper towel		
T-shirt material		
Bath towel material		
100 grit sandpaper		
150 grit sandpaper		
400 grit sandpaper		
Fuzzy side of Velcro		
Hooked side of Velcro		

Table W9.2 Ghosting and Drying Time

Drying Time (min)	Extent of Ghosting (Minimal, Moderate, Nearly Complete)
1	
5	
30	

W9.3 Exercise 2: Angularity of Blood

When blood leaves the body or an object, such as when it is cast off a moving object (a knife), it will impact the surface and leave an elongated pattern depending on the impact angle.

W9.3.1 Procedure

Insert a ceramic tile into the slots of a precut wooden form (the slots are cut at specific angles). Each slot has a defined angle, the angle of incidence, which is labeled on the side of the form.

- Drop individual droplets onto the inserted board from about 1½ ft. above the form—one droplet for each slot.
- Measure the width/diameter and length of each droplet.
- Calculate the impact angle [arc sine (w/l) as a guide a $w/l = 0.5$ is a 30° angle) and the angle of incidence (90° angle of impact).
- Fill in Table W9.3
- Determine the error using the known angle of incidence (written on the side of the form) as the "known" angle.
- Show the filled-out table to an instructor for grading.

W9.4 Exercise 3: Blood Trails

Blood dripping from a moving object/person will leave a trail of blood that indicates the direction of travel.

Table W9.3 Angularity of Blood: Measuring Impact Angles

A "Known" Angle of Incidence (Written on Form)	B "Known" Impact Angle (90-A)	C Bloodstain Width (w)	D Bloodstain Length (l)	E Calculated Angle of Impact (arc sine (w/l))	F Error $(B - E)/B \times 100$
80					
70					
60					
50					
40					
30					
20					
10					
0 (Flat)					

Table W9.4 Blood Trails: Direction of Travel

Trail Designation	Beginning and End of Trail (First Identifiable Stain and Last Stain in Trail)
Inside Trail 1	
Inside Trail 2	
Outside Trail 1	
Outside Trail 2	

W9.4.1 Procedure

- Fill a dropping bottle with blood. Holding the dropping bottle upside-down vertically, allow the blood to drip from the bottle while squeezing gently. Create three trails: one walking, one walking fast, and one running. Examine the resulting trails looking for the telltale signs of direction.
- Unknown trails have been placed on a floor inside the building and one on the outside along a sidewalk. Examine these and label the direction in Table W9.4
- Photograph diagnostic droplets from each trail.
- Show the table and photographs to an instructor for grading.

W9.5 Exercise 4: Blood Dripping from Objects

A blood-covered object will drip blood until the blood dries or there is insufficient blood to overcome the force of gravity.

W9.5.1 Procedure

- Dip several objects into blood and allow the blood to drip onto the floor. Observe how many drops it takes for blood to stop dripping passively from the object. Try knives, spoons, wooden spoons, and so on. Use your imagination, as the more objects you test, the better the "feel" you will have for interpreting events at scenes of crimes.
- Measure the diameter of droplets from various items and record the values on a sheet of paper.
- Photograph each drip pattern and place the photo into a catalog or album of photos. Also photograph the bloody object.
- Label each entry with the measurement of the diameter of the droplets that formed.
- Show the diameters measured and the photographs to an instructor for grading.

W9.6 Exercise 5: Bloody Footprints

This exercise is to determine how far someone can walk and still leave a blood trail. This experiment will be done as a group.

W9.6.1 Procedure

- Place several droplets on the floor
- Have someone walk through the droplets
- Examine the bloody footprints

- Darken the room
- Prepare for BlueStar enhancement of the footprints
- Follow procedure in Exercise W6.3.2
- Show photographs to an instructor for grading

W9.7 Exercise 6: Other Patterns: Swipes, Cast Off, Dragging (Hair), and Crawling

W9.7.1 Swipes and Wipes

Patterns of blood also occur when a bloody object comes into contact with a surface and moves across it. This is known as a swipe pattern (Chapter 14).

W9.7.1.1 Procedure

- Bloody an object such as a hand, a piece of fabric, and so on.
- Swipe the object along a wall.
- Notice the starting and ending point of the wipe. Notice how the end is more "feathered" than the beginning of the swipe which is usually more defined.
- Four swipe patterns have been placed on a wall. Identify the beginning and end of each pattern.
- Fill in Table W9.5 and show it to an instructor for grading.

W9.7.2 Exercise 7: Cast-Off Pattern

The purpose of this exercise is to illustrate what happens to blood when it leaves an object that is in motion.

W9.7.2.1 Procedure

- Dip an object (knife, fork, bat, hand) into a bowl of blood.
- Swing the object across a wall.
- Observe the pattern carefully ensuring to understand how and why the pattern changes as it moves away from the initial cast-off point.
- Photograph the pattern and put it into the photo album of bloodstain patterns. Show the photographs to an instructor for grading. In the album, note which object was used to create the pattern.
- For a hand and a fork, examine how the pattern changes, depending on the surface from which the cast-off pattern occurs. For example, if the fingers of the hand face the cast-off surface, droplets from each finger can be seen on the wall. However, if the side of the hand faces the cast-off surface, only a moderately broad pattern is observed.
- Be sure to photograph all patterns.

Table W9.5 Swipe Patterns: Direction of Movement

Pattern Designation	Designate the Beginning of the Pattern (Right or Left)
1	
2	
3	
4	

W9.7.3 Exercise 8: Dragging (Hair)

Bloody hair leaves an extremely thin line of blood when it contacts a surface. An interesting way to observe this is to have a volunteer lie on the floor and place the head in pool of blood. Someone else can pull the person some distance. The pattern that forms is characteristic of someone being dragged through blood. The characteristic hair pattern is also present. Photograph the patterns using midrange and close-up photographs. Show the photographs to an instructor for grading.

W9.7.4 Exercise 9: Crawling through Blood

Another characteristic pattern occurs when someone crawls through blood. The features readily apparent are the patterns that the knees, elbows, and hands make as the person moves through the blood. Have someone crawl through a pool of blood. Examine the pattern closely and then photograph it. Show the photograph to an instructor for grading.

Workshop 10: Bloodstain Patterns—Impact Spatter and Area of Origin

W10.1 Introduction: Area of Origin of Impact Spatter

In the first bloodstain pattern workshop, we determined the impact angle of blood hitting a sloped surface. We discussed both the angle of impact and the angle of incidence, where the former is determined by dividing the width of a resulting stain by its length and then calculating angle of impact using trigonometric functions. Determining the spatial origin of an impact spatter pattern requires such a process. The trigonometric function used is after dividing the width (w) of a bloodstain by its length (l) and then taking the arc sine function of the fraction. The arc cosine will give the angle on incidence.

W10.1.1 Exercise 1: The String Method—Determining Area of Impact Manually

An instructor will demonstrate how to use strings to analyze the individual bloodstains resulting from an impact.

- *Procedures*
  - Create an impact spatter from a pool of blood and allow the blood to dry.
  - Triangulate the area of origin by measuring appropriately to fix the origin spatially.
  - Choose 10 stains that are well formed and that appear to have traveled linearly before impacting on the surface.
  - Measure the width (W) and length (L) of each of the 10 stains and determine the impact angle of each using a calculator. Record these on graph paper.
  - Using a small piece of masking tape, fix a string to the point where the stain impacted the wall.
  - In the plane of the stain's trajectory and using a zero-edge protractor, draw the string out at that angle and fix it to a nonmoveable object—wall, floor, chair, tripod, etc.
  - Repeat the step above for all 10 stains.

- Triangulate the impact point (actually an area) for the stain. Remember, the calculated impact points might be higher than an original impact location.
- Photograph the result.
- Show the completed stringing to an instructor for grading.

W10.1.2 *Exercise 2: The String Method—Using the Laser to Determine Area of Impact*

A second way of determining the area of impact is also a string method. Instead of tracking the string at the impact angle along the zero-edge protractor, a laser attached to the protractor does this for you. The point where the laser beam hits a fixed object is where the string is affixed. The process of selecting an appropriate stain and calculating the impact angle is the same.

- *Procedures*
  - After determining the area of impact manually, move to an impact spatter pattern created by someone else in the class and determine the area of impact using a laser.
  - Compare your area of impact with that determined by the first group who did it manually.
  - Show your results to an instructor for grading.

W10.2 Exercise 3: Multiple Blows—2D Area of Convergence

Four impact patterns have been placed on the white boards attached to walls in several rooms. Use the 2D point of convergence method (Chapter 14) to determine how many impacts make up the patterns.

- *Procedures*
  - Examine the pattern and choose approximately 20–30 stains that appear to be traveling linearly. Do not choose stains that have begun to form an arc or are moving downward.
  - Using a pencil, draw lines through the origins of these droplet stains by back projecting through the axis of the stain toward the area of convergence. This is in two dimensions, which means that the spatial origin (area of impact) is not being determined.
  - Photograph your back projection drawing.
  - Determine the minimum number of impact areas based on the number of cross-points observed.
  - Fill in Table W10.1

Table W10.1 Determining the Number of Blows

Impact Number	Number of Convergence Points	Minimum Number of Blows
1		
2		
3		
4		

W10.3 Questions

- In 500 words or less, discuss the characteristics of an appropriate droplet stain that should be used for determining area of impact and 2D points of convergence. Use photographs that you took of your results to illustrate your response.
- In 1000 words or less, discuss cast-off patterns from the perspective of using impact angles to determine the spatial origin of the blood being cast off a weapon.

Mass Fatality Events, Bioweapons, and Microbial Forensics

15

We've been hit. Hit hard. How hard, we don't yet know. The loss of life . . . is greater than any of us can possibly bear. In 1940, when London was being bombed—every night, night after night—Londoners scrawled a message on the rubble the next morning: "We can take it," they wrote. Well, New Yorkers are made of the same tough stuff. So can we! New York, and the United States, are stronger than any group of barbaric terrorists. The city is still here. It will be here tomorrow morning. It's going to be here forever.*

15.1 Mass Fatality Events: An Introduction

Mass fatality events occur for many reasons. Some are from natural causes and others from man's intervention, and they run the gamut from hurricanes, tsunamis, fires, and building explosions to terrorist events. A recent position paper by the U.S. Department of Homeland Security (DHS) [2] says that all human remains are to be recovered and that "complete documentation and recovery of human remains and items of evidence must be completed." The directives stress that mass disaster scenes are to be considered crime scenes and that the customary rules of evidence and chain of custody apply.

This section concentrates on defining mass fatality events and illustrating the chaos and mayhem they bring to society. The discussion also briefly touches on identifying the missing or dead as it relates to scene investigation.

15.1.1 Defining Mass Fatality Events

Mass fatality events are just that—the loss of multiple lives. These occur for several reasons (Table 15.1). War certainly claims lives as do terrorist events and natural events such as hurricanes, earthquakes, and tsunamis. Recent examples are all too vivid. The most recent rush of terrorist events began with the bombing of the World Trade Center (WTC) in New York City in 1993 and the bombing of the federal building in 1995 in Oklahoma City that claimed 168 lives including 19 children [3]. After the 2001 WTC attacks and the related wars in Iraq and Afghanistan, terrorism has become part of our daily consciousness.

Although human-inspired events are horrific, natural mass fatality events occur frequently enough. The 2004 and 2010 earthquake-triggered tsunamis in Indonesia, the killer Hurricane Katrina's destruction of the Louisiana and Mississippi coast lines in 2005 [4], and the 7.0 magnitude 2010 Haitian earthquake on January 12 that claimed 230,000 lives [5], injured approximately 300,000, and left 1,000,000 homeless are dramatic examples of the destruction caused by natural forces.

* Rudy Giuliani, during a press conference, a few hours after the 9/11 attacks [1].

Table 15.1 Causes and Recent Examples of Mass Fatality Events

Multiple Deaths	Recent Examples
• War	• WTC bombing—1993
• Apartment building collapse—fire	• Oklahoma bombing—1995
• Airline crashes	• WTC attacks 2001
• Multicar accidents	• Iraq–Afganistan war—ongoing
• Terrorist events	• Flight 587—2001
• Natural events	• Rhode Island bar fire—2003
	• Earthquake and tsunami in Indonesia—2004
	• Katrina—2005
	• Haitian earthquake—2010
	• Japan earthquake–tsunami 2011

Natural and man-inspired events, the latter including wars, bombings, and so on, are mass fatality events that seemingly occur daily. Another, much more insidious megafatality potential comes from bioweapons. Biological weapons are silent, deadly, and fully capable of killing millions. Their effects are not relegated solely to human affliction—disease. They are capable of contaminating water supplies and the food chain thereby wreaking havoc in other insidious ways. In some respects, bioweapons are more deadly and destructive than bombings or natural megafatality events because their effects can be more far reaching and encompassing, as the example of the 2001 anthrax mailings showed.

Defining mass fatality events can be tricky because they are more than simply explosions, hurricanes, or even the release of anthrax spores [6]. Is there a cut off between a few deaths, multifatality scenes, and megafatality scenes? With the exception of the 2001 anthrax mailings, these events fall into the megafatality category. But which category does the 2003 Rhode Island nightclub fire fall into where approximately 100 people died [7]?

For the purposes of this discussion, we define mass fatality events arbitrarily in terms of the resources required. If local resources are overwhelmed and the governor of the state seeks federal help, then the event, automatically, is a megafatality or potentially megafatality event (not all deaths would have been recorded just after the event occurred). If local resources, for example, the police, emergency medical technicians, medical examiners, and so on, are adequate, then the event falls into the multifatality event category.

15.1.2 The Anatomy of Mass Fatality Events

The anatomy of mass fatality events has two main parts: (i) the loss of life and structure, and (ii) the aftermath. We consider these in terms of rescue (of the injured), recovery (of the deceased and missing), and cleanup (cleaning the rubble or an area exposed to weapons of mass destruction, for example, explosions, radiation, chemicals, and bioweapons).

15.1.2.1 Loss of Life and Structure

With the exception of the 2001 WTC attacks, most megafatality events have a deceased/injured/inconvenienced pyramidal structure.* This means that the number of people injured

* Shiya Ribowsky, personal communication. Former director of medicolegal investigator for the WTC at the office of Chief Medical Examiner in New York City.

and affected by an event outweighs the number of people who perish, for example as in an airliner crash. Consider, for example, the 265 people who died aboard American Airlines Flight 587 in November 2001. Everyone aboard the airliner died, but the number of those affected, such as families, businesses, properties, and so on, was much larger than the number who perished. The 1995 bombing of the federal building in Oklahoma City is also an example. In that event, 168 people died, a horrific number, certainly, and approximately 500 were injured. Still, the number of people who were inconvenienced and/or affected was in the millions. In fact, the entire nation was affected.

The pyramidal structure of most megafatality events is illustrated in Figure 15.1 on the left. Other events can change the pyramid into an hourglass, such as the structure of the 2001 WTC attacks shown in Figure 15.1 on the right. Here, the number of people directly involved who died exceeded the number physically injured but paled in contrast to those who were affected, as the event had a worldwide impact.

Anyone studying Figure 15.1 might argue that an airliner crash rarely has 95% of the passengers injured. In fact, most perish. The pyramid structure remains because the number of people who are affected or inconvenienced is significantly larger than the number of people who perish.

15.1.2.2 The Human Consequences of Mass Fatality Events

The pyramidal and hourglass structures described above are objective statistical accounts of mass fatality events from loss of life, economic, and emotional perspectives. Not accounted for is the on-going human struggle that continues well after these events. In fact, the anatomy of mass fatality events goes much deeper and can occur in sequence over long periods. For most, the reality of the event itself and the aftermath never go away. The loss of life is tragic and it affects the immediate family forever. The long-term effects extend to the surrounding area and the public at large. Americans will never forget the 2001 attacks on the WTC in New York City, the Pentagon in Washington, DC, or the crash of Flight 93 in Pennsylvania. Nor do we forget the attack on Pearl Harbor on December 7, 1941 or the occurrence of Hurricane Katrina in 2005.

These events and others are entrenched in our collective psyche. Each has an anatomical structure that can be thought of as primary, secondary, and tertiary, and perhaps deeper effects that begin at a point in time but never end. The anatomical structure begins with the initial event, that which is the most visible, the headline event. The follow-on effects for are

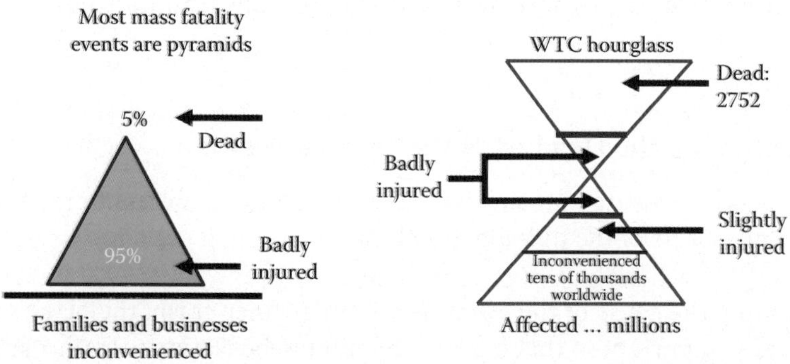

Figure 15.1 Structure of mass fatality events.

Table 15.2 Anatomy of the 2001 World Trade Center (WTC) Attacks

Event	WTC Example
Primary effect	Planes hit the buildings
Secondary effect	The kill zone
Tertiary effect	Building collapse
Quaternary effect	Posttraumatic stress
Quinternary effect	Lung disease—mental illness

not as visible, at least to the public. Table 15.2 shows the sequence of effects for the WTC attacks that builds over time.

The primary effect is the most visible, where there is an immediate loss of life, for example, planes hitting the WTC towers in 2001, the tsunami hitting the coast in Indonesia in 2004, Hurricane Katrina smashing into the Louisiana coastline in 2005, or the Haitian earthquake in 2010. In the bombing of the federal building in Oklahoma City, the primary effect was the bombing itself.

The secondary effect is the kill zone where lives are lost secondary to the primary event, for example, the people on the floors where the planes hit in the WTC buildings, the explosion and the collapsed building in Oklahoma City during the explosion and after the bombs went off, the loss of life after Hurricane Katrina, and so on. The tertiary effect in the WTC attacks occurred when the buildings collapsed and additional lives were lost. For other events, the tertiary effect might equate with the quaternary effect (Table 15.2), and might not be as visual as buildings collapsing but instead people dying who are trapped in already collapsed buildings.

After the immediate and near-immediate loss of life, the long-term effects begin. The quaternary and "quinternary" (to coin a term) effects reflect the emotional toll and possibly subsequent disease that the primary event triggered. These effects are long-lasting and might never be resolved.

The anatomy of a bioweapon event is similar. There will be primary, secondary, tertiary, and quaternary events, at least. The primary event is the release of the bioweapon. The secondary effect is the kill zone, which could be localized to a specific area or building, such as a bombing, but it could spread across a much wider area. The tertiary effect will be people becoming ill and possibly succumbing to disease caused by a primary bioevent. If the event is a bombing, people will die or become permanently disabled. The quaternary event relates to those who are emotionally traumatized by the primary event.

15.1.3 Identifying the Dead in Mass Fatality Events

After first responders ensure that survivors are safe and have access to medical attention, three important aspects of the investigation begin.

- Determining the cause of the event: If it is an airliner crash, the plane's parts will be critically important so that it can be rebuilt by the National Traffic Safety Board (NTSB), an independent U.S. federal government agency. If it is a bioevent, the bioweapon must be found, isolated, and identified.

- Recovering victims and their personal belongings (critical for identifying those who perished).
- Identifying the dead (which requires collecting as much biological tissue as possible): In the United States, if the event is an airliner crash, the NTSB has jurisdiction. If the event is criminal in nature, the FBI takes custody of the scene. This is what happened in the case of the 9/11 crash of Flight 93 in Pennsylvania.
- If the event is caused by a bioweapon (Table 15.2), the Center for Disease Control and the FBI assume the lead in the investigation.

Depending on the type of event, the FBI and/or the NTSB are responsible for nonhuman evidence at the scene. The recovery and interpretation of human remains become the responsibility of the local medical examiner/coroner. If the medical examiner does not have the capacity or the capability to identify large numbers of victims, s/he can solicit the services of federal agencies, such as the Federal Emergency Management Agency (FEMA) and the Disaster Mortuary Operational Response Team (DMORT, a volunteer organization that has expertise in handling the identification of individuals in mass disasters). DMORT was active in the aftermath of the 9/11 attacks and during the 2005 Hurricane Katrina disaster.

Although this discussion concerns body identification, it is not an in-depth conversation of the topic. The intent is to acquaint crime scene investigators with the issues pertaining to identifying the dead or missing. Investigators should be aware of the typical death investigation scene and the ingredients necessary for identifying the missing.

15.1.3.1 The Ingredients Necessary for Identification

Whether the person died in a mass fatality event or is an unknown person lying in an abandoned building in the Bronx, New York, the identification process is the same. Specific kinds of information/data are required to make an unequivocal identification.

15.1.3.1.1 Metadata Metadata usually cannot make a definitive identification per se, but it can help in the process. Metadata is information obtained from multiple sources used to identify a deceased individual. Typically, metadata includes paperwork that yields investigative leads, such as a wallet with an ID card, address of an apartment or house, letters, credit cards, and so on. Other data, such as physical description, medical prostheses, clothing last worn, photographs, and so on, are obtained from family members. Finding and collecting this information can be critical to compiling a list of missing persons.

15.1.3.1.2 Dental Records Comparison of the teeth of a deceased individual with dental records of the person while still alive can be a positive and/or confirmatory identification. After a body is recovered, if teeth are present, a mold can be taken that can be compared with the dental records of the person while still alive. Even individual teeth found at a mass fatality event can be important because they are a good source of DNA.

15.1.3.1.3 Fingerprints Fingerprints of a deceased individual can be compared with fingerprints of a known person. This can be a positive or confirmatory identification.

15.1.3.1.4 Tattoos and Other Body Decorations Tattoos, piercings, and other body decorations can help the process of identification, not as specific proof of identification but, like metadata, can help confirm identification.

15.1.3.1.5 DNA Testing DNA testing, like dental record comparisons and fingerprinting, can provide absolute proof of identity. There are caveats, however. There are two types of DNA in the human body, Genomic and mitochondrial. Only genomic DNA testing can provide the most definitive results for identifying missing or deceased individuals.

There are two types of genomic DNA tests used for making identifications: direct and indirect testing.

15.1.3.1.5.1 Direct DNA Testing The direct test involves a comparison of DNA from the deceased with DNA from known sources belonging to the deceased/missing person. A DNA profile is obtained from the missing person (bone, tissue, teeth, hair, etc.) and that is compared with the DNA profile of a sample obtained from a known source from the missing person (toothbrush, blood bank specimen, tissue paper, underwear, razor blades, electric razor clippings, etc.). If the profiles match and the match statistics are sufficiently robust, the identification is unequivocal.

15.1.3.1.5.2 Indirect DNA Testing The indirect DNA test is essentially a paternity test. A DNA profile is obtained from the missing person and from close biological relatives (mother, father, brothers, and sisters) of the missing person. Since there is a genetic relationship, the probability of paternity can be calculated. If the probability is sufficiently robust, the identification is unequivocal. This how the United States government identified Osama Bin Laden's body.*

15.1.3.1.5.3 Mitochondrial DNA Testing Mitochondrial DNA (mtDNA) is maternally inherited, which means the mtDNA from a deceased/missing person will have the same mtDNA profile as the mother, grandmother, great grandmother, and so on. This testing is not as definitive as direct or indirect genomic testing described above, but it can help confirm the identification when both tests are combined. Given sufficiently robust statistics, this method can be a way to make unequivocal identifications.

15.1.3.1.5.4 Y Chromosomal Testing Another genomic DNA test takes advantage of the DNA present on the Y chromosome. This DNA is inherited in the male lineage and can also help with the identification process. If sufficient numbers of Y chromosome markers are tested for successfully, the identification can be made.

15.1.3.1.5.5 Combining DNA Testing Sometimes the DNA is degraded, which means its quality is poor. This occurs for several reasons, the most common being decomposition of a body or exposure to the elements. In these circumstances, one DNA test type might not be sufficient and multiple testing is necessary. This means testing for genomic markers, mitochondrial markers, and/or Y chromosomal DNA markers to make a single identification.

15.1.3.1.6 Other Modalities Other modalities are also used to identify the bodies in mass fatality and other events. Dental records obtained from the missing can be compared with the dentition of the recovered body. Medical intervention identified by x-rays of the recovered body can reveal old injuries (healed bones) or medically inserted material into the body (pacemakers, metallic plates, etc.).

* Madison Park and Sabriya Rice, CNN HEALTH. May 3, 2011. http://www.cnn.com/2011/HEALTH/05/02/bin.laden.body/index.html (accessed July 24, 2011).

15.2 Introduction to Bioweapons and Microbial Forensics

In our complex world, especially since the September 2001 attacks on the WTC in New York and the Pentagon in Washington, DC, bioweapon attacks are all too familiar. A stark example is the November 2001 mailing of letters in the United States containing *Bacillus anthracis* (anthrax) spores that claimed five lives and infected 17 others. This single example confirms that it was only the latest in what will be an ongoing threat. Bioweapons are not single-dimensional, that is, they are not solely related to diseases, but they can target water and food supplies. For these reasons, being familiar with the general characteristics of biocrimes is important. Using biological agents, bioweapons, as a means to harm or cause havoc is terrorism, which has been defined by Budowle et al. [8] as

> An attack or threat of an attack on the innocent to create fear, intimidate, inflict harm, and/or affect economic as well as well-being. (p. 2)

Alternatively, bioterrorism or biocrimes have been defined as

> Biocrime or bioterrorism is the threat or use of microorganisms, toxins, pests, prions,* or their associated ancillary products to commit acts of crime or terror [10].

If history is a guide, bioterrorism investigations will likely involve multiple points of attack, as the 2001 anthrax mailings dramatically illustrated. The components of these investigations are similar to but decidedly different from traditional scenes of crimes. The similarities include those components essential to all scene investigations, that is, finding probative forensic evidence through competent management, archiving, searching, and so on. The differences, however, are stark.

In traditional scenes—homicides, sexual assaults, burglaries, robberies, hit-and-runs cases, and so on—the investigative paradigm is rooted in the Locard Exchange Principle, which predicts a transfer of evidence, for example, trace evidence, among the participants of the crime who meet in time and space. Consider a homicide scene where the murderer and the victim struggle during which they exchange physical evidence between themselves and the scene. This is typically how evidence originates (Chapter 4). Bioterrorism or bioweapon scenes have a different operational paradigm.

- The participants might never meet in time and space because the spread of bioweapons does not require direct contact with the place(s) of death or the victim(s).
- Bioweapon scenes pose a significant health risk to investigators and the public, while traditional scenes are not classified as general health risks. At traditional scenes, investigators wear PPE appropriate to protect against bloodborne pathogens, which might not be appropriate for bioweapon scenes.
- With the exception of seriously ill individuals or dead bodies, bioweapon scenes might not have a significant macroscene of traditional forensic evidence. That is,

* Prion: "A proteinaceous infectious particle, or prion, (pronounced/pri:on) is an infections agent composed primarily of protein unlike viruses, which consist of two or three parts: a helical molecule, protein coat and sometimes a viral wrapper. The word prion, coined in 1982 by Dr. Stanley B. Prusiner, is a portmanteau derived from the words *protein* and *infection*. Prions are the cause of a number of diseases in a variety of mammals, including bovine spongiform encephalopathy (BSE, also known as 'mad cow disease') in cattle and Creutzfeldt–Jakob disease (CJD) in humans. In general usage, prion refers to the theoretical unit of infection" [9].

> there might be nothing visible to suggest that a crime took place, such as what is usually observed in a more traditional crime. In fact, the target of the bioweapon might be in the hospital.

A typical bioweapons attack scenario suggests that people will become ill. Reports from physicians and health-related institutions to the Centers for Disease Control and Prevention (CDC) will trigger a public health investigation. If the information suggests a bioweapon attack, the law enforcement, specifically the FBI, will become involved. There are two biocrime scenarios: overt and covert [11]. The former automatically triggers law enforcement and is characterized by something at the scene that automatically raises suspicion, for example, white powder, suspicious envelopes or packages, and so on. Secondarily, the public health mechanism kicks in, and its concern is epidemiological. If the bioevent is covert, characterized by an apparent outbreak of disease, the initial concern is for public health. Secondarily, law enforcement becomes involved and proceeds to establish a legal framework for the case.

What if multiple incidences of illness do not occur and there is no health-related report to the CDC? What if deaths occur at a single location? Could this happen in a bioweapons attack? Arguably, it happened in the 2001 anthrax mailings. The first victim became ill in Florida. He was diagnosed with inhalation anthrax and unfortunately died on October 5, 2001. In total, 11 individuals are believed to have contracted inhalation anthrax as a result of the mailings [12,13].

Could this happen again? Yes, certainly. Assume terrorists learned important lessons from the 2001 anthrax mailings, for example, that anthrax spores can leak from envelopes, contaminate mail handling equipment, and infect innocent mail handlers [14]. Assume, too, that a bioweapon can be contained and carried into the United States undetected. The FBI's Dr. Beecher, however, would disagree that this is possible. He believes that it would be impossible to prevent the contamination of the outside of an envelope even if the inside could secure the bioweapon [14]:

> . . . it appears that it is virtually impossible to intentionally place dried spores inside a standard envelope without heavily contaminating its outside surfaces. Even if it were possible to perfectly seal a spore-laden envelope so that no spore could escape from the inside, the outer surface would be so heavily contaminated that spores shed from the surface would present a hazard. Significant contamination of a facility would likely occur simply by carrying such a letter to the containment device in which it is to be opened. (p. 5309)

Beecher confirms that it is possible for a bioweapon to be stashed inside luggage (or a mailing box) inside a bioweapon-impenetrable material. The concealed bioweapon might be invisible to current counter-terrorist measures. Once inside the target country, it would be available for widespread distribution or to target selected individuals, religious groups, or important VIPs. If selectively released, the bioweapon could be transmitted from person to person, a process that could occur over several days, weeks, or months. Millions might become ill and/or die according to the terrorist's schedule.

A scenario not often considered concerns the terrorists themselves. What if, for instance, there is sloppy handling of bioweapons? Someone would find them, even a colleague who might not be aware of the risk, and become exposed and then carry the bioagent to another location. Their death scenes would be treated, initially, like any death investigation.

Bioweapon death scenes are different from routine death scene investigations because the "usual" macroscene elements are missing: no struggle, no blood resulting from traditional bloodletting sources, no forced entry, and so on. Investigators or the medical examiner might move a body (never a wise procedure without a physician present) to observe injuries. Each intrusion, even touching the body, increases the risk. The bottom line is that a bioweapon death scene is an insidious environment of death. This is not like a typical death scene, which certainly has the potential of bloodborne pathogens. This is true even though the victims and the assailant never met. They were never at the same place at the same time and probably did not know each other.

The absence of an obvious macroscene in a death investigation should send a signal that something is not right: multiple bodies, no apparent struggle, no blood, locked doors, and so on. If sufficient time has passed, the bodies might show signs of fatal disease. See Table 15.4 later in this chapter for examples of the effects of biological infection that could signal a bioweapon-related infection. If those infected had sought medical help, the death investigation would be more like a typical bioweapon scenario with reports from physicians to the CDC. But what if an inadvertently infected terrorist chose not to act like the normal person and does not go to a physician? Assuming that a terrorist is going to act like a normal person is an assumption without a factual basis. Might not the terrorist choose instead to die without alerting authorities about a bioweapon attack that had been planned? Would that not be more terrorist-like? In multiple death investigations where the macroscene "does not add up," investigators should always consider that a bioweapons attack had taken place and should initiate a search for telltale signs.

Throughout this text, there has been a constant emphasis on the scientific method as the only logical method to ensure a successful investigation. This model still applies to bioweapon scenes. Terrorism scenes are the responsibility of federal investigators, and the discipline emerging from the 2001 anthrax mailings has become known as microbial forensics. Perhaps, a more apt name is bioweapon forensics or bioforensics because bioweapons are not necessarily microbial or viral in origin.

15.3 Microbial Forensics

Microbial forensics can be defined as [15]

> A scientific discipline dedicated to analyzing evidence from a bioterrorism act, biocrime, or inadvertent microorganism/toxin release for attribution purposes. (p. 1)

Laying the foundation for the discipline of microbial forensics has become the responsibility of the Scientific Working Group on Microbial Genetics and Forensics (SWGMGF). The organization has focused on defining quality assurance guidelines for laboratories, establishing criteria for development and validation of methods, prioritizing efforts on those pathogens and toxins most likely to be used, understanding and enhancing microbial population genetic data, and establishing design criteria for information databases [15]. It is clear that microbial forensics encompasses more than a single discipline.

From the crime scene investigator's perspective, the SWGMGF has little impact because the on-scene investigator deals with what is happening at the current time, and whether the National Biodefense Analysis and Countermeasures Center (NBACC) or the National Bioforensics Analysis Center (BFAC) supported by the DHS works in partnership with the FBI and other federal agencies and laboratories [15] is of little importance to the first responder or crime scene unit that finds itself faced with a bioevent crime. The problem becomes exacerbated if a biocrime scene is not recognized correctly as a bioevent.

Public health officials, especially the CDC, are primary investigators for disease outbreaks. It's mission is to assess the potential risk for disease and its spread. The forensic aspect of a bioweapon investigation involves other, no less important, considerations. But the forensic mission is different because it encompasses more than simply identifying the pathogen involved.

Both investigations occur simultaneously and hopefully cooperatively. Both need to identify the microorganism or agent responsible. But that is where their similarities end. The forensic investigation collects and preserves evidence for subsequent presentation in a legal proceeding. The public health aspect of the investigation is concerned only with the location, identification, and spread of the biological hazard. From a forensic perspective, preserving evidence for a downstream prosecution and the presentation of biological evidence in court has a more stringent standard: Evidence preservation, chain of custody, validation of testing procedures, quality assurance, and testimony in court, different from that required for public health considerations.

The forensic biocrime investigation demands careful controls. The data produced and forensic validation and evaluation of appropriate technologies must meet legal standards that scientists can evaluate. In the 2001 anthrax attacks, creating new methods of detecting and identifying microorganisms was a necessary and integral part of the investigation because appropriate methods did not exist. Still, the data resulting from the investigation had to meet legal standards. The FBI understood these legal challenges, and it researched new genetic testing methods to differentiate different strains of anthrax.

Certainly, the investigation concerning public risk and that of the forensic aspect of these cases are at odds. Thus, any microbial evidence, for example, anthrax spores that can potentially link to a particular suspect, must meet legal and scientific standards.

15.3.1 Bioterrorism Terminology

In the wake of the 2001 anthrax mailings, terms related to bioterrorism are commonplace, and for the remainder of this discussion, the definitions in Table 15.3 apply [16].

15.3.2 Bioweapons

For Americans, bioweapons invoke reminders of the anthrax attacks of October 2001 that followed the wake of the airliner attacks on the WTC in New York City and the Pentagon in Washington, DC. Thoughts logically extend to the terrible consequences these weapons evoke: disease, suffering, and death. Unfortunately, anthrax is not the only bioweapon, not by a long shot. Tables 15.4 through 15.5 list the most important bioweapon categories, bacteria, viruses, and toxins. Law enforcement officials are crime scene investigators should review these tables to better understand the severity of becoming infected and to generally

Table 15.3 Bioterrorism Terminology

Term	Definition
Biocrime	A crime committed using biological weapons.
Bioweapon	A biological agent used as a weapon.
Bacteria	A single-celled microorganism.
Virus	Protein/nucleic acid parasites that invade living cells, take over the cell's metabolic apparatus, and replicates, which causes the cell to burst and release new viral particles.
Biological toxins	Biological molecules obtained from biological agents.
Bioscene(s)	Places that are the focus of bioterrorism events, which can include the target, the point of dissemination, or the point of manufacture of a bioweapon.
Bioevidence	Bioweapon collected as evidence during an official investigation.

know the postmortem signs bodies could exhibit to signal that a bioweapon might have been involved.

15.3.2.1 Bacterial Pathogens

Bacteria are ubiquitous in nature and are invisible. Thus, from the scene investigative perspective, they are part of the microscene. They come in various forms—rods (bacilli), spheres (cocci), and comas or spirals (spirilla). They may or may not be motile and may or may not form spores, a dormant state that allows them to survive for decades. The 2001 anthrax mailings is an example of dormant spores of the bacterium *B. anthracis*.

Bacteria, as bioweapons, can create havoc in multiple ways. They can be directly lethal and/or incapacitating and they can contaminate the food supply, plants, and animals. Table 15.4 lists potential bacterial bioweapons aimed at humans [17]. Others can target plants (*Clavibacter michiganensis*—potatoes and *Liberobacter asiaticus*—citrus plants, among others) or animals (*Mycoplasma capricolum*—goats and *Mycoplasma mycoides mycoides*—cattle). Most bacteria that attack humans also attack animals.

Table 15.5 lists additional potential bacterial bioweapons, taking into consideration the bacterial agent, the effects of infection, and the lethality (see pp. 9–10 in Reference [16]).

15.3.2.2 Viral Pathogens

Viruses are extremely small particles and are the simplest type of common microorganism. They consist of a protein shell inside of which is a nucleic acid, either RNA or DNA. Smaller than bacteria, a virus is a tiny parasite that invades a living cell and takes over the cell's metabolic apparatus, where it replicates, causes the cell to burst, and releases new viral particles. These newly formed viruses infect other cells until the host organism—a human—dies or is incapacitated. Like bacteria, they act to kill and/or to incapacitate. They invade tissues and cause disease by producing toxins. Also, like bacteria, viruses attack people, animals, and plants.

Table 15.6 lists potential viral bioweapons (see pp. 9–10 in Reference [16]). Like Table 15.4, it considers the likely method of dissemination, whether it is transmissible person to person, or duration of the illness, or incubation period, or lethality, or vaccine efficacy, or symptoms and effects, or treatment and potential as a biological bioweapon.

Table 15.4 Examples of Potential Bacterial Bioweapons

Bacterial Bioweapon	Anthrax	Brucellosis	*Escherichia coli*	Tularemia	Cholera	Diptheria	Glanders	Melioidosis	Bubonic/ Pneumonic Plague	Typhoid Fever
Method of dissemination	1. Spores in aerosol 2. Sabotage (food)	1. Aerosol 2. Sabotage (food)	Water/food supply contamination	1. Aerosol 2. Rabbits or ticks	1. Aerosol 2. Sabotage (food and water)	Unknown	Aerosol/ cutaneous	1. Food contamination 2. Inhalation 3. Insect bites 4. Direct contact with infected animals	Infected fleas Aerosol (pneumonic)	1. Contact with infected person 2. Contact with contaminated substances
Person to person	No (except cutaneous)	Unknown	Yes: In daycare or nursing homes	No	Rare	High	High	No	High (pneumonic)	High
Incubation period	1–43 days	1–3 weeks to months	Unknown	2–10 days	3–5 days	2–5 days	3–5 days	Days	1–3 days	7–14 days
Duration	3–5 days (usually fatal)	Unknown	5–10 days (most cases)	>2 weeks	>1 week	Unknown	Unknown	4–20 days	1–6 days (usually fatal)	Unknown
Lethality	*Contact or cutaneous anthrax*: fatality rate of 5–20% *Inhalational anthrax*: almost 100% unless caught early	Low	0–15% if hemolytic uremic syndrome (HUS) develops; 5% if thrombotic thrombocytopenic purpura (TTP) develops	Moderate if left untreated	Low (<1%) with treatment; high (>50%) without	5–10% fatality	50–70%	Variable	5–10% if treated *Bubonic*: 30–75% if untreated *Pneumonic*: 95% if untreated	<1% if treated 10–14% if untreated
Vaccine efficacy (aerosol exposure)	Currently no human data	Vaccine under evaluation	No vaccine	No commercially available vaccine	No data on aerosol	DPT vaccine 85% effective; booster recommended every 10 years	No vaccine	No vaccine	Vaccine not available	Oral vaccine (Vivotif) and single-dose injectable vaccine (capsular polysaccharide antigen); both vaccines are equally effective and offer 65–75% protection against the disease

Symptoms and effects	Flu-like, upper-respiratory distress; fever and shock in 3–5 days, followed by death	Irregular prolonged fever, profuse sweating, chills, joint and muscle pain, persistent fatigue	Gastrointestinal (diarrhea, vomiting) dehydration; in severe cases, cardiac arrest and death.	Chills, sustained fever, prostration, tendency for pneumonia, enlarged, painful lymph nodes, headache, malaise, anorexia, nonproductive cough	Sudden onset with nausea, vomiting, diarrhea, rapid dehydration, toxemia, and collapse	Local infection in respiratory passages; damage to heart, kidneys, and central nervous system	Skin lesions, ulcers in skin, mucous membranes, and viscera; inhaled, upper respiratory tract involvement	Cough, fever, chills, muscle and joint pain, nausea, and vomiting; progressing to death	Enlarged lymph nodes in groin; septicemic (spleen, lungs, meninges affected)	Prolonged fever; ulceration of intestines; enlargement of spleen; rose-colored spots on skin; constipation or diarrhea
Treatment	Vaccine available for cutaneous and inhalation, anthrax. *Cutaneous* responds to antibiotics and immune serum. *Pulmonary anthrax* responds to immune serum in initial stages. *Intestinal* is same as for pulmonary	Antibiotics	Antibiotics available; most recover without antibiotics within 5–10 days	Vaccination using live attenuated organisms	Replenish fluids and electrolytes.	Antitoxin effective	Drug therapy somewhat effective	Antibiotics	Doxycycline (100 mg twice a day for 7 days); ciprofloxicin also effective	Antibiotics shorten period of communicability and cure disease rapidly
Potential as biological agent	High; Iraqi and U.S.S.R. biological programs worked to develop anthrax as a bio weapon	Unknown	Unknown	Highly infectious, 90%–100%	Not appropriate for aerosol delivery	Very low	Unknown	Moderate	High	Not deployed via aerosol; more likely for covert contamination of water or food

The use of information from the Department of Justice is appreciated.

Table 15.5 Additional Examples of Potential Bacterial Bioweapons

Bacterial Bioweapon	Effects of Infection	Lethality
Clostridium botulinum	Botulism. Paralysis that starts with the muscles of the face and spreads to the limbs and eventually to the breathing muscles and thus to respiratory failure and death.	
Escherichia coli O157:H7	Enterohemorrhagic. Causes hemorrhage in the intestines.	Mortality rate <15%
Salmonella	Severe diarrhea, typhoid fever.	
Shigellosis	Shigellosis. Abdominal pain, cramps, diarrhea, fever, bloody diarrhea, dysentery, rectal bleeding and possibly sepsis, seizures, convulsions, and renal failure.	Mortality rate <15–50%
Clostridium tetani	Lockjaw. Muscle rigidity spreads from and facial muscles to extensor muscles of the limbs.	Mortality rate <90%
Legionella pneumophila	Legionnaire's disease. Anorexia, malaise, myalgia, headache progressing to fever, mild cough to fatal pneumonia.	Mortality rate <25%

Table 15.7 lists additional potential viral bioweapons (see pp. 527–591 in Reference [17]), taking into consideration only the bioweapon and where it has been identified, the effects of infection, and prognosis.

15.3.2.3 Other Bioweapon Categories

Although bacteria and viruses represent large categories of biological agents that could be used as bioweapons, they are not the end of the story. Other potential organisms that are not as easily recognized by the general public include rickettsial and fungal pathogens.

15.3.2.3.1 Rickettsial Pathogens These are single-cell mircroorgansims that produce fewer diseases than bacteria and are easily killed by heat and dehydration. As bioweapons, they can be lethal or simply incapacitating, and can be freeze-dried into an easily dispersible powder. Their danger is that they are only detectible by epidemiological investigation of disease patterns. They can be dispersed in letters like those in the 2001 anthrax attacks, although they would likely contaminate the mail routes—similar to the 2001 anrthax attacks—because they are sized midway between bacteria and viruses. They can also be dispersed by local insects. A few examples of rickettsial agents include:

- Typhus (*Rickettsial prowazekki*—40% mortality)
- Rocky mountain spotted fever (*Rickettsia rickettsii*—25% mortality)
- Scrub typhus (*Rickettsia tsutsugamushi*—60% mortality) (see pp. 527–591 in Reference [17])

15.3.2.3.2 Fungal Pathogens Fungi are unicellular or multicellular organisms of the plant kingdom that include molds, mildew, smuts, rusts, and yeast. They reproduce by forming spores, which, unlike bacterial spores, are not a protective mechanism. Like bacterial spores, however, fungal spores can lie dormant for decades, germinating on or in a host. Their main use as bioweapons would be to wreak havoc with the agricultural food

Table 15.6 Examples of Potential Viral Bioweapons

Viral Bioweapon	Marburg Virus	Junin Virus	Rift Valley Fever Virus	Smallpox	Venezuelan Equine Encephalitis	Yellow Fever Virus	Dengue Fever Virus	Ebola Virus	Congo-Crimean Hemorrhagic Fever Virus
Method of dissemination	Aerosol	Not known	1. Mosquito 2. Aerosols or droplets	Aerosol	1. Aerosol 2. Infected vectors	Mosquito-borne	Mosquito-borne	1. Direct contact 2. Aerosol	Unknown
Person to person	Unknown	Unknown	Unknown	High	No	No	No	Moderate	Yes
Incubation period	5–7 days	7–16 days	2–5 days	10–12 days	1–6 days	3–6 days	3–15 days	4–16 days	7–12 days
Duration of illness	Unknown	16 days	25 days	4 weeks	Days to weeks	2 weeks	1 week	Death between 7 and 16 days	9–12 days
Lethality	25%	18%	<1%	20–40%	1–60%	10–20% death in severe cases; full recovery after 2–3 days	5%	1. High for Zaire strain; 2. Moderate with Sudan	15–20%
Vaccine efficacy	No vaccine	No vaccine	Inactivated vaccine—limited quantities	Vaccine protects against infection within 3–5 days of exposure	Experimental only	Vaccine available; confers immunity for >10 years	Vaccine available	No vaccine	No vaccine available
Symptoms and effects	Sudden onset of fever, malaise, muscle pain, headache, and conjunctivitis, followed by sore throat, vomiting, diarrhea, and rash. Internal and external bleeding. Liver function may be abnormal and platelet function may be impaired	Hemorrhagic syndrome, chills, sweating, exhaustion and stupor	Febrile illness, sometimes abdominal tenderness	Sudden onset of fever, headache, backache, vomiting, marked prostration, and delirium; Small blisters form crusts which fall off 10–40 days after first lesions appear	Sudden illness with malaise, spiking fevers, rigors, severe headache, photophobia, and myalgias	Sudden onset of chills, fever, prostration, aches, muscular pain, congestion, severe gastrointestinal disturbances, liver damage, and jaundice; hemorrhage from skin and gums	Sudden onset of fever, chills, intense headache, pain behind eyes, joint and muscle pain, exhaustion, and prostration	Mild febrile illness, then vomiting, diarrhea, rash, kidney and liver failure, internal and external hemorrhage (begins on 5th day); petechiae	Fever, easy bleeding, petechiae, hypotension and shock; flushing of face and chest, edema, vomiting, and diarrhea

continued

Table 15.6 (Continued) Examples of Potential Viral Bioweapons

Viral Bioweapon	Marburg Virus	Junin Virus	Rift Valley Fever Virus	Smallpox	Venezuelan Equine Encephalitis	Yellow Fever Virus	Dengue Fever Virus	Ebola Virus	Congo-Crimean Hemorrhagic Fever Virus
Treatment	No specific treatment exists	No specific therapy	No studies	Vaccinia immune globulin (VIG) and supportive therapy	Supportive treatments only	No specific treatment	No specific therapy	No specific therapy	No specific treatment
Potential as viral bioweapon	High Weaponized by former Soviet Union	Unknown	Difficulties with mosquitoes as vectors	Possible U.S.S.R. offense bioprogram	High U.S. and U.S.S.R. offensive biological programs Weaponized liquid and dry forms for aerosol distribution	High, if efficient dissemination device is used	Unknown	Developed by former Soviet Union	Unknown

The use of information from the Department of Justice is appreciated.

Table 15.7 Additional Examples of Potential Viral Bioweapons

Biological Agent	Effects of Infection	Prognosis
Orthomyxoviridae: Worldwide—wild birds	*Highly pathogenic avian influenza*: Abrupt onset of fever with chills, sore throat, muscle pain, frontal headache, sensitivity to light burning in the eyes, cough, chest pain, and difficulty breathing.	Mortality rate <50%
Herpesviridae: Worldwide, BSL-2 agent	*Cercopithecine herpes-1 virus*: Fever, headache, encephalitis, vesicular skin lesions at site, and variable neurological patterns.	Mortality rate <80%
Togaviridae	*Eastern equine encephalitis*: Headache, nausea, vomiting, confusion, seizures, weakness cranial verve palsies, photophobia, fever, chills, diarrhea, sore throat, and severe joint pain.	Mortality rate <90%
Flaviviridae: Japan, Southeast Asia, Indian subcontinent and parts of Oceania; BSL-3 agent	*Japanese encephalitis*: Mild fever and headache progresses to high fever, chills, nausea, vomiting, photophobia, and objective neurologic signs. Can lead to seizure disorders, movement disorders, and mental retardation.	Mortality rate <60%
	Murray Valley encephalitis	Mortality rate <40%
	Powassan encephalitis: Mild fever and headache to high fever, headache, stupor, disorientation, tremors, meningoencephalitis, convulsions, spastic paralysis, and coma.	Mortality rate <60%
	West Nile fever: Asymptomatic or nonspecific flu-like symptoms. Can progress to encephalitis and/or meningitis, seizures, and coma.	Mortality rate <11%
Paramyxoviridae: Australia; BSL-3 level agent	*Hendra virus*: Flu-like symptoms progressing to pneumonia, respiratory failure, renal failure blood clots, and cardiac arrest.	Mortality rate "High"
Rhabdoviridae: Europe Africa, Middle East, Asia, and Americas; BSL-3 agent	*Rabies*: Headache, fever progressing to delirium, psychosis, thrashing, muscular seizures, and aphasia.	Mortality rate <99%

chain, specifically to attack wheat, corn, and rice (see pp. 593–602 in Reference [17]). A few examples of fungal pathogens include:

- Coccidioidomycosis (*Coccidiodides immitis*—50% mortality)
- Coffee berry disease (*Colletotrichum coffeanum* variant virulans—20–80% loss)
- Philippine downy mildew (*Peronosclerospora philippinensis*—early plants stunted)
- Wheat cover smut (*Tilletia indica*—targets wheat)

15.3.2.3.3 Toxins Toxins are poisonous substances produced by animals, plants, or microorganisms. Table 15.8 gives examples of potential toxin bioweapons and considers the likely method of dissemination (person to person), duration of the illness, incubation period, lethality, vaccine efficacy, symptoms and effects, treatment, and potential as a biological bioweapon (see p. 12 in Reference [16]).

Table 15.8 Examples of Potential Toxin Bioweapons

Toxin Bioweapon	Botulinum Toxin	Staphylococcal Enterotoxin B	Tricothecene Mycotoxins	Ricin (Castor Bean)	Saxitoxin
Likely method of dissemination	1. Aerosol 2. Sabotage (food and water)	1. Aerosol 2. Sabotage (food supply)	1. Aerosol 2. Sabotage	1. Aerosol 2. Sabotage (food and water)	1. Contaminated shellfish 2. Inhalation 3. Toxic projectile
Person to person	No	No	No	No	No
Incubation period	Hours to days	3–12 h	2–4 h	Hours to days	5 min to 1 h
Duration of illness	Death in 24–72 h; months if not lethal	Hours	Days to months	Days; death within 10–12 days for ingestion	Death in 2–12 h
Lethality	5–60%, untreated <5% treated	<1%	Moderate	100%, without treatment	High without respiratory support
Vaccine efficacy	Botulism antitoxin	No vaccine	No vaccine	No vaccine	No vaccine
Symptoms and effects	Ptosis; weakness, dizziness, dry mouth and throat, blurred vision and diplopia, flaccid paralysis	Sudden chills, fever, headache, myalgia, nonproductive cough, nausea, vomiting, and diarrhea	Skin—pain, pruritis, redness and vesicles, sloughing of epidermis Respiratory—nose and throat pain, discharge, sneezing, coughing, chest pain, hemoptysis	Weakness, fever, cough, pulmonary edema, severe respiratory distress	Light headedness, tingling of extremities, visual disturbances, memory loss, respiratory distress, death
Treatment	Antitoxin	Mild cases—pain relievers and cough suppressants Severe cases—mechanical breathing and fluid replenishment	No antidote or therapeutic regimen is available	Oxygen Drugs to reduce the inflammation and support cardiac and circulatory functions Ingested—empty stomach and intestines replace lost fluids	Induce vomiting, provide respiratory care, including artificial respiration
Potential as toxin bioweapon	Not toxic via aerosol Lethal if delivered orally Covert poisoning indistinguishable from natural botulism Poisoning limited use	Moderate—could be used in food and limited amounts of water LD50 is sufficiently small to prevent detection	High—used in aerosol form (“yellow rain”) in Laos, Kampuchea, and Afghanistan (through 1981)	Has been used in 1978—Markov Included on prohibited Schedule I chemicals list for Chemical Weapons Convention High potential for aerosol form	Moderate; aerosol form is highly toxic

The use of information from the Department of Justice is appreciated.

15.3.3 The Bioscene

The bioscene was defined in Table 15.3 as

> Places that are the focus of bioterrorism events, which can include the target, the point of dissemination, or the point of manufacture of a bioweapon.

The good news is that most local law enforcement crime scene investigators will not encounter people who are carriers of bioweapons, bodies that succumbed because of a bioweapon attack, or a place that was the target of a bioweapon attack. The reason is that the usual investigations involving local law enforcement include burglaries, homicides, sexual assaults, and so on, crimes that traditionally have little connection with biocrime perpetrators.

The bad news is that there is no guarantee that the status quo will continue. One can envision local law enforcement entering a scene, believing it to be a burglary, and suddenly being in a place where bioweapons are being manufactured. The possibility exists that a speeding car stopped by police is carrying bioweapons. And, of course, as mentioned previously, there could be the death scene where dead bodies were the target of a bioweapon attack or a terrorist inadvertently became infected. The following discussion focuses on the steps the local law enforcement crime scene investigator should initiate when faced with a potential biocrime. The key to identifying the danger is learning to recognize when things don't add up, which might be a body without traditional evidence, powder without drug paraphernalia, suspicious packages, laboratory equipment, or subtle but strange odors.

15.3.3.1 Powder or Suspicious Envelopes/Packages at the Scene

Suspicious packages and unknown powders are potential threats, and they should be respected by crime scene investigators. Entering a scene and finding an unknown powder, which could well be sugar or cocaine, but no signs of drug paraphernalia or manufacture should raise a red flag. Suspicious envelopes and packaging should also raise flags. Learning to recognize these is critical.

15.3.3.1.1 Suspicious Envelopes/Packages Packaging that should trigger suspicion for letters or packages have the following characteristics. If an envelope/package does not have these characteristics, it could still harbor a bioweapon.

- Postage issues: excessive, none, or noncancelled
- Return address: none, fictitious
- Handwriting: suspicious, "altered"
- Unexpected: envelopes/packages from foreign countries
- Postmark: location different from return address
- Packaging: excessive (tape/string), unprofessionally wrapped or marked "fragile," "rush," "personal," "confidential," and so on, without reason

The United States Postal Service (USPS) has guidelines on its Web site for identifying the suspicious packages (Table 15.9) [18].

Table 15.9 Suspicious Mail. The Use of Information from the United States Postal Service is Greatly Appreciated

If You Receive a Suspicious Letter or Package

1. Handle with care. Dont't shake or bump.
2. Isolate it immediately.
3. Dont't open, smell, touch, or taste.
4. Treat it as suspect. Call local law enforcement authorities.

Look for

1. No return address
2. Restrictive markings
3. Sealed with tape
4. Misspelled words, addressed to title only, incorrect title, badly typed or written
5. Oily stains, discolorations, or crystalilzations on wrapper
6. Strange odor
7. Excessive tape
8. Rigid or bulky
9. Lopsided or uneven

If You Suspect the Mail May Contain

A bomb: Evacuate immediately, call police, contact postal inspectors, and call local fire department/HAZMAT Unit.

A radiological threat: Limit exposure—don't handle, evacuate area, shield yourself from object, call police, contact postal inspectors, and call local fire department/HAZMAT Unit.

A biological or chemical threat: Isolate—don't handle, evacuate immediate area, wash your hands with soap and warm water, call police, contact postal inspectors, and local fire department/HAZMAT Unit.

The envelopes in the anthrax mailings had at least one and sometimes two of these characteristics. The Leahy letter (Figure 15.2) recovered from the Capitol Mail room is an example [19]. Its lettering was block-like (altered) and it had a false return address, which would not be known at the crime scene. The danger in handling envelopes and other packages is that anthrax spores are small enough to penetrate the pores of the paper [11], which means that anyone handling the letters without proper PPE will be exposed, as will anyone

Figure 15.2 Anthrax letter mailed in 2001 to Senator Leahy. The use of information from the Department of Justice and the FBI is appreciated.

in the area. In fact, the PPE will be effectively contaminated [11,14], which involves issues of downstream decontamination.

15.3.3.1.2 Handling Suspicious Envelopes/Packages Bioweapon threats occur frequently. Thankfully, most are hoaxes. Most are empty letters but some have contained powdery substances. The following are suggestions for handling such material.

- Do not touch, sniff, taste, open, shake, empty, or look closely at the envelope/package or its contents.
- Do not touch, taste, smell, or sniff packaging contents that might have spilled.
- Place envelope/package on stable surface.
- Alert others that a potential hazard exists.
- Leave the area taking preventative action to ensure that potentially infectious material is not exposed to the face or skin.
- Call medical personnel for exposed or potentially exposed individuals.
- Obtain a list of persons who were in the area when the suspicious envelope/package arrived. Include in the list those who came into contact with the suspicious object.

15.3.3.1.3 On-Scene Investigative Guidelines for Nonhazardous Materials Personnel

15.3.3.1.3.1 First Responder First responders are at risk because there is no way to know what danger exists at the scene. If the response is to an incident involving the alleged use of anthrax, hazardous materials (hazmat) officials should respond. Although most incidents are hoaxes, each must be treated as real. Whether or not anthrax is present, the hoax itself is a criminal event, and it must be investigated. The following list is meant to educate first responders [20]. These and other specific procedures should be part of comprehensive training programs.

- Arrive at the scene wearing appropriate scene investigative protective gear and decontamination supplies (including dilute bleach*), water, plastic bags, and coveralls (for affected persons who need fresh clothing, etc.).
- Secure the area to minimize the spread of contamination and protect the crime scene (for later evidence collection) to decontaminate those persons affected and to remove them for medical treatment. Decontamination procedures for affected persons will vary depending on the degree of exposure, which is not known at the scene. Anyone at the scene is at risk. The person who opened the envelope and any others who came into direct contact with the envelope after it was opened are at the greatest risk.
- Affected persons should be assisted to
    - Wet clothing with water or dilute bleach (e.g., with a low-pressure garden sprayer—not a hose) to reduce the risk of secondary aerosols.
    - Remove clothing and personal items (e.g., watches, rings, keys) and place them in marked plastic bags.

* Dilute bleach: One part bleach plus nine parts water.

    - Wash hands and then face and head.
    - Change into fresh clothing.
    - If a shower is available in the building, take a thorough shower with soap and water and change into a second set of fresh clothing.
- If no shower is available, transport the affected persons to a hospital for decontamination and treatment. Affected persons must be seen by a physician. Antibiotic treatment should be provided immediately. The U.S. Food and Drug Administration (FDA) approved the use of Ciprofloxacin for the treatment of inhalational anthrax [21]. Some personal items that may have been contaminated can be decontaminated using dilute bleach (see earlier footnote on "dilute bleach").

15.3.3.1.3.2 Accidents at the Scene What happens if there is an accident? Assume you or someone inadvertently touches or moves an envelope that has an unknown powder. Assume the powder is anthrax or some other bioweapon. Whether weaponized or not, anthrax spores are easily dispersed [14], which means that you have contaminated not only the area (floor, tables, etc.), but also yourself (skin—hands, face, hair, etc., clothing, shoes) and anyone in the immediate vicinity. The key to controlling the situation is not to panic. Immediately limit the exposed area and the number of people who might have been inadvertently exposed. The following is a checklist of how to handle the situation [20].

- Remember, there is no immediate danger. Relax and remain calm. Contain the contamination by not touching your face, eyes, nose, or mouth.
- Do not disturb the suspect material—letter or package—anymore. Do not pass it around. Do not try to clean up the powder or brush it off your clothing.
- Stay where you are. Keep coinvestigators with you. Do not allow anyone to leave the premises.
- Quarantine the area and stop others from entering.
- Call for backup and hazmat services.
- If facilities are close, wash your hands and wet your clothing to prevent aerosols.
- If possible, shut down the building's ventilation system and turn off fans or equipment that circulates air around the area.
- Wait for help to arrive.

The following guidelines are meant to educate the responders. They are not meant to be hard-and-fast rules. All on-scene activity in bioweapon crime investigations falls under the jurisdiction of the DHS, the FBI, and the CDC.

Crime scene investigative units typically wear PPE that is appropriate for routine investigations. These offer some protection, but there can be instances when local law enforcement responds to a scene without expecting to find bioweapons or other weapons of mass destruction (WMD) and finds them or not, but they are there. Regardless of the purported scenario, the guideword is caution.

Enter the scene slowly and cautiously. Walk through carefully and focus not only on the obvious crime, but also on signs that indicate that bioweapons or other WMD could be present. Even the run- of- the-mill homicide scene could be where bioweapons or WMD are manufactured and/or distributed. Because such threats are increasing, the first order of business is to ascertain whether a biothreat is present. This might be obvious to someone versed in the science, but two questions must be answered for any scene.

- Is laboratory equipment present and what kind is it? If the answer is "yes," it could mean one of three things: bioweapons or WMD are being manufactured; it is a clandestine laboratory; or there is an innocent explanation. Never assume the latter.
- Are suspicious envelopes or packages visible (see Section 15.3.3.1.1)? If "yes," assume the scene is contaminated with bioweapons (even if the package is sealed), the package contains a bioweapon or the package contains an explosive device. Call for immediate and appropriate backup. Secure the scene. If "no," treat the scene like any crime scene investigation but remain vigilant. Follow the guidelines in Chapter 3 for managing the scene.

15.3.3.1.3.3 Apparent Threat: The Answer to the Last Question Is "Yes." If the answer to the question—whether there are suspicious envelopes or packages visible—Is "yes," consider four assumptions to be fact.

- The scene contains bioweapons or other WMD.
- The scene is contaminated with the bioweapon.
- The first responder has been contaminated.
- Anyone who is or was at the scene has also been contaminated.

The first responder has immediate responsibilities.

- Detain anyone at the scene so that bioweapon contamination is contained at the scene.
- Assume that bioweapons are present and assume the contamination listed above.
- Without touching anything, attempt to ascertain whether the envelope/package has been opened. *Note*: the envelope/package might appear contained, but dispersed bioweapons are typically invisible, even to the usual eye-aided scene visualizing techniques such as flashlights and the ALS. Never forget that extremely small bioweapons, anthrax, can penetrate envelopes [14].

15.3.3.1.3.4 No Apparent Threat If there is no apparent threat, for example, verbal, written, packaging, envelopes, and so on, and there is no reason to believe bioweapons materials are present, secure the scene and wait for appropriate personnel to arrive. Do not touch anything, such as powders, normal evidence, or solid waste. If there is a reasonable explanation for the powder, for example, coffee creamer, sugar, corn starch, and so on, treat the powder like any other nonhazardous evidence. Treat unopened packages as though they contain explosives or bioweapons. Never open sealed packages at the scene.

If no threat exists but suspicious materials have been received by someone or an organization that could be a potential terrorist target, consider that the area is a bioweapon scene. Call appropriate agencies. Detain anyone present until appropriate personnel arrive. Threats will be verified after scientific analysis. If the threat is verified, the premise must be decontaminated by appropriate personnel. The first officer and the responding crime scene team should also be treated and decontaminated.

15.3.3.1.3.5 General Scene Guidelines With respect to what to do at scenes, understanding how agencies interact is important but so is having a set of guidelines to follow when unexpectedly encountering a bioscene.

- Consider suspicious powders, envelopes, and packages as high threats. *Note*: By the time investigators arrive, aerosolized bioweapons should have fallen onto surfaces at the scene—tables, chairs, floors, and so on. The threat still exists because investigative activity can re-aerosolize the bioweapons.
- Wear appropriate PPE. If the bioweapon is verified, the scene investigation automatically becomes a joint operation of CDC and law enforcement.
- Call appropriate health and hazmat officials for examination and collection of specimens.
- Collect specimens for bioweapon identification and dispersal characteristics.
- Coordinate the health-related investigation with the traditional crime scene investigative activity.
- Decontaminate equipment and personnel after the investigation.
- If a threat is verified or if contact occurs, individuals at the scene and those who have come in contact should be treated by medical personnel.

15.4 Collecting Bioagents at the Scene

If the scene has been identified as a bioevent, the responsibility for collecting samples falls under the purview of federal agents. If the scene has not been identified as a bioevent, local law enforcement will not be collecting the bioagents but will begin the investigation as a routine criminal case.

Fortunately, some studies concerning collecting biomaterial from crime scene locations have been studied for anthrax. Table 15.10 presents selected examples from the *NIJ Guide 101-00* of the National Institute of Justice [16]. The data show how the surface

Table 15.10 Anthrax Recovery from Various Surfaces versus Method of Recovery

Testing Method	Surface	Recovery (%)
Moist cotton swab	Nonporous	6.2–24
	Porous	0–10
Moist polyester swab	Nonporous	2–10
	Porous	0–6
Moist wipe	Nonporous	2–13
	Porous	1–8
Sample collection and recovery devices (SCRDs)	Nonporous	2–8
	Porous	0.5–4
Contact plates (BA, TSPBA, and PLET agar)	Nonporous	12–76
	Porous	1.5–15

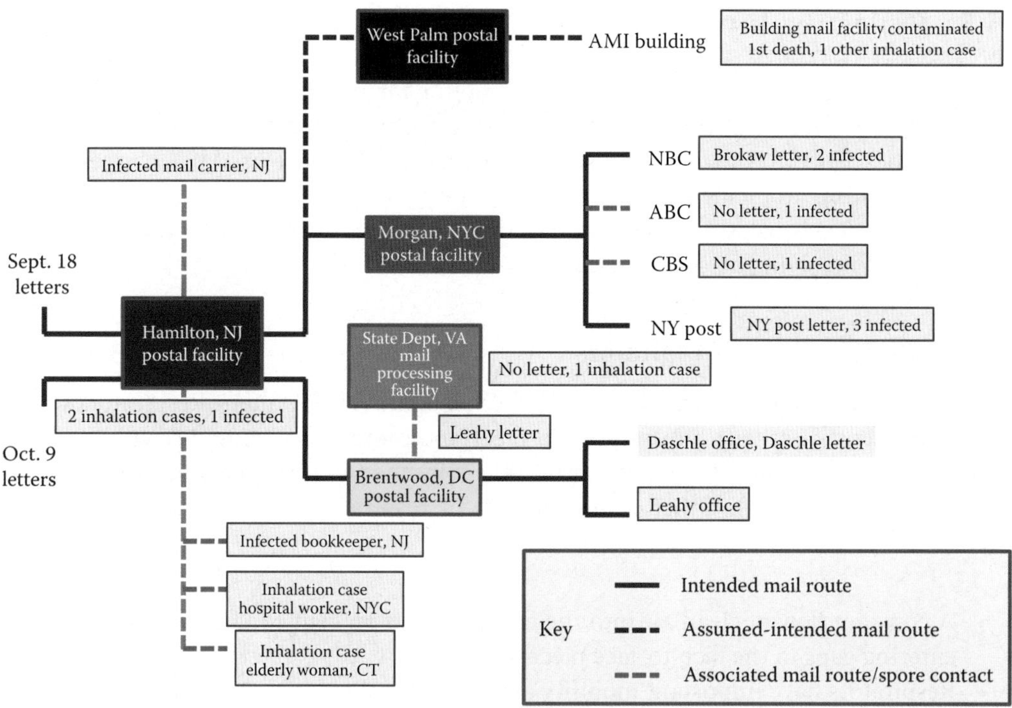

Figure 15.3 Distribution of anthrax spores after the mailings in 2001. The use of public information from the United States Postal Service is appreciated.

and the collection method can dramatically affect the ability of investigators to collect the bioweapon evidence. Even after CDC and/or the FBI have completed their investigations and have left the scene, the area must be considered contaminated.

The collection of anthrax spores from mailroom facilities where anthrax was located after the 2001 anthrax mailings showed that premoistened wipes and a high-efficiency particulate air (HEPA) vacuum sock (87% and 80% recovery, respectively) were more efficient than wet swabs (54%) and dry swabs (14%) for collecting the spores [22].

The relevant lesson learned from the 2001 anthrax mailings is that anthrax spores are easily spread to those who are not direct targets. In all 22 people were infected, five of whom died from the letters (11 with inhalation anthrax). Figure 15.3 shows the distribution of anthrax spores to the intended victims and the relationship of the mail routes to those who were infected or died but were likely not primary targets. The range of the anthrax spread is obvious. Two letters were sent to New York, two to Washington, DC, and presumably one to the American Media, Inc. building in Florida, believed to be sent by the same sender [23].

The implication of the 2001 anthrax mailings proves the point made above. That is, pockets of deceased individuals can occur. Fortunately, the nature of cutaneous anthrax infection, lesions, and so on means that it is easily diagnosed. But it can also be missed. To cite a case in point: It is believed that one of the 2001 terrorists might have been infected with cutaneous anthrax. Had medical personnel recognized it sooner, law enforcement could have been alerted and perhaps 9/11 avoided [24].

15.5 Protecting Investigators Performing Environmental Sampling

Anyone doing environmental (crime scene) sampling for anthrax spores is at risk for exposure and must wear PPE, including respiratory devices, protective clothing, and gloves. The items described in the following sections are similar to those used by emergency personnel responding to incidents involving letters or packages. Emergency responders need to use greater levels of protection in responding to incidents involving unknown conditions or those involving aerosol-generating devices.

15.5.1 Air-Purifying Respirators

Air-purifying respirators should have a full face piece and HEPA filters. Respirators should be used in accordance with a respiratory protection program that complies with the respiratory-protection standard (29 CFR 1910.134) set by the Occupational Safety and Health Administration (OSHA). Other characteristics of respirators include those outlined by CDC [25].

- A constant flow of clean air into the face pieces to prevent contaminated air from entering gaps in the face-to-face piece seal.
- Respirators have important mobility and field of vision.
- Respirators should be assigned to individuals after a quantitative fit testing. This is important because it will reduce inhalation exposures by 98% of what they would be without wearing this type of respirator.

15.5.2 Disposable Protective Clothing: Integral Hood and Booties

The 2001 anthrax investigation showed that anthrax spores will be on the surface of the PPE of investigators [14]. It was shown that the routine PPE worn by crime scene investigators protects the skin-covered areas [26]. Dust particle masks do not protect the face or the possibility of inhaling anthrax spores, which can lead to the most dangerous form of anthrax infection, inhalation anthrax.

- Outerwear
  - Wearing protective clothing does not *only* protect the skin.
  - PPE does not eliminate the possibility of transferring a bioagent to locations other than the immediate scene.
  - Disposable rubber shoe coverings with ridged soles, worn over the booties of the disposable suit, reduce the likelihood of slipping on wet or dusty surfaces.
  - PPE should be decontaminated immediately after leaving a potentially contaminated area.
  - Protective clothing should be removed and discarded before removing the respirator.
- Disposable gloves
  - Disposable gloves made of lightweight nitrile or vinyl protect the hands from contact with potentially contaminated dusts without compromising dexterity.
  - Double gloving is a necessary safeguard.

Table 15.11 Mass Fatality Internet Resources

Agency	URL	Description
National Traffic Safety Board (NTSB)	http://www.ntsb.gov/Family/family.htm	*Federal Family Assistance Plan For Aviation Disasters*: The NTSB Office of Transportation Disaster Assistance provides family/victim support coordination, family assistance centers, forensic services, communication with foreign governments, and interagency coordination to assist the communities and commercial carriers in the event of a major transportation disaster. There are also links on this site to the full version of the Aviation Disaster Family Assistance Act of 1996 (Public Law 104-264), the Foreign Air Carrier Family Support Act of 1997, and amendments to both laws.
	http://www.ntsb.gov/Family/LEO_brochure.pdf	*Responding to an Aircraft Accident—How to Support the NTSB (For Police and Public Safety Personnel).*
Interpol Disaster Victim Identification Guide	http://www.interpol.int/Public/DisasterVictim/guide/default.asp	A resource for general information on disaster victim identification primarily used in Europe and the Middle East. Designed to encourage the compatibility of procedures across international boundaries, this guide gives practical advice on major issues of victim identification, underlining the importance of preplanning and training
	http://www.interpol.int/Public/DisasterVictim/Forms/Default.asp	Disaster victim identification (DVI) forms are for use in cases of major disaster for Interpol, and are reflective of the antemortem information typically collected from family members. The Interpol DVI forms are available in English, French, Spanish, and Arabic.
National Association of Medical Examiners Mass Fatality Plan	http://www.thename.org/Library/NAME%20Mass%20Fatality%20Plan%20with%20appendices.pdf	Mass Fatality Plan is a template for jurisdictions creating a plan. Many of the forms are similar to those in use by DMORT.
Disaster Mortuary Operational Response Team (DMORT)	www.dmort.org	Disaster Mortuary Operational Response Team (DMORT), within DHS/FEMA/NDMS.
	http://www.dmort.org/DNPages/DMORTDownloads.htm	Morgue protocol from the DMORT response to the crash of United Flight 93 on September 11, 2001. The criminal nature of this event caused DMORT to alter some of its morgue operations, and this protocol was adopted for this response.
World Health Organization/Pan American Health Organization	http://www.who.int/water_sanitation_health/hygiene/emergencies/emergencies2002/en/	*Environmental Health in Emergencies and Disasters: A Practical Guide* is an extensive book dealing mostly with medical issues. Chapter 14, titled "Mortuary Services and Handling of the Dead," is relevant to mass fatality response.
	http://www.paho.org/english/dd/ped/ManejoCadaveres.htm	The overview site for *Management of Dead Bodies in Disaster Situations*. This guide is a very comprehensive guide to a variety of issues in mass fatality situations. Chapters include preparedness for mass death response, medicolegal work, health considerations in mass fatalities, sociocultural issues, psychological aspects, legal concepts, and several case studies from recent South and Central American disasters. Direct download in PDF format is available at: http://www.paho.org/English/DD/PED/DeadBodiesBook.pdf

continued

Table 15.11 (Continued) Mass Fatality Internet Resources

Agency	URL	Description
	http://publications.paho.org/english/dead_bodies.pdf	"Infectious disease risks from dead bodies following natural disasters" is an important report indicating that dead bodies from disasters do not pose a risk for infection.
Department of Defense (DOD)	http://www.dtic.mil/doctrine/jel/new_pubs/jp4_06.pdf	*Joint Tactics, Techniques and Procedures for Mortuary Operations in Joint Operations* (149 pp, August 1996). An extensive guide to the search, recovery, transport, and tentative identification of remains in theaters of military operation.
	http://chppm-www.apgea.army.mil/documents/TG/TECHGUID/TG195a.pdf	*Guidelines for Protecting Mortuary Personnel from Potential Infectious Material* (28 pp, October 2001). A useful synopsis of the major issues relative to the handling of infectious remains.
	http://hld.sbccom.army.mil/downloads/cwirp/guidelines_mass_fatality_mgmt.pdf	*Guidelines for Mass Fatality Management During Terrorists Incidents Involving Chemical Agents* (46 pp, November 2001). Developed by the U.S. Soldier Biological Chemical Command, Military Improved Response Program, this guide addresses the variety of issues that medical examiners, coroners, law enforcement, and first responders will need to deal with in a chemical fatality incident.
	http://hld.sbccom.army.mil/downloads/reports/coroner_guide.pdf	*Medical Examiner/Coroner Guide for Mass Fatality Management of Chemically Contaminated Remains* (2 pp). A condensed version of the above guide, in checklist form.
	http://chppm-www.apgea.army.mil/documents/FACT/36-004-0202.pdf	*Dealing with the Stress of Recovering Human Dead Bodies*: A two-page overview of expectations for disaster responders in the handling of dead bodies. Produced by the U.S. Army Center for Health Promotion and Preventive Medicine.
	http://www.afip.org/Departments/oafme/	The Office of the Armed Forces Medical Examiner conducts scientific forensic investigations for determining the cause and manner of death of members of the Armed Forces on active duty or on active duty for training and, under specific circumstances, civilians who die in areas of exclusive federal jurisdiction.
	http://www.afip.org/Departments/oafme/dna/index.html	The Armed Forces DNA Identification Laboratory provides worldwide scientific consultation, research, and education services in the field of forensic DNA analysis to the Department of Defense and other agencies. The DOD DNA Registry provides DNA reference specimen collection, accession, and storage of U. S. military and other authorized personnel.
DOD: U.S. Coast Guard	http://www.uscg.mil/hq/g-o/g-opr/nsarc/nsp.pdf	*Guidance for Mass Rescue Operations*: This document guidance should be considered by search and rescue (SAR) authorities (particularly rescue coordination centers), emergency and disaster response authorities, ship and aircraft owners and operators, and other government and industry persons responsible for planning for mass rescue operations.

- A thin cotton glove can be worn inside a disposable glove to protect against dermatitis from prolonged exposure of the skin to moisture caused by perspiration.

15.6 Mass Fatality Internet Resources

Table 15.11 contains contact information for those interested in agencies that are concerned with bioweapon attacks (see p. 12 in Reference [16]).

References

1. *Rudy: The Rudy Guiliani Story* (TV movie). 2003. Available at: http://www.imdb.com/title/tt0323849/quotes (accessed December 6, 2010).
2. U.S. Department of Homeland Security (DHS). 2007. *National Preparedness Guidelines.* Available at: http://www.dhs.gov/xnews/releases/pr_1189720458491.shtm (accessed February 27, 2011).
3. *Wikipedia.* Oklahoma city bombing. Available at: http://en.wikipedia.org/wiki/Oklahoma_City_bombing (accessed December 6, 2010).
4. *Wikipedia.* Hurricane Katrina. Available at: http://en.wikipedia.org/wiki/Hurricane_Katrina (accessed December 6, 2010).
5. *Wikipedia.* 2010 Haiti Earthquake. Available at: http://en.wikipedia.org/wiki/2010_Haiti_earthquake (accessed December 6, 2010).
6. FBI. Amerithrax or anthrax investigation. Available at: http://www.fbi.gov/about-us/history/famous-cases/anthrax-amerithrax/amerithrax-investigation (accessed December 7, 2010).
7. CNN (U.S.). 2003. At least 96 killed in nightclub inferno. Available at: http://articles.cnn.com/2003-02-21/us/deadly.nightclub.fire_1_attorney-general-patrick-lynch-nightclub-stampede-rhode-island-nightclub?_s = PM:US (accessed December 6, 2010).
8. B. Budowle, M. R. Wilson, J. P. Burans, R. G. Breeze, and R. Chakraborty. 2005. Chapter 1: Microbial forensics. In: R. G. Breeze, B. Budowle, and S. E. Schutzer (eds), *Microbial Forensics.* London, UK: Elsevier Academic Press, p. 2.
9. *Wikipedia.* Prion. Available at: http://en.wikipedia.org/wiki/Prion (accessed November 18, 2010).
10. Scientific Working Group on Microbial Genetics and Forensics. 2003. Quality assurance guidelines for laboratories performing microbial forensic work. *Forensic Science Communications,* 5(4). Available at: http://www2.fbi.gov/hq/lab/fsc/backissu/oct2003/2003_10_guide01.htm (accessed July 24, 2011).
11. B. Budowle, E. Schutzer, M. S. Asher, R. M. Atlas, J. P. Burans, R. Chakraborty, J. J. Dunn et al. 2005. Toward a system of microbial forensics: From sample collection of interpretation of evidence. *Applied and Environmental Microbiology,* 71(5):2209–2213.
12. L. R. Ember. 2006. Anthrax sleuthing: Science aids a nettlesome FBI criminal probe. *Chemical and Engineering News,* 18(49):47–54.
13. L. A. Cole. 2009. *The Anthrax Letters: A Bioterrorism Expert Investigates the Attacks that Shocked America.* New York, NY: Skyhorse Publishing, p. 197.
14. D. J. Beecher. 2006. Forensic application of microbiological culture analysis to identify mail intentionally contaminated with *Bacillus anthracis* spores. *Applied and Environmental Microbiology,* 72(8):5304–5310.
15. B. Budowle, S. E. Schutzer, A. Einsein, L. C. Kelly, A. C. Walsh, J.A. L. Smith, B. L. Marrone, J. Robertson, and J. Campos. 2003. Building microbial forensics as a response to bioterrorism. *Science,* 301:1852–1853.
16. A. A. Fatah, J. A. Barrett, R. D. Arcilesi, Jr., K. J. Ewing, C. H. Lattin, and T. F. Moshier. 2001. *An Introduction to Biological Agent Detection Equipment for Emergency First Responders,* NIJ Guide

101-00. Washington, DC: National Institute of Justice, Office of Justice Programs, U.S. Department of Justice, pp. 7–8, 9–10, 12.
17. D. H. Ellison, 2008. *Handbook of Chemical and Biological Warfare Agents*, 2nd edn. Boca Raton, FL: CRC Press, pp. 493–525, 527–591, 593–602.
18. United States Postal Service (USPS). Suspicious mail. Available at: http://www.usps.com/cpim/ftp/bulletin/2004/html/pb22119/suspicious.htm (accessed February 15, 2011).
19. FBI. 2008. Photo gallery: Amrithrax case/anthrax evidence. Available at: http://www.fbi.gov/about-us/history/famous-cases/anthrax-amerithrax/the-envelopes-4 (accessed January 10, 2011).
20. T. B. Anderson. Anthrax letters: Background information and response guidelines. Available at: http://www.zoology.ubc.ca/zoology/anthrax.html (accessed July 25, 2011).
21. U.S. Food and Drug Administration (FDA). 2009. Cipro (Ciprofloxacin hydrochloride) for inhalation anthrax—Message to physicians and health practitioners on Cipro. Available at: http://www.fda.gov/Drugs/EmergencyPreparedness/BioterrorismandDrugPreparedness/ucm130746.htm (accessed February 15, 2011). Last updated April 30, 2009.
22. W. T. Sanderson, M. J. Hein, L. Taylor, B. D. Curwin, G. M. Kinnes, T. A. Seitz, T. Popovic et al. 2002. Surface sampling methods for *Bacillus anthracis* endospore contamination. *Emerging Infectious Diseases*, 8:1145–1151.
23. United States Postal Service (USPS). 2004. United States Postal Service response to the General Accounting Office recommendations on the anthrax attacks of 2001. Available at: http://www.usps.com/communications/news/security/final_gao.htm (accessed February 15, 2011).
24. W. J. Broad and D. Johnston. 2002. A nation challenged: Bioterrorism; report linking anthrax and hijackers is investigated. *New York Times*, March 23. Available at: http://www.nytimes.com/2002/03/23/us/nation-challenged-bioterrorism-report-linking-anthrax-hijackers-investigated.html (accessed February 15, 2011).
25. Centers for Disease Control and Prevention (CDC). 2001. Protecting investigators performing environmental sampling for *Bacillus anthracis*: Personal protective equipment. Available at: http://emergency.cdc.gov/agent/anthrax/environment/investigatorppe.asp (accessed February 15, 2011). Last updated November 6, 2001.
26. D. A. Frawley, A. M. Samaan, R. Bull, J. M. Robertson, A. J. Mateczun, and P. C. B. Turnbull. 2008. Recovery efficiencies of anthrax spores and ricin from nonporous or noabsorbent and porous or absorbent surfaces by a variety of sampling methods. *Journal of Forensic Sciences*, 53(5):1102–1107.

Forensic Entomology
Bugs and the Postmortem Interval

16

These summer flies have blown me full of maggot ostentation.*

16.1 Forensic Entomology: Introduction

According to Byrd, "Forensic Entomology is the use of the insects, and their arthropod relatives that inhabit decomposing remains to aid legal investigations. The broad field of forensic entomology is commonly broken down into three general areas: medicolegal, urban, and stored product pests" [1].

- *Medicolegal*: Typically, the need is to determine the postmortem interval (PMI) or the time since death occurred. This involves the collection of necrophagous feeding insects at the scene followed by ascertaining the stage of the insects' life cycles.
- *Urban*: This aspect of entomology has two aspects: civil and legal. The former reflects the damage that insects cause to property and crops. From a legal perspective, the insects leave bite marks that must be interpreted correctly.
- *Stored products*: This relates to insects found in foodstuffs.

This chapter does not consider PMI estimations made by medical examiners based on post-death signs. The premise of this discussion is that insects play an important role in determining the PMI in death investigations. The reason is that in death investigations, the time since someone died can provide important information for the successful completion of the investigation, and is a factor medical examiners, scene scientists/investigators, prosecutors and defense attorneys commonly take into consideration. Scene scientists/investigators should be aware of the processes taking place after someone dies: decomposition and the sequential appearance of entomological signs at the scene. Students and novice scene scientists/investigators need to understand this as well.

Why do insects play such an important role in estimating the PMI? The reason is that their life cycles predictably move from the egg to an adult in a process known as metamorphosis.† This well-studied process can be correlated fairly accurately when environmental conditions are known so that which means that medical examiners and/or forensic entomologists can use the metamorphosis timeline to ascertain how long someone had been dead. Entomological PMI estimates are particularly helpful when the body has completed the usual postdeath medical signals (rigor mortis, liver mortis, etc.) commonly used by medical examiners to determine the PMI. The list in Table 16.1

* Shakespeare. *Love's Labour's Lost,* Act V, Scene 2, 409–410.
† Metamorphosis: "Typically marked and more or less abrupt developmental change in the form or structure of an animal (as a butterfly or a frog) occurring subsequent to birth or hatching" [2].

Table 16.1 Entomology-Related Evidence

The Entomological Crime Scene
Decomposing body
Flies/fly infestation
Necrotic insects
Temperature
Footprint/tire tracks
Maggots/maggot trails
Animal-distributed bones
Hidden/discarded weapons
Firearms evidence—bullets/cartridges
Disturbed soil as evidence of additional burials

shows the type of evidence that might be expected at scenes requiring entomological analysis. Some of this evidence would be also found in routine homicide or burglary scenes.

It is also important to realize that entomological PMI estimates are just that, *estimations*. What is really measured is the time it takes from insect colonization to the formation of the adult insect. Figure 16.1 illustrates the process.

After someone dies, such as in a murder case, insects colonize the body soon after death. As shown in Figure 16.1, this is time from when the person is murdered to when colonization begins. Although this length of time should be included in PMI calculations, it is not because it is unknown. The only information available to forensic entomologists is the time from colonization, based on the physical presence of eggs, to the presence of the adult insect. Thus, calculations for PMI utilize the timeline of the insects' life

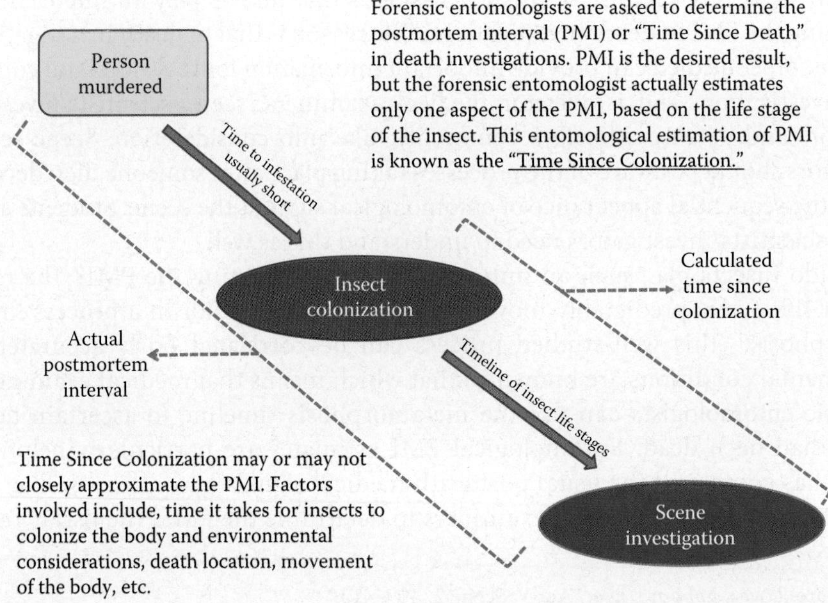

Figure 16.1 Postmortem interval: time since colonization.

stages to determine the time it took from colonization to the beginning of the scene investigation. These estimates are based on the entomological information gathered at the scene.

Forensic entomologists require specific types of information to make PMI calculations (see Figure 16.2). Sometimes, the only people on the scene capable of providing some of this information are the first ones present, which could be the first responder or even someone not associated with the police but instead a passerby. Obtaining this information is important, though. The appropriate information should be obtained by a trained forensic entomologist or someone from the medical examiner's office who is trained to collect the data.

Still, scene scientists/investigators need to learn to recognize the stages of decomposition and the insects associated with each. By understanding metamorphosis and the insects of interest, they will have the intellectual tools to know where to look for insects associated with decomposition and they will be in a better position to protect the appropriate evidence at the scene.

So, to what extent should the scene scientist/investigator know or understand forensic entomology? The answer is simple. Scene investigators are probably neither forensic entomologists nor medical examiners, and they should never make the calculations involved in PMI estimations from the entomological data because there are too many variables that can affect the PMI calculations. Also, it should not be assumed they will ever know how to identify the specific insects, except in the very broad sense. However, they can understand the fundamental approach forensic entomologists take to investigating a scene and thus can protect entomological evidence from damaging effects stemming from the investigation. And, with specific training, they can learn to obtain relevant data for subsequent use. Thus, their role can be a crucial spoke in the wheel of the PMI estimation process.

From Figure 16.2, it is apparent that most of the data necessary for PMI estimations are collected at the scene: obtaining the appropriate temperatures, capturing adult insect species, larvae, and pupae. If forensic entomological expertise is not available, the scene scientist/investigator should immediately recognize the need to obtain these important

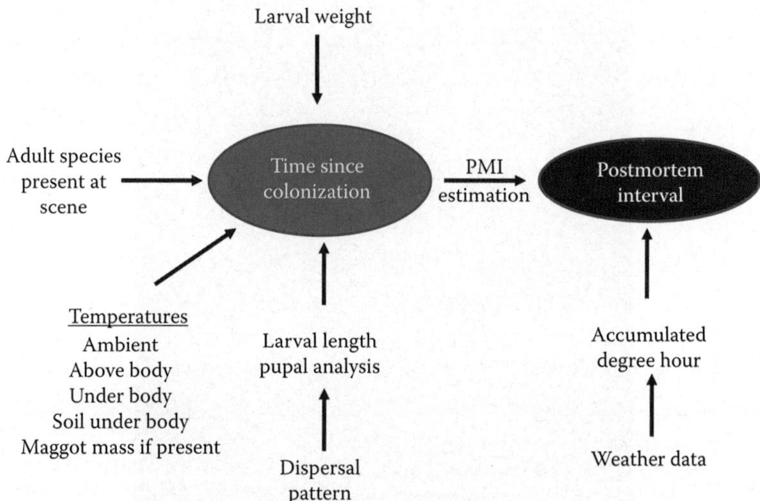

Figure 16.2 Data needed to calculate the postmortem intervals (PM1).

items of evidence. This begins with an understanding of the death–decomposition sequence and the insects associated with each stage.

16.2 What Happens after Death

Understanding the stages of decomposition a body undergoes after death is an important first step in determining the PMI and the role insects play in that process. Importantly, insects are an integral part of decomposition. From an understanding of the stages of decomposition, the scene scientist/investigator can learn to associate the number and types of insects present in each. Thus, by associating insects with the physical state of the body, the entomological evidence has a better chance of being preserved.

Finding the appropriate entomological evidence is critical but tedious, and mistakes can happen. For example, in a scene investigation in the woods where bodies were found, investigators trampled a maggot trail so badly that the location of the largest larvae and pupae was not possible. Since larval length is an important consideration for estimating PMI (Figure 16.1), the resulting calculations were, at best, poor estimates. Had the investigators known what they should have been looking for, they would have located the maggot trail and preserved it. Figure 16.3 shows students marking a maggot trail in the woods.

Figure 16.4 shows a spoon with larvae and soil collected from the larvae trail. The generally accepted stages of decomposition are shown in Table 16.2 [3].

16.3 PMI and Life Cycles

The reason why flies and other insects are used to determine the PMI, or more precisely, the time since colonization, is that their life cycles have been extensively studied and are

Figure 16.3 Searching for a maggot trail. (Photograph by Robert C. Shaler.)

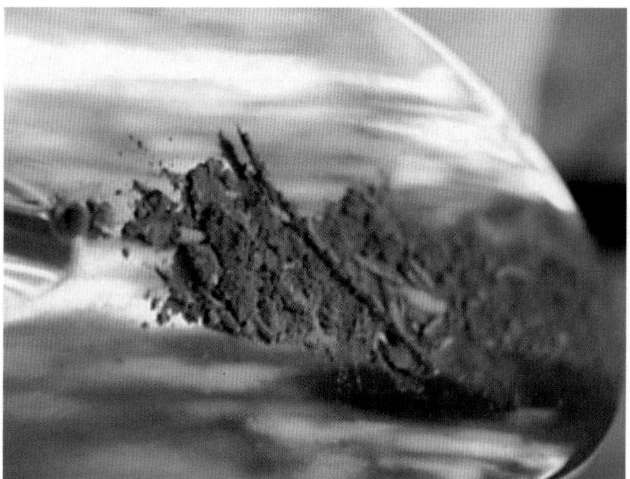

Figure 16.4 Larvae and soil collected from maggot trail. (Photograph by Robert C. Shaler.)

fairly accurately predicted. The reason is that a dead body presents insects with a continually changing food source that supports a succession of organisms ranging from bacteria, fungi, and vertebrate scavengers. The group of organisms that are of interest to forensic entomologists is the arthropods of which the main element of interest is the insects. When insects infest a body, they begin a biological clock that allows for the estimation of the PMI [3,4,5].

Although life-cycle analysis is well studied, estimations of PMI are just that, *estimations.* This does not imply that forensic entomology is not a science. It is, but given the varying environmental conditions at outdoor crime scenes, the calculation of PMI is only as good as the data collected from the scene and from existing and relevant weather data. If it is cold, the life cycle will be longer than when it is warm. Forensic entomologists certainly understand this and try to account for varying conditions, but precise up-to-the-minute determinations are not possible.

In arriving at PMI estimations, the forensic entomologist studies the arthropods present at the scene. A list of insects typically considered for PMI estimations is shown in Table 16.3 [3].

In the first group in Table 16.3 (necrophagous species), the most common insect activity found early on dead bodies and soon after death come from the bottle fly Calliphoridae, of which there are two types—blue and green. Another early arriver is the flesh fly (Sarcophagidae). When these flies "smell" a dead body, they are drawn to it and begin laying their eggs, usually in orifices and open wounds. This process can take minutes or more depending on factors such as concealment, time of the day, presence of drugs in the cadaver/carcass, etc. [3,4].

The presence of eggs on a body marks the first visible stage of insect development, and it begins the progression from egg to adult, a process called metamorphosis or life stages. For the bottle fly, there are four distinct stages: egg–larvae–pupae–adult. These are illustrated in Figure 16.5. The diagram shows the progression of the development from larvae to pupae to adult.

Learning to recognize the manifestation of a decomposing body, that is, the stages of decomposition, and to associate those with insects present at that stage requires knowledge

Table 16.2 Stages of Decomposition

Stage of Decomposition	Description	Insect Activity
First stage	• Begins at moment of death until onset of bloating • Characterized by early stages in decomposition: algor morits and livor mortis [4]	• First insects are blow flies (Calliphoridae) and flesh flies (Sarcophagidae) • Eggs are deposited around natural body openings and open wounds
Bloated stage	• Putrefaction begins. Gases from anaerobes cause inflation of abdomen • Temperature of carcass rises from putrefaction and metabolic activity of Diptera larvae • Fluids seep from openings • Soil under body becomes alkaline from larvae under carcass • Normal soil fauna under body leaves	• Blow flies are strongly attracted to remains during this stage • Attraction reaches a maximum when the body reaches its peak inflation • Some predatory Staphylinidea may be present
Decay stage	• Begins when skin breaks (sometimes classified as wet decomposition [5]) • Gases escape • Remains deflate	• Diptera larvae are prevalent in large feeding masses • Coleoptera arrive • Blow fly and flesh fly larvae complete development and depart • Necrophagous and predatory insects are in later parts of decay stage • Diptera larvae will have removed most of the flesh by the end of the decay stage
Postdecay stage	Remains reduced to skin, cartilage, and bones (sometimes classified as dry decomposition [5])	• Diptera no longer predominate group • Various coleoptera predominate throughout this stage • Diversity of this taxa will predominate • Increase in number of parasites and predators of beetles
Skeletal stage	Only bones and hair remain	• No obvious carrion-frequenting taxa present • Gradual return of normal soil fauna to area beneath remains • No definite end point to this stage • Changes in soil composition may last for an extended period depending on local conditions

of entomology and training. For example, if flies are in the area and rice-like particles (eggs) are present in the body's orifices—arrow in Figure 16.6 points to eggs—the following facts can be determined:

- The body is in the fresh stage of decomposition.
  - Other physical manifestations, such as body cooling (algor mortise), blood settling (livor mortis), or rigor (joint stiffening) should be noted and photographed.

Table 16.3 Insects Considered for Postmortem Interval (PMI) Estimations

Arthropod Group	Value in Estimating PMI
Necrophagous species • Diptera (Calliphoridae and Sarcophagidae) • Flies	Probably most important isolatable taxa for PMI estimations
Predators and parasites of necrophagous species • Coleoptera • Parasites of Diptera larva (necophages in early decomposition become predators in later larval development)	The second most important group for PMI estimations
Omnivorous species • Wasps, ants, beetles • Feed on corpse and arthropods	Can adversely affect PMI estimations by removing (eating) necrophagous species
Adventive species • Use corpse as extension of normal habitat • Collembola, spiders, centipedes • Acari: fungi feeders	Not as important for PMI estimations

- Fly eggs are present in the animal's orifices and two bottle flies can be seen.
- At this stage, larvae have not yet begun to form or, if they have, they have not dispersed far from the body.
  - The eggs should be collected appropriately.
- The checklist in Table 16.4 should be followed to ensure that no evidence is lost.

And depending on resources available and training, the important entomological specimens and information should be collected.

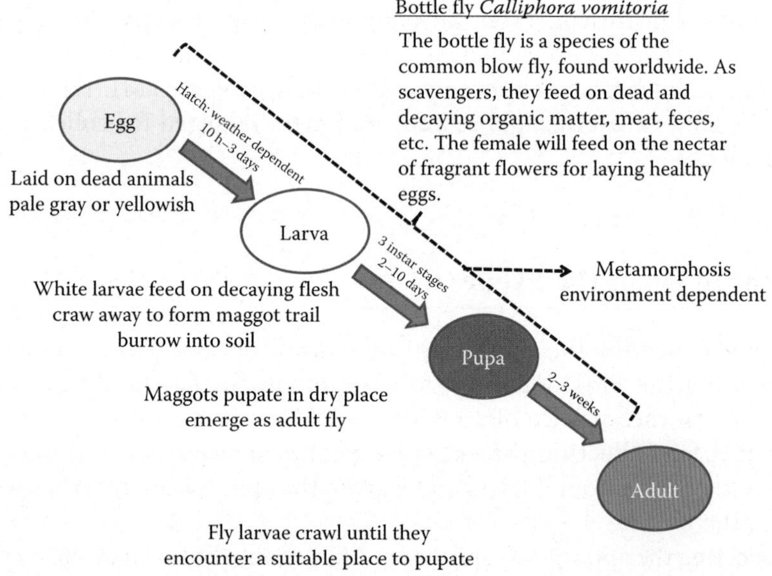

Figure 16.5 Four stages of metamorphosis.

Figure 16.6 Fly eggs in body orifices. (Photograph by Robert C. Shaler.)

If the stage of decomposition is more advanced, a larger number and species of insects will be expected. Identifying them (at least photographically) is important, so it is the responsibility of the investigative team to capture them properly. Ideally, again, the scene scientist/investigator should collect all the different species present. The supplies and equipment required to do this are not expensive and should be easily attainable.

16.4 Equipment/Reagents Required for Collecting Entomological Evidence

When the crime scene unit is dispatched to a scene, no one really knows what challenges the scene will present. From an entomological perspective, ideally, the crime scene mobile unit should have sufficient supplies and equipment to collect the critical entomological data and specimens necessary for calculating the PMI. Table 16.4, adapted from Byrd [7], shows a list of supplies and equipment required for collecting the entomological evidence.

16.5 What to Do at the Scene

Identifying and collecting the entomological data and specimens at the scene are critical for estimating the PMI. Ideally, a forensic entomologist should be called to the scene. However, in the absence of a readily available entomologist, Table 16.5 can be used as a guide for collecting the entomological evidence to ensure that nothing is overlooked so that the entomologist can be given the appropriate information required to determine the PMI.

After collecting the appropriate specimens, they should be taken to the medical examiner's office, which will ensure they are delivered to a forensic entomologist who works with the medical examiner.

Table 16.4 Equipment and Supplies for Collecting the Insects and Larvae

Item	Reason
Aerial or sweep net: 15–18 in. with 24–36 in. collapsible metal handles	For collecting flies around area of dead body
Collection vials: Screw cap-type vials with neoprene cap inserts (4-dram size) or wide-mouth jar. Jars filled with 1/2 in. of powdered plaster, paper towel, or cotton balls to absorb ethyl acetate	Kill jars for collecting the maggots
Feather-weight (or light-touch) forceps: These are commercially available from most biological supply houses. Using normal forceps is risky because, if too much force is used, larvae can be killed	For collecting without damaging delicate and soft fly larvae
Plastic "yogurt" or "bait" containers: 16–64 oz. in size	For collecting and shipping the larvae
Aluminum foil	To hold live larvae and food source during shipment (precut potato wrappers work well)
Vermiculite (or dirt from scene)	For filling bottom of the larval containers to allow for migration, and to absorb excess fluids during shipment
Plastic specimen containers: 4–8 oz. size	Additional collection containers
Paper labels (nonadhesive, heavy bond paper)	*Nonadhesive*: Used to label inside of preserved and live specimen containers *Adhesive*: For labeling outside of containers
Graphite pencil	For making labels (preservation fluids will cause ink to smear)
Small hand trowel or garden spade	For sampling soil and digging for migrating larvae or pupae in outdoor death scenes
Thermometers: Digital	Used for taking temperature of area around body and maggot mass
Photographic equipment (including scales)	Need to capture forensically relevant photographs: establishing, midrange and close-ups (of insects)
Chemicals: ethyl acetate, ethanol, KAA	Used to kill insects
Paper towels	For kill jars, cleaning utensils, and drying hands after disinfecting
Disposable gloves	For personal protection
Sifting screens	Used to process soil samples for collecting the insects and insect artifacts
Form for death scene investigation	For record keeping
Shipping containers: Styrofoam containers with lids are best because they are insulated. Corrugated cardboard boxes are cheap and commonly used	Used to ship collected specimens to appropriate experts

16.6 Arson and Entomological Survival

Experimental work has been done that shows that important entomological evidence can survive house fires. So, it is clear that even intense fires might not destroy forensic evidence. Fire does not prevent insect colonization or the ability of the entomologist to determine the elapsed time since death. However, there are caveats, and one is to be expected: Fires will speed colonization rates by between 1 and 4 days, which could impact calculating the PMIs [5,6].

Table 16.5 Guidelines for Archiving and Collecting the Entomological Evidence

Activity	Method/Equipment Needed	Reason
Archiving: photography and video	Establishing, midrange, and close-up photographs of all areas where insects and larvae/eggs are found. Also video record area and insect/ larvae relationships with body.	Showing relationship of body to area and close up photos of larvae and other insects present. Video is a good way to show the relationship of area to body and location of larvae and other insects.
	Use scales in each photograph with millimeter/inch ruling.	Captures detail.
	Do not use flash to photograph larvae.	Washes out detail.
	Photograph and video: a. Maggot mass and temperature readings taken of mass and under body. b. Detail of body structure changes. c. Bite marks on living people.	Proper archiving procedure to capture close-up photographs and video.
Ascertain decomposition stage	Recognize decomposition signs at each stage. Understand the specific insects that should be present.	Important that entomological data is not lost.
Use collection net to capture flying insects	Wave the collection net over body in figure eight pattern to capture flying insects. Place insects into collection jars.	Important to know which species are predominate.
Take temperatures • Ambient air • Under body • Soil under body • Maggot mass • Body temperature	Use a normal digital thermometer.	Temperatures are important for making degree-day calculations.
Collecting the maggots	Collect one spoonful of larvae from at least three maggot areas on corpse and at scene. In collection jars, place half of collected larvae in solvent (ethanol—not isopropanol or formalin; kill first with hot water if possible) and rest in cloth covered jars (for breathing). Label with date, initials, location, and time.	Needed to identify the species of insect. Live larvae needed to determine the time to next stage of development.
Search for dispersed pattern of larvae. Collect larvae and pupae at dispersal points along the trail [5]. Locate center of dispersal (usually cadaver or carcass) and measure the distance up to 6 m. Divide distance into 1.5 m segments. Divide circumference into four quadrants with a radius of 6 m. Remove 10 cm of soil for up to 1.5 m from center of dispersal. In another quadrant, remove 1.5–3.0 cm soil up to 6 m. Alternate between odd and even quadrants.	Since individuals will bury themselves, it will be necessary to dig and then sift soil. Place larvae in collection jars.	As larvae mature, they move away from body so they can pupate. The largest larvae will be at the end of the larval trail. Need to find reasonable number of pupae and larvae for accurate PMI.
Collect the soil from under body.	Place spoonful of soil from various locations (documented photographically) in collection jar and cover with cloth.	Identification of buried larvae.

References

1. J. H. Byrd. Forensic entomology: Insects in legal investigations. Available at: http://www.forensicentomology.com/definition.htm (accessed April 19, 2010).
2. *Merriam-Webster Online Dictionary*. Metamorphosis. Available at: http://www.merriam-webster.com/dictionary/metamorphosis (accessed September 15, 2010).
3. M. L. Goff. 1993. Estimation of postmortem interval using arthropod and successional patterns. *Forensic Science Review* 5(2):82–94.
4. S. C. Voss, S. L. Forbes, and I. R. Dadour. 2008. Decomposition and insect succession on cadavers inside a vehicle environment. *Forensic Science, Medicine, and Pathology* 4:22–32.
5. L. Gomes, W. Godoy, and C. J. Von Zuben, 2006. A review of postfeeding larval dispersal in blowflies: Implications for forensic entomology. *Naturwissenschaften* 93:207–215.
6. G. S. Anderson, 2005. Effects of arson on forensic entomology evidence. *Canadian Society of Forensic Science Journal* 38(2):49–67.
7. J. H. Byrd. Forensic entomology: Insects in legal investigations. Available at: http://www.forensicentomology.com/equipmentlist.html (accessed July 25, 2011).

Microscenes and Trace Evidence

V

Microscenes
Hair and Fibers

17

Anyone can be confident with a full head of hair. But a confident bald man—there's your diamond in the rough [1].

17.1 Introduction

Chapter 4 discussed the origin of evidence as it relates to the two fundamental principles in forensic science: the principle of divisible matter and the Locard Exchange Principle. The relationship between the macroscene and microscene elements was covered in some detail. This chapter expands on the concept of trace evidence and explores hair and fiber evidence as examples of microscene elements commonly found at crime scenes.

Although fibers represent a vast array of trace evidence and are generally different chemically and structurally (except for wool and cotton which are natural fibers) from hair, they will not be discussed from the crime scene perspective individually because collecting hairs and fibers at the scene involves fundamentally the same procedures. In fact, many consider hairs and fibers as a class of "fibers," and often the term "hair fiber" is mentioned during an investigation. Certainly, the term makes little sense, but this is lexicon that has become ingrained over time. Because they are collected at the same time from the same items of evidence, they are considered similarly and rightfully as classes of trace evidence. However, if this was a criminalistics or forensic science textbook, fibers would occupy a separate chapter.

17.2 Hair and Fibers as Evidence

Hair and fibers are common and seemingly ubiquitous categories of crime scene evidence and should be a focus of macroscene and microscene scene investigations. From a search perspective, hair and fibers are visible or can be made visible using light sources. As the microscene was defined in Chapter 4, hair and fibers straddle the macroscene and microscene sphere. However, they are considered trace evidence in this chapter because they are examined microscopically in the laboratory and have traditionally been considered by criminalists as a class of trace evidence. They are also collected in the same way as trace evidence.

Hair at the scene can come from animals or humans—fibers from plants or manufactured synthetically—and are a source of associative physical evidence. The problem is that there is too much; they are everywhere. Deciding where to find them and then which to collect can be daunting. With respect specifically to hair, there is so much because people and animals are continuously shedding, which means wherever we go, we leave traces of hair. The same is true for fibers, with certain caveats. Essentially, we leave a trail of fibers, too, but to a lesser extent.

Someone might say, "Well I don't. I'm bald."

Consider this. Most people have hair on their bodies, even bald men: body, armpit (axillary), head hair, pubic hair, and beard hair. During a violent physical encounter, hair is lost quite easily through shedding and/or pulling, which is why it has always been a common type of physical evidence encountered in criminal investigations. Importantly, it is category of evidence that is readily collected, identified, and compared. The same is nearly true for fibers because the contact that occurs during a struggle creates an energy that fosters the transfer of fibers. "Compared" is the operative word for what happens in the laboratory and for the importance of hair and fiber evidence in the court during testimony. The laboratory criminalist has the responsibility to compare scene-collected hair and/or fibers with exemplars collected from individuals, suspects, witnesses, victims, and/or their clothing.

Historically, hair evidence has enjoyed an elevated status in the courts and with juries because it has been presented as scientific evidence having an infallible ability to make matches. In fact, some court testimony about hair matches has had the strength of essentially determining guilt—in the minds of the jury and lawyers—being death sentences as a result [2]. Such testimony with respect to the subjective strength of microscopic hair comparisons has come under fire in recent years, and the scientific underpinning of these comparisons has been called into question, notably by the 2009 NAS report [3]. In the aftermath of the NAS report, the forensic value of microscopic hair analysis has been tempered. In fact, the NAS recommends using microscopic hair comparisons as a prescreen for follow-on mitochondrial DNA (mtDNA) typing.

Although the NAS report [3] did discuss fibers (see pp. 161–162), as evidence it did not offer the same poor review. The reason is that fiber analysis is not nearly as subjective as microscopic hair analysis and testimonial opinions have not been based on an examiner's experience. Instead on the objective results of scientific analysis. Also, fiber evidence has not typically been a court tool used to specifically identify someone. More traditionally, and not without exception, fiber evidence has been used by the legal system as a form of associative evidence that can tilt the scale toward or away from guilt rather than pointing a finger directly at an individual.

Because hair testimony has been used to point an accusing finger at an individual, the NAS report gave significant space to hair evidence (see pp. 155–161 in Reference [3]). Does that mean the NAS is saying that hair analysis has no forensic value? No! Normally, microscopic comparison of hairs usually does not identify a specific person, but, like fiber evidence, it has intrinsic investigative value. For example, it can

- Demonstrate that there may have been an association between a suspect and a crime scene or a suspect and a victim.
- Demonstrate that no evidence exists for an association between a suspect and a crime scene or a suspect and a victim.

Both statements illustrate the associative value of hair evidence and although microscopic hair comparisons have been discredited through testimony and follow-up exonerations by DNA analysis, it can still be important to help exculpate or inculpate. The NAS report aside, microscopic examination of hair continues to have important forensic value, as shown in Table 17.1.

Table 17.1 Importance of Microscopic Hair Evidence

- Elimination prescreen for mtDNA analysis
  - This might not be absolutely reliable
- Identify body location of hair
  - Head
  - Pubic
  - Beard and moustache
  - Axillary (armpit)
  - Eyelash and eyebrow
  - Body
- Identify the ethnicity of scene-found hair
- Differentiate the animal versus human
- Identify the treated hair
- Not reliable as a source of attribution

The above discussion illustrates that hair can be used to provide important investigative information. But the true contemporary forensic value of hair remains. Aside from identifying a hair's structural characteristics microscopically and using them as a basis of comparison, the importance of hair lies in the fact that it contains DNA, because cellular material forms its root, which becomes trapped in the hair shaft as it grows.

Certainly, fiber analysis is much simpler in concept because the analysis of fiber evidence can only identify the type of fiber, for example, rayon, cotton, wool, and so on, and the dyes used in its manufacture. Other forensic information can identify other characteristics, for example, whether it was burned, cut, pulled, and so on, which can help substantiate or repudiate witness statements or other soft, factual evidence in a case. But synthetically manufactured fibers do not have the gold standard of evidence that DNA enjoys.

17.2.1 DNA in Hair

The basic structure of hair, from a DNA perspective, is simple. But to understand hair from that perspective, it is necessary to describe its growth cycle. From a scene investigative perspective, a quick look at the root end of a found hair can tell a lot about its potential forensic value. This single observation can reveal a lot about what will happen to the hair in the forensic laboratory and how valuable it will be as evidence. The reason is that the diagnostic physical features of hair are easily observed with a magnifying glass, which can help ascertain whether the these are present. First, we examine the growth cycle of human hair.

17.2.1.1 The Growth Cycle of Hair

Hair's growth cycle has three phases: anagen, catagen, and telogen. Each has important forensic consequences with respect to subsequent DNA analysis, which defines its ability to identify the source of the hair. The growth phases are described in the following sections.

17.2.1.1.1 Anagen or Growth Phase of Hair The anagen phase of hair growth is the longest, usually lasting between 2 and 6 years. During this phase, the hair grows and dead cells of the protein keratin are pushed out through the scalp. The sebaceous glands produce sebum, an oily substance that helps to condition and protect the hair. At any one time, approximately 80–90% of the hairs on a human head are in the anagen phase [4].

During a struggle, hair in the anagen growth phase can be yanked from the head. A strong tug will forcibly remove the hair with a group of cells attached to the root end. Typically, there is an abundance of these root sheath cells visible with a magnifying glass. A follicular papilla might also be attached. Importantly, these cells have nuclei, and there should be sufficient cellular material to perform genomic DNA testing, the DNA typically analyzed to identify someone. Roots can appear dark and fleshy and can have pigmentation. Sometimes even brushing one's hair pulls out root sheath cells. Yanking almost guarantees that root might have its root elements attached [5]. The adhering root sheath cells are fragile and easily lost, and though looking at them with magnifying glass is acceptable, extreme care must be taken to preserve them.

17.2.1.1.2 The Catagen or Transitional Phase of Hair Growth After the anagen growth phase, the hair enters the catagen or transitional phase. At this stage, the sebaceous glands produce less oily sebum and the hair stops growing. The root stops growing and forms a blunt club-like appearance. This "club hair" attaches to the hair shaft, and prevents the hair from receiving nourishment from the blood supply. After 1 to 2 weeks, the hair enters the telogen phase. At any time, approximately 2% of head hairs are in the catagen phase [4].

17.2.1.1.3 The Telogen or Inactive Phase of Hair Growth The telogen phase lasts approximately 3 months. The hair remains attached to the head but is not growing. In essence, it is resting and inactive. The hair follicle stops producing keratin and the club end is fully formed, which is a hard white lump. When the inactive or resting phase is complete, the hair is shed. At any one time, approximately 10–18% of head hairs are in the telogen phase and approximately 100 head hairs are shed daily [4].

17.2.1.2 DNA and the Structural Parts of the Hair

Hair contains two types of DNA: genomic and mitochondrial. Genomic DNA is the DNA that is preferentially analyzed to identify the absolute source of scene-related biological evidence, for example, blood, semen, saliva, and so on. It is found in the nucleus of the cell and consists of equal contributions from the mother and the father. DNA is different structurally and genetically. It is inherited from the mother, the father has no contribution, and, although analyzing mtDNA can be important, it typically does not have the identifying power of genomic DNA. That does not mean the mtDNA has no forensic value. It does. In the absence of genomic DNA, it is the next best thing, and it can provide strong inculpatory evidence and it can exculpate absolutely. Table 17.2 shows the type and relative amount of both types of DNA in hairs found at a crime scene.

Table 17.2 illustrates the general success investigators might expect from the DNA analysis of hairs found at a crime scene. Since the shaft of a hair contains minimal amounts of genomic DNA, the hair's growth cycle determines whether genomic DNA testing will be successful. The shaft usually has sufficient mtDNA to obtain a mitotype.

Finding anagen hairs is important for two reasons: (i) The hair is in its active growth stage, which means it should have the maximum amount of genomic DNA present.

Table 17.2 Structural Parts of Hair and DNA Present

Structural Part of Hair	Anagen Hair	Catagen Hair	Telogen Hair
Shaft	Minimal genomic DNA mtDNA present	Minimal genomic DNA mtDNA present	Minimal genomic DNA mtDNA present
Root with root sheath cells	Large amount of genomic DNA present mtDNA present	Not present	Not present
Root without sheath cells	Genomic DNA present mtDNA present	Minimal genomic DNA mtDNA present	Minimal genomic DNA Minimal/No mtDNA
Club end hair root	Not present	Minimal genomic DNA mtDNA present	Minimal genomic DNA Minimal mtDNA present

As mentioned, because these hairs are actively growing, they are firmly attached to their follicules. When found, then, it means that it took a force to remove them from the scalp. As they are yanked out, they usually have root sheath cells attached, which is a good source of genomic DNA, the type of DNA that has the best chance of identifying the source of the hair. (ii) The importance of DNA testing aside, finding anagen hairs could have investigative significance because it means that the hair might have been yanked from someone's head, for example, a handful of perpetrator's hair in homicide victim's hand. Certainly, there can be innocent reasons for found hairs to be in the anagen phase, for example, the hair got caught on something.

Finding catagen hairs means that hair growth had slowed or stopped and the hair was in its resting phase. Hairs of this type have a root but no adhering root sheath cells, which limits the amount of genomic DNA present. Still, mtDNA should be present. Telogen hairs are at the end of the growth cycle and are typically found as shed hairs. Since they comprise 10–18% of the hairs in the head, finding them at a scene is highly probable. As a source of DNA, they are not the best, but mtDNA will be present in the shaft and in the root. Genomic DNA is likely not to produce meaningful results unless newer typing approaches are used.

17.3 Transfer and Persistence of Hair

Transfer and persistence of hairs are topics related to the Locard Exchange Principle (Chapter 4). Though this is an important topic for scene-related microscene investigations, relatively few studies have been done concerning either the persistence or the transfer of hairs. Several studies have been done concerning the persistence of fibers, however.

17.3.1 Transfer of Hair at the Scene

Locard believed that there would always be a transfer of trace evidence, whether hairs, dust, or fibers. That does not imply that the evidence will always be found because it could be too small to detect or it might have been lost for whatever reason. Still, finding hair should be a concern during the investigation. Typical evidence transfers will be primary, which occur during the commission of the crime. Secondary transfers are also possible; although not the object of the crime scene search, they can take place and can deposit non-crime-related evidence. The typical primary transfers, that can take place, include the following:

- From the perpetrator to the scene
- To the perpetrator from the other participants, for example, the victim(s)
- To the perpetrator from the scene
- From the other participants to the scene

The first is the most important from the perspective of showing that an arrested person was at the scene. The probability that transferred hair evidence is present should be fairly high. So, knowing that the evidence should be there means formulating a search strategy to locate it followed by applying the appropriate techniques to collect it. Logic is the mechanism for finding the hair (and fibers). Mostly, it would be in areas where the probability of the transfer is the highest. According to Locard, the area of a struggle would be where energy was expended. Logically, then, this is where there is the highest likelihood of finding anagen hairs, those having the highest potential for DNA analysis.

Logic also dictates other areas where hair evidence might be found, for example, ski masks are a common type of evidence and the clothing of the victim is another source of hair evidence. With respect to collecting hair and fiber evidence, the rule of thumb is that, if there is a possibility of losing the evidence during transfer to the laboratory, the medical examiner's office, or the property clerk, the evidence should be collected at the scene. For example, if there are hairs on the clothing of the deceased in a death investigation, it is prudent to collect the hairs at the scene, after archiving.

17.3.2 Persistence of Hair

The persistence of hairs on garments is important because of the probability of finding them on the clothing of arrested suspects. When a suspect is arrested, the clothing should be collected and packaged so that no trace evidence is lost. From an investigative perspective, the persistence of this evidence is important. Recently, Dachs et al. [6] studied hair persistence on cotton, polycotton, cotton/acrylic, polyester, and wool. Their results are summarized below. Included in this list below is similar work with animal hairs [7].

- Neither artificial dyes nor the presence or absence of roots had statistically significant effects on the persistence of hair.
- The type of fabric had a major impact and it was found that, generally, hairs persist longer on rougher fabrics.
- The rate of loss of hairs from nonwoolen fabrics during normal wear follows an exponential decay curve.
- The rate of loss from woolen garments was linear, which means the loss of hair from wool is even over time. This suggests a different mechanism for hairs leaving nonwoolen fabrics.
- The speed at which hair was lost from fabrics decreased in the following order: polyester, cotton/acrylic, polycotton, cotton, smooth wool, and rough wool.
- For animal hairs, the fabric type and the structure of the garment were integral to the mechanism of hair persistence; this included yarn or knit tightness for the retention of the animal hair on a particular garment.

- Also for animal hairs, wool garments had a shallower initial decay. After 30 min, 82% of hairs remained compared with polyester garments that exhibited a deeper initial decay where only 25% of the hairs remained. This means that most hair is lost within the first 30 min of transfer.

17.4 Collecting and Preserving Hair at the Scene

The process of collecting and preserving trace evidence is every bit as crucial as finding the evidence in the first place. Extreme care must be taken to guarantee that the evidence is not contaminated or lost. Additionally, the proper legal procedures must be taken into account so that the evidence is not lost for a legal proceeding. The Scientific Working Group on Materials Analysis (SWGMAT) promulgated guidelines for the collection and preservation of trace evidence [8]. The document is divided into several sections that are summarized and paraphrased for on-scene considerations in the following sections.

17.4.1 Documentation

17.4.1.1 Create a Case File for the Specific Case

The file must contain the case documentation for the length of time required by the prevailing laws and nonconflicting agency policy. For a reminder of how to prepare case files, see Chapter 7.

17.4.1.2 Record Important Case-Specific Information

- Date and time, when appropriate, of the collection
- Name of person(s) collecting the evidence
- Description of items collected
- Assign a unique identifier for each item collected
- Record location of each item (documented by notes, sketches, measurements, photographs, or a combination)

17.4.1.3 Contamination and Loss

- Be cognizant of and use appropriate procedures to evidence contamination and loss.
- Confer with other scene investigators to ensure that trace evidence is not lost as a result of testing or collection of other evidence.
- General principles and practices to avoid evidence contamination and loss, applicable to both laboratory and nonlaboratory settings, include the following:
    - Restrict contact between items and personnel before the trace evidence has been secured.
    - Wear appropriate protective apparel, for example, laboratory coats and disposable gloves, to prevent contamination.
    - Change apparel as necessary to avoid contamination or transfer between evidentiary items, locations, and personnel.
    - Handle trace evidence as little as possible to minimize the loss and exposure to contaminants.
    - Collect, package, and seal the items individually in appropriate packaging.
    - Keep items in a secure, sealed package until processed in a controlled environment.

  - Use clean equipment during collection and examination.
  - Adhesive lifting materials used to collect and/or store must be uncontaminated.
  - Ensure that tape edges do not contact unclean surfaces.
  - Ensure there is adequate lighting for locating, packaging, and preserving the evidence.
  - If possible, package evidence in an area that has no excessive air currents, static electricity, or excessive foot traffic.
- Document in the case file instances where contamination or loss occurred or could have occurred.

17.5 Trace Evidence Collection and Preservation Techniques

The constant theme of this text has been to apply logic through the scientific method with respect to activity at the scene. This applies to finding, collecting, and preserving trace evidence. One aspect is the need to consider the scene from a holistic perspective, which means considering everything the scene has to offer: the particulars of the incident case and the conditions at the scene and/or the surrounding area. Deciding which collection technique is most appropriate is part of the decision tree concerning collecting, packaging, and preserving the evidence.

Here, specific questions need answers. These include: What is the best method for collecting the evidence? Will collecting the evidence compromise the integrity of the evidence and thus the laboratory's ability to analyze it? How should it be packaged and preserved until it gets to the laboratory? These questions deserve careful consideration before deciding on an appropriate strategy for moving forward. The following sections can be used as a check-off for ensuring the integrity of the evidence.

17.5.1 Record Keeping

Record on an appropriate form, the scene location of the evidence and the techniques used for detection, collection, and preservation.

17.5.2 Collection Techniques

Methods used for detecting trace evidence include, but are not limited to, visual searches assisted by different types of illumination, such as oblique lighting with flashlights and ALSs (UV, laser, high intensity), and assisted by magnification.

Protecting the evidence is critical, so recovering and collecting the trace evidence should be as least intrusive as possible. The usual collection techniques include picking (with tweezers), lifting (with tape), scraping, vacuuming, combing, and clipping. For on-scene work, the most common is picking, tape-lifting, and vacuuming. If a dead body is present, the medical examiner will determine whether trace evidence from fingernails will be collected at the scene or during the autopsy. If the decision is to collect the samples during the autopsy, the hands of the victim (deceased) should be bagged using paper bags. If samples are collected at the scene, the hands should still be bagged to protect what might have been missed.

Collection techniques are presented in the sections below. Consider each separately for its possible role in the overall collection strategy. Some techniques can be performed in sequence, that is, as a cascade. For example, the first technique discussed, "Picking (Hunt and Peck)," should be the first in the sequence because it is most amenable for lifting surface evidence that is easily visualized by the naked eye or by a light source. Next in the sequence is tape lifting, which picks up the more embedded evidence. Finally, vacuuming is the last in the sequence because it picks up the tiny bits of material. It is also the least favorite to examine in the laboratory.

17.5.2.1 *Picking (Hunt and Peck)*

Trace evidence can be separated from an item, for example, clothing, using clean forceps or other implements. The collected samples should be immediately protected against loss or contamination. Figure 17.1 summarizes the techniques that can be used. It illustrates the placement of a hair fiber into an evidence envelope.

The sequence is to first use the naked eye using a flashlight or the white setting on the ALS to locate hair or other trace evidence, for example, fibers, dirt, debris, and so on. Next is to use the ALS's other wavelengths in the following order, depending of the specific ALS being used: UV (300–400 nm), CSS (if using the MiniScope™), 415 nm, and 535 nm. Each wavelength will highlight the trace evidence having different spectral characteristics.

17.5.2.2 *Tape Lifting*

An adhesive-bearing tape is firmly patted or rolled over an item. The tape picks up loosely adhering the trace evidence. It should not be overloaded. The tape is placed with the collected material on a transparent backing, for example, clear plastic sheeting, glass slides, and clear plastic or glass Petri dishes. The clear protective material protects against contamination and permits samples to be easily viewed and removed for further comparison in the laboratory. Table 17.3 summarizes the important considerations for tape lifting.

17.5.2.3 *Scraping*

A clean spatula or similar tool is used to dislodge the trace evidence from an item onto a collection surface, for example, clean paper, and so on. The collected debris is packaged immediately to avoid the sample loss. This is usually a laboratory method because it is a controlled environment that reduces the risk of contamination or loss of evidence.

- Hunt and peck-picking
  - High intensity light source
    - Flashlight or ALS white light setting
    - Direct and oblique lighting
  - Using the ALS
    - White light
    - CSS setting

Figure 17.1 Picking microscene elements at the scene. (Photograph by Robert C. Shaler.)

Table 17.3 Tape Lifting Microscene Elements at the Scene

Collecting Microscene Elements Tape Lifting

- Tape lifting
  - Not all tapes are appropriate
    - Fiber: 3MM evidence tape
    - Other commercially available trace evidence lift tape
    - Use fingerprint lift tape as last resort
  - Apply tape to evidence in overlapping sections
  - Do not overload tape
    - Change tape frequently
- Preserving tape lifts
  - Seal sticky side of tape lift
    - Clear plastic or plastic wrap
    - Tape to bottom of cardboard box

17.5.2.4 Vacuuming

A vacuum cleaner equipped with a filter trap is used to recover the trace evidence from an item or area. The filter and its contents should be immediately packaged to avoid sample loss. The appropriate vacuum components, the filter and trap, must be changed and rigorously cleaned between each vacuuming to avoid contamination. This method is subsequent to other collection techniques. It is indiscriminate and can result in the collection of a large amount of extraneous material (see Table 17.4).

17.5.2.5 Combing

Combing is used to recover the trace evidence from the hair of witnesses, suspects, and victims. A clean comb or brush should be used for each combing. The combings should be packaged with the combing device in the same package.

17.5.2.6 Clipping and Scraping Fingernails

Trace evidence can be recovered from fingernails by nail clipping, scraping, or both. Fingernails from the right and left hands are packaged separately, which does not preclude

Table 17.4 Vacuuming Microscene Elements at the Scene

Collecting Microscene Evidence Vacuuming

- Collect visible hairs/fibers prior to vacuuming
- Common vacuuming applications
  - Vehicle floorboards
  - Carpets
  - Clothing
- Check area after vacuuming for missed evidence
- Using light sources
  - ALS
  - Bright white light–oblique
- Drawbacks
  - Collects material not related to the crime
    - Consumes too much of crime lab analyst's time

collecting each nail separately from the others, such as a nail with obvious damage. Fingernails should be clipped with clean scissors or clippers and packaged in clean paper.

Clean implements should be used to collect the debris from under the fingernails. The collected debris and the scraping device should be packaged together in clean paper and sealed appropriately.

17.5.2.6.1 Procedure for Packaging Fingernail Clipping or Scrapings and Larger Items of Evidence

- Use packaging that prevents loss and contamination.
- Seal packages properly so that edges do not have openings. Do not use saliva to seal adhesive on packaging.
- Secure small or loose evidence in clean, unused primary containers such as paper packets, Petri dishes, or appropriate vials.
- Seal the Primary container in an envelope or paper bag, which is also sealed and labeled appropriately.
- Secure large items, such as whole garments, individually and in clean, unused packaging.
- Air dry wet clothing before packaging in a location that is free from excessive air currents and foot traffic.
- Place paper under the drying clothing to catch trace evidence that might fall off.
- Package intact visible and firmly attached small or manageable items.
- Document, collect, and package visible but easily lost evidence.
- Document and collect evidence from items impractical to transport.
- Always consider the possibility of physical matches when examining trace evidence. These matches should be documented and the item(s) collected and packaged properly.

17.6 Evidence Security

- Store trace evidence in a secure, controlled-access area. The evidence must have a documented and continuous chain of custody from the time it was collected at the scene until it is admitted into court or the case has been disposed and the evidence is no longer needed. Even then, new evidence can warrant a reinvestigation of the case, which means that someone might need to reanalyze the evidence.
- ASTM Standard Practice E 1492–92 (Standard Practice for Receiving, Documenting, Storing, and Retrieving Evidence in a Forensic Science Laboratory) has standards for evidence handling in a forensic laboratory. These standards represent good forensic and laboratory practice, and they are fundamentally applicable to the crime scene and the laboratory.

References

1. L. David. Hair quotes. Available at: http://www.brainyquote.com/quotes/keywords/hair_2.html (accessed November 19, 2010).
2. J. Grisham. 2006. *The Innocent Man*. New York, NY: Doubleday.
3. Committee on Identifying the Needs of the Forensic Science Community, Committee on Science, Technology and Law Policy and Global Affairs, Committee on Applied and Theoretical

Statistics, Division on Engineering and Physical Sciences, National Research Council of the National Academies. 2009. *Strengthening Forensic Science in the United States: A Path Forward.* Washington, DC: The National Academies Press, pp. 155–161, 161–162.
4. M. M. Houck. 2007. *Forensic Science: Modern Methods of Solving Crime.* Westport, CT: Praeger Publishers, p. 79.
5. H. Harding and G. Rogers. 1999. Physiology and growth of human hair. In: J. Robertson (ed.), *Forensic Examination of Hair.* London: Taylor and Francis Group.
6. J. Dachs, I. J. McNaught, and J. Roberston. 2003. The persistence of human scalp hair on clothing fabrics. *Forensic Science International,* 138(1):27–36.
7. A. E. Boehme, E. Brooks, I. J. McNaught, and J. Robertson. 2009. The persistence of animal hairs in a forensic context. *Australian Journal of Forensic Sciences,* 41(2):99–112.
8. SWGMAT Evidence Committee. 1998. Trace evidence recovery guidelines. Available at: http://www.swgmat.org/Trace%20Evidence%20Recovery%20Guidelines.pdf (accessed November 20, 2010).

Workshop 11: Every Touch Leaves a Trace—Hairs and Fibers

W11.1 Introduction

Each crime scene represents a complex interaction of what might be thought of as subject subscenes—fingerprints, bodies, footprints, and so on, each of which is an integral part of the whole. To understand what a scene is saying, a complete understanding of the relationships among the evidence present is critical. In homicide cases, the body, although important, represents a scene unto itself which is only part of the whole. The same is true for sexual assaults. Here, the victim is one scene and the location of the attack is another. In shooting scenes, bullet path trajectories are part of the scene but only an integral part of the larger overall scene. In bludgeoning cases, bloodstain patterns may be important as is their interpretation, though this is only a part of the puzzle. Their interpretation requires knowledge of the whole, and vice versa. Impression evidence, such as fingerprints and/or footwear and tire tracks, represents yet another category. In this text, these subscene parts have been classified into two categories: macroscene and microscene elements. The macroscene elements are visible, and there may be many at each scene: the body, the bullet hole in the window, wet residue footprints, and so on.

Although a macroscene element or the macrocrime scene is visible evidence, some macroscene evidence might be visible only after the enhancement, such as latent prints. Inconspicuous and buried within this macro or visual scene is a type of evidence that is not as visually apparent and is not easily made visible through enhancement. As its name implies, trace evidence embodies the essence of the Locard Exchange Principle—Locard Elements—that represents a class that also comprises a subscene of its own, the microscene. Trace evidence can be anything classified as evidence. Within its framework there are multiple categories: hairs, fibers, glass shards, dust, microbes, and so on. Trace evidence is critical evidence because it can connect someone to a location even if visible evidence is missing or lacking.

W11.1.1 Considerations

W11.1.1.1 Reference Samples Standard reference samples should always be collected.

- When collecting the reference samples, make certain that a representative sample to sufficiently represent all variations is present. That is, when collecting a sample from a multicolored carpet, collect several examples of each color present. The collected evidence must be packaged and preserved properly. If the evidence is fibers from a sofa, collect several representative samples. If one area of the sofa has been "bleached" because it has been exposed to sunlight over a period of years and another area keeps its "vibrant" colors because that area was in the shade, collect exemplars from both areas.

- Document the location from which each exemplar was collected and give a unique item number to the sample. In the sofa example above, the sofa itself might be Item 1, but the sample from the "vibrant" area might be labeled Item 1A and that from the "bleached" area might be Item 1B.
- Collect a standard sample and label all items examined.
- Patterned marks or impressions may be encountered that require additional documentation and specialized collection and/or documentation procedures, such as 1:1 or close up photography.
- Consider the appropriate enhancement techniques: oblique lighting, powder dusting, and so on.
- Consider collection and preservation techniques: adhesive lifting, casting, packaging.

Always consider the possibility of a physical match between a fractured, broken, torn, or cut portion of an object to its source. In these instances, collect the entire item in question as well as the suspected source item, if available. In packaging, protect the edges to reduce the possibility of deformation. When the possibility of a physical match exists, always package the unknown item separately from the source item.

W11.2 Finding Trace Evidence: Locard Elements

Finding trace evidence, Locard Elements, can be tedious and usually requires a visual aid, which may be a common method of illumination, such as oblique lighting using the flashlight or the ALS. The ALS is often helpful using the white light, the CSS, or the UV settings. The CSS and/or UV settings may cause some fibers or other trace evidence to fluoresce. The UV setting can also be helpful. Sometimes, it is necessary to use magnification, such as magnifying goggles. Generally, there are three methods to find trace evidence at the scene.

W11.2.1 Picking (Hunt and Peck)

In this method, trace evidence is separated from an item using clean forceps or other implements. The collected samples are immediately placed into an evidence envelope. The location of the evidence should be documented.

W11.2.2 Tape Lifting

An adhesive-bearing substrate such as tape is repeatedly and firmly patted or rolled over the item. Loosely adhering trace evidence will stick to the tape. When using this method, grid the item to ensure that the collecting tape does not become overloaded. Tape lifts are typically placed on a transparent backing, for example, clear plastic sheeting, glass slides, and clear plastic or glass Petri dishes, which protects the evidence against contamination. It also allows an examiner to make a visual comparison easily.

W11.2.3 Vacuuming

A vacuum cleaner is equipped with a filter trap that traps the trace evidence. The vacuum should be used in a grid pattern otherwise the filter will become overloaded. After vacuuming, the filter should be immediately packaged in an evidence envelope, which is labeled to document where the sample was collected. The filter should be changed when a new grid is vacuumed. All evidence envelopes should be documented with the location of the sweepings. Vacuuming is a last-resort collection technique except for areas where picking and tape lifting are inconvenient, that is, vehicle carpets, because the amount of material collected can be overwhelming for a laboratory examiner.

W11.2.3.1 Finding Trace Evidence In this exercise, students working in pairs will use the picking, tape lifting, and vacuuming methods to search for trace evidence on various items of furniture. An instructor will demonstrate state each collection technique.

- *General Procedures*
  - Grid the furniture using masking tape. Photograph the furniture with the grid in place. Label each grid with a unique identifier.
  - Using a flashlight and then an ALS (white light setting) use the picking method to locate hairs and fibers (another items) that could be evidence in a crime. Package these items in an evidence pouch, label it appropriately, and show it to an instructor for grading.
  - Using the ALS of the long UV setting (300–400 nm), search the area again, picking any fluorescent or newly highlighted potential evidence. Package the evidence as above. Show it to an instructor for grading.
  - Next, use evidence collection tape (3) to tape the same gridded area.
  - Place each tape in a cardboard box, cover with a plastic wrap, and affix the tape to an evidence collection box.
  - Show the box to an instructor for grading.
  - Finally, use an evidence vacuum to clean the gridded areas. Before vacuuming, show an instructor how you set up the vacuum.
  - Vacuum the area.
  - Collect the debris from the filter holder and package appropriately in an evidence pouch.
  - Label appropriately and show it to an instructor for grading.

W11.2.3.2 Exercise 1: Learning the Basics

W11.2.3.2.1 Procedure After a demonstration of the three the common techniques for collecting the trace evidence, these methods should be practiced. For this exercise, work in pairs.

- Picking (Hunt and Peck)
  - In pairs, grid an area of a segment of a carpet.
  - Search using the flashlight held at an oblique angle.
    - Find trace evidence on a carpet segment.
    - Package the evidence in an evidence envelope and label it appropriately.
  - Search using the white light of the ALS.
    - Repeat the flashlight experiment.

  - Search using the CSS setting on the ALS.
    - Repeat the flashlight experiment.
- Tape Lifting
  - On the same grid, use the tape lifting method to find the trace evidence.
  - After collecting, cover the tape with a clear plastic wrap to preserve the evidence.
- Vacuuming
  - Vacuum the same grid using the vacuum cleaner designed to collect the trace evidence.
- Compare the evidence collected by each of the methods.
- Which would you prefer to sort through if you were a crime lab analyst? Which is the most effective way of collecting the trace evidence?
- Show the evidence collected to an instructor for grading.

W11.2.4 Combing

The combing method is typically used for collecting the evidence from pubic hair/pubic region. In this method, a clean comb or brush is used to recover trace evidence from the hair of an individual. After combing (brushing), the comb (brush) and the collected evidence should be combined in the same evidence package.

W11.2.5 Scraping

A clean spatula or razor blade is used to dislodge trace evidence from an item onto a collection surface such as clean paper. The debris should be packaged into an evidence package and labeled to document its location. Typically, this is a laboratory technique, and has found increasing utility in recent years to collect the epithelial cells for DNA analysis.

W11.2.6 Clipping

Clipping is typically used to obtain trace evidence from the fingernails of homicide and sexual assault victims. In addition to clipping, the fingernails should be scraped to collect the evidence trapped under the fingernails.

Clipping should be done with clean scissors or clippers and packaged in clean paper. When scraping, too, a clean implement should be used to collect the debris from under the fingernails. The clipped fingernails and the scraped debris should be packaged in a single evidence package. Commonly, fingernails from the right and left hands are packaged separately. Some investigators collect each nail separately from all others. An example of this would be when a nail has obvious damage.

W11.3 Exercise 2: The Locard Exchange Principle

In this exercise, you will work in teams of two. The objective is to find trace evidence on a piece of furniture on which there has been a struggle. The fibers collected from the furniture should be compared with fibers lifted from several items of clothing (that you collect as exemplars) and the items of clothing that had been in contact with the furniture should be identified. The exercise also involves examining exemplar clothing that was in contact with the item of furniture. The trace evidence collected from the furniture should be compared with the tape lifts taken from the items of exemplar clothing. Eight items of clothing will be possible exemplar candidates.

Table W11.1 Demonstrating the Locard Exchange Principle

Description of Fibers from Furniture	Description of Fibers from Clothing	Does the Fiber from the Furniture Match the Fiber from the Clothing?

W11.3.1 Procedure

- Section a piece of furniture into grids. Collect trace evidence from the furniture using the tape lift method.
- Tape lift fibers from several items of clothing.
- After collecting the evidence, compare the trace evidence collected from the furniture with that from the clothing.
  - Be sure to use white light, UV light, and the CSS search setting on the ALS to examine the fibers collected.
- Determine which items of clothing had been in contact with the furniture you examined.
- After completing the exercise, fill out Table W11.1

W11.4 Questions

- In 1000 words or less, describe the two fundamental principles relating to evidence transfer: the principle of divisible matter and the Locard Exchange Principle. Explain why transfer occurs sometimes and not as readily at other times.
- In 1000 words or less, discuss the trace evidence you might expect to find at a homicide scene. Include in your discussion a plausible reason why the deceased and the other areas of the scene are considered separate crime scenes.

Glass
A Multitasking Class of Evidence

18

18.1 Introduction

Like impression evidence, glass is an important class of associative evidence found in multiple crime types. From the smallest of splinters to a window with bullet holes, glass is evidence that tells a story about its relationship to the crime. Assume a burglar wants to rob a house. He looks around and figures out that a particular house is alarmed but that the basement windows are not. Perhaps, the owners decided that the basement did not need an alarm system, rationalizing that the windows were too small for someone to crawl through. Perhaps, it was because of financial constraints. The burglar thus breaks a window in the basement and climbs through. Inadvertently, he is providing tangible evidence of the crime and is creating a potential source of evidence that could lead to his conviction, if caught. Although he might leave other evidence, the broken glass can provide investigative information, such as the direction of the break and the location of the entry point of the burglar. The glass itself is also important. For example, maybe the robbery had been staged by the people living at the house. Inspecting the glass in such case will reveal the direction of the break, outside-in or inside-out. If the break had been inside-out, it narrows the possibilities to two, assuming the window had not been broken prior to the burglary: (i) the people living in the house broke the window to stage the burglary, or (ii) this was how the burglar left the house.

This chapter considers glass from the perspective of its value as forensic evidence, how to find it at the scene and how to collect, package, and preserve it for further analysis. While subsequent laboratory analyses can differentiate one type of glass from another, the scene investigator is not concerned with anything other than finding the evidence, making important and critical on-scene determinations and interpretations, and collecting and preserving it. First, though it is instructive to have an understanding of the composition of glass and the different types of glass and their uses.

18.1.1 What Is Glass?

Everyone knows what glass is. Or, they think they do. The *Merriam-Webster Online Dictionary* defines glass as any amorphous material that forms while melting and then forms a rigid structure without crystallizing after cooling.* This means a glass is not necessarily made of silicon, and plastics and resins fall into the category of a "glass."

Other than knowing that something broken at a scene is glass, why should the scene investigator be interested in the composition of glass? The reason is simple. Knowing

* Glass: "Any of various amorphous materials formed from a melt by cooling to rigidity without crystallization: as **a**: a usually transparent or translucent material consisting typically of a mixture of silicates **b**: a material (as obsidian) produced by fast cooling of magma" [1].

that different types of glass have different purposes and thus different chemical compositions can be valuable because it can give information about how to search for it. Certain types of glass that appear uncolored and transparent to the unaided eye have elemental compositions that can make them colored or fluoresce under UV or other wavelengths of light. Tables 18.1 and 18.2 show the types of glass, their general composition, and uses. The first table shows the general categories listed by their common chemical composition. The second table lists the varying types of glass classified by common names and uses [2,3].

The glass types listed in Table 18.1 are not all-inclusive. Other glass compositions are also manufactured, such as aluminum silicate and lead borate (Table 18.2) [3].

18.2 Glass as Evidence

Now that we know that all glass is constructed the same way, why is it forensically important? Importantly, glass is an example of multitasking, associative evidence. That is, not only does it have many uses, it occurs in many crime types to provide forensic information that can significantly help the on-scene investigation. Figure 18.1 is an overview.

In crimes against persons and property—homicides, burglary, sexual assault, and so on—glass can suggest origin by linking glass shards on an assailant/burglar with those at the scene. This is an example of associative evidence. It "associates" the suspect with the

Table 18.1 Common Types of Glass and Their Uses

Category of Common Glass	Common Uses
Soda-lime glass	Flat glass used for containers and light bulbs: >90% of all glass. Contains 60–75% silica, 12–18% soda, and 5–15% lime and other minor ingredients.
Soda-lead glass	Called crystal or lead. Lead oxide used is often glass used for cut glass decanters, vases, and bowls. The lead gives the glass a brilliance which makes it suitable for decorative glass. This type is typical of the collectable antique glass characteristic of the brilliant glass period in the mid to late 1800s into the early twentieth century. Importantly, leaded glass fluoresces a blue-white color under UV light.
Borosilicate glass	Heat-resistant glass used for ovenware and laboratory glass—beakers, test tubes, and so on, 3X better than soda-lime glass; known as Pyrex and Kimax. Contains about 80% silica, 4% sodium oxide, 2% alumina, and 13% boric oxide.
Fused silica glass	Highly heat-shock resistant, used for laboratory glassware and optical fibers. Can be heated to extremely high temperatures and put into cold water without cracking. Made of 100% silica.
96% silica glass	Resists heat nearly as well as fused silica glass. It is less expensive. Contains a borosilicate glass and is sold under the trade name Vycor.
Colored glass	Glass gets color from various metal oxides added during its manufacture. Nickel oxide—from yellow to purple. Cobalt oxide—blue and gold. Copper or selenium—red glass. Some yellow antique glass contains uranium oxide (it is radioactive) that fluoresces a bright yellow-green under UV light.

Table 18.2 Glass Categorized by Usage

Type of Glass	Uses	Type of Glass	Uses
Flat glass	Windows, mirrors, room dividers, furniture, and windshields.	Glass containers	Packaging food, medicines, chemicals, jars, bottles.
Optical glass	Eyeglasses, microscopes, telescopes, and camera lenses.	Fiberglass	Fine, solid rods of glass. Insulation, glass yarn, tape, cloth and mats, electrical insulation, chemical filtration firefighters suits, automobiles, airplanes.
Laminated safety glass	Alternating layers of flat glass and plastic and windshields.	Bullet-resistant glass	Thick, multilayer laminated. Windshields, bank teller windows, military windshields, aircraft.
Tempered safety glass	Single piece and stronger than flat glass. All-glass doors, side and rear windows of automobiles, basketball backboards. Breaks into small cubes of glass.	Colored structural glass	Heavy plate glass. Building exterior facing, interior walls, partitions, and tabletops.
Opal glass	Small particles in the glass that disperses light making it appear milky. Contains fluorides and is used for lighting fixtures and tableware.	Foam glass	Filled with many cells of gas. Light and floats on water. Heat insulation in buildings, steam pipes. Can be cut with a saw.
Glass building blocks	Two hollow sections sealed at high temperature. Insulation made into walls and other structures.	Heat-resistant glass	Contains boric oxide. Withstands temperature changes. Cookware and resistance to chemical attack.
Laboratory glass	Withstands rapid change in temperature. Laboratory ware.	Glass for electrical uses	Electrical applications. Resistant to flow of electric current and seals tightly to metals without cracking. Light bulbs, TV picture tubes.
Glass optical fibers	Transmit information as pulses of light, control board displays.	Glass tubing	Made from different types of glass. Fluorescent lights, neon signs, glass piping, chemical tubing.
Radiation-absorbing and radiation-transmitting glass	Transmits, modifies or blocks heat, light, x-rays, and other radiant energy. UV light absorbs UV. Polarized glass cuts glare of brilliant light. One-way glass coated (can see only one way).	Laser glass	Contains small amount of substances that allow it to generate laser beams.
Invisible glass	Coatings on cameras and eyeglasses. Chemical film that decreases normal loss of light by reflection.	Photochromic glass	Darkens when exposed to UV light. Sunglasses, windows, instrument controls.
Photosensitive glass	Exposed to UV light and heat and reproduces pattern or photograph in the body of the glass.	Heavy metal fluoride glass	Transparent glass used in optical fibers that absorb IR rays.
Chalcogenide glass	Made from elements of the chalcogen group—selenium, sulfur, and tellurium. Transparent to IR light. Semiconductor in electronic devices.	Sol-gel glass	Used as protective coating on solar collectors or as insulating material.

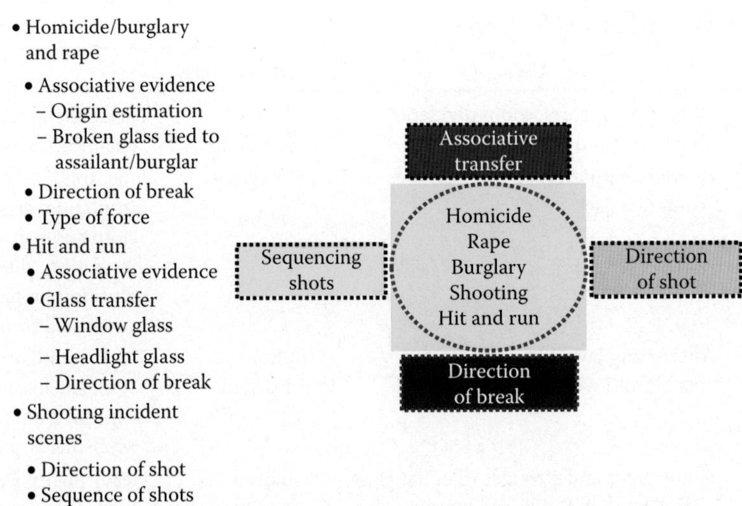

Figure 18.1 Glass: multitasking evidence.

scene. Thus, glass from a broken window (see Section 18.1) can provide valuable probative information. Additionally, the distribution and size of the shards produced from the broken window can indicate the type of force used to break the window. For example, a bullet tends to create smaller shards while a baseball bat will create small and larger shards. In hit-and-run cases, glass can be important evidence if the windshield or headlight glass collected from the scene compares favorably with glass from a suspect vehicle. In shooting scenes, glass can provide diagnostic information of the sequence of shots through a window or windshield or by showing the direction of the shot from the structure of the bullet hole in the glass.

18.2.1 Direction of Force

Understanding how glass breaks gives insight into how to determine the direction of the force that broke the glass, say a window. Figure 18.2 illustrates the breaking process. After a striking force, glass first bends and then begins to fracture beginning with the formation of radial fractures, R1. As the stress on the glass continues, concentric fractures form, C1, and fracturing continues with alternating radial (R2) and concentric (C2) fractures until the process ends.

When the first radial fracture begins, stress occurs along the edges closest to the point of impact, and stress lines form called conchoidal fractures. Since these stress lines or fractures form right angles opposite the side from where the force is applied, they give investigators and laboratory analysts a mechanism with which to determine the direction of the applied force. The initial steps necessary to understand the direction of the force are

- Locate the inner and outer surfaces (determine the outside and inside surfaces of the glass). Sometimes examining features other than the glass can help, such as the location of putty and paint on the glass.

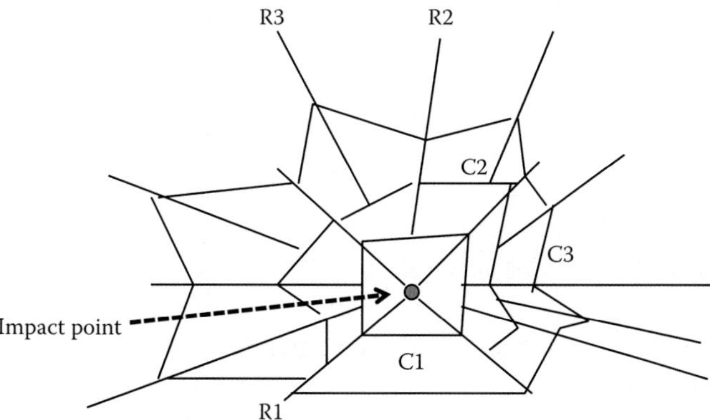

Figure 18.2 How glass fractures.

- Reconstruct as much of the window as possible, if necessary using physical matches; fitting glass together as though building a jigsaw puzzle is an approach that works.
- Find the appropriate radial fracture(s) and examine the edge.
- Locate the perpendicular of the conchoidal stress fractures on the edge of the radial fracture.
- The side opposite the perpendicular is the origin of the force on the glass.

The schematic in Figure 18.3 lists the steps to determine the direction of the force. Start by examining the edge of the primary radial fracture and then find the conchoidal stress fracturs along that edge. On one side of the radial edge, the conchoidal fractures form right angles, that is, form a perpendicular with the edge. The side opposite the perpendicular is where the force was applied and, because of the way glass breaks, a cone (as shown in Figure 18.4) produced on the opposite side of where the

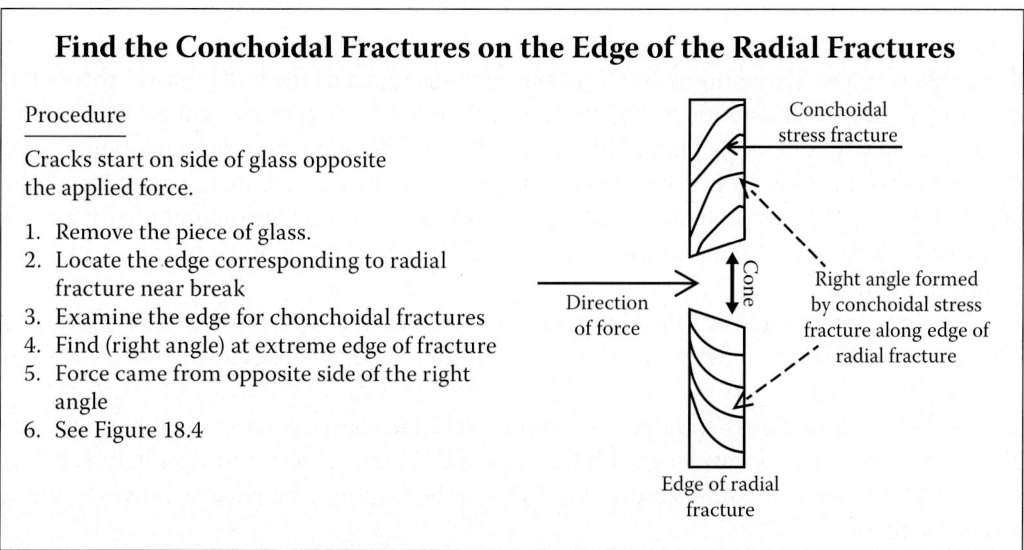

Figure 18.3 Determining the direction of force.

Table 18.3 When Directionality from Conchoidal Fractures Does Not Work

Direction of Break

- Tempered glass
  - Not easily reconstructed
  - Dices without forming ridges
- Laminated glass—automobile glass
  - Both sheets have restricted movement
    - Remains bulged
    - Determining the direction isn't always straightforward
- Thermal glass
  - Fracture is curved and has smooth edge
  - No indication of point of origin

force was applied—the same side as the perpendicular formed by the conchoidal stress fracture.

The procedure described above generally holds, but there are exceptions as shown in Table 18.3. In tempered glass, it dices quickly, which makes determining the location of conchoidal fractures impossible. Often, the glass falls apart making reconstruction difficult. Laminated glass is two glasses sandwiched between and stuck to a plastic material. When this glass fractures, the laminate interferes with the interpretation. One is that the glass panes on either side of the laminate fracture individually and are restricted by the laminate. It is important, then, to carefully examine each pane individually. Also, the laminate can be confusing because a force can make it bulge, which can confuse the determination of the direction of an impact because the bulge can be toward or away from the origin of the force. Thermal glass fragments differently from other glass because the fractures are curved and there is no point of origin.

18.2.1.1 Bullet through a Window

Under some circumstances, a bullet passing through a window might not cause it to shatter, leaving instead a hole; Figure 18.4 illustrates what happens when a bullet passes through a window. The window fractures but remains intact as the bullet passes through it carrying shards of glass with it. On its travel, it removes a cone-like chunk of window, leaving an empty cone in its place. This cone forms on the opposite side of the bullet path, the exit side of the bullet path. The shape of the cone can help elucidate the direction of the bullet. A perfectly shaped (symmetrical) cone indicates a straight-through bullet path [4]. A skewed (asymmetric) cone forms when the bullet path is at an angle to the window, as shown in Figure 18.4.

The direction of force as well as an approximation of the impact angle of a bullet going through a window can be determined by locating the trail of small shards/splinters a bullet carries with it when it exits the window. The procedure requires the scene scientist/investigator to locate these shards/splinters using whatever light source seems to best highlight the glass; whether a certain wavelength on the ALS, a UV light, or a simple flashlight is determined by the chemical composition of the glass. The trail may be elusive, however, but it should be there.

The impact angle can be roughly approximated by tracking the shard trail (Figure 18.5). As Figure 18.5 illustrates, the bullet creates the shard trail by carrying

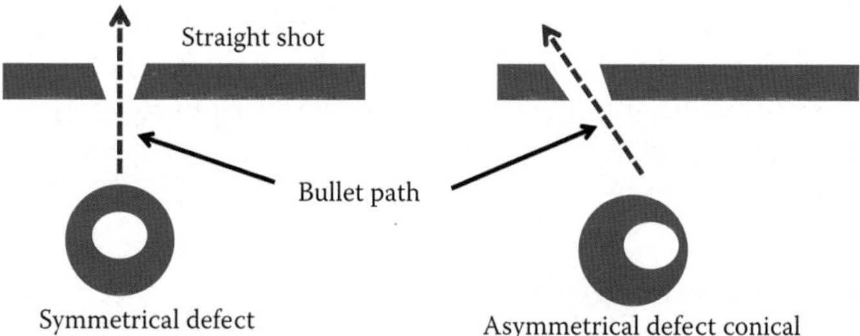

Figure 18.4 Bullet direction through plate glass window. (Adapted from D. H. Garrison, Jr. 2003. *Practical Shooting Scene Investigation*. Boca Raton, FL: Universal Publishers, pp. 91–104. With permission.)

splinters of glass with it after it passes through the window. This shard trail follows the bullet's path at the same angle that it hit the window. After locating the trail, place a clear, zero-edge protractor directly under the window such that the zero degree line is directly under the exit and the edge of the protractor is parallel with the window pane. Place markers, for example, string or laser beam, along the shard trail and across the protractor. The string crosses the protractor at an angle, which is approximately the same as the impact angle of the bullet. The angle determined is only an approximation because the shard trail is wider than a narrow line. Still, knowing the bullet's direction should help in locating it in situations where the bullet cannot be located easily or was a fatal bullet and is still in the deceased's body.

Determining the approximate
angle of impact of bullet through window

Procedures

1. Locate the glass shard trail using ALS, flashlight and/or UV light source.
2. Measure the distance the smallest shards/splinters traveled.
3. Using zero edge protractor, determine the approximate angle bullet exited from the window.
5. Confirm approximate angle by measuring the length and width of the bullet hole and calculating angle using sine function.
6. Check location of fine spray of shards on objects in vicinity. Shards on the right indicate a right twist bullet.

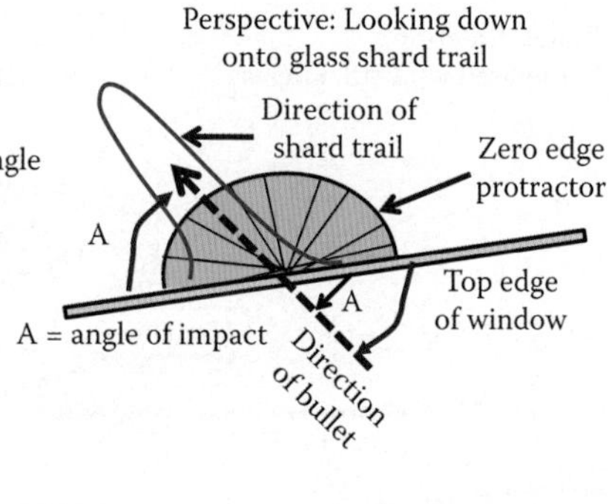

Figure 18.5 Approximating impact angle using debris track. (Adapted from D. H. Garrison, Jr. 2003. *Practical Shooting Scene Investigation*. Boca Raton, FL: Universal Publishers, pp. 91–104. With permission.)

With angled shots through glass, the spin of the bullet creates a backward spray of glass shards that can be found on objects in the vicinity of the bullet hole and on the impact side. If shards are on the right, it indicates the bullet had a right twist. If they are on the left, the bullet had a left twist [4].

18.2.2 When the Radial Edge Fails

The radial edge technique does not work with all types of glass. Tempered glass is not easily reconstructed. Actually it is a daunting task. Simply seeing the hundreds or thousands of similar-looking chunks of sharp-edged glass makes the mission appear impossible. It is possible, though. It just takes time, perseverance, and perhaps the promise of a libation at the end of the trail! Laminated glass or automobile windshields have their own problems because of the plastic lamination holding the sandwiched glass together. Thus, the radial edges are not free to examine because they are held together by this plastic laminate. Determining the direction requires understanding how the bullet hole forms when the bullet passes through the glass (Figure 18.6).

18.2.3 Direction through a Windshield

A gunshot though a windshield passes through the first pane of glass, the laminate, and then the second pane of glass, respectively, before exiting. When a bullet strikes a single pane of glass, the glass bends before fracturing. The bullet passes through, taking a chunk of glass and leaving a cone shape on the opposite side of its entrance point, indicative of is direction. The laminate holding the two panes of glass together changes the dynamics of this process by restricting the usual bending movement of the glass and altering the visual shape of the cone on the exit side of the glass. In fact two cones form. Fortunately, they have subtle, unique visual characteristics that can be identified at the scene. This is illustrated in Figure 18.6.

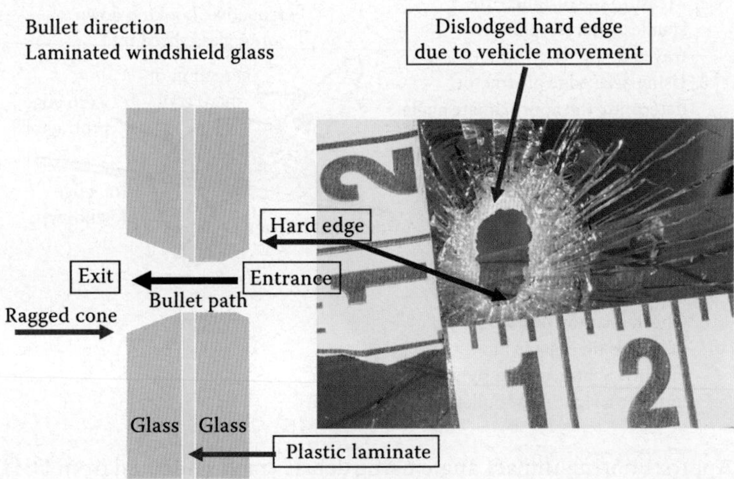

Figure 18.6 Bullet direction through laminated glass. (Photograph by Robert C. Shaler.)

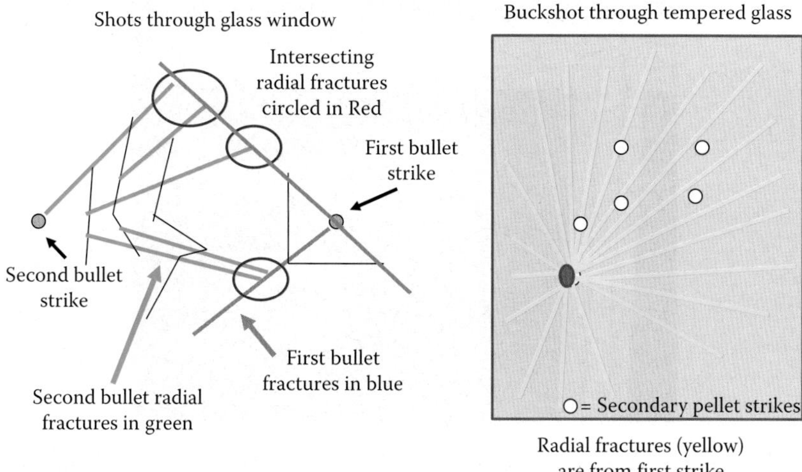

Figure 18.7 Sequencing the bullet shots in glass.

On the entrance side, the bullet forms a cone in the punctured glass, the visible characteristic of which is a hard edge. The red cone's edge on the entrance side is different from that on the exit side which is ragged. The red arrow in Figure 18.6 points out the hard edge, which identifies this as the entrance side (see also Figure 18.7 for another example). As a result of the vehicle being in motion, the cone in the photo has a ragged edge at the top of the entrance hole. This points out how tenuous some interpretations can be if artifacts are present and not identified.

18.2.3.1 Sequencing Bullet Shots in Plate Glass

Determining which bullet passed through the glass first is as simple as locating the radial fractures and tracing them to their endpoint. If the radial fracture from, say bullet 1, ends at a radial fracture from another bullet, say bullet 2, then bullet 1 entered the glass second. This is illustrated diagrammatically on the left side in Figure 18.7. The radial fractures (green) fired by the second bullet—on the left—were stopped from continuing by the radial fractures coming from the bullet hole on the right (blue radial fractures). Unless there is reason to believe these radial fractures are artifacts, such as elongation of radial fractures because the car had been moved, the radial fractures in green (second bullet) impacted second.

Another example is shown diagrammatically in Figure 18.8. The circles in red illustrate where the radial fractures from the two shots intersect. Determining which of the shots impacted the window is a matter of identifying the intersecting radial fractures and determining which were "stopped" by the radial fractures from the other shot. In this case, the shots were fired into laminated windshield glass. A close inspection of the windshield shows fractures in glass on both sides of the laminate. Thus, care must be taken to ensure the fractures from only one side of the glass are tracked to find the intersecting fractures. Also, artifacts from movement of the car or from the laminate are possible, so always consider them in the determination of shot sequence. Also in the picture, the hard edge along the bullet hole (arrow) is visible. This is an indication that the bullet was moving from the outside to the inside of the vehicle.

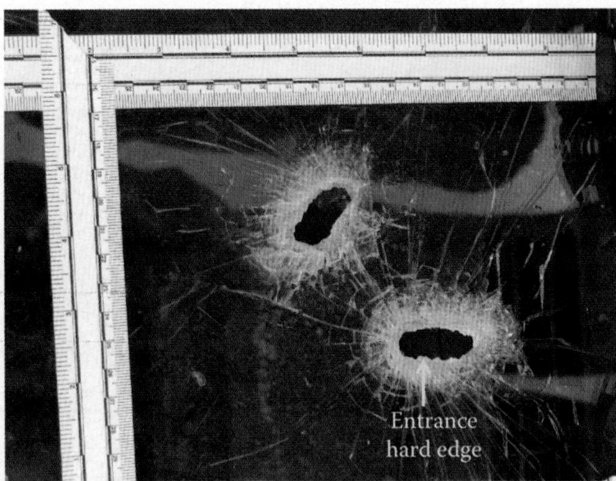

Figure 18.8 Sequencing shots through laminated windshield. (Photographs by Robert C. Shaler.)

Bullets shot though tempered or hardened automobile glass presents problems because of a tendency of the glass to shatter. When that happens, reconstructing the bullet path(s) is difficult because it means reconstructing the window from shards collected at the scene. Determining which shot impacted the glass first is illustrated diagrammatically on the right side of Figure 18.7. The diagram shows pellets from a shotgun impacting tempered glass. As with the windshield example above, it is necessary to track the radial fractures in order to identify which pellet first impacted the glass. In tempered glass, the first strike creates virtually all of the radial fractures. This means that in Figure 18.7 (the right side) the first pellet striking the window is on the lower left. Close examination of the radial fractures will quickly reveal that most, if not all, of the visible radial fractures originate from a single location—the first strike. The other pellet strikes were created by secondary pellets. Sequencing them is impossible.

18.3 Collecting, Packaging, and Preserving Glass Evidence

The first step in preserving glass evidence is to understand how it fractures and the distribution it can take at the scene. The distribution will depend largely on the type of break. If the break results in a bullet hole, the glass distribution will be along the path of the bullet and behind depending on twist [4]. If the break results in a broken window, the distribution pattern will be more spread out within a 360° circle around the point of impact. See Chapter 4, Figures 4.9 and 4.10. There could be a void or break in the distribution pattern where the perpetrator stood. The distribution can be as great as 10 ft. with most shards occurring closer to the point of impact.

The operative rule for collecting, packaging, and preserving glass evidence is common sense and understanding the type of break. The objective is to prevent alteration of the evidence in any way during packaging and transit. This means being extremely careful when collecting the evidence so that damage does not occur. It also means archiving the evidence at the scene before packaging. For example, the tempered glass in Figure 18.7

is extremely fragile. In fact, it would be appropriate to tape both sides of the glass to prevent its becoming a mass of glass nuggets during transit. There is, however, a chance that even after taping, the glass fragmentation pattern will be destroyed. The best way to ensure capturing the pattern intact is to photograph it properly before it falls apart, because if the glass shatters during transit the photograph is available for reconstructing the bullet path(s). It is essential to archive the fracture patterns at the scene by sketching, photography, and/or video.

Another caution is important: protect sharp edges from chipping. This not only protects the person handling the evidence in the laboratory or at the police department, but also protects the integrity of the evidence. A rule of thumb is to refrain from using tweezers because they can chip fragile edges. Large pieces can present handling problems. These should be placed between two pieces of rigid cardboard, and the cardboard and sides taped together. The taped cardboard should be placed into a larger container and secured to prevent the movement. Placing small shards in a proper container, such as a glass vial or a small cardboard box, ensures they cannot shift during transit. The interior and exterior sides of glass, for example, window glass, should be marked before packaging. This helps the laboratory identify the direction of the force, if not done at the scene. Generally, glass is placed inside a container of appropriate size (between two pieces of cardboard) and then that is placed inside a larger container. The edges of glass are taped for safety and evidence protection. The larger outer container is labeled "GLASS FRAGILE" and also with the appropriate case identification information. Table 18.4 gives more specific instructions for preserving the glass evidence.

Table 18.4 Collecting and Packaging the Glass Evidence

Always Handle Glass Evidence with Gloves

Glass remaining at a scene

- Collect an appropriate amount of glass from the point of breakage.
- Place in container to prevent crushing during transport.
- Secure to prevent movement that damages edges of fragment.

Larger items

- Broken headlights, tail lights, light bulbs, bottles, etc. sent to the laboratory intact.
- Label fragments or objects containing biological evidence "BIOHAZARD."
  - Dry before packaging.

Fingerprints recovered from glass

- Handle using the gloves.
- All fragments of glass should be collected to determine the angle or point of impact.
  - Place small items in plastic vials and stabilize. Do not allow fragments to rub together.

Fragments removed from a frame

- Each fragment should be labeled: interior or exterior and relative position in frame.
  - Example: "Bottom left corner."

Small fragments

- *Do not use tweezers:* Can be damaged by tweezers during collection.
- Use tape when the pieces are very small.
- Place clothing and footwear in a paper bag, seal, and label.
  - Ensure the bag will not tear.

References

1. *Merriam-Webster Online Dictionary*. Glass. Available at: http://www.merriam-webster.com/dictionary/glass (accessed July 25, 2011).
2. S. W. Martin. 2001. Glass. Discovery Channel School, original content provided by World Book Online. Available at: http://www.discoveryschool.com/homeworkhelp/worldbook/atozscience/g/225740.html (accessed July 11, 2010).
3. Lenntech. 2010. Glass: What is glass and how is it produced? Available at: http://www.lenntech.com/glass.htm (accessed on July 11, 10).
4. D. H. Garrison, Jr. 2003. *Practical Shooting Scene Investigation*. Boca Raton, FL: Universal Publishers, pp. 91–104.

Workshop 12: Glass as Evidence

W12.1 Introduction: Glass at the Scene

Like blood, glass evidence has the potential of supplying an investigator with more than one piece of investigative information. The following are examples of the type of information that can be obtained from glass at the scene.

- Direction of force
- Sequence of shots in window
- Associative evidence through shard analysis

This workshop concentrates on two of the above: direction of force and distribution of glass shards. The aim of this exercise is to determine the direction of the force that broke glass in a window and then to examine the resulting shards of glass in order to determine the extent of shard dispersal.

W12.2 Point of Impact

When a window breaks, it does so under a force of some kind. When a force hits a window, the glass bends and then fractures forming radial and concentric fractures that are diagnostic of the impact site on the glass. Figure 18.2 (Chapter 18) illustrates how glass typically fractures. Glass fractures from the opposite side of the impact force. Radial fractures form first followed by concentric fractures. Also, conchoidal stress fractures form along the edge of the radial fracture. Because the process is well understood, it is possible to determine the direction of the force by examining the appropriate radial fractures.

The procedure for identifying the direction of the force or point of impact requires finding the radial fracture closest to the impact point, if possible. The radial edge should be examined for conchoidal fractures as shown in Figure 18.2. The presence of conchoidal fractures means that the fragment chosen was close to the impact point. The diagram in Figure 18.2 (Chapter 18) of a radial section of broken glass shows the relative positioning of conchoidal fractures with respect to the impact point.

The side of the radial fracture in which the conchoidal fracture is perpendicular to the edge should be located. It can be determined that the force, then, came from the opposite side.

W12.3 Exercise 1: Direction of Force

In this exercise, to determine the direction of force, we will break a window with a hammer. (Wear goggles, long sleeves, gloves, shoes, and long pants.)

- Procedures
  - Grid a room into eight sections with masking tape as shown in Figure W12.1
  - Set the unbroken window on the center point of the grid and mark the location with tape pasted to the floor.
  - Photograph the setup.
  - Break the window with a hammer.
  - Photograph the broken window in place.
  - Remove the broken window and large shards and take to a remote location for reconstructing the window.
  - Find the fracture closest to the impact point and examine the edge of the radial fracture. Use a magnifying lens to help see the detail of the edge.
  - Find the perpendicular conchoidal fracture along the edge of the radial fracture. The impact point is on the opposite side of the edge. Ascertain whether the impact came from the inside or outside.
  - Show your work to an instructor for grading.

W12.4 Distribution of Glass Shards

After glass breaks, extremely small, sharp shards are distributed around the break point. When a bullet goes through a window, it carries shards of glass with it, which is diagnostic of the projectile's direction. Additionally, a cone forms on the exit side of the glass (Chapter 18).

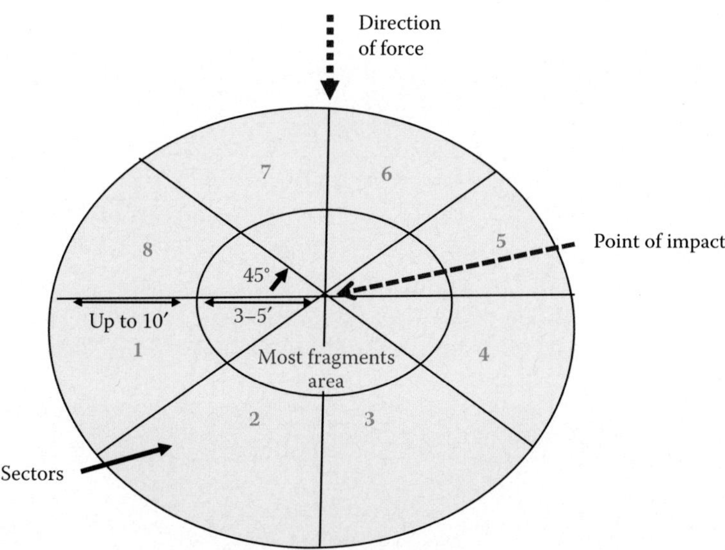

Figure W12.1 Floor grid pattern for Exercises 1 and 2.

W12.4.1 Exercise 2

This exercise is a continuation of Exercise 1. After breaking the double pane basement casement window, the aim of this exercise is to examine the distribution of the glass shards.

- Procedures
  - Use an ALS to map the shard distribution area on the impact and exit sides of the broken window.
  - Count the number of shards in each section.
  - Measure the width and distance of shards from the break point.
  - Diagram/record (enter the numbers in each grid section) the density of chards on a piece of graph paper (as shown in Figure W12.1).
  - Photograph the distribution of shards backward and forward of the impact site.
  - Show the photographs and the graph paper to an instructor for grading.

W12.5 Questions

- In 1000 words or less, explain where glass shards are likely to be found after a burglar breaks a basement double pane casement window.
- Explain the difference between radial and concentric fractures.
- Explain what role conchoidal fractures play in the determination of the direction of force used to break a window.
- Explain how to sequence shots of bullets through a window pane.
- Explain why laminated windshield glass makes determining the direction of the shot difficult.

Soil and Paint as Evidence

19

19.1 Soil: An Introduction

> If a healthy soil is full of death, it is also full of life: worms, fungi, microorganisms of all kinds . . . Given only the health of the soil, nothing that dies is dead for very long [1].

Soil is a category of physical evidence that, like hair and fibers, is ubiquitous. And like hair and fibers, it is a category of trace evidence, even though it, too, is visible. What makes it trace evidence is how it is collected at the scene and analyzed in the laboratory, the latter requiring microscopic, instrumental, and biological testing methods to identify the various mineral, organic, microbiological, botanical, manufactured, and other biological components. Soil varies greatly throughout the world, and it forms for various reasons [2]. The following list was adapted from [2]

- *Parent material*: This is the material that forms the basis of soil. It can be bedrock, organic material, an old soil surface, or a deposit from water, wind, glaciers, volcanoes, and so on.
- *Climate*: The environment changes from day to day, month to month, and season to season. This means that temperature, weather, wind, sunshine, and other environmental forces work on the parent material to change it over time.
- *Biological material*: Plants and animals living in or on the soil affect decomposition of waste materials and how soil materials move around in the soil profile. The dead remains of plants and animals become organic matter which enriches the soil. Humans affect the soil through the use of fertilizers, construction, and manufacturing.
- *Topography*: The location of soil can affect how climatic processes impact it. Soils at the bottom of a hill will get more water than soils on the slopes, and soils on the slopes that directly face the sun will be drier than soils on slopes that do not.

Certainly scene investigators are not concerned with how soil forms or its composition but more with how a particular soil sample at the crime scene can lead to the conviction of a suspect. Still, it is important that they understand some of the questions that interest forensic scientists and those that have legal implications.

19.2 The Forensic Premise: Location Diversity of Soil

From a forensic (and legal) perspective, this refers to whether soil in one location is different from soil in another and whether that diversity can be proven and can withstand scientific scrutiny. Answering this query requires three separate discussions (none of which is appropriate to discuss in depth here): Can science reliably differentiate soil samples, do soil samples vary significantly from location to location, and is there a statistical standard with which to assign probabilistic estimates of soil matches? A final question might also be: If the above cannot be demonstrated satisfactorily, does soil analysis have forensic investigative and legal value as evidence?

19.2.1 Can Science Differentiate Soil Sufficiently for Forensic Investigations?

A priori, one would expect that soil taken from impression evidence dirt should be scientifically identical as that obtained from the shoes or trousers of a suspect who made the original scene impression. This means that scientific analysis of soil from the same sources always give identical test results, within an acceptable measurement error. Although not new to forensic investigations, the science of soil analysis is gaining in popularity, and wide-ranging disciplines have an interest because of the varied content of soil and its potential in forensic applications. Some of the interested disciplines include chemistry, geology, molecular biology, pedology,* archeology, mineralogy, and forensic science [4]. It seems that science is up to the task of sufficiently characterizing soil for forensic purposes. Although not for forensic investigations, the U.S. Department of Agriculture categorizes soil into 12 major types and compiles statistics on soil diversity covering 95% of the United States [5]. Generally, the forensic analysis of soil includes the analysis of minerals (primary and clay), organic matter, microorganisms including bacteria, inorganic matter, pollen and other botanicals, diatoms, fossils, and dust [6]. The answer to the question is, yes, science is up to the task of scientifically differentiating one soil sample from another.

19.2.2 Do Soil Samples Differ from Location to Location?

This question concerns the variability of soil in a fairly small and possibly confined area versus that in a larger area. For example, if footwear impressions in soil are found outside a burglarized house, does the soil in that impression differ significantly from other soil in the immediate surrounding area? The crime scene unit will collect representative samples in the immediate area including samples from the impression, so the laboratory will answer the question for that specific area. It is generally believed, although this has not been proven rigorously, that soil samples differ even if they are within a few feet of each other. Recent research suggests this might be true [7,8]. But from a single case perspective, the real question concerns the differences in soil in the immediate surrounding area of the scene. We already know that science can differentiate different soil samples, so it is not whether the analysis and the scientific comparisons can be made, but what the comparisons mean. If the soil samples taken from a wide area around the scene, say several blocks away or from backyards in the next street, give the same scientific analysis, within reasonable measurement error, the probative value of the soil as evidence is significantly diminished.

19.2.3 Is There a Statistical Standard for Soil Matches?

Another question concerns the statistical strength of soil "matches." In fact, is it even possible to assign probabilities to these matches? This is a problem for the courts and not for

* "Soil science" [3].

scene investigators. There will always be the issue of statistics and their meaning concerning match criteria. At the time of this writing, the validity of statistical inferences has not been proven, and the numbers used to show the strength of a match are as fallacious as the crime scene investigator who testifies that two soil samples, one from a suspect's shoe and the other from soil outside a crime scene house, came from the same source. Making such source attributions are not yet scientifically valid.

19.3 Forensic Value of Soil

The fact that soil is everywhere and that it can be transferred easily renders it important as potential forensic evidence. But with the foregoing discussion—statistical matches are not verified in research—what is the forensic and legal value of soil analysis and comparison? The worn-out example is that soil found on the suspect's shoe, tire, or clothing that got muddy during the commission of a crime matches an exemplar taken from the scene. The following consider examples of soil having forensic value.

19.3.1 Soil Taphnomy

One aspect of forensic soil analysis concerns soil taphonomy, specifically the soil at grave sites and the detritusphere—soil surrounding the cadaver. This is becoming important in forensic applications because the soil contains the aftermath of how it affects decomposition. The burial environment is complex, a dynamic system of biological, chemical, and physical processes that are affected by a decomposing body [9].

19.3.2 Associative Evidence: Similarities in Soil Composition

Certainly demonstrating that soil samples collected from the crime scene are similar to soil samples found on the clothing of a suspect has important associative value as evidence. Although this does not mean or even suggest that the two soil samples have a common origin, it is not possible to categorically state that they do but scientific similarities suggests a common origin and thus a forensic association.

19.3.3 Exculpatory Evidence: Dissimilarities in Soil Composition

Unlike the match scenario in Section 19.2.2, if the analysis of an exemplar soil sample compared with that taken from the clothing or vehicle of a suspect shows that the two samples are scientifically dissimilar, it is reasonable to conclude that they do not have a common origin.

19.3.4 Sequence of Deposition: Layering of Soil

When a vehicle goes through mud puddles and other areas where mud and/or dirt can be deposited on or under a vehicle, the position of different soils can suggest a sequence of deposition. That is, the bottom most layer was likely deposited first. Comparing this bottom layer favorably with that of the scene suggests a common association.

19.4 Collecting and Preserving Soil

From the crime scene investigative perspective, collecting soil might seem as simple as using a digging utensil, such as a small scoop, to collect some of the soil and place it into an appropriate container. In a sense, it is that simple. There are guidelines, however.

19.4.1 Logic

First and foremost, the logic of knowing where to collect soil samples is the most important. This is something that is defined by the case. If it is a hit-and-run case, soil might be expected to be on the body, assuming the vehicle ran over the victim and left a tire imprint in dirt on the clothing. If the scene is from a stalker, footwear impressions might be in dirt outside a window. A body that had been dumped but had been murdered in a field would have clues to the actual murder location from the mud and debris on the clothing. Thinking one's way through the evidence is the first step in collecting the evidence because that is how to know where to find it, how to sample the area, and how to package it to ensure its security.

19.4.2 Packaging Soil Evidence

Packaging is important because improperly collected and packaged soil can quickly be overgrown with mold or other fungi that can compromise or obviate subsequent scientific analysis. Generally, soil must "breathe," which is why it is collected in paper or cardboard. Do not package soil in glass or plastic. Generally, 3 tbsp of soil should be collected from the first 1/4 in. of an impression or from an exemplar soil site. The packaging should be secured with evidence tape but should not be airtight.

All packaging must be properly labeled with the date, initials of the investigator, the case number, the exact location of evidence (this means measurements and photographs), a description of the evidence, a unique identifier, and the method of collection.

19.4.3 Soil from a Cast

Soil should remain on the cast of impression evidence for at least 24 h to give the cast time to cure. After that, the cast can be cleaned and the soil packaged as described in Section 19.4.2.

19.4.4 Exemplar Soil Samples

Exemplar soil samples are collected from the immediate area around samples collected from impression evidence. Generally, samples are collected in a logical, geometric pattern. Certainly, several samples should collected from a single area. The number, per se, is not important, but a sufficient number must be collected so that a representative sampling of the area is available. This is important so that appropriate inferences can be made concerning the soil diversity in that area. An example of but one variation for an open area is shown in Figure 19.1.

The pattern illustrated in Figure 19.1 is an example of one method for ensuring that representative samples in an open area are collected. As an example it is not meant to be

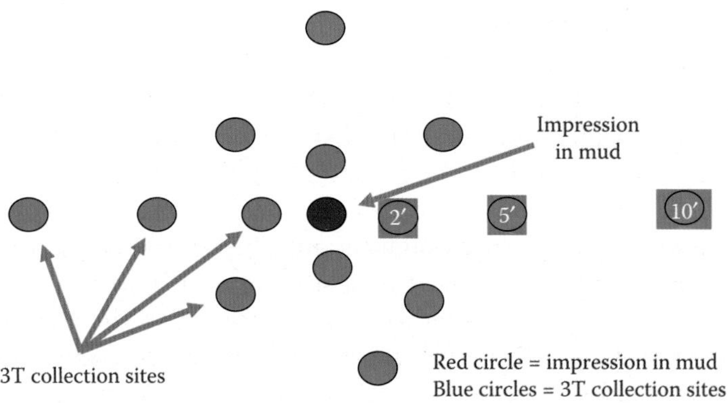

Figure 19.1 Collecting exemplar soil samples in open areas.

the only way to collect exemplar soil samples at a scene, as it would not be appropriate for all scenes. The scene will dictate which method should be used. Importantly, sampling vertically and horizontally is important (see p. D-176 in Reference [6]). With respect to collecting exemplars, the following should be kept in mind:

- Each collected sample must have a unique identifier.
- Each packaged sample must have the unique identifier on the outside of the package.
- A sketch of the collection pattern, including measurements, should be made.
- A photograph of the collection area with evidence markers in place will be important for presentation in court, if the question of representative sampling comes up during testimony.

19.4.5 Samples from Vehicles

Vehicles can have significant soil deposited in the vehicle (e.g., floors, seats, etc.) and on it. It is critically important that all areas are sampled. Importantly, too, samples should not be mixed, even if they are in close proximity, and the texture of the soil on the vehicle should be preserved (see p. D-176 in Reference [6]). Areas from which samples should be collected include:

- Exterior and inner surface of the front bumper and grill
- All wheel wells and tires
- Engine compartment including carburetor housing and air filter
- Rocker panels
- Control arms/A-frames and leaf springs
- Tops of mufflers and condensers
- Interior of passenger compartment and trunk
- Exterior and inner surfaces of rear bumper
- Rain gutter paths and windshield trim
- Swab exterior painted body surface
- Other sites that seem important

19.5 Paint: An Introduction

All streets in our contemporary world offer a visual insight into how ingrained science and technology has become in our everyday space. Stop, look around, and reflect on the vast array of colors assaulting your senses. The paint on the automobiles, taxi cabs, and buildings is a tribute to the science of polymer chemistry. With so much of it in what seems like every nook and cranny covering wood, ceramic, metal, and plastic surfaces, it is little wonder that paint is an important class of associative forensic evidence. For example, paint chips transferred from one car to another or from the car to the victim are important because it can show that a particular vehicle was involved in the crime. The paint transfer can also involve embedding it into the fabric weave of the victim's clothing, which can sometimes identify the hit-and-run vehicle's make and model. Tools used in burglaries can have microscopic flakes of paint that can be analyzed and compared with toolmark damage at a scene even if the toolmark itself is unusable.

19.5.1 What Is Paint?

We usually think of paint esthetically and/or functionally. Esthetically it is decorative. Functionally—technically it is a surface coating—it is designed to protect the surface on which it lies. We rarely think of paint in scientific terms because its components only concern us tangentially; it does what we want it to do. Scientifically, however, it is a complex mixture of pigments, modifiers, extenders, and binders. The pigments give the paint its color; blue and green pigments are usually organic compounds while reds, yellows, and whites are often inorganic. Modifiers control the properties of the paint such as gloss, flexibility, toughness, and durability. Extenders add bulk and covering capacity and are usually inorganic. Binders are natural or synthetic resins that stabilize the mixture and form a film when it is spread. Topcoat, primer, and undercoat have different chemical compositions. Samples collected from the scene can be expected to be contaminated from exposure to dirt and other environmental materials. The Scientific Working Group on Materials Analysis (SWGMAT) has a Paint Subgroup that defines methods for the forensic analysis of paint. The group's definitions for terms used for paint constituents is shown in Table 19.1 [10].

The crime scene perspective cares not about the composition of paint but only about the forensic value paint might have in a particular investigation.

Table 19.1 Definition of Paint Components by the Scientific Working Group on Materials Analysis

Paint Component	Definition
Binder	A nonvolatile portion of the liquid vehicle of a coating, which serves to bind or cement the pigment particles together.
Coating	A generic term for paint, lacquer, enamel, or other liquid or liquefiable material that is converted to a solid, protective, or decorative film or a combination of these types of films after application.
Pigment	A finely ground, inorganic or organic, insoluble, and dispersed particle. Besides color, a pigment may provide many of the essential properties of paint such as opacity, hardness, durability, and corrosion resistance. The term pigment includes extenders.
Additive (modifier)	Any substance added in a small quantity to improve properties. Additives may include substances such as driers, corrosion inhibitors, catalysts, ultraviolet absorbers, and plasticizers.

19.5.2 Forensic Value of Paint Evidence

Forensic paint evidence is found on a variety of objects (e.g., clothing, tools, vehicles, etc.) typically collected as evidence in crime scene investigations. We need to examine how important it is, in the general context, as evidence. Several attributes of paint as evidence is listed as follows:

- Links an object (e.g., weapon, tool, vehicle, etc.) to the crime scene
- Links an object (e.g., vehicle, weapon, tool, etc.) to a victim
- Physical matches (e.g., paint chips to a chipped/damaged surface) provide strong evidence of an original source
- Analysis of OEM paint, for example, from a vehicle or evidence can help to identify the make, model, and year of an automobile
- Analysis of layers can provide strong evidence of an original source

It is obvious, thus, that collecting paint from a scene, whether from a toolmark or debris from a hit-and-run scene, can be critically associative and sometimes evidence of attribution.

Paint can chip, which makes it suitable for making physical matches, such as physically fitting a collected paint chip into a void made in the original surface as a result of the crime. This is like fitting a piece into a jigsaw puzzle. Such physical matches elevate the strength of the comparison to possibly one of attribution.

If the paint is a flake, then microscopic analysis (or examination with a hand lens) can show the presence of layers. The greater the number of layers, the more discriminating the paint chip. Combined with the chemical and instrumental analyses of the layers, the stronger subsequent attribution will be. Microscopic analysis of the paint layer has been a staple in crime laboratories for decades. The following was taken from a Philadelphia laboratory report from a 1964 analysis of a deceased's blue dungarees:

> Chips of paint composed of three . . . layers in the following sequence, salmon pink, aqua and brown and chips composed of light green with a layer of brown varnish, and chips composed of aqua and brown which are similar in all physical characteristics to the paint from inside and outside of the cellar door, Specimen #2 [11].

Paint analysis was used to help convict British serial rapist Malcolm Fairley, also known as "The Fox," in 1985. After one attack, investigators found minute specks of yellow paint on a tree branch around 45 in. (114.3 cm) from the ground. The paint was analyzed and identified as a type of car paint used on a single automobile model, the Austin Allegro, between 1973 and 1975. The police went to an address in North London to interview a suspect and found a young man was cleaning a yellow Austin Allegro. Scratches were found on the paint about 45 in. from the ground that matched the paint flakes found at the scene. On this, and other evidence, Fairley was convicted on several accounts of indecent assault, rape, and burglary and given six life sentences [12].

Although paint is visible, like hair and fibers, it is considered a category of trace evidence. Analyzing paint for forensic comparative purposes requires extremely sophisticated scientific instrumentation [10]. Like most trace evidence, paint is an example of associative evidence, which means that it is not used to make specific attributions, but it has value in

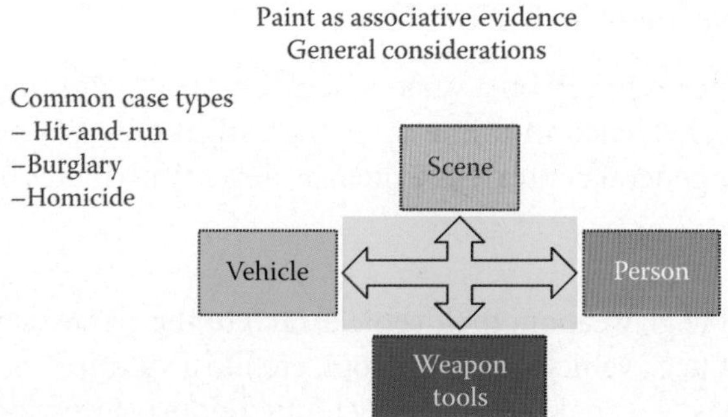

Figure 19.2 Case types with paint evidence.

substantiating alleged facts. Because it is fairly ubiquitous, it occurs in a wide variety of crimes, often in crimes where DNA is not available as evidence.

Figure 19.2 illustrates the relationship of paint transfer in cases in general. The diagram shows transfer of paint between vehicles, weapons/tools, the scene, and people. The diagram is purposefully general to present the transfer concept as associative evidence. There are, however, instances when paint evidence can be so rare that it can be used to make attributions. Figure 19.3 illustrates when paint evidence can be extremely strong.

However, although paint can be associated with almost any crime, considering each individually would be impossible. Therefore, the following discussion considers only three crime types: hit-and-run cases and burglaries.

19.5.2.1 Hit-and-Run Cases

Hit-and-run cases involve injuries, death, and property damage. They are typically difficult crimes to solve and bring to trial because there are several proofs necessary. In essence, these are legal issues, ones that should only concern the crime scene team to the extent that the appropriate evidence is collected and submitted for analysis. Two of the most

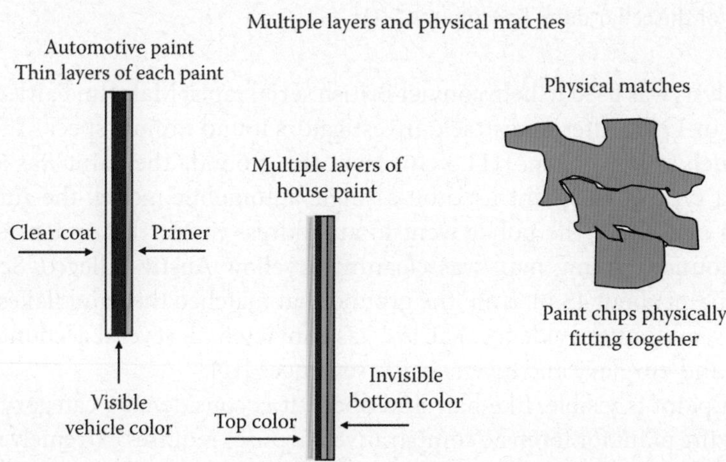

Figure 19.3 Source attribution from paint evidence.

Table 19.2 Paint Other Evidence in Hit-and-Run Cases

Vehicle-to-Person

- Victim to vehicle
  - Blood
  - Fabric impression
- Vehicle to clothing of victim
  - Macroscene elements
    - Imbedded into surface of fabric
    - Color of car
      - Part of car in contact with victim
      - Manufacture of car and year
      - Broken plastic at scene can help ID car
    - Whole chips of paint
      - May contain several layers
        May allow for physical match
      - e.g. fender/grill of car, etc.
  - Microscene elements
    - Smears
    - Small flakes

- Vehicle-to-vehicle
  - One-to-other paint transfer
    - Paint from each vehicle transferred
- Vehicle-to-object
  - Transfer from vehicle to inanimate object at scene
    - Telephone poles
    - Road barriers
    - Road Surface

important legal proofs are identifying the vehicle and the driver. Each requires identifying the appropriate evidence at the scene.

Table 19.2 shows the three common categories of hit-and-run cases: vehicle to person, vehicle to vehicle, and vehicle to object. Each can involve the transfer of paint from the vehicle in question to a person, to another vehicle, or to an inanimate object. In the first, the vehicle is a pedestrian, for example, and transfers paint to the victim's skin or clothing. In the second, a dual transfer, transfer could occur where each vehicle transfers paint. In the third, the vehicle transfers paint to an inanimate object, for example, a telephone pole, house, guard rail, and so on, and there is transfer of paint, possibly two ways.

In these cases, finding and collecting the evidence is critical to identifying the culprit vehicle. Although there will likely be a lot of debris from the collision, for example, paint chips, plastic, glass, and so on, as always, the first step in locating important, probative evidence is thinking though the scene, capturing it in its entirety, and determining what is important and potentially probative. This means carefully, systematically, and logically examining the scene for evidence and evidence transfer. Flashlights and/or an ALS (if appropriate electrical connections are available) will be an important aid. In victim-associated crimes, the clothing would be removed from the body at the morgue. If paint transfer is observed at the scene, this should be documented in notes and photographed. The medical examiner should be made aware that paint evidence is available.

When the suspect vehicle is located and brought to the police precinct, examining it in light of what was found at the scene will be critical. No part of the vehicle should be ignored. The obvious areas of damage need to be scrutinized for missing parts and possible physical matches from collected scene evidence.

19.5.2.2 Burglaries

Burglaries are another category where paint transfers can and do occur. Consider the burglar who jimmies a car trunk open. Expect a paint transfer to the tool from the

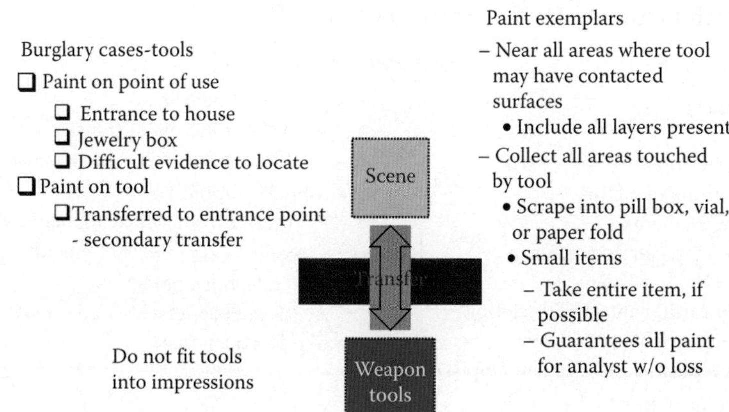

Figure 19.4 Paint evidence in burglary cases.

automotive paint. If the tool, for example, a crowbar, had paint on it, small flecks of paint might be adhering to the area of the tool had been inserted into the trunk of the car. There any number of scenarios where a tool might be the subject of a paint transfer, for example, windows, doors, safes, or other transfers, such as varnish from a wooden cabinet, and so on. Figure 19.4 lists some examples.

19.5.3 Collecting Paint Evidence

Before considering any approach for collecting and packaging paint evidence, consider carefully the evidence and its possible associative or attributive value. As discussed above, certain types of paint evidence (e.g., multilayered and chips) has the inherent potential of being attributive, and, the collection strategy should take this into consideration. Paint chips having multiple layers must be preserved so that they will not be damaged. Similarly, chips having physical match potential must likewise be protected. If possible, photograph the physical match *in situ*.

The following has been adapted from SWGMAT's guidelines for collecting and packaging paint evidence [10].

19.5.3.1 Scene Samples

Samples at the scene having paint can include "tools, floors, walls, glass fragments, hair, fingernails, roadways, adjacent structures, transfers or smears on vehicles, or transfers to or from individuals such as damaged fabric with paint inclusions" [10]. The collection guidelines in Chapter 17, Section 17.5, apply to trace evidence in general. There are specifics with respect to paint.

- Package items having paint transfers in their entirety for examination, if possible.
- Remove paint evidence manually *before* using tape lifts to collect other types of evidence.
- Avoid collecting paint evidence with tape, if possible. Tape adhesives present manipulation problems and can contaminate the sample.

- Collect the entire item when paint is smeared because they could represent a mingling of components from several layers or films. Because of the difficulties associated with collecting smeared or abraded samples, the entire object bearing the questioned paint should be submitted to the laboratory whenever possible.
- Always consider cross-transfers. When suspected, collect samples from both surfaces.

19.5.3.2 Exemplar or Known Samples

Exemplars (known samples) are necessary in order to make appropriate comparisons. The important aspect of collecting exemplars is to ensure that the area sampled is representative of what is being compared. If, during a hit-and-run accident, paint transfers from suspect (fleeing) vehicle to the victim vehicle, collecting exemplars from the victim vehicle and the transferred paint from the suspect vehicle is important. The transferred paint from the suspect vehicle must be compared with exemplars from that vehicle once it is recovered. Exemplars from the victim vehicle must be compared with transferred paint from the victim to the suspect vehicle. If the suspect vehicle hit the victim vehicle on the driver's side fender, appropriate samples must be collected inside the crash zone as well as from representative locations surrounding the crash zone. This way, there will be a sufficient number of samples with which to make the comparison. The transferred paint to the victim vehicle is used to compare with the exemplars collected from the suspect vehicle. The following guidelines are appropriate:

- Collect from areas as close as possible to, but not within, the point or points of damage or transfer. These damaged areas are usually not suitable sources of known samples.
- Collect all layers of the undamaged paint film.
- Account for variations in thickness and layer sequences over short distances, which happens in architectural paint and automotive films where the curves, corners, and edges are often impact points and may have been subjected to previous damage, sanding, or over painting.
- Collect several exemplars from an area to obtain representative samples of the damaged area.
- Package exemplars collected from different areas separately and label appropriately.
- Collect an example of the underlying transfer area when possible. Areas adjacent from walls, ceilings, doors, windows, handles, and automobile doors, fenders, and hoods can be valuable for assessing scene and exemplar differences and for evaluating the cross-transfers of trace materials.
- Remove paint flakes from parent surfaces carefully. Methods could include lifting or prying loosely attached flakes, cutting samples of the entire paint layer structure using a clean knife or blade, or dislodging by gently impacting the opposite side of the painted surface. If cutting, insert the blade down to the parent surface.
- Consider the method for collecting paint flakes. No one method is suitable for all situations.

Table 19.3 is an overview to use as a general guide for collecting the paint evidence.

Table 19.3 General Guidelines for Collecting the Paint Evidence

From Vehicles	From Garments

• Document collection areas photographically
• Collect transferred paint
• Collect exemplar paint
• Collect generous samples
  • 1/4" × 1/4"
  • Remove paint in flakes if possible
    – Sometimes can bend the metal a bit to get this done
  • Scrape if flaking doesn't work
    – Clean scrapping tool first
      – Use disposable scalpel blades
    – Scrape into druggist fold
  • Never combine samples
  • Put individually collected paint samples into separate containers
• Paint on one area may differ from damaged area
  • Color might appear the same
    – Repaired vehicles that are repainted
	• Collect entire garment
	  • LAB removes paint imbedded into fabric
	• DRY Damp or bloody garments
	  • Package in paper bags—not plastic
	  • Wrap separately by rolling in paper
	    – Avoid flakes from escaping
	    – Avoid flakes transferring to other part of evidence
	  • Seal bags with tape
	    – Ensure that flakes cannot escape through the seams
	  • Label appropriately

References

1. W. Berry. 1977. The unsettling of America. Available at: http://www.gardendigest.com/earth.htm#Quotes (accessed December 1, 2010).
2. C. Spector. Secrets hidden in soil. Available at: http://soil.gsfc.nasa.gov/forengeo/secret.htm (accessed November 30, 2010).
3. *Merriam-Webster Online Dictionary*. Pedology. Available at: http://www.merriam-webster.com/dictionary/pedology (accessed December 1, 2010).
4. R. W. Fitzpatrick. 2008. Nature distribution and origin of soil materials in the forensic comparison of soils. In: M. Tibbett and D. O. Carter (eds), *Soil Analysis in Forensic Taphonomy: Chemical and Biological Effects of Buried Human Remains*. Boca Raton, FL: CRC Press, pp. 1–6.
5. U.S. Department of Agriculture (USDA). 2010. Keys to soil taxonomy, 11th edn. Available at: ftp://ftp-fc.sc.egov.usda.gov/NSSC/Soil_Taxonomy/keys/2010_Keys_to_Soil_Taxonomy.pdf (accessed December 1, 2010).
6. N.A. 2001. Forensic examination of soil evidence. *13th Interpol Forensic Science Symposium, Lyon, France*, October 16–19, pp. D-176, D1-180–D1-187.
7. L. E. Heath and V. A. Saunders. 2006. Assessing the potential of bacterial DNA profiling for forensic soil comparisons. *Journal of Forensic Sciences*, 51:1062–1068.
8. A. Morrisson, S. McColl, L. Dawson, and M. Brewer. 2009. Chapter 6: Characterization and discrimination of urban soils: Preliminary results from the Soil Forensics University Network. In: K. Ritz, L. Dawson, and D. Miller (eds), *Criminal and Environmental Soil Forensics*. New York, NY: Springer, pp. 75–86.
9. M. Tibbett and D. O. Carter. 2008. Preface. In: M. Tibbett and D. O. Carter (eds), *Soil Analysis in Forensic Taphonomy: Chemical and Biological Effects of Buried Human Remains*. Boca Raton, FL: CRC Press, pp. vii–viii.

10. Scientific Working Group on Materials Analysis (SWGMAT) Paint Subgroup. 1999. Forensic paint analysis and comparison guidelines. *Forensic Science Communications*, 1(2), Section 7.2.1.
11. Police Laboratory Report of Agnes Mallattratt. Lab. No. 20,714, 10/21/64.
12. Paint Analysis. Available at: http://www.enotes.com/forensic-science/paint-analysis (accessed December 2, 2010).

Bang! It's a Shooting Incident Scene

VI

Introducing Shooting Scene Investigations

20

> Nancy Ordway (Peggy Ann Garner): Would you mind saying just a word or two to me?
> Peter Denver (Van Heflin): On what subject?
> Nancy Ordway (Peggy Ann Garner): I don't think it really matters. It's just that my mother always told me that, "If a girl could be at a party for 30 minutes without getting a man to talk to her, she might as well go home and shoot herself" [1].

20.1 Introduction

Shooting incidents are, unfortunately, a common occurrence in our society. The classic image is Film Noir-ish or gangster-related, the Capone gang spraying bullets inside the SMC Cartage Company garage on Valentine's Day in 1929 [2] or Eliot Ness' band of Prohibition Bureau Agents peppering kegs in one of Capone's breweries, their amber stream of illegal booze flooding the room. Modern society offers a different image, though. The troubled Virginia Tech student who shoots-up a campus classroom killing multiple innocents [3], Vice President Cheney accidentally shoots lawyer Harry Whittington in the face with a shotgun [4], or Army Major Nidal Malik Hasan murders his fellow soldiers at Fort Hood [5]. These may seem like extreme examples, but shooting incidents fill the tabloids with spectacular headlines almost daily. Generally, we classify shooting incidents into one of the following categories:

- Suicide
- Accidental discharge of a weapon—hunting incidents/stray bullets
- Homicide
- Drive-by shootings
- Terrorist activity
- Emotionally disturbed incidents

Understanding and reconstructing the shooting incidents means identifying, interpreting, and preserving all critical forensic evidence. There are specific scene-dependant activities and considerations necessary to ensure a comprehensive scene investigation and subsequent reconstruction. From a forensic perspective, this means understanding how firearms work and how projectiles interact with targets, the ammunition used and its chemistry, and determining bullet flight paths.

20.2 On-Scene Considerations and Activity

It is unnecessary to be an expert in forensic ballistics, perform bullet matches or muzzle-to-target experiments, to be a competent shooting scene investigator. However, it is necessary to thoroughly understand the principles. It is also necessary to be an experienced scene scientist/investigator with a thorough understanding of how to conduct a comprehensive and competent scene investigation. Certainly a prerequisite is to reason appropriately and understand how to apply the scientific method properly. See Chapter 2.

Once at the shooting incident scene, thinking should center on what happened and its implications. For example, if a ricochet is suspected (see discussion in Section 20.9), an important question concerns what one would expect to see if it was indeed a ricochet mark. Certainly, this is an experience-based question, but it is an important one because knowing what to expect can lead to finding firearms-related evidence, such as an original impact site or defect, a bullet terminus, the bullet, or understanding the victim's wounds and/or holes in clothing. The thought process should logically concentrate on what physical evidence is known to the investigation, for example, damage to the recovered projectiles, wound characteristics, bullet hole/ricochet characteristics (size, chemistry, trace evidence), and how it relates to the overall scene characteristics. Information might well be in dispute, such as the specifics of the event, but this should not be the prime consideration, especially at first. Many questions will be answered later, such as after experimentation for determining muzzle-to-target distances. The medical examiner will answer other shooting-related questions, such as distance from a wound based on stippling or fouling on a victim's skin. The entire investigation should be based on applying the scientific method using appropriately validated scientific protocols and standards (see Chapters 6–12 in Reference [6]).

Shooting scenes are somewhat unique because they involve understanding bullets, their marks, and recovery. But this only a part of the usual good crime scene investigative practice discussed in Chapter 3. The successful investigation of a shooting incident requires a diligent effort to obtain specific firearms-related information within the context of the usual practice of archiving, sketching, managing, and so on.

As with most scenes, all of the information required to complete the investigation will not be available immediately. Some witness statements obtained during the initial investigation can be important, especially with shooting scenes, because each witness could have seen the incident from a different perspective. The composite of views might give a better overview of what happened. An example is the witness who claims to have heard multiple shots, say five, but another heard just three. Gunshots can echo, and the first witness may have interpreted the echo as gunshots. The second witness might have been in a different location, one that did not have an echo. What if the investigating team finds four bullets? Does this mean that the first witness was incorrect or is there a bullet missing? Differences in witness accounts can be confusing, but the team must attempt to sort them out at the scene, if possible. The resolution might require returning to these scene(s) and firing weapons using blank ammunition in different locations with investigators recording the retorts from different perspectives. Certainly, there will be differences in traffic, weather, humidity, and so on, from when the incident occurred.

An open-minded investigation is critical to ascertaining the ground truth of what happened as closely as possible. This means an objective gathering of critical facts. The following is an example of a list of information that should be obtained (note that this list is not all-inclusive) (see Chapters 6–12 in Reference [6]):

- Number of individuals involved—shooters and nonshooters
- Number of witnesses and their relative locations and sight lines
- Lighting/weather conditions

- Bullet/defect identification and chemical analysis
- Bullet flight path(s) angular component determinations
- Muzzle-to-target distances, if necessary
- Number of shooters
- Identification of shooters
- Position of shooters
- Location and type of trace evidence
- Collection of all firearms evidence
- Artifacts created by emergency medical technicians, witnesses, investigators
- Categorization of victims
    - Wounds—anatomical location, tracks, entrances, and exits
    - Locations and position of victims at the scene
- Collection of fragile evidence

20.2.1 Fragile Evidence

This is an important category of evidence that is present in all scenes, including shooting incidents. Particular to shooting scenes, however, is evidence unique to the discharge of a firearm. The following details the type of fragile evidence that might be found at shooting scenes and requires special attention.

20.2.1.1 Gunshot Residue

GSR is composed of easily dislodged particles. Anything that might contain GSR must be located expeditiously, collected, and preserved properly. The list of places where GSR might be found depends on the specific investigation, but common places include the hands and clothing of victims and shooters, bullets, ricochet, defects, and bullet holes. When collecting evidence, such as clothing, packaging is critical. Generally, clothing should be carefully folded, much as for preserving bloodstain evidence (Chapter 13), to avoid inappropriate transfer of the GSR from one part of the clothing to another. It is also important to package each item separately. Protecting areas where GSR might have fallen or was deposited, such as pockets, arms, or where a shooter stood, is critical [7].

20.2.1.2 Cartridge Cases

Cartridge cases are important because they can pinpoint the area from where a weapon had been discharged (semiautomatics). They contain ejection marks, firing pin marks, and so on, and have important comparative forensic value, which means protecting them from further damage (other than the marks made after ejection from the weapon). In addition to the cartridge cases, the pattern they form after ejection from the weapon is a separate category of fragile evidence. These patterns must be archived photographically because cartridge cases are easily moved—kicked (see p. 199 in Reference [6]).

20.2.1.3 The Usual Fragile Evidence

In addition to shooting-scene-specific fragile evidence, the usual fragile evidence associated with all scenes may also be important. These include footprints, tire tracks, fingerprints, and so on.

20.2.1.4 *Bullets*

Bullets will be discussed in more detail in Section 20.5, but the following underscores information available immediately to the investigation (see pp. 187–196 in Reference [6]).

- Deformation to ascertain angle of impact and strike surface characteristics
- Fragmentation and their location
- Rifling and twist to help identify specific weapons
- Number of lands and grooves visible
- Adherent trace evidence
- Blood

20.2.1.5 *Bullet/Projectile Marks and Holes*

Resulting from a bullet impact, projectile marks, and holes can have fragile trace evidence critical to identifying what a bullet struck on its path to its terminus. Although there is minimal risk of the bullets being ruined like footwear impressions, the marks they produce have important microscene elements, which means seriously considering how to preserve them. Certainly, blindly performing tests on a bullet hole can ruin the trace evidence present. The sequence of testing must be considered carefully, chemical analysis being last. First, document the defect photographically. Preserving the trace evidence present is the next consideration. A way to do this is to tape lift it on to cast the defect/hole with silicone casting material. The casting material captures the trace evidence and forms a mold of the defect, which preserves its structure.

Not all shooting scenes are single-shot occurrences, so it is critical to account for all firearm evidence. The following is a checklist of the evidence that should be obtained (see pp. 187–196 in Reference [6]):

- Categorize all bullets from all weapons, at the scene or from recovered weapons.
- Determine the number of missing bullets from all weapons.
- Identify the number of cartridge casings recovered versus the number that should have been recovered.
- Locate and count the number of identifiable bullet holes (entry versus exit), ricochet marks, or other defects at the scene as well as those in victims (from autopsy x-rays).
- Locate and inventory all bullet strikes and deflections.
- Identify the number and types of wounds.
- Obtain witness accounts of shots fired.

The presence of firearms evidence creates a new set of investigative challenges, such as the additional fragile evidence discussed above. The usual sexual assault requires a search for biological and trace evidence. However, if that case also involves a shooting, the scene's complexity goes up several notches. If it also involves a vehicle, the scene complexity increases yet again because bullets do weird things inside the vehicles (Chapter 21).

20.3 Basic Facts and Definitions

As with any new topic, students need to understand that shooting scenes and forensic ballistics have their own language, and being familiar with it is important for investigators to communicate effectively. The following discussion introduces students to the nuances of shooting scenes, presenting them as both different and the same as other scene types. It will not cover firearms in particular or provide an in-depth discussion of ammunition or forensic ballistics, except as they serve as examples or represent specific scene issues. It does discuss specific aspects of shooting scene investigations pertaining to the discharge of a weapon, how the projectile interacts with targets, and why discharged bullets are prime examples of the Locard Exchange Principle (see p. 9 in Reference [6]). First, though, it is important to introduce the language of the shooting scene investigation.

20.3.1 Ammunition

The following discussion introduces students to the terminology and definitions of common types of ammunition and its components. It is not a comprehensive discussion of the topic, which is available elsewhere [8,10].

20.3.1.1 Small Arms Ammunition

Scene scientists/investigators do not need to be ballistics experts but they should be familiar with the forensic aspects of ammunition and the information it has to offer to an investigation. From a forensic perspective, small arms ammunition consists of a cartridge case, primer, propellant, and a bullet. Essentially, there are three common types that are manufactured: rimfire, center fire, and caseless. Some terms are defined in Table 20.1 (see pp. 43–99 in Reference [8]).

Table 20.1 Description/Definition of Ammunition-Related Terms

Term	Description and/or Definition
Primer	The mechanism for igniting the propellant. 1. *Rimfire ammunition*: firing pin crushes a soft hollow rim of the cartridge to explode the primer. 2. *Center fire ammunition*: Primer held in a cup in the base of the cartridge. Primer crushed by firing pin.
Propellant	A mixture of chemicals that must be ignited from a primer. Ignited propellant produces gases that propel the bullet down the barrel of the firearm.
Cartridge case	A holder for the propellant and primer (not the bullet).
Straight case	Diameter is constant along length.
Bottle-necked case	Long case narrows to hold the bullet.
Tapered case	Old European style; wide-based case gradually reduced.
Bullet	A missile that is either fired or unfired.
Pellets	Individual lead or steel balls for shotgun ammunition
Shot	Another term for pellets (e.g., "lead shot").
Rimfire ammunition	Short brass, generally with a diameter of 0.22 in. Closed end is a flat head with a hollow rim with primer. Firing pin strikes rim which crushes and explodes the primer. The resulting flame ignites the propellant.
Center fire ammunition	Brass; the head is thick and heavy with a central recess or pocket for primer cap. A hole goes from the primer pocket to the cartridge, allowing flash to reach the propellant.
Caseless ammunition	The propellant surrounds the bullet as a single solid piece. No cartridge. The primer is usually at the rear of the propellant. Not typically associated with shooting incident scenes.

Table 20.2 Short List of Bullet Types and Descriptions

Type of Bullet	Description
Wadcutter	Flat-nosed with a sharp shoulder. Designed to produce clear holes in paper targets.
Spitzer	Elongated ogival bullet with a sharp point.
Soft point or semijacketed	A jacketed bullet with the jacket cut to reveal a lead core.
Hollow point	Usually semijacketed with a cavity, which expands on impact with soft targets; increases wounding effect of bullet.
Dum-dum	0.303 in. rifle bullet. The Mark II version is fully jacketed. Outlawed by the Hague Convention for military use but not for police use. Often mislabeled as a hollow point.
Rifled slug	Lead (steel and lead or plain steel) for smooth bore shotguns. Designed for hunting, it is also used by police. Outside of slug has helical ribs.
Saboted bullet	Subcaliber, plastic-coated bullet. High velocities due to smaller diameter. Plastic is shed when bullet leaves the barrel.
Flechette	Thin projectile stabilized by fins. Designed for military in the 1950s, inaccurate.

It seems that the list of bullet types is almost endless. Table 20.2 contains a short list of the most common types and their descriptions (see pp. 43–99 in Reference [8]).

20.3.1.2 *Shotgun Ammunition*

Shotgun shootings are also common and like other types of ammunition, it has its own language. With shotgun ammunition the bore or gauge, such as 0.410 in., refers to the number of lead balls of the same diameter as the inside of the barrel that weighs 1 lb. Thus, a 12-gauge shotgun has a barrel of 0.729 in. and 12 round balls 0.729 in. in diameter that weigh 1 lb. Unlike rifled weapons, shotguns have a smooth barrel that fires pellets, a single ball, or dust shot (see pp. 43–99 in Reference [8]).

Shotgun pellets are traditionally composed of lead and a small amount of antimony. Other materials also include: soft steel with a copper coating and bismuth alloyed with iron and/or tungsten. The single projectiles used in shotguns are called slugs, which can be round balls, also known as pumpkin shot. The type of shot depends on its shape. Examples include Brenneke, Foster, or Sabot slugs. Other specialized single projectile rounds include police ammunition called Hatton rounds (also known as a breaching round—designed to shatter deadbolts, door locks, and hinges [9]) and tear gas rounds (see pp. 43–99 in Reference [8]).

20.3.2 Primer Compounds and Their Composition

Priming compounds are a shock-sensitive mixture of chemicals that explode when struck by an object such as a firing pin. The debris resulting from that explosion is what is known as primer powder or GSR. One concern is ammunition in a fire because primer compounds in the ammunition are heat and shock sensitive. Temperatures ranging from 190°C to 260°C can cause spontaneous combustion which can ignite the propellant. While there is certainly the possibility of accidental discharge of bullets in fires, in fact, this is slim. The soft brass of the cartridge case relaxes its grip on the bullet which prevents a build-up of pressure. Nevertheless, in any fire, this should be a concern.

20.3.2.1 Lead-Based Primers

Until 2000, the most common components of priming compound were lead-based. Typically, they included explosive ingredients (lead styphenate and tetrazine), an oxidizer (barium nitrate), and a fuel to promote burning (antimony sulfide). Powdered glass was added to increase the friction and to assist in the detonation. Aluminum and magnesium were added to high-powered magnum pistols or rifles.

20.3.2.2 Lead-Free and Nontoxic Primers

There has been a move to replace the poisonous lead in primers with lead-free equivalents. The development of explosive chemicals such as dinitrodihydroxydiazobenzene (diazinate), dinitro-benzofuroxan salts, potassium dinitro-benzofuroxan, perchorate or nitrate salts, diazo, trizole, and tetrazaole compounds, and others. New oxidizers include zinc oxide, potassium nitrate, strontium nitrate, and zinc peroxide, and the fuel components might include boron, metallic powders, carbon, silicon, and metal sulfides.

20.4 Forensic Ballistics

There are four categories of ballistics: internal, intermediate, exterior, and terminal. Anyone working on shooting scenes should understand the differences among them. The following short discussion introduces the concepts important to scene investigators. For that reason, intermediate is not discussed except to indicate that it refers to what happens in the GSR cloud as the bullet exists the barrel of the weapon (also see Chapter 14, pp. 267–278, in Reference [10]).

20.4.1 Internal (Interior) Ballistics

This is the study of what happens in the barrel of a weapon, specifically what happens from when the firing pin strikes the primer to when the bullet or projectile exits the barrel of the weapon. A number of topics interest to individuals who study this area of ballistics, including primer ignition, barrel pressures, velocity, time the bullet remains in the barrel, recoil, and so on.

20.4.2 External Ballistics

This is the study of bullet flight after it leaves the muzzle, also known as the bullet path or, incorrectly, the trajectory. For most shootings, distances are short, which means the maximum range of the firearm is not a serious consideration. However, depending on the scene, long-distance shots could become a part of the investigation. In these instances, appropriate expertise should be sought. The subject is complex involving calculations that include bullet shape, sectional density, atmospheric pressure, and possibly the rotation of the earth (see pp. 213–234 in Reference [6] and pp. 274–278 in Reference [10]).

20.4.3 Terminal Ballistics

This refers to what happens when the bullet interacts with targets. Examples include what happens when it causes wounds as well as its interaction with inanimate objects such as water, soil, concrete, wood, and other materials (see pp. 278–281 in Reference [10]).

20.5 Bullets—The Locard Exchange Principle in Action

Bullets not only pack a wallop, but they and the defects they produce can be chuck-full of forensic information, depending on the importance of that particular bullet in the context of the shooting incident. If that bullet has forensic value, other than pinpointing the weapon that shot it, which is certainly important, the truckload of forensic information potentially is staggering. A list of the possible evidence that could be obtained is below:

- Bullet holes—caliber (an approximation) and ammunition type
- Bullet flight path—what it hit
- Bullet path component angles
- Position of the shooter
- Bullet strike surface characteristics
- Ricochet(s) interpretation

For these reasons, bullets must be found, collected, and preserved because protecting the forensic information is critical. So, in addition to human injury, an obvious aftermath of firearm discharge is the mark its bullets and projectiles leave on surfaces at the scene. Like all topics, bullets and defects—bullet impact marks—have a language with which the scene scientist/investigator should be familiar. These are defined in Table 20.3 [11].

A bullet found at the scene has potential forensic value, and the question of how to best capture it is an important one. The forensic value a bullet might hold is astounding, as shown by the specifics listed below.

Table 20.3 Firearms-Related Terms

Bullets, Projectiles, and Defects (Marks)	Definition
Target	An object struck by a projectile
Terminus or "final target"	The place where a bullet stops
Intermediary target	Object struck by bullet on way to terminus
Defects	a. Bullet impact marks b. May or may not be aligned to a bullet's path to its terminus
Bullet marks	a. Deflection defect: Bullet grazes a target b. Skip or skid: Bullet leaves a brief shallow mark c. Furrow or trench: Bullet leaves longer deeper mark d. Chunk-out: Piece of target knocked out
Secondary projectile	Piece of target dislodged and becomes a projectile
Secondary projectile defect	Secondary projectile leaves a mark on an object
Sympathetic fracture	Occurs not directly from the bullet impact
Bullets	a. Intact: Bulled recovered whole b. Deformed: Shape is altered because of hitting the final or intermediate targets c. Bullet or jacket fragment: Piece of the bullet resulting from contact with a target d. Metallic fragment: Possible bullet fragment that is not readily identifiable

- Chemical analysis to help identify the type of bullet
- Size to help categorize the caliber
- Trace evidence to identify intermediate targets
- Blood to identify injured people

20.5.1 Identifying Bullet Strikes

Bullets strike targets in various ways, and, like bullets, their defects, and marks have a language of their own. Figure 20.1 illustrates bullet marks [11] for bullets striking a wall.

The on-scene identification of which holes/defects result from a bullet strike is important because, if misinterpreted, the investigation can result in an incorrect and flawed reconstruction of the sequence of events.

20.5.2 Chemical Analysis of Bullet Holes and Other Defects

Bullets and their holes and other defects can be treasure troves of forensically important physical evidence. Unlocking these secrets requires a marriage of on-scene chemical and subsequent laboratory microanalyses. The reason is that a bullet can interact with multiple targets, collecting parts of whatever it hits and leaving physical material behind as it speeds along its way. This repertoire of forensic loot includes microtraces (Locard Elements) such as elements from the barrel of the weapon and from the primer discharge. A particularly impressive photograph of this as well as the Schlieren patterns can be seen in Reference [12]. It shows a bullet exiting from the GSR cloud after leaving the barrel of the gun. Logically, then, the bullet carries these microscene elements (trace evidence) with it and leaves traces in the hole/defect it creates after hitting an object; it leaves traces of itself as well (see pp. 32–39 in Reference [6]).

Term	Meaning	Illustration
Perforation	Bullet enters and exits target	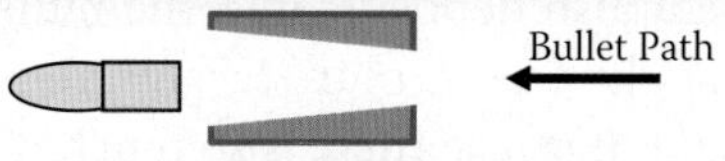 Bullet Path
Penetration	Bullet enters target but does not exit	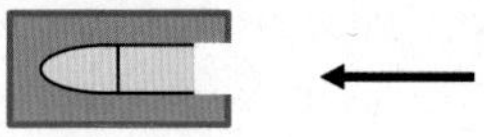
Imbed	Bullet just enters target but is not completely inside	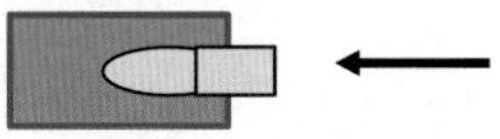
Spall	Bullet enters target and punches debris on exit side without exiting	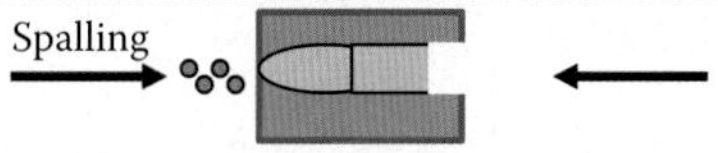 Spalling
Deflection	Bullet hits target and then changes direction, not entering the target	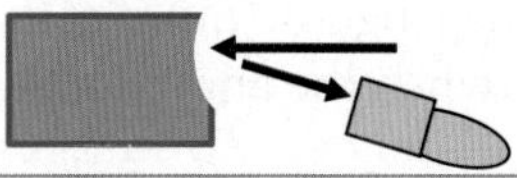

Figure 20.1 Illustration of common bullet mark terminology. (Adapted from D. H. Garrison. 2003. *Practical Shooting Scene Investigation: The Investigation & Reconstruction of Crime Scenes Involving Gunfire*. Boca Raton, FL: Universal Publishers. With permission.)

Together, the bullet and its holes/defects are classic examples of the Locard Exchange Principle in action, making them a potentially sacred class of physical evidence potentially capable of providing a variety of evidence details. They can tell an investigator what the gun was and who and/or what it struck along the way. The astute scene scientist/investigator, although not normally carrying a microscope (relatively powerful hand-held digital microscopes are available), must carefully examine recovered bullets visually, if for no other reason than to see what it has collected during its short-lived journey.

A careful visual inspection of the bullet and the hole/defect is necessary because bullets and the places they strike contain physical evidence that transfers to the bullet surface. This is followed by microchemical and instrumental analyses in the laboratory. On-scene chemical analysis of the holes/defects take place only after collecting the trace evidence that might be present.

First, however, it is necessary to identify those "holes or defects" made by a bullet, which is not necessarily straightforward. This is requires by a close visual inspection of the defect followed by chemical testing for lead or other primer components. However, to know what one is looking for requires an understanding of what happens to bullets from the beginning to the end of their journey. Bullets strike many surfaces, perforating some and grazing, ricocheting, or embedding in others. Clarifying which defects are from bullets is a critical part of the scene investigation. The first step is a simple visual examination of the hole/defect using a magnifying glass with the unaided eye and using a hand-held microscope at a magnification of about 40×, if available. The purpose is to find what is known as "bullet wipe."

20.5.3 Bullet Wipe

As a bullet travels down the barrel of a gun, its surface becomes contaminated with material from previous discharges of the weapon, some of which is carbonaceous material and condensed GSR. After leaving the barrel, the bullet flies though a cloud of rapidly condensing GSR, which also deposits onto the bullet's surface. After leaving the GSR cloud, the bullet might strike one or more targets, depositing surface contamination and part of its metallic content. Because there is so much material that can be transferred from the bullet to the defect, it is important to visually check the defect to get a "feel" for what is present. If bullet deposit—bullet wipe—is present, there is a good chance the hole/defect was made by a bullet. So, what is bullet wipe? Heard defines it as [8]

> Mixture of bullet lubricant, mouth sealant and carbonaceous material picked up by the bullet whilst traveling down the bore, which is deposited on any material through which it passes. (p. 226)

For practical purposes, a black or gray ring around the hole is diagnostic of bullet wipe. The larger the ring, the more carbonaceous material was present on the bullet. Don't stop here! This is when the analytical work begins.

20.5.4 Trace Evidence

The second visual test is to search for trace evidence: fibers, fragments of metal from the bullet's travel down the barrel, debris from other intermediate targets, and blood. Next, chemical spot tests can help identify the composition of the bullet. This completes the on-scene analysis. Note that trace evidence in the hole/defect could be removed by tape lifting or casting, although this might also remove some of the bullet wipe and could (probably not) compromise chemical testing to identify the composition of the striking projectile (see pp. 41–62 in Reference [6]).

20.5.5 Testing for Lead

After the explosion of the primer powder and ignition of the propellant, the cartridge releases the bullet allowing it to travel the length of the barrel where it exits and flies through a cloud of volatilized primer powder—GSR—containing vaporized lead, antimony, and barium (depending on the composition of the primer). A small portion of this vaporous milieu quickly condenses onto the surface of the bullet, which is ultimately transferred to whatever surface it strikes. Finding lead around a suspect hole or defect in a wall or through clothing, while presumptively positive for lead, is also presumptively positive for a bullet strike.

A common presumptive test for lead takes advantage of the reaction of sodium rhodizonate with lead. The sodium rhodizonate reaction results in a lead–rhodizonate complex that is a deep purple/pink color (see Figure 20.2). The test is simple to perform and gives nearly instantaneous results. Barium and antimony test similarly tested, but a positive rhodizonate test for lead is a reddish-purple-pink color that turns blue/purple after spraying with a solution of 5% hydrogen chloride. A summary of the reaction of lead with sodium rhodizonate is shown in Figure 20.2 (see pp. 41–62 in Reference [6]).

A step-wise procedure for presumptive testing for lead at the scene is shown below:

- *Procedures*
  - Press a dilute acetic acid (or tartrate)-moistened swab or piece of gauze against a surface to be tested—a suspected bullet hole on metal or a wall or on clothing.
  - Check for color formation.
  - If there is no color change, place a drop of the aqueous sodium rhodizonate (dilute solution in dilute acetic acid) onto the swab.
  - If the swab or gauze turns a bright reddish-purple, the test is positive. A positive test means that it is likely—not confirmed—that lead might be present, which is consistent with the presence of a bullet hole.

Test for lead

Sodium rhodizonate for Pb

- Tested directly on the object or lift
  - 15% acetic acid (or 2.8 M Tartrate) solution of sodium rhodizonate
    - Prepared fresh
    - Overspray with 5% HCl
      - Differentiates Pb from Ba and Sr, which give similar color
      - Pb will turn blue/purple after 5% HCl spray

Sodium rhodizonate $\xrightarrow{\text{15\% Acetic Acid}}$ Pb-conjugate—pink-purple/blue in acid solution

Figure 20.2 Reaction of lead with sodium rhodizonate.

- *Alternate procedure for larger surfaces*
  - Moisten a piece of filter paper in tartrate solution and press it against a suspected bullet impact mark for several seconds.
  - Remove the paper and spray it with a dilute solution of sodium rhodizonate.
  - A reddish-purple/pink color is a positive test (see p. 44 in Reference [6]). At the scene, there may initially be a question whether the mark on the brick came from the ricochet of the bullet. Testing for lead can give the answer.

A true bullet defect (or bullet impact mark) should give a positive test for lead if it was made by a bullet. Sometimes a lead bullet will disintegrate after a low impact angle strike, its lead vaporizing from the force of the impact and friction. The vaporized lead quickly condenses back onto the surface in a pattern showing the direction of the impact. This condensed lead is known as "lead splash" and it flows in the direction the projectile was moving. It is not always visible until treated with rhodizonate (see p. 44 in Reference [6]). Often there is a gray defect on the surface, which, from an investigative perspective, should not be labeled as a bullet impact mark or strike until after obtaining a positive sodium rhodizonate test.

Bullet-hole chemistry does not stop with the rhodizonate lead test because bullets are not always lead-only projectiles. In fact, many are jacketed with copper or nickel, the former the more prevalent. By identifying the presence of either copper or nickel as a component of the bullet wipe, more information about the bullet is obtained. Knowing whether the bullet defect was caused by a jacketed bullet can help narrow the choices among bullets that could have caused the defect, especially when some shooters are using copper-jacketed ammunition and others are not.

20.5.6 Testing for Copper

When a bullet hits intermediate and final targets, it leaves chemical traces on the outer edges of the hole or the defect. One component is GSR lead in the form of bullet wipe, as discussed in Section 20.5.5. Another will be the metallic trace of the bullet's surface, lead if it is unjacketed or copper or nickel if it is jacketed. If the jacket is copper, those traces should be detectable.

There are two tests for detecting the traces of copper associated with bullet holes. One test, the dithiooxamide (DTO) test reagent (rubeanic acid) which complexes with copper to yield a mossy green/charcoal color (see pp. 41–62 in Reference [6]). Performing the test is almost identical to that discussed for lead except that the reagents are different. The DTO test for copper uses a 0.2% w/v ethanol solution in dilute base—ammonium hydroxide. Although the test is more sensitive than the sodium rhodizonate test for lead, when lead splash is present, the lead can mask the copper which, in terms of the amount present, will not be as prevalent.

Consider, too, that copper is a much harder metal than lead (Mohr hardness of 1.5 for lead vs. 2.8 for copper). This means that copper is less likely to leave a deposit than lead. So, although the DTO test is more sensitive than the sodium rhodizonate test for lead, there is less copper present. The DTO test for copper is summarized in Figure 20.3 (see pp. 41–62 in Reference [6]).

The other test for copper uses 2-nitroso-4-naphthol (2-NN) as the color-producing reagent. 2-NN complexes with copper to give a light pink color. It also reacts with

Testing for copper

DTO—Dithiooxamide (Rubeanic acid)

- **Test for copper**
  - Mildly basic solution (NH_4OH)
  - More sensitive than sodium rhodizonate test for lead
    - Sensitivity compromised by
      - Hardness and higher boiling point of Cu versus lead
      - Ability of exposed lead to overwrite underlying Cu
      - Color produced can be difficult to see
- **Always assume both lead and copper present**
  - DTO test done before rhodizonate test
    - Mild acidic soln. used to transfer Pb residues also transfer copper
    - Pb test removes the copper
  - No such thing as copper splash

Dithiooximide —(Ammonium Hydroxide)→ Dark Mossy Green-charcoal

Figure 20.3 DTO presumptive test for copper.

iron and zinc to form green and orange colors, respectively. The test is summarized in Figure 20.4.

Importantly, investigators do not necessarily have to choose which test to use because they can be performed sequentially (see pp. 41–62 in Reference [6]). Figure 20.5 illustrates the testing sequence.

20.5.7 Testing for Nickel

Some bullets have nickel jackets. Knowing this at the scene can help pinpoint the type of ammunition used. Finding nickel can be important, especially if the projectile is not found, because most bullets are not nickel plated. The reaction of nickel with dimethylglyoxime (DMG) is shown in Figure 20.6 (see pp. 41–62 in Reference [6]).

Testing for copper

2-NN: 2-nitroso-1-naphthol

- Test for copper
  - 2NN—Gives pink color
- Easier to see against dingy backgrounds
  - False positives eliminated by drying "lift" and over-spraying with DTO
  - Used like DTO test
  - DTO and 2-NN Tests can be done in sequence, with the 2-NN test first.

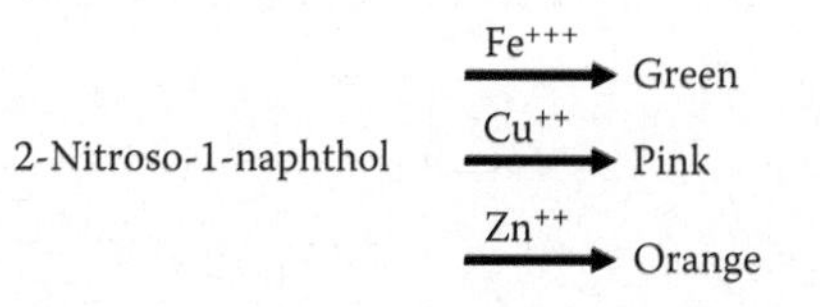

Figure 20.4 2-NN test for copper.

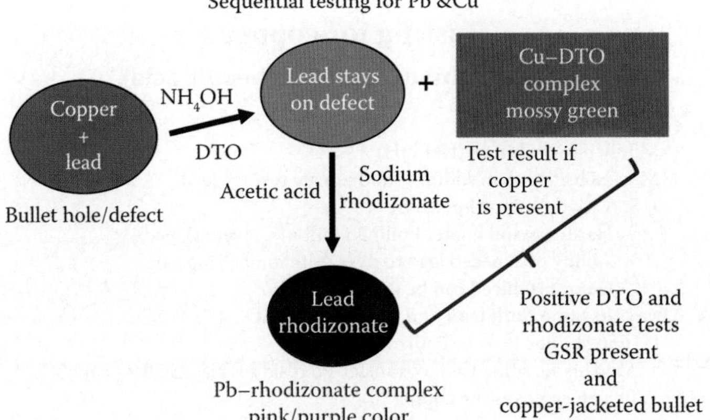

Figure 20.5 Sequential testing for copper and lead.

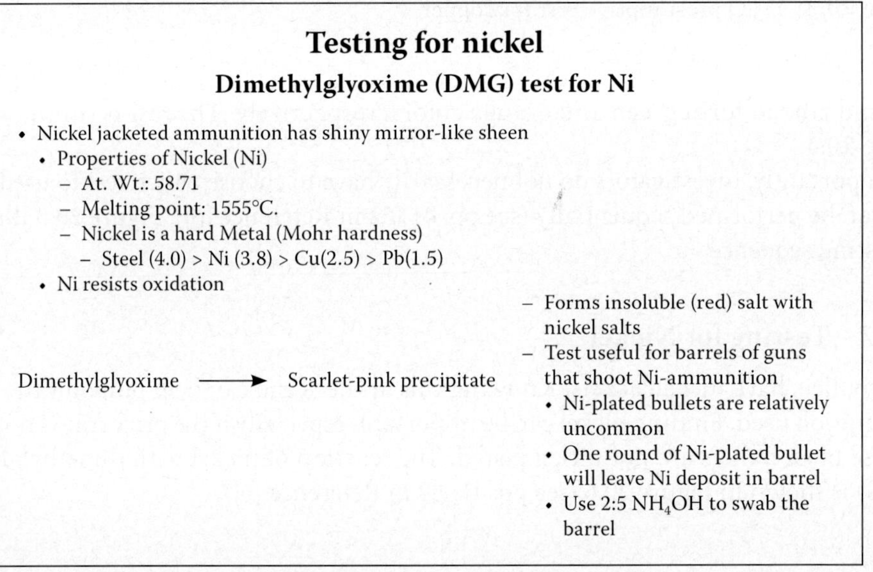

Figure 20.6 Dimethylglyoxime test for nickel.

20.6 Bullet Holes and Caliber

Heard defines caliber as [8]

> A numerical value, included in the cartridge name, to indicate the approximate diameter of the missile. (p. 48)

Haag defines caliber as [6]

> The diameter of a projectile, commonly expressed in hundredths or thousandths of an inch in the United States, when discussing small arms, although it may also be expressed in metric units. Caliber may also refer to bore or groove diameter, again, in either inches

> or millimeters. A term also used to designate the specific cartridge(s) for which a firearm is chambered. May be used as a unit of measure. For example, a bullet can be described as three calibers in length, when its length is three times its diameter. (p. 304)

One might expect that a bullet would leave a hole/defect representative of its width, which should also represent or be an estimation of its caliber. This is not necessarily true (see pp. 177–210 in Reference [8]), as discussed below for various targets.

- *Skin*: Skin is elastic, which makes the determination of the bullet caliber nearly impossible because attempts to regain its original shape. For round-nosed and hollow-point bullets, the hole diameter is much smaller than the bullet caliber. The bullet wipe diameter, too, will be smaller.
- *Fabrics*: Much like skin, fabric bullet holes are smaller than the caliber. The only diagnostic information is torn fibers, which can indicate the direction of travel.
- *Wood*: The caliber can be approximated by placing a piece of strong white paper over the wood surrounding the hole. Rubbing the surface over the hole with a lead pencil should give a white circle that approximates the caliber—the diameter of the bullet.
- *Vehicle tires*: These are almost self-healing, so determining the caliber of the bullet is impossible.
- *Vehicle body metal*: Semijacketed hollow-point bullets can leave a large entry hole. If stripped of its jacket, these same bullets can leave a smaller hole. High-velocity bullets can leave larger holes making the entrance seem more like an exit hole.

Other factors come into play as well. One is the velocity of the bullet and how it is made. Sheet metal is an important consideration because of the large number of vehicular shootings. A full metal-jacketed bullet interacts with sheet metal and deforms it depending on the impact velocity. If the impact velocity is low, it typically leaves holes smaller than the diameter of the bullet, but at higher velocities the hole becomes progressively larger, eventually becoming larger than the diameter of the bullet. This happens because the metal is slightly elastic. At low bullet velocities, the metal relaxes (contracts) and has time to relax and deform. At higher velocities, the metal expands and has little time to stretch, which results in less deformation. Lead and alloy bullets produce larger holes than the bullet. The reason is that the softer lead expands on contact before the metal can deform (see pp. 94–95 in Reference [6]). Determining a deformation ratio could be used to differentiate between bullets at the scene—based on differences in bullet velocities—because of how different bullets deform the metal. Identifying these differences could signal that different weapons and/or ammunition were used.

20.7 Trace Evidence and Bullet Holes

After the bullet leaves the barrel of the gun and travels to its terminus, it can strike a number of intermediate targets, among which will be surfaces made from different materials—glass, plaster, skin, fabric, and so on. If the Locard Exchange Principle holds true—energy is needed to create a fracture (principle of divisible matter), a bullet's surface should reflect its journey.

If the bullet went through a red plaid shirt, the fibers could be imbedded on the ogive.* If it was the second projectile through tempered glass, it might have a scored surface from the sharp edges of the already fractured glass. If it passed through human tissue, blood should be present. A bullet passing through the head of an individual might have adherent blood, hair, and/or bone particles. Thus, evidence adhering to a bullet is fragile evidence and it must be treated with the reverence it deserves. This means handling bullets carefully in order to preserve whatever fragile trace evidence is present (see pp. 123–126 in Reference [10]).

The rifling in the gun barrel can tear small fragments from the bullet. These fragments can also adhere to the bullet until it strikes a target. Tape lifting or casting the bullet hole and the surrounding area can capture these microscopic fragments, which when analyzed might lead to the identity of bullet type and/or its country of origin. This analysis is *not* the same as that for volatilized GSR lead on the surface of the bullet. Structurally, these two types of evidence are different: GSR is characteristically spherical, is examined by scanning electron microscopy and x-ray fluorescence (SEM/EDX), and can have smooth contours. Torn fragments by the rifling of the barrel of the weapon are rough and easily distinguished from GSR. The lift of this evidence should be protected like any trace evidence.

20.7.1 Blood from Bullets and Bullet Holes

A bullet passing through human flesh should have that person's blood on it (see p. 124 in Reference [10]). Theoretically, if it hits two people, the blood from both—a mixture of DNA—should be present. The caveat, however, is that the first person's blood could be diluted after passing through the second person, and detecting it might be beyond the capabilities of current technology. That does not mean that it will not or cannot be detected. If it is detected, the first person's blood should be the minor contributor to the mixture, which can be important reconstruction information, although the actual results will be case specific. Not finding a second contributor does not necessarily mean the bullet failed to pass through a second person.

An example is a shooting during a robbery. The bullet exiting the intended victim goes through a second person. Subsequent DNA analysis of the bullet using today's technology might show only the second person's blood. It is possible, even likely, that a minor DNA component is present but had not been detected, that is, there is mixture of DNA. If it had been detected, the minor component should be the blood of the first person injured. Newer DNA sequencing technology has the potential of identifying these mixtures. This layering of DNAs through concentration differences might help reconstructing the sequence of events of a shooting by the relative positioning of people in the projectile's path.

20.8 Bullet Flight Paths

Determining the path a bullet takes from the time it leaves the muzzle of the gun to its final target is important for understanding what happened during the event. The terminology can be confusing because bullet flight paths are sometimes erroneously referred to as

* Ogive: "An *ogive* is the roundly tapered end of a two-dimensional or three-dimensional object. In ballistics or aerodynamics, an ogive is a pointed, curved surface mainly used to form the approximately streamlined nose of a bullet or other projectile" [13].

trajectories (see p. 147 in Reference [6]). For the short distances involved in most shootings, this is a misnomer because what is being determined in most shooting incidents is not a trajectory but instead a flight path in a straight line. A true trajectory is a curved path, usually occurring over long distances, that is affected by gravity, diminishing velocity of the bullet, and other factors. That discussion is beyond the scope of this chapter. In fact, determining the true trajectory of a bullet requires an understanding of the physics of trajectories and gravity, the velocity, caliber of the weapon, the ammunition used, muzzle velocity, wind characteristics, and so on. For most shooting incidents, true trajectory analysis is irrelevant because of the short distances involved—estimated to average 25 yards [14]. For most scenes, critical information needed to complete the investigation is listed below:

- Identification of intermediate targets
- Identification of fatal bullets
- Determination of the number of weapons fired
- Identification of shooter position(s)
- Determination of bullet flight path angular components

20.8.1 Intermediate Targets

Identifying intermediate targets requires an investigation of the scene to ascertain what objects were hit. Recovered bullets might help identify other intermediate targets based on the trace evidence present on the bullet's surface. Thus, gentle handling of bullets while examining their surface carefully is a critical first step after recovering a bullet. Secondarily, packaging it properly to preserve its trace evidence for subsequent laboratory analysis is essential.

20.8.2 Fatal Bullets

Some fatal bullets may be recoverable at the scene but others will be identified during the autopsy. Recovering bloody bullets at the scene does not mean that it was a fatal projectile because it might have passed through someone's arm or other soft tissue. The medical examiner will determine which bullets were fatal.

20.8.3 Number of Weapons Fired

Determining the number of weapons requires extensive on-scene work and injury analysis by communicating with hospital physicians and the medical examiner, if the shooting resulted in live-victim injuries or was also a death investigation. The investigation must identify and collect all firearms evidence. Only then can the number of weapons fired be determined. If a bullet is unaccounted for based on the number of bullet strikes, reconstruction data will be missing, which can compromise the final interpretation of the events.

20.8.4 Shooter Position

Determining shooter position(s) depends on a number of factors. First is the preservation of fragile evidence, for example, footwear impressions, cartridge case ejection patterns, and so on. Second is the accuracy of on-scene bullet path angular component (coordinates) measurements. If these measurements are erroneous, determination of the bullet path will be incorrect as will the determination of shooter positions.

20.8.5 Bullet Flight Path Angular Components

Bullet flight paths are defined by their angular components, vertical and azimuth. It is impossible to determine shooter positions in the absence of other physical evidence (footwear impressions, cartridge casings, etc.). Even with other investigative information, defining the bullet's flight path accurately is critical to the reconstruction of the shooting events.

20.8.6 Bullet Flight Paths into Fixed Objects

Bullet flight paths occur as either ending in fixed objects (walls, vehicles, furniture, etc.) or are unfixed, such as passing through objects without a final terminus identified. In those fixed objects where trajectory rods are appropriate, determining a bullet's flight path is fairly straightforward. Generally, the bullet flight path's angular components represent the cocoon within which one describes a particular bullet's final journey, and they are an essential part of the shooting incident reconstruction. There are several ways to determine these angles (see pp. 147–159 in Reference [6]).

20.8.7 Trajectory Rods

One common way is to use trajectory rods inserted into the bullet hole (assuming it has already been determined that a bullet made the hole). Trajectory rods should be the last step in the analysis of bullet holes because inserting something into the hole can dislodge or ruin the trace evidence present. These rods work well for perforating bullet strikes in fixed objects where there are two points of bullet contact: an entrance and an exit. The trajectory rod spans the gap between the entry and the exit.

Trajectory rods tell investigators where a bullet could not have come from (see p. 37 in Reference [11]). However, if these rods are used improperly, the bullet flight path will be inaccurate; the result is a faulty determination of the location of shooter position(s) and likely a flawed reconstruction. Placing trajectory rods properly is essential. There is good and bad technique. Bad techniques include sticking anything into a hole before trace evidence is collected and chemical analysis is complete, shoving something larger into the hole, such as a pen or pencil ruins the hole and leads to an erroneous bullet path determination. Not centering the rod in the hole using a carefully and gently placed centering method, such as a rubber or cork with a center hole for the rod also leads to errors.

The characteristics of the material suitable for trajectory rods are important. These rods should be resistant to bending and to weather conditions, and should be able to be linked together and to be attached to lasers. Forensic supply houses sell trajectory rod kits. These typically contain metal rods that can be screwed together and to attach a laser. A caveat with these kits, in addition to their expense, is that metal rods tend to get bent over time. When they are out of round, they are useless for accurately determining the bullet paths. Wooden dowels can be made into rods having diameters that closely mimic the bullet calibers. These can be sealed against moisture so that they do not warp. Stiff plastic rods are also commercially available in multiple colors. Drinking straws can be used if the circumstances are correct, but these are short. They can, however, be used as a conduit for a laser beam.

Using trajectory rods properly is critical, regardless of the probe diameter. The reason is that there are more diameters of holes than there are rods. The most important aspects of using a trajectory rod is that

- The rod should be smaller than the hole.
- The rod should be centered in the hole, which means using a centering device without destroying the edges of the hole.

20.8.8 Angular Components of the Bullet Flight Path

Bullet flight paths are defined with respect to its two important angular components which can sometimes be determined at the scene: For vehicular shooting incidents, these are best determined at an off-site facility. The angular components are vertical and horizontal (azimuth): up-down and side to side. The vertical component is the north/south (up or down) path, and the azimuth is the horizontal east/west (left or right) path. Describing each is critical because bullets travel in 3D planes—up or down and left to right or right to left. If their path is neither up or down or left to right or right to left, they have no angular component (see pp. 150–159 in Reference [6]).

20.8.8.1 Vertical Component

Haag [6] defines the vertical component of the bullet path, vertical angle, as

> The vertical component of a projectile's reconstructed flight path. This angle is given a minus sign if the path followed by the projectile is downward and appositive sign if upward. A flight path that parallels a level surface has a vertical angle of 0.0° (p. 333).

Figure 20.7 shows how to determine the vertical angle of a bullet's flight path from a trajectory rod inserted into a bullet hole. Generally, there are two ways. Both methods use trajectory rods. The first uses a print out of a photograph of the trajectory rod inserted into the bullet hole. To make the calculation, the hypotenuse of a right triangle formed with a

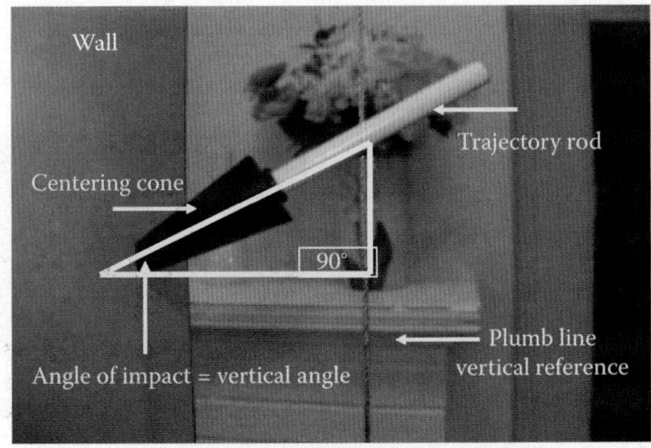

Use scale to measure sides of triangle
calculate angle using trigonometric functions

Figure 20.7 Determining vertical angular component photographically. (Photograph by Robert C. Shaler.)

plumb line is used, as shown in Figure 20.7. The angle is calculated using trigonometric functions.

After printing the photograph, the following steps should be applied:

- Draw a right triangle on the printed photograph using the plumb line as the vertical reference.
- Measure the three sides of the triangle using a ruler.
- Using these measurements, calculate the angle of impact using trigonometric functions for a right triangle.

The second method uses an inclinometer placed on the trajectory rod, as shown in Figure 20.8. The vertical angular component of the bullet flight path is read from the dial. The inclinometer should always be photographed. This is illustrated in Figure 20.8 (see pp. 150–154 in Reference [6]).

20.8.8.2 Azimuth or Horizontal Angular Component

The horizontal angular component is determined using a zero-edge protractor (see pp. 154–159 in Reference [6]). The 90° line on the protractor is placed in the center of the hole under the trajectory rod. Haag [6] defines the azimuth as

> An angle or bearing lying in the horizontal plan usually described on the basis of compass directions or with north, south, east, west descriptors. In shooting reconstruction, an arbitrary north-south or east-west reference line may be chosen as a reference or azimuth angles related to that line. (p. 299)

The procedure for measuring the azimuth from a bullet hole in a windshield is shown in Figure 20.9. This photograph, taken from under the zero-edge protractor, shows the position of the bullet hole in the window, the perpendicular (90° mark) on the protractor, and the position where the plumb line touches the protractor. The angle is read from the perpendicular to where the plumb line touches the protractor. After placing a horizontal (the inclinometer is leveled to zero), the zero-edge protractor is put into place—the 90° line is under the center of the bullet hole (under the trajectory rod), and a plumb line is dropped

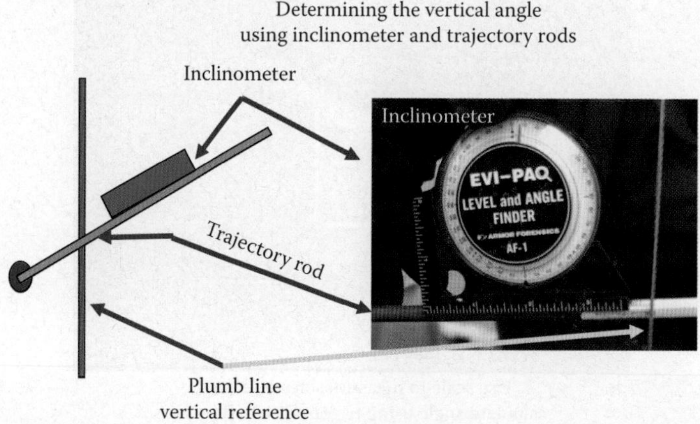

Figure 20.8 Determining the vertical angular component using inclinometer. (Photograph by Robert C. Shaler.)

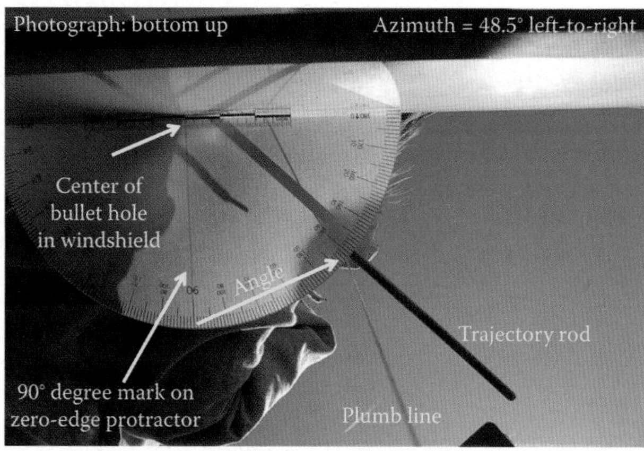

Figure 20.9 Determining the azimuth using a zero-edge protractor. (Photograph by Robert C. Shaler.)

against the outside edge of the trajectory rod so that it just touches the outer edge of the protractor. The angle from where the vertical plumb line just touches the protractor is read. For example, if the line touches the protractor at the 75° mark, the azimuth is computed by subtracting from 90 (90 – 75 = 15°) and the azimuth is recorded as 15° right to left.

20.8.8.3 Bullet Flight Paths through Unfixed Objects

Sometimes bullets go through a window without a noticeable second strike, such as when an intermediate target moves during a struggle or an intermediate target is not available. Determining the accurate bullet flight paths under these circumstances is nearly impossible. The key word is accurate. Sometimes "ball park" estimates are possible. Situations occur when an unfixed intermediate target can move, such as curtains, clothing, and so on. Approximating a bullet flight path might be possible using witness statements, obvious signs of moved furniture, footprints, and obstructions that confine the bullet path to a narrowed or loosely defined area. In these instances, and others, it might be possible to define a bullet's possible area of origin and estimate an approximate path.

Consider a situation where someone sitting in a car is struck in the head with a bullet. The bullet exits the passenger's side of the car, which is open, without hitting anything inside the car. If the bullet hit the driver in the temple without going through the driver's side window or hitting anything inside the vehicle, there are no points of reference with which to determine its path. Assume that the driver's side window was half raised (Figure 20.10). The black vertical line represents the closed part of the driver's side window, which restricts the possible entry points of the bullet since it was not impacted. The light blue vertical lines represent openings on the passenger's and driver's side. Although the general path of the bullet is confined to the upper part of the driver's window, it is broad as defined by the maximum positive and negative vertical angular components (orange arrows in Figure 20.10), which would put a shooter in an unreasonable position. A more likely path is defined between the two purple arrows, the highest horizontal path and the lower path above the edges of each open window. The driver's precise position is unknown because he is a moving target. In this scenario, it may be impossible to position the driver's head accurately and thus determine an approximate bullet path. The medical examiner would provide the bullet trajectory through the victim, which might further narrow the possibilities for the bullet path and possibly the shooter's position.

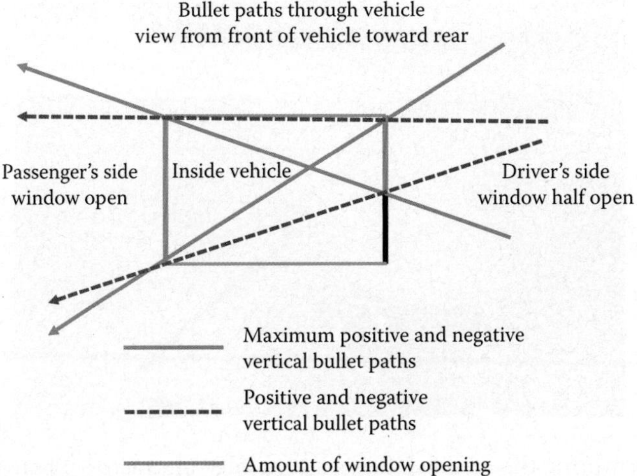

Figure 20.10 Flight path through open windows in vehicle.

The situation changes if the passenger's side window is rolled up to the same height as the driver's side, as shown in Figure 20.11, which effectively restricts the bullet path, the location of the driver's head, and the position of the shooter. How much restriction depends on how open are the two windows. In this example, each is about halfway. The shooter's location is less ambiguous—more straight-on—as paths represented by the hatched purple arrows. The orange arrows still represent an extreme for the shooter's position, especially the upward path.

A third possibility occurs when a bullet actually perforates the driver's side window. The entry point is known and the position of the passenger's side window restricts the path even more depending on how open it is. If the bullet perforates the passenger's side window, the bullet path is defined, which also positions the victim's head. If the window is completely down, as in Figure 20.12, the bullet path remains unknown but restricted. The bullet path through the deceased will be defined by the medical examiner which can help narrow the bullet path further. Still, the shooter's location is not yet precisely defined, which means other information is needed.

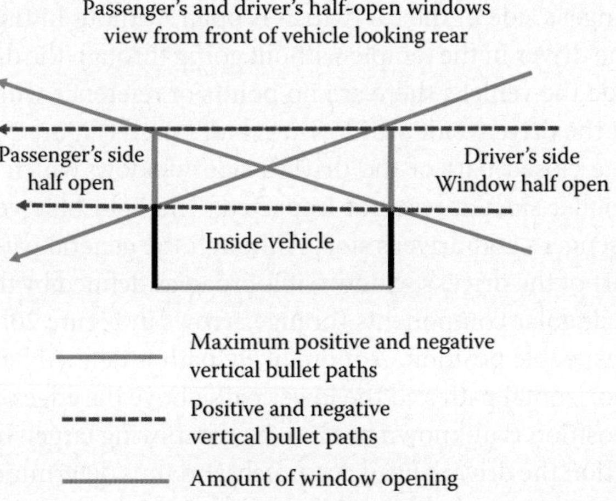

Figure 20.11 Bullet path through partially open passenger's and driver's windows.

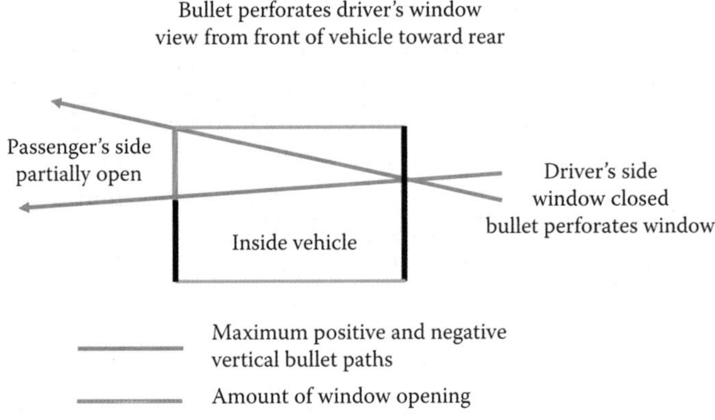

Figure 20.12 Bullet perforates driver's side window.

20.9 Ricochet

In most crime scenes, bullets travel in straight lines until they hit something. When that happens, several things might take place before the bullet finds its terminus.

- The bullet can enter the object
- It can go through the object
- It can bounce or ricochet off the object

The point at which the bullet ricochets off an object is determined by the following factors:

- The structure and velocity of the bullet
- The physical characteristics of the surface
- The angle at which the bullet strikes the surface

Generally, ricochet occurs at shallow angles of impact. However, as the impact angle becomes more acute, a point is reached when the bullet no longer ricochets and enters the object. That angle is called the critical angle, and it is illustrated in Figure 20.13.

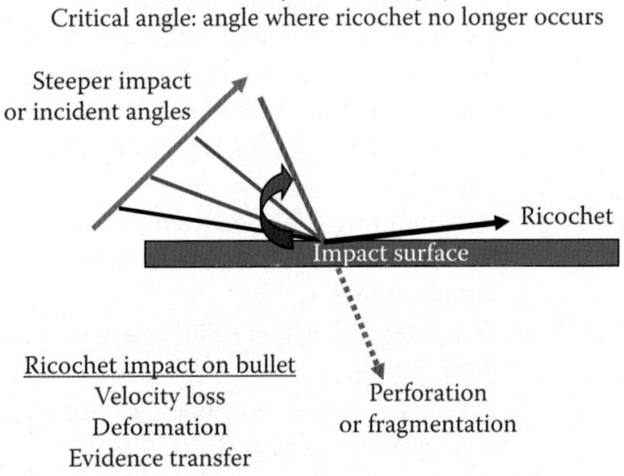

Figure 20.13 Illustration of the critical angle.

As with most fields of study, the concept of ricochet has its own language. Without understanding these concepts and the lexicon, students and novice investigators would have difficulty communicating with professionals in the field. Table 20.4 provides the definitions of important terms, as defined by other authors, which sometimes differ. One glaring discrepancy is the concept of incident and impact angles. For some practitioners, the angle at which the bullet strikes the surface is the angle of incidence while for others it is the angle of impact. It is important to understand that these are the same concept in forensic bullet path terminology (see pp. 116–118 in Reference [6], pp. 203–204 in [8], and pp. 195–196 in [10]).

Table 20.4 Bullet Ricochet Terminology

Term	Definition
Angle of incidence	The angle at which a missile strikes a surface before ricocheting [8]. The intercept angle described by the preimpact path of the projectile and the plane of the impact surface at the impact site when viewed in profile—differs from the NATO method. To convert, subtract 90° minus the forensic angle defined above[6].
Angle of impact	The angle of incidence of the impinging bullet or pellet to the substrate [8].
Angle of ricochet	The angle at which a missile leaves a surface after ricocheting [8]. The angle formed between the path of the departing projectile subsequent to impact and the plane of the impacted surface [6].
Critical angle	The actual degree at which a bullet will ricochet from a surface [8]. Angle at or below which a ricochet would be expected for a given bullet or pellet and a given substrate [10]. The incident (intercept) angle above which the particular projectile at a given impact velocity no longer ricochets from the impacted surface [6].
Ricochet	The deflection of a missile after impact [8]. A change in angle and/or direction of a fired bullet or pellet as a result of impact with a substrate [8]. The continued flight of a rebounded projectile and/or major projectile fragments after a low angle impact with a surface or object [6].
Ricochet mark	A two-dimensional effect without discernible depth (such as a ricochet off an automobile windshield without surface penetration) [8].
Ricochet crease	A three-dimensional effect with discernible depth (such as a ricochet off an automobile hood) [10].
Deflection—as opposed to ricochet	A deviation in a projectile's normal path through the atmosphere as a consequence of an impact with some object [6].
Deflection—as a consequence of ricochet	Any lateral component of the ricocheted projectile's departure path relative to the plane of the impacted surface as viewed from the shooter's position and with the plane of the surface normalized to a horizontal attitude [6].
Deflection—as a consequence of perforating or striking an object	Deviations in any direction from the projectile's normal flight path as a consequence of perforating or striking an object rather than rebounding off surfaces [6].
Angle of deflection	Lateral deflection (left or right) of a ricocheting bullet or pellet as it leaves a substrate [8].
Frangible surface	Surface that is subject to crumbling or breaking upon application of force, e.g., asphalt or concrete [8].
Nonfrangible surface	Surface that tends to bend or stretch upon application of force, e.g., sheet metal [8].

20.9.1 Tendencies to Ricochet

Why does a bullet ricochet? The simple answer is that it hits a target at an angle less than the critical angle for that surface and type of ammunition. *A priori,* it is impossible to know whether a bullet will ricochet. However, there are characteristics of bullets that seem to foster ricochet (see p. 121 in Reference [6]).

20.9.1.1 Nature of the Bullet

The way the bullet is constructed such as hardness, weight, center of gravity, and metallic components will impart, more or less, a tendency to ricochet.

20.9.1.2 Shape of the Bullet

The shape of the bullet is also important. For example, round-nosed bullets tend to ricochet more than flat ones. Full metal jacket rounds ricochet easier than lead or lead alloy bullets.

20.9.1.3 Response of the Surface

A hard unyielding surface versus a surface in which the bullet can enter also affects how a bullet ricochets.

20.9.1.4 Velocity

Generally, low-velocity projectiles ricochet more often than high-velocity ones.

20.9.2 Surface Characteristics and Ricochet Angles

As discussed above, when a bullet strikes a surface, it will either ricochet or penetrate/perforate. As shown above, the nature of the bullet, its velocity, and angle will have something to do with whether or not it ricochets. Another consideration is the surface structure. For this discussion, surfaces are classified as yielding, unyielding, and frangible.

20.9.2.1 Soft or Yielding Surfaces

Soft or yielding surfaces are soft enough for the bullet to enter the surface's matrix, for example, sheetrock, wood, automotive metal, and so on. How a projectile interacts with these surfaces is illustrated in Figure 20.14, which was adapted from various sources (see p. 116 in Reference [6], pp. 195–211 in [10], and pp. 122–125 in [15]). The light green arrow shows the bullet's incident path. The color changes to red as it enters the matrix of the surface. For these surfaces, the impact/incident angle is generally smaller than the ricochet angle. Said another way, the ricochet angle is typically greater than the angle at which the bullet strikes the surface, although this is not always true (see p. 116 in Reference [6] and pp. 195–211 in [10]).

So, why is it important to know the ricochet angle? The reason is that all projectiles must be collected and knowing that a particular surface is yielding—obvious from a gouged-out strike—can help locate the bullet if it is not immediately obvious. Theoretically, the angle of impact can be approximated for some surfaces using by dividing the width of the defect by its length and then taking the arc sine of the fraction (see Figure 20.16) (see pp. 195–211 in Reference [10]). From this, the bullet impact angle and its path can be *inferred*. Also a bullet/projectile striking a soft or yielding surface loses velocity quickly and might not be as deformed as the same bullet/projectile striking a hard or unyielding surface.

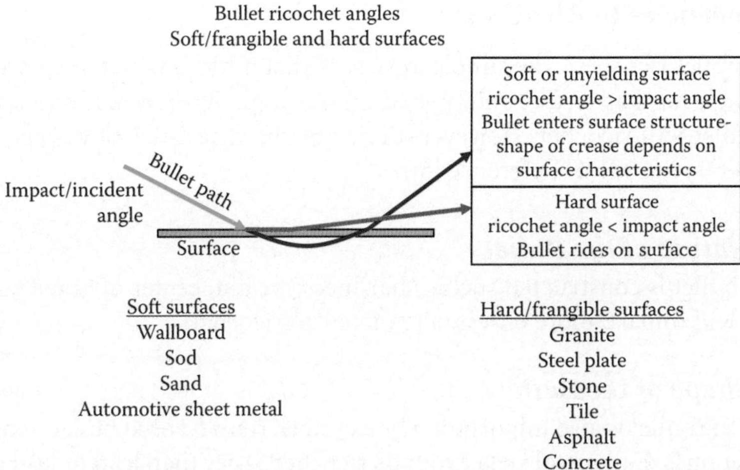

Figure 20.14 Ricochet from soft and hard surfaces. (Adapted from Haag, L. C., *Shooting Incident Reconstruction*, Elsevier Academic Press, Amsterdam, 2006, p. 116; Hueske, E. E., *Practical Analysis and Reconstruction of Shooting Incidents*, CRC Press, Boca Raton, FL, 2006, pp. 195–211; and Jauhari, M., Approximate relationship between the angles of incidence and ricochet for practical application in the field of criminal investigation, *Journal of Criminal Law, Criminology, and Police Science*, 62(1):122–125, 1971.)

20.9.2.1.1 Direction of Travel The direction a bullet is traveling can be determined by examining the physical characteristics of the ricochet mark. This is an important on-scene activity. This is not difficult because the bullet strikes the surface and either enters or indents it. As the bullet travels along the indentation it forms, its shape "pushes" the surface material to form a "ramp" from which it can exit. The ramp that forms is steeper than the entry angle, which means the projectile will exit at a larger angle than that at which it struck. From painted surfaces, such as painted automotive sheet metal, the direction of travel can also be determined using other characteristics of the defect: pinch point, lead in, fracture lines. An example shown in Figure 20.15 is a bullet striking automotive sheet metal.

Bullets striking painted sheet metal display certain diagnostic characteristics. These can indicate direction of travel by showing the place where the bullet struck the surface. Sometimes,

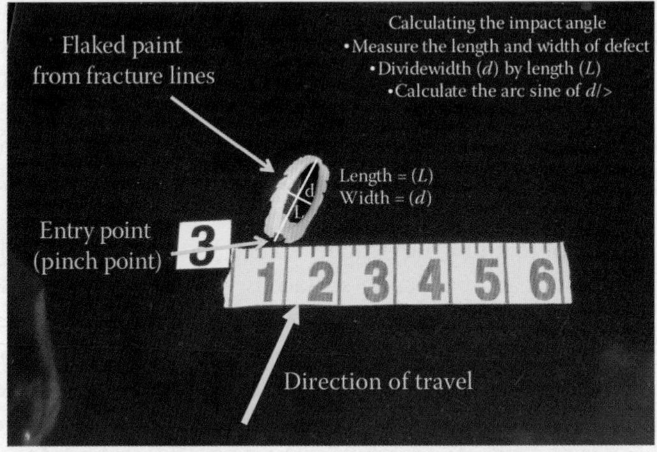

Figure 20.15 Bullet striking automotive sheet metal. (Photograph by Robert C. Shaler.)

the paint forms a visible knob (pinch point, arrow in Figure 20.15), where the projectile struck the painted surface. Sometimes, too, fracture lines on the edge of the mark form on painted surfaces. These are small stress cracks that occur when the bullet moves along the surface and either ricochets or penetrates/perforates it. The fracture lines point backward to the direction from which the projectile was traveling, much like the wake of a boat. Sometimes, the fracture lines cause the paint to flake off, as shown in Figure 20.15. It is possible to visualize otherwise invisible fracture lines by powder dusting the defect and then lifting the powder with fingerprint lifting tape or by casting using a silicone-casting material (a better method), which also captures the physical characteristics of the ricochet/hole.

Another directional clue is what is known as a lead-in mark at the entry point of the ricochet mark/hole. Like fracture lines and pinch points, the lead-in mark appears much like the area leading from the pinch point in Figure 20.15 except that the pinch point is not present.

20.9.2.2 Hard or Unyielding Surfaces

Bullets that do not penetrate or perforate hard or unyielding surfaces can also ricochet. When it happens, the bullet strikes the surface, skims on top of it for awhile, and then exits as a ricochet. Because the bullet rides the surface, the forensic information available is different from that of a soft or yielding surface. Figure 20.15 illustrates how a projectile interacts with an unyielding surface (see p. 116 in Reference [6], pp. 195–211 in [10], and pp. 122–125 in [15]). The light green arrow shows the bullet's incident path. When it strikes the surface (dark green arrow in Figure 20.15), it rides along the surface and exits, ricochets. Its ricochet angle is typically less than its impact angle or angle of incidence.

20.9.2.2.1 Twist Bullet twist refers to the spin imparted to the bullet by the lands and grooves of the barrel of the gun, right or left as it heads to a target. When the bullet hits a hard unyielding surface, it rides along the surface longer tilted on its twisting side. If it has a right twist, that is, it is spinning to the right when it hits the surface, it will leave a mark visibly elongated on the right side. The process is illustrated in Figure 20.16. On the

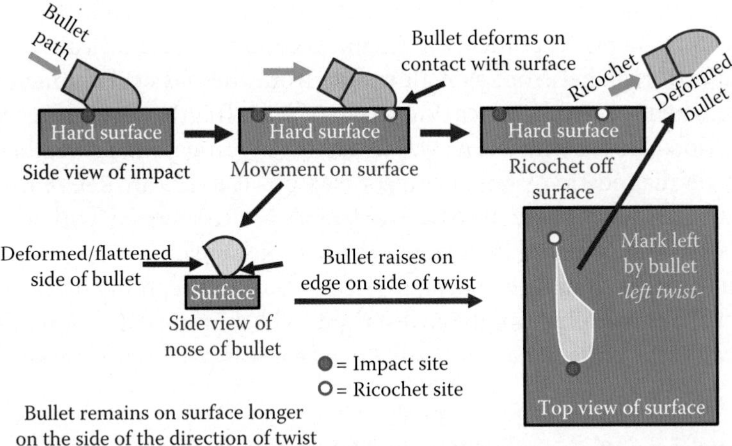

Figure 20.16 Identifying the twist from bullet impact marks. (Adapted from E. E. Hueske. 2006. *Practical Analysis and Reconstruction of Shooting Incidents*. Boca Raton, FL: CRC Press, p. 204; Reprinted from *Shooting Incident Reconstruction*, L. C. Haag, Copyright 2006, with permission from Elsevier.)

top set of diagrams, the bullet strides the surface, rides along the surface, and then exits as a ricochet. The bottom two diagrams illustrate what happens to the bullet as it runs on the surface and then ricochets. When the bullet impacts the surface, it deforms or flattens. The twist of the bullet causes it to rise up on its twisting side (see p. 204 in Reference [10]). In the side view diagram, the bullet is coming at the reader. If the twist is to the left, as in this diagram, the bullet is raised on its left side, which raises the right side off of the surface. When the bullet exits (right bottom diagram in Figure 20.16), the mark it leaves is longer on the side of the twist, in this case the left side. Certain marks have an elongation because the bullet stays on the surface for a relatively long time. This elongation is known as a "Chisum trail" after criminalist Jerry Chisum (see p. 116 in Reference [6] and pp. 195–211 in [10]).

When a bullet leaves the barrel of a gun, it is spinning because of the grooves in the barrel. This twist can be identified on painted and glass surfaces. These surfaces are the "negatives of the bullet surface" (see pp. 195–211 in Reference [10]). The twist can also be identified on hard or unyielding surfaces. This provides information about the bullet, even if the bullet is never recovered. If, in a shooting incident, two bullets were recovered, one with a right twist and the other a left twist, and both ricocheted off of a hard surface, the twist information from the ricochet mark will tell investigators which bullet struck which surface.

20.9.2.3 Direction

The way in which bullets strike a surface can help determine the direction in which the bullet was moving. In Figure 20.16, the ricochet mark clearly shows where the bullet hit and how it moved along the surface. Since it stayed on the surface longer, its tail (the elongated part of the mark) points toward the direction in which the bullet was traveling. In this figure, all bullets are traveling bottom to top.

20.9.2.3.1 Semihard or Semiyielding Surfaces With respect to ricochet, additional surface characteristics must be considered. In addition to soft and hard surfaces, there are two other classifications, semihard and semiyielding. An example is road asphalt. On asphalt, forensic testing and other indicators can fail; these can include directional indicators such as lead-in or pinch points and chemical tests for metals (lead splash). A more reliable indicator of ricochet from asphalt results from the physical characteristics of the mark or crease when it is fresh, appearing sharp or with fragile edges. If recognized early in the investigation before being worn away by traffic, investigators, or weather, these characteristics can be diagnostic of bullet impact (see pp. 128–129 in Reference [6]). Bullets striking asphalt can have characteristic trace evidence associated with those surfaces: front-to-back striations, mineral inclusions, and tar-like smears.

Because of the uneven nature of asphalt, ricochet and deflection angles are unpredictable. The bullet striking asphalt might have a right twist, but the deflection might be to the left simply because the bullet struck a small stone that was part of the physical integrity of the asphalt.

20.9.2.3.2 Surfaces with Frangible (Crushable) Materials Typically, these surfaces have materials that tend to crumble when struck by a bullet/projectile. Examples include cinder blocks and bricks and stones cast from mortar. These tend to react like hard or unyielding surfaces until the combination of the impact velocity and the incident/impact angle causes the material to shatter below the impact site, making the ricochet angle sometimes less than the incident angle—much like a hard surface (see pp. 128–129 in Reference [6]).

20.9.2.4 Effects of Ricochet

When a bullet/projectile impacts a surface, many things can happen. Examples are summarized in the list below (see pp. 120–121 in Reference [6]):

- Bullet/projectile loses velocity, more so in yielding surfaces.
- Bullet/projectile departs surface at an angle other than its incident angle, which varies depending on the specific surface.
- Bullet/projectile may deform or fragment, the amount of which depends on the surface characteristics. Yielding surfaces may not deform the bullet at all.
- The struck surface may deform or breakup, such as with frangible materials, resulting in ricochet.
- Mutual evidence transfers take place between bullet/projectile and impact surface.
- Impact surfaces are categorized as yielding, unyielding, semihard or semiyielding, or frangible. Each has characteristics that affect ricochet.

20.9.2.5 Deflections

Essentially, a deflection occurs when a bullet/projectile deviates from the plane of its incident/impact angle. This happens as a result of ricochet or because of how the bullet/projectile interacts with the surface. An example was discussed for semihard surfaces such as asphalt. The bullet/projectile strikes the asphalt and interacts with the surface. If the bullet strikes something hard in the asphalt, such as a stone, it can deflect unpredictably.

At other times, a bullet/projectile can perforate a surface and then exit in a plane that is not the same as the incident plane. That is, deflection occurs to the right, left, up, or down. In these instances, the direction of the deflection can be related to the twist of the bullet. For instance, when the bullet enters the material, it is spinning. When it exits it will do so in a manner that reflects its spin. Given the correct conditions, if the bullet has a right twist, it will deflect to the right. The caveat is that the bullet must be in contact with the interior of the material for a period of time, depending on the material, to allow it to "grab" the texture of the surface sufficiently for it to change the direction. For those materials that are thin, such as sheet metal, there will be little or no deflection (see pp. 140–141 in Reference [6]).

20.9.2.6 Why Ricochets Are Important

Just as bullets should be thought of as the poster children of the Locard Exchange Principle, ricochet marks, too, can be the source of transfer of trace evidence. And as discussed above, they can possess information in addition to trace evidence; this information reflects the bullet's direction and its twist.

20.10 Packaging/Preserving Firearms Evidence

Protecting evidence collected from a shooting incident scene is critical. Most firearms evidence falls into specific categories: firearms, bullets, cartridge cases, ammunition, powder and shot patterns, GSR, serial number restorations, bullet holes, ricochet marks, and other defects. Each of these will be discussed separately.

20.10.1 Firearms

Firearms at the scene can provide important evidence other than that obtained from the ballistics examination. All firearms should be treated as though they might have blood and fingerprints because these are individualizing types of evidence that might identify the shooter and/or the victim. Still, the logistics of preserving that evidence and other ballistics evidence must take into consideration the necessary steps to render the firearm safe. For scene investigators, this presents a potential problem because there is always the impulse to handle and examine the weapon as closely as possible. Most shooting scene investigators understand that it is bad practice to stick anything into the barrel to examine the weapon. The following specific sequential steps are necessary in handling the weapon:

- Archive the position of the weapon at the scene through sketches and photography.
- Carefully pick up the weapon using a gloved hand by holding it at the extreme end of the barrel and the area of the handle not usually touched when firing the weapon.
- Render the weapon safe by ensuring the safety is on.
- Inspect the chamber for live rounds and remove any present and package carefully as described below for bullets.
  - For semiautomatics, remove the magazine, leaving the rounds inside. Package it separately for subsequent fingerprint analysis by securing it between cardboard in an evidence box, ensure that it will not shift during transit.
  - For revolvers, photograph or record the relative position of each round in the cylinder.
- Record weapon-specific information: serial number, make, model, and caliber of the weapon.
- Mark all the weapons with an identifying evidence number, the initials of the collecting officer, and the date. Ensure that it is marked in an area that will not destroy the evidence.
- Place all firearms in evidence boxes designed to carry firearms, ensuring that the weapon cannot shift during transit.
- Do not attempt to clean the bore or chamber before packaging the weapon.
- Do not ship firearms that have bullets in the chamber.

20.10.2 Bullets

The focus on shooting incidents is usually on bullets. This is understandable because they can be a treasure trove of important forensic information. For this reason, finding, collecting, and preserving bullets are critical parts of the scene investigation. The following list is an overview of how to handle bullets at the scene. All bullets should be collected because each individual bullet might not have sufficient rifling characteristics to make a specific identification of the firearm used.

- Recover all bullets and archive their position through sketches and photography. Each bullet should have a unique evidence identification number.
- Never touch a bullet with an ungloved hand.
- Never touch the ogive area of a bullet because it might remove important fragile trace evidence, such as hairs or fibers, and so on.
- Handle bullets with nonmetallic tweezers because metallic tweezers can put scratches on the bullet that can interfere with the interpretation of their meaning and importance with respect to reconstruction of the incident.
- Never mark bullets to identify them for the same reason as above.
- Wrap bullets in soft paper or tissue and seal in separate pill boxes or envelopes. Pack the pill box with paper to ensure that the bullet will not move during transit.
- Label and seal the container appropriately.

20.10.3 Cartridge Cases

Cartridge cases also carry important forensic information, such as markings from the breech clock, firing pin, ejector, and so on. Therefore, it is important to ensure that the they are not marked further during the investigative process. The following is a checklist for preserving cartridge case evidence.

- Archive cartridge case evidence through sketches and photography. Each should have its own evidence identification number.
- Handle cartridge cases with gloved hands by picking them up at the ends of the case. This will ensure that any fingerprint evidence on the barrel of the case is preserved as much as possible.
- Do not mark brass cartridge cases. Fired shotgun shells can be on the inside or the outside of the paper or plastic.
- Package each cartridge case in a separate container prepared as described above for bullets.

20.10.4 Ammunition

All unused ammunition not inside weapons should be recovered, whether from the vehicles of suspects, clothing, houses, and so on. Preserving this ammunition is important and it should be treated as described above for bullets. If unused ammunition is in boxes, the outside of the box should be marked appropriately.

20.10.5 Powder and Shot Patterns

Generally, powder patterns are found on the skin of victims (fouling and/or stippling) or on clothing. Preserve these patterns photographically and if possible collect the evidence, for example, clothes, at the scene, and package sufficiently well so that there is no transfer of evidence from one part to another. The most appropriate way to package the GSR on clothing is to wrap it in paper as though preserving bloodstain evidence. See Chapter 13.

References

1. N. Johnson (dir./prod.). 1954. *Black Widow* [motion picture]. Beverley, CA: Fox Productions.
2. New World Encyclopedia contributors. Saint Valentine's Day Massacre. *New World Encyclopedia*. Available at: http://www.newworldencyclopedia.org/entry/Saint_Valentine%27s_Day_Massacre (accessed November 8, 2010).
3. C. Hauser. 2007. Virginia Tech shooting leaves 33 dead. *The New York Times (U.S.) Online*, April 16. Available at: http://www.nytimes.com/2007/04/16/us/16cnd-shooting.html (accessed November 8, 2010).
4. A. E. Kornblut. 2006. Cheney shoots fellow hunter in mishap on a Texas ranch. *The New York Times (Washington) Online*, February 13. Available at. http://www.nytimes.com/2006/02/13/politics/13cheney.html (accessed November 8, 2010).
5. R. D. McFadden. 2009. Army doctor held in Ft. Hood rampage. *The New York Times (U.S.) Online*, November 5. Available at: http://www.nytimes.com/2009/11/06/us/06forthood.html (accessed November 8, 10).
6. L. C. Haag. 2006. *Shooting Incident Reconstruction*. Amsterdam: Elsevier Academic Press.
7. A. J. Schwoeble and D. L. Exline. 2000. Chapter 1: Gunshot residue as forensic evidence. In: *Current Methods in Forensic Gunshot Residue Analysis*. Boca Raton, FL: CRC Press, pp. 1–9.
8. B. J. Heard. 2008. *Handbook of Firearms and Ballistics: Examining and Interpreting Forensic Evidence*, 2nd edn. Sussex, UK: John Wiley & Sons Ltd.
9. *Wikipedia*. Hatton or breaching round. Available at: http://en.wikipedia.org/wiki/Breaching round (accessed November 8, 2010).
10. E. E. Hueske. 2006. *Practical Analysis and Reconstruction of Shooting Incidents*. Boca Raton, FL: CRC Press.
11. D. H. Garrison. 2003. *Practical Shooting Scene Investigation: The Investigation & Reconstruction of Crime Scenes Involving Gunfire*. Boca Raton, FL: Universal Publishers.
12. G. S. Settles, T. P. Grumstrup, L. J. Dodson, J. D. Miller, and J. A. Gatto. 2004. Full-scale high-speed Schlieren imaging of explosions and gunshots. In: D. L. Paisley (ed.), *Proceedings of the 26th International Conference on High-Speed Photography and Photonics, Alexandria, VA*, September 20–24, SPIE Paper No. 5580-174.
13. *Wikipedia*. Ogive. Available at: http://en.wikipedia.org/wiki/Ogive (accessed November 8, 2010).
14. Firearms staff, FBI Academy. October 1969, revised March 1974. Bouncing Bullets. FBI Law Enforcement Bulletin.
15. M. Jauhari. 1971. Approximate relationship between the angles of incidence and ricochet for practical application in the field of criminal investigation. *Journal of Criminal Law, Criminology, and Police Science*, 62(1):122–125.

21 Vehicles as Shooting Incident Crime Scenes

21.1 Introduction

This chapter is not meant to create instant experts in how to examine vehicles involved in shooting incidents. It is, though, designed to acquaint students with the complexities and some of the issues involved.

Vehicles are an indispensable and thus integral and critical part of our modern society. So, it should not be surprising that they are involved in various crime types such as hit-and-run cases, kidnappings, homicides, sexual assaults, shootings, and so on. Although it is tempting to examine vehicles associated with each crime category, it makes more sense to concentrate on vehicles involved in shooting incidents. The reason is that shooting incidents are associated with most crime types and vehicles are often involved. A shooting incident involving a vehicle can involve all of categories of evidence already covered in this text: firearms (Chapter 20), biological (Chapters 13–16), trace (Chapters 4, 17–19), fingerprints (Chapters 9 and 10), and footwear and tire track impressions (Chapters 11 and 12). As with all scenes, vehicles must be archived (Chapters 6–8), searched (Chapter 5), and the scenes managed (Chapter 3). In investigating vehicle shooting incidents, these lessons learned must be applied. Additionally, the specific lessons of ricochet, deflection, and angular components of the bullet path that were discussed in Chapter 20 apply equally to vehicle shooting incidents.

It is apparent, then, that vehicle-involved shootings are extremely complicated. In fact, the vehicle, even one found at a homicide scene, must be considered by the investigating unit as a scene unto itself, as is the body. And like a dead body, several analytical issues must be considered and evaluated carefully before a definitive statement about what happened can be rendered. Without question, the successful investigation of a shooting incident requires rigid application of the scientific method; unless done properly, the final interpretation of the events that took place will likely be erroneous.

21.2 Two Scenes in One

It is safe to say that vehicle scenes are several scenes in one. Because of the extraordinary issues involving vehicles, these scenes present problems not typical of other scenes. First, the macroscene/microscene comprises two parts: the outside of the vehicle and the inside. This is similar to the inside and outside of a house in which a homicide took place. Each is important and each has macroscene and microscene evidence. Second, the exterior and interior of vehicles do not provide a lot of working area, especially the interior, which can complicate the investigation from an efficiency perspective. Generally, the outside of the vehicle (except for establishing shots of bullet holes/defects on the vehicle) should be examined at the scene. The interior of the vehicle should be examined in a controlled environment [1].

21.2.1 Outside the Vehicle

The outside of the vehicle is the conduit to the inside, so by Locard standards anyone who touched the vehicle had to have left behind evidence. The macroscene elements associated with the exterior of the vehicle include, for example, footwear impressions, tire track impressions, paint transfers, bullet holes, blood and tissue, glass, cartridge cases, and so on. Microscene elements associated with the exterior can include fibers, fingerprints, trace evidence associated with bullet holes, and so on. What matters is that this evidence is not forgotten in the haste to track bullets through the vehicle. It would be helpful for the reader to review the scene scenario discussion (Section 4.6) in Chapter 4.

The outside of the vehicle must be investigated first so that fragile evidence is not lost. This does not include sticking trajectory rods into bullet holes. The sequence of a vehicle investigation is illustrated in Figure 21.1.

The on-scene activity must be accomplished in a systematic and logical sequence. As with any scene investigation, archiving takes precedence. Archiving vehicles requires collecting as much information about the vehicle as possible, which includes still photography and video of the vehicle including all four sides and license plates. Depending on the type of crime, other information should also be obtained: VIN number, tire manufacturer and size, damage to the body of the vehicle, bullet holes, impressions in the paint (hit-and-run case involving a pedestrian), blood and fibers adhering to glass (windshield), and tissue and blood on the undercarriage and tires (see Table 21.1). After photographing and video recording, search for fibers and fingerprints. Bullet holes should be treated with reverence by examining them for trace evidence (Chapter 20) before attempting to determine the bullet path.

Investigation sequence
Check for live/injured victims
Treat the vehicle as a separate crime scene
Follow a normal scene investigative sequence

Investigate the outside of the vehicle first
Search for macroscene and microscene elements

Initial on-scene considerations
Archive the vehicle—photography/videography
Treat the bullet holes as locard elements before analyzing the paths
Use ALS to search for fibers and fingerprints
Dust/enhance the fingerprints
Search for and collect the blood and tissue evidence
Photograph and lift the impression imprints on vehicle

Figure 21.1 Investigating the outside of the vehicle.

21.2.2 Inside the Vehicle

After investigating the outside of the vehicle, it is time to archive the inside (Figure 21.2). This begins with establishing shots (and video) of the interior looking outside-in from all exterior points of the vehicle and then with midrange shots through the windows and doors. Live victims might have been removed, a process that can compromise evidence. Deceased victims might still be inside the vehicle, and their positions must be documented. Other macroscene evidence inside the car is also important: location and pattern of bloodstains, bullet holes, bullets and bullet fragments, cartridge cases, broken glass, and so on. There is also the question of who was where, especially if the driver and passengers are not present. The position of blood and bloodstain patterns, fingerprints, and biological material on air bags can be an important mechanism for obtaining this information.

21.2.3 Vehicle Checklist

Vehicles have an abundance of information to share with investigators, and it is simply a matter of obtaining it. Table 21.1 is a list of investigative information required in vehicle-related incidents (see p. 269 in Reference [2]).

Notice in Table 21.1 that some of the information is vehicle-specific and the rest investigative. Certainly, the vehicle-specific information is readily available. But the other information will require investigative activity, such as the positioning of the seats at the time of the shooting (seats can be moved to remove victims) or height or positions of windows and door openings. Most of the information is available from inspecting the vehicle while archiving the exterior and interior. Additional information that should be obtained is shown in the following list:

- Manufacturer's diagram of vehicle can help with sketching the vehicle. Sometimes diagrams are available on the Internet or from manufacturer's advertising records. These diagrams will also have dimension data that can be helpful.

Investigation sequence
Archiving: Macroscene elements
Establishing shots from all outside perspectives
Midrange and close-up shots of important evidence
Microscene elements
Search microscene elements

Inside on-scene activity
Photography/videography
Use ALS to search for fibers and fingerprints
Fingerprints
Blood and tissue
Track bullet paths into and out of the vehicle

Figure 21.2 Investigating the inside of the vehicle.

Table 21.1 Vehicle Data Checklist

• Make/model/color	• Angle of windshield relative to horizontal plane
• Vin/plate/engine	• Interior dimensions
• Transmission	• Position of seats
• Front/rear/all wheel drive	• Front and back
• Suspension characteristics	• Head rests
• Height changes w/load	• Seat backs
• Tires—sizes/description	• Door locks
• Height of vehicle above ground	• Marking vehicle at scene—paint
• Height/positions of window and door openings	• Position of:
• Positions of windows	• Tires—make, size, inflated/flat
• Method of operation	• Shifting lever
• Documentation of glass collected	• Parking brake
• Location	• Center arm rest/console hatch
	• Glove box: locked/unlocked

- Behavior of vehicle in motion is important. Knowing how the vehicle will react in specific circumstances can also be helpful. If it is an older vehicle, it will likely not react as though it was fresh from the dealer. This information is only available through experimentation.
- Nature of scene terrain can be obtained by surveyor records or by analysis after the event. Some of the information, such as road contour, is obtained during the scene investigation.
- Effects of scene terrain, such as its effect on the determination of bullet paths, are important to ensure that the paths determined are accurate (see Figure 21.3).

21.3 Bullets and Vehicles

Vehicles pose significant problems in shooting incidents, specifically for determining bullet paths into and out of the vehicle. Generally, two separate activities take place when vehicles are involved in shooting incidents: on and off-scene activities. The former takes place at the scene of the shooting and typically involves the archiving process, dusting/developing fingerprints, locating other impression evidence, blood, tissue, glass, and cartridge cases. The latter takes place at a controlled facility, such as a police-secured garage, where an intense investigation of the bullet paths and the interior of the vehicle begin. Here, two factors are involved: the different materials that comprise vehicles and the issue of the vehicle in motion.

21.3.1 Issues in the Determination of Bullet Paths

21.3.1.1 Vehicle Composition

Vehicles are composed of various classes of structural material. These can be divided into structural material that holds the vehicle together, for example, frame, axles, and so on, nonstructural material that, although structural in that it has form and shape, is more practical and decorative instead of maintaining the integrity of the vehicle, for example, dashboard, seats, interior door panels, and so on. Table 21.2 lists various

Table 21.2 Composition of Vehicles

Wide Variety of Material and Surfaces

- Frangible materials
  - Laminated glass in windshields
  - Tempered glass in side and rear windows
- Malleable (yielding) surfaces
  - Sheet metal
- Heavy unyielding metal structures
  - Axels
  - Support members
    - Frame
    - Engine
- Composites
  - Plastic
  - Fiber
  - Rubber moldings
  - Insulation
- Tires
- Painted and unpainted surfaces
- Varied shapes and curvatures

materials that make the process of determining bullet paths in vehicles extremely complicated (see p. 267 in Reference [2]).

21.3.1.2 Vehicles in Motion

In addition to the material composition of vehicles, the fact that they can be or are in motion at the time of the shooting can also present problems that complicate the investigative process to the point where some of the investigative questions investigators might not have immediate answers. An important consideration is precisely when and where bullets impacted the vehicle. Some of this information can be retrieved from statements of live victims or witnesses. The position of broken glass on the ground can be an important clue. With respect to determining a bullet path, bullets through a windshield can help, and that might provide information concerning where the vehicle was when the windshield was struck (Chapter 20). Eventually, the vehicle will stop and the aftermath of the shooting is reflected by the damage incurred. Tires are an issue because bullet strikes can deflate them slowly. Once flat, the vehicle is cocked at an angle that was not there before the shooting. This simply means that all considerations must be taken into account because an erroneous bullet path determination will lead to an incorrect reconstruction of the events. Table 21.3 lists some complicating investigative issues that can occur in vehicle-related shooting incidents (see p. 267 in Reference [2]).

21.3.2 On-Scene Activity

21.3.2.1 Positioning the Vehicle

One of the first activities of the on-scene investigation is to position the vehicle. Since this is an outside activity, it occurs simultaneously with the archiving process. But what does

Table 21.3 Complicated Investigative Issues

- Vehicles in motion or not on level surfaces
  - Final resting place surface different from when struck by bullets
  - Stuck location or orientation when struck difficult or impossible to determine
  - Relative position of doors and windows
    - Can change during or after incident
  - Shattered glass can be lost after incident
  - Laminated glass cracks continue postevent
  - Tires deflate slowly and go flat at location other than where shooting took place

positioning mean? Four aspects can affect reconstruction efforts and determination of bullet paths.

21.3.2.1.1 Anchoring the Vehicle at the Scene Being able to recreate the final resting position of the vehicle is important for reconstructing the shooting incident. One effective way of doing this is to spray a fluorescent line of paint starting at the midpoint of all four tires (the axles) and moving onto the pavement. This effectively anchors the vehicle to that location on the roadway which remains for postevent analysis. Additionally, the fluorescent paint on the pavement, which is semipermanent, marks the position of the vehicle's four tires at the original scene. This allows investigators and reconstructionists to know exactly where the vehicle originally came to rest.

21.3.2.1.2 Determining the Tilt of the Vehicle Vehicles are not always perfectly horizontal to the roadway on which they came to rest after a shooting incident. An inclinometer placed on the trunk and/or hood of the vehicle (if it was an automobile) gives the resting angle of the vehicle. Certainly, a tilt can be the normal resting position for the vehicle for any number of reasons, such as, worn structural components, or it might be the consequence of the shooting incident, for example, flattened tires [3].

21.3.2.1.3 Contour of Roadway Roads are not generally perfectly flat. In fact, the process of building roads requires making them higher in the middle than on the sides. This allows drainage to minimize hydroplaning for vehicles traveling in wet weather. If a roadway is assumed to be flat or nearly so, the bullet paths that are eventually determined will be erroneous. Figure 21.3 illustrates the point by three vehicles positioned along the contour of the road. Each of the three vehicles has a different tilt—red line above each. If a bullet is fired into each of the vehicles horizontally (green arrows), the path it takes will be determined by the tilt at which the vehicle lies. This means that each path can be different depending on which part of the roadway the vehicle sits, which can have serious consequences for reconstructing the incident. In Figure 21.3, the two vehicles on the left have similar bullet paths (green arrows) but these are different from the paths for the vehicle on the right A banked roadway will give a different tilt to the vehicle [4].

21.3.2.1.4 Tire Tracks The final resting place of the vehicle is not necessarily where the shooting began, which means investigators must attempt to determine where the shooting started. Sometimes tire tracks, such as skid marks, can help determine where this happened because they indicate where the driver might have lost control, applied the brakes, or swerved. This information along with the determination of bullet paths and positioning of the shooter can go a long way toward reconstructing the shooting incident.

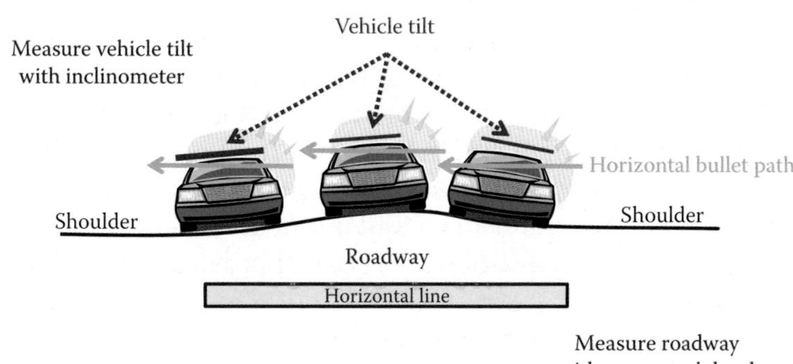

Figure 21.3 Effect of roadway contour on bullet paths. (Adapted from D. H. Garrison. 2003. In *Practical Shooting Scene Investigation: The Investigation & Reconstruction of Crime Scenes Involving Gunfire.* Boca Raton, FL: Universal Publishers, pp. 86–87. With permission.)

21.3.3 Post–On-Scene Activity

21.3.3.1 Measuring the Vehicle

Measuring the vehicle refers to determining those vehicle-related measurements discussed in Chapter 12, for example, wheelbase calculation, turning diameter, and so on, as well as those specific to the shooting incident. The latter refers to measuring the vehicle to create reference points that describe the bullet impact marks outside or inside. Generally, this activity takes place after the on-scene activity at a location that gives investigators space and time to investigate the bullet paths correctly. The post–on-scene activity requires documenting bullet holes and defects, and describing bullet holes and defects with respect to a reference point(s).

21.3.3.1.1 Documenting Bullet Holes/Defects Documenting bullet holes and defects refers to taking midrange and close-up photographs. This activity takes place before anyone touches the impact mark, such as determining the bullet paths. As with all forensic photographs, the close-up photos must have scales. For bullet impact marks or holes, the scale is important. Only millimeter scales should be used because of the accuracy required. As Figure 20.15 (Chapter 20) shows, determining the impact angle is essentially the same process as that used to determine the impact angle of bloodstains (Figure 14.11, Chapter 14). Figure 20.15 shows how to measure the length and width; however, the scale in the photograph is inappropriate and improperly placed.

21.3.3.1.2 Describing Bullet Holes/Defects After establishing photos, the next step is to take midrange and close-up shots of damage to the vehicle—impact points, bullet holes, defects, and so on, and then describing then so that anyone examining the case at a later time can understand the positioning of the bullet holes/defects. In effect, this means creating artificial vertical and horizontal reference points, a process that requires several measurements. In addition, the bullet holes/defects must be archived and measured. These processes are listed below:

- Referenced to a standard vertical and horizontal artificial point—the reference point.
- Measure the length and width of the hole/defect to calculate the impact angle.

The purpose of relating bullet holes/defects to a standard reference point is to create reference points to which all descriptions of defects can be related. One method would be to use fixed points on the vehicle as reference points for each defect measured, for example, trim, molding, hook lines, and so on [1]. For example, a bullet hole in the driver's side door could be described (on a diagram of the door) as being 6 in. below the door handle and 21.5 in. to the right of the horizontal line drawn to the front edge of the driver's side door. Photographs would be necessary to properly understand the placement of the bullet hole. Describing a bullet hole in this manner in a wall in a house makes sense, but not for vehicles because reference points on vehicles are not easily translated simply because of the way in which vehicles are built.

With respect to creating a standard reference point for all bullet/defect measurements, there are two accepted methods: the Haag method and the Moran method.

21.3.3.1.2.1 The Haag Method The Haag method, called "squaring the vehicle" (see pp. 170–171 in Reference [2]), is an attempt to place the vehicle into a square box using tripods, tape measures, and string. After the vehicle is removed from the scene and transported to a secured location and the initial archiving completed, the process of squaring the vehicle can begin. The process involves encompassing the vehicle inside an artificial box created using horizontally placed strings attached to tripods or other immovable objects (Figure 21.4). One horizontal measure is along the side of the vehicle and the other in the front (and/or back). These two horizontal references meet at a point at a right angle (the standard reference point) in space. All bullet hole/impact mark measurements are made to this reference point. Figure 21.4 illustrates this process. The process takes place in a controlled environment on a smooth-level surface, and three measurements are taken in order to precisely position the hole/defect.

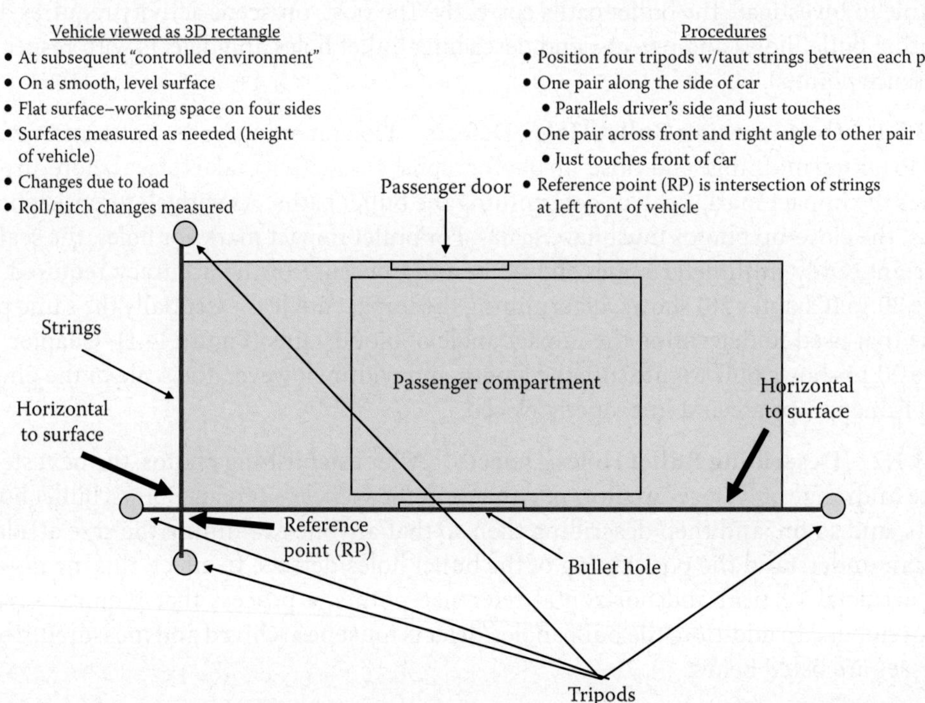

Figure 21.4 Haag method for determining the standard reference points.

- Height of reference point.
- Angle from bullet hole/defect to reference point.
- Height off the ground of the bullet hole/defect on the vehicle.

21.3.3.1.2.2 The Moran Method The Moran method for creating a standard reference point for bullet holes/defects accomplishes the same thing, only differently. The process also takes place in a controlled environment on a smooth level surface. The standard reference point is determined by placing tape on the floor a set number of inches away from the vehicle determined by a specific distance from axle location on each tire. A vertical reference is tape-placed vertically on the vehicle. Measurements from bullet holes/defects are related to the height and distance from the hole to the horizontal and vertical references (see pp. 270–279 in Reference [3]).

21.4 Perforating Strikes to Vehicles

When bullets perforate vehicles, it seems that anything can happen because of the structural composition that complicates the determination of bullet paths. As the bullet enters the vehicle, whether through the windshield, a door, the trunk, or any other place, it encounters obstacles. These obstacles can fragment the bullet, creating secondary projectiles or simply alter its path (deflections and/or ricochet). For these reasons, tracking bullets through vehicles is a tedious process, and it often requires dismantling parts of the interior. An example is shown in Figure 21.5. In this example, the incorrect bullet path and hence shooter positions would have been determined—left side of Figure 21.5—if the

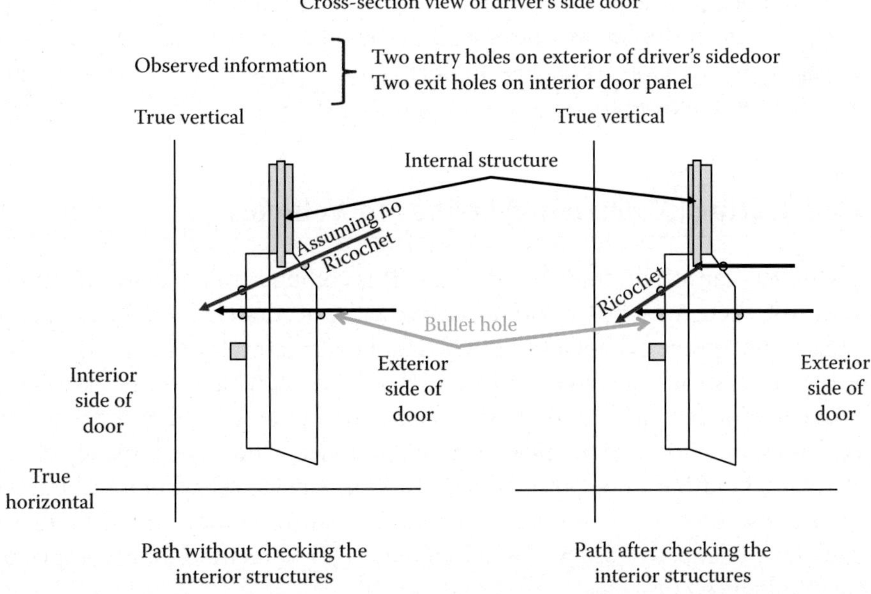

Figure 21.5 Bullet ricochet from internal door structure. (Adapted from D. H. Garrison. 2003. In: *Practical Shooting Scene Investigation: The Investigation & Reconstruction of Crime Scenes Involving Gunfire*. Boca Raton, FL: Universal Publishers, pp. 72–73; Reprinted from *Shooting Incident Reconstruction*, L. C. Haag, Copyright 2006, with permission from Elsevier.)

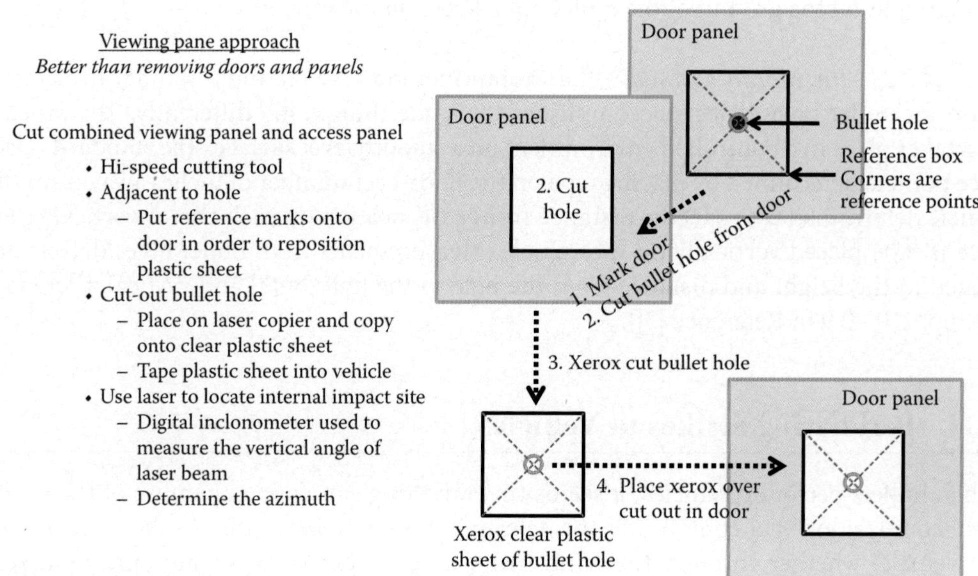

Figure 21.6 Examining the internal structures of the door panels. (Adapted from L. C. Haag. 2006. *Shooting Incident Reconstruction*. Amsterdam: Elsevier Academic Press, p. 160.)

investigator neglected to identify whether the bullet struck an internal structural element of the door. Here, the bullet paths, one at an acute angle and another nearly horizontal, suggest two shooters or at least one shooter firing from two different angles. The right side of Figure 21.5 shows the bullet ricocheting off of the internal structure and indicating that the bullet paths of both shots were close to horizontal and probably fired by the same person (see p. 172 in Reference [2]).

21.5 Penetrating (Nonexiting) Strikes to Vehicles

In vehicles, bullets can strike, enter, but not exit. This complicates the determination of bullet paths because there must be two points of contact to accurately identify a bullet path. In vehicles, the second point of contact might be inside a structural element. Figure 21.5 is an example. The bullet struck the internal structure of the door, which would have been determined by tearing the seat apart and observing and then photographing the mark made by the bullet. Sometimes "seeing" the place where the bullet struck is technically challenging because it requires cutting a hole into, perhaps, a door panel to see where the bullet hit. The viewing panel or window method is a convenient mechanism for locating the bullet and for determining the bullet paths (see p. 174 in Reference [2]). A method for accomplishing this is illustrated in Figure 21.6.

In this approach, a box is drawn on the door around the bullet hole. Next the box is cut keeping the reference corners on the door. The cutout is photocopied onto clear acetate, the acetate placed over the open hole on the door and then fixed to the door panel. The clear plastic provides a view inside the door panel so that the impact point can be observed and the bullet path determined.

References

1. D. H. Garrison. 2003. Chapter 7: Vehicle shootings. In: *Practical Shooting Scene Investigation: The Investigation & Reconstruction of Crime Scenes Involving Gunfire*. Boca Raton, FL: Universal Publishers, pp. 72–73.
2. L. C. Haag. 2006. *Shooting Incident Reconstruction*. Amsterdam: Elsevier Academic Press, pp. 160, 170–171, 172, 174, 267, 269.
3. B. R. Moran. 2007. Chapter 8: Shooting incident reconstruction. In: W. J. Chisum and B. E. Turvey (eds), *Crime Reconstruction*. San Diego: Elsevier Academic Press, pp. 270–279, 281.
4. D. H. Garrison. 2003. Chapter 8: Road structure as it affects vehicle shootings. In *Practical Shooting Scene Investigation: The Investigation & Reconstruction of Crime Scenes Involving Gunfire*. Boca Raton, FL: Universal Publishers, pp. 86–87.

Miscellaneous Considerations and Specialized Scenes

VII

Fire Scenes
A Scientific Method Investigation

22

22.1 Introduction

This chapter is designed to introduce students to the process of investigating fire scenes and is not meant as a definitive or comprehensive guide to on-scene practice. This is available from the National Fire Protection Association (NFPA) [1]. Other references as well as agencies are available (see Section 22.6). Local jurisdictions usually have a fire marshal and the fire department might have investigators. Additionally, insurance companies will dispatch a fire investigator to work on the investigation. Certification of fire investigators is important, as it is for all certified professions but it is only a piece of paper indicating that someone has passed a test. Though this conveys a certain amount of knowledge, there is no guarantee that the person is a competent investigator.

Fires happen for a number of reasons, but regardless of the cause, they destroy property and families and cost taxpayers billions of dollars annually. Whether the fire was started accidently or deliberately, it must be put out and its cause and origin identified. Certainly, fire scene investigations are also among the most complicated and dangerous. The most comprehensive manual of fire investigation has been published by the NFPA [1], which is an essential guide for all fire scene investigators. In addition to determining the agency responsible for the fire investigation (fire services and/or law enforcement), there are fundamental reasons why fire investigations are complex (see pp. 2–4 in Reference [2]).

- The origin of the fire is not necessarily obvious. Thus, determining the cause and origin of the fire requires considerable time, extensive data collection, and rigorous application of the scientific method (see pp. 16–17 in Reference [1]). It is an effort requiring experience, technology, science, and knowledge.
- The fire can compromise evidence because it can consume evidence, which means that sufficient data to establish the origin and cause might not survive.
- Such destruction of evidence can be exacerbated by normal rescue, suppression, and salvage tasks.
- There is the threat a major fire presents to the health and safety of the community, the public, and the investigators.
- There is always the threat that a fire can spread to adjoining structures.

22.2 The Scientific Method in Fire Investigations

The underlying premise of this text is that crime scene investigation is a scientific and investigative endeavor (Chapter 1), which means that the scientific method is the primary investigative tool. Few investigative texts outline how the scientific method is to be used, but the NFPA goes to great lengths to explain how and why the scientific method is the only appropriate method for investigating fires. In recommending the use of a systematic approach to fire investigations as part of the basic fire investigative methodology, the NFPA [1] writes,

> The systematic approach recommended is that of the scientific method . . . This method provides for the organizational and analytical process desirable and necessary in a successful fire investigation. (Section 4.2, p. 16 in Reference [1])

Concerning the scientific method, the NFPA [1] says,

> The scientific method is a principle of inquiry that forms a basis for legitimate scientific and engineering process, including fire incident investigation. (Section 4.3, p. 16 in Reference [1])

The NFPA discusses the scientific method for fire investigations by illustrating how each step fits into the investigative sequence, which is essentially the process of applying the scientific method to any crime scene investigation (see Chapter 2).

- Recognize that a fire has occurred.
- Define a process for solving the problem by determining its origin and cause through data collection, scene analysis, scientific analysis, and witness and/or expert interviews.
- Collect the empirical data through observation or experimentation.
- Use inductive reasoning to develop a hypothesis based on the data collected to explain the fire using fire-related criteria: burn patterns, fire spread, origin determination, ignition sequence, and so on.
- Use deductive reasoning to test the hypothesis against all known facts to disprove the hypothesis. If the hypothesis cannot be disproved, then it is deemed proven.

The NFPA [1] summarizes its use of the scientific method:

> All collected and available data should be analyzed using the principles of the scientific method. . . . hypotheses should be developed and tested explaining the origin, ignition sequence, fire spread, fire cause or causes of damage or casualties, or responsibility for the incident. (Section 4.4.5, p. 17 in Reference [1])

22.3 Essential Fire Science

The chemistry of combustion and the nature of fires, what causes them and what sustains them, have been studied and are well understood. A fire requires four ingredients to burn, and the components of the combustion reaction are referred to as the fire tetrahedron (see p. 18 in Reference [1]). The properties of each side of the tetrahedron are listed below. A break in any one of the four categories causes the fire to go out.

- *Fuel*: A substance that can undergo combustion.* Generally, fuels are organic substances, such as kerosene, gasoline, plastics, wood, alcohol, and natural gas, but

* Combustion takes place when a fuel source becomes vaporized after heating. Heating causes vapors or pyrolysis products to be released into the atmosphere where they can burn if an ignition source is present. Gaseous fuels do not require a heat source (p. 18 in Reference [1]).

there are also inorganic fuels that include substances such as magnesium and sodium.

- *Oxidizing agent*: A substance that can provide oxygen to the combustion mixture. An obvious oxidizer is the atmosphere, but potent chemical oxidizers, such as ammonium nitrate, potassium nitrate, and hydrogen peroxide, are capable of releasing oxygen during the reaction.
- *Heat*: The heat source causes the fuel to release vapors, which is a requirement for ignition. Heat sources are normally calibrated in terms of intensity or heating rate (kilowatts) or as the total heat energy received over time (kilojoules). In a fire, the heat source produces vapors causing ignition and promoting growth and spread of the fire.
- *Uninhibited classical chain reaction*: The combustion reaction is complex set of chemical reactions. It results in the rapid oxidation of a fuel, produces heat and light. Importantly, a self-sustained combustion happens when the exothermic reaction produces sufficient heat radiating back to the fuel. This produces vapors and causes ignition even in the absence of the original ignition source. In these instances, as long as there is a fuel source, the combustion reaction will continue.

22.3.1 Scientific Complexities of a Fire

Understanding the relationship of the rate and pattern of fire development as a complex relationship among the chemistry of a burning fuel and the surrounding environment is paramount to understanding the cause and spread of a fire (see pp. 35–36 in Reference [1]). Fire chemistry is complex. For example, phase changes and thermal decomposition are essentially the response of fuels to heat going from a solid or a liquid phase to a gas phase involving processes of melting, charring, sublimation, and vaporization (p. 18 in Reference [1]). For thermal decomposition these changes are typically irreversible due partly to pyrolysis, which can produce flammable gases. An example is polyurethane that decomposes to a liquid and flammable gases and vapors (see p. 19 in Reference [1]).

22.3.1.1 Combustion Products

Combustion happens in two ways. Premixed burning is where the oxidizer and the fuel are already mixed (gasoline in air), and diffusion burning is where the fuel and oxidizer come together to cause the combustion. This is the typical way in which fires start.

Combustion products vary depending on whether there is complete or incomplete combustion, but they include the three states of matter: solid, liquid, and gas. The most visible product of combustion is smoke, which increases in the later stages of the fire. Ash is an example. Incomplete combustion also produces carbon monoxide, which is dangerous, and small tarry droplets or aerosols can condense on surfaces producing smoke patterns. Investigators use these patterns to help identify the origin and spread of the fire.

The presence of a smoke deposit is evidence that the smoke engulfed the surface, whereas the absence of a smoke deposit shows that engulfment might not have happened. This, however, is not necessarily true, and the absence has the same meaning as all absent evidence: the absence of evidence is not evidence of absence. The amount of smoke is determined by the specific type of fuel; some are clean burning (natural gas) and others are not (fuel oil) (see pp. 19–20 in Reference [1]). The color of the smoke is not necessarily an indicator of what was burning.

22.3.1.2 Heat Transfer or Heat Flux or Energy Flow

Heat movement, or transfer, occurs by movement of heat from a hotter to a cooler surface. This process occurs in three ways: conduction, convection, or radiation. Importantly, heat transfer affects the ignition, the growth, the spread, and the extinction of a fire. It produces much of the physical evidence used by investigators to identify the origin and cause of fires.

22.3.1.2.1 Conduction and Thermal Inertia Conduction is a mechanism of fire spread via the transfer of heat in a solid material, and it has a direct impact on ignitibility and flame spread. The rate of this transfer (energy transfer) is known as the thermal conductivity of the material. A related term is the heat capacity (c) which is the amount of energy required to raise the temperature of the material by 1° (Celsius or Kelvin) under specified conditions. Another term is the density which is related to the mass of the material.

The thermal inertia of a solid is determined by multiplying the thermal conductivity, density of the material, and heat capacity together. This is the property that is most important in the initiation and early stages of a fire.

22.3.1.2.2 Convection Convection is the transfer of heat energy from heated liquids or gases to a cooler part of the environment. This typically happens when there are temperature differences, such as heat transferred to a cooler solid from hot gases. The rate of this transfer is directly related to the temperature difference between the two materials. In the early stages of a fire, convection plays a role in heating the surfaces exposed to hot gases (see pp. 21–22 in Reference [1]).

22.3.1.2.3 Radiation Radiation is the transfer of heat from a hot to a cool surface using electromagnetic waves without an intervening medium. This type heat is transferred in a straight line, although it can be interrupted by interfering surfaces. The smoke and hot gases that collect at the ceiling during a compartment fire are the source of radiation that can lead to ignition of other materials. The rate of heat transfer from a radiating source is proportional to that material's absolute temperature, so that doubling the absolute temperature creates a 16-fold increase in the radiant heat (pp. 21–22 in Reference [1]).

Radiant heat is one of the factors instrumental in causing flashover in a compartment fire, which occurs when an upper-layer gas temperature reaches 590°C (1100°F). When this happens, all combustible materials exposed to upper-layer radiation will ignite (pp. 35–36 in Reference [1]).

22.3.1.3 Fuel Load

Fuel load describes the amount of fuel present. It has no effect on the rate of growth of a specific fire in its preflashover phase (pp. 22–23 in Reference [1]).

22.3.1.4 Heat Release Rate

The heat release rate (HRR) has its maximum effect in the preflashover phase due to the burning of individual fuel sources. The HRR increases during the growth phase, reaches a peak, and then declines, producing an idealized shape much like a bell curve in statistics. The HRR occurs in three phases, each related to the amount of fuel source remaining. During the growth phase, the HRR increases because of the increasing flame spread over the fuel source. At its peak, the fire is characterized by full involvement of the fuel source. The decay phase reflects the reduction in fuel and the fuel area to burn (see pp. 22–23 in Reference [1]).

22.3.1.5 *Properties of Flames*

Anyone who has seen a fire immediately notices the color of the flame. It is tempting to relate flame color to the temperature and the material that is burning, but such a correlation is not necessarily accurate. The size of the flame is expressed as the flame height and the fire dimensions (length and width diameter). The flame height of a fire fluctuates over time, and there are three visual measures used to describe its appearance.

- *Continuous flame height*: the height over which flames are visible at all instances
- *Average flame height*: the height over which flames are visible 50% of the time
- *Flame tip height*: the greatest height over which flames are visible at any time

A fire has three regions defined by the flame height, which can be observed in a frame-by-frame inspection of a video of the fire.

- *Continuously flaming region*: lower portion of the visible flame
- *Intermittently flaming region*: upper portion of the visible flame
- *Plume region*: above the visible flame

At a fire scene, the flame height in corners is usually higher than that against walls or in open areas, which are essentially the same. Flame heights higher than the ceiling results in flame extensions along the ceiling, which can be longer than if the ceiling was not present (see pp. 24–25 in Reference [1]).

22.3.1.5.1 Thermal Structure of a Flame The maximum time-averaged temperatures of flames in the continuously flaming region occur at the centerline of the fire with temperatures approximating 1000°C (1632°F). Generally, the type of fuel has only a moderate effect on temperature; flame temperatures for accelerants are not higher than for fuels such as wood or plastic (see pp. 24–25 in Reference [1]). The temperature of the intermittent flame region is similar but falls to approximately 300°C (572°F) in the plume region.

22.3.1.5.2 Flame Spread Flame spread, the concept of a flame spreading over fuel sources, relates to the direction of the flame compared with the direction of the gas flow, and it occurs by two mechanisms: concurrent flame spread or counterflow flame spread. Counterflow flame spread occurs when the flame spreads over a horizontal surface or downward on a vertical surface. This type of flame spread is generally slow. Concurrent flame spread—wind-aided flame spread—is rapid and occurs when the flame spread is in the same direction as the gas flow. An example would be the upward spread of flame on a wall (see p. 32 in Reference [1]).

22.3.1.6 *Ignition*

For a fire to begin, a fuel source must catch fire. In other words, it must be ignited. To be ignited, the source material must be in either the gaseous or vapor state and the temperature of the heat source must be raised above the material's ignition temperature. Ignition varies considerably depending on several factors: gas, liquid, or solid phase, chemical properties of the fuel, and the form and intensity of heating. Ignition occurs in several ways: smoldering, flame, and piloted (ignition from small flames, sparks, hot surfaces), or autoignition.

22.3.1.7 Fire Effects and Fire Patterns

Fires produce effects and thus patterns that are visible or measureable (see pp. 39–59 in Reference [1]). Many such effects and patterns exist, and over time fire scene investigators have used them to determine whether a fire had been deliberately set, the philosophy being that these patterns only occur if an accelerant had been used to start the fire. As fire scene interpretations have come into question, their reliability as indicators of arson has become the subject of a great deal of controversy. The two concepts are different. As defined by the NFPA, fire effects are, "Changes in materials due to fire" (p. 39), and fire patterns are, "Visible or measureable physical changes or shapes formed by a fire effect or group of fire effects" (p. 47). Table 22.1 is a noninclusive list of fire effects that have been used by fire investigators to ascertain facts about a fire.

As defined above, fire patterns are visual or measureable changes formed by a fire effect. As such they reflect the way that the three mechanisms of heat transfer (conduction, convection, and radiation) produce fire effects and the nature of flame, heat, and smoke within a structure. Patterns form from heat, deposition, and consumption (see p. 48 in Reference [1]), defined by the dynamics of the fire. They are used to find the heat source of a fire and sometimes to define the heat intensity (heat/fuel) or spread (movement). Generally, there are two basic types of fire patterns: movement and intensity. These are important because the systematic analysis of these patterns can lead to the heat source.

In fire spread or movement patterns, heat, flame, and smoke produce patterns as a result of the growth of the fire and the growth, spread, and flow of the products of combustion away from an initial heat source. Because they are moving away from the initial heat source, an logical and systematic analysis of these patterns can lead back to the original heat source (see pp. 58–59 in Reference [1]).

Heat or intensity patterns occur as a materials respond to flames and hot gases producing lines of demarcation. These can help determine the characteristics and quantities of fuel materials as well as the direction of fire spread. Table 22.2 is a noninclusive list of fire patterns, their causes, and uses.

22.4 First Responder

The first responder to fire scenes has responsibilities similar to those broadly outlined in Chapter 3. For fire scenes, there are specific responsibilities related to fire investigation. Table 22.3 is an overview of some of the important responsibilities of the first responder. At some point, the first responder will hand over the scene to an investigator in charge. At that time, there will be a formal debriefing. A more comprehensive list of the first responder's responsibilities is available [1,2].

22.5 The Fire Scene Investigation

After obtaining the legal right to investigate the fire, victims taken care of, and the fire suppression efforts completed, the critical aspect of the fire scene investigation begins: determining the origin and cause of the fire. The sequence of the investigation is determined by the team leader, which typically moves from areas of lesser to greater fire damage, documenting fire-related patterns, marking evidence, and so on. Chapter 3 covered

Table 22.1 Fire Effects

Fire Effect	Description	Use
Temperature estimation	Temperatures in structural fires rarely exceed 1900°F.	Analysis of melted materials to establish minimum temperature in specific areas.
		Laboratory and expert analysis should be done on collected samples.
Mass loss of material	Fires consume material during the course of combustion.	Used as indicator of the duration and intensity of the fire—not valid in all situations.
Char	Caused by pyrolysis of wood during burning—leaves mostly carbon residue. Char shrinks as it forms and develops cracks and blisters.	Large shiny blisters (alligator charing) not diagnostic of liquid accelerant. Time of burning not determined solely on depth of char.
		No scientific evidence relates char to accelerant or the growth rate of a fire.
		Char can indicate direction of fire flow.
Spalling	Loss of surface material resulting from cracking, breaking, or chipping in concrete, masonry, rock, or brick.	Caused by many factors (heat, freezing, chemicals, etc.).
		Not solely determinative of presence of liquid accelerant. Burning accelerant not normally cause of spalling beneath surface of liquid.
		Heat liquid can cause spalling on adjacent surfaces. Resulting fire causes spalling on surface after liquid burns away.
Oxidation: A chemical process product of combustion. Refers to oxygen reaction with metals, rock, soil or acidic smoke aerosols and fire suppressant material (dry or wet chemicals).	Color and texture change. The higher the temperature and exposure, the more pronounced the effects. Postfire oxidation due to ambient humidity and exposure time. Materials oxidize according to their chemical properties.	Noncombustible material oxidation produces lines of demarcation and fire patterns Useful to fire scene investigators.
Color changes	Heat causes dyes to change color. Fabrics can show gradations of color depending on exposure to heat.	Information relating to the exposure of materials to temperature. Color changes occur for nonfire reasons (sun/chemicals).
Melting of material: Physical change caused by heat. Substances have melting temperature range: yellow brass, 1710°F; stainless steel, 2600°F; insulating brick, 3000°F; porcelain, 2820°F; silver, 1760°F; pot metal, 562–752°F; plastics—PVC, 167–221°F; nylon, 349–509°F; PE, 251–275°F.	Boundary between melted and unmelted can produce demarcation lines of heat and temperature.	Metals give information on temperature. Glass softens over a range of temperatures can give useful information on temperatures. Plastics can give useful information on temperature but in areas of hot gases and not flames.

continued

Table 22.1 (Continued) Fire Effects

Fire Effect	Description	Use
Smoke on surfaces: Occurs by settling and deposition.	Smoke from smoldering fires accumulates on walls, windows, and cooler surfaces.	Chemical analysis of the smoke deposits indicates nature of fuel.
Clean burn	Clear areas on noncombustible surfaces where soot and smoke condensed and was subsequently burned off.	Indicative of high heat, clean burn areas are not, solely, demonstrative of areas of origin.
Calcination: Chemical change in gypsum (wallboard) to anhydrite. Process of heating drives water out of gypsum leaving calcined product on surface.	The deeper the calcinations (plotted as graph), the more the heat exposure (heat flux duration). Calcined and noncalcined areas show lines of demarcation.	Gypsum has predictable response to heat. Color differences and depth of calcination can be indicator to establish areas of greater or lesser heat exposure—area of origin, ventilation, and fuel load.
Breaking of glass (crazing): A temperature difference of 126°F between the center of pane of glass and its protected edge can cause cracks. Without edge protection from radiated heat, glass breaks at higher temperature.	Crazing refers to complicated pattern of short cracks in glass—straight or crescent shaped. Claimed to be the result of very rapid heating on one side of glass. This is not true. Pressures developed in fires are not sufficient to either break glass windows or to force them from their frames.	There is no scientific basis for claim that crazing occurs in fires.

Source: National Fire Protection Association (NFPA), Chapter 4: Basic methodology, In: *NFPA 921 Guide for Fire and Explosion Investigations*, NFPA, Quincy MA, 2008, pp. 35–59.

the basics of how to manage a scene including how to incorporate the scientific method into the process. This should be reviewed at this point.

After the origin or origins of the fire have been determined, the cause of the fire can be considered. This involves a scientific approach requiring analysis of the evidence, postulating hypotheses, testing the hypotheses, and deriving conclusions and opinions. A very simple example concerns a short-circuited electrical box. Once the cause of the fire is known, the only question remaining is why the short circuit occurred, for example, was the wiring not up to relevant, local fire codes? An investigation includes the collection of evidence, which might in this example be as simple as taking the breaker box and examining the wiring, making a hypothesis of why the short circuit occurred, testing the hypothesis by examining the codes and drawing a conclusion. If the codes were not been violated, the test of the hypothesis fails and another hypothesis must be postulated and another round of testing begins. A short circuit does not necessarily require the involvement of law enforcement because a crime might not have been committed. However, if the origin of a fire is a sofa in the living room of a house, the question "how did the fire start?" becomes significant. Was the cause a lit cigarette or an accelerant used? If the former, it might be a tragic accident associated with property loss and possibly one or more lives. If the latter, the fire might be an arson, which would require the involvement of law enforcement.

The fire scene investigation generally follows the same sequence as any scene investigation, with usual scene investigative components of managing, archiving, searching, and so on, applied to specific requirements of fire scene investigations. Fire scenes are different

Table 22.2 Fire Patterns

Fire Pattern	Description	Use
Lines or areas of demarcation	Caused by differences in heat or smoke effects on substances in the fire.	Used to infer differences in heat or smoke in specific areas of a fire. Interpretation can be difficult.
Plume-generated patterns	Generated by 3D fire plumes. Effectively lines of demarcation created by the 3D (conical) shape of the fire plume after being interrupted by a 2D structure (wall, ceiling). The rate of heat release of burning fuel affects the shape of fire pattern.	Gives insight into fire development. The lack of a pattern after the fire does not mean that pattern was not present earlier in the fire's growth. Progress of fire can change pattern: final pattern observed might evolve from cone evolving to columnar pattern and then "V," "U," or hourglass pattern.
Location of patterns	On any surface exposed to effects of the fire or its by-products. Can occur on interior, external, structural members, walls, machinery, roofs, doors, windows, ceilings, floors, gutters, and so on.	Determine height at which burning began in the structure. *Walls*: Lines of demarcation and underlying of structure can show patterns. Most commonly "V," "U," hourglass, and spalling patterns. Surfaces behind wall can also have patterns. *Ceilings and under surface of tables or shelves*: Typically circular or partial circles. *Floors*: Transition through flashover to full-room involvement is associated with radiant heat flux that can modify or obliterate patterns. Burning between seams or cracks or around door thresholds might not signify use of ignitable liquid. Curling of vinyl floor tiles is not necessarily from use of ignitable liquid, but scientific analysis can identify the liquid.
Heat shadowing	From object blocking travel of radiant heat. Can change, mask, or inhibit production of lines of demarcation.	Can assist in reconstruction of origin area.
"V" patterns on vertical surfaces	Created by flames, convective or radiated heat from a hot fire, and/or gases or smoke in the fire plume.	The angle of the "V" does not indicate the speed of the fire growth or the rate of heat released.
Inverted cone (triangular pattern)	Caused by vertical flame plumes not reaching the ceiling.	Indications of relatively short-lived or low heat release rate fires: not floor-to-ceiling. Not necessarily associated with ignitable liquid fuels.
Irregular patterns	Curved or pool-shaped patterns on floors and floor coverings.	Should not be identified as coming from ignitable liquids.
Trailers	Caused by intentionally distributed ignitable liquids, solids, or combinations.	Found along floors to connect separate fire sets or upstairs.

Source: National Fire Protection Association (NFPA), Chapter 4: Basic methodology, In: *NFPA 921 Guide for Fire and Explosion Investigations*, NFPA, Quincy MA, 2008, pp. 35–59.

Table 22.3 First Responder Responsibilities

First Responder Responsibility [2]	Interpretation	Examples
Initial responsibilities	Provide critical investigatory information, which might provide the starting point for evidence collection and preservation efforts.	• The type of occupancy and conditions of structure (lights on; fire through the roof; walls standing; open, closed, or broken windows and doors). • Conditions around scene (e.g., blocked driveways, debris, damage to other structures). • Presence of victims and witnesses. • Vehicles leaving the scene. • Bystanders or unusual activities. • Flame and smoke, unusual observations (containers, exterior burning or charring, absence of normal contents, unusual odors, fire trailers). • Weather conditions. • Fire suppression techniques: ventilation, forcible entry, utility shutoff measures. • Fire alarms, security alarms, sprinklers.
Scene safety	Safety of civilians and public safety personnel. Identify, evaluate, and mitigate the scene hazards. Establish the safety zones for evacuated victims.	• Evaluate the scene for safety hazards (e.g., structural collapse of the building; smoke; electrical, chemical, or biological hazards; other health risks). • Establish the safety/hazard zones. • Communicate the hazards to other personnel arriving at the scene. • Use the tools and personal protective equipment appropriate to the task during all operations.
Preserve the fire scene	Recognize the future evidentiary value items and protect them from damage from fire suppression or rescue efforts.	• Observe and note the evidence that may be present at the scene (fire patterns, burn injuries, trailers, ignitable liquids, furniture pushed together, papers piled up). • Incendiary/ignition/explosive devices (matches, lighters, timing devices). • Usual scene evidence: impression evidence, glass, broken windows, tool marks on doors and windows, discarded clothing, blood, bodies, witnesses, and so on.
	Recognize the threats to evidence: movement, removal, contamination, or destruction.	• Fire suppression activities, activities that destroy fire patterns, salvage activities that involve moving or removing potential physical evidence, weather conditions that affect transient evidence, and contamination from external sources, such as fuel-powered tools or equipment. • Personnel walking through the scene, witnesses, and victims leaving the scene, medical intervention, and treatment of victims (e.g., by damaging evidence at the scene or destroying victims' clothing). • Premature removal or movement of bodies. • Vehicles at the scene (e.g., that introduce fluid to the scene through vehicle leaks or destroy other evidence, including shoe prints and tire impressions).
Security and control	Establish the control of the scene. Initiate the archiving of the scene.	• Establish up a security perimeter using barrier tape, fire line, sentry, vehicles). • Control the access into/out of the scene through security perimeter. • Initiate the archiving of the scene.

primarily in that the investigation requires significant fire investigative expertise. Other differences are also apparent. See Chapter 6, Section 6.7.8, and Tables 6.8a and b, which lists what should be photographed at fire scenes and the reason for the photograph (see also Section 22.5.1 below).

22.5.1 Archiving the Fire Scene

Although Tables 6.8a and b (Chapter 6) were an overview for archiving fire scenes, certain nuances of fire scene investigation are worthy of additional consideration. The goal is to accurately record the sequence of the investigation. Importantly, too, as already discussed in Chapter 6, archiving is a mechanism for study at a later time and also for helping to locate missed evidence during the initial investigation. For fire scene archiving, color photography should be the main archiving mechanism. Video can be important in helping to ascertain the flame height (see 22.3.1.5) (see pp. 124–125 in Reference [1]). Fire scenes are dark, so having an external light source, such as a floodlight, a detachable flash, or a strobe, is critical. The following list gives a general overview of fire scene archiving.

- The exclusive use of video is not recommended, but video would include scene and topic videos (Chapter 7).
- Generally, filters should not be used.
- Establishing photographs are shot using a maximum DOF.
- After-the-fire photographs should begin on the outside and work toward the inside, ending at the point of origin. The rationale is to document the entire fire scene, not just the point of origin.
- Sequential photographs illustrate the relationship of scene details to the overall scene.
- Photo diagrams should be prepared to show the location of the camera when the photo was taken.

In addition, the photographer should capture suppression efforts, the cause, and the origin when they are determined (identification of code violations, use of ignitable liquids, etc.) as the investigation progresses. Thus, the archiving process should be contemporaneous with the investigation. The responsibility of the fire department to suppress the fire is an important activity that should be captured (fire hydrants, attack line locations, engine company positions, etc.). The reason is to be able to explain at a later time how the suppression activities related to the investigation and suppression success. While the fire is burning, it is also important to capture how it progresses as well as to capture the fire department activities.

Exterior photographs will fix the location of the fire and document the burning structure, its surrounding area including street signs and automobiles (including license plates). These can be invaluable for conducting postscene investigation. The photographs of the external structure of the building should include all sides, corners, exterior angles, fire patterns, and structural failures (windows, roofs, walls, etc.) (see p. 125 in Reference [1]). Fires attract crowds, and those standing in the crowd should be captured for possible future contact.

Interior photographs are important to track the fire's travel backward to the origin. Ventilation points and smoke, heat, and burn patterns should be captured. Rooms in the immediate area of the origin should be photographed, even if there is no damage. All heat-producing appliances or equipment (furnaces, fire places) should be photographed to document what role these might have played in the fire or to eliminate them as potential contributors. All furniture, the position of doors and windows, fire and smoke alarms, air conditioning and other dampers, and clocks should be photographed too. Other potential sources of fires, such as gas appliances, circuit breaker panels, electrical cords, and outlets in the area of the fire's location, should be documented. If the fire is arson, traditional forensic evidence should be photographed: establishing, mid-range, and close-up photographs. If possible, victims and witnesses and witness perspectives of the fire should be photographed (see p. 125 in Reference [1]).

With respect to lighting, the fire scene is dark, which means an external light source is required. Adjusting the ISO to increase the sensitivity of the digital processor is not a good idea because that will only add noise to the final photograph. Oblique lighting might be important, so a detachable flash unit will be necessary. A ring flash for close-up photography can reduce the glare without the use of UV filters, which would be useless inside a burned structure. Because of the darkness, the technique known as painting with light or using slaves might be helpful to illuminate extremely dark areas (Chapter 6). Bracketing shutter speed is a good idea to ensure better exposures. Also, all photographs should be shot using the RAW file format, and JPEG photographs should be backups (many digital cameras take a RAW and JPEG image simultaneously). Sufficiently large memory cards are needed to store RAW photographs as these are usually large files.

Sometimes IR photography reveals information that visible light photography cannot. Some digital cameras can respond to IR light by using special IR filters making the digital camera a dual-purpose tool. Using the filters requires a tripod because some of the exposures can be lengthy.

Videotaping the fire scene has an advantage over still photography: it allows the stepwise documentation of the flame height. It is possible to objectively narrate the video process, which can highlight specific areas of the investigation.

Note-taking is also an important exercise that complements sketches, photography, and video. Notes capture important information, such as names and addresses, serial numbers, statements and interviews, photo logs, evidence and chain of custody logs, materials encountered, measurement data for CAD programs, and investigator observations (fire effects and patterns, building conditions, position of switches and controls) (see p. 127 in Reference [1]). The NFPA has developed specific forms for fire investigations.

Sketches are the final cog, but not necessarily the last completed, in the archiving wheel. Most fire scene sketches are plan and elevation sketches. Exploded sketches illustrate the detail of the fire involvement in a single room with the walls and ceiling-folded flat. If the structure does not survive, design and construction drawings might be available. Final drawings should include fire patterns. Others might have details that show char depth at various points—isochar graphs (see p. 132 in Reference [1]).

22.5.2 Evidence at Fire Scenes

The concept of evidence at fire scenes is more complicated than that occurring in the usual crime scene investigation (homicide, sexual assault, burglary). Also, preserving evidence at fire scenes is inherently difficult, which is made more difficult because the fire can consume the evidence, and suppression efforts to put out the fire can damage, obliterate, or destroy it. Additionally, physical evidence at a fire scene is significantly different from that found at the more routine crime scenes. The evidence at fire scenes is relevant to ascertain the origin, the cause, the spread, the reason for the fire and to identify perpetrators, if applicable. The evidence at routine crime scenes is relevant to identify who was at the scene and who was responsible for committing the crime.

A further difference lies in the efforts required to preserve the evidence present. At routine crime scenes (weather issues certainly play a part sometimes), the evidence is usually contained and efforts must be made to protect the fragile evidence. At a fire scene, all evidence is potentially fragile. Thus, every effort should be made to preserve fire scene evidence, and, when it is found during any phase of the fire investigation, it should be photographed *in situ*, protected from loss, movement, or destruction, and preserved.

Unlike most scenes where evidence is collected during the investigation, the cause of a fire will not usually be known until near or at the end of the investigation. In fact, evidence collection will not begin until fire suppression efforts are complete. According to the NFPA [1], this means that "the entire fire scene is considered physical evidence and should be preserved" (p. 134). Unlike routine crime scenes where evidence is collected by law enforcement, at fire scenes, the fire scene investigator and insurance company investigators might collect evidence, which can include not only the usual evidence (fingerprints, footwear and tire track impressions, body fluids, weapons) but also arson-related or incendiary evidence: the physical structure, its contents, materials ignited, or material on which the fire appeared (see p. 135 in Reference [1]). Other evidence includes fire patterns and artifacts (remains of material first ignited or other items related to the fire development or spread such as consumption of combustibles, smoke, soot, oxidation, charring, etc.).

22.5.3 Collecting Evidence

Collecting evidence from fire scenes can be broken into two components: that which is accelerant-related and that which is not. From a fire scene perspective, collection methods are determined by the physical state of the evidence (solid, liquid, or gas), its physical characteristics (size, shape, and weight), its fragility (broken, damaged, or altered), and volatility (evaporation possibility). With respect to collecting fire-related evidence, the ASTM guidelines apply* [3].

Previous chapters discussed guidelines for collecting and preserving the traditional forensic evidence. In fire scenes, cans or containers used to carry accelerants might be left at the scene and tools used to open containers or gain entry might also be present. These must be collected, packaged, and preserved for laboratory analysis.

Accelerants (a fuel or oxidizer used to initiate a fire or increase the rate of growth or speed the spread of a fire) are typically associated with fire scene evidence (see p. 137 in Reference [1]). Liquid accelerant characteristics, as listed below, are important with respect to collecting them for laboratory analysis:

- Absorbed by structural components, interior furnishings, and other fire debris
- Float when in contact with water (not alcohol)
- Survive when trapped in porous material

* ASTM E 1387, Standard Test Method for Ignitable Liquid Residues in Extracts from Fire Debris Samples by Gas Chromatography; ASTM E 1618, Standard Test Method for Ignitable Liquid Residues in Extracts from Fire Debris by Gas Chromatography-Mass Spectrometry.

22.5.3.1 *Liquid Accelerants*

In the liquid state, accelerants can be collected using a variety of methods that can pick up the liquid without contaminating it (eye dropper, siphoning device, new syringe). The liquid is placed into an appropriate container. The liquid can also be absorbed onto cotton or gauze pads. If so, the absorbed liquid is placed into an airtight container.

22.5.3.2 *Liquid Evidence Absorbed by Solid Materials*

Liquid accelerants are readily absorbed by materials at the scene (solid material, soil, or sand), which preserves them for future laboratory analysis. Areas to sample include raw unsealed or sawed edges, ends, nail holes, cracks, knot holes, soil, sand, and concrete. For deeply absorbing substances, sampling deep into the material will be necessary. Sometimes it might be necessary to reabsorb the accelerant using diatomaceous earth, lime, or non-self-rising flour. Place the reabsorbed accelerant into an airtight container. An appropriate container is a clean paint can or other containers suggested by laboratory personnel.

22.5.3.3 *Solid Samples*

Solid samples are common household materials or dangerous chemicals, and they should be packaged after receiving the instructions from laboratory personnel.

22.6 Tools, Equipment, and PPE

The safety of investigators is a primary concern that begins with ensuring that anyone officially at the fire scene has the appropriate equipment and PPE with which to work.

22.6.1 Personal Protective Equipment

The list of tools necessary to fight a fire and to ensure that each investigator has the appropriate equipment is large. Generally, the NFPA [1] recommends PPE that is typically used in routine crime scene investigations, including eye protection, flashlights, gloves, helmet/hard hat, appropriate respiratory equipment, safety boots or shoes, and turnout gear or overalls (pp. 119–120).

22.6.2 Tools and Equipment

The tools recommended by the NFPA [1] for investigators includes some that is used in routine crime scene investigations (lighting, compass, soap/hand cleaner, tape measure, tongs, tweezers, water, writing/drawing supplies, evidence labels, evidence-collecting containers, rulers, pen knife, marking pens). Other equipment recommended is included in a well-equipped crime scene van (hand tools, hatchet, magnet, paper towels/wiping cloths, claw hammer, pen knife, screwdrivers, rope, saw, twine, sieve, Styrofoam cups, tongs, tweezers, voltmeter-ohmmeter, ladder). Other equipment is more directly fire-related (absorption material, axe, broom, paint brushes, rake, hydrocarbon detector, pliers/wire cutters) (pp. 119–120).

Table 22.4 Fire Investigation Resources

Resource	Website	Phone Number
Interfire	http://www.interfire.com	+ 1-877-INTERFIRE
International Association of Arson Investigators	http://www.fire-investigators.org	+ 1-314-739-4224
International Fire Service Training Association	http://www.ifsta.org	+ 1-405-744-5723
National Association of Fire Investigators	http://www.nafi.org	+ 1-312-427-6320
National Center for Forensic Science	http://ncfs.ucf.edu	+ 1-407-823-6469
National Fire Protection Association	http://www.nfpa.org	+ 1-617-770-3000

Table 22.5 Fire Investigation Points of Contact

Point of Contact	Website	Phone Number
Bureau of Alcohol, Tobacco, and Firearms Headquarters	Enforcement Operations Center http://www.atf.treas.gov	+ 1-888-ATF-FIRE
	Arson and Explosives National Repository	+ 1-800-461-8841; +1-202-927-4590
	Arson and Explosives Programs Division	+ 1-202-927-7930
	National Laboratory	+ 1-301-762-9800
Chemical Transportation Emergency Center (CHEMTREC®)	http://www.chemtrec.org	+ 1-800-262-8200
Federal Bureau of Investigation Chemistry Division	http://www.fbi.gov	+ 1-202-324-4318
Federal Emergency Management Agency U.S. Fire Administration	http://www.usfa.fema.gov	+ 1-301-447-1000
National Institute of Standards and Technology Building and Fire Research Laboratory	http://www.bfrl.nist.gov	+ 1-301-975-6850

22.7 Fire Resources and Contacts

For more detailed or specific information, Table 22.4 lists organizations that are involved who are involved in fire investigations (see pp. 58–61 in Reference [2]).

Table 22.5 lists points of contact for fire scene investigative organizations (see pp. 58–61 in Reference [2]).

References

1. National Fire Protection Association (NFPA). 2008. Chapter 4: Basic methodology. In: *NFPA 921 Guide for Fire & Explosion Investigations*. Quincy MA: NFPA.
2. Office of Justice Programs. 2000. *Fire and Arson Scene Evidence. A Guide for Public Safety Personnel.* Washington, DC: U.S. Department of Justice.
3. ASTM International. Available at http://astm.org (accessed July 26, 2011).

Quality at the Crime Scene

23

23.1 Introduction

Providing quality service is the management's responsibility toward its customers. For a crime scene investigative unit, this means providing high-quality crime scene investigations for the community it serves. Quality assurance programs, also called the quality system, have similar attributes: standard operating procedural manual, quality manual, employment criteria, employee training, employee safety, appropriate facilities, peer review, and so on. For this discussion, quality assurance at the scene is the prime focus, and this begins with the crime scene investigative unit's approach to quality.

23.2 A Comprehensive Quality Program for Crime Scene Investigative Units

All crime scene units should establish, follow, and maintain a documented quality system that is appropriate to the activities of the agency and the crime scene investigative unit. All quality systems should be documented in a manual that includes or references the following aspects, as adapted from the FBI's quality guidelines for DNA laboratories [1].

23.2.1 Goals and Objectives

This is the mission statement of the organization and the functional unit. It enunciates the responsibility of the unit to the public and its dedication to high quality and service. The section should delineate the jurisdiction served.

23.2.2 Organization and Management

Management is responsible for the quality system. It must ensure that the objectives and goals of the unit reflect the needs of the community. This section should include an organizational chart starting with the highest levels of command or management.

23.2.3 Personnel

Here, the personnel and their backgrounds are listed. Each person's education, experience, certificates, and so on are maintained. As these change or personnel change, this section must be updated.

23.2.4 Facilities

The investigative unit should have an appropriate facility designed to ensure the integrity of the analyses and the evidence. This means a detailed description of the facilities, which includes work areas, break areas, evidence storage, reagent and chemical storage, and equipment storage.

23.2.5 Evidence Control

Evidence control is an important function in any forensic organization. The crime scene unit must document how it controls evidence from the time it is found at the scene to when it is transported to the police department to wherever it travels in the criminal justice system. All procedures must be written and signed off on. Generally, the following should be documented in written format.

- Evidence should be marked with a unique identifier on the evidence package. The unit should clearly define what constitutes evidence and what constitutes work product. The laboratory should have and follow a written method to distinguish each item throughout processing, such as evidence pattern evidence enhancement, fingerprinting, bullet comparisons, and so on, that may not require the assignment of unique identifiers or individual evidence seals for each specimen.
- Chain of custody for all evidence shall be documented and maintained in hard copy or electronic format. The chain of custody shall include the signature, initials or electronic equivalent of each individual receiving or transferring the evidence, the corresponding date for each transfer, and the evidentiary item(s) transferred.
- The unit must have a documented policy and follow procedures designed to minimize the loss, contamination, and/or deleterious change of evidence.
- There must be secure, controlled access areas for evidence storage and work in progress.

23.2.6 Validation

Each procedure and each piece of equipment employed must be validated for use. Validation is defined by the FBI for forensic DNA laboratories but is equally applicable to crime scene investigative units [1].

> *Validation* is a process by which a procedure is evaluated to determine its efficacy and reliability for forensic casework analysis and includes the following:
>
> 1. Developmental validation is the acquisition of test data and determination of conditions and limitations of a new or novel DNA methodology for use on forensic samples.
>
> 2. Internal validation is an accumulation of test data within the laboratory to demonstrate that established methods and procedures perform as expected in the laboratory (p. 8).

23.2.7 Analytical Procedures

Analytical procedures refer to any testing using chemical or other procedures used to locate, enhance, collect, or preserve the evidence at the crime scene. The unit shall have and follow written procedures approved by the team leader. These standard operating procedures should be reviewed annually by the team leader. Each procedure in the unit should have written standard protocol that specifies reagents, their preparation, and their quality control. Written procedures apply to commercial reagents and those prepared in-house. Commercial reagents should be labeled with the identity of the reagents and the expiration dates provided by the manufacturer. In-house prepared reagents shall be labeled with the identity of the reagent, the date of preparation and/or expiration, and the identity of the individual preparing the reagent.

23.2.8 Equipment Calibration and Maintenance

All equipment must be calibrated and maintained to ensure that it is providing the service necessary for a competent scene investigation. An example would be the ALS, which must be tested on a set schedule to ensure that it is working properly and visualizes the evidence consistently. All equipment should be suitable for the methods used by the unit, and there should be a documented program of performance checks and calibration of instruments and equipment. The unit should also have and follow a documented program that ensures that instruments and equipment are properly maintained. Examples of equipment and tools necessary for BPA are shown below. These must be maintained by the unit.

- BPA measurement, illumination, photographic and marking equipment, and tools
    - Single-stain measurement devices (e.g., dividers, calipers, magnifying loupe, computer software)
    - Angle of impact devices (e.g., level and angle finder, protractor, geometric triangle, computer software)
    - Ruler and tape measure
    - Plumb bob
    - Strings in different colors
    - Adhesive tape
    - Dowel rods
    - String support pole or tripod
    - Scientific calculator
    - Lasers (e.g., levels, distance measuring)
    - High-intensity light sources
    - Forensic light source and appropriate eyewear
    - Flashlights
    - Extension cords
    - Power supply
    - Camera and media generally accepted for crime scene documentation
    - Interchangeable lenses
    - Flash equipment (e.g., speed light, ring flash)
    - Digital memory cards or film
    - Cable release or remote IR shutter triggering device
    - Batteries
    - Video camera and media
    - Tripod
    - Color balance card
    - Self-adhesive labels (e.g., arrows, rulers, numbers, or letters)

- Metric scales (e.g., photo evidence scales, folding scales, adhesive scales, fluorescent scales, L-shaped scales)
- Compass with 360° scale
- Number, letter, or arrow placards
- Crime scene flags
- Note-taking and sketching materials (e.g., notebook, graph paper, pencils, markers)
- Audio recorder and media

Additional equipment would be added to the list depending on the activities of the unit. This could include casting or supeglue fuming equipment and others.

23.2.9 Reports

Each crime scene investigation should require a written report and the reporting guidelines written in the quality manual. Examples of statements that are acceptable as well as those that are unacceptable for various procedures should be included. There should be written procedures for taking and maintaining casework notes used to support conclusions drawn during an investigation. Casework reports should including the following:

- Case identifier
- Description of evidence examined
- Description of the technology
- Results and/or conclusions
- Disposition of evidence
- Signature and title of the person accepting responsibility for the content of the report

23.2.10 Review

A mechanism should be documented concerning peer review. This should include a review of the procedures, interpretations, reports, and testimony. But for crime scene investigations, there should be a mechanism for reinvestigating or visiting the scene if for no other reason than to reevaluate the work done by the original investigative unit. The review should include technical and administrative review of the work product. The individual conducting technical reviews should be or have been a certified crime scene investigator. The review should include all case notes, worksheets, photographs, and other electronic data, written or printed information supporting the investigative conclusions. If possible, the initial scene should be a part of the review.

23.2.11 Proficiency Testing

Proficiency testing for crime scene investigative units could include oral and/or written exams reviewed by outside agencies or consultants. This could include, among others, technical issues relating to fingerprinting, pattern evidence, bloodstain patterns, DNA, and so on. It could also include hands-on testing to demonstrate competency. The best proficiency tests are those that mimic real-world situations. Generally, personnel should undergo semiannual external proficiency testing in each technology performed to the full extent in which they participate in scene investigations. For purposes of tracking compliance, the unit should, document, and maintain all proficiency test records. The unit should maintain the following records.

- Test set identifier
- Identity of the investigator
- Date of analysis and completion
- Copies of all data and notes supporting conclusions
- Proficiency test results
- Any discrepancies noted
- Corrective actions taken

All proficiency test participants shall be informed of the final test results and such notification must be documented. The unit should use an external proficiency test provider, if available. As an example, the Scientific Working Group for Bloodstain Pattern Analysis (SWGSTAIN) has published the requirements for a BPA proficiency testing program whose intent is to evaluate a BPA analyst's continued competency [2]. The components of the program include:

- Pattern recognition
- Angle of impact determination
- Area of convergence/origin determination
- Clothing examination
- Possible mechanism determination
- Stain selection and sampling for biological analysis
- Sample integrity
- Photography
- Analysis/reporting
- Chemical enhancement
- Agency procedures relating to documentation, technical review, evidence handling, and related administrative actions

23.2.12 Corrective Action

The unit should establish and follow a corrective action plan to address discrepancies in proficiency tests and on-scene investigations. The corrective action plan should define what level/type of discrepancies and identify (when possible) the cause/effect the discrepancy might have, corrective actions taken, and preventative measures taken. When mistakes occur they must be acknowledged by the unit, immortalized in a log, and corrective action taken. Corrective action and the procedures used must be documented in the quality manual. Whether the action results in retraining, a review of the literature or whatever, the procedure must be written.

23.2.13 Audits

Any competent unit will not shy away from having an outside agency audit its work product. These should be conducted annually to ensure that a quality system is operating.

Checklists should be used so that nothing is missed. In addition to in-house audits, external audits are also a mandatory part of a quality system. Here, outside experts review the unit's quality system, reports, selected cases, testimony, and quality control testing. An audit report is submitted to the agency which can trigger a more intrusive investigation. The purpose of the audit is not to be punitive but instead to pinpoint the issues that affect the service the unit provides.

23.2.14 Safety

Safety is one of the prime concerns of the unit. Personnel must have PPE that is appropriate for the work they are doing. The quality manual must detail the PPE required for specific operations as well as the proper use of chemicals, instrumentation, and so on, if there is a safety issue.

Each crime scene investigator must wear PPE before entering a documented crime scene. The type of PPE will be determined by the type of scene. All PPE is disposable and must be suitable for biohazard investigations (e.g., coveralls, gloves, shoe covers), and must protect both the investigator from biohazards at the scene as well as the scene from the investigator. Typical requirements include:

- Respiration protection
- Eye protection
- Disinfecting agents (e.g., towelette, antibacterial solution)
- Stepping plates
- Paper roll
- Barrier tape
- Biohazard waste containers
- First aid kit

23.2.15 Outsourcing

Outsourcing by crime scene investigative units can include, among others, bloodstain pattern experts, crime laboratory scientists, anthropologists, odontologists, and entomologists. The qualifications of these experts should be documented in the quality manual as well as the instances when they are required.

23.2.16 Written Records

The investigative unit should maintain and follow a written procedure regarding document retention that addresses proficiency tests, corrective action, audits, training, continuing education, case files, and court testimony monitoring.

23.2.17 Organization and Management

23.2.17.1 Management Staff

- Managerial staff must have the authority and resources needed to discharge their duties.
- The crime scene team leader is accountable for the technical operations.

- The crime scene unit must have sufficient investigators to ensure quality at all scene investigations.
- A manual/guide that specifies and documents the responsibility, authority, and interrelation of all personnel who manage, perform, or verify work affecting the validity of the scene investigation.

23.2.17.2 Personnel

- Personnel must have the education, training, and experience commensurate with the examination and testimony provided. The unit should have written job descriptions augmented by additional documentation that defines responsibilities, duties, and skills.
- A documented training program is necessary for qualifying all investigative and analytical personnel.
- The training program should include a training manual covering procedures used by the unit.
- The training program should teach and assess the technical skills and knowledge required to perform the crime scene investigations.
- The training program requires an individual's demonstration of competency. The unit should maintain documentation of the successful completion of such competency test(s).
- When hiring experienced personnel, the team leader is responsible for assessing their previous training and ensuring it is adequate and documented. Modification to the training program may be appropriate, which is documented by the technical leader.
- Personnel, regardless of previous experience, must successfully complete competency tests covering the routine methods used prior to participating in independent investigative work. In those instances, the individual can be a member of an investigative team but without reporting responsibilities.
- Personnel should have access to continuing education to ensure that the unit is delivering a quality service and to ensure that the qualifications of its personnel are maintained. If continuing education is conducted internally, the title of the program, a record of the presentation, date of the training, attendance list, and the presenter's curriculum vitae should be verified and retained. If the continuing education is conducted externally, documentation of attendance must be maintained appropriately such as through certificates, program agenda/syllabus, or travel documentation.
- The unit should have a program of review of the technical and scientific literature that documents its personnel's ongoing reading of the literature. The unit should maintain or have physical or electronic access to a collection of current books, reviewed journals, or other applicable literature.

23.3 Defining Quality at the Scene

As a consequence of the report of the National Research Council of the National Academies [3], accreditation of crime scene units is a growing concern. A trademark of accreditation is the unit's quality assurance program which ensures that its work product meets minimum quality standards. In addition to written standard procedures, a critical part of quality assurance programs is its quality testing program of testing reagents and procedures used at the crime scene. This is also known as "quality control" testing of reagents, Chapter 13.

Most testing reagents lose sensitivity and, less likely, specificity over time. Since these testing reagents are used to investigate crimes, all reagents used should produce consistent results from one crime scene to the next, and the lifetime or each reagent should be defined and related to a known standard. To ensure the quality at the scene, testing reagents must be quality checked regularly against established quality guidelines, which means that all reagents used in the field must meet established quality standards. For example, if a presumptive chemical testing reagent routinely detects dried blood diluted say, 10,000 times, it should not be used if it stops meeting that standard. It should be removed from service and replaced.

A related topic is the sensitivity of a particular reagent compared with other reagents that test for the same analyte—suggested in the example above. All testing reagents have a sensitivity threshold, which means that if one reagent detects blood at the 1 in 10,000 level and the other at 1 in 100,000 it should come as no surprise that the second reagent will give a positive test long after the first. Scene scientists/investigators must know the on-scene characteristics of their testing reagents.

23.3.1 Quality Control of Testing Reagents

Establishing a quality assurance program for all aspects of the team's work product is essential, and one part of that program must be devoted to reagent testing. The following procedure is an example of how a crime scene unit can use quality testing to check its testing reagents for sensitivity and/or specificity. Reagent preparation (even commercially purchased reagents) and the results of quality testing should be maintained in a spreadsheet or notebook and archived.

The standard operating procedure for testing should be part of a quality manual and labeled as, perhaps, "Presumptive reagent quality testing." Such a quality check for blood testing reagents is described in the following section. Each testing reagent used at the scene must have a quality checking procedure as well as a documented, signed-off standard procedure for using it in the field.

23.3.1.1 Standard Operating Procedure for Blood Testing Reagents

- Prepare a stock solution of blood by adding 100 μL of whole blood to 900 μL distilled water (1:10 dilution).
- Serially dilute 100 μL aliquots of the above solution until the final solution is 1:1,000,000.
- Place 10 μL aliquots onto the tip of the same cotton swab used to swab blood at the crime scene and allow it to dry.
- Test the cotton swab with testing reagent as though it was taken at a crime scene.
- A running record of all quality testing can be kept in a tabular format in a spreadsheet. A hard copy should also be archived as a record after each testing. An example of such a tabular record is shown in Table 25.1.

Table 23.1 Quality Control Testing of Kastle–Meyer Reagent

Reagent: Test Date	1:10,000	1:100,000	1:1,000,000	Comments
Kastle–Meyer: 4/15/09	+	+	Weak	Cut off at 100,000
Kastle–Meyer: 9/15/09	+	+	Weak	Cut off at 1,000,000
Kastle–Meyer: 1/15/10	+	Weak	=	*Does not meet standard*
Kastle–Meyer: 1/15/10	+	+	=	Fresh reagent—meets standard

Reagents must never be used after they fail—the 1/15/10 test in Table 23.1. Fresh reagents should be made, and these must meet predetermined quality standards. Reagents should also be quality checked for specificity—if that is part of what the reagent is supposed to do—and the results should also be recorded in a table much like the one referred to above. This is a matter of preparing a series of stains on cotton swabs from various body fluids—semen, saliva, urine, blood—and then testing them periodically, perhaps at the same time as the sensitivity check.

23.3.2 Standard Operating Procedures

Each test used at the scene must be documented in a manual. The procedure must contain guidelines for its use. This would include interpretation guidelines, limitations of its use, and safety guidelines. An example for semen testing reagents is shown in the procedure below.

23.3.2.1 Performing the AP Test on Fresh Semen Stains

23.3.2.1.1 Quality Assurance and Control Testing of the AP Test for Semen Before using the AP test for semen at the scene, test a known semen stain (positive control) and a negative reagent control (distilled water) to ensure the reagents meet minimum standards [2]. These results must be archived (as discussed for blood testing reagents above). If either control fails, do not proceed until the problem has been resolved or new reagents meet minimum standards. If the results of the test are positive, a substrate control (if available) must also be tested, unless the stain is on a cotton swab, and the results of the testing must be documented. It is not necessary to test the submitted control swabs.

- *Procedures*
  - Lightly moisten sterile swab with distilled water and press or gently rub it against the suspected stain.
  - Add one to two drops of sodium *a*-naphthyl AP solution.
  - Add one to two drops of *o*-dianisidine dye solution.
  - The development of a blue/purple color within 10–15 s is indicative of AP levels consistent with semen.
  - For samples giving inconclusive results (longer color development times), semen must be confirmed microscopically or by showing the presence of p30.
- *Interpretation of results*
  - Positive reaction: Blue/purple color within 10–15 s.
  - Negative reaction: No color development, slight/slow color development.
  - Inconclusive reaction: Slow moderate to strong color development longer than 15 s and not longer than 30 s.

References

1. FBI. 2009. Quality assurance standards for forensic DNA testing laboratories. Available at: http://www.cstl.nist.gov/strbase/QAS/Final-FBI-Director-Forensic-Standards.pdf (accessed February 28, 2011).
2. The ASCLD-LAB Proficiency Review Program. 2008. Available at: http://www.ascld-lab.org/documents/alpd1002.pdf (accessed April 14, 2010).
3. Committee on Identifying the Needs of the Forensic Science Community, Committee on Science, Technology and Law Policy and Global Affairs, Committee on Applied and Theoretical Statistics, Division on Engineering and Physical Sciences, National Research Council of the National Academies (NRC). 2009. *Strengthening Forensic Science in the United States: A Path Forward*. Washington, DC: National Academies Press.

Collection and Preservation of Evidence

24

24.1 Introduction

Chapters in this text discuss various evidence types—biological, impression, trace, and so on—including the collection and preservation techniques. While these comprise the most common evidentiary categories, many are not included because they are beyond the scope of an introductory text. And while it is impossible to anticipate all the evidence that might be encountered during any individual investigation, it might be valuable for investigators to have a more comprehensive list of evidence types including those discussed in the chapters. The following list covers many evidence categories, but there are rules of thumb that apply to all evidence types that have not been presented previously as a specific topic.

24.2 Rules of Thumb for Packaging Evidence

- Labeling should be on the evidence, if possible, with a unique identifier for the specific item. Labeling should also be on the outside packaging. In situations, where it is not possible to label the evidence directly, for example, bullets or cartridge cases, labeling should be placed on the outside packaging. The specific information needed includes: the name of the person collecting the evidence, a unique identifier for that evidence, the date, location where the evidence was found, and a description of the evidence. (A description such as blue jeans is not acceptable. Descriptions should be sufficiently detailed so that anyone handling the jeans will have no difficulty knowing that this is the correct pair of blue jeans based on the description, for example, pair of Dockers blue jeans, size 32 × 29, rip in crotch area, bloodstains on front and rear, etc.)
- Evidence packaging should be sealed with evidence tape.
- The initials of the collector and the date of collection should span the evidence tape onto the packaging.
- The outside packaging should have a description of the item inside the package and should be labeled with the name of the collector, date, and so on, as described above. The chain of custody or a copy of it should be attached to the bag.
- There should be only one item of evidence per package.
- For evidence where the transfer of trace or other evidence from one part of the evidence (garment) to another is not warranted (e.g., blood, GSR, fibers, hairs, etc.), the item should be laid flat, covered with paper, and the evidence folded so that each fold is protected with paper.

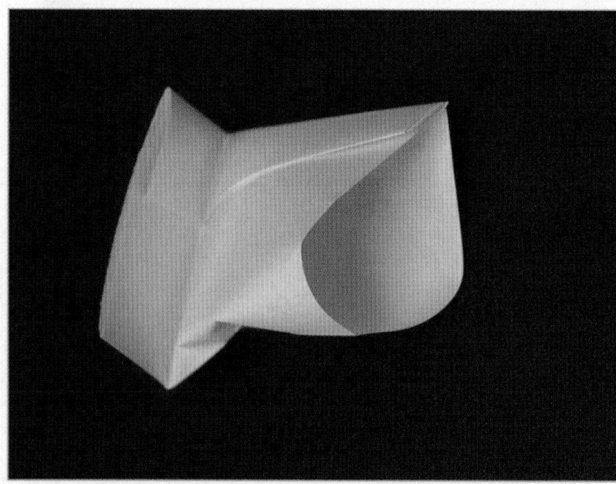

Figure 24.1 Example of druggist fold.

- A chain of custody form must be filled out for each item of evidence that is collected.
- Trace evidence should be collected in druggist folds, not envelopes, and then placed inside an evidence collection envelope and labeled appropriately. An example of a druggist fold is shown in Figure 24.1.
- Liquids should be placed inside leak-proof containers appropriate for that type of evidence.
- Biological evidence (bloodstains, semen, etc.) should be dried before packaging.

24.3 List of Evidentiary Categories

Table 24.1 is meant to fill the evidentiary gaps in a single look-up source. Many of the items have been discussed either directly or tangentially in individual chapters. For evidence that was discussed, the chapters are included in the list. For items of evidence not discussed, there is no chapter designation. What will become readily apparent when comparing the information below with recommendations given in the chapters is that the chapters often have specific or more detailed packaging or preservation instructions. The information in Table 24.1 is usually more general. As part of its quality assurance program, each crime scene unit should develop collection and preservation procedures for the types of evidence commonly encountered and have a mechanism in place for obtaining that information for those categories of evidence not usually encountered.

Table 24.1 Evidence Collection and Preservation

Evidence Type	Chapter Number	Amount	Collection and/or Preservation Method
Adhesive tape	10	Collect at least 1 ft. of material or all of the available evidence.	Cover the sticky side with waxed paper, cellophane, or plastic wrap. Tape to the bottom of cardboard box (smooth side down) and cover, for example, see packaging electrostatic lifts. Seal the box and submit to Latent Print Section.
Ammunition (live)	20	Collect all firearms-related evidence—all available rounds.	Package each separately. Label or tag outside of container. Show the type of material, date obtained, investigator's initials, case name, and number. Do not mail. Place in small containers. Prevent the shifting of the evidence while in transit.
Arson debris	22	Follow recommendations in NFPA 921 (2008) and ASTM 3 1387 and ASTM E 1618.	Package in clean metal (paint) cans, glass jars, or coffee cans covered with aluminum foil. Seal with tape. Do not use plastic bags.
Blasting caps		Consult laboratory.	Consult laboratory and/or bomb squad. Follow the directions for collecting and packaging given at that time.
Blood and body fluids—stains	13	*Blood*: Collect as much stain as possible, ideally entire stain, especially if small. If a large stain, cut at least 1 in.^{2} Dry completely before packaging. Do not use excessive heat. Submit entire stained object. If not possible, use a lightly moistened swab and concentrate as much of the evidence as possible onto small area of swab. *Saliva*: For areas suspected of having saliva, swab area, dry and submit as for any swab. *Semen*: Use sexual assault evidence kit. If not possible or appropriate, transfer entire item as described for garments. If evidence is too large, cut stained area (highlighted by ALS)—labeled appropriately—and package as any biological evidence.	Package each stain separately and label appropriately. Do not allow stained parts of garments to contact unstained areas. On packaging, include specimen type, date obtained, investigator's initials, case name and number, and from where the sample was taken. Place garments in paper bags. Fold stained (and dried) garment over paper to ensure no part of stained areas come into contact with unstained areas. Ensure all folds sealed on evidence envelopes are sealed. Always use paper—*never plastic.* Package the swabs in evidence boxes specifically designed for swabs.

continued

Table 24.1 (Continued) Evidence Collection and Preservation

Evidence Type	Chapter Number	Amount	Collection and/or Preservation Method
Blood and body fluids for toxicology		When possible, use standard DUI or Coroner's kit, as appropriate. Fill out provided labels (name of subject, date/time collected, officer's name, and agency). Fill out case history form provided with the kit. Instruct clinicians to collect two 10-mL gray stopper vacutainers and two red top tubes (for body fluids). (Standard DUI kits contain potassium oxalate and sodium fluoride.)	Package in designated blood mailing containers and label appropriately.
Caps, bottles, cups		Submit entire container. If not possible, collect saliva by swabbing drinking area with sterile cotton swabs moistened with distilled water.	Collect and package all swabs as for any biological evidence.
Building materials		Collect all possible evidence.	Seal in pillbox or paper bag to prevent loss. Mark the container appropriately.
Bullets	20	Collect all fragments. Do not mark or clean.	Place on tissue soft paper. Place in pill, powder, or match box. Do not pack in cotton or gauze. If wet, avoid plastic containers. Pack to prevent shifting in transit. Seal in container and mark container—not mark projectile. Place crime scene investigation or investigator's initials, date, case name, and number on container.
Cartridge cases (empty rounds)	20	Collect all firearms evidence. When fingerprint evidence is possible, do not remove from weapon. Carry to latent print laboratory.	Package and mark appropriately as described for bullets above. Package to prevent shifting.
Casts from impression evidence*	11	Allow to dry 24 h before packaging, if possible. If not, carefully lift cast and place in box and support well in a rigid container. Use layers of newspaper. Do not clean. *Do not use plastic.*	On back of casts and on the outside of container indicate the type of material (dental stone, etc.), date obtained, investigator's initials, and case name and number. Label packaging "FRAGILE." *Take photos of impressions before casting.

Clothing	13, 20	Collect only pertinent items and do not handle with bare hands. Leave clothing intact. Do not cut out stains or cut through bullet holes. If wet, dry before packing. Never package in plastic bags.	Wrap each article individually with identification written on outside of package. Place in paper evidence bags—*never plastic.* Label clothing using evidence tag and also label outside of container. Fill out chain of custody—garment type, date obtained, investigator's initials, and case name and number.
Chemicals—acids		Contact appropriate laboratory chemists for instructions. Collect all that is appropriate but not <1 oz. No special preservation conditions are necessary.	Contact the appropriate laboratory chemists. Package in glass container with plastic lid. If hydrogen fluoride is suspected, do not package in glass. Package in plastic container (hydrogen fluoride dissolves glass). Label "DANGER: ACID, CORROSIVE."
Chemicals—alkalies		Contact appropriate laboratory chemists for instructions. Collect as much as appropriate but not <1 oz.	Contact the appropriate laboratory chemists. Package in glass bottle with plastic cap for liquids or pillboxes for solids. Seal to prevent the loss. Label outside of container to indicate the type of material—if known—date obtained, investigator's initials, and case name and number. Label the container "ALKALI, GLASS, CORROSIVE."
Cosmetics		Collect all that are appropriate	Seal in glass container.
Documents		Collect all original material and original envelope (if appropriate). Determine whether document should be treated for latent fingerprints.	Place in plastic envelope, which is then placed inside manila envelope. Insert the stiff backing to prevent bending or folding. Seal and mark appropriately. Wrap securely. If burned and/or brittle, obtain instructions from laboratory. Label packaging before inserting evidence. Do not write on packaging after evidence is inside.

continued

Table 24.1 (Continued) Evidence Collection and Preservation

Evidence Type	Chapter Number	Amount	Collection and/or Preservation Method
Documents—typewritten		Examine ribbon for evidence message thereon. For carbon paper samples either remove the ribbon or place in stencil position. Obtain at least one copy in full word-for-word order of questioned typewriting. Include partial copies in light, medium, and heavy degrees of touch. Include standard carbon paper samples of every uppercase and lowercase character on the keyboard.	Package as described above for documents. Include serial number, make, and model of typewriter on same side as samples of the typewriting. If possible, drugs and packaging materials should be separated and packaged separately for drug chemistry/latent print cases. Consult with laboratory scientists. Label outside of container appropriately.
Drugs		Contact laboratory chemists for instructions. *Liquids*: All to 1 pt. Not <15 cc, or ½ oz., if available. If bottle has no stopper, transfer liquid contents to glass stopped bottle and seal with adhesive tape and wax. Mark "FRAGILE." Determine alleged normal use of drug and, if prescription given, check with druggist to determine supposed ingredients. *Powders*: Amount slightly over maximum penalty amount. Seal with tape to prevent any loss.	
Dynamite and other explosives		Contact the laboratory scientists for instructions.	Contact the laboratory scientists for packaging instructions.
Electrostatic dust lifts	11	Take the photos of impressions before lifting. Make a second lift of the impression if the first lift has excessive dust/debris. Photograph the lifted impression.	Secure the edges inside suitably sized, high-quality cardboard box, or specialized evidence box, for electrostatic lifts. Avoid the surface abrasion. Seal the outer package. Label outside of container appropriately.
Fibers	17	Submit the entire article if possible. Collect the trace evidence specimens as discussed in Chapter 17.	Place the fibers in druggist fold and seal the edges to prevent the loss. Individual envelopes are inappropriate.

Firearms	20	Collect all available firearms. Do not place anything barrel. Attach the tag with pertinent data, crime scene investigation or investigator's initials, and case name and number. Keep from rusting If in water, do not dry. Package in original water source if possible.	Unload all weapons before shipping; otherwise, hand-carry the loaded weapon. Advise if firearms are to be for malfunction or accidental discharge exam; do not unload unless absolutely necessary. Wrap in paper, wooden, or cardboard box or specially designed firearms evidence container. Label package to identify the contents of package and whether firearm is loaded. Indicate direction of barrel. Prevent shifting while in transit. If unloaded, mark position of cylinder and note location of cartridges. If wet, package in capped 6 in. plastic pipe of appropriate length containing original water source.
Fuses		Collect all available evidence or up to 1 ft.	Place in manila envelope, box, or suitable container.
Gasoline/kerosene or other flammable liquids		Collect as much as possible, but at least ¼ to ¾ cup.	Package in metal fireproof container. Pack container in wooden box. Label "GASOLINE" or appropriately.
Gelatin lifts	11	Photograph the impressions before lifting. Label the back of lift before lifting. Photograph the gelatin lift after lifting.	Seal and secure the uncovered in a shallow box (see electrostatic lifters). Do not replace the acetate cover. Avoid the high heat or extreme cold. Label outside of container appropriately.
Glass fragments	18	*Window glass*: Mark inside and outside, if known. Collect as many representative samples as possible. Collect radial fractures near point of impact. Label as such. Collect all large items—headlights, and so on, for comparisons.	Wrap each piece separately. Pack in box to prevent the shifting and breakage. Identify the contents. Avoid the chipping when packaging Mark "GLASS FRAGILE."
Grease/motor oil		Collect as much as possible to 1 qt.	Metal or glass container with tight screw top.
Grease/motor oil in dirt		Collect all dirt/grease/oil. Collect the exemplar soil that does not have grease/oil present.	Package the contaminated soil and exemplar soil separately in glass container. Label appropriately.

continued

Table 24.1 (Continued) Evidence Collection and Preservation

Evidence Type	Chapter Number	Amount	Collection and/or Preservation Method
Gunshot residue (on clothing)	20	Collect all appropriate garments. Do not handle with bare hands.	Fold fabric flat. Wrap so there is clean paper between folds to ensure that residue is not transferred to other areas of garment or is lost. If wet, dry before packaging. Avoid the shaking. Package in paper bags separately. Do not package in plastic bags. Do not cut through bullet holes or tears on garments.
Hair	17	Collect the standards for microscopic comparison. In sexual assault cases, exemplars should be collected at hospital by *sane* nurses. Use the fingers to pull exemplar hairs, not tweezers. *Do not cut.*	Package in druggist fold. Seal the edges and openings with evidence tape and initial across tape. Single envelope is unsatisfactory.
Impressions (dental stone)	11, 17	Photograph the impression before casting. Cast 2 ft. of tire track if possible for all four tires. Do not use wood or twigs for reinforcement. Do not clean lifted cast.	Before stone hardens, place initials, date and case number on back side of cast. Surround cast with packing material in box to prevent shifting or breakage. Avoid sealing in plastic bags. Label "CAST FRAGILE." Do not clean.
Ink		*Liquid*: Collect at least 1 tsp. *Ink on paper*: Collect as for documents. Collect writing utensils and pens as exemplars.	Package in glass-sealed container. Package as for documents.
Fingerprints: latent print lifts	10	*Tape lifts*: Collect lifts onto coated lift backings (fingerprint lift cards). *Mikrosi or silicone cast lifts*: Tape onto back of fingerprint lift card. *Gel lifts*: Cover lift with acetate cover and tape onto fingerprint lift card. Label back of lift appropriately in case it becomes detached. Always wear gloves.	Label each lift to include exact location, date, and name of person taking lift. Submit multiple lifts collectively in a sealed and properly labeled envelope. Automated fingerprint identification system processing requires the submission of elimination prints.
Fingerprints: nonporous items	10	Collect all items that are appropriate.	Use cardboard boxes and paper bags. Package to prevent movement. Avoid the surface contact inside the packaging.
Items in water		Whenever possible, keep wet. Do not air dry.	Use the plastic containers and place the items in original water.

Matches		Collect one or two books of paper matches or a full box of wooden matches.	Package in metal container. Place container in larger package to prevent the shifting. Put the loose matches in box or metal container. Keep away from heat/fire. Label "KEEP AWAY FROM FIRE."
Paint	19	*Liquid*: Collect as much as possible up to ¾ pt. *Solid/chips*: Collect as much as possible or at least ½ in.^{2}.	Package in friction top paint can or large-mouth screw-top jars; if glass, pack inside container such as heavy corrugated paper or wooden box to prevent the breakage. If small amount, package inside pillbox or small glass vial with screw top. Envelopes not satisfactory. Do not pack paint chips in cotton. Secure with only evidence tape—not scotch tape or adhesive tape.
Paraphernalia (drug)		Collect all that applies. Empty liquid from smoking devices into a separate glass container.	Pack glass items to prevent the breakage. Package syringes in approved sharps containers. Label "BIOHAZARD." Package large smoking paraphernalia in cardboard secured by packing material.
Safe insulation	17	Collect 1 lb or up to 1 cup if possible.	Packaged in pillbox or paper bag. Seal the edges with evidence tape and corners to prevent any loss. Do not use glass containers. Label outside of container appropriately.
Sharp objects (knives, axes, etc.)	13	Collect all that applies. If blood-covered, dry and protect as described for dried blood evidence.	Use the evidence packaging designed for specific types of sharp objects. If not available, pack in cardboard box with appropriate backing to prevent the shifting, or use the plastic cylinders. If blood evidence present, do not package in plastic.
Soil	19	*Casts*: Do not clean. Soil exemplars: Collect from 3 tbsp to 1 cup of top ¼ in. of soil in geometric pattern from selected areas around impression. *Vehicles*: Collect from multiple areas. Do not mix samples and retain texture.	Package the cast and adhering soil together. Package collected soil in paper. Do not use plastic or glass. Seal with evidence tape and label appropriately: location, initials, date, case number, and so on.

continued

Table 24.1 (Continued) Evidence Collection and Preservation

Evidence Type	Chapter Number	Amount	Collection and/or Preservation Method
Stomach contents	13	Collect all available samples whether dry or wet. *Wet samples* Dry vomitus	Place in glass container. Seal container with evidence tape. Wrap in paper or soft packaging. Place in suitable mailing package to prevent the breakage or spillage. Refrigerate until mailed. Label "STOMACH CONTENTS." Scrape from floors and place in evidence glass or plastic container. If on furniture or clothing, submit entire item, if possible. If not possible, cut area from item, package as for any biological evidence.
Tires	12	Collect all appropriate tires. Photograph tire. Since tires are generally large and cumbersome and are more easily handled independently, they need not be packaged unless preservation of trace evidence is a concern. Prepare the inked (or petroleum-based) test of prints of tires onto art board while tires are on vehicle. Alternately prepare inked acetate impressions. Photograph the inked impressions. Consider whether or not spare tire may have been involved.	Label or tag tires. Identify the vehicle from which they were removed, owner of vehicle if known, date of recovery, crime scene investigation or detective's initials, and case name and number. Package the inked exemplar impressions so that inked impressions or petroleum-based impressions are not smeared by packaging. Ensure that inked or petroleum exemplars are marked appropriately with marks on tires to ensure appropriate tire comparisons.
Tools	11	Collect all tools that apply. *Never* use tool to collect the suspect marks.	Cover the end or edges with paper bag to catch trace evidence. Do not place tape directly on edge. Wrap each tool in paper. Use appropriate evidence container available from forensic supply sources. If not available, use a strong cardboard or wooden box and package tool to prevent the shifting.

Toolmarks	11	Identify all toolmarks at scene. Photograph toolmark before collecting. If it cannot be collected, cast using a silicone casting material. Photograph the resulting cast. Cover cut ends of toolmark, for example, cut wire. Wrap with paper. Do not use tape on cut ends. *Wire*: 1 ft. or more.	Mark packaging or tag attached on opposite end of toolmark. Package casts to prevent the movement. Tape onto cardboard backing. Place in box and pack to prevent the shifting. Package exemplar toolmarks or tools separately from evidence. Mark the ends cut while collecting the suspect marks.
Unknown material		Size is important. Collect as much as possible.	*Dry*: Use the paper folds, paper bags, and cardboard boxes. *Liquid*: Package in glass container with plastic screw top. Seal with evidence tape to prevent loss and label appropriately.
Urine (toxicology)	13	*Note*: If submitting for a sexual assault case, a release form must be signed by the victim and submitted. Keep questioned specimens separate from known standards.	Use the standard DUI kit. Fill out completely. Refrigerate the sample until mailed. Collect the urine in two 30 ml plastic bottles. Place in DUI kit and seal with provided seals.
Wood		Collect at least 1 ft., if possible.	Wrap securely to prevent the friction, shifting, breakage, or contact. Separate unknown items from exemplars.

Scientific and Technical Working Groups

25

25.1 Introduction

Since the FBI convened the Technical Working Group for DNA Methods (TWGDAM), now the Scientific Working Group (SWG) for DNA Methods (SWGDAM), the forensic community has formed several working groups. The intent of these groups is to bring together practitioners in the field from crime laboratories, federal and local agencies, and industry. One common purpose of these groups is to begin an open dialogue concerning the philosophy relating to each SWG and to review and update the methods used to examine the evidence. For the more mature groups, such as SWGDAM, the work product has resulted in the endorsement of specific methods for analyzing the DNA in forensic evidence. Other SWGs are not that far along. For example, the work product of SWGSTAIN has been the development of a standard list of terminology so that all bloodstain pattern analysts can speak the same language (Chapter 14).

What these working groups lack, unfortunately, is the authority to enforce their recommendations. The SWGs create, prepare, and publish standards and guidelines for their constituents. Importantly, though, the documents they produce provide a basis for operational requirements. Enforcement of the guidelines is left to the appropriate governing agency and their internal policies. In essence, the guidelines that the SWGs create have no force of law [1]. Table 25.1 is a list of active scientific and technical working groups [1,2].

Table 25.1 Technical/Scientific Working Groups

Scientific/Technical Working Group	Full Name	Contact Information
SWGIT	Scientific Working Group on Imaging Technology	http://www.theiai.org/guidelines/swgit/index.php
SWGDE	Scientific Working Group on Digital Evidence	http://www.swgde.org/
TWGED	Technical Working Group for Education and Training in Digital Forensics	http://www.ncjrs.gov/pdffiles1/nij/grants/219380.pdf
SWGTREAD	Scientific Working Group on Shoeprint and Tire Tread Evidence	www.swgtread.org/
SWGFAST	Scientific Working Group on Friction Ridge Analysis, Study, and Technology	www.swgfast.org/
FISWG	Facial Identification Scientific Working Group	www.fiswg.org/FISWG_overview_v1.0_20090618.pdf
SWGSTAIN	Scientific Working Group on Bloodstain Pattern Analysis	www.swgstain.org/

continued

Table 25.1 (Continued) Technical/Scientific Working Groups

Scientific/Technical Working Group	Full Name	Contact Information
SWGGUN	Scientific Working Group for Firearms and Toolmarks	www.swggun.org/
SWGDOC	Scientific Working Group for Forensic Document Examination	www.swgdoc.org
SWGMAT	Scientific Working Group for Materials Analysis	None
SWGDAM	Scientific Working Group for DNA Analysis Methods	www.cstl.nist.gov/strbase/mtDNA.htm
SWGDOG	Scientific Working Group on Dog and Orthogonal Detector Guidelines	www.swgdog.org
SWGDRUG	Scientific Working Group for the Analysis of Seized Drugs	www.swgdrug.org
SWGANTH	Scientific Working Group for Forensic Anthropology	www.swganth.org
SWGTOX	Scientific Working Group on Toxicology	www.swgtox.org
TWGFEX	Technical Working Group for Fire and Explosives	ncfs.ucf.edu
SWGCBRN	Scientific Working Group for the Forensic Analysis of Chemical, Biological, Radiological, and Nuclear Terrorism	None
SWGGSR	Scientific Working Group on Gun Shot Residue	None

References

1. Committee on Identifying the Needs of the Forensic Science Community, Committee on Science, Technology and Law Policy and Global Affairs, Committee on Applied and Theoretical Statistics, Division on Engineering and Physical Sciences, National Research Council of the National Academies (NRC). 2009. Chapter 7: Strengthening Oversight of Forensic Science Practice. In: *Strengthening Forensic Science in the United States: A Path Forward*. Washington, DC: National Academies Press, pp. 201–206.
2. FBI. Scientific Working Groups. Available at: http://www.fbi.gov/about-us/lab/swgs (accessed March 1, 2011).

Glossary

Acid phosphatase (AP): An enzyme found in high levels in semen.

Acid violet 17, Amido black, Coomassie blue: Protein-staining reagents used to enhance the bloodstained fingerprints and footwear impressions at crime scenes.

Active archiving: The intellectual approach to creating a scene's archive.

Alternate light source (ALS): An instrument that can deliver various wavelengths of light and is used to find biological and trace evidence at the crime scene.

Ammunition: See Chapter 20.

Amylase : Specifically AMY 1, alpha amylase is an enzyme found in high levels in saliva.

Anagen growth phase: The longest growth phase of hair usually lasting between 2 and 6 years. During this phase, the hair grows and dead cells of the protein keratin are pushed out through the scalp.

Aperture: The hole to the outside that allows light to reach the digital sensor.

Apocrine glands: Glands associated with hair but are mainly found in the groin region.

Archiving: The process of creating the historical record of the scene investigation.

Ardrox, basic yellow 40, rhodamine 6G: Fluorescent stains used to develop superglue fumed fingerprints.

Bacterial pathogens: Bacteria that can attack humans, animals, or plants

Barrier filters: Filters that block specific wavelengths of reflected light.

Baseline measurement method: Measuring items at a scene using the perpendicular dropped to a fixed line.

Basic violet 3: Fingerprint developing reagent for acrylic-based adhesives.

Bioscene: Places that are the focus of bioterrorism events, which can include the target, the point of dissemination, or the point of manufacture of a bioweapon.

Bioterrorism: Biocrime or bioterrorism is the threat or use of microorganisms, toxins, pests, prions, or their associated ancillary products to commit the acts of crime or terror.

Bloodstain pattern analysis (BPA): The interpretation of blood patterns.

Bloodstain terminology: See Chapter 14.

BlueStar™: Enhanced formulation of luminol that gives a blue-white luminescence with blood.

Bullet twist: The spin of the bullet imparted to it while it is in the barrel of the weapon.

Bullet types: See Chapter 20.

Bullet wipe: Mixture of bullet lubricant, mouth sealant, and carbonaceous material picked up by the bullet while traveling down the bore, which is deposited on any material through which it passes.

Case file: The location, virtual or otherwise, where the investigative record is maintained.

Catagen or transitional phase of growth: Growth phase after the anagen phase. The hair stops growing and forms a club-like appearance at the root.

Centripetal force: A force directed toward the center of the path of the moving object.

Chain of custody: Also known as the "chain," this is the historical and signature record of an item of evidence.

Chemical presumptive testing: Chemical tests used to presumptively determine whether blood might be present

Close-up photographs: Photographs that capture the detail of specific items of evidence.

Combustion reaction: A complex set of chemical reactions that results in the rapid oxidation of a fuel, and produces heat and light.

Common bullet mark terminology: See Chapter 20.

Concentric fractures: Secondary fractures that connect radial fractures.

Conchoidal fractures: Stress fractures that are perpendicular to the opposite side of the force in radial fractures and on the same side of the direction of force in concentric fractures.

Conduction: A mechanism of fire spread by the transfer of heat in a solid material.

Convection: The transfer of heat energy from heated liquids or gases to a cooler part of the environment.

Correct forensic exposure: The combination of light and perspective that captures the story the scene is telling.

Crime scene: The place where the participants meet in time and space or where the instrument of the crime (biological, explosive, etc.) is prepared and delivered regardless of the route it takes.

Criminalistics: A discipline that embraces a holistic philosophy, the principles of science, the scientific method, and logic as it relates to the analysis and interpretation of evidence and its relationship to a set of alleged facts.

Cross projection or exploded sketch: Flattened or exploded view of the sketch designed to capture the evidence on surfaces other than the floors.

Cyanoacrylate monomer: An ester of cyanoacrylate used in superglue fuming to develop fingerprints.

Deductive reasoning: Works from the general to the more specific and is often referred to as a "top-down" process of logic.

Deflection: Occurs when a bullet/projectile deviates from the plane of its incident/impact angle as a result of ricochet or because of how the bullet/projectile interacts with the surface.

Dental records: Antemortem dental records used to identify the missing or deceased individuals.

Dental stone: Gypsum-based casting material, used to capture 3D impression detail from tire tracks and footwear impressions.

Depth of field (DOF): Determines what is in focus in a photograph.

Detritusphere: Soil surrounding the cadaver.

Direct DNA testing: The direct comparison of a DNA profile obtained from the tissue or bone of a body with the profile obtained from an exemplar of the missing or deceased individual.

DNA: Deoxyribonucleic acid—the biological molecule of life that is inherited half from the mother and half from the father.

Dry residue impression: Impression evidence created from dirt, dust, or some other contaminant on a shoe imparted to a flat hard surface.

Eccrine sweat gland: Glands that are found covering the entire body but are the only sweat glands associated with friction ridge skin. The secretions are water soluble.

Edmond Locard: French scientist credited with the phrase "Every touch leaves a trace."

Elevation sketch: Side views of part of a scene.

Electrostatic lifter: An instrument that creates a static electric charge as a mechanism to lift dry residue impressions.

Equivalent exposures: Different camera settings of aperture, shutter speed, and ISO that allow the same amount of light to reach the digital sensor.

Establishing or overall photographs: The overview of the scene or specific areas of the scene.

Evidence: Anything associated with a crime scene, incident, or argument; whether or not it has been collected, described, photographed, analyzed scientifically, or reasoned about and which might be introduced into a legal proceeding in order to ascertain the truth of an issue.

Evidence dynamics: Influence that "changes, relocates, obscures, or obliterates the physical evidence, regardless of the intent.

Exculpatory evidence: Evidence that points to the innocence of someone.

Exterior ballistics: The study of bullet flight after it leaves the muzzle, also known as the bullet path or, incorrectly, the trajectory.

Faunal succession: The sequence of infestation.

Fingerprint development cascade: A step-wise sequence of fingerprint enhancement methods.

Fingerprint dusting brushes: A variety of material used to coat the fingerprints with dusting powder.

Fingerprint dusting powder: A powder that sticks to the fingerprint emulsion.

Fingerprint residue: An emulsion consisting of mainly sebaceous oils, epithelial cells, eccrine secretions, and external contaminants.

Fire patterns: Visual or measurable changes formed by a fire effect.

Flame spread: The concept of a flame spreading over fuel sources, which occurs by two mechanisms: concurrent flame spread or counterflow flame spread.

Fluid mechanics: The study of fluids (liquids, gases, and plasmas) and the forces that act on them.

Focal length: Relates to the distance needed to capture something in full frame.

Forensic entomology: The use of insects, and their arthropod relatives, that inhabit decomposing remains to aid legal investigations.

Forensic photography: Principles of photography applied to forensic investigations.

Forensic science: A discipline where member and a broad groups of professionals who employ and adhere to the rigorous standards of their respective professions, who consider matters under consideration in order to ascertain the truth of a set of alleged facts, criminal or civil.

Forensic sketching: A marriage of drawing and making measurements of crime scene elements, the final rendering of which is a perspective that renders the scene understandable to the lay public and provides information to investigators.

Forensic trajectory analysis: The mathematical description of the path taken by a projectile or a droplet of blood.

Forensic videography: The documentary video of the crime scene.

Forensics: A broad term whose members are professionals who apply accepted investigative and/or scientific techniques to questions related to the criminal justice system.

Forms: Fill-in worksheets to capture important scene-related information.
Friction ridge detail: Ridges and grooves of the fingerprint.
Front and rear track widths: The distance between the middle of the leading edge of the front-and-back tires, respectively.
Fuel: A substance that can be oxidized.
Fuel load: A term that describes the amount of fuel present.
Fungal pathogens: Unicellular or multicellular organisms. Their main use as bioweapons would be to attack the agricultural food chain, specifically wheat, corn, and rice.
Gel lifter: A gelatin-glycerol-based sticky gel used to lift dry and wet residue impression, and useful for lifting the fingerprints on mildly textured surfaces. Also known as Gellifter.
Grid search method: Searching two times in one direction followed by searching the other on a perpendicular.
Ground truth: The actual truth of what happened.
Gunshot residue (GSR): Shock-sensitive mixture of chemicals that explode when struck by an object such as a firing pin. The resulting debris is known as primer powder or gunshot residue.
Heat and humidity (H&H) superglue methods: The use of a heat source to vaporize the cyanoacrylate monomer in the presence of water vapor.
Heat release rate (HRR) : A term relating to the amount of heat released during its three phases of growth depending on the availability of a fuel source.
Heat source: Causes a fuel to release vapors.
Hypothesis testing: The intellectual interpretation of evidence that leads to experiments to test the validity of a hypothesis.
IAI: International Association of Identification.
Impression evidence: An impression in a softer surface that leaves a pattern. Also known as pattern. Examples include fingerprints, footwear and tire track impressions, cartridge case ejection marks, bite marks, and tool marks.
Inculpatory evidence: Evidence pointing to the guilt of someone.
Indirect DNA testing: A paternity-like test used to identify the missing or deceased individuals.
Inductive reasoning: Begins with an observation and moves to a testable tentative hypothesis, which is more open-ended. This is considered a bottom-up process.
Interior ballistics: The study of what happens in the barrel of a weapon, specifically when the firing pin strikes the primer to when the bullet or projectile exits the barrel of the weapon.
Investigation : The process of observing and studying as part of a systematic inquiry.
Investigative questions: Pertinent questions that the investigation should answer.
International Standards Organization (ISO): Refers to the sensitivity of the digital sensor to light. The higher the ISO, the more sensitive.
Laminated glass: Two pieces of glass held together by plastic. This is the usual construction of automotive windshields.
Latent fingerprints: Invisible fingerprints left at a crime scene.
Lateral flow immunochromatography: An immunological technique for identifying the blood, semen, and saliva at crime scenes.
Line search method: A one-time search of a scene using a parallel line of individuals.

Link search method: An intellectual approach to searching that utilizes the linkage theory as the basis for the search.
Locard Exchange Principle: The transfer of material among the participants of a crime.
Logic: The science that evaluates arguments.
Luminol: See BlueStar™.
Macroscene: The individual visible or visualizable elements of the crime scene, each of which is a part of the whole.
Macroscene elements: Visible parts of the scene.
Maggot trail: The trail of maggots leading to the place of pupation.
Metadata: Ancillary information collected to help identify the missing or deceased individuals.
Metering: The process of measuring the light entering the camera. Most modern single-lens reflex (SLR) cameras have through-the-lens (TTL) metering.
Microbial forensics: A scientific discipline dedicated to analyzing the evidence from a bioterrorism act, biocrime, or inadvertent microorganism/toxin release for attribution purposes.
Microscene: Invisible, microscopic, or latent traces intimately associated with the macroscene and commonly called trace evidence but could be defined as Locard Elements.
Microscene elements: Microscopic evidence, also trace evidence or Locard Elements.
Mikrosil™: Silicone-based casting material, used to capture impression evidence detail and to lift fingerprints.
Midrange photographs: Photographs that highlight specific areas and the relationship of evidence in those areas.
Nonporous surfaces: Surfaces that do not absorb fingerprint residue.
Oxidizing agent: Substance that provides oxygen to a mixture.
Parallel search method: Essentially the same as the line search method.
Passive archiving: The mindless approach to creating a scene's archive.
Patent fingerprints: Visible fingerprints left at a crime scene.
Persistence of trace evidence: The characteristic of an item to retain the trace evidence over a period of time.
Perspective sketch : 3D rendering of the scene.
Photogrammetry: Method for converting multiple photographs of a scene into a 3D rendering using specialized software.
Picking method of trace evidence collection: The process of picking visible traces of trace evidence, such as hair and fibers, from an object.
Point-to-point search: A logical method that utilizes found evidence to determine where to search.
Polar coordinate measuring method: Fixing items at a scene off a virtual line created using the cardinal coordinates.
Porous surfaces: Surfaces that can absorb fingerprint residue readily.
Postmortem interval (PMI): The time since death occurred.
Primary transfer: The first transfer of trace evidence between items.
Principle of divisible matter: The process of matter being divided through an energetic process leaving one part at the crime scene and the other at the original source.
Probative evidence: Evidence that has potential value in ascertaining the ground truth of an issue.
Processing: A series of actions or operations leading to a finished product.

Quality assurance: A program instituted by an agency that ensures that its work product meets minimum quality standards.

Quality testing: Testing of reagents to ensure that they meet predefined standards or performance.

Radial fracture: The first fracture (crack) to form when glass breaks. These fractures initially radiate from the point of impact.

Radiation : The transfer of heat from a hot to a cool surface using electromagnetic waves without an intervening medium.

Responding officer: The first officer on the scene.

Ricochet: A change or deviation in a bullet's initial flight path.

Rickettsial pathogens: Single-cell microorganisms that produce diseases and are easily killed by heat and dehydration. As bioweapons, they can be lethal or simply incapacitating.

Rubeanic acid (dithiooxamide—DTO): Copper testing reagent to give a mossy green-charcoal color.

Reflected ultraviolet imaging system (RUVIS): An instrument that uses reflected ultraviolet light to highlight the impression evidence such as fingerprints, footwear impressions and superglue fumed fingerprints.

Scene processing cascade: A processing scheme for managing a crime scene investigation.

Scene security: Protecting the scene through three levels of security.

Scene video: A video overview of the scene.

Scientific method: The method used by scientists to verify the observations.

Searching : The process of looking for evidence logically using intellectual assessment of the scene, management, and archiving.

Sebaceous sweat gland: Glands mainly associated with hair. They are not associated with friction ridge skin. They secrete oils and other substances. Mixed with eccrine secretions, they are responsible for the oily component of the fingerprint emulsion left at crime scenes.

Secondary transfer: The subsequent transfer of primary transferred material to a second object.

Semen: The male ejaculated fluid.

Semiporous surfaces: Surfaces that slowly absorb fingerprint residue.

Sketches: Draft and final renderings of the crime scene.

Single-lens reflex (SLR) cameras: Cameras that utilize the removable lenses to capture the scene-specific information.

Smudged fingerprints: Latent or patent fingerprints without friction ridge detail.

Snow print wax: A spray wax used to form a wax mold of impressions in snow.

Sodium rhodizonate: Lead testing reagent that gives a reddish-purple color with lead in an acidic solution.

Soil taphonomy: Soil at grave sites.

Squaring the vehicle—Haag method: Creating reference points by placing the vehicle into a virtual box using tripods, tape measures, and string.

Squaring the vehicle—Moran method: Creating reference points of a vehicle using vertical surfaces of the vehicle and the ground as a horizontal reference.

Subteams: Individual working units at the scene having specific responsibilities.

Superglue fuming: A fingerprint development method that uses the fumes of cyanoacrylate monomer to polymerize on the surface of fingerprint ridges.

SWGMAT: Scientific Working Group on Materials Analysis.
SWGSTAIN: Scientific Working Group on Bloodstain Pattern Analysis.
Systematic : Something that is purposefully regular.
Tape lift method: Using tape to lift/collect hairs, fibers, and other trace evidence from objects.
Telogen or inactive phase: Lasts approximately 3 months. Hair remains attached but is not growing.
Terminal ballistics: The study of the interaction of bullets with its target.
Terminal velocity: The velocity attained when acceleration due to the downward force of gravity equals the upward force of drag.
Plan sketch : An overview or bird's-eye view of the crime scene.
Three-dimensional (3D) impression evidence: Impressed patterns in a soft surface.
Time since colonization: The time frame from when someone is murdered to the time it takes for colonization to begin.
3,3′,5,5′-Tetramethybenzidine (TMB), Kastle–Meyer (KM): Heme-reacting chemicals used to presumptively identify the blood.
Topic video: A video of specific areas of the scene to show the relationship of evidence to each other and to the scene.
Toxins: Poisonous substances produced by animals, plants, or microorganisms.
Tread depth: The depth of an impression based on the manufacturer's nonskid design of the tread.
Triangulation measurement method: Measuring items at a scene using two fixed points.
Turning diameter: The diameter of the circle made when the vehicle is driven in a circle.
Two-dimensional (2D) impression evidence: Extremely shallow impressions on a flat hard surface.
2% 5-Sulfosalicylic acid: Blood fixing reagent.
Vacuum method of trace evidence collection: Using a vacuum to collect hairs, fibers, and other trace evidence from objects.
Vacuum superglue method: The use of a vacuum to vaporize the cyanoacrylate monomer.
Vertical and azimuth angles: Angular components of bullet flight path.
Viral pathogens: Viruses that attack humans, animals, or plants.
Walkthrough: When the first officer hands over the scene to the team leader.
Wet residue impression: Impression evidence created from dirt or dust on a wet shoe.
WetWop, sticky-side powder, TapeGlo™: Commercially available reagents used to develop the fingerprints on the sticky side of tapes, specifically rubber-based adhesives.
White balance (WB): A measure of color temperature in degrees Kelvin that the camera uses to "see" white.
Worksheets: Anything relevant to the investigation filled out, prepared, or recorded: investigative notes or thoughts, typed into a computer, including draft and final sketches.
Zone search method: Prioritizing the search by dividing the scene into zones and then searching each separately.

Index

Note: n = Footnote

B

C

D

E

I

P

T

U

V

W

Z